CIMA Official
Learning System

CIMA
PUBLISHING

Strategic Level, Performance Pillar

P3 — Performance Strategy

**Paul M. Collier
Sam Agyei-Ampomah**

ELSEVIER

AMSTERDAM   BOSTON   HEIDELBERG   LONDON   NEW YORK   OXFORD
PARIS   SAN DIEGO   SAN FRANCISCO   SINGAPORE   SYDNEY   TOKYO

CIMA Publishing is an imprint of Elsevier
Linacre House, Jordan Hill, Oxford OX2 8DP, UK
30 Corporate Drive, Suite 400, Burlington, MA 01803, USA

First edition 2008

Permissions may be sought directly from Elsevier's Science and Technology Rights
Department in Oxford, UK: phone (+44) (0) 1865 843830; fax (+44) (0) 1865 853333;
e-mail: permissions@elsevier.com. Alternatively you can visit the Science and Technology
Books website at www.elsevierdirect.com/rights for further information

Notice
No responsibility is assumed by the publisher for any injury and/or damage to persons
or property as a matter of products liability, negligence or otherwise, or from any use
or operation of any methods, products, instructions or ideas contained in the material
herein.

British Library Cataloguing in Publication Data
A catalogue record for this book is available from the British Library

Library of Congress Cataloguing in Publication Data
A catalogue record for this book is available from the Library of Congress

ISBN: 978-1-85617-795-5

For information on all CIMA publications
visit our website at www.elsevierdirect.com

Typeset by Macmillan Publishing Solutions
(www.macmillansolutions.com)

Printed and bound in Italy

09 10 11   11 10 9 8 7 6 5 4 3 2 1

Contents

9 Information Systems Control and Auditing   267

The CIMA
Learning System

Acknowledgements

Every effort has been made to contact the holders of copyright material, but if any here have been inadvertently overlooked the publishers will be pleased to make the necessary arrangements at the first opportunity.

How to use your CIMA *Learning System*

This *Performance Strategy Learning System* has been devised as a resource for students attempting to pass their CIMA exams, and provides:

- a detailed explanation of all syllabus areas;
- extensive 'practical' materials, including case studies and real-life examples;
- generous question practice, together with full solutions, many drawn from past examination papers;
- an exam preparation section, complete with exam standard questions and solutions.

This Learning System has been designed with the needs of home-study and distance-learning candidates in mind. Such students require very full coverage of the syllabus topics, and also the facility to undertake extensive question practice. However, the Learning System is also ideal for fully taught courses.

The main body of the text is divided into a number of chapters, each of which is organised on the following pattern:

- *Detailed learning outcomes*: This is expected after your studies of the chapter are complete. You should assimilate these before beginning detailed work on the chapter, so that you can appreciate where your studies are leading.
- *Step-by-step topic coverage*: This is the heart of each chapter, containing detailed explanatory text supported where appropriate by worked examples and exercises. You should work carefully through this section, ensuring that you understand the material being explained and can tackle the examples and exercises successfully. Remember that in many cases knowledge is cumulative: if you fail to digest earlier material thoroughly, you may struggle to understand later chapters.
- *Question practice*: The test of how well you have learned the material is your ability to tackle exam standard questions. Make a serious attempt at producing your own

answers, but at this stage do not be too concerned about attempting the questions in exam conditions. In particular, it is more important to absorb the material thoroughly by completing a full solution than to observe the time limits that would apply in the actual exam.

- *Solutions*: Avoid the temptation merely to 'audit' the solutions provided. It is an illusion to think that this provides the same benefits as you would gain from a serious attempt of your own. However, if you are struggling to get started on a question you should read the introductory guidance provided at the beginning of the solution, and then make your own attempt before referring back to the full solution. However, the answers provided are often more detailed than would be expected from examination candidates. Also, different approaches to answering questions are often possible. The solutions provided to past examination questions are those published for examination candidates to help with revision. Examiners have more detailed marking guides than ensure candidate performance is properly marked, even where answers are different to the published ones.

Having worked through the chapters you are ready to begin your final preparations for the examination. The final section of this CIMA *Learning System* provides you with the guidance you need. It includes the following features:

- A brief guide to revision technique.
- A note on the format of the examination. You should know what to expect when you tackle the real exam, and in particular the number of questions to attempt, which questions are compulsory and which optional, and so on.
- Guidance on how to tackle the examination itself.
- A table mapping revision questions to the syllabus learning outcomes allowing you to quickly identify questions by subject area.
- Revision questions. These are of exam standard and should be tackled in exam conditions, especially as regards the time allocation.
- Solutions to the revision questions. As before, these indicate the length and the quality of solution that would be expected of a well-prepared candidate.

 If you work conscientiously through this CIMA *Learning System* according to the guidelines above you will be giving yourself an excellent chance of exam success. Good luck with your studies!

Guide to the Icons used within this Text

🔑 Key term or definition

π Equation to learn

✏️ Exam tip to topic likely to appear in the exam

✋ Exercise

❓ Question

✅ Solution

❗ Comment or Note

Study technique

Passing exams is partly a matter of intellectual ability, but however accomplished you are in that respect you can improve your chances significantly by the use of appropriate study and revision techniques. In this section we briefly outline some tips for effective study during the earlier stages of your approach to the exam. Later in the text we mention some techniques that you will find useful at the revision stage.

Planning

To begin with, formal planning is essential to get the best return from the time you spend studying. Estimate how much time in total you are going to need for each subject that you face. Remember that you need to allow time for revision as well as for initial study of the material. The amount of notional study time for any subject is the minimum estimated time that students will need to achieve the specified learning outcomes set out earlier in this chapter. This time includes all appropriate learning activities, for example, face-to-face tuition, private study, directed home study, learning in the workplace, revision time, etc. You may find it helpful to read *Better Exam Results* by Sam Malone, CIMA Publishing, ISBN: 075066357X. This book will provide you with proven study techniques. Chapter by chapter it covers the building blocks of successful learning and examination techniques.

The notional study time for Strategic level *Performance Strategy* is 200 hours. Note that the standard amount of notional learning hours attributed to one full-time academic year of approximately 30 weeks is 1,200 hours.

By way of example, the notional study time might be made up as follows:

	Hours
Face-to-face study: up to	60
Personal study: up to	100
'Other' study – e.g. learning at the workplace, revision, etc.: up to	40
	200

Note that all study and learning-time recommendations should be used only as a guideline and are intended as minimum amounts. The amount of time recommended for face-to-face tuition, personal study and/or additional learning will vary according to the type of course undertaken, prior learning of the student, and the pace at which different students learn.

Now split your total time requirement over the weeks between now and the examination. This will give you an idea of how much time you need to devote to study each week. Remember to allow for holidays or other periods during which you will not be able to study (e.g. because of seasonal workloads).

With your study material before you, decide which chapters you are going to study in each week, and which weeks you will devote to revision and final question practice.

Prepare a written schedule summarising the above – and stick to it!

The amount of space allocated to a topic in the study material is not a very good guide as to how long it will take you. For example, 'Risk and Internal Control' has a weight of 20% in the syllabus. However, the principles of risk and control are covered throughout each chapter and so the 20% weighting is only a guide. In the P3 syllabus, each topic area is inter-related.

It is essential to know your syllabus. As your course progresses you will become more familiar with how long it takes to cover topics in sufficient depth. Your timetable may need to be adapted to allocate enough time for the whole syllabus.

Tips for effective studying

1. Aim to find a quiet and undisturbed location for your study, and plan as far as possible to use the same period of time each day. Getting into a routine helps to avoid wasting time. Make sure that you have all the materials you need before you begin so as to minimise interruptions.
2. Store all your materials in one place, so that you do not waste time searching for items around the house. If you have to pack everything away after each study period, keep them in a box, or even a suitcase, which won't be disturbed until the next time.
3. Limit distractions. To make the most effective use of your study periods you should be able to apply total concentration, so turn off the TV, set your phones to message mode and put up your 'do not disturb' sign.
4. Your timetable will tell you which topic to study. However, before diving in and becoming engrossed in the finer points, make sure you have an overall picture of all the areas that need to be covered by the end of that session. After an hour, allow yourself a short break and move away from your books. With experience, you will learn to assess the pace you need to work at. You should also allow enough time to read relevant articles from newspapers and journals, which will supplement your knowledge and demonstrate a wider perspective.
5. Work carefully through a chapter, making notes as you go. When you have covered a suitable amount of material, vary the pattern by attempting a practice question. Preparing an answer plan is a good habit to get into, while you are both studying and revising, and also in the examination room. It helps to impose a structure on your solutions, and avoids rambling. When you have finished your attempt, make notes of any mistakes you made, or any areas that you failed to cover or covered only skimpily.
6. Make notes as you study, and discover the techniques that work best for you. Your notes may be in the form of lists, bullet points, diagrams, summaries, 'mind maps', or the written word, but remember that you will need to refer back to them at a later date, so they must be intelligible. If you are on a taught course, make sure you highlight any issues you would like to follow up with your lecturer.
7. Organise your paperwork. There are now numerous paper storage systems available to ensure that all your notes, calculations and articles can be effectively filed and easily retrieved later.

Learning and verbs

At each stage of the CIMA syllabus, different verbs are used in questions. These verbs determine the type of answer which is expected of candidates. A definition of the verbs is contained in the following Table.

Learning objective	Verbs used	Definition
1. **Knowledge** What you are expected to know	List State Define	Make a list of Express, fully or clearly, the facts of Give the exact meaning of
2. **Comprehension** What you are expected to understand	Describe Distinguish Explain Identify Illustrate	Communicate the key features of Highlight the key differences between Make clear/state the meaning of Recognise, or select after consideration Use an example to describe or explain
3. **Application** How you are expected to apply your knowledge	Apply Calculate/compute Demonstrate Prepare Reconcile Solve Tabulate	To put to practical use To ascertain mathematically To prove with certainty To get ready for use To prove consistent Find an answer to Arrange in a table
4. **Analysis** How you are expected to analyse the detail of what you have learned	Analyse Categorise Compare and contrast Construct Discuss Interpret Produce	Examine in detail Place into a defined class Show the similarities and differences To build or compile To examine by argument Translate into intelligible terms Create or bring into existence
5. **Evaluation** How you are expected to use your learning to evaluate, make decisions or recommendations	Advise Evaluate Recommend	Counsel, inform or notify Appraise or assess the value of Advise on a course of action

The learning objectives form a hierarchy. As the verbs move through the learning objectives, the answer required of candidates under successively higher verbs is more demanding. For example, list is a simple requirement to recall facts, whilst recommend involves analysis in interpreting facts and making specific suggestions as a result of applying knowledge to the facts of a scenario and presenting a logical argument with evidence to support your suggestions.

Paper P3 – Performance Strategy

Syllabus overview

Two key issues underpin Paper P3 – what risks does the organisation face and how can those risks be managed and controlled? The scope of the paper includes both financial and non-financial risks. The management strategies covered extend to the use of financial instruments, and more general strategies of risk identification and management, involving establishing and monitoring appropriate systems of internal control. With the growing importance of 'new' sources of risk, the paper pays particular attention to risks arising from governance, ethical and social/environmental issues.

Syllabus structure

The syllabus comprises the following topics and study weightings:

Topics	Study Weighting
(A) Management Control Systems	10%
(B) Risk and Internal Control	25%
(C) Review and Audit of Control Systems	15%
(D) Management of Financial Risk	35%
(E) Risk and Control in Information Systems	15%

Assessment strategy

There will be a written examination paper of 3 hours, plus 20 minutes of pre-examination question paper reading time. The examination paper will have the following sections:

Section A – 50 marks
A maximum of four compulsory questions, totalling 50 marks, all relating to a pre-seen case study and further new unseen case material provided within the examination. (Note: The pre-seen case study is common to all three of the Strategic level papers at each examination sitting i.e. paper E3, P3 and F3.)

Section B – 50 marks
Two questions, from a choice of three, each worth 25 marks. Short scenarios will be given, to which some or all questions relate.

Learning outcomes and syllabus content
P3 – A. Management Control Systems (10%)

Learning Outcomes

Lead	Component	Indicative Syllabus Content
1. Evaluate control systems for organisational activities and resources. (5)	(a) Evaluate and recommend appropriate control systems for the management of an organisation (b) Evaluate the appropriateness of an organisation's management accounting control systems (c) Evaluate the control of activities and resources within an organisation (d) Recommend ways in which identified weaknesses or problems associated with control systems can be avoided or solved.	● The ways in which systems are used to achieve control within the framework of an organisation (e.g. contracts of employment, policies and procedures, discipline and reward, reporting structures, performance appraisal and feedback). (A–D) ● The application of control systems and related theory to the design of management accounting control systems and information systems in general (i.e. control system components, primary and secondary feedback, positive and negative feedback, open- and closed-loop control). (A–D) ● Structure and operation of management accounting control systems (e.g. identification of appropriate responsibility and control centres within the organisation, performance target setting, avoiding unintended behavioural consequences of using management accounting controls). (A–D) ● Variation in control needs and systems dependent on organisational structure (e.g. extent of centralisation versus divisionalisation, management through strategic business units). (A–D) ● Assessing how lean the management accounting system is (e.g. extent of the need for detailed costing, overhead allocation and budgeting, identification of non-value adding activities in the accounting function). (A–D) ● Cost of quality applied to the management accounting function and 'getting things right first time'. (A–D)

P3 - B. Risk and Internal Control (25%)

Learning outcomes

Lead	Component	Indicative Syllabus Content
1. Identify and discuss evaluate types of risk facing an organisation (5)	Identify risks facing an organisation: (a) Discuss ways of identifying, measuring and assessing the types of risk facing an organisation, including the organisation's ability to bear such risks (b) Produce a report on evaluate risks facing an organisation, including appropriate representations of risk exposure (e.g. a risk map).	• Types and sources of risk for business organisations: financial, commodity price, business (e.g. from fraud, employee malfeasance, litigation, contractual inadequacy, loss of product reputation), technological, external (e.g. economic and political), and corporate reputation (e.g. from environmental and social performance or health and safety) risks. (A) • Fraud related to sources of finance (e.g. advance fee fraud and pyramid schemes). (A) • Risks associated with international operations (e.g. from cultural variations and litigation risk, to loss of goods in transit and enhanced credit risk). (Note: No specific real country will be tested). (A) • Quantification of risk exposures (impact if an adverse event occurs) and their expected values, taking account of likelihood. (A) • Information required to fully report on risk exposures. (B) • Risk map representation of risk exposures as a basis for reporting and analysing risks. (B)
2. Discuss and evaluate risk management strategies and internal controls. (5)	(a) Discuss the purposes and importance of internal control and risk management for an organisation (b) Evaluate risk management strategies (c) Evaluate the essential features of internal control systems for identifying, assessing and managing risks (d) Evaluate the costs and benefits of a particular internal control system.	• Purposes and importance of internal control and risk management for an organisation. (A) • Issues to be addressed in defining management's risk policy. (B) • The principle of diversifying risk. (Note: Numerical questions will not be set.) (B) • Minimising the risk of fraud (e.g. fraud policy statements, effective recruitment policies and good internal controls, such as approval procedures and

separation of functions, especially over procurement and cash). (B, C)

- The risk manager role (including as part of a set of roles) as distinct from that of internal auditor. (C)
- Purposes of internal control (e.g. safeguarding of shareholders' investment and company assets, facilitation of operational effectiveness and efficiency, contribution to the reliability of reporting). (C)
- Elements in internal control systems (e.g. control activities, information and communication processes, processes for ensuring continued effectiveness etc.). (C)
- Operational features of internal control systems (e.g. embedding in company's operations, responsiveness to evolving risks, timely reporting to management). (C)
- The pervasive nature of internal control and the need for employee training. (C)
- Costs and benefits of maintaining the internal control system. (D)

3. Discuss and evaluate governance and ethical issues facing an organisation. (5)

(a) Discuss the principles of good corporate governance, particularly as regards the need for internal controls

(b) Evaluate ethical issues as a source of risk to the organisation and recommend control mechanisms for their detection and resolution.

- The principles of good corporate governance based on those for listed companies (the Combined Code), e.g. separation of chairman and CEO roles, appointment of non-executive directors, transparency of directors' remuneration policy, relations with shareholders, the audit committee. Other examples of recommended good practice may include The King Report on Corporate Governance for South Africa, Sarbanes-Oxley Act in the USA, The Smith and Higgs Reports in the UK, etc). (A)
- Recommendations for internal control (e.g. The Turnbull Report). (A)
- Ethical issues identified in the CIMA *Code of Ethics for Professional Accountants*, mechanisms for detection in practice and supporting compliance. (B)

P3 – C. Review and Audit of Control Systems (15%)

Learning Outcomes

Lead	Component	Indicative Syllabus Content
1. Discuss the importance of management review of controls. (5)	(a) Discuss the importance of management review of controls.	• The process of review (e.g. regular reporting to management on the effectiveness of internal controls over significant risks) and audit of internal controls. • Major tools available to assist with a review and audit process (e.g. audit planning, documenting systems, internal control questionnaires, sampling and testing).
2. Discuss and evaluate the process and purposes of audit in the context of internal control systems and produce a plan for such an audit. (5)	(a) Discuss and evaluate the process of internal audit and its relationship to other forms of audit (b) Produce a plan for the audit of various organisational activities including management, accounting and information systems (c) Analyse problems associated with the audit of activities and systems, and recommend action to avoid or solve problems associated with the audit of activities and systems (d) Recommend action to improve the efficiency, effectiveness and control of activities (e) Discuss the relationship between internal and external audit work.	• Role of the internal auditor and relationship of the internal audit to the external audit. (A) • Relationship of internal audit to other forms of audit (e.g. value-for-money audit, management audit, social and environmental audit). (A) • Operation of internal audit, the assessment of audit risk and the process of analytical review, including different types of benchmarking, their use and limitations. (B, C) • Particular relevance of the fundamental principles in CIMA's *Ethical Guidelines* to the conduct of an impartial and effective review of internal controls. (B, C) • Detection and investigation of fraud. (B, D) • The nature of the external audit and its process, including the implications of internal audit findings for external audit procedures. (E)
3. Discuss and evaluate corporate governance and ethical issues facing an organisation. (5)	(a) Discuss the principles of good corporate governance for listed companies, for conducting reviews of internal controls and reporting on compliance. (b) Discuss the importance of exercising ethical principles in conducting and reporting on internal reviews.	• The principles of good corporate governance for listed companies, for the review of the internal control system and reporting on compliance. (A) • Application of the CIMA *Code of Ethics for Professional Accountants* to the resolution of ethical conflicts in the context of discoveries made in the course of internal review, especially section 210. (B)

P3 – D. Management of Financial Risk (35%)

Learning Outcomes

Lead	Component	Indicative Syllabus Content
1. Identify and evaluate financial risks facing an organisation. (5)	Identify financial risks facing an organisation. (a) Evaluate financial risks facing an organisation.	• Sources of financial risk, including those associated with international operations (e.g. hedging of foreign investment value) and trading (e.g. purchase prices and sales values). (A) • Transaction, translation, economic and political risk. (A) • Quantification of risk exposures, their sensitivities to changes in external conditions and their expected values. (A)
2. Identify and evaluate alternative risk management tools. (5)	(a) Identify and evaluate appropriate methods for managing financial risks (b) Evaluate the effects of alternative methods of risk management and make recommendations accordingly (c) Explain discuss exchange rate theory and demonstrate the impact of differential inflation rates on forecast exchange rates (d) Recommend risk management strategies and discuss their accounting implications.	• Minimising political risk (e.g. gaining government funding, joint ventures, obtaining local finance). (A) • Operation and features of the more common instruments for managing interest rate risk: swaps, forward rate agreements, futures and options. (Note: Numerical questions will not be set involving FRA's, futures or options. See the note below relating to the Black Scholes model.) (A, B, D) • Operation and features of the more common instruments for managing currency risk: swaps, forward contracts, money market hedges, futures and options. (Note: The Black Scholes option pricing model will not be tested numerically, however, an understanding of the variables which will influence the value of an option should be appreciated.) (A, B, D) • Illustration and interpretation of Simple graphs depicting cap, collar and floor interest rate options. (B) • Theory and forecasting of exchange rates (e.g. interest rate parity, purchasing power parity and the Fisher effect). (C) • Principles of valuation of financial instruments for management and financial reporting purposes (IAS 39), and controls to ensure that the appropriate accounting method is applied to a given instrument. (D) • Quantification and disclosure of the sensitivity of financial instrument values to changes in external conditions. (D) • Internal hedging techniques (e.g. netting and matching). (D)

P3 – E. Risk and Control in Information Systems (15%)

Learning Outcomes

Lead	Component	Indicative Syllabus Content
1. Evaluate the benefits and risks associated with information-related systems. (5)	(a) Evaluate and advise managers on the development of information management (IM), information systems (IS) and information technology (IT) strategies that support management and internal control requirements. (b) Identify and evaluate IS/IT systems appropriate to an organisation's needs for operational and control information (c) Evaluate benefits and risks in the structuring and organisation of the IS/IT function and its integration with the rest of the business (d) Evaluate and recommend improvements to the control of IS (e) Evaluate specific problems and opportunities associated with the audit and control of systems which use IT.	• The importance and characteristics of information for organisations and the use of cost-benefit analysis to assess its value. (A, B) • The purpose and content of IM, IS and IT strategies, and their role in performance management and internal control. (A, B) • Data collection and IT systems that deliver information to different levels in the organisation (e.g. transaction processing, decision support and executive informative systems). (A, B) • The potential ways of organising the IT function (e.g. the use of steering committees, support centres for advice and help desk facilities, end user participation). (B, C, D) • The arguments for and against outsourcing. (B, C, D) • Methods for securing systems and data back-up in case of systems failure and/or data loss. (B, C, D) • Minimising the risk of computer-based fraud (e.g., access restriction, password protection, access logging and automatic generation of audit trail). (B, C, D) • Risks in IS/IT systems: erroneous input, unauthorised usage, imported virus infection, unlicensed use of software, theft, corruption of software, etc. (B, C, D) • Risks and benefits of Internet and Intranet use by an organisation. (B, C, D) • The criteria for selecting outsourcing/facilities management partners and for managing ongoing relationships, service level agreements, discontinuation/change of supplier, hand-over considerations. (C, D) • Controls which can be designed into an information system, particularly one using information technology IT (e.g. security, integrity and contingency controls). (D) • Control and audit of systems development and implementation. (E) • Techniques available to assist audit in a computerised environment (computer-assisted audit techniques e.g. audit interrogation software). (E)

Introduction to Performance Strategy

Introduction to Performance Strategy

1.1 Introduction

Two key issues underpin P3 *Performance Strategy*:

1. What risks does an organisation face?
2. How can those risks be managed and controlled?

The main purpose of this chapter is to help candidates see *Performance Strategy* as an integrated subject. Whilst the syllabus (see *The CIMA Learning System* that precedes Chapter 1) has five separate elements, each with its own learning outcomes and syllabus content, to understand *Performance Strategy* properly is to see all the elements of the syllabus as inter-related.

1.2 Risk management in 2009

This chapter is being written early in 2009 as the effects of the global financial crisis affect most organisations and individuals. Share markets have suffered major falls, the value of pension funds has fallen as a result. There is little confidence in the regulators of financial markets, or in the large investment banks (some of which have failed) or in credit rating agencies. Huge companies like General Motors and Chrysler have asked for funds from the US government to keep them afloat. Individuals are concerned about the falling values of their homes, whether they will keep their jobs and many economies have fallen into recession. Commentators argue that this is the most serious financial crisis to face the world since the Great Depression that commenced in 1929 and continued well into the 1930s.

1.2.1 Case study: Global financial crisis

The global financial crisis commenced in 2007 and continued into 2008 as a result of falling US house prices and defaults on 'sub-prime' mortgages. The sub-prime market supported loans to those with poor credit histories. These loans enabled US homeowners to borrow up to the full value of their homes, with low initial repayments. However, homeowners were unable to refinance when interest rates increased and the fall in US housing prices led to many homeowners being unwilling or unable to repay their mortgages. In the US, the structure of these loans was that owners could walk away, return their keys to their lender, and avoid responsibility or repay their debts (a practice which is impossible in the UK and most other countries). The subsequent sale of houses at a loss led to further falls in the housing market.

The impact on global financial markets has been to a large extent a result of the securitisation of debts like these. Securitisation involves the pooling of debts, making them available to a wider range of investors, which in turn provides more money for lending. The resulting security often received a higher credit rating, and attracted a lower rate of interest. The portfolios of many financial institutions contained investments with assets derived from bundled home mortgages which had received overly favourable credit ratings. A congressional committee in the US has claimed that credit rating agencies were fully aware that their conflicts of interest were giving unduly high scores to risky assets, threatening the stability of the entire financial system.

Part of the securitisation package was the creation of derivatives known as Credit Default Swaps (or CDS). A CDS is like an insurance policy, under which a buyer makes a payment (a kind of premium) to a seller, and receives an amount of money if there is a default in the underlying debt repayment. Many commentators have argued that the financial system was vulnerable because of the use of these derivatives. There has been criticism of the US Treasury, Federal Reserve, and the SEC for being opposed to increasing regulation of derivatives trading.

Derivatives are very powerful methods of risk management (Chapters 11–14 of the Learning System covers financial risks like these in detail) but can be misunderstood and misused. In an interview with the BBC in 2003, Warren Buffett, one of the world's most astute – and successful – investors, said that "the rapidly growing trade in derivatives poses a 'mega-catastrophic risk' for the economy … such highly complex financial instruments are time bombs and 'financial weapons of mass destruction' that could harm not only their buyers and sellers, but the whole economic system."[1]

The effects of the sub-prime crisis were subsequently felt throughout the world in terms of reduced credit availability and higher interest rates. In response, governments and central banks announced interest rate cuts, capital injections, and lending guarantees to restore liquidity.

---

[1] http://news.bbc.co.uk/2/hi/business/2817995.stm

In September 2007, Northern Rock plc experienced a bank run by its customers with the UK government providing 'lender of last resort' funding and guarantees for the bank's depositors. In 2008, Northern Rock was nationalised by the UK government.

Bear Stearns, one of the largest US brokers and investment banks collapsed and was subsequently sold to J P Morgan Chase. The US Government intervened by imposing a 'conservatorship' to protect mortgage giants Fannie Mae and Freddie Mac from insolvency. Lehman Brothers filed for bankruptcy after the Federal Reserve Bank refused to provide it with financial support and J P Morgan subsequently took over part of their business. Similarly, Merrill Lynch was sold to Bank of America. American Insurance Group (AIG) also suffered a liquidity crisis and had to be supported by the US Federal Reserve. Washington Mutual Bank, the sixth largest bank in the US closed and went into receivership, making it the largest bank failure in US history.

In Europe, Fortis was broken up and Hypo Real, Germany's second largest mortgage lender, was bailed out by the government. In the UK, Bradford and Bingley also had to be nationalised.

Even whole countries were affected. Iceland was especially affected due to its banks' debts being six times that country's gross domestic product. Iceland's three largest commercial banks were taken over by the Icelandic government to avoid their collapse. Interest rates were increased to 18% under the terms of a loan provided by the International Monetary Fund. The result has been a serious impact on the country's economy with sharp falls in the value of its currency and the suspension of its foreign currency exchange market. The Icelandic stock exchange has fallen in value by over 75%.

Stock markets around the world have fallen, as the global economy faces recession and unemployment in what many commentators have called the most serious financial crisis since the Great Depression. The US government passed the Emergency Economic Stabilisation Act and many European central banks injected capital into their banking systems. The Troubled Asset Relief Program (TARP) enabled the US government to purchase what have become known as 'toxic assets' from financial institutions. In November 2008, TARP was scrapped with funds being reallocated to help relieve pressure on consumer credit, including car and student loans, and credit cards. At the time of writing there are major concerns for the car industry, especially General Motors, Ford and Chrysler in the US who have called on the US government for assistance.

1.3 The emergence of risk, governance and control

Risk management has evolved from various separate functional areas: occupational health and safety; insurance; the hedging of financial risks (foreign exchange and interest rates); credit risk; and project management. The first two were largely the focus of risk managers in organisations, whilst the third and fourth were the province of financial and treasury managers, the fifth being the responsibility of operational managers. Risk management also had links with quality management and the international standard ISO9000.

There have been two major developments in risk management as it affects accountants:

1. Sarbanes-Oxley legislation
2. The Basel Committee on Banking Supervision

The introduction of the US Sarbanes-Oxley (SOX) Act in 2002 was the legislative response in the US to the financial and accounting scandals of Enron and WorldCom and the misconduct at the accounting firm Arthur Andersen. Its main aim was to deal with issues of transparency, integrity and oversight of financial markets. SOX as it is called requires the certification of annual and quarterly financial reports by the chief executive and chief financial officer of all companies with US securities registrations, with criminal penalties for knowingly making false certifications. SOX is criticised for having increased corporate costs as a result of the greater emphasis on internal controls and the audit of financial reporting.

The notion of risk in relation to financial derivatives in the banking industry was first formulated by the Basel Committee on Banking Supervision (1994). For banks and regulated financial institutions, the Basel Committee has had an important impact, particularly as it affects risk and internal control. Part of the Bank for International Settlements, the objectives of the Basel Committee include enhancing the understanding of key supervisory issues and improving the quality of banking supervision worldwide. Basel II is the second group of Accords from the Basel Committee. It contains international standards for banking laws and regulations aimed at helping to protect the international financial system from the results of the collapse of a major bank or a series of banks. Basel II established rigorous risk and capital management requirements to ensure each bank holds reserves sufficient to guard against its risk exposure given its lending and investment practices.

Risk came to be seen on a much wider basis through the publication of books such as *Risk Society* (Beck, 1986, 1992 in translation); *Risk* (Adams, 1995) and *Against the Gods* (Bernstein, 1998). These books highlighted the social and cultural aspects of risk management.

In the UK, high profile corporate failures led to a series of reports, beginning with that by Sir Adrian Cadbury on corporate governance (Cadbury Code, 1992) and culminating in the Combined Code on Corporate Governance (Financial Reporting Council, 2003). In Australia, the first risk management standard was produced in 1999 as AS4360.

In the US the Treadway Commission produced *Internal Control – Integrated Framework* (Commitee of Sponsoring Organizations of the Treadway Commission (COSO), 1992) but the critical legislation impacting organisations, particularly in relation to risks associated with financial reporting, followed the scandals of Enron and WorldCom and the enactment of the Sarbanes-Oxley Act (SOX) in 2002. Chapter 4 describes the background of corporate governance in detail.

The relationship between risk and reward, with risk coming to be seen both in terms of upside and downside is now well established (International Federation of Accountants, 1999). As risk management became more widespread and took on the mantle of enterprise risk management (Commitee of Sponsoring Organizations of the Treadway Commission (COSO), 2003; see Chapter 5), the role of internal audit, previously an essentially accounting role became transformed into a broader risk-based audit, with the Institute of Internal Auditors becoming the predominant body, rather than the accounting profession. Risk-based approaches have also been adopted by external auditors, particularly those subject to SOX. Chapter 7 describes the internal audit in detail.

Management controls have always existed, in order to control the behaviour of employees with the purpose of ensuring that organisational objectives are achieved. Many of these controls were accounting controls, such as budgets, standard costs, variance analysis, etc. (discussed in detail in Chapter 3). As organisations became more sophisticated, non-financial controls were added. These controls included targets such as quality, waste, delivery lead time, customer satisfaction, etc. When other controls, such as those in respect of personnel, information systems, corporate policies, working practices, etc. are added, the result is a system of management control, although often the components of the 'system' lead to different behaviours. Chapter 6 describes internal control in detail.

Good governance (e.g. Financial Reporting Council, 2003) requires that boards of directors review the effectiveness of internal controls in response to the risks facing the organisation. The risk-based approach to control, as for audit, should lead to the development of controls that are a response to risks, rather than being developed incrementally over time (International Federation of Accountants, 2006) often for political purposes unrelated to risk.

Standards for risk management are now international, and remarkably consistent in their focus (Commitee of Sponsoring Organizations of the Treadway Commission (COSO), 2004; Institute of Risk Management, 2002; Standards Australia, 2004). As Michael Power explains in his recent book *Organized Uncertainty* (Power, 2007), risk has become very important in the language of managers and a major element of accountability.

The relevance of risk to accountants has been reflected in CIMAs *Performance Strategy* syllabus. *Performance Strategy* is a strategic level subject that brings together enterprise risk management, governance, internal control and audit in relation to both financial and non-financial risks. The title 'Performance Strategy' is important, because the syllabus is not just concerned with what things might go wrong – so-called downside risks but also with the risk of not achieving the organisational strategy and goals, that is, the risk of not achieving the desired level of performance. Governance, internal control and audit should therefore be directed at achieving performance goals through using risk management as an important tool.

1.4   What is corporate governance?

Corporate governance is the system by which companies are directed and controlled. Boards of directors are responsible to their shareholders and have a stewardship function for the governance of the company. The responsibilities of Boards include setting the company's strategic goals, providing the leadership to put those goals into effect, supervising the management of the business and reporting to shareholders. This role involves the management of risk and the review of the effectiveness of internal control. Corporate governance is covered in Chapter 4.

CIMA has produced a model of enterprise governance (Chartered Institute of Management Accountants and International Federation of Accountants, 2004) that emphasises the importance of the two dimensions of conformance and performance. Conformance is about satisfying good governance, whilst performance focuses on strategy to improve shareholder value.

1.5   What is risk management?

Risk management is the process of understanding and managing risks that the organisation faces in attempting to achieve its objectives. Perhaps the best definition of risk management is that in relation to enterprise risk management (or ERM, discussed in Chapter 5). ERM aligns risk management with business strategy and embeds a risk management culture into the business. It encompasses the whole organisation and sees risks as opportunities as much as hazards.

In managing risk, organisations should follow a well-established process, although the level of detail they go into may vary quite significantly. While there are different models for risk management (discussed in detail in Chapter 5), the following 7 step process contains the essential ingredients:

1. *Identify the risk*: Risks are an everyday part of life, so organisations need a system to identify all the risks they face. This involves collecting information from a variety of sources: individuals, reports, observation and environmental assessments. Common methods of collecting data that identify risks include workshops, scenarios, brainstorming, surveys, etc. These may be linked with consultations with stakeholders, environmental analyses, strategic plans, etc.

2. *Assess the risk impact*: Once risks have been identified, some assessment needs to be made of their likely impact. This involves quantifying the risk in some way. We might carry out market surveys, computer simulations, cost–benefit analyses, use a Delphi technique or apply probabilities, statistical tests or sensitivity analysis. Alternatively, we may rely on subjective judgements.

3. *Risk mapping*: This involves prioritising the most critical risks by mapping the likelihood (or probability) of the risk eventuating against its consequences (or impact) if it does eventuate. Organisations may use a simple high–medium–low scale for both likelihood and consequences or map risks against a more complex scale. Whichever method is used, prioritisation is important because organisations will typically face hundreds or even thousands of risks, and only the most significant ones can be managed.

4. *Record risks in a risk register*: The risk register contains a listing of risks that have been identified, together with the likelihood and consequence of the risk occurring. This is a comprehensive register that ensures that risks are continually evaluated and managed, with most emphasis given to the greatest risks.

5. *Risk evaluation*: Risks are evaluated against the organisation's appetite for risk. This appetite is a balance between risk and return and must ultimately be a judgement that is made by the board of directors. This is really a question of setting the parameters for whether particular risks should be accepted, rejected or managed in some way.

6. *Risk treatment*: Also called risk response, this involves decisions as to whether particular risks should be avoided, reduced, transferred or accepted. Avoidance involves exiting from high risk activities. Risk reduction involves mitigating either the likelihood or impact of risks by introducing various internal control mechanisms. Sharing or transferring risk can take place through methods such as outsourcing, insurance or hedging while the acceptance of risk implies that no action is necessary in relation to risks evaluated as low.

7. *Risk reporting*: Risk reporting will explain the method of risk management, how risks are identified and assessed. The highest risks (in terms of likelihood and consequences) will be reported rather than all those in the risk register and the risk response will be identified for each. Risk reports should show both the gross risk (before controls are introduced) and the net risk (after the effect of controls is taken into account) to demonstrate the cost effectiveness of those controls.

1.6 What is internal control?

Internal control is the whole system of financial and other controls established to provide reasonable assurance of effective and efficient operation; internal financial control and compliance with regulation. An internal control system comprises five elements: a control environment, risk assessment, control activities, monitoring, and information and communication.

The control environment is the attitude and awareness of the Board and managers regarding the importance of internal controls and comprises culture and values – the background against which specific controls are introduced. Risk assessment was described in Section 1.5 above. Control activities are the policies and procedures that help ensure that objectives are achieved. Importantly, these controls are not just accounting controls but include quantitative (but non-financial) controls as well as qualitative (i.e. non-numeric) controls (see the discussion of management controls in Section 1.3 above). Monitoring continually evaluates the whole control system. Reviewing the effectiveness of internal control is one of the Board's responsibilities. Information and communication includes the need to capture relevant information about the organisation's environment and to communicate this information within the organisation. Internal control is covered in Chapter 6.

1.7   What is audit?

Audit is a systematic examination of the activities and status of an organisation based primarily on investigation and analysis of its systems, controls and records. The main types of audit are the external audit, the primary function of which is to form an opinion on the truth and fairness of financial statements; and the internal audit, the role of which is to examine and evaluate, add value and improve the operations of the organisation. It does so by helping an organisation achieve its objectives by improving the effectiveness of risk management, control and governance processes.

The audit committee is a committee of the board of directors, the primary function of which is to review the system of internal control, the external audit process, the work of internal audit and the financial information provided to shareholders. The role of audit is covered in Chapter 7 whilst the audit committee is covered in Chapter 4.

1.8   A model of governance, risk and control

It is important to understand the links between governance, risk management and internal control and the interaction between the board of directors, the audit committee, external and internal auditors, as this is the foundation of the *Performance Strategy* syllabus. This relationship is shown in Figure 1.1.

The Reading to Chapter 7 provides a case study of ABC, an example of these relationships.

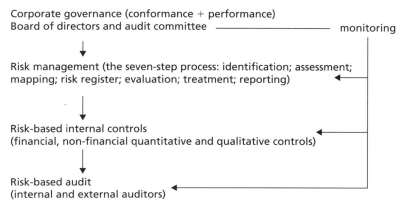

Figure 1.1   A model of governance, risk and control

1.9 Fraud, information systems and financial risk

The preceding discussion does not differentiate between different types of risk. However, the *Performance Strategy* syllabus addresses three specific risks: fraud (Chapter 10); information systems (Chapters 8 and 9) and financial derivatives (interest and exchange rate risks, covered in Chapters 11–14). Information systems risk comprises 15% of the syllabus and financial risk 35%. It is important therefore, to understand not only the general principles of governance, risk and control in Chapters 1–7 but also the specific risks covered in Chapters 8–14. Importantly, all the general principles apply to the specific risks, as well as to all other risks that are not identified in the syllabus. These unspecified risks therefore represent about 50% of the syllabus. It should also be remembered that many organisations will face general risks as well as specific information systems and financial risks. In interpreting Figure 1.1 therefore, it is important to remember that risks may be general, information systems or financial.

1.10 Summary

- The links between governance, risk management and internal control and the interaction between the board of directors, the audit committee, external and internal auditors is the foundation of the *Performance Strategy* syllabus.
- Corporate governance is the system by which companies are directed and controlled.
- Risk management is the process of understanding and managing risks that the organisation faces in attempting to achieve its objectives. Enterprise Risk Management aligns risk management with business strategy and embeds a risk management culture into the business, seeing risks as opportunities as much as hazards.
- Internal control is the whole system of financial and other controls established to provide reasonable assurance of effective and efficient operation; internal financial control and compliance with regulation. It comprises five elements: a control environment, risk assessment, control activities, monitoring, and information and communication.
- Audit is a systematic examination of the activities and status of an organisation based primarily on investigation and analysis of its systems, controls and records. The role of internal audit is to examine and evaluate, add value and improve the operations of the organisation, by helping an organisation achieve its objectives by improving the effectiveness of risk management, control and governance processes.
- The audit committee is a committee of the board of directors, the primary function of which is to review the system of internal control, the external audit process, the work of internal audit and the financial information provided to shareholders.
- The *Performance Strategy* syllabus addresses three specific risks: fraud, information systems and financial derivatives (interest and exchange rate risks). Information systems risk comprises 15% of the syllabus and financial risk 35%. Unspecified risks represent the balance of about 50% of the syllabus. Many organisations will face general risks as well as specific information systems and financial risks.

References

Adams, J. (1995), *Risk*. London: UCL Press.

Basel Committee on Banking Supervision (1994), *Risk Management Guidelines for Derivatives*. Basel: Bank for International Settlements.

Beck, U. (1986, 1992 in translation), *Risk Society*. London: Sage.

Bernstein, P.L. (1998), *Against the Gods: The Remarkable Story of Risk*. New York: John Wiley.

Cadbury Code (1992). Report of the Committee on the Financial Aspects of Corporate Governance: The Code of Best Practice, London: Professional Publishing.

Chartered Institute of Management Accountants and International Federation of Accountants (2004). Enterprise Governance: Getting the Balance Right. New York: CIMA/FIAC. http://www.ifac.org/MediaCenter/files/EnterpriseGovernace.pdf.

Committee of Sponsoring Organizations of the Treadway Commission (COSO) (1992). Internal Control – Integrated Framework. New York: COSO.

Committee of Sponsoring Organizations of the Treadway Commission (COSO) (2003). Enterprise Risk Management Framework. New York: COSO.

Committee of Sponsoring Organizations of the Treadway Commission (COSO) (2004). Enterprise Risk Management – Integrated Framework. New York: COSO.

Financial Reporting Council (2003). The Combined Code on Corporate Governance.

Institute of Risk Management (2002), *A Risk Management Standard*. London: IRM.

International Federation of Accountants (1999). Enhancing Shareholder Wealth by Better Managing Business Risk. *Rep. International Management Accounting Study No. 9.* New York: IFAC.

International Federation of Accountants (2006). Internal Controls – A Review of Current Developments, Professional Accountants in Business Committee, New York.

Power, M. (2007), *Organized Uncertainty: Designing a World of Risk Management*. Oxford: Oxford University Press.

Standards Australia (2004). Australian and New Zealand Risk Management Standard AS/NZS 4360:2004, 3rd edition. Sydney: Standards Australia.

Management
Control Theory

Management Control Theory

2

LEARNING OUTCOMES

After completing this chapter you should be able to:

► Evaluate appropriate control systems for the management of an organisation.

► Evaluate the control of activities and resources within an organisation.

► Recommend ways in which identified weaknesses or problems associated with control systems can be avoided or solved.

2.1 Introduction

In this chapter and in Chapter 3, we are mainly concerned with Section A of the *Performance Strategy* syllabus: Management Control Systems. The main purpose of this and the following chapter is to introduce students to the theory of management control. Whilst this section of the syllabus accounts for only 10% of the study weighting, the principles in this chapter underlie all the other chapters in the Learning System. The chapter introduces organisation theory, systems theory, environmental change, feedback and feed forward, and open and closed systems as a framework for understanding organisational control. Various theories of management control are introduced as well as typologies (or classifications) of different types of management control. The chapter also contains a brief summary of different organisation structures and responsibility centres.

2.2 Organisation theory

Organisations are collectives of people who join together in common pursuit of shared goals. People form organisations because they are unable to achieve their goals as individuals without marshalling other resources (money, people, materials, etc.). Organisations have a high degree of structure or formality. They are 'social' in the sense that they comprise people, but the organisation of resources requires some rules and the assignment of roles to individuals. Goal-orientation and formalisation of structure distinguishes organisations from other collectives such as families and social groups.

2.3 Systems theory

Systems theory developed from the work of a biologist, von Bertalanffy, whose work has been classified by nine different levels of complexity. The main level of relevance to us is the cybernetic system. The cybernetic system is capable of self-regulation, for which the example of the thermostat is most commonly used (see below). Systems theory has been the foundation for much of the theory of management accounting control systems as well as non-financial performance measurement (see later in this chapter).

Systems theory emphasises the importance of hierarchy in complex systems. Systems are composed of multiple sub-systems. For example, organisations are complex systems broken up into strategic business units, divisions, geographic areas, departments and teams. Sub-systems may also exist for different aspects of business activity such as purchasing, production, distribution, administration.

2.4 Environmental change

Organisations exist in an environment of markets for products and services where resource suppliers, producers and customers meet. However, the environment is also composed of political, economic, technological, environmental, and social and cultural factors that organisations must consider. It is from the environment that much of the risk facing organisations emerges.

Systems theory separates the organisation from its environment. These boundaries are not always clear as organisations carry out a lot of boundary-spanning activity such as market research, lobbying with government, benchmarking with competitors, working with community groups, all at least to some extent aimed at reducing risk.

The environment presents opportunities as well as risks, a subject that we describe in more detail in the chapter on risk and risk management. However, the unpredictability of the organisation's environment leads to management introducing a set of controls, in order to respond to organisational risk (including taking advantage of opportunities) and achieve organisational purposes.

2.5 Open and closed systems

A closed system is a set of inter-related components that is separate from its environment. An example of a simple control system is the room thermostat which contains a number of components:

- A measurement device to detect the room temperature.
- A target temperature that has been pre-set as the comfortable level that is desired by the occupants.
- A mechanism by which the room temperature can be adjusted, either by cooling or heating to achieve the target temperature.

The 'dumb' thermostat is a closed system of inter-related components.

Open systems are capable of self-regulation when they have more than one part and contain a programme. In simple terms, a programme is pre-determined information that guides subsequent behaviour. A programme exercises control through the processing of information and decision-making.

The key component in maintaining a comfortable room temperature is the programme that enables self-regulation. The thermostat becomes an open system when it is capable of being programmed by a person, who sets (and may re-set) the desired temperature level.

However, that person is not part of the control system. We can call that person the 'controller' as s/he makes decisions about the desired temperature level (the target).

Organisations are open systems composed of sub-systems of interdependent activities which may be tightly or loosely linked together but are bound by goal-orientation and formalisation of structure.

2.6 Organisational control

An organisation as a cybernetic system contains three levels:

1. *Target-setting level*: Targets and performance standards are set in response to environmental demands and constraints, such as customer demand for products and services. The goals are sent to the operations level.
2. *Operations level*: Where inputs (money, materials, labour, etc.) are converted into outputs (products and services).
3. *Control level*: Which monitors the outputs and compares them with the targets and performance standards established at the target-setting level.

2.6.1 Target-setting

Organisations establish targets in order to achieve their goals and objectives. These targets for a business organisation will typically be related to the achievement of shareholder value or a financial measure such as Economic Value Added (EVA™), Return on Investment (ROI) or Return on Capital Employed (ROCE). These financial targets will usually be reflected in budgets and standard costs.

Other targets may be set which are non-financial, such as market share, customer satisfaction, productivity. In addition, various performance standards may be established such as on-time delivery, product quality, employee morale, investment in research and development. Non-financial performance measures may be established and reflected in a measurement tool such as the Balanced Scorecard (see Chapter 3).

2.6.2 Operations

The operation of a business is concerned with converting inputs into outputs as shown in Figure 2.1.

Inputs are all the resources that go into the business: money; raw materials; labour; skills, technology and expertise; information; etc.

Processes are the activities carried out to convert inputs into outputs. The aim of these processes is to add value to the inputs. These processes will vary as to whether an organisation is a service provider, retailer or manufacturer. The processes variously include purchasing, storage, materials handling, manufacturing, service delivery, information processing, distribution, etc.

Figure 2.1 Input–process–output model

Outputs are the finished products or services that are sold and delivered to customers. The price charged to customers for the outputs must exceed the cost of the inputs and the cost of processing if the business is to make a profit.

The same principle applies to public sector and not-for-profit organisations, the only difference is that the conversion process does not result in a profit but in the expenditure of the least possible amount of money to achieve the best possible circumstances, an approach called 'value for money' or 'best value'.

2.6.3 Control

Control may be carried out through:

- a system in which there is provision for corrective action applying either a feedback or feed forward process; or
- a system which includes no provision for corrective action, as no human action is involved.

An example of a closed loop system is an inventory control system that enables management action such as the ordering of needed stock and the identification of surplus stock. An open loop example would provide inventory records which were not used for ordering. We typically refer to organisational controls in the context of closed loop systems.

A control is a method of ensuring that targets are achieved and performance standards attained. Control as it is used in the context of a 'control system' is the power of directing or restraining; a means of regulation; a standard or comparison for checking.

This type of control is a cybernetic system because goals exist and the control system is aimed at reducing deviations. However, feedback and feed forward processes do not work for non-cybernetic systems, because objectives are ambiguous, outputs not measurable or the effects of interventions unknown. Consequently, non-cybernetic control is through intuition, judgement and the exercise of power and influence (see later in this chapter).

2.7 Corrective action

In the cybernetic system, variations between targets and actual achievements are detected and result in corrective action, either through feedback or feed forward processes.

2.7.1 Feedback

> Feedback control is the measurement of differences between planned outputs and actual outputs achieved, and the modification of subsequent action and/or plans to achieve future required results (CIMA *Official Terminology*). Feedback typically takes place through comparing actual with standard costs, and actual performance with budget. In non-financial performance measurement, targets and actual performance are compared. In both cases, corrective action is taken after the event.

Positive feedback refers to a deviation from target that has a positive impact on the organisation, for example, a higher than expected income, which does not require corrective action, although it can lead to valuable learning so that it can be repeated.

Negative feedback refers to a deviation from target that is detrimental to the organisation, with corrective action being required to meet the target, for example, an overspend on an expense budget.

Double loop (or secondary) feedback indicates that it is the target that is incorrect rather than behaviour. Corrective action is to the plan, for example, where standard costs need to be adjusted to reflect changes in purchasing prices or working methods.

2.7.2 Feed forward

 Feed forward control is the process of forecasting differences between actual and planned outcomes, and the implementation of action, before the event, to avoid such differences (CIMA *Official Terminology*). Feed forward can take place during the budget process when forecasts – prior to approval – are reviewed as to whether they will contribute to organisational objectives.

2.7.3 Standards for control

There are five major standards against which performance can be compared:

1. Previous time periods
2. Similar organisations
3. Estimates of future organisational performance *ex ante*
4. Estimates of what might have been achieved *ex post*
5. The performance necessary to achieve defined goals.

Performance can only be judged against a standard and it is important to understand what the standard is against which performance will be judged.

2.8 Management control

Within organisations, the control of operations through target setting, operation and control involving feedback and feed forward processes using standards of comparison is referred to as a management control system. This is a cybernetic model of control; however, there are other perspectives through which we can understand management control, and these are described later in this chapter, and in the next chapter.

To begin, some definitions from CIMA's *Official Terminology* are relevant here:

Control is:

The ability to direct the financial and operating policies of an entity with a view to gaining economic benefits from its activities.

Management control is:

All of the processes used by managers to ensure that organisational goals are achieved and procedures adhered to, and that the organisation responds appropriately to changes in its environment.

> Control environment is:
>
> The overall attitude, awareness and actions of directors and management regarding internal controls and their importance to the entity … [it] encompasses the management style, and corporate culture and values shared by all employees. It provides a background against which the various other controls are operated.
>
> Control procedures:
>
> Those policies and procedures in addition to the control environment which are established to achieve the entity's specific objectives.

There are some important aspects of control that can be derived from these definitions:

- Control is not limited to financial control but extends to operational and other forms of control.
- Control is linked to goals and environmental change.
- Control is a set of procedures, but also a set of values or attitudes which need to be embedded in the culture of the organisation.

An appreciation of control in its broadest sense is essential in understanding the subject matter of the *Performance Strategy* syllabus.

2.8.1 Anthony's theory of control

In his seminal work on the subject, Anthony (1965) defined management control as:

The process by which managers assure that resources are obtained and used effectively and efficiently in the accomplishment of the organization's objectives.

Anthony's (1965) classic categorisation of control was at three levels: strategic, management and operational, which he saw as linked.

1. *Strategic control* exists at the board and chief executive level. This level is linked with the control environment. It includes strategic planning, governance procedures, determining the organisation structure, corporate policies and monitoring. Strategic control involves environmental information such as competitor analysis, market trends, economic forecasts and calculations of customer or product/service profitability. Information is high level financial information emphasising shareholder value measures and some key non-financial performance data.
2. *Management control* takes place at the middle management level. It is concerned with implementing strategy and procedures and monitoring performance to ensure it is consistent with strategy and achieves performance targets. It is concerned with the effective use of resources and the efficiency with which objectives are achieved. Control is exercised via responsibility centres through management accounting (typically budget reports) and non-financial information systems (see Chapter 3) which are aggregated at the responsibility centre level.
3. *Operational control* takes place at the task level of day-to-day activity, where structured and repetitive activities take place. Control is via short-term data such as workloads, volume of processing and output data. Information will be detailed and summarised in non-financial terms, emphasising volume, productivity and capacity utilisation.

In Anthony's work, management control was seen as the interface between strategic planning and operational control such that management control ensured that day-to-day operations were consistent with overall strategy and that strategy was implemented through day-to-day activities.

2.8.2 Otley and Berry's model of control

Otley and Berry (1980) defined management control as monitoring activities and then taking action in order to ensure that desired ends are attained. They developed their model of a management control system as a cybernetic control process that involved four conditions:

1. The existence of an objective which is desired.
2. A means of measuring process outputs in terms of this objective.
3. The ability to predict the effect of potential control actions.
4. The ability to take actions to reduce deviations from the objective.

Their model is shown in Figure 2.2.

The input–process–output model shown in Figure 2.1 has been included within Figure 2.2; however, there are now some additional elements:

- A predictive model of the process, which is the set of assumptions held about the cause–effect, input–output or action–outcome relationships that are contained within the business model underlying how every business works.
- Outputs are compared with objectives (targets and performance standards): this is the performance gap.
- A mis-match between expectation and achievement leads to the evaluation of alternative courses of action to bring achievement in line with expectation.
- The preferred corrective action is implemented.

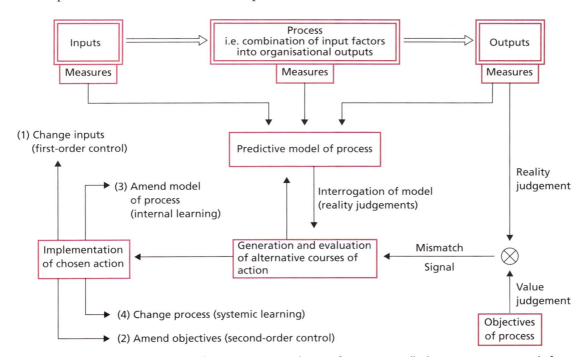

Figure 2.2 Outline scheme of necessary conditions for a controlled process (Reprinted from Accounting, Organizations and Society, Vol. 5, No. 2, D.T. Otley & A.J. Berry, Control, organization and accounting, pp. 231–44, Copyright 1980, Elsevier Science)

The corrective action could result in any of:

- a change to the inputs (first order control) which causes behaviour to alter;
- a change in the objectives or the standards to be attained (second order control);
- amending the predictive model (internal learning) on the basis of past experience and the measurement and communication processes associated with it;
- changing the nature of the system itself inputs, outputs and predictive models (systemic learning).

However, there are practical problems in the management control model, as Otley and Berry (1980) recognised:

Organizational objectives are often vague, ambiguous and change with time … measures of achievement are possible only in correspondingly vague and often subjective terms … predictive models of organizational behaviour are partial and unreliable, and … different models may be held by different participants … the ability to act is highly constrained for most groups of participants, including the so-called 'controllers'.

2.8.3 Simon's strategy, control and learning

Simons (1990) developed a model of the relationship between strategy, control systems and organisational learning in order to reduce strategic uncertainty. The model is reproduced in Figure 2.3. Simons argued that management control systems were the methods by which information could be used to maintain or alter patterns in organisational activity. His research suggested that management control systems could be used to learn and then use that learning to influence strategy. Management has limited time and capacity to process all available information. Simons found that the choice by top managers to make certain control systems interactive provided signals to organisational participants about what should be monitored and where new ideas should be proposed and tested. Programmed or automated management controls could be differentiated from 'interactive' controls, that is, those which top managers used to actively monitor and intervene in the decisions of subordinates. This signal activated organisational learning.

Simons' model can be summarised as:

- The intended business strategy creates strategic uncertainties that top managers monitor.
- Top managers make selected control systems interactive to personally monitor the strategic uncertainties.
- The choice to make certain control systems interactive (while programming others) provides signals to organisational participants about what should be monitored and where new ideas should be proposed and tested.
- This signal activates organisational learning and through interactive management control, new strategies emerge.

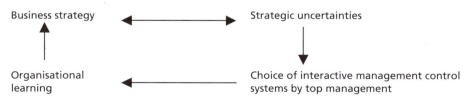

Figure 2.3 Process model of relationship between business strategy and management control systems (Reprinted from Accounting, Organizations and Society, Vol. 15, No. 1/2, R. Simons, The role of management control systems in creating competitive advantage, pp. 127–43, Copyright 1980, Elsevier Science)

2.9 Organisational structure

Organisations operate through a variety of organisational forms. The form of structure that is adopted (functional, divisionalised, matrix, network) will determine the type of control exercised over operational management. This will be reflected in reporting relationships in an organisation chart. Emmanuel et al. (1990) described organisational structure as:

A potent form of control because, by arranging people in a hierarchy with defined patterns of authority and responsibility, a great deal of their behaviour can be influenced or even pre-determined.

The influential business histories written by Chandler (1962, 1990) demonstrated that structure follows strategy. Galbraith and Nathanson (1976) suggested that the choice of organisational form was the result of choices about five design variables: task, people, structure, reward systems and information and decision processes. These choices need to be consistent with the firm's product-market strategy, that is, there should be 'fit' or 'congruence' between them.

2.9.1 Functional structure

The functional structure (sometimes called the U-form or unitary organisation) locates decision-making at the top of the organisational hierarchy, with functional responsibilities for marketing, operations, human resources, finance, etc., allocated to departments. In the functional structure, departments must communicate with each other and find mechanisms for co-operation. Control is largely top-down as decisions must be referred up the organisational hierarchy from the departmental to corporate level and down again.

In the functional structure, service departments such as accounting provide a staff function to the line functions, those concerned with the marketing, production and distribution of products and services. Accounting knowledge tends to be centralised in the accounting department, which collects, produces, reports and analyses accounting information on behalf of its (internal) customer departments.

The functional structure may be suitable for smaller organisations with a narrow geographic spread and a limited product/service range, but it is not generally suitable for larger organisations.

2.9.2 Divisionalised structure

The divisional structure (sometimes called the M-form or multidivisional organisation) is based on a head office with corporate specialists supporting the chief executive, with divisions established for major elements of the business. These divisions may be based on geographic territories or different products or services. Each division will typically have responsibility for all the functional areas: marketing, operations, human resources and accounting. In the divisionalised structure, operational control is located in each division, subject to the overall strategy and management controls imposed by head office.

Divisionalisation makes it easier for a company to diversify, while retaining overall strategic direction and control. Performance improvement is encouraged by assigning individual responsibility for divisional performance, typically linked to executive remuneration (bonuses, profit-sharing, share options, etc.).

The advantage of the divisional structure is that while planning is centrally co-ordinated, the implementation of plans, decision-making and control are devolved to local management who should have a better understanding of their local operations. The divisions are often referred to as 'strategic business units' to describe their devolved responsibility for a segment of the business. These business units are, in accounting, termed responsibility centres.

2.9.3 Matrix structures

Matrix structures are a combination of functional and divisional forms, with dual reporting to a functional manager as well as a product or service group manager. A matrix structure may be appropriate when an organisation has a wide geographic spread (and hence is organised along country lines) but where co-ordination of product development, marketing, production and distribution needs to take place on a global basis.

2.9.4 Network structures

Networks comprise partnerships or collaborations of organisations with different ownership, but who agree to co-operate in pursuit of common business goals. Examples include partnerships between retailers and logistics suppliers or between organisations and their outsourced IT functions. Networks emerge from the pursuit of core competence and the desire to work with other specialist organisations who can provide the technology and skills for support services.

2.10 Responsibility centres

Decentralisation implies the devolution of authority to make decisions. Divisionalisation adds to decentralisation the concept of delegated profit responsibility. Departments (in a functional structure) or divisions (in a divisionalised structure) are established for accounting purposes as responsibility centres.

Responsibility centres, through their managers, are accountable for achieving certain standards of performance. There are three main types of responsibility centres:

1. *Cost centres*: which are responsible for controlling costs.
2. *Profit centres*: which are responsible for achieving profit targets.
3. *Investment centres:* which are responsible for achieving an adequate return on the capital invested in the division.

 Financial control in divisionalised businesses is

the control of divisional performance by setting a range of targets and the monitoring of actual performance towards these targets (CIMA *Official Terminology*)

Management within each division (responsibility centre) will carry out a significant function in analysing and interpreting financial information, typically supported by locally based accounting support staff. Accounting influences, and is influenced by, the structure adopted and the extent of managerial responsibility for business unit performance.

One of the earliest writers on divisional performance, Solomons (1965), highlighted three purposes for financial reporting at a divisional level:

1. to guide divisional managers in making decisions;
2. to guide top management in making decisions;
3. to enable top management to appraise the performance of divisional management.

2.11   Divisional performance management

The most common accounting measures of divisional performance are return on investment (for profit centres) and residual income (for investment centres).

At divisional level, management control ensures that the division is efficient and effective. Controls will include:

- Departmental budgets
- Production planning or capacity utilisation systems
- Staff appraisals
- Financial and operational controls, (e.g. credit control, stock control).

At corporate level, the aim is to ensure that divisions help to contribute to corporate goals. Controls will include:

- Measures of financial performance (e.g. profits, cash flow, return on investment, residual income)
- Strategic planning systems
- Human resource controls (e.g. meetings, management development, corporate culture).

The appraisal of divisional performance should take place in accordance with the principle of controllability.

2.12   Controllability

The principle of controllability according to Merchant (1987) is that individuals should only be held accountable for the results they can control. One of the limitations of operating profit as a measure of divisional performance is the inclusion of costs over which the divisional manager has no control. The need for the company as a whole to make a profit often demands that corporate costs be allocated to divisions so that these costs can be recovered in the prices charged. However, research by Merchant concluded that the controllability principle was not found in practice.

One of the particular control problems for organisations is a result of the transfer pricing problem whereby divisions sell their intermediate products or services internally within the organisation. The price at which the transfer takes place may be dysfunctional for particular divisions or for the organisation as a whole. Care needs to be exercised when holding managers accountable for results that are heavily influenced by internal transfer prices.

However, there are problems with divisionalised performance evaluation. Roberts and Scapens (1985) have argued that in a divisionalised company there is distance between the division and the head office such that the context in which accounting information is gathered (the division) will often be quite different from the context in which it is interpreted (the head office). This may result in manipulating the accounting reports or in a partial or misleading portrayal of divisional performance.

2.13   A broader perspective on management control

Management controls the behaviour of people within the organisation through a variety of mechanisms. Many studies have recognised that a management control system consists of the formal, information-based and procedure-driven elements of control plus the informal elements of control based on social relationships.

Ouchi (1977) argued that there are only two forms of control because only two things can be observed: behaviour and the outputs that result from behaviour. Ouchi further argued that there were three mechanisms for control:

1. the *market* in which prices convey the information necessary for decisions;
2. *bureaucracy*, characterised by rules and supervision;
3. an informal social mechanism, called a *clan* which operates through socialisation processes which may result in the formation of an organisational culture.

Management control is also a reflection of the power held by one group in the organisation over another. Typically this is the management hierarchy; however, there are different types of power. In some organisations, accountants dominate structures of power, in others it is engineers and in others marketing and sales people.

Controls can be understood as falling within three broad categories:

1. Financial controls
2. Non-financial quantitative controls
3. Non-financial qualitative controls.

While financial controls express financial targets and spending limits and non-financial quantitative controls present a 'Balanced Scorecard' of customer, process and innovation targets, the day-to-day control of most employees is through a preponderance of qualitative controls. Employees are subject to formal and informal processes by which they are recruited, trained and socialised into the organisation. Supervision and management, underscored by financial and non-financial targets and constraints, will aim to influence people's behaviour by formal rules such as organisation charts, policies and procedures, reinforced by performance appraisal, rewards (remuneration and promotion), disciplinary measures as well as by informal methods represented in organisational or departmental cultures and accepted ways of doing things, reinforced by the relative power of different people and groups within the organisation.

2.13.1 Financial controls

 Internal financial controls are established:

to provide reasonable assurance of:

- the safeguarding of assets against unauthorised use or disposition;
- the maintenance of proper accounting records and the reliability of financial information used within the business or for publication. (CIMA *Official Terminology*)

Budgets are one of the most visible forms of control. Budgets are established in line with strategy and a view can be taken for each budget year as to whether the budget will contribute to achieving the strategy (feed forward). Budgets hold managers accountable for achieving financial targets (revenue, cost, profit, return on investment, etc.). Managers must explain variances between actual and budget performance (feedback). Management style will influence the level and extent of budgetary control. The use of budgets, standard costs and variance analysis, and the limitations of these as controls will be discussed at length in Chapter 3.

Financial control dominates the thinking of accountants because of their association with financial reporting and audit, but Johnson and Kaplan (1987) in their influential book *Relevance Lost: The Rise and Fall of Management Accounting* argued that non-financial measures were better predictors of long-term profitability and that more operational measures of performance were the origin of management accounting systems. Kaplan with Norton went on to develop the Balanced Scorecard while Kaplan with Cooper were instrumental in the early development of activity-based costing.

Accounting controls are discussed in the next chapter.

2.13.2   Non-financial quantitative controls

Non-financial measurement is increasingly common in most organisations. These are typically methods by which performance can be measured and monitored in order to achieve improvement in financial results.

Given the limitations of financial reports, performance measurement through a *Balanced Scorecard*-type approach (Kaplan and Norton, 2001) has become increasingly popular. Targets are set to cover a variety of aspects of business performance (in the Balanced Scorecard, measures cover customer, internal business process, and learning and growth dimensions as well as the more traditional financial measures). As for all systems of internal control, it is important to set targets, measure actual results, compare actual results with target and take corrective action. Performance may then be judged relative to

Improvements over time (i.e. trend);

Achievement of targets;

Benchmark comparisons with world-class organisations, competitors or industry averages.

Although these are beyond the cope of this syllabus, students should recognise:

- Balanced Scorecard – or a similar non-financial performance measurement system
- Activity-Based Management – both costing and budgeting
- Total Quality Management – whether through a sophisticated system such as Six Sigma or by recognising the cost of quality or through the ISO 9000 generic standards or a system such as the European Foundation for Quality Management (EFQM) Business Excellence model.

Non-financial performance *management* (which can be contrasted with performance *measurement*) requires accountants to have a better understanding of the operational activities of the business and build this understanding into control systems design; target setting; connecting control systems with business strategy and focusing on the external environment within which the business operates. The basic principles of control (whether financial or non-financial) are described through this Chapter.

The maxim 'what gets measured gets done' is true of both financial and non-financial performance evaluation, and hence both are powerful forms of control. However, these two broad categories of control need to be considered in more detail through the variety of forms of control that are available to organisations.

Johnson and Kaplan (1987) also criticised the excessive focus on financial performance measures. The limitations of financial measures are largely due to their focus on short-term financial performance. Financial measures are usually recognised as lagging indicators, they inform us about performance after it has happened. By contrast, non-financial measures (which are quantitative but expressed in non-monetary terms) are leading indicators of performance. They inform us about what is happening now in the business, and give a good indication of what the likely future financial performance will be.

Non-financial indicators can provide better targets and predictors for the firm's long-term profitability goals. These targets can be used effectively for control purposes, through feedback and feed forward processes. As well as monitoring target achievement, indicators can also be shown as trends, to determine whether performance is improving or deteriorating over longer time periods than is usually disclosed in financial reports. Finally, non-financial indicators can be benchmarked to internationally-recognised 'best practice', to competitor organisations and to industry averages. This is to some extent a return to the operations-based measures that were the origin of management accounting systems.

Examples of non-financial performance measurement include performance on research and development, marketing and promotion, distribution, quality, production cycle time, waste, human resources and customer relations, all of which are vital to a company's long-term performance.

The development of the **Balanced Scorecard** by Kaplan and Norton has received extensive coverage in the business press and is perhaps the best known framework for non-financial indicators. It presents four different perspectives and complements traditional financial indicators with measures of performance for customers, internal processes and innovation/improvement. These measures are grounded in an organisation's strategic objectives and competitive demands. Kaplan and Norton (2001) argued that the Scorecard provided the ability to link a company's long-term strategy with its short-term actions, emphasising that meeting short-term financial targets should not constitute satisfactory performance when other measures indicate that the long-term strategy is either not working or not being implemented well. Kaplan and Norton did not specify particular measures, but argued that the measures chosen must be those that are relevant to each particular business, its strategy, competitive position, nature of industry, etc. Performance measures need to mirror operational complexity, but must be kept simple to be understood.

A further model which has been widely adopted is the 'Business Excellence' model developed by the European Foundation for Quality Management (EFQM). This is an integrated self-assessment tool comprising nine elements that are weighted and divided into two groups: results and enabling criteria. The results criteria are business results, people satisfaction, customer satisfaction and impact on society. The enablers are processes, people management, policy and strategy, resources and leadership.

The management control paradigm may still be dominated by management accounting and non-financial performance measurement is isolated from, rather than integrated with, management accounting. Research continues to show that most companies tend to make decisions primarily on financial monitors of performance. Boards, financiers and investors place overwhelming reliance on financial indicators such as profit, turnover, cash flow and return on capital. Managers tend to support the view that non-financial performance information should only be used internally.

There are dysfunctional consequences of non-financial performance measures. In his public sector study, Smith (1995) found the following unintended consequences of performance measurement:

- Tunnel vision: the emphasis on quantifiable data at the expense of qualitative data.
- Sub-optimisation: the pursuit of narrow local objectives at the expense of broader organisation-wide ones.
- Myopia: the short-term focus on performance may have longer term consequences.
- Measure fixation: an emphasis on measures rather than the underlying objective.
- Misrepresentation: the deliberate manipulation of data so that reported behaviour is different from actual behaviour.
- Misinterpretation: the way in which the performance measure is explained.
- Gaming: an employee can pursue a particular performance standard when that is what is expected of him/her, even though s/he knows that this is not in the organisation's best interests in terms of its strategy.
- Ossification: performance measurement can inhibit innovation and lead to paralysis of action.

2.13.3 Non-financial qualitative controls

There is a wide variety of non-financial qualitative controls. Some of these are:

- Formal structures
- Informal structures
- Rules, policies and procedures
- Physical controls
- Strategic plans
- Incentives and rewards
- Project management
- Personnel controls.

These controls influence behaviour by requiring certain policies and procedures or standard instructions to be implemented in order to ensure that behaviour is legally correct, co-ordinated and consistent throughout the organisation; linked to objectives; secure; efficient and effective; fair and equitable.

Formal structures

Formal structures are represented on an organisation chart, reflecting the reporting relationships in an organisation: who is responsible for what, who reports to whom, etc. The organisational hierarchy will make plans, stipulate priorities, determine decisions and resource allocations, all of which will flow down through the management structure.

Control through formal structures takes place as part of day-to-day business activities, through supervision and management, reinforced by the power and authority of the supervisor or manager. This is evident in the assignment of work, meetings to discuss progress and managerial monitoring of the progress and completion of work and whether targets and milestones have been achieved.

Informal structures

Often allied with management style and culture, informal structures represent the 'hidden' organisation chart: those people with the power to influence and change what happens in the organisation. Informal or social methods may be used to control behaviour outside the normal channels. Informal structures may compete with or complement the formal organisation structure.

The organisation culture is particularly powerful in socialising individuals to particular values, norms and beliefs held by organisations, business units or departments (which is described in more detail in this chapter). A variation is the professional culture, which socialises, for example accountants, through their education and training. The culture is often most evident in discussions over a coffee or lunch, informal gossip and during after-work social events where the formal structures may be reinforced or eroded.

Rules, policies and procedures

These may come in a variety of guises: standing orders, manuals, standard operating procedures, job descriptions, policies, guidelines, codes of conduct, authority levels for spending, etc. By definition rules are written and guide behaviour, often in very prescriptive ways.

In all organisations, these rules dictate behaviour, by prescribing forms to be completed, procedures to be followed, etc. Failure to follow these rules often results in an organisational sanction: doing the work again, a reprimand, even dismissal where failure is repetitive.

Physical controls

Control may be exercised over physical access to buildings or rooms by security guards, computer access control systems, keys, computer passwords, CCTV surveillance, checking of bags of employees (especially in retail businesses).

Whereas other controls are dependent on compliance, physical controls absolutely prevent access through the erection of barriers.

Strategic plans

Strategy is an important element of control because it sets the organisation's longer- term vision through a focus for future action: by identifying objectives, assigning resources, implementing plans and policies, and providing a framework within which budgets are set are non-financial performance targets are established.

Strategy provides a powerful unifying device for an organisation's members, who are expected to be committed to common goals. Often, personal incentives are linked to achieving these imposed goals.

Incentives and rewards

If 'what gets measured gets done', then it is equally (or even more true) that 'what gets rewarded gets done'. While it has been common for sales people to receive commission for orders, organisations are increasingly rewarding managers and other employees through profit-related pay, bonuses and share options; and linking employee rewards to sustainable long-term performance through deferred compensation schemes. Such rewards may be based on profits, shareholder value or a combination of these.

Project management

Projects are a set of activities intended to accomplish a specified end result that is typically an important part of implementing strategy. Examples of projects are relocations, new computer systems implementation, new product launches, new production facilities, etc. Projects are self-contained and cannot be controlled through standard financial and non-financial performance reporting. The most common method of controlling projects is through three-way monitoring on project quality, cost and time. The first is established by comparing performance with a pre-determined standard, the second by comparing the project budget with actual spend, and the third by monitoring progress against predetermined milestone dates.

Personnel controls

Personnel controls cover the spectrum of recruitment, contracts of employment, induction, training, job design, promotion, coaching and mentoring, performance appraisal and remuneration. Personnel controls also cover disciplinary action against employees including dismissal procedures, a sanction of last resort.

The illusion of control

Marshall et al. (1996) suggested that failures of risk management in Barings, Kidder Peabody and Metallgesellschaft were due to dysfunctional culture, unmanaged organisational knowledge and ineffective controls. Marshall et al. (1996) argued that an emphasis on internal control systems was insufficient while they can provide information, decision-makers need knowledge to interpret that information, and an excess of controls can produce:

An illusion of control; hiding the very real risks that lie in those areas where much that is not quantifiable or constant must be factored into a decision (p. 90).

Berry et al. (2005) argued that the risk of control existed in two ways:

1. If controls are prescriptive, organisational participants may have less room to manoeuvre, leading to insufficient flexibility to cope with the unexpected.
2. The existence of controls may themselves lead managers to believe that risks are well controlled, and unforeseen circumstances may arise or opportunities may be missed.

2.14 Case study: low cost airlines

Before the introduction of low cost airlines, the business model for airlines was fairly similar, pricing reflected little competition and the only real differentiators between airlines were around reputation, largely a result of airline safety records. An early attempt to change the business model by Sir Freddie Laker (Laker Airlines) failed.

Applying the management control model to a conventional airline, first order control would be exercised through cost control over employment costs, fuel prices, the cost of acquiring aircraft, maintenance expenses, etc., and changing working conditions to improve efficiency, that is, through changing the inputs.

Where or not these controls improve performance, second order control can be exercised, typically through changing objectives or standards, such as varying prices, altering financial and non-financial targets.

Amending the predictive model is a form of learning from past experience. Certain routes are more profitable and some less profitable or unprofitable, so resources are shifted towards the more profitable routes. Learning leads to the introduction of yield management, or selling different seats at different discounted prices to fill capacity. The business model is therefore modified rather than being wholly changed.

Systemic learning is changing the nature of the system itself, comprising the inputs, outputs and predictive models. The introduction of low cost airlines such as EasyJet and Ryanair has changed the business model for airlines completely. Some of the changes introduced have been:

- Selling seats via the Internet rather than through travel agents.
- Yield management with variable prices depending on capacity utilisation.
- Using lower cost, out-of-town airports.
- No printed tickets, seat allocations, or free meals and drinks.
- No exceptions policies to reduce the cost of handling exceptions (e.g. no flexibility for passengers who arrive late).
- Fast turnaround times for aircraft to improve utilisation.

These changes have reduced costs (inputs); changed processes such as turnaround times and yield management for pricing; and the predictive model that perceived that customers would only book through travel agents, fly from central airports, demand seat allocations and meals, etc., has been dramatically altered.

EasyJet and Ryanair have focused on the short-haul market which has grown as a result of lower prices, rather than compete head-on with the major long-haul airlines. It is the latter market segment that has been significantly affected by the reduction in international travel over recent years. Consequently, the profit declines in the major airlines are contrasted with the generally successful performance of the low cost airlines, although in the last year even these airlines have begun to come under increasing competitive pressure from each other and Ryanair's financial performance has deteriorated.

2.15 Summary

- Systems theory emphasises the importance of hierarchy in complex systems but systems are composed of multiple sub-systems.
- The cybernetic system is capable of self-regulation, for which the example of the thermostat is most commonly used. In the cybernetic system, variations between targets and actual achievements are detected and result in corrective action, either through feedback or feed forward processes.
- Performance can only be judged against a standard (e.g. previous time periods, similar organisations, estimates of future organisational performance, estimates of what might have been achieved, and the performance necessary to achieve goals).
- Control is not limited to financial control but extends to operational and other forms of control; it is linked to goals and environmental change and it is a set of procedures, but also a set of values or attitudes which need to be embedded in the culture of the organisation.
- Anthony's categorisation of control was at three levels: strategic, management and operational.

- Otley and Berry defined management control in terms of the existence of an objective which is desired; a means of measuring process outputs in terms of this objective; the ability to predict the effect of potential control actions and the ability to take actions to reduce deviations from the objective. However, each of these had practical problems.
- Feedback and feed forward processes do not work for non-cybernetic systems, because objectives are ambiguous, outputs not measurable or the effects of interventions unknown. Consequently, control is through intuition, judgement and the exercise of power and influence.
- The form of structure that is adopted (functional, divisionalised, matrix, network) will follow strategy and determine the type of control exercised over operational management. Responsibility centres may be cost centres, profit centres or investment centres. The most common accounting measures of divisional performance are return on investment (for profit centres) and residual income (for investment centres).
- The appraisal of divisional performance should take place in accordance with the principle of controllability.
- There are different mechanisms by which management control can be exercised: market, bureaucracy and clan (Ouchi).
- Internal controls can be understood as falling within three broad categories: financial controls; non-financial quantitative controls and non-financial qualitative controls.
- Many examples are provided for accounting controls and non-financial qualitative controls in this chapter.
- Non-financial performance measures such as the Balanced Scorecard provide the ability to exercise management control through the monitoring of target achievement, improving trends and benchmarking to best practice, competitors or industry averages.
- Management accountants can have a significant role to play in developing and implementing risk management and internal control systems within their organisations.

References

Anthony, R.N. (1965), *Planning and Control Systems: A Framework for Analysis*. Boston, MA: Harvard Business School Press.

Berry, A.J., Collier, P.M., Helliar, C.V. (2005), Risk and control: the control of risk and the risk of control. In *Management Control: Theories, Issues and Performance*, ed. A.J. Berry, J. Broadbent, D. Otley, pp. 279–99. Basingstoke: Palgrave Macmillan.

Chandler, A.D.J. (1962), *Strategy and Structure: Chapters in the History of the American Industrial Enterprise*. Cambridge, MA: Harvard University Press.

Chandler, A.D.J. (1990), *Scale and Scope: The Dynamics of Industrial Capitalism*. Cambridge, MA: Harvard University Press.

Emmanuel, C., Otley, D. and Merchant, K. (1990), *Accounting for Management Control*. London: Chapman & Hall.

Galbraith, J.R. and Nathanson, D.A. (1976), *Strategy Implementation: The Role of Structure and Process*. St. Paul: West Publishing Company.

Johnson, H.T. and Kaplan, R.S. (1987), *Relevance Lost: The Rise and Fall of Management Accounting*. Boston, MA: Harvard Business School Press.

Kaplan, R. S. and Norton, D. P. (2001), *The Strategy-Focused Organization: How Balanced Scorecard Companies Thrive in the New Business Environment*. Boston, Mass.: Harvard Business School Press.

Marshall, C., Prusak, L. and Shpilberg, D. (1996), 'Financial Risk and the Need for Superior Knowledge Management.' *California Management Review*, Vol. 38, pp. 77–101.

Merchant, K.A. (1987), how and why firms disregard the controllability principle. In *Accounting and Management: Field Study Perspectives*, eds. W.J. Bruns and R.S. Kaplan. Boston, MA: Harvard Business School Press.

Otley, D.T. and Berry, A.J. (1980), 'Control, Organisation and Accounting'. *Accounting, Organizations and Society*, Vol. 5, pp. 231–44.

Ouchi, W.G. (1977), 'The Relationship between Organizational Structure and Organizational Control'. *Administrative Science Quarterly*, Vol. 22, pp. 95–113.

Roberts, J. and Scapens, R. (1985), 'Accounting Systems and Systems of Accountability – Understanding Accounting Practices in Their Organizational Contexts'. *Accounting, Organizations and Society*, Vol. 10, pp. 443–56.

Simons, R. (1990), 'The Role of Management Control Systems in Creating Competitive Advantage: New Perspectives'. *Accounting, Organizations and Society*, Vol. 15, pp. 127–43.

Smith, P. (1995), 'On the Unintended Consequences of Publishing Performance Data in the Public Sector.' *International Journal of Public Administration*, Vol. 18, pp. 277–310.

Solomons, D. (1965), *Divisional Performance: Measurement and Control*. Homewood, IL: Richard D. Irwin.

Revision Questions

2

❓ Question 1

The following question was the 50-mark case study in the pilot examination for Risk and Control Strategy.

Crashcarts IT Consultancy PLC is a £100 million turnover business listed on the stock exchange with a reputation for providing world class IT consultancy services to blue chip clients, predominantly in the retail sector. In 2000, Crashcarts acquired a new subsidiary for £2 million based on a P/E ratio of 8, which it renamed Crashcarts Call Centre. The call centre subsidiary leased all of its hardware, software and telecoms equipment over a 5-year term. The infrastructure provides the capacity to process 3 million orders and 10 million line items per annum. In addition, maintenance contracts were signed for the full 5-year period. These contracts include the provision of a daily backup facility in an off-site location.

Crashcarts Call Centre provides two major services for its clients. First, it holds databases, primarily for large retail chains' catalogue sales, connected in real time to clients' inventory control systems. Second, its call centre operation allows its client's customers to place orders by telephone. The real-time system determines whether there is stock available and, if so, a shipment is requested. The sophisticated technology in use by the call centre also incorporates a secure payment facility for credit and debit card payments, details of which are transferred to the retail stores' own computer system. The call centre charges each retail client a lump sum each year for the IT and communications infrastructure it provides. There is a 12-month contract in place for each client. In addition, Crashcarts earns a fixed sum for every order it processes, plus an additional amount for every line item. If items are not in stock, Crashcarts earns no processing fee.

Crashcarts Call Centre is staffed by call centre operators (there were 70 in 2001 and 80 in each of 2002 and 2003). In addition, a management team, training staff and administrative personnel are employed. Like other call centres, there is a high turnover of call centre operators (over 100% per annum) and this requires an almost continuous process of staff training and detailed supervision and monitoring.

A summary of Crashcarts Call Centre financial performance for the last 3 years:

	2001	*2002*	*2003*
Income			
Contract fixed fee	400,000	385,000	385,000
Order processing fees	2,500,000	3,025,000	3,450,000
Line item processing fees	600,000	480,000	390,000
Total income	£3,500,000	£3,890,000	£4,225,000
Expenses			
Office rent & expenses	200,000	205,000	210,000
Operator salaries & oncosts	1,550,000	1,920,000	2,180,000
Management, administration & training salaries	1,020,000	1,070,000	1,120,000
IT & telecoms lease & maintenance expenses	300,000	310,000	330,000
Other expenses	150,000	200,000	220,000
Total expenses	£3,220,000	£3,705,000	£4,060,000
Operating profit	£280,000	£185,000	£165,000

Non-financial performance information for the same period is as follows:

	2001	*2002*	*2003*
No. of incoming calls received	1,200,000	1,300,000	1,350,000
No. of orders processed	1,000,000	1,100,000	1,150,000
Order strike rate (orders/calls)	83.3%	84.6%	85.2%
No. of line items processed	3,000,000	3,200,000	3,250,000
Average no. of line items per order	3.0	2.9	2.8
No. of retail clients	8	7	7
Fixed contract income per client	£50,000	£55,000	£55,000
Income per order processed	£2.50	£2.75	£3.00
Income per line item processed	£0.20	£0.15	£0.12
Target number of orders per operator	15,000	15,000	15,000
Number of operators required	66.7	73.3	76.7
Actual number of operators employed	70.0	80.0	80.0

Requirements

NOTE: ALTHOUGH THE WHOLE QUESTION IS REPRODUCED HERE, STUDENTS OF P3 WILL ONLY BE ABLE TO ANSWER QUESTION (D) AT THIS TIME. HOWEVER, CANDIDATES SHOULD RETURN TO THIS QUESTION AFTER THEY HAVE STUDIED CHAPTER 5.

(a) Discuss the increase in importance of risk management to all companies (with an emphasis on listed ones) over the last few years and the role of management accountants in risk management. (**10 marks**)

(b) Advise the Crashcarts Call Centre on methods for analysing its risks. (**5 marks**)

(c) Apply appropriate methods to identify and quantify the major risks facing Crashcarts at both parent level and subsidiary level. (**20 marks**)

(d) Categorise the components of a management control system and recommend the main controls that would be appropriate for the Crashcarts Call Centre. (**15 marks**)

Total = 50 marks

Question 2 EasyJet

Read again the example of low cost airlines in this chapter (Section 2.14).

EasyJet, the low cost airline, floated on the stock exchange in late 2000, flying 30 aircraft to 19 destinations. EasyJet acquired Go in 2002 for £374 million to become Europe's largest low cost carrier.

	1998	1999	2000	2001	2002 incl. Go	2003 incl. Go
Passengers (m)	1.72	3.07	5.63	7.1	11.4	20.3
Passenger load factor (%)	71.9	76.2	81.5	81.5	84.8	84.1
Operating revenue (£m)	77	140	264	357	552	932
Pretax profit (£m)	5.9	1.3	22.1	40.1	72.0	52.0
No. of aircraft			30	32	35	68
Average fare					£46.37	£43.28

Low cost airlines have increased their share of the intra-European market from 2% in 1998 to 7% in 2001 and are expected to reach 14% by 2007. EasyJet's costs per available seat kilometre are 7.1p compared with 12.0p for the top three international flag carriers and 4.5p for Ryanair.

Requirements

(a) From the above information and your knowledge of low cost airlines (gained from personal experience or reading the business press), evaluate what you think are the sources of EasyJet's cost advantages.

(b) Recommend appropriate performance measures for EasyJet to use in its management control system.

(c) Evaluate the importance of shareholder value, culture and power for EasyJet.

Solutions to Revision Questions

2

NOTE: CANDIDATES WILL ONLY BE ABLE TO ANSWER QUESTION (D) AT THIS TIME. HOWEVER, CANDIDATES SHOULD RETURN TO THIS QUESTION AND THE SOLUTION AFTER THEY HAVE STUDIED CHAPTER 5.

✔ Solution 1

(d) Categorise the components of a management control system and recommend the main controls that would be appropriate for the Crashcarts Call Centre

Components of MCS

The main elements of an MCS are input, process, output, measurement, comparison to target, corrective action and predictive model (see diagram).

Necessary conditions for control

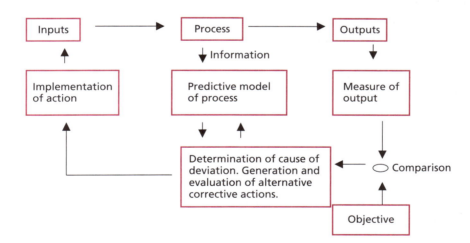

Source: Otley and Berry (1980)

Management control can be considered in relation to both feedback (taking corrective action *ex post*) and feed forward (taking action *ex ante*).

One feature of relevance to MCS design is the use of appropriate responsibility centres and the centralisation/decentralisation of responsibility to those centres. There is no information about the controls that the Group exercises over the subsidiary but the main board and the audit committee need to oversee the subsidiary's operations and performance.

Main controls:

As risks – or rather the causes of risk – should drive controls, the main elements of the control system in Crashcarts should include (but not be limited to):

- Number of clients (especially increases and potential losses).
- Non-financial performance, especially key performance statistics on calls received, orders and line items processed.
- Financial performance compared with target.
- Client contract performance, contract review and client satisfaction.
- Systems failure appears to be managed through maintenance agreements for all infrastructure, however supplier performance needs to be monitored.
- Employment procedures, training, performance appraisal and monitoring of staff to reduce staff turnover and improve morale.
- Strategic plan, budgets, targets, management reporting (financial and non-financial), expenditure authorisation.
- Insurance.
- Procedure manuals (e.g. access, password protection, data validation, virus protection, data back up, transaction audit trails and so on).
- Health and safety (e.g. fire safety, ergonomics, stress-related illness and so on).
- Use of risk consultants, internal audit, external audit.
- Reporting to the main boards' audit committee should take place.
- Embed risk management in culture.

☑ Solution 2 EasyJet

(a) Sources of EasyJet's cost advantages
- Lower general administration costs (e.g. no ticketing, no seat allocations)
- Direct sales, no third party reservation systems or travel agent commissions
- No free catering or in-flight amenities (therefore reduces costs)
- Cost reductions through avoidance of 'expectations' that incur overheads (e.g. unaccompanied children, pets, no flexibility with late check-ins)
- Lower crew costs (cabin crew staff and salary levels) and higher productivity (more hours flown)
- Lower airport costs through use of secondary airports
- Higher seat density (more seats per plane)
- Use of marginal pricing and yield management to maximise capacity utilisation
- Cheaper aircraft (EasyJet pitched Boeing and Airbus in a battle to be its supplier)
- Fast on-ground turnaround so greater utilisation of aircraft capacity (but less flexibility where delays occur).

(b) EasyJet's performance measures
- Control of fixed costs
- Average revenue (per route, per seat, per flight, etc.)
- Capacity utilisation (i.e. load factor)
- Turnaround time (double the daily use of BA aircraft)
- Each of the above by route (i.e. destination) which is the main profit centre
- Sales growth year on year
- Market share
- Number of passengers.

(c) Shareholder value, culture and power

- The listing of EasyJet in 2000 brought it into the shareholder value arena; prior to this Stelios Haji-Ioannou did not have to meet market expectations.
- Power is still exercised by Stelios as the single largest shareholder, although this is likely to be behind the scenes after his retirement as Chairman following stock market pressure for a more 'conventional' (to the City) chairman.
- Culture is customer oriented but a 'no exceptions' policy applies (see the television documentaries on EasyJet) and has a low cost focus throughout.

Accounting Controls

Accounting Controls

3

LEARNING OUTCOMES

After completing this chapter you should be able to:

▶ Evaluate appropriate control systems for the management of an organisation.

▶ Evaluate the appropriateness of an organisation's management accounting control systems.

▶ Evaluate the control of activities and resources within an organisation.

▶ Recommend ways in which identified weaknesses or problems associated with control systems can be avoided or solved.

3.1 Introduction

As for Chapter 2, we are mainly concerned here with section A of the *Performance Strategy* syllabus: Management Control Systems. The main purpose of Chapters 2 and 3 is to introduce students to the theory of management control. Whilst this section of the syllabus accounts for only 10% of the study weighting, the principles in this chapter underlie all the other chapters in the Learning System. In Chapter 2, we described management control systems generally. This chapter overviews the main accounting controls and overviews and critiques the main management accounting controls and evaluates lean accounting systems.

3.2 Accounting controls

Accounting controls are important in all organisations. They include control over:

- Cash
- Debtors
- Inventory

- Investments and intangibles
- Non-current assets
- Creditors
- Loans
- Income and expenses.

3.2.1 Cash

Cash controls ensure that:

- Monies received by the organisation are banked
- Bank accounts exist and are properly safeguarded
- Bank accounts, especially foreign accounts, are properly authorised
- Signatories for bank accounts are authorised and sufficient
- Payments are properly authorised
- Transfers between bank accounts are properly accounted for
- Adequate cash forecasting is carried out to ensure that commitments are recorded and overdraft limits are not exceeded.

3.2.2 Debtors

Debtor controls ensure that:

- Invoicing of customers is properly recorded in debtor accounts
- Money collected from customers are properly recorded in debtor records
- Bad debts are written off and adequate provision is made for doubtful debts
- Debtor accounts are regularly reconciled
- Appropriate credit checking procedures are in place
- Collection activity is ongoing and effective
- Credit notes and write-offs are properly authorised
- Investigations take place in relation to all disputed amounts with customers
- Customers verify the balances on their accounts.

3.2.3 Inventory

Inventory controls ensure that:

- Physical inventory is periodically checked by counting and compared with inventory records
- Inventory is valued in accordance with accounting principles
- Adequate procedures exist to record receipts of stock from suppliers and issue of stock to production/distribution
- Inventory is stored adequately to avoid loss and secured from theft and damage and that insurance cover is adequate
- Inventory is usable; obsolete, excess or damaged stock is identified for provisions and that authorisation is given prior to disposal of stock
- Adequate procedures exist to record stock in transit.

3.2.4 Investments and intangibles

Investment controls ensure that:

- There is physical evidence of ownership of investments and that this evidence is held in safe custody
- Periodic reviews are carried out of all investments to determine whether they should be retained or disposed of
- Investments are valued in accordance with accounting standards
- Acquisitions and disposals are properly authorised
- Income from investments is properly accounted for
- Charges for amortisation are appropriate and consistent with accounting standards.

3.2.5 Non-current assets

Non-current asset controls ensure that:

- Assets are recorded in an Assets Register
- Assets are periodically checked to ensure they exist
- Acquisitions and disposals are properly authorised
- Assets are secured as far as possible against theft, damage or misuse and appropriate insurance cover exists
- Assets are depreciated over reasonable periods of time and assets are valued in accordance with accounting standards
- Assets that are obsolete, worn out or damaged are identified for appropriate accounting treatment.

3.2.6 Creditors

Creditors' controls ensure that:

- Purchases are properly authorised
- Receipts of goods and services are in accordance with the purchase order
- Invoices received from suppliers are checked against the receipt of goods or services, the price and the invoice calculations
- Adequate documentation exists to support all invoices and invoices are authorised
- Invoices are properly recorded in creditor accounts
- Payments to suppliers are authorised and properly recorded in creditor accounts
- Creditor accounts are periodically reconciled
- Investigations take place in relation to all disputed amounts with suppliers.

3.2.7 Loans

Loan controls ensure that:

- Amounts owed are properly recorded
- Loans are properly authorised
- Interest obligations are satisfied
- Loan provisions are being met.

3.2.8 Income and expenses

Income and expense controls ensure that:

- Sales of goods and services are properly documented (invoice, cash receipt, etc.) immediately after the transaction occurs
- Costs are properly recorded and classified (e.g. expense, inventory, fixed asset, etc.)
- Income and expenses are matched and relate to the appropriate accounting period and accrual and prepayments, etc. are properly recorded to adjust between periods
- Expenses are properly authorised.

Specific controls may exist in relation to certain expenses, such as:

- Payroll
- Personnel-related expenses.

3.2.9 Payroll controls

- Employees have been properly recruited in accordance with Personnel/Human Resource policies, with adequate pre-employment checks being carried out
- New employees have been authorised by the appropriate department manager and the Personnel/Human Resource department
- Rates of pay are in accordance with Personnel/Human Resource policies
- Time worked is properly recorded
- Annual leave, sick or maternity leave, overtime, etc. are properly authorised
- Employees who terminate employment are removed from the payroll
- All employees on the payroll exist (payroll 'ghosts' are a common method of fraud)
- Payroll calculations are checked for calculation errors and unusually high (or low) payments before payment is made
- Payroll deductions are all properly authorised by employees
- Employee benefits (e.g. health fund) are properly authorised.

3.2.10 Personnel-related expenses

Many personnel incur expenses as part of their employment. These expenses include, but are not limited to:

- Use of motor vehicle (capital cost, often by lease payment; mileage; fuel; maintenance; accident damage; fines; etc.)
- Mobile telephone
- Office telephone, fax, email, Internet use
- Travel and accommodation
- Entertainment.

Such expenses may be paid personally by employees and then reimbursed by the organisation, or may be charged to the company by purchase order or by corporate credit card.
   All such expenses must be:

- Documented
- Authorised
- Necessary for business purposes
- Not private expenditure which the employee seeks to have paid for by the organisation.

Similarly, organisations need to establish policies and processes to recover business expenditure used for private purposes, for example, private mileage, use of business telephones for personal calls.

3.3 Management accounting controls

There are various management accounting tools by which control is exercised. Candidates will have studied these management accounting controls in previous subjects in the CIMA syllabus. However, the focus on accounting controls in this section is to reiterate the assumptions underlying these controls and the limitations inherent in their use.

The main management accounting controls which will be covered here are:

- Standard costing
- Capital investment appraisal
- Overhead allocation
- Transfer pricing
- Budgeting
- Budgetary control and variance analysis.

While these accounting controls are generally accepted by accountants, they can be criticised on a number of grounds. For example, standard costing assumes a static high volume manufacturing environment, something which is no longer an important feature of Western economies. Capital investment appraisal has techniques that are applied to often subjective 'guesses' of future cash flows. Overhead allocation involves assumptions that are often quite misleading for management decisions and transfer pricing can result in divisionalised businesses acting contrary to the corporate interest. Budgeting has been criticised as being overly constraining of action and variance analysis, like standard costs focus narrowly on costs rather than overall efficiencies.

3.3.1 Standard costing

Standard costing is a control technique which compares standard costs and revenues with actual results to obtain variances which are used to stimulate improved performance (CIMA *Official Terminology*).

The standard cost is the planned cost of the product/service produced in a period. Standard costs are typically based on a bill of materials (the components that go into a finished product) and a labour routing (the labour steps or processes that are used to produce a product or service). Standard costs are developed by considering past experience, known changes in technology or process improvements, and known changes in labour or supplier rates. Standard quantities are multiplied by standard costs to produce a standard cost per unit of product or service, which can then be compared with the actual cost (see variance analysis later in this chapter).

Traditional costing supports the traditional mass production model that seeks economies of scale to obtain the lowest unit cost of production. This leads to a highly automated factory capable of producing large production runs and profit follows from reducing the per unit cost. While this may be a reasonable proposition for large scale manufacturing, it does not work where production is geared around flexibility and customisation, which are increasingly evident in markets, or in service industries, where standard costs only apply to labour and again, do not reflect flexibility and customisation.

3.3.2 Capital investment appraisal

> Capital investment or capital expenditure means spending money now in the hope of getting it back later through future cash flows. Most investment appraisals consider decisions such as: whether or not to invest; whether to invest in one project or one piece of equipment rather than another; whether to invest now or at a later time.

There are three main methods of evaluating investments: accounting rate of return; payback and discounted cash flow (DCF). For any project, investment appraisal requires an estimation of future incremental cash flows, that is, the additional cash flow (net of income less expenses) that will result from the investment, as well as the cash outflow for the initial investment. Depreciation is of course an expense in arriving at profit which does not involve any cash flow. Cash flow is usually considered to be more important than accounting profit in investment appraisal because it is cash flow that drives shareholder value.

Despite the apparent sophistication of techniques (particularly DCF), capital investment decisions are often made subjectively and then justified after the event by the application of financial techniques. This is particularly so for emergent strategies, rather than planned or deliberate strategies. Despite the usefulness of these techniques, the assumption has been that future cash flows can be predicted with some accuracy. This is of course very difficult to do in practice and the assumptions behind estimated cash flows are very subjective.

3.3.3 Overhead allocation

> Overhead allocation is the process of spreading production overheads (i.e. those that cannot be traced directly to product/services) equitably over the volume of production. The overhead allocation problem is a significant issue as most businesses produce a range of product/services using multiple production processes.

The most common form of overhead allocation used by accountants has been to allocate overhead costs to product/services in proportion to direct labour or machine hours. However, this may not accurately reflect the resources consumed in production. For example, some processes may be resource intensive in terms of space, machinery, people or working capital. Some processes may be labour intensive while others use differing degrees of technology. The cost of labour, due to specialisation and market forces, may also vary between different processes. Further, the extent to which these products consume the (production and non-production) overhead of the firm can be quite different. The allocation problem can lead to overheads being arbitrarily allocated across different product/services, which can lead to misleading information about product/service profitability.

In their book *Relevance Lost*, Johnson and Kaplan (1987) emphasised the limitations of traditional management accounting systems which failed to provide accurate product costs. Management accounting, according to these writers, had failed to keep pace with new technology and had become subservient to the needs of external financial reporting. Johnson and Kaplan also argued against the focus on short-term reported profits and instead for short-term non-financial performance measures that were consistent with the firm's strategy and technologies.

In a later book, Kaplan and Cooper (1998) describe how activity-based cost (ABC) systems

emerged in the mid-1980s to meet the need for accurate information about the cost of resource demands by individual products, services, customers and channels. ABC systems enabled indirect and support expenses to be driven, first to activities and processes, and then to products, services, and customers. The systems gave managers a clearer picture of the economics of their operations (p. 3).

Activity-based costing is an attempt to identify a more accurate method of allocating overheads to product/services. Cost pools accumulate the cost of business processes, irrespective of the organisational structure of the business. The cost driver is the most significant cause of the activity and is used to measure each product's demand for activities. The actual cost pools and cost drivers used will be contingent on the circumstances of each business. Cross-subsidisation can be hidden in traditional methods (i.e. direct hours methods) of overhead allocation where a business sells a mixture of high-volume and low-volume product/services. The ABC method allocates costs based on cause-and-effect relationships, while the traditional direct hours method is based on an arbitrary allocation of overhead costs which assumes a relationship between direct hours and overhead incurrence.

However, ABC can be costly to implement because of the need to analyse business processes in detail; the collection of costs in cost pools as well as cost centres and the identification of cost drivers and the extent to which individual product/services consume resources. ABC also requires a computer system that accumulates costs vertically for cost/profit centre reporting, and horizontally for business processes.

3.3.4 Transfer pricing

When decentralised business units conduct business with each other, an important question is what price to charge for in-company transactions, as this affects the profitability of each business unit. However, transfer prices that are suitable for evaluating divisional performance may lead to divisions acting contrary to the corporate interest (Solomons, 1965). In practice, many organisations adopt negotiated prices in order to avoid demotivating effects on different business units. In some Japanese companies it is common to leave the profit with the manufacturing division, placing the onus on the marketing division to achieve better market prices.

The political process inherent in transfer pricing between divisions is also evidenced in many multi-national corporations, where transfer pricing is more concerned with how to shift profits between countries so as to minimise income taxes on profits and so maximise after-tax profits to increase shareholder value. While this is undoubtedly in the interests of individual companies and does need the approval of taxation authorities, it does raise issues of the ethics of transfer pricing when multi-nationals minimise their profits and taxation in relatively high tax countries such as the UK.

In the UK, transfer pricing rules have now been extended by the 2004 Finance Act from UK-foreign transactions to include transactions between entities in the UK. This means that transactions between UK companies must, for tax purposes, be conducted on an 'arm's length' basis, although smaller companies are partially exempt from the rules. This has an impact on reported profits of divisions of companies, whose profits may be affected (increased or decreased) by these taxation rules.

3.3.5 Budgeting

Emmanuel et al. (1990) identified three purposes of budgets: as forecasts of future events, as motivational targets and as standards for performance evaluation. They further noted four assumptions made in the budget process:

- Budget preparation followed the organisational pattern of authority and responsibility.
- The organisational structure determined whether responsibility centres were treated as cost, revenue, profit or investment centres.
- Budget preparation for production activities was based on standard costing.
- Budgets for profit centres required estimates of prices and quantities that depended on real market conditions.

Budgets provide a control mechanism through both the feed forward and feedback loops. In feed forward terms, budgets can be reviewed in advance, to ensure that they are consistent with organisational goals and strategy. If they do not contribute to goals, changes can be made to the budget before it is approved. Using feedback, variations between budget and actual performance can be investigated and monitored and corrective action taken for future time periods.

Although the tools of budgeting and cash forecasting are well developed and made easier by the widespread use of spreadsheet software, the difficulty of budgeting is in predicting the volume of sales for the business, especially the sales mix between different products or services and the timing of income and expenses.

There are however, problems with budgets that cause problems in its role as a control mechanism. For example:

- *Gaming*: Low targets are set because managers believe these will be readily achieved. They are consequently more the result of negotiation rather than of detailed planning.
- *Creative accounting*: Manipulating results so that targets are achieved, particularly where these are linked with performance bonuses.
- *Achievement motive*: Once targets are achieved, managers may no longer be motivated to continue their efforts, particularly as this may result in higher targets being set in the future.

Lowe and Shaw (1968) studied the process for sales budgeting in a retail chain. Three sources of forecasting error were identified: unpredicted changes in the environment (event related); inaccurate assessment of the effects of predicted changes (information related) and forecasting bias (human adjustment, event and information related). The sources of bias in estimation were found to be: the reward system; the influence of practice and norms and the insecurity of managers. Biasing was a common phenomenon due to 'the desire to please superiors in a competitive managerial hierarchy'.

One of the most common methods used by employees in the budgeting process is the creation of 'slack' resources, that is, asking for more than what is required. The practice of reducing budgets where they have not been spent has been a feature of both public and private sector organisations, and has led to managers spending their budget allocations at year end, whether the expenditure is needed or not, to avoid budget cuts in the following year. Similarly, managers bid for more budget resources than they need in the knowledge that their bid will be reduced by more senior managers. Budget expectations perceived to be unfair or exploitative are not internalised by employees and can lead to lower motivation and performance. The manipulation of data or its presentation to show performance in the best possible light is another common behaviour.

3.3.6 Budgetary control and variance analysis

> Variance analysis involves comparing actual performance against plan, investigating the causes of the variance and taking corrective action to ensure that targets are achieved. Variance analysis can be carried out for each responsibility centre, product/service and for each line item.

Flexible budgets provide a better basis for investigating variances than the original budget, because the volume of production may differ from that planned. If the actual activity level is different from that budgeted, comparing revenue and/or costs at different (actual and budget) levels of activity will produce meaningless figures. A flexible budget is a budget that is flexed, that is, standard costs per unit are applied to the actual level of business activity.

In the non-manufacturing sector, overheads form the dominant part of the cost of producing a service and so price and usage variance analysis has a limited role to play. However, organisations can use variance analysis in a number of ways to support their business strategy, most commonly by investigating the reasons for variations between budget and actual costs, even if those costs are independent of volume. These variations may identify poor budgeting practice, lack of cost control or variations in the usage or price of resources that may be outside a manager's control.

Standard costing, flexible budgeting and variance analysis can be criticised as tools of management because these methods emphasise variable costs in a manufacturing environment. While labour costs are typically a low proportion of manufacturing cost, material costs are typically high and variance analysis has a role to play in many manufacturing organisations.

However, even in manufacturing the introduction of new management techniques such as just-in-time is often not reflected in the design of the management accounting system. *Just-in-time (JIT)* aims to improve productivity and eliminate waste by obtaining manufacturing components in the right quality, at the right time and place to meet the demands of the manufacturing cycle. It requires close co-operation within the supply chain and is generally associated with continuous manufacturing processes with low inventory holdings, a result of eliminating buffer inventories – considered waste – between the different stages of manufacture. Many of these costs are hidden in a traditional cost accounting system. Variance analysis has less emphasis in a JIT environment because price variations are only one component of total cost. Variance analysis does not account, for example, for higher or lower investments in inventory.

3.4 Beyond Budgeting

Budgeting has continued to be criticised in recent years. It is argued that budgeting disempowers the front line, discourages information sharing, and slows the response to market developments. Hope and Fraser (2003) suggest that budgets should be replaced with a combination of financial and non-financial measures, with performance being judged against world-class benchmarks. Business units can also measure their performance against comparable units in the same organisation. This, it is argued, shifts the focus from short-term profits to improving competitive position year after year.

The Beyond Budgeting Round Table (http://www.bbrt.co.uk/) has identified 10 reasons why budgets cause problems. Budgets:

1. Are time consuming and expensive
2. Provide poor value to users
3. Fail to focus on shareholder value
4. Are too rigid and prevent fast response
5. Protect rather than reduce costs
6. Stifle product and strategy innovation
7. Focus on sales targets rather than customer satisfaction
8. Are divorced from strategy
9. Reinforce a dependency culture
10. Can lead to unethical behaviour.

Compared with the traditional management model, 'beyond budgeting' has two fundamental differences. First, it is a more adaptive way of managing. In place of fixed annual plans and budgets that tie managers to predetermined actions, targets are reviewed regularly and based on stretch goals linked to performance against world-class benchmarks and prior periods. Second, the 'beyond budgeting' model enables a more decentralised way of managing. In place of the traditional hierarchy and centralised leadership, it enables decision-making and performance accountability to be devolved to line managers and creates a self-managed working environment and a culture of personal responsibility. This leads to increased motivation, higher productivity and better customer service.

CIMA and ICAEW have produced a report on Better Budgeting (CIMA and ICAEW, 2004) following a round table discussion between practitioners and academics. Budgeting appeared to be alive and well in organisations, although they have undergone significant changes over the last 20 years, particularly with forecasting or high-level plans often seen as more important than detailed budgets. There has also been a shift from a top-down, centralised process to one that is more participative and bottom-up.

3.5 Case study: Svenska Handelsbanken

Source: **Jan Wallander, *Scandinavian Journal of Management*, 1999, pp. 405–21. © Elsevier Science.**

Jan Wallander is an executive director of Handelsbanken. He was appointed to the role when the bank, the largest commercial bank in Sweden, faced a crisis. Although at the time, Swedish banks did not use budgets, Handelsbanken had started to instal a sophisticated budgeting system.

Wallander (1999) was very critical of budgeting commenting:

You can make forecasts very complicated by putting a lot of variables into them and using sophisticated techniques for evaluating the time series you have observed and used in your work. However, if you see through all this technical paraphernalia you will find that there are a few basic assumptions which determine the outcome of the forecast (p. 408).

Wallander argued that there are two reasons to abandon budgeting:

1. If there is economic stability and the business will continue as usual, we use previous experience to budget. Therefore, we do not need an intricate budgeting system, because people will continue working as they presently are. Even when conditions are not normal, the expectation is that they will return to normal.
2. If events arise that challenge economic stability then budgets will not reflect this because we have no ability to foresee something of which we have no previous experience.

Wallander concluded that traditional budgeting is:

An outmoded way of controlling and steering a company. It is a cumbersome way of reaching conclusions which are either commonplace or wrong (p. 419).

Importantly, Wallander did not reject planning outright. He argued that it is important to have an 'economic model' which establishes the basic relationships in the company, such as the ability to plan production. He described this as the type of planning that is going on all the year round but that it had nothing to do with the annual budget.

Handelsbanken has an information system which is focused on the information needed to influence actual behaviour. It incorporates both financial and 'balanced scorecard' measures at the profit centre level, and performance is benchmarked externally and internally. The bank rewards its staff through a profit-sharing scheme. Despite its abandonment of budgeting, Handelsbanken remains a very successful bank. Wallander concluded that:

Abandoning budgeting, which was an essential part of the changes, had no adverse effect on the performance of the bank compared to other banks, which all installed budgeting systems during the period (p. 407).

3.6 The cost of quality

Quality is concerned with conformance to specification; ability to satisfy customer expectations and value for money. Recognising the cost of quality is important in terms of continuous improvement processes. The cost of quality is:

The difference between the actual costs of producing, selling and supporting products or services and the equivalents costs if there were no failures during production or usage (CIMA *Official Terminology*).

There are two broad categories of the cost of quality: conformance costs and non-conformance costs.

Conformance costs are those costs incurred to achieve the specified standard of quality and include *prevention costs* such as quality measurement and review, supplier review and quality training (i.e. the procedures required by an ISO 9000 quality management system). Costs of conformance also include the *costs of appraisal*: inspection or testing to ensure that products or services actually meet the quality standard.

The cost of *non-conformance* includes the cost of internal and external failure. The *cost of internal failure* is where a fault is identified by the business before the product/service reaches the customer, typically evidenced by the cost of waste or rework. The *cost of external failure* is identified after the product/service is in the hands of the customer. Typical costs are warranty claims, discounts and replacement costs.

Identifying the cost of quality is important to the continuous improvement process as substantial improvements to business performance can be achieved by investing in conformance and so avoiding the much larger costs usually associated with non-conformance.

3.7 Social and environmental costs

Corporate social and environmental reporting (CSR) attempts to highlight the impact of organisations on society. Until recently, there has been limited support for broader social accounting because accountants and managers have generally seen themselves as the agents of owners. Social reporting was seen as undermining the power of shareholders and the foundation of the capitalist economic system. There was a dominant belief among business leaders that government and not business has the responsibility to determine what is reported.

Recently, global warming has modified this attitude. Global warming is commonly associated with the poor use of technology and short-term management thinking. Reducing pollution and harmful carbon emissions through better technology will almost always lower cost or raise product value in the long term which will offset the cost of compliance with environmental standards, although doing so may require innovation. Carbon trading may be an advantage in forcing companies to address their level of emissions.

Part of the appeal of environmental accounting now is that issues of energy efficiency, recycling and reductions in packaging have cost-saving potential and therefore profits and social responsibility have come to be seen as not mutually exclusive.

Management accounting is concerned with recognising costs for decision-making. Environmental management accounting is concerned with collecting, measuring and reporting costs about the environmental impact of an organisation's activities. It is similar in principle to methods used for measuring quality costs. These costs can be broken down into four types:

1. Prevention costs, to avoid environmental damage. This could include the cost of equipment to reduce pollution and the training of employees.
2. Measurement costs, to determine the extent of the organisation's environmental impact. This could include testing, monitoring and external certification.
3. Internal failure costs, where remedial action has to be taken (e.g. cleaning up spillages or leakages, or employee health and safety-related damages).
4. External failure costs, such as penalties incurred for environmental damage.

Continuous environmental improvement is likely to result from an investment in preventive measures and measurement to enable corrective action, rather than in after-the-event remedying the cost of failure. Failure costs can involve substantial costs, both financial and reputational (e.g. the 1984 Bhopal chemical accident, the 1986 Chernobyl nuclear disaster, and the 1989 Exxon Valdez oil spillage off the Alaskan coast).

3.8 Emerging management accounting techniques

Several new techniques have been introduced to make management accounting more relevant to modern production methods. These include:

- Strategic management accounting
- Life cycle costing
- Target costing
- Kaizen.

3.8.1 Strategic management accounting

In their book *Relevance Lost*, Johnson and Kaplan (1987) argued that management accounting and control systems could not cope with the information demands of the new manufacturing environment and the increased importance of service industries. The notion of strategic management accounting (SMA) is linked with business strategy and maintaining or increasing competitive advantage.

The term strategic management accounting was coined by Simmonds (1981). Simmonds defined SMA as the provision and analysis of management accounting data about a business and its competitors which is of use in the development and monitoring of the strategy of that business. Simmonds argued that accounting should be more outward looking and help the firm evaluate its competitive position relative to its competitors by collecting and analysing data on costs, prices, sales volumes and market share, cash flows and resources for its main competitors. Simmonds emphasised the learning curve through early experience with new products that lead to cost reductions and lower prices. Bromwich (1990) suggested that SMA should consider product benefits and how the cost of providing these benefits related to the price the customer was willing to pay.

Lord (1996) summarised the characteristics of SMA:

- collection of competitor information: pricing, costs, volume, market share;
- exploitation of cost reduction opportunities: a focus on continuous improvement and on non-financial performance measures;
- matching the accounting emphasis with the firm's strategic position.

Lord (1996) argued that firms place more emphasis on particular accounting techniques depending on their strategic position. Dixon (1998) argued that strategy formulation and implementation

is carried out using the techniques and language of the management accountant. In turn, the strategic decision-making process can influence the procedures of management accounting and the design of management control systems (p. 273).

However, Lord (1996) questioned the role of accountants in strategic management accounting, arguing that firms successfully collect and use competitor information without any input from the management accountant. Dixon (1998) argued that

the costs of capturing, collating, interpreting and analysing the appropriate data out-weighs the benefits … [and] that the collection and use of competitor information for strategic purposes can be achieved without implementing a formal SMA process (p. 278).

Despite these conflicting views, organisations collect and analyse information that extends the traditional boundaries of management accounting information by:

- Looking beyond the accounting period of 12 months.
- Extending beyond the organisation to the whole supply chain to include suppliers and customers.
- Benchmarking performance with competitors.

The TNA case study provides a good example of how management accounting information can be used strategically.

3.8.2 Case study: TNA

TNA is a multinational but family-owned company that developed a new type of packaging machine for use by major food manufacturers. The design of the machine resulted in international patents and the company has captured a significant market share through the competitive advantage achieved by its technology and commitment to export market development, and research and development. The company outsourced the manufacture of its machines, although all final assembly of components and installation was carried out by TNA's staff. Annual sales have increased from $6 million in 1991 to $100 million in 2007.

Interestingly, the company did not appoint an accountant until 1998 when sales were $30 million. The owner found that he had little use for product costing or management accounts that were backward-looking. The company only used financial reporting for statutory purposes. The owner argued that traditional accounting was unhelpful because of the lumpiness of capital equipment sales in the industry (there may be no sales for 6 months and then an order for 20 machines from a single customer) and the extensive upfront research and development (R&D) and export market development costs the company incurred, often years in advance of sales being generated, making the annual accruals basis of accounting largely meaningless. The outsourced production cost of equipment was a relatively small proportion of the selling price, which was high given the superior operating characteristics of the TNA machine compared with its competitors. Non-financial measures were used minimally, with the main attention given to the number of units sold and market share. However, qualitative aspects were important, particularly customer satisfaction, product quality and continual innovation through R&D.

The main form of management control used by the owner was a spreadsheet model which the owner – an engineer – developed and maintained on a laptop computer which accompanied him on his frequent overseas travel to develop export markets and maintain customer satisfaction. Over a period of 10 years, the spreadsheet developed continually, but went through two major versions.

The first version of the spreadsheet, when the company was relatively small, was a cash-based accounting system that extended to production planning and cash forecasting. It was developed as a result of cash flow problems in the early years of the business. The spreadsheet contained the expected number of units sold, revenue (progress payments), purchases, operating expenses, capital expenditure, taxes, and loan repayments, all updated on at least a weekly basis. The spreadsheet also provided forecasted cash balances, inventory levels, unearned income (i.e. deposits taken against future deliveries), and forecast profit for tax purposes.

The spreadsheet had three functions. It was a historical record, recording what was achieved on a cash flow basis, updated from actual monthly sales and purchases. Second, it was a forecasting device, containing milestones. Enquiry and order status was continually monitored through regular communication with the company's overseas marketing offices. Cash flow needs were also identified. Third, it was a decision-making tool. The spreadsheet was updated with actual orders. This information was input to the build program (for the assembly of equipment) and component purchasing and was used in supplier negotiations.

As the company grew, increasing market share rather than cash flow became the focus of the owner's attention. A second version of the spreadsheet was then developed. This spreadsheet was industry focused, providing a top-down analysis of markets and competitors gained through 'marketing intelligence'. The spreadsheet contained estimates of the machine base by market segment, with market growth and anticipated customer replacement plans, adjusted by the relative performance of TNA's equipment compared with that of its competitors. The spreadsheet resulted in TNA targeting the customers of weaker competitors, many of whom manufactured their equipment in-house and had significant under-utilised capacity. The spreadsheet information also led to strategic developments in new products. The second version of the spreadsheet was an example of strategic management accounting.

Apart from these more formal controls, TNAs owner exercised a 'social control'. Through continual overseas travel and telephone contact with his offices 24/7 (at least one of the company's offices was always open across international time zones) the owner maintained close contact with employees, customers and suppliers. Social events were a regular part of the way the company did business, providing an opportunity for the owner to gain market knowledge, understand problems and at the same time communicate his strategy and expectations to his employees.

Even after the company employed an accountant, the owner's spreadsheet, together with his social control, were the main forms of management control used in the company. Traditional accounting was marginalised. Budgets were mainly cash-flow based with the only real targets being for sales. Monthly accounting reports were used only minimally, and then only for expense control. Costing was not used other than for financial reporting and negotiations with suppliers. TNA's owner developed a relevant management control system that was consistent with his own values and the unique circumstances of his business, one which continually developed over time in reaction to business circumstances.

A full copy of the research in relation to TNA is in Collier P M (2005) Entrepreneurial cognition and the construction of a relevant accounting. *Management Accounting Research*, Vol. 16, no. 3, pp. 321–39.

3.8.3 Life cycle costing

All products and services go through a typical life cycle, from introduction, through growth and maturity to decline. Over time, sales volume increases, then plateaus and eventually declines. Management accounting has traditionally focused on the period after product design and development, when the product/service is in production for sale to customers. However, the product design phase involves substantial costs that may not be taken into account in product/service costing. These costs may have been capitalised or treated as an expense in earlier years. Similarly, when product/services are discontinued, the costs of discontinuance are rarely identified as part of the product/service cost.

Life cycle costing estimates and accumulates the costs of a product/service over its entire life cycle, from inception to abandonment. This helps to determine whether the profits generated during the production phase cover all the life cycle costs. This information helps managers make decisions about future product/service development and the need for cost control during the development phase.

The design and development phase can determine up to 80% of costs in many advanced technology industries. This is because decisions about the production process and the technology investment required to support production are made long before the product/services are actually produced. Consequently, efforts to reduce costs during the production phase are unlikely to be successful when the costs are committed or locked-in as a result of technology and process decisions made during the design phase.

3.8.4 Target costing

> Target costing is concerned with managing whole of life costs *during the design phase*. The technique was developed in the Japanese automotive industry and is customer-oriented. Its aim is to build a product at a cost that could be recovered over the product life cycle through a price that customers would be willing to pay to obtain the benefits (which in turn drive the product cost).

Target costing has four stages:

1. Determining the target price which customers will be prepared to pay for the product/service.
2. Deducting a target profit margin to determine the target cost which becomes the cost to which the product/service should be engineered.
3. Estimating the actual cost of the product/service based on the current design.
4. Investigating ways of reducing the estimated cost to the target cost.

Target costing is equally applicable to a service. The design of an Internet banking service involves substantial upfront investment, the benefits of which must be recoverable in the selling price over the expected life cycle of the service.

3.8.5 Kaizen

> Kaizen is a Japanese term – literally 'tightening' – for making continuous, incremental improvements to the production process. While target costing is applied during the design phase, kaizen costing is applied during the production phase of the life cycle when large innovations may not be possible. Target costing focuses on the product/service. Kaizen focuses on the production process, seeking efficiencies in production, purchasing and distribution.

Like target costing, kaizen establishes a desired cost reduction target and relies on team work and employee empowerment to improve processes and reduce costs. This is because employees are assumed to have more expertise in the production process than managers. Frequently, cost reduction targets are set and producers work collaboratively with suppliers who often have cost reduction targets passed onto them.

The investigation of cost reduction is a cost-to-function analysis that examines the relationship between how much cost is spent on the primary functions of the product/service compared with secondary functions. This is consistent with the value chain approach of Porter (1985). Such an investigation is usually a team effort involving designers, purchasing, production/manufacturing, marketing and costing staff. The target cost is rarely achieved from the beginning of the manufacturing phase. Japanese manufacturers tend to take a long-term perspective on business and aim to achieve the target cost during the life cycle of the product.

3.9 Lean management accounting

The idea of lean management accounting has been developed out of lean manufacturing and in particular the work of Womack and Jones (2003) in their book *Lean Thinking*. Lean management accounting is about relevant accounting, performance measurement and control techniques to support lean manufacturing and sustain a lean enterprise.

Lean thinking is a development from some of the value chain principles of Porter (1985), the business process re-engineering approach of Hammer and Champy (1993) and *Relevance Lost* of Johnson and Kaplan (1987). It has five principles:

1. Value provided to customers is reflected in the price by using a target costing approach.
2. Value stream: managing the business through processes or value streams rather than traditional departmental structures.
3. Flow of products and services through the value stream while eliminating waste.
4. Pull to enable flow of products and services based on customer demand rather than push through production processes.
5. Perfection through quality improvement which is both continuous and breakthrough.

Lean thinking does not rely on benchmarking but savagely eliminates waste within value streams. The target is not comparison with other companies but how much waste can be eliminated.

Lean management accounting methods must also be lean and not contribute to waste. The problems of traditional costing systems in lean manufacturing are that it:

- provides no useful improvement information;
- is organised by departments rather than value streams;
- leads production to produce large batches and build inventories to reduce unit costs;
- hides waste in overhead;
- creates waste through detailed transaction recording systems.

Lean management accounting:

- Provides the value stream leader with performance measurement information to both control and improve the value stream.
- Provides information for performance measurement and cost reporting.
- Provides relevant cost information for financial reporting purposes.

Lean management accounting does not use sophisticated manufacturing resource planning systems or production scheduling and tracking but instead uses visual methods like kanbans. Instead of reporting detailed transactions for materials and labour as they occur backflushing is used. Backflush costing is:

> 🔑 A method of costing, associated with a JIT (Just in Time) production system, which applies cost to the output of a process. Costs do not mirror the flow of products through the production process, but are attached to output produced (finished goods stock and cost of sales), on the assumption that such backflushed costs are a realistic measure of the actual costs incurred (CIMA *Official Terminology*).

This is considered to be a reliable method in lean manufacturing because inventory movements are reduced to a minimum. The method of costing used is value stream direct costing, in which all costs incurred by the value stream are pooled and the product cost is the average cost of the value stream for the quantity produced for the period. This has similarities to process costing because the focus on production flow through the value stream begins to look like process manufacturing.

3.10 The changing role of management accountants

Management accounting is:

> 🔑 The application of the principles of accounting and financial management to create, protect, preserve and increase value so as to deliver that value to the stakeholders (CIMA *Official Terminology*).

Management accounting is concerned with information used in:

- Formulating business strategy
- Planning and controlling activities
- Decision-making
- Efficient resource usage
- Performance improvement and value enhancement
- Safeguarding tangible and intangible assets
- Corporate governance and internal control.

Consequently, either explicitly or implicitly, management accountants are involved in internal control mechanisms.

Chartered Institute of Management Accountants (1999) report on *Corporate Governance: History, Practice and Future* viewed the role of management accountants in corporate governance as providing the information to the chief executive and the board which allows their responsibilities to be effectively discharged.

A study of changing management accounting practice by Scapens et al. (2003) on *The Future Direction of UK Management Accounting Practice* identified a change in the way management accounting was being used in organisations, from a traditional monitoring and control perspective to a more business and support-oriented perspective.

The research by Scapens et al. identified how many routine management accounting tasks either were being done by computer systems or by small, specialist groups:

The challenge for the management accounting profession is to ensure that their members have the knowledge, skills and capabilities to take advantage of the opportunities that are undoubtedly there (p. ix).

Scapens et al. identified the changes in the business environment that have impacted on management accounting during the 1990s:

- Globalisation, increasing competition, volatile markets and the emergence of more customer-oriented companies.
- Technological change in production and information technology and the nature of work and information flows as a consequence of enterprise resource planning systems and personal computers.
- Changing organisational structures, such as demergers and focusing on core competencies and the outsourcing of non-core activities.
- The feeling in top management that change is necessary and the changing management information needs.

The impact on management accountants identified by the Scapens et al. research study have included:

- Database technologies have facilitated the storage of vast quantities of information that is easily accessible and analysable. Transaction processing and routine management information is now computerised in most organisations.
- Decentring of accounting knowledge to non-financial managers who need to be aware of the financial consequences of their decisions. Cost management is increasingly seen as a management rather than an accounting task.
- Budgets are increasingly being used as flexible rather than static plans, being updated with rolling forecasts by managers for performance monitoring purposes.

These factors have led to a shift in the 'ownership' of accounting reports, from accountants to business managers.

Scapens et al. argued that a key role for management accountants in the twenty-first century is:

Integrating different sources of information and explaining the interconnections between non-financial performance measures and management accounting information … because it enables individual managers to see the linkages between their day-to-day operations, how these operations are presented in the monthly management accounts, and how they link to the broader strategic concerns of the business as reflected in the non-financial measures (p.15).

The Scapens et al. research identified the diverse range of tasks in which management accountants are becoming proactively involved:

- assessment of the financial implications of operational decisions, including risk assessment;
- short-term tax considerations;
- assisting managers to make short-run profits on currency dealings;
- establishing new contracts;
- assisting in decisions over potential acquisitions and outsourcing decisions;
- supporting research and development decisions;
- assisting with regulatory issues.

Although Scapens et al. did not address the management accountant's role in risk management, each of the above areas is involved to a greater or lesser extent in identifying and managing risk. In an earlier study, Parker (2001) specifically noted the role of accountants in risk management.

CIMA's Fraud and Risk Management Working Group produced a guide to good practice in risk management (Chartered Institute of Management Accountants, 2002). The report argues that:

Management accountants, whose professional training includes the analysis of information and systems, performance and strategic management, can have a significant role to play in developing and implementing risk management and internal control systems within their organisations (p. 3–4).

3.11 The impact of changes in business practices on accounting controls

The desire to reduce waste, including non-productive accounting practices, brings into question some of the accounting controls that accountants have come to rely on.

Standard costing and variance analysis are criticised because in lean organisations, they reduce volumes produced to the level required by market demand, as inventory is considered wasteful. This results in negative variances (higher expenses) and higher per unit overhead allocations. This then impacts on selling prices (which should be higher) or profits (which will be lower if prices remain unchanged).

Traditional costing supports a mass production model relying on economies of scale, but mass production is in decline in Western economies, By contrast, lean production aims to make products one at a time to satisfy customer needs, generating profits by flowing increasing volumes of production through the resources. Whereas mass production relies on labour and machine utilisation, variance analysis and achieving budgets, lean production focuses on throughput, cycle time, quality, inventory turn and the value stream (rather than the department).

An important consequence of the changes described in this chapter:

- Changes to transfer pricing rules for tax purposes;
- Questions over the value of traditional budgeting processes and the increasing attention to 'Beyond Budgeting'; and
- The value of standard costing and variance analysis as a result of lean production approaches.

is that organisations may be unable to rely as much on budgeting, costing systems and management reporting systems as they once were.

The emergence of greater attention to longer-term approaches such as life cycle and target costing, and broader supply chain and competitor analyses encompassed by strategic management accounting may also influence the value of traditional accounting tools and encourage use of different approaches.

For students of *Performance Strategy*, the decline in use, or at least questioning, of some traditional accounting techniques has important implications for control purposes as accounting techniques may have a reduced role to play in future assurances about effective management control.

3.12 Summary

- There are a number of accounting techniques that are part of management control systems, such as capital investment appraisal, overhead allocation, transfer pricing, budgeting and variance analysis.

- Despite the apparent sophistication of capital investment appraisal techniques (particularly DCF), decisions are often made subjectively and then justified by the application of financial techniques. Despite the usefulness of these techniques, the assumption has been that future cash flows can be predicted with some accuracy.

- Traditional management accounting systems have serious limitations in providing accurate product costs as a result of the overhead allocation problem.

- Transfer pricing can have demotivating effects on business units when used for evaluating divisional performance and may lead to divisions acting contrary to the corporate interest. Consequently, many organisations adopt negotiated prices in order to avoid these effects. In multinationals, transfer pricing may be more concerned with how to shift profits between countries so as to minimise income taxes than on its value for management control.

- Budgets provide a control mechanism through both the feed forward and feedback loops. There are however, problems with budgets that cause problems in its role as a control mechanism, such as gaming, manipulating results and no longer being motivational. There are real difficulties in future financial projections and the Beyond Budgeting movement has criticised budgeting as a management tool.

- Flexible budgets provide a better basis for investigating variances than the original budget if the standard costs are applied against actual volumes before the variance is calculated. Feedback is more meaningful than comparisons against the original budget. However, JIT and TQM environments limit the value of variance analysis because price variations are only one component of total cost and will tend to emphasise following standard work instructions rather than encouraging employees to adopt an innovative approach.

- The cost of quality comprises conformance and non-conformance costs. Identifying the cost of quality is important to the continuous improvement process as substantial improvements to business performance can be achieved by investing in conformance and so avoiding the much larger costs usually associated with non-conformance. A similar approach can be applied to social and environmental accounting.

- New management accounting techniques have been developed in response to modern production methods. These include strategic management accounting, life cycle costing, target costing and kaizen.

- Strategic management accounting is the analysis of management accounting data about a business and its competitors which is of use in business strategy. This includes collection of competitor information; exploitation of cost reduction opportunities and matching the accounting emphasis with the firm's strategic position. However, there are significant costs in collecting and analysing this information.

- Life cycle costing estimates and accumulates the costs of a product/service over its entire life cycle, from inception to abandonment. This helps to determine whether the profits generated during the production phase cover all the life-cycle costs. This is important because decisions about the production process and the technology investment required to support production are made long before the product/services are actually produced.

- Target costing is concerned with managing whole of life costs during the design phase. Its aim is to build a product at a cost that could be recovered over the product life cycle through a price that customers would be willing to pay to obtain the benefits.

- Kaizen is a process for making continuous, incremental improvements to the production process when large innovations may not be possible.

- Lean management accounting is about relevant accounting, performance measurement and control techniques to support lean manufacturing and sustain a lean enterprise. Lean thinking does not rely on benchmarking but savagely eliminates waste within value streams. Lean management accounting reduces transaction processing costs by using visual methods like kanbans and uses backflushing to record the cost of materials and labour.

- The decline in use, or at least questioning, of some traditional accounting techniques has important implications for control purposes as accounting techniques may have a reduced role to play in future assurances about effective management control.

References

Bromwich, M. (1990), 'The Case for Strategic Management Accounting: The Role of Accounting Information for Strategy in Competitive Markets.' *Accounting, Organizations and Society*, Vol. 15, pp. 27–46.

Chartered Institute of Management Accountants (1999), *Corporate Governance: History, Practice and Future*. London: CIMA Publishing.

Chartered Institute of Management Accountants (2002), *Risk Management: A Guide to Good Practice*. London: CIMA Publishing.

CIMA and ICAEW (2004), 'Better Budgeting: A report on the better Budgeting forum from CIMA and ICAEW'.

Collier, P.M. (2005), Entrepreneurial Cognition and the Construction of a Relevant Accounting. *Management Accounting Research*, Vol. 16, no. 3, pp. 321–39.

Dixon, R. (1998), Accounting for Strategic Management: A Practical Application. *Long Range Planning* Vol. 31, pp. 272–9.

Emmanuel, C., Otley, D. and Merchant, K. (1990), *Accounting for Management Control*. London: Chapman & Hall.

Hammer, M. and Champy, J. (1993), *Reengineering the Corporation: A Manifesto for Business Revolution*. London: Nicholas Brealey Publishing.

Hope, J. and Fraser, R. (2003), Who Needs Budgets? *Harvard Business Review*, 108–15.

Johnson, H.T. and Kaplan, R.S. (1987), *Relevance Lost: The Rise and Fall of Management Accounting*. Boston, MA: Harvard Business School Press.

Kaplan, R.S. and Cooper, R. (1998), *Cost & Effect: Using Integrated Cost Systems to Drive Profitability and Performance*. Boston, MA: Harvard Business School Press.

Lord, B.R. (1996), 'Strategic Management Accounting: The Emperor's New Clothes?' *Management Accounting Research*, Vol. 7, pp. 347–66.

Lowe, E.A. and Shaw, R.W. (1968), 'An Analysis of Managerial Biasing: Evidence from a Company's Budgeting Process.' *Journal of Management Studies*, October, pp. 304–15.

Porter, M.E. (1985), *Competitive Advantage: Creating and Sustaining Superior Performance*. New York: Free Press.

Scapens, R.W., Ezzamel, M., Burns, J. and Baldvinsdottir, G. (2003), *The Future Direction of UK Management Accounting Practice*. Oxford: Elsevier.

Simmonds, K. (1981), 'Strategic Management Accounting.' *Management Accounting*, Vol. 59, pp. 26–9.

Solomons, D. (1965), *Divisional Performance: Measurement and Control*. Homewood, IL: Richard D. Irwin.

Wallander, J. (1999), Budgeting – An Unnecessary Evil. *Scandinavian Journal of Management*, Vol. 15, pp. 405–21.

Womack, J.P. and Jones, D.T. (2003), *Lean Thinking: Banish Waste and Create Wealth in your Corporation*. London: Free Press.

Revision Questions

3

? Question 1

This question is a modified version taken from a question in the November 2005 examination for P3.

VCF is a small listed company that designs and installs high technology computer numerical control capital equipment used by multinational manufacturing companies. VCF is located in one Pacific country, but almost 90% of its sales are exported. VCF has sales offices in Europe, Asia, the Pacific, Africa, and North and South America and employs about 300 staff around the world.

VCF has annual sales of $200 million but the sales value of each piece of equipment sold is about $2 million so the sales volume is relatively low. Sales are always invoiced in the currency of the country where the equipment is being installed. The time between the order being taken and the final installation is usually several months. However, a deposit is taken when the order is placed and progress payments are made by the customer before shipment and upon delivery, with the final payment being made after installation of the equipment.

The company has international patents covering its technology and invests heavily in research and development (R&D, about 15% of sales) and marketing costs to develop export markets (about 25% of sales). VCF's manufacturing operations are completely outsourced in its home country and the cost of sales is about 20%. The balance of costs is for installation, servicing and administration, amounting to about 15% of sales. Within each of these cost classifications, the major expenses (other than direct costs) are salaries for staff, all of whom are paid well above the industry average, rental of premises in each location and travel costs. Area managers are located in each sales office and have responsibility for achieving sales, installing equipment and maintaining high levels of after-sales service and customer satisfaction.

Although the head office is very small, most of the R&D staff are located in the home country, along with purchasing and logistics staff responsible for liaising with the outsource suppliers and a small accounting team that is primarily concerned with monthly management accounts and end of year financial statements.

VCF has a majority shareholding held by Jack Viktor, an entrepreneur who admits to taking high risks, both personally and in business. The Board of four is effectively controlled by Viktor who is both Chairman and Chief Executive. The three other directors were appointed by Viktor. They are his wife, who has a marketing role in the business, and two non-executive directors, one an occasional consultant to VCF and the other a long time family friend. Board meetings are held quarterly and are informal affairs, largely led by by Viktor's verbal review of sales activity.

Viktor is a dominating individual who exercises a high degree of personal control, often by-passing his area managers. Because the company is controlled by him, Viktor is not especially concerned with short-term profits but with the long-term. He emphasises two objectives: sales growth to generate increased market share and cash flow; and investment in R&D to ensure the long-term survival of VCF by maintaining patent protection and a technological lead over its competitors.

Viktor is in daily contact with all his offices by telephone. He travels extensively around the world and has an excellent knowledge of his competitors and customers. He uses a limited number of non-financial performance measures, primarily concerned with sales, market share, quality and customer satisfaction. Through his personal contact and his twin objectives, Viktor encourages a culture committed to growth, continual innovation, and high levels of customer satisfaction. This is reinforced by high salary levels, but Viktor readily dismisses those staff not committed to his objectives.

The company has experienced rapid growth over the last 10 years and is very profitable although cash flow is often tight. A high margin is achieved because VCF is able to charge its customers premium prices for its equipment. This enables faster production and better quality than VCF's competitors can offer.

Viktor has little time for traditional accounting. Product costing is not seen as valuable because the cost of sales is relatively low and most costs incurred by VCF, particular R&D and export marketing costs are incurred a long time in advance of sales being made. R&D costs are not capitalised in VCF's balance sheet.

Although budgets are used for expense control and monthly management accounts are produced, they have little relevance to Viktor who recognises the fluctuations in profit caused by the timing of sales of low volume but high value capital equipment.

Viktor sees little value in comparing monthly profit figures against budgets because sales are erratic. However, Viktor depends heavily on a spreadsheet to manage VCF's cash flow by using sensitivity analysis against his sales and cash flow projections. Cash flow is a major business driver and is controlled tightly using the spreadsheet model.

The major risks facing VCF have been identified by Viktor as:

- competitor infringement of patents, which VCF always meets by instituting legal actions;
- adverse movements in the exchange rate between the home country and VCF's export markets, which VCF treats as an acceptable risk given that historically, gains and losses have balanced each other out;
- the reduction in demand for his equipment due to economic recession;
- a failure of continued R&D investment to maintain technological leadership; and
- a failure to control costs.

Viktor addresses the last three of these risks by his policy of outsourcing manufacture, and continuous personal contact with staff, customers and competitors.

Requirements
Identify and evaluate the

(a) existing accounting controls, and
(b) the use of non-financial performance measures.

within VCF.

Question 2

This question is a modified version taken from a question in the May 2006 examination for P3.

CDE is a manufacturer of almost one hundred different automotive components that are sold in both large and small quantities on a Just-in-Time (JIT) basis to the major vehicle assemblers. Business is highly competitive and price sensitive. The company is listed on the stock exchange but CDE's share performance has not matched that of its main competitors.

CDE uses a sophisticated computer system to control production scheduling, inventory movements and stock control, and labour and machine utilisation. A large accounting department carries out a detailed annual budgeting exercise, determines standard costs for labour and materials, and allocates production overhead on the basis of machine utilisation. Strict accounting controls over labour and material costs are managed by the detailed recording of operator and machine timesheets and raw material movements, and by calculating and investigating all significant variances.

While the information from the computer system is useful to management, there is an absence of integrated data about customer requirements and suppliers. Some information is contained within Excel spreadsheets and Access databases held by the Sales and Purchasing departments respectively. One result of this lack of integration is that inventories are higher than they should be in a JIT environment.

The managers of CDE (representing functional areas of sales, production, purchasing, finance and administration) believe that, while costs are strictly controlled, the cost of the accounting department is excessive and significant savings need to be made, even at the expense of data accuracy. Managers believe that there may not be optimum use of the production capacity to generate profits and cash flow and improve shareholder value. CDE's management wants to carry out sensitivity and other analyses of strategic alternatives, but this is difficult when the existing management accounting system is focused on control rather than on decision support.

Requirement

Critically evaluate CDE's management accounting systems and make recommendations for improvement, given the business conditions being faced by CDE and the desire of management to reduce the cost of accounting.

 # Question 3

This question is a modified version taken from a question in the November 2007 examination for P3.

VWS is a company manufacturing and selling a wide range of industrial products to a large number of businesses throughout the country. VWS is a significant local employer, with 2,500 people working out of several locations around the region, all linked by a networked computer system.

VWS purchases numerous components from 750 local and regional suppliers, receiving these into a central warehouse. The company carries about 10,000 different inventory items, placing 25,000 orders with its suppliers each year.

The Accounts Payable Department of VWS has six staff who process all supplier invoices through the company's computer system and make payment to suppliers by cheque or electronic remittance.

Requirement

Discuss the purposes and value of an internal control system for Accounts Payable to a company like VWS. (**10 marks**)

Solutions to
Revision Questions

3

✔ Solution 1

(a) Financial controls

Costing: as cost of sales represents only 20% of selling price, and other costs are period costs, often incurred more than a year in advance of sales taking place, it can be understood that product costing is not especially helpful. Indeed, lean accounting suggests that using techniques that do not add value is to be avoided.

Flexible budgeting is unlikely to be helpful in reconciling actual and target performance due to the high proportion of fixed, period costs. However, even 20% of sales is significant and there ought to be a comparison between standard cost and actual cost charged by the outsource supplier to ensure that variances are identified and investigated and if necessary, corrected or at least used to modify the selling price.

Budgets: These are used by VCF in a limited manner. Budgets can be used for feed forward and feedback purposes. Viktor uses budgets for feed forward although this is limited to cash forecasting, and for feedback purposes in relation to expense control. This use could be expanded to integrate sales forecasts for cash purposes with budgets for control purposes so that area managers are held responsible for achieving sales targets as well as controlling costs, and so have profit responsibility. The cash forecast used by Viktor would then be integrated with profit reporting.

However, the 'Beyond Budgeting' movement has recognised the limitations of traditional budgeting and recommends a more adaptive method of managing through targets linked to stretch goals and a more decentralised management style (contrasted with the centralisation of VCF through Viktor).

(b) Non-financial performance measures

The Balanced Scorecard recognises the need for non-financial measures around customers, processes and innovation. VCF appears to use a small number of non-financial measures: sales, market share, quality and customer satisfaction. Three of these are customer measures. Given the importance of export sales, measures could also be expanded around the relative effectiveness of generating sales per head or per dollar spent in each area (country) with benchmarking of managers against each other. Quality is the only process measure and given the long lead time, cycle time between order and installation may be a useful measure as well as rework, customer complaints, installation problems, etc. Given the importance of employees to VCF, measures should be implemented to expand on the relatively simplistic percentage of sales spent on R&D. These could include employee retention, training costs, employee satisfaction/morale, etc.

Solution 2

CDE's management accounting system relies on budgeting, standard costs, overhead allocation, detailed time and material recording and variance analysis. While these accounting controls are generally accepted by accountants, they can be criticised as they apply to the business needs of CDE.

Budgets provide a valuable control mechanism, both through feed forward (in which budgets are reviewed in advance to determine whether corporate goals will be achieved) and feedback (in which variations between actual and budget performance can be investigated and monitored and corrective action taken). However there are problems with budgets. This can include gaming responses by managers who may set low targets, manipulating results so that targets are achieved (particularly where this is linked with performance bonuses), and reducing efforts once targets are achieved. The difficulty in budgeting is predicting sales levels and sales mix for a multi-product business like CDE in a competitive and price sensitive marketplace.

Overhead allocation involves the process of spreading production overheads over the volume of production, a difficult process where a large variety of products with different volumes are manufactured, as in CDE. The assumption used by CDE that overhead can be allocated based on machine hours can be quite misleading for management decision-making and result in issues of cross-subsidisation of products. An activity-based costing approach might eliminate the subsidisation problem and improve pricing, sales mix and profitability by allocating costs to cost pools and allocating overheads to products from those cost pools based on the consumption of overheads by each product as measured by cost drivers.

Standard costing is used to determine the planned cost of a product produced in a period, typically based on a bill of materials (the components that go into a finished product) and a labour routing (the labour steps or processes that are used to produce a product or service). They are developed by considering past experience, known changes in technology or process improvements, and known changes in labour or supplier rates. However, in a modern manufacturing environment, there are often trade-offs between the quality and availability of materials, the skill and experience of labour, and the prices that must be paid for those resources. It is not always helpful in decision-making that variance analysis focuses narrowly on costs rather than overall efficiencies.

Traditional costing approaches support the mass production model that seeks economies of scale by producing large production runs to obtain the lowest unit cost of production. However, such an approach is unlikely to be effective in a Just-in-Time environment where production is geared around flexibility and customisation. Time and material recording leads to the ability to carry out detailed variance analysis by comparing actual performance against plan, investigating the causes of the variance and taking corrective action to ensure that targets are achieved.

JIT aims to improve productivity and eliminate waste by obtaining manufacturing components of the right quality, at the right time and place to meet the demands of the manufacturing cycle. It requires close co-operation within the supply chain and is generally associated with continuous manufacturing processes with low inventory holdings, a result of eliminating buffer inventories which are considered waste. Many of these costs are hidden in a traditional cost accounting system. Variance analysis has less emphasis in a JIT environment because price variations are only one component of total cost. Variance analysis does not account, for example, for higher or lower investments in inventory. Managers should therefore consider the total cost of ownership rather than the initial purchase price.

A lean manufacturing approach involves the pull of products and services through the value stream (rather than a departmental structure) based on satisfying customer orders, rather than a pull approach to satisfy inventory. It focuses on eliminating waste. Lean management accounting methods must not contribute to waste. Traditional management accounting methods provide little useful improvement information; are organised by departments rather than value streams; leads to the production of large batches and builds inventories to reduce unit costs; hides waste in overhead; and creates waste through detailed transaction recording systems.

Lean management accounting does not use sophisticated manufacturing resource planning systems or production scheduling and tracking but instead uses visual methods like kanbans. Instead of reporting detailed transactions for materials and labour as they occur, backflushing is used. Like process costing, value stream direct costing pools all costs incurred by the value stream in which the product cost is the average cost of the value stream for the quantity produced for the period. This is considered to be a reliable method in lean manufacturing because inventory movements are reduced to a minimum.

The costs of accounting in CDE could be significantly reduced by eliminating much of the detailed transaction recording and variance analysis carried out and replacing this with a lean management accounting system consistent with the JIT environment in which it operates. Budget processes should be reviewed to eliminate as far as possible unintended consequences. Standard costs would still be required for pricing purposes but overhead allocation needs to be improved, perhaps through an activity-based costing approach.

Such an approach to reducing the cost of accounting is consistent with more sophisticated IT systems (see Chapter 8) that would provide a more holistic, rather than accounting-dominated control and decision-support system.

☑ Solution 3

An internal control system comprises the policies and procedures that an organisation implements to achieve its objectives, efficiently and effectively conduct its business, safeguard its assets, prevent and detect fraud, and ensure the accuracy and completeness of accounting records in order to produce reliable financial statements. In relation to Accounts Payable, internal controls ensure that suppliers are paid accurately and on time in order to ensure continuity of supply. Because the payment of money is involved, the safeguarding of cash resources is critical to the Accounts Payable function and the opportunity for fraud by employees or suppliers must be minimised. As the processing of supplier invoices has a material impact on the accuracy of financial statements, approval and end of financial period cut-off procedures need to be effective. The control environment within a company like VWS must be supportive of these controls.

The purposes of controls over Accounts Payable are that:

- purchases are properly authorised through an effective purchase ordering system;
- goods are received or services supplied, and that these are in accordance with that purchase order;
- the price on invoices is checked, and that calculations are correct;
- invoices are properly authorised for payment with supporting evidence;
- invoices are correctly posted to creditor accounts in the accounting period in which goods are received or services provided;

- payments are made to suppliers in accordance with trading terms, are properly authorised and recorded in creditor accounts;
- creditor accounts are regularly reconciled with supplier statements; and
- a thorough investigation of any disputed amounts takes place.

The value of controls may be seen in their functioning as directive, preventative, detective and corrective. Some controls are directive. Training or policies and procedures show employees what should be done. In Accounts Payable, training and policies would provide the parameters in which the department would carry out the transaction processing of invoices and payment. For example, staff would not be permitted to use the system unless they had been properly trained and were made aware of the Accounts Payable Department's written policies and procedures.

4

Corporate
Governance and
the Audit
Committee

Corporate Governance and the Audit Committee

4

LEARNING OUTCOMES

After completing this chapter you should be able to:

► Discuss the principles of good corporate governance particularly as regards the need for internal controls.

4.1 Introduction

The main purpose of this chapter is to describe the emergence of corporate governance in the UK (with some international comparisons) and to identify in some detail the principles of corporate governance based on the Combined Code. The main learning outcome is contained in Section B of the *Performance Strategy* syllabus. The role of the audit committee is described in detail together with its basis in the Combined Code and the Smith and Higgs Guidance. The role of the audit committee is covered in relation to internal control and relations with external auditors. It concludes with the emerging area of enterprise governance and the benefits of corporate governance.

4.2 Models of corporate governance

There are two models of corporate governance:

- Shareholder value/agency model
- Stakeholder model.

Each represents a different means by which the functioning of boards of directors and top management can be understood. Research by Cooper et al. (2001) presents an interesting contrast between performance measurement for stakeholder and shareholder value.

In UK company law, there is no doubt that shareholders are in a privileged position compared with other stakeholders. Hence, corporate governance in the UK is founded on the shareholder value/agency model. However, as will be seen later in this chapter, other models of governance take a broader view, for example that found in South Africa.

The corporate governance framework in the UK operates at a number of levels:

- through legislation particularly the Companies Act, 2006, which came into effect in 2008;
- through regulation and in particular for listed companies through the Stock Exchange Listing Rules, which are the responsibility of the Financial Services Authority (FSA);
- through the Combined Code on Corporate Governance, which is the responsibility of the Financial Reporting Council. The Combined Code is appended to the FSA's Listing Rules.

4.3 Governance, risk management and internal control

> It is important to understand the links between governance, risk management and internal control and the interaction between the board of directors, the audit (and/or risk committees), external auditors and internal auditors. This is the foundation of the *Performance Strategy* syllabus as was introduced in Chapter 1. This chapter sets the scene in terms of governance while the following chapters are concerned with risk management and internal control.

Even before the spate of corporate governance reports culminating in the *Combined Code* on Corporate Governance (Financial Reporting Council, 2003), a growing number of institutional investors were starting to encourage greater disclosure of governance processes and emphasising the quality and sustainability of earnings, rather than short-term profits alone. For example, a survey published by KPMG in 2002 reported that 80 per cent of fund managers would pay more for the shares of a demonstrably well-governed company, with the average premium being 11 per cent. Research by management consultants McKinsey has also shown that an overwhelming majority of institutional investors are prepared to pay a significant premium for companies exhibiting high standards of corporate governance.

The media has also increased its reporting of governance practices. The high-profile failures of companies, notably the press coverage given to Enron and WorldCom, brought corporate governance to worldwide attention. The September 11 attacks in the United States also resulted in an increase in attention to risk. This increased attention to corporate governance has been a global one, which has been highlighted even further by the global financial crisis and its effect on national economies, global industries and individual companies (see Chapter 1).

4.4 Historical perspective

Policy concern with corporate governance has been driven in recent years – well before the 2008/9 global financial crisis – by a series of corporate scandals and failures in a number of countries, not just due to cyclical events but also to systemic weaknesses.

Major corporate collapses have been a feature of recent business history in the UK and elsewhere.

In the UK:

- the Maxwell publishing group,
- Bank of Commerce & Credit International (BCCI),
- Asil Nadir's Polly Peck, and
- Marconi.

In Germany:

- Holtzman,
- Berliner Bank, and
- Babcok.

In France:

- Credit Lyonnaise, and
- Vivendi.

In Italy:

- Pasminco.

In Australia:

- the insurer HIH,
- Ansett Airlines, and
- OneTel.

In the United States:

- Enron,
- WorldCom, and
- Tyco.

There have also been failures in many Japanese and Korean financial institutions. The OECD's interests in corporate governance emerged after the Asian financial crisis in 1997 and led to the publication in 1999 of the *OECD Principles of Corporate Governance.*

The emergence of corporate governance can be put down to:

- an enforcement exercise in relation to past misdeeds,
- changing financial markets including the rapid rise of institutional investors and their increasing desire to be more active investors, and
- the growth of savings for pensions in most member countries and the dependence of an ageing population on pensions and savings which have been affected by declining confidence in stock markets.

4.5 Corporate governance developments in the UK

In the UK, a series of reports has had a marked influence on the development of corporate governance. The first report, by Sir Adrian Cadbury, followed a number of high-profile corporate failures including Polly Peck (1990), BCCI (1991), and pension funds in the Maxwell Group (1991).

The Cadbury Report (Cadbury Code, 1992) was in relation to *Financial Aspects of Corporate Governance*. The Greenbury report was published in 1995 on Directors' Remuneration. The Hampel report was published in 1998 and followed from the Committee on Corporate Governance which was set up to review the implementation of the Cadbury Code. It was responsible for the *Corporate Governance Combined Code* which was published in 1998 and incorporated the recommendations of the Cadbury, Greenbury and Hampel Committees.

The Turnbull Guidance on internal control (Institute of Chartered Accountants in England & Wales, 1999) was subsequently incorporated into the *Combined Code*, as was the Higgs report on the role of non-executive directors and the Smith report on the role of audit committees, both published in 2003. In 2001, the relationship between institutional investors and companies was addressed by the Myners Review, 'Institutional Investment in the UK'. In 2002, the *Directors' Remuneration Report Regulations* were introduced to further strengthen the powers of shareholders in relation to directors' pay. The Higgs and Smith Reports followed by the Tyson Report on the recruitment and development of non-executive directors. In 2004, the Financial Reporting Council established the Turnbull Review Group to determine whether the guidance needed to be updated. *Internal Control: Revised Guidance for Directors on the Combined Code* was published by the Financial Reporting Council in October 2005.

A report produced in 2007 by King's College, London for the Department of Trade and Industry considered the key drivers of good corporate governance and how appropriate the policy environment was in the UK to promote good governance practices. The report[1] identified 18 key mechanisms for corporate governance, ranging from board independence to shareholder activism, information disclosure, audit and internal control effectiveness, executive remuneration, takeovers and stakeholder involvement. The researchers identified gaps in government policy that supported these mechanisms, mainly relating to executive remuneration, employees and stakeholders generally. The report also found that it was important to balance and recognise trade-offs between mandatory regulations and 'soft law' such as codes based on comply or explain principles (such as the Combined Code on Corporate Governance) and the self-regulation of professional groups. The cost of regulation must also be considered.

Between July and October 2005 the FRC carried out a review of how the Combined Code was being implemented. The results of that review were published in January 2006 (Financial Reporting Council, 2006). At the same time the FRC began consultation on a small number of possible amendments to the Code.

Respondents agreed that there had been an improvement in corporate governance since the introduction of the Combined Code; and that the dialogue between boards and their main shareholders had become more constructive. However, a concerned expressed during the review was that the Combined Code was a rigid set of rules. The FRC's response was that the 'comply or explain' approach acknowledged different circumstances, but for that approach to work, companies needed to provide meaningful explanations to investors.

The review found that investors considered the overall quality of disclosure to have improved, but believed that there was more scope for corporate governance statements to become more informative.

---

[1] The full report including a detailed description of the 18 drivers can be downloaded from www.berr.gov.uk/files/file36671.pdf

The review found that major changes to the Code were not necessary, however there was support for two potential changes:

1. To amend the provision relating to the composition of remuneration committees to enable the chairman to sit on the committee where s/he was considered independent; and
2. Providing shareholders voting by proxy at an annual general meeting with the option of withholding their vote, and to encourage companies to publish details of proxies on some votes.

During 2007, the Financial Reporting Council (FRC) conducted a further review of the UK Combined Code on Corporate Governance and found that it was working effectively and needed no major changes[2]. However, two amendments were proposed. The first change is to remove the restriction on an individual chairing more than one FTSE company. The second is to allow the chairman of a smaller listed company to be a member of the audit committee where s/he is considered independent on appointment. Revisions to the Code were made in June 2008. The latest version of the Code can be downloaded from the FRC website at http://www.frc.org.uk/corporate/combinedcode.cfm.

4.6 International developments

The U.S. Committee of Sponsoring Organizations of the Treadway Commission (COSO, 1992) report (see below) had an important influence on the Cadbury committee in the UK and on developments in Canada, the Netherlands, Australia, New Zealand, France, Italy, and South Africa.

4.6.1 The United States

Corporate governance emerged in the United States with the Treadway Commission's Report on *Fraudulent Financial Reporting* in 1987. The report affirmed the important role played by audit committees in governance. The Treadway Commission report was later reinforced by the Securities and Exchange Commission in its listing requirements.

A sub-group of the Treadway Commission, the Committee of Sponsoring Organisations (COSO) developed *Internal Control – Integrated Framework* in 1992 (Committee of Sponsoring Organizations of the Treadway Commission, 1992) and in 2003 a report was published on *Enterprise Risk Management* (Committee of Sponsoring Organizations of the Treadway Commission, 2003).

The introduction of the Sarbanes-Oxley Act in 2002 was the legislative response to the financial and accounting scandals of Enron and WorldCom and the misconduct at the accounting firm Arthur Andersen. Its main aim was to deal with core issues of transparency, integrity and oversight of financial markets. Sarbanes-Oxley introduced the requirement to disclose all material off-balance sheet transactions. The Act requires the certification of annual and quarterly financial reports by the chief executive and chief financial officer of all companies with US securities registrations, with criminal penalties for knowingly making false certifications.

---

[2] Current news on governance and internal control is available from the Financial Reporting Council at http://www.frc.org.uk/corporate/

A further requirement is for the CEO and CFO to give assurances regarding the effectiveness of internal controls. Section 404 of Sarbanes-Oxley requires companies to state the responsibility of management for establishing and maintaining an adequate internal control structure and procedures for financial reporting; and to make an assessment of the effectiveness of the internal control structure and procedures for financial reporting. External auditors are required to report on management's assessment.

The Sarbanes-Oxley legislation focuses more on the role of the audit committee than on the responsibilities of the board. However, there are no provisions relating to the internal audit function or its role in risk and control. An independent Public Company Accounting Oversight Board was also established with responsibility for setting standards for auditing, quality control and independence.

The US Securities and Exchange Commission (SEC) has identified the Turnbull guidance as a suitable framework for complying with US requirements to report on internal controls over financial reporting, as set out in Section 404 of the Sarbanes-Oxley Act 2002 and related SEC rules.

4.6.2 South Africa

The King Report on Corporate Governance in South Africa provides an integrated approach to corporate governance in the interest of all stakeholders, embracing social, environmental and economic aspects of organisational activities. It therefore takes, to some extent at least, a broader stakeholder model of governance. The King Report relies heavily on disclosure as a regulatory mechanism.

The South African changes emphasised increasing the accountability and independence of boards, noting that delegation to committees does not absolve the board of its responsibilities.

The King Report philosophy is that in presenting financial information, openness and substance is more important than form. Internal control is part of the risk management process for which the board is responsible. The internal audit function has its main focus on risk and control.

It is interesting to compare the different approaches taken to corporate governance in the United States and South Africa. A detailed comparison of Sarbanes-Oxley and the King Report is contained in PricewaterhouseCoopers (2003).

The King Committee on Corporate Governance developed the King Report on Corporate Governance for South Africa, 2002 (King II). King II acknowledges that there is a move away from the single bottom line (that is, profit for shareholders) to a triple bottom line, which embraces the economic, environmental and social aspects of a company's activities.

4.6.3 Other international developments

In 1995 the Canadian Institute of Chartered Accountants through the Criteria of Control Committee (that has become known as 'CoCo') published *Guidance for Directors – Governance Processes for Control*. This emphasised the role of the board in understanding the principal risks facing companies and ensuring a proper balance between risks incurred and the potential returns to shareholders.

In France, the Vienot Report in 1995 proposed that boards should not simply aim to maximise share values but to safeguard the prosperity and continuity of the business.

In Australia, the Australian Stock Exchange has a Corporate Governance Principles and Recommendations. There is also a series of standards that have been issued by

Standards Australia relating to governance, risk and control. AS8000 of 2003 covers Good Governance Principles, supported by a number of practical handbooks. AS8000 covers best practice for the Board charter, Board protocol, a statement of matters reserved for the Board, Board delegations of authority, letters of appointment for board members, and a code of conduct for board members.

In 2004, the OECD published their principles of Corporate Governance (OECD, 2004). The principles were:

1. Ensuring the basis for an effective corporate governance framework by promoting transparent and efficient markets, being consistent with the rule of law and clearly articulating the division of responsibilities among different authorities.
2. Protecting and facilitating the exercise of the rights of shareholders.
3. Ensuring the equitable treatment of all shareholders, who should have the opportunity to obtain effective redress for violation of their rights.
4. The rights of shareholders is established by law and active co-operation between companies and shareholders should be encouraged in creating wealth, jobs and the sustainability of financially sound enterprises.
5. Ensuring timely and accurate disclosure on all material matters regarding the financial situation, performance, ownership and governance of the company.
6. The strategic guidance of the company, effective monitoring of management by the board and the board's accountability to the company and its shareholders.

4.7　Basel Committee and operational risk

For banks and regulated financial institutions, the Basel Committee on Banking Supervision has had an important impact, particularly as it affects risk and internal control. Part of the Bank for International Settlements, the objectives of the Basel Committee are to enhance the understanding of key supervisory issues and improve the quality of banking supervision worldwide. Guidelines and standards are developed. Important guidelines for students of Risk and Control include:

Basel Committee on Banking Supervision (1994). *Risk Management Guidelines for Derivatives*. Basel: Bank for International Settlements.

Basel Committee on Banking Supervision (1998). *Framework for the Evaluation of Internal Control*. Basel: Bank for International Settlements.

Basel Committee on Banking Supervision (2001). *Sound Practices for the Management and Supervision of Operational Risk*. Basel: Bank for International Settlements.

Further information is available from the bank's website www.bis.org/bcbs/

A particular focus of attention is the latest version of Basel II. These are international standards for banking laws and regulations aimed at helping to protect the international financial system from the results of the collapse of a major bank or a series of banks. Basel II establishes rigorous risk and capital management requirements to ensure each bank holds reserves sufficient to guard against its risk exposure given its lending and investment practices.

Regulators require banks to measure their market risk using a risk measurement model which is used to calculate the Value at Risk (VaR). VaR is based on the assumption that investors care mainly about the probability of a large loss. The VaR of a portfolio is the maximum loss on a portfolio occurring within a given length of time with a given small probability. Banks can measure their value at risk through models developed internally or by a standardised approach using a risk-weighting process developed by the Basel Committee on Banking Supervision.

VaR calculates the maximum loss expected (or worst case scenario) on an investment, over a given time period and given a specified degree of confidence. Calculating VaR involves using three components: a time period, a confidence level and a loss amount or percentage loss. VaR is covered in more detail in chapter 11.

Basel II has raised operational risk management to the top of the agenda of financial institutions around the world. Operational risk includes systems risks, such as hardware or software failure, issues over availability and integrity of data, and utility failures, and external events (e.g. computer hacking, terrorist attack, vandalism or supplier failure.), clear strategies and oversight by the Board of Directors and senior management, a strong operational risk culture and internal control culture (including, among other things, clear lines of responsibility and segregation of duties), effective internal reporting, and contingency planning were all identified as crucial elements of an effective operational risk management framework for banks of any size and scope.

However, the global financial crisis has identified substantial problems with banks' governance processes in terms of understanding operational risk and applying risk measurement models like VaR, emphasised by the number of banks that have failed or required government support (in UK, Northern Rock and Bradford & Bingley, in the US Bear Sterns, Washington Mutual, IndyMac, Fannie Mae and Freddie Mac, etc.)

4.8 Principles of corporate governance

 Corporate governance is

The system by which companies are directed and controlled. Boards of directors are responsible for the governance of their companies. The shareholders' role in governance is to appoint the directors and the auditors and to satisfy themselves that an appropriate governance structure is in place. The responsibilities of the board include setting the company's strategic aims, providing the leadership to put them into effect, supervising the management of the business and reporting to shareholders on their stewardship. The board's actions are subject to laws, regulations and the shareholders in general meeting (CIMA *Official Terminology*).

The *Combined Code on Corporate Governance* (Financial Reporting Council, 2003) superseded the earlier Combined Code issued by the Hampel Committee in 1998. It incorporates the Turnbull Guidance on internal control, the Smith Guidance on audit committees and good practice guidelines from the Higgs report on the role of non-executive directors.

The Combined Code applies for reporting years beginning on or after 1 November 2003. Stock Exchange Listing Rules require listed companies to disclose how they have applied the principles in the Code; and to confirm either that the company complies with the Code's provisions or, if it does not comply, to provide an explanation. This approach is known as 'comply or explain'. The comply or explain approach can be contrasted with the far more prescriptive approach adopted in the United States, which applies to foreign companies with shares listed in that country.

The London Stock Exchange and RSM Robson Rhodes (2004) has produced a practical guide to corporate governance and the Combined Code which addresses issues of board development, managing risk, the audit committee, etc.

The Department of Trade and Industry in the UK published 'Building Better Boards' in December 2004. This best practice guide offered the following recommendations to help companies improve recruitment and performance in the boardroom.

- Building Better Boards is about companies thinking more systematically about the effectiveness of their boards, their recruitment processes and the way in which they develop their own people.
- Boards, which have the scope to consider a wider range of perspectives, and generate richer, more informed discussion of the issues facing the company, are more likely to anticipate problems and produce high quality solutions.
- Board members with diverse experiences and backgrounds bring varied and complementary perspectives, contribute in the making of strong and dynamic boards and lead to companies that can compete successfully in the global economy.
- Diversity isn't about tokenism. It's about getting the right skills mix on the board. There are real business benefits, which companies can derive from broadening the base of their boards and bringing in fresh minds with different skills and new perspectives to contribute to the growth and development of the business.
- Provides managers with an overview of the scope of development available for their talented executives, enabling them to make a positive contribution in a boardroom in the future.
- Provides an overview for aspiring executives as to the skills required to secure a position on the board of a UK company. It also includes a range of case studies demonstrating how individuals and businesses have pursued their own and their staff's development.
- Good corporate governance is ultimately about people. The key to building better boards is a commitment from the top down to the dynamic development of the board in the best interests of the company.

The main principles of corporate governance found in the Combined Code are in relation to:

- Directors
- Remuneration of directors
- Accountability and audit
- Relations with shareholders
- Institutional shareholders
- Disclosure.

The main principles are described in more detail below (references, e.g. A1, B2, C3) are to the relevant sections in the Combined Code.

4.8.1   Directors

- Every company should be headed by an effective board, which is collectively responsible for the success of the company (A1).
- There should be a clear division of responsibilities at the head of the company between the running of the board and the executive responsibility for the running of the company's business. No one individual should have unfettered powers of decision-making (A2).
- The board should include a balance of executive and non-executive directors (and in particular independent non-executive directors) such that no individual or small group of individuals can dominate the board's decision-making (A3).

- There should be a formal, rigorous and transparent procedure for the appointment of new directors to the board (A4).
- The board should be supplied in a timely manner with information in a form and of a quality appropriate to enable it to discharge its duties. All directors should receive induction on joining the board and should regularly update and refresh their skills and knowledge (A5).
- The board should undertake a formal and rigorous annual evaluation of its own performance and that of its committees and individual directors (A6).
- All directors should be submitted for re-election at regular intervals, subject to continued satisfactory performance. The board should ensure planned and progressive refreshing of the board (A7).

4.8.2 Remuneration

- Levels of remuneration should be sufficient to attract, retain and motivate directors of the quality required to run the company successfully, but a company should avoid paying more than is necessary for this purpose. A significant proportion of executive directors' remuneration should be structured so as to link rewards to corporate and individual performance (B1).
- There should be a formal and transparent procedure for developing policy on executive remuneration and for fixing the remuneration packages of individual directors. No director should be involved in deciding his or her own remuneration (B2).

4.8.3 Accountability and audit

- The board should present a balanced and understandable assessment of the company's position and prospects (C1).
- The board should maintain a sound system of internal control to safeguard shareholders' investment and the company's assets (C2).
- The board should establish formal and transparent arrangements for considering how they should apply the financial reporting and internal control principles and for maintaining an appropriate relationship with the company's auditors (C3).

4.8.4 Relations with shareholders

- There should be a dialogue with shareholders based on the mutual understanding of objectives. The board as a whole has responsibility for ensuring that a satisfactory dialogue with shareholders takes place (D1).
- The board should use the annual general meeting to communicate with investors and to encourage their participation (D2).

4.8.5 Institutional shareholders

- Institutional shareholders should enter into a dialogue with companies based on the mutual understanding of objectives (E1).
- When evaluating companies' governance arrangements, particularly those relating to board structure and composition, institutional shareholders should give due weight to all relevant factors drawn to their attention (E2).
- Institutional shareholders have a responsibility to make considered use of their votes (E3).

4.8.6 Disclosure

Schedule C of the Combined Code provides for the disclosure of corporate governance arrangements in the annual reports of listed companies. The annual report should contain:

- A statement of how the board operates, including a 'high level; statement of the types of decisions that are taken by the board and those that are delegated to management'.
- The names of the chairman, deputy chairman, chief executive, senior independent director and chairmen and members of the nomination, audit and remuneration committees.
- The number of meetings of the board and the committees listed above and individual attendance by directors.
- The names of the non-executive directors whom the board determines to be independent, with reasons where necessary.
- Other significant commitments of the chairman.
- How performance evaluation of the board, its committees and its directors has been conducted.
- The steps the board has taken to ensure that directors develop an understanding of the views of major shareholders about the company.
- A description of the work of the nomination, remuneration and audit committees.

4.8.7   Case study: Equitable Life

During the 1960s to 1980s the 242-year-old Equitable Life had sold thousands of policies with guaranteed returns, some as high as 12 per cent. The company ran into problems in 2000 when it closed to new business after years of excessive returns to special policy holders had left the company with no money to absorb a deterioration in the value of its stock market investments. It had a 'black hole' in its finances estimated at £4.4 billion because it had been paying out more to policy holders than it held in reserves. Equitable lost a case in the House of Lords in 2000 that led to a further deterioration in its financial position of £1.5 billion.

A report by Lord Penrose published early in 2004 said that the former management was primarily culpable for Equitable's near collapse, aided by the failure of regulators to identify the mutual insurer's financial position. The autocratic former Chief Executive and chief actuary Roy Ranson was blamed for keeping regulators and the board of Equitable in the dark about the precarious state of Equitable's financial position throughout the 1990s. The Penrose report also said that there had been weaknesses in the way that insurance companies were supervised throughout that period. The 'light touch' approach to regulation had not been changed to meet the requirements of an increasingly sophisticated and risky investment industry.

The Penrose report said that management had been dominated by 'unaccountable' actuaries, a board of non-executives who had no idea what was going on at the company they were charged with overseeing and a regulator that failed to act as any kind of protector for policy holders.

Lord Penrose said, The board at no stage got fully to grips with the financial situation faced by the Society. Information was too fragmented [and], their collective skills were inadequate for the task.

4.9 Board effectiveness

The supporting principle for Code A1 states:

The board's role is to provide entrepreneurial leadership of the company within a framework of prudent and effective controls which enables risk to be assessed and managed. The board should set the company's strategic aims, ensure that the necessary financial and human resources are in place for the company to meet its objectives and review management performance. The board should set the company's values and standards and ensure that its obligations to its shareholders and others are understood and met.

Board effectiveness is largely a consequence of:

- Effective splitting of the roles of chairman and chief effective;
- The role of non-executive directors;
- The role of committees of the board: remuneration; nomination and audit.

4.9.1 Roles of Chairman and Chief Executive

The chairman is responsible for the leadership and effectiveness of the board and effective communication with shareholders. The roles of chairman and chief executive should not be exercised by the same individual (Code provision A2). A chairman should be independent and it should be exceptional that a chief executive should become chairman. Boards should contain a balance of executive and non-executive directors and a balance of skills and experience. Except for smaller companies (defined by the Code as those below the FTSE 350), at least half the board, excluding the chairman, should comprise non-executive directors determined by the board to be independent. A smaller company should have at least two independent non-executive directors. The board should appoint one of the independent non-executive directors to be the senior independent director, who should be available to shareholders if they have unresolved concerns.

4.9.2 Non-executive directors

Non-executive directors should be independent in judgement and have an enquiring mind, but they also need to build in recognition by management in the contribution they are able to make, so as to be well informed about the company and its environment, able to have a command of the issues facing the business. Non-executives need to insist that information provided by management is sufficient, accurate, clear and timely.

The Higgs Suggestions for Good Practice identified the role of non-executive directors in relation to:

- *Strategy*: constructively challenging and helping to develop proposals on strategy.
- *Performance*: scrutinise management's performance in meeting agreed goals and monitor performance reporting.
- *Risk*: satisfy themselves about the integrity of financial information and that financial controls and systems of risk management are robust and defensible.
- *People*: determining appropriate levels of remuneration of executive directors, and a prime role in appointing and removing executive directors, and in succession planning.

For the purposes of Code provision A3, independence is unlikely if a director

- Has been an employee of the company within the last 5 years;
- Has had a material business relationship with the company within the last 3 years;

- Has received additional remuneration, participates in share options, performance-related pay or is a member of the company's pension scheme;
- Has close family ties with the company's advisers, directors or senior employees;
- Holds cross-directorships with other directors;
- Represents a significant shareholder;
- Has served on the board for more than 9 years.

A research report produced by Independent Remuneration Solutions and reported in the Financial Times of 10th January 2005 suggests that non-executive directors do not believe that they have sufficient collective power to control a chairman or chief executive with a large shareholding in the company.

The same research found that non-executive directors of the largest companies (those with a turnover of more than £1 billion) spent an average of 38 days each year on their duties for which the average fee level was £35,000 per annum. Almost all now hold shares in the company, which aligns their interests with those of other investors.

4.9.3 Higgs Guidance

In 2006 the Financial Reporting Council published Good Practice Suggestions from the Higgs Report. The report can be downloaded from http://www.frc.org.uk/corporate/combinedcode.cfm. Although there were many recommendations, key recommendations concerned the roles of the Chairman and non-executive directors.

The chairman is pivotal in creating the conditions for overall board and individual director effectiveness, both inside and outside the boardroom. Specifically, it is the responsibility of the chairman to:

- run the board and set its agenda;
- ensure that the members of the board receive accurate, timely and clear information, in particular about the company's performance, to enable the board to take sound decisions, monitor effectively and provide advice to promote the success of the company;
- ensure effective communication with the shareholders and ensure that the members of the board develop an understanding of the views of the major investors;
- manage the board to ensure that sufficient time is allowed for discussion of complex or contentious issues, where appropriate arranging for informal meetings beforehand to enable thorough preparation for the board discussion. It is particularly important that non-executive directors have sufficient time to consider critical issues and are not faced with unrealistic deadlines for decision-making;
- take the lead in providing a properly constructed induction programme for new directors that is comprehensive, formal and tailored, facilitated by the company secretary;
- take the lead in identifying and meeting the development needs of individual directors, with the company secretary having a key role in facilitating provision. It is the responsibility of the chairman to:
  - address the development needs of the board as a whole with a view to enhancing its overall effectiveness as a team;
  - ensure that the performance of individuals and of the board as a whole and its committees is evaluated at least once a year; and
  - encourage active engagement by all the members of the board.

Non-executive directors should constantly seek to establish and maintain confidence in the conduct of the company. They should be independent in judgement and have an enquiring mind. To be effective, non-executive directors need to build a recognition by executives of their contribution in order to promote openness and trust. To be effective, non-executive directors need to be well-informed about the company and the external environment in which it operates, with a strong command of issues relevant to the business. A non-executive director should insist on a comprehensive, formal and tailored induction. Once in post, an effective non-executive director should seek continually to develop and refresh their knowledge and skills to ensure that their contribution to the board remains informed and relevant. Best practice dictates that an effective non-executive director will ensure that information is provided sufficiently in advance of meetings to enable thorough consideration of the issues facing the board. The non-executive director should insist that information is sufficient, accurate, clear and timely.

4.10 Remuneration committee

The role of the remuneration committee is to determine and agree with the board the framework for the remuneration of the chief executive, the chairman and other members of executive management that the board considers should be considered by this committee.

The Code provides that the remuneration committee should consist exclusively of independent non-executive directors and should comprise at least three or, in the case of smaller companies two such directors.

The committee should:

- determine and agree with the board the framework or broad policy for the remuneration of the chief executive, the chairman of the company and such other members of the executive management as it is designated to consider. The remuneration of non-executive directors shall be a matter for the chairman and executive members of the board. No director or manager should be involved in any decisions as to their own remuneration;
- determine targets for any performance-related pay schemes operated by the company;
- determine the policy for and scope of pension arrangements for each executive director;
- ensure that contractual terms on termination, and any payments made, are fair to the individual and the company, that failure is not rewarded and that the duty to mitigate loss is fully recognised;
- determine the total individual remuneration package of each executive director including, where appropriate, bonuses, incentive payments and share options;
- ensure that provisions regarding disclosure of remuneration, including pensions, as set out in the Directors' Remuneration Report Regulations 2002 and the Code, are fulfilled.

Source: http://www.icaew.co.uk

4.11 Nomination committee

The role of the nomination committee is to identify and nominate candidates to fill board vacancies when they arise, by evaluating the balance of skills, knowledge and experience on the board and preparing a description of the role and capabilities required for an appointment (Higgs Suggestions for Good Practice).

A majority of members of the committee should be independent non-executive directors. The chairman or an independent non-executive director should chair the committee, but the chairman should not chair the nomination committee when it is dealing with the appointment of a successor to the chairmanship.

The committee should:

- be responsible for identifying and nominating for the approval of the board, candidates to fill board vacancies as and when they arise;
- before making an appointment, evaluate the balance of skills, knowledge and experience on the board and, in the light of this evaluation;
- prepare a description of the role and capabilities required for a particular appointment;
- review annually the time required from a non-executive director. Performance evaluation should be used to assess whether the non-executive director is spending enough time to fulfil their duties;
- give full consideration to succession planning in the course of its work, and what skills and expertise are therefore needed on the board in the future;
- regularly review the structure, size and composition (including the skills, knowledge and experience) of the board;
- keep under review the leadership needs of the organisation, both executive and non-executive, with a view to ensuring the continued ability of the organisation to compete effectively in the marketplace;
- make a statement in the annual report about its activities and the process used for appointments; and
- ensure that on appointment to the board, non-executive directors receive a formal letter of appointment setting out clearly what is expected of them in terms of time commitment, committee service and involvement outside board meetings.

Source: http://www.icaew.co.uk

4.12 Audit committees and the Combined Code

 Code C3 of the Combined Code (Financial Reporting Council, 2003) states:

The board should establish an audit committee of at least three, or in the case of smaller companies[3] two, members, who should all be independent non-executive directors. The board should satisfy itself that at least one member of the audit committee has recent and relevant financial experience.

 An audit committee is

A formally constituted sub-committee of the main board which should normally meet at least twice a year. Membership of the committee should comprise at least three directors, all non-executive. A majority of the committee members should be independent of the company. The primary function of the audit committee is to assist the board to fulfil its stewardship responsibilities by reviewing the systems of internal control, the external audit process, the work of internal audit and the financial information which is provided to shareholders (CIMA Official Terminology).

---

[3] Below FTSE 350

The main role and responsibilities of the audit committee should be established in the terms of reference but should include:

- Monitoring the integrity of the company's financial statements; significant judgements made in relation to the financial statements; and formal announcements made by the company to the stock exchange.
- Reviewing the company's internal control and risk management systems (although in some cases financial controls may be the responsibility of the audit committee while non-financial controls and risk management may be the responsibility of a separate risk committee of the board, in which case the principles in Code provision C.3.1 should also apply to the risk committee).
- Monitoring and reviewing the effectiveness of the internal audit function.
- Making recommendations to the board for the board to place a resolution before shareholders in an annual general meeting for the appointment, re-appointment and removal of the external auditor and to approve the terms of engagement and remuneration of the external auditor.
- Reviewing and monitoring the external auditor's independence and objectivity and the effectiveness of the audit process.
- Developing and implementing policy on the engagement of the external auditor to supply non-audit services in order to maintain auditor objectivity and independence.

The audit committee should report to the board, identifying any matters where it considers action or improvement is needed and making appropriate recommendations.

The audit committee should also review arrangements by which staff may confidentially raise their concerns about possible improprieties in matters of financial reporting and, more generally, how those investigations take place and are followed up with appropriate action (Code provision C.3.4).

The audit committee should have terms of reference tailored to the needs of the company, which must be approved by the board. The audit committee should review its terms of reference and its own effectiveness annually. The board should also review the effectiveness of the audit committee annually.

4.12.1 Smith Guidance

The Combined Code Guidance on Audit Committees is referred to as the Smith Guidance. The Smith Guidance states that the chairman of the company should not be a member of the audit committee. Appointments to the audit committee should be made by the board on the recommendation of the nomination committee in consultation with the audit committee chairman. Appointments should be for a period of up to 3 years, extendable by no more than two additional 3-year periods, so long as members continue to be independent.

At least one member of the audit committee should have recent and relevant financial experience. The Smith Guidance states that it is desirable that this person should have a professional qualification from one of the professional accountancy bodies. The nature of the company will determine the degree of financial literacy required. Appropriate induction and training of audit committee members is essential, and the board must make available adequate resources for the audit committee to fulfil its responsibilities.

The arrangements for audit committees should be appropriate to the scope of their responsibilities and the size, complexity and risk profile of the company. The audit committee has a role to act independently of management 'to ensure that the interests of shareholders are properly protected in relation to financial reporting and internal control' (Smith Guidance, para. 1.4).

All directors remain equally responsible for the company's affairs as a matter of law, under the principle of the 'unitary board'. The audit committee is a committee of the board and disagreements must be resolved at board level. A section of the company's annual report should describe the work of the audit committee.

The Smith Guidance emphasises that

a frank, open working relationship and a high level of mutual respect are essential, particularly between the audit committee chairman and the board chairman, the chief executive and the finance director. The audit committee must be prepared to take a robust stand, and all parties must be prepared to make information freely available to the audit committee, to listen to their views and to talk through the issues openly (para. 1.7).

4.13 Role of the audit committee

It is not the duty of the audit committee to carry out functions that belong to others, such as management in the preparation of financial statements, or auditors in the planning and conduct of audits. Audit committees need to satisfy themselves that there is a proper system and allocation of responsibilities for the day-to-day monitoring of financial controls but they should not seek to do the monitoring themselves. However, this oversight function may lead to more detailed work if there are signs that something is wrong.

The Smith Guidance states that there should be no less than three audit committee meetings each year, held to coincide with key dates in the financial reporting and audit cycle as well as board meetings. Between meetings, the chairman of the audit committee will maintain contact with the board chairman, chief executive, finance director, external audit lead partner and the head of internal audit.

The audit committee should review the significant financial reporting issues and judgements made in connection with the preparation of the company's financial statements, interim reports, preliminary announcements and other related statements. Although it is management's responsibility to prepare financial statements, the audit committee should consider significant accounting policies, any changes to those policies and any significant estimates and judgements. Management should inform the audit committee of the methods used to account for significant or unusual transactions where the accounting treatment is open to different approaches. Taking the advice of the external auditors, the audit committee should consider whether the company has adopted appropriate accounting policies and made appropriate estimates and judgements. The audit committee should review the clarity and completeness of disclosures made in the financial statements.

There are two other important roles for the audit committee:

1. reviewing the effectiveness of internal controls (which is covered in Chapter 6); and
2. liaising with the external auditors (which is covered in Chapter 7)

4.13.1 Case study: Royal Dutch/Shell

In January 2004 the Anglo-Dutch company announced that it had remove 3.9 billion barrels of oil and gas from its 'proven' reserves in its balance sheet. This represented one-fifth of the company's proven reserves. The US Securities and Exchange Commission (SEC) have clear guidelines on what constitutes proven reserves: a reasonable certainty that the reserves can be delivered. These rules appeared to have been broken and the SEC launched an investigation. There were also indications that US investors are preparing a class action law suit for damages.

The announcement by Shell resulted in a fall in its share price which reduced its market capitalisation by £2.9 billion.

In responding to criticism after the announcement, Sir Philip said 'The group has made, and is continuing to make, significant enhancements to the internal controls surrounding the booking and reporting of reserves at all levels of the organisation' (reported in *The Times*, 6 February 2004).

The announcement led to the forced resignation of the chairman, Sir Philip Watts, and his deputy for exploration and production. The resignations followed an internal report from the group's audit committee to its board. New chairman Jeroen van der Veer was reported as saying 'The reason they went was because the board believed, based on the facts of the audit committee, that a change in the leadership was necessary … The work on the reserves recategorisation is continuing so I am not going to speculate if there was anything illegal' (reported in *The Sunday Times*, 7 March 2004).

The complex governance structure of Royal/Dutch/Shell also came under criticism for having two boards – with different board members – based in the Netherlands and the UK and calls were being made by analysts for a unified board structure.

In August 2004, the Financial Services Authority fined the Royal Dutch/Shell group of companies £17 million for committing market abuse and breaching stock exchange listing rules. The fine was a result of the 'unprecedented misconduct' in relation to misstatements of proven oil and gas reserves, despite indications and warnings between 2000 and 2003 that these reserves were false or misleading.

The US Securities and Exchange Commission (SEC) provides clear guidelines on what constitutes proven reserves: a reasonable certainty that the reserves can be delivered. These rules appeared to have been broken and the SEC launched an investigation. Following the ruling, the US Securities and Exchange Commission fined Shell US$120 million (£65 million). A class-action lawsuit in the US against Shell by investors was settled in 2008 for US$ 352 million.

4.14 Enterprise governance

In a report published by Chartered Institute of Management Accountants and International Federation of Accountants (2004), Enterprise Governance: Getting the Balance Right, enterprise governance was described as constituting the entire accountability framework of the organisation, with two dimensions:

- Conformance, and
- Performance.

These dimensions need to be in balance.

Conformance is what is generally referred to as corporate governance, covering board structures, roles and remuneration. Codes such as Turnbull address the conformance dimension through compliance, audit assurance and oversight such as the audit committee.

Performance focuses on strategy, resource utilisation and value creation, helping the board to make strategic decisions, understand its appetite for risk and the key performance drivers. Performance does not fit easily with codes and audit and oversight.

The CIMA/IFAC report presents a number of case studies. There were four key corporate governance issues that underpinned success and failure:

- Culture and tone at the top;
- The chief executive;
- The board of directors;
- Internal controls.

In the case of success, a virtuous circle was based on good governance being taken seriously because it was good for the company, not because it was required by law or codes of practice. In the case of failure, poorly designed executive remuneration packages distorted behaviour in the direction of aggressive earnings management and, in some cases, fraudulent accounting as in Enron and WorldCom.

However, good corporate governance was necessary but insufficient for success. While bad governance can damage an organisation, good governance cannot on its own ensure success.

The CIMA/IFAC report identified four key strategic issues that underpinned success and failure:

- Choice and clarity of strategy;
- Strategy execution;
- Ability to respond to sudden changes and/or fast moving market conditions;
- Ability to undertake successful mergers and acquisitions (M&A).

Unsuccessful M&A was the most significant issue in strategy-related failure.

The case studies in the CIMA/IFAC report identified no equivalent mechanism to the audit committee in its conformance role to ensure adequate oversight of the performance dimension. A recommendation of the report was the establishment of a strategy committee to undertake regular reviews of strategy and to better inform the full board's discussions about strategic decisions.

The CIMA/IFAC report identified the key priorities for attention as enterprise risk management; the acquisition process and board performance. The report recommended a 'Strategic Scorecard' with four components: strategic risks; strategic options; strategic position and strategic implementation.

The full report is available from the CIMA website.

4.15 Benefits of good corporate governance

The benefits of applying good corporate governance are to:

- Improve decision-making
- Reduce stock price volatility and cost of capital
- Improve stakeholder and shareholder communication
- Identify, mitigate and manage risks
- Identify opportunities for performance improvement

- Improve access to capital markets
- Enhance the marketability of product/services by creating confidence among stakeholders
- Demonstrate transparency and accountability
- Raise the organisation's reputation.

There are also benefits for national economies in good governance through stability and economic performance. The global financial crisis of 2008–9 has raised awareness of how lower standards of governance (see Chapter 1) contribute to economic problems on a national and global basis.

4.16 Summary

- Despite the primacy of the shareholder value/agency model of corporate governance, broader approaches exist (notably in the South African King Report).
- There are important links between governance, risk management and internal control and the interaction between the board of directors, the audit (and/or risk committees), external auditors and internal auditors.
- The emergence of corporate governance can be traced to institutional investors encouraging greater disclosure of governance processes; media reporting of governance practices; the high-profile failure of major business organisations in many countries and the dependence of an ageing population on savings and pension funds affected by declining confidence in stock markets.
- The emergence of corporate governance in the UK has followed a succession of reports: Cadbury, Greenbury, Hampel, Turnbull, Higgs and Smith, all culminating in the Combined *Code on Corporate Governance* which applies to listed companies.
- Companies are required to comply with the Combined Code's provisions or to provide an explanation. This approach is known as the 'comply or explain' approach.
- The Sarbanes-Oxley Act in 2002 was the legislative response in the United States which is very prescriptive. The King Report in South Africa takes a broader stakeholder approach to governance. There are important differences of emphasis in the two approaches.
- Corporate governance is the system by which companies are directed and controlled.
- The main principles of corporate governance found in the Combined Code are in relation to directors; remuneration of directors; accountability and audit; relations with shareholders; institutional shareholders and disclosure.
- The board's role is to provide entrepreneurial leadership of the company within a framework of prudent and effective controls which enables risk to be assessed and managed. Board effectiveness is largely a consequence of the effective splitting of the roles of chairman and chief executive; the role of non-executive directors; and the role of remuneration, nomination and audit committees of the board.
- The audit committee is a committee of the main board. The primary function of the audit committee is to assist the board to fulfil its stewardship responsibilities by reviewing the systems of internal control, the external audit process, the work of internal audit and the financial information which is provided to shareholders.
- The Combined Code states that a board should establish an audit committee of at least three, or in the case of smaller companies, two members, who should all be independent non-executive directors. The board should satisfy itself that at least one member of the audit committee has recent and relevant financial experience.

- The Smith guidance is that the chairman of the company should not be a member of the audit committee. Appointments to the audit committee should be made by the board on the recommendation of the nomination committee in consultation with the audit committee chairman.
- Enterprise governance constitutes the entire accountability framework of the organisation, comprising both conformance and performance, which need to be kept in balance. Good corporate governance is necessary but not sufficient for success. Conformance is what is generally referred to as corporate governance. Performance focuses on strategy, resource utilisation and value creation, helping the board to make strategic decisions, understand its appetite for risk and the key performance drivers.
- The benefits of good corporate governance include improved decision-making, reduced stock price volatility and cost of capital; improved stakeholder and shareholder communication; better risk management; performance improvement; improved access to capital markets; enhanced marketability of product/services; demonstrated transparency and accountability, and enhanced reputation.

References

In particular, students will find it beneficial to consult the *Combined Code on Corporate Governance*. Although this chapter highlights the main points, the Code is more detailed and in this single source incorporates the recommendations of the Turnbull, Smith and Higgs reports.

Cadbury Code (1992), *Report of the Committee on the Financial Aspects of Corporate Governance: The Code of Best Practice*. London: Professional Publishing.

Chartered Institute of Management Accountants and International Federation of Accountants (2004), *Enterprise Governance: Getting the Balance Right*.

Committee of Sponsoring Organizations of the Treadway Commission (COSO) (2003), *Enterprise Risk Management Framework*.

Committee of Sponsoring Organizations of the Treadway Commission (COSO) (1992), *Internal Control – Integrated Framework*.

Cooper, S., Crowther, D., Davies, M. and Davis, E.W. (2001), *Shareholder or Stakeholder Value: The Development of Indicators for the Control and Measurement of Performance*. London: Chartered Institute of Management Accountants.

Financial Reporting Council (2003), *The Combined Code on Corporate Governance*.

Financial Reporting Council (2005). *Internal Control: Revised Guidance for Directors on Internal Control*.

Financial Reporting Council (2006). *Review of the 2003 Combined Code: The findings of the Review*.

Financial Times (2005). *Non-execs say time demands outstrip pay*. 10th January, p. 3.

Institute of Chartered Accountants in England & Wales (1999), *Internal Control: Guidance for Directors on the Combined Code* (Turnbull Report).

London Stock Exchange & RSM Robson Rhodes (2004), *Corporate Governance: A Practical Guide*. London.

OECD (2004), *OECD Principles of Corporate Governance*. Paris: Organisation for Economic Co-Operation and Development.

PricewaterhouseCoopers (2003), *Corporate Governance in South Africa: A Comparison of The King*. Report 2002 and The Sarbanes-Oxley Act of 2002.

Revision Questions

? Question 1

This question has been adapted from the November 2007 examination for P3.
"Effective internal control, internal audit, audit committee and corporate governance are all inter-related". Discuss this statement with reference to the role of an audit committee in promoting good corporate governance.

(9 marks)

? Question 2

This question has been adapted from the November 2008 examination for P3.
HFD is a registered charity with 100 employees and 250 volunteers providing in-home care for elderly persons who are unable to fully take care of themselves. The company structure has no shareholders in a practical sense although a small number of issued shares are held by the sponsors who established the charity many years previously. HFD is governed by a seven-member Board of Directors. The Chief Executive Officer (CEO) chairs the board which comprises the chief financial officer (CFO) and five independent, unpaid non-executive directors who were appointed by the CEO based on past business relationships. You are one of the independent members of HFD's board.

The CEO/Chair sets the board agendas, distributes board papers in advance of meetings and briefs board members in relation to each agenda item. At each of its quarterly meetings the Board reviews the financial reports of the charity in some detail and the CFO answers questions. Other issues that regularly appear as agenda items include new government funding initiatives for the client group, and the results of proposals that have been submitted to funding agencies, of which about 25% are successful. There is rarely any discussion of operational matters relating to the charity as the CEO believes these are outside the directors' experience and the executive management team is more than capable of managing the delivery of the in-home care services.

The Board has no separate audit committee but relies on the annual management letter from the external auditors to provide assurance that financial controls are operating effectively. The external auditors were appointed by the CEO many years previously.

HFD's Board believes that its corporate governance could be improved by following the principles applicable to listed companies.

Requirements

(a) Recommend how HFD's Board should be restructured to comply with the principles of good corporate governance. (**16 marks**)

Solutions to Revision Questions

✔ Solution 1

Corporate governance has increased in importance on the corporate agenda as a result of the Combined Code (in the UK), Sarbanes-Oxley (in the US) and similar reforms throughout the world, as a response to major corporate collapses of Enron and WorldCom (in the US) and many other large companies in many countries. Institutional investors have also promoted improved governance processes as part of the move to encourage sustainability of earnings.

Corporate governance is the method by which companies are directed and controlled through Boards of Directors which establish corporate aims, provide leadership, supervise management and reporting to shareholders. The board's role is to provide entrepreneurial leadership within a framework of controls that enable risk to be managed.

The Combined Code recommends that board's appoint an audit committee of independent non-executive directors to assist the board in fulfilling its stewardship function by reviewing systems of internal control, the external audit process, the work of internal auditors and external auditors and financial reporting to shareholders. The Board will appoint and remunerate non-executive directors, some of whom will be appointed to the audit committee. The role of appointing and remunerating board members is normally a function of a Nominations or Remuneration Committee of the Board.

The main roles of the audit committee are:

- monitoring the integrity of financial statements;
- reviewing internal control and risk management systems;
- monitoring and reviewing the effectiveness of internal audit;
- appointing, monitoring and reviewing the effectiveness of external audit.

Importantly, the audit committee is a committee of the board and should have its own terms of reference. Although the Board delegates its authority to the audit committee, it retains its responsibility. The audit committee reports to the board and makes recommendations appropriate to its responsibilities. It is the board's responsibility to review the effectiveness of internal control (and not just financial control) on a continuous basis. The Board makes an annual assessment of internal control which forms part of the board's reporting to shareholders. In this assessment the board must acknowledge that it is responsible for the internal control system and for reviewing its effectiveness. In making this assessment, the audit committee and Board will rely to some extent on the reports from its external auditors. In the US, Sarbanes-Oxley has a particular emphasis on internal control over financial reporting and does not give the same prominence to the role of the audit committee as does the Combined Code. For companies listed in the US, external auditors report on management's assessment, but this is not a feature of UK legislation. The board should review the audit committee's effectiveness annually.

By monitoring risk management and internal controls, the audit committee and the Board itself contribute to good corporate governance, the benefits of which can include: improved decision-making, reduced stock price volatility and cost of capital; improved stakeholder and shareholder communication; better risk management; performance improvement; improved access to capital markets; enhanced marketability of product/services; demonstrated transparency and accountability, and enhanced reputation.

 Solution 2

The principles of corporate governance that are in the Combined Code are equally applicable to public sector and third sector (not-for-profit) organisations. They are applicable whether a charity is limited by shares or limited by guarantee. There are 6 categories of corporate governance in the Combined Code: directors, remuneration, accountability and audit, relations with shareholders, institutional shareholders, and disclosure. The main principles applicable to HFD are in relation to directors, accountability and audit and disclosure. Remuneration and relations with shareholders are not relevant to HFD.

Good corporate governance requires that a company be headed by an effective board with a clear division of responsibilities between running the board and running the company/charity with no individual having unfettered decision-making power. There should be a balance of executive and non-executive directors so that no individual or group can dominate the board. There should be a formal and rigorous process for the appointment of directors who should receive induction training. Information should be supplied in a timely manner to board members so that the board can discharge its duties. The board should then evaluate its performance both individually and collectively each year.

These principles do not seem to be applied for HFD as it is dominated by the chief executive who also acts as chair and appears to dominate the board through his appointment of non-executive directors and his control over the agenda. To meet the principles of good corporate governance, HFD should:

- separate the roles of chief executive and chairman with the chairman being a non-executive director;
- ensure that all directors are independent of influence by the chief executive. Positions should be advertised with interviews being conducted, perhaps initially by an independent person. Appointments should be for a defined period, after which directors should stand for re-election;
- provide induction training to new board members in the goals and operations of the charity;
- annually evaluate the performance of each director and the board as a whole.

Accountability and audit principles of good corporate governance require that a board should be able to present a balanced and understandable assessment of the company's position and prospects, should maintain a sound system of internal control and maintain an appropriate relationship with the company's auditors.

HFD's board does not seem to be able to make a balanced and understandable assessment of the company's position and prospects, given the narrow confines of what the CEO/Chair allows it. The CEOs relationship with the external auditors is not appropriate.

To meet the principles of good corporate governance, HFD should:

- set an agenda for board meetings that encompasses a wide variety of strategic matters including the charity's strategy, operations, risk management, internal controls and not be limited to financial reports and proposals for funding;
- consider meeting more frequently than quarterly;
- obtain an independent assessment of the company's internal controls by appointing a firm to act as (outsourced) internal auditor;
- affirm the reporting relationship of the external auditors to the board as a whole, and not to the CEO. The external auditors may need to be changed if they are unwilling to accept this changed relationship;
- although it is good practice, it is not necessary to have a separate audit committee, but if not, the functions of the audit committee should be carried out by the full board itself.

5

Risk and Risk
Management

Risk and Risk Management

5

LEARNING OUTCOMES

After completing this chapter you should be able to:

► Discuss ways of identifying, measuring and assessing the types of risk facing an organisation, including the organisation's ability to bear such risks.

► Evaluate risks facing an organisation.

► Discuss the purposes and importance of risk management for an organisation.

► Evaluate risk management strategies.

5.1   Introduction

The main purpose of this chapter is to define risk and identify different types of risk and to look at risk from a variety of perspectives. The chapter then looks at risk management in detail through its architecture, strategy and the risk management process which includes risk assessment, reporting and treatment.

This is a long chapter but it contains a great deal of data about the entire risk management process, together with a number of case studies. It is focused primarily on section B of the *Performance Strategy* syllabus but the principles of risk management apply through Part D (Financial Risk) and Part E (Information Systems Risk). As risk management is at the core of the syllabus for *Performance Strategy*, students will be expected to be able to apply the concepts in this chapter to any area of risk.

5.2   Risk

A typical dictionary definition of risk is 'a chance or possibility of danger, loss, injury, or other adverse consequences'.

Discussions of risk in management accounting texts have been linked to concepts of probability and sensitivity, primarily in the context of capital budgeting. In most accounting text books, risk has been considered in decision-making through techniques such as decision trees, probabilities, standard deviation and portfolio analysis.

In finance texts risk is often considered in terms of hedging techniques, discount rates for the cost of capital in capital investment evaluations, and beta analysis in the capital-asset pricing model.

Both of these approaches are consistent with CIMA's *Official Terminology*, which defines risk as:

A condition in which there exists a quantifiable dispersion in the possible outcomes from any activity.

By contrast, uncertainty is:

The inability to predict the outcome from an activity due to a lack of information about the required input/output relationships or about the environment within which the activity takes place (CIMA *Official Terminology*).

The distinction between risk and uncertainty dates back to Knight's classic work *Risk, Uncertainty and Profit*, published in 1921. According to Knight, risk was not knowing what future events will happen, but having the ability to estimate the odds, while uncertainty was not even knowing the odds. While the first was calculable, the second was subjective.

However, various researchers have noted a general lack of consensus about the definition of risk both in the management literature and in practical use in organisations (see later in this chapter). We need to start therefore with some categorisation of different types of risk.

5.3   Types of risk

Risks can be classified in a number of ways, for example:

- *Business or operational*: relating to the activities carried out within an organisation;
- *Financial*: relating to the financial operation of a business;
- *Environmental*: relating to changes in the political, economic, social and financial environment;
- *Reputation risk*: caused by failing to address some other risk.

It is important to recognize that there is no one widely-accepted set of categories, they will vary according to the nature of the business and its industry. What is important is that risks are classified in some way that is relevant to the needs of the business. The advantages of risk classification are that:

- The list of individual risks facing an organisation is potentially endless. By grouping them into categories, they can be managed in common by the use of similar controls.
- The identification of risks needs to begin at a senior level within the organisation. Categorisation forces managers to be more pro-active in their attitude to risk management. Boards of directors need to consider 'big picture' risks rather than the detail.
- Once a risk has been identified, it becomes possible to think of tools that may be used to measure and control them. Categorisation helps managers to identify how they can use their past experience.
- Risk categorisation provides a framework that can be used to define who is responsible, design appropriate internal controls and assist in simplified risk reporting.
- The development of a sound risk management system would be difficult without grouping risks into categories. Such a systematic approach may help organisations identify related risks in the same category.
- Categorisation may also assist in recognising which risks are inter-related.

For the purposes of explanation, we consider risk under these categories: business (or operational), financial, environmental or reputation. However, separate categories may well be identified for specific industries, such that credit risk may be particularly appropriate for a bank, technology risk for a call centre, or compliance risk for a regulated utility.

5.3.1 Business or operational risk

Business or operational risk relates to the activities carried out within an organisation, arising from structure, systems, people, products or processes. Business or operational risks include business interruption, errors or omissions by employees, product failure, health and safety, failure of IT systems, fraud, loss of key people, litigation, loss of suppliers, etc. These are generally within the control of the organisation through risk assessment and risk management practices, including internal control and insurance.

In banking, operational risk has a particular meaning, as defined by the Basel Committee on Banking Supervision. Operational risk is defined as 'the risk of loss resulting from inadequate or failed internal processes, people and systems or from external events'. This definition includes legal risk but excludes strategic and reputational risk. Operational risk, which is largely subjective, is distinguished from the more quantifiable credit, liquidity, interest rate and market risks.

5.3.2 Financial risk

Financial risk relates to the financial operation of a business, such as credit risk, liquidity risk, currency risk, interest rate risk and cash flow risk. Some of these risks arise from cultural and legal differences between countries, such as the demand in some countries for cash payments to arrange local sales. Obtaining money from customers in other countries or recovering the cost of lost goods in transit may also be difficult due to different legal or banking regulations. While these are typically outside the organisation's control, organisations can take action to mitigate those risks, for example, by credit control procedures, hedging, export insurance. These risks can be classified as transaction, translation, economic and political (see below).

5.3.3 Environmental risk

Environmental risk relates to changes in the political, economic, social and financial environment over which an organisation has little influence. Environmental risks include legislative change, regulations, climate change, natural disasters, loss of business, competition, economic slowdown and stock market fluctuations. These are outside the organisation's control but can be mitigated to some extent through environmental scanning and contingency planning.

5.3.4 Reputation risk

Reputation risk is caused by failing to address some other risk. This is within the organisations' control but requires the organisation to take a wider view of its role in society and to consider how it is seen by its customers, suppliers, competitors and regulators. The failure of accountants Arthur Andersen was a direct result of its loss of reputation following its audit and other work on behalf of WorldCom and Enron.

There have been changes to conceptions of risk in recent years, perhaps the most important one being the recognition that in considering risk, we should not just be concerned with 'downside' loss, but also with 'upside' opportunity.

5.4 International risk

Financial risks associated with international operations deserve special treatment, and are covered in more detail in Chapters 11 to 14, so the treatment here is brief. Financial risks in international operations can be classified as transaction, translation, economic and political. Although financial techniques such as hedging against movements in currency exchange rates and interest rate movements are the subject of later chapters (transaction and translation risk), there are some basic principles of managing risk in international transactions. In this section we are concerned with

- economic risk, and
- political risk

arising from international transactions.

5.4.1 Economic risk

Economic risk arises before transactions take place. These risks require a thorough knowledge of the organisation's competitive position on a global basis. Examples include:

- Dealing only in the home currency, risking customers and suppliers doing business with competitors who are prepared to deal in local currencies.
- Increasing inventory purchased from another country in anticipation of price increases, which may be offset by changing relative exchange rates.
- Bidding for new business on a fixed price basis without knowing when the bid will be taken up.
- Investing in a marketing campaign in another country in competition with local competitors, a decision which is subsequently affected by changes in relative exchange rates.
- Investing in capital equipment located in another country for local supply, a decision which is subsequently affected by changes in relative exchange rates.
- Investing in the home country, a decision which is subsequently affected by changes in relative exchange rates between the home country and a competitor located in another country.

5.4.2 Political risk

Political risk refers to the detrimental consequence of political activities in other countries that have an effect on the organisation. Examples include:

- Discrimination against foreign businesses.
- Nationalisation or expropriation by government of property.
- Regulations requiring specified use of local materials or labour.
- Exchange controls that limit transfers of funds or exchange into foreign currencies.
- Changes in taxation regulations or rates of tax.
- Restrictions on access to local loans.

5.5 Threat, uncertainty and opportunity

Risk can be understood in a number of different ways:

- Risk as hazard or threat
- Risk as uncertainty
- Risk as opportunity.

5.5.1 Risk as hazard or threat

Risk as hazard or threat is what managers most often mean when they talk about risk, referring mainly to negative events. Managing risk in this context means using management techniques to reduce the probability of the negative event (the downside) without undue cost. Risk as hazard is typically a concern of those responsible for conformance: financial controllers; internal auditors and insurance specialists.

5.5.2 Risk as uncertainty

Risk as uncertainty is the notion reflected in the CIMA *Official Terminology* referring to the distribution of all possible outcomes, both positive and negative. Managing risk in this context means reducing the variance between anticipated and actual outcomes. Risk as uncertainty concerns chief financial officers and line managers responsible for operations.

5.5.3 Risk as opportunity

Risk as opportunity accepts that there is a relationship between risk and return and usually, the greater the risk, the greater the potential return, but equally, the greater the potential loss. Managing risk in this context means using techniques to maximise the upside while minimising the downside. Risk as opportunity is the outlook of senior managers and corporate planners.

5.5.4 Risk: from threat to opportunity

Shareholders understand the risk/return trade-off as they invest in companies and expect boards to achieve a higher return than is possible from risk-free investments such as government securities. This implies that they expect boards and managers to be entrepreneurial, but that risks taken will be considered and managed within the accepted risk profile of the organisation.

Building on work by the International Organization for Standardization (ISO/IEC Guide 73), *The Risk Management Standard* (Institute of Risk Management, 2002) defined risk as the combination of the probability of an event and its consequences, with risk management being concerned with both positive and negative aspects of risk.

International Federation of Accountants (1999) published an important study on *Enhancing Shareholder Wealth by Better Managing Business Risk*. The IFAC report defined risks as

Uncertain future events which could influence the achievement of the organization's strategic, operational and financial objectives but shifted the focus of risk from a negative concept of hazard to a positive interpretation that managing risk is an integral part of generating sustainable shareholder value. The report argued that business risk management

establishes, calibrates and realigns the relationship between risk, growth and return.

Similarly, the Turnbull report (Institute of Chartered Accountants in England & Wales, 1999) defined risk as any event that might affect a listed company's performance, including environmental, ethical and social risks.

There is a natural progression in managing risk:

- from managing the risk associated with compliance and prevention (the downside);
- through managing to minimise the risks of uncertainty in respect of operating performance; and
- moving to the higher level of managing opportunity risks (the upside) which need to be taken in order to increase and sustain shareholder value.

This natural progression requires answers to two questions:

(a) What are the drivers of value?
(b) What are the key risks associated with these drivers of value?

The IFAC report argued that these questions could be answered by mapping the business processes that drive value; and then identifying and analysing the business risks and establishing the appropriate responses that will have the most impact on the value drivers. This is the process of risk management.

5.6 Drivers of value and risk

We know from the value chain (Porter, 1985) that various business activities add value that is reflected in prices. Value drivers may be purchasing power, production economies, distribution efficiency, after-sales service, etc. We also know that each of these value drivers also has cost drivers and it is important to recognise that the price able to be charged for the added value must exceed the cost of the activity that adds the value. However, we can take this one step further by recognising that each driver has associated with it particular risks. For example, if after-sales service is a value driver, this requires trained and experienced staff with good attitudes towards customer service. There is a cost of providing the staff, training them and monitoring the service they deliver. However, there are also risks associated with this. Employees may leave, standards of service may slip relative to competitors, information systems may fail, or customer expectations may change.

The risks facing an organisation can result from factors both external and internal to the organisation, although these drivers can overlap. Figure 5.1 contains examples of the drivers of key risks.

The Institute of Risk Management model shown in Figure 5.1 categorises risk in terms of financial; strategic; operational and hazard. Some of these risks are driven by external factors (competition, interest rates, regulations, natural events) and some are driven by internal factors (research and development, cash flow, information systems, etc.). Some risks have both external and internal drivers (e.g. employees, supply chains, products and services, and merger and acquisitions).

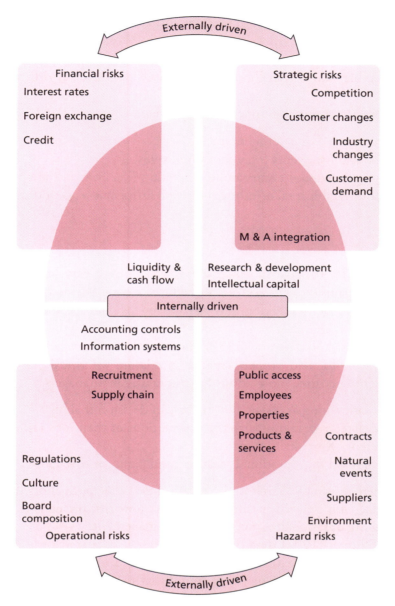

Figure 5.1 Risk drivers

Source: Institute of Risk Management (2002), *A Risk Management Standard*, reproduced with permission.

5.7 A wider view of risk

In chapters 2 and 3, we considered different methods of management control (including financial, quantitative and qualitative controls) and the limitations of some of the traditional management accounting techniques. These issues are important in gaining an understanding of risk.

Earlier in this chapter, we identified various categorisations of risk and some different examples of risk within those categories. Together with approaches that emphasise calculation, that is, probability, sensitivity, hedging, insurance (itself based on probabilities), discount rates, etc., the assumption was that risks can be assessed, measured and managed via feedback- and feed forward-type loops.

However, many risks are not objectively identifiable and measurable but subjective and qualitative. For example, the risks of litigation, economic downturns, loss of key employees, natural disasters, loss of reputation are all subjective judgements. Risk is therefore to a considerable extent 'socially constructed' and responses to risk reflect that social construction.

Risk can be thought about and understood by reference to:

- the existence of internal or external events;
- information about those events (i.e. their visibility);
- managerial perception about events and information (i.e. how they are perceived); and
- how organisations establish tacit/informal or explicit/formal ways of dealing with risk.

5.7.1   Managers and risk

Bettis and Thomas (1990) have shown that researchers have very little knowledge about how managers in organisations perceive and take risks or of the commonalities or differences between individual risk taking and risk taking by managers in the organisational context.

Research by March and Shapira (1987) suggested that managers were insensitive to probabilities but were focused on performance in relation to critical performance targets. These authors identified three motivations for risk taking by managers.

1. Managers saw risk taking as essential to success in decision making;
2. Managers associated risk taking with the expectations of their jobs rather than with any personal preference for risk;
3. Managers recognised the 'emotional pleasures and pains' of risk taking.

As a result of their research, March and Shapira noted that both individual and institutionalised (i.e. taken for granted within the organisation) risk preferences were important in understanding organisational responses to risk management.

Weber and Milliman (1997) described risk preference as a trait on a continuum from risk avoiding to risk taking, with risk factors being based on the magnitude of potential losses and their chances of occurring. They found that risk preference may be a stable personality trait, but the effect of situational variables on choice may be the result of changes in risk perception. These situational variables may exist at both national and organisational levels.

At the organisational level, Douglas and Wildavsky (1983) explained risk perception as a cultural process, commenting that

each culture, each set of shared values and supporting social institutions is biased toward highlighting certain risks and downplaying others.

5.7.2   Risk and organisational culture

There are three ways in which risk and organisational culture can interact:

1. A major shock or crisis, for example, a fire in a critical manufacturing site, in which culture is changed towards risk management before changing any processes.

2. Corporate governance changes are accepted as a result of legislation or regulation but without any cultural change. Processes are implemented but culture may change very gradually over time.

3. Compliance is not necessary (such as for a small, privately owned business), but where those in control can see benefits in risk management and this leads to a gradual change in both process and culture.

5.7.3 Risk and national culture

Uncertainty avoidance was one of the dimensions in the study on national cultural differences among IBM employees carried out by Hofstede (1980). The characteristic of uncertainty avoidance indicated the extent to which members of a society felt threatened by uncertainty and ambiguity. This was associated with seeing uncertainty as a threat, but compensated for by hard work, written rules and a belief in experts.

In a comparative study of four cultures (American, German, Polish, and Chinese), Weber and Hsee (1998) found that the majority of respondents in all four cultures were perceived to be risk averse. These authors proposed a 'cushion hypothesis' because in some countries (notably Chinese), collectivism cushions members against the consequences of negative outcomes. This in turn affects the subjective perceptions of the riskiness of options.

5.7.4 Risk and society

In an acclaimed book, Beck (1986, 1992 in translation) argued that we lived in a *Risk Society* (the title of his book) and that all risk was socially constructed.

Adams (1995) also adopted a 'cultural theory' perspective and differentiated the formal sector of risk management, with its concern with risk reduction, from the informal sector of individuals seeking to balance risks with rewards. Adams, like others, also contrasted the distinction between objective, measurable risk and subjective, perceived risk.

Adams presented four rationalities of risk, shown in Figure 5.2.

Adams identified four distinctive world views that have important implications for risk. Adams' 'four rationalities' (together with some possible implications for seeing risk) are:

1. Fatalists
2. Hierarchists
3. Individualists
4. Egalitarians.

Fatalists have minimal control over their own lives and belong to no groups that are responsible for the decisions that rule their lives. They are resigned to their fate and see no point in trying to change it. Managing risks is irrelevant to fatalists.

Hierarchists inhabit a world with strong group boundaries with social relationships being hierarchical. Hierarchists are always evident in large organisations with strong structures, procedures and systems. Hierarchists are most comfortable with a bureaucratic risk management style using various risk management techniques.

Individualists are enterprising, self-made people, relatively free from control by others, but who strive to exert control over their environment. Entrepreneurs in small–medium enterprises fit into this category. Risk management to individualists is typically intuitive rather than systematic.

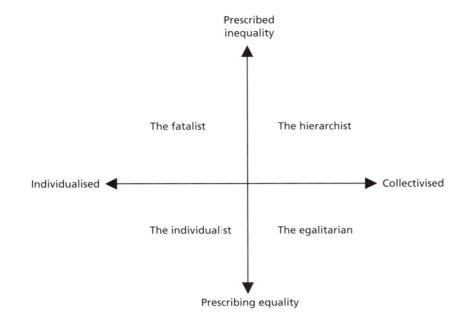

Figure 5.2 The four rationalities

Source: J. Adams, *Risk*, London: UCL Press, p. 35, reproduced with permission © Taylor and Francis.

Egalitarians have strong group loyalties but little respect for externally imposed rules and group decisions are arrived at democratically. Egalitarians are more commonly found in public sector and not-for-profit organisations whose values are oriented to social concerns. Egalitarians are most comfortable in situations of risk sharing through insurance, hedging or transfer to other organisations.

Collier, Berry & Burke (2007) carried out an extensive research project, funded by CIMA, into risk management and the impact on management accountants. The research found that fatalists are those who do not see risk management as being important or having any consequences. This group comprised only 7% of the respondents. Individualists agree that risk management is about positive consequences but disagreed or were neutral about negative consequences, perhaps reflecting them as a risk seeking group. Hierarchists disagreed or were neutral in relation to positive consequences but agreed in relation to negative ones. This is the risk-avoiding group. The egalitarians were risk aware, being balanced between risk management's role in achieving both positive and avoiding negative consequences. The Collier, Berry & Burke research suggested that this might be the group that would embed risk in culture and decision-making.

This research has important implications as it reflects the differences between individuals and groups in how they see risk and controls put in place to respond to risk.

5.8 Implications for risk management

The foregoing discussion has important implications for risk management because it demonstrates that not everyone, even in the same organisation, will see risk in the same way, and risks will almost certainly be seen differently by people in different organisations, even in the same industry.

This leads us to define some important risk terms: risk appetite and risk culture.

5.8.1 Risk appetite

Risk appetite is the amount of risk an organisation is willing to accept in pursuit of value. It is directly related to an organisation's strategy and may be expressed as the acceptable balance between growth, risk and return. Risk appetite may be made explicit in organisational strategies, policies and procedures. Alternatively, it may be implicit, needing to be derived from an analysis of organisational decisions and actions taken.

5.8.2 Risk culture

Risk culture is the set of shared attitudes, values and practices that characterise how an entity considers risk in its day-to-day activities. This may be determined in part from the organisational vision and/or mission statement and strategy documents but will be mainly derived from an analysis of organisational practices, notably rewards or sanctions for risk-taking or risk-avoiding behaviour.

5.8.3 Risk thermostat

Adams (1995) developed the notion of the 'risk thermostat' to illustrate how

- Everyone has a propensity to take risks;
- The propensity to take risks varies from person to person;
- The propensity to take risks is influenced by the potential rewards of risk taking;
- Perceptions of risk are also influenced by experience of 'accidents' that cause losses;
- Individual risk taking represents a balance between perceptions of risk and the propensity to take risks;
- Accident losses are a consequence of taking risks.

Figure 5.3 shows the risk thermostat with cultural filters (the ellipses) that influence each of the above factors.

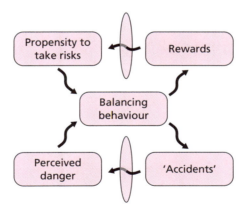

Figure 5.3 The risk thermostat with cultural filters

Source: J. Adams, *Risk*, London: UCL Press, p. 15, reproduced with permission © Taylor and Francis.

5.9 Risk management

The traditional view of risk management has been one of protecting the organisation from loss through conformance procedures and hedging techniques. This is about avoiding the downside. The new approach to risk management is about 'seeking the upside while managing the downside'. Figure 5.4 shows how risk management can reconcile the two perspectives of conformance and performance.

The conformance and performance dimensions are part of the Enterprise Governance approach supported by CIMA and described in Chapter 4.

 Risk management is defined as:

The process of understanding and managing the risks that the organization is inevitably subject to in attempting to achieve its corporate objectives (CIMA *Official Terminology*).

The Institute of Risk Management provides a more detailed definition of risk management as

The process by which organisations methodically address the risks attaching to their activities with the goal of achieving sustained benefit within each activity and across the portfolio of all activities. The focus of good risk management is the identification and treatment of these risks. Its objective is to add maximum sustainable value to all the activities of the organisation. It marshals the understanding of the potential upside and downside of all those factors which can affect the organisation. It increases the probability of success, and reduces both the probability of failure and the uncertainty of achieving the organisation's overall objectives.

Through these definitions, risk management can be seen as

- Linked closely with achieving business objectives;
- Addressing both 'upside' and 'downside' risks;
- Involving the identification and treatment of risks;
- Reducing both uncertainties and the probability of failure.

The risk management process is to manage, rather than eliminate risk. This is most effectively done through adopting a risk culture.

Figure 5.4 Risk management reconciles conformance and performance

Source: International Federation of Accountants (1999), *Enhancing Shareholder Wealth by Better Managing*.

World class risk management encompasses a framework of:

- *Risk management structure*: to facilitate the identification and communication of risk;
- *Resources*: to support effective risk management;
- *Risk culture*: to strengthen decision-making processes by management;
- *Tools and techniques*: to enable the efficient and consistent management of risks across the organisation.

5.9.1 Risk management and shareholder value

Ernst and Young (2001) have developed a model of shareholder value in which

Shareholder value = Static NPV of existing business model + Value of future growth options

which more simply put is 'the sum of the value of what a company does now and the value of what they could possibly do in the future'.

Good risk management allows businesses to exploit opportunities for future growth while protecting the value already created. By aligning risk management activity to what the shareholders consider vital to the success of the business, the shareholders are assured that what they value is protected.

Ernst and Young identify four stages:

(a) Establish what shareholders value about the company – through talking with the investment community and linking value creation processes to key performance indicators.
(b) Identify the risks around the key shareholder value drivers – the investment community can identify those factors that will influence their valuation of the company. All other risks will also be considered, even if not known by investors.
(c) Determine the preferred treatment for the risks – the investment community can give their views on what actions they would like management to take in relation to the risks. The risk/reward trade-off can be quantified by estimating the change in a company's market valuation if a particular risk treatment was implemented.
(d) Communicate risk treatments to shareholders – shareholders need to be well informed, as a shared vision is important in relation to the inter-related concepts of risk management and shareholder value.

Ernst and Young link enterprise risk management to shareholder value. This involves:

- Protecting existing value: the traditional role of risk management.
- Optimisation of risk: creating value by maximising the return for the level of risk the organisation is willing to accept. Real options analysis is one method of risk optimisation.
- Financial engineering of risk and capital: this alters the nature of risk itself, by improving the difference between return on investment and the weighted average cost of capital. Shifting off-balance sheet transactions back on to the balance sheet can result in a higher market valuation as a result of the perceived risk that may be attached to off-balance sheet transactions.

5.9.2 Benefits of risk management

The benefits of effective risk management include:

- being seen as profitable and successful;
- being seen as predictable, with analysts comfortable with what the organisation is saying;

- not issuing profit warnings, or having major exceptional items to report to shareholders;
- mergers and acquisitions are managed proactively;
- goodwill is not impaired;
- there is an excellent brand reputation;
- being seen to adopt corporate social responsibility and a good corporate citizen;
- having a well-managed supply chain;
- having a good credit rating.

The benefits of enterprise risk management are:

- Aligning risk appetite and strategy
- Linking growth, risk and return
- Enhancing risk response decisions
- Minimising operational surprises and losses
- Identifying and managing cross-enterprise risks
- Providing integrated responses to multiple risks
- Seizing opportunities
- Rationalising capital.

5.9.3 Limitations of risk management

No matter how well designed and implemented it may be, risk management is only able to provide reasonable assurance to management and the Board of Directors about the achievement of organisational objectives. This is because future events are inherently uncertain and therefore unpredictable. Whilst risk management can alert managers and directors to the degree to which the organisation is meeting its objectives, it cannot provide assurance that those objectives will be achieved. Risk management can fail because of poor judgement, mistake, negligence, collusion or fraud, or by deliberately ignoring or circumventing risk management processes and controls. Risk management can also be costly to implement and maintain, especially if it becomes a 'tick box' process aimed at achieving legitimacy rather than actually changing behaviour (it can be argued that the actions of some banks and financial institutions in the lead up to the global financial crisis of 2008–9 may have exhibited this kind of behaviour).

5.10 Enterprise risk management

CIMA's Fraud and Risk Management Working Group produced a *Risk Management: Guide to Good Practice* report (Chartered Institute of Management Accountants, 2002) revealing that risk management is evolving from a reactive response to a crisis (or a 'tick-box' exercise) into a proactive activity which forms a key part of strategic management.

Enterprise risk management aligns risk management with business strategy and embeds a risk management culture into business operations. It encompasses the whole organisation and sees risks as opportunities to be grasped as much as hazards. It is generally agreed among professional risk managers that the future management of risk will be fostering a change in the risk culture of the organisation towards one where risks are considered as a normal part of the management process.

In 2003, the Committee of Sponsoring Organizations of the Treadway Commission (COSO) (2003) published *Enterprise Risk Management Framework*. COSO defined enterprise risk management. This was updated in COSO's *Enterprise Risk Management – Integrated Framework* (COSO, 2004). Enterprise risk management (ERM) is defined as

A process, effected by an entity's board of directors, management and other personnel, applied in strategy setting and across the enterprise, designed to identify potential events that may affect the entity, and manage risk to be within its risk appetite, to provide reasonable assurance regarding the achievement of entity objectives.

ERM has four categories of objectives:

1. *Strategic*: high level goals which are aligned with the organization's mission;
2. *Operations*: efficient and effective use of resources
3. *Reliability of reporting*;
4. *Compliance with laws and regulations*.

These categories may be the responsibility of different executives and address different needs of the entity.

ERM also consists of eight inter-related components:

1. *Internal environment*: the tone of the organization, which sets the basis of how risk is viewed, including the risk management philosophy and risk appetite.
2. *Objective setting*: a process to set objectives that are aligned with the organization's mission and are consistent with its risk appetite.
3. *Event identification*: internal and external events affecting achievement of objectives must be identified, distinguishing between risks and opportunities.

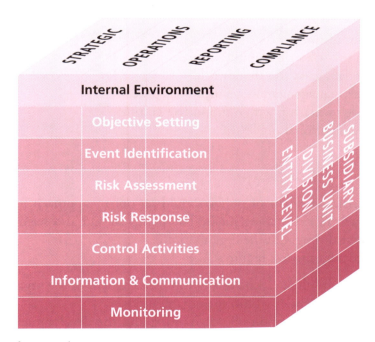

Figure 5.5 ERM framework

Source: COSO (2004) Enterprise Risk Management – Integrated Framework.

4. *Risk assessment*: Risks are analyzed, considering likelihood and impact, as a basis for determining how they should be managed, both on an inherent (gross) and residual (net) basis. Gross and net risk are described later in this chapter.
5. *Risk response*: Management decides whether to avoid, accept, reduce or share risk, developing a set of actions to align risks with its risk appetite.
6. *Control activities*: policies and procedures help ensure the risk responses are effectively carried out.
7. *Information and communication*: Relevant information is identified, captured and communicated that enables people to carry out their responsibilities.
8. *Monitoring*: The entire ERM is monitored through ongoing management activities and separate evaluations and modified made where necessary.

The COSO ERM comprises a three dimensional matrix in the form of a cube, which reflects the relationships between objectives, components, and different organisational levels. The COSO ERM 'cube' is shown in Figure 5.5

5.11 Risk management strategy

Whichever model of risk management is applied, organisations should develop a risk management strategy. Such a strategy will encapsulate:

- the risk profile of the organisation (i.e. the level of risk it finds acceptable);
- the risk assessment and evaluation processes the organisation practices;
- together with its preferred options for risk treatment (e.g. retention, avoidance, reduction, transfer);
- who is responsible in the organisation for risk management; and
- how reporting and monitoring processes will take place.

Effective risk management requires:

- management commitment
- integration with the strategic planning process
- using a common language and framework
- acceptance of risk management as a continuous process
- organisation-wide ownership with a supportive culture
- embedded in organisational processes.

5.11.1 Risk management policy

An organisation's risk management policy should set out its approach to and appetite for risk and its approach to risk management. The policy should also set out responsibilities for risk management throughout the organisation.

The risk management process requires:

- commitment from the chief executive and top management of the organisation;
- assignment of responsibilities within the organisation;
- allocation of the necessary resources for training and the development of an enhanced risk awareness by all stakeholders.

5.12 Risk management roles and responsibilities

A risk management framework needs to be established, reflecting the policy and guidelines for the organisation. Particular roles and responsibilities need to be established within the organisation. This includes assigning responsibility to:

- The Board, or its audit committee
- A risk management group
- The chief risk officer
- Internal audit
- External audit
- Line managers
- All employees, through the organisation's culture.

5.12.1 Role of the Board

The Board has responsibility for determining the strategic direction of the organisation and for creating the environment and the structures for risk management to operate effectively. This may be through an executive group, a non-executive committee, an audit committee or such other function that suits the organisation's way of operating and is capable of acting as a 'sponsor' or 'champion' for risk management.

5.12.2 The risk manager

The chief risk officer (CRO) or risk manager works with other managers in establishing and maintaining effective risk management throughout the organisation. The effectiveness of the CRO will be based on how well the CRO is able to instill a risk-aware culture throughout the organisation and delegate the detail of risk management to each organisational level. This is more an internal championing and consulting role for the CRO, which is unlikely to be effective if risk management is centralised.

The CRO has cross-functional responsibility for risk, with responsibility for developing and implementing a risk strategy, providing the overall leadership and strategic direction for ERM, establishing the framework in which ERM takes place, developing policies and procedures, clarifying with the Board of Directors the organisational risk appetite, implementing methods for the identification and assessment of risk, risk recording through risk registers, monitoring of risk events and their consequences, coordinating risk mitigation strategies and risk reporting.

5.12.3 Risk management group

The risk management group will advise the Board (and/or audit and risk committees) on risk management strategy and processes and will be the body which implements the Board's strategies and policies.

The risk management group should include:

- Chief risk officer (see above)
- Internal auditor

- Chief information officer (responsible for IT)
- Chief executive or chief operations officer
- Line managers representing each business unit
- Functional managers responsible for areas with high risk exposure (e.g. health and safety, environmental protection, quality control, insurance and so on)

The risk management group may also include the Chief Financial Officer and/or legal counsel.

5.12.4 Business unit responsibility

Business units should have primary responsibility for risk management on a day-to-day basis, including responsibility for promoting risk awareness within their operations, within the organisation's overall risk management policy. Risk management groups will often be duplicated within each business unit. Each group will have responsibility for the risk identification, assessment and evaluation process through to recording in the risk register for their business unit and reporting risks and risk treatment (consistent with organisational policy) to higher levels of management and ultimately to the Board.

5.13 Approaches to risk management

Various approaches exist to managing risk. These include:

- COSO's ERM framework (described above)
- CIMA's risk management cycle
- The Institute of Risk Management standard
- Australia/New Zealand Standard AS/NZS 4350
- HM Treasury's Orange Book

There are also other models available from professional consultancies, as well as those developed by various organisations for their internal use. However, the principles in all these approaches (or models) are virtually the same.

5.13.1 CIMA risk management cycle

CIMA's risk management cycle is shown in Figure 5.6. It can be observed that the risk management cycle is a development from the feedback loop and management control systems generally.

5.13.2 IRM risk management standard

Figure 5.7 shows the risk management process developed by the Institute of Risk Management (2002).

Figure 5.7 contains three elements:

- Risk assessment comprises the analysis and evaluation of risk through processes of identification, description and estimation. The purpose of risk assessment is to undertake risk evaluation. Risk evaluation is used to make decisions about the significance of risks to the organisation and whether each specific risk should be accepted or treated.

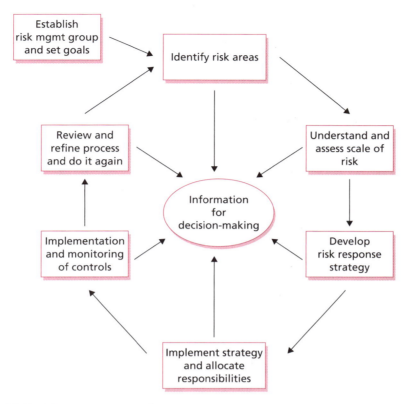

Figure 5.6 CIMA risk management cycle

Source: Chartered Institute of Management Accountants (2002), *Risk Management: A Guide to Good Practice*, CIMA.

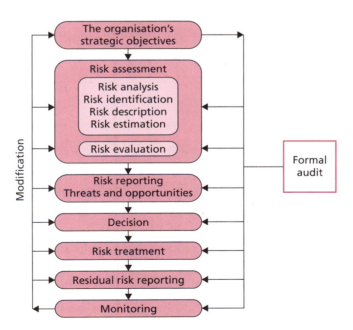

Figure 5.7 Risk management process

Source: Institute of Risk Management (2002), *A Risk Management Standard*, p. 4, reproduced with permission © Institute of Risk Management 2002.

- Risk reporting is concerned with regular reports to the Board and to stakeholders setting out the organisation's policies in relation to risk and enabling the monitoring of the effectiveness of those policies.
- Risk treatment (also called risk response) is the process of selecting and implementing measures to modify the risk. This may include risk control/mitigation, risk avoidance, risk transfer, risk financing (e.g. insurance), etc. Following risk treatment, there will be residual risk reporting.

5.13.3 Australia/New Zealand Standard AS/NZS 4360: 2004

AS/NZS 4360 (Standards Australia, 2004) was first published in 1995 and revised in 1999 and again in 2004. The Standard provides a generic guide for managing risk which can be applied to a wide range of activities in public, private or community enterprises. The Standard specifies the elements of the risk management process, but it is generic and independent of any specific industry or economic sector. It recognises that the design and implementation of an organisation's risk management system will be influenced by its varying needs, objectives, and its products and services.

The Standard has been applied far wider than in Australia/New Zealand. It has many similarities with the COSO model, the Institute of Risk Management's Risk management Standard and with the CIMA risk management cycle. However, AS/NZS 4360 is in process of being taken over by the International Standards Association and the standard will be released as an International Standard within the ISO framework.

The Standard comprises five steps:

1. Establish the goals and context for risk management.
2. Identify risks.
3. Analyse risks in terms of likelihood and consequences and estimate the level of risk faced.
4. Evaluate and rank those risks.
5. Treat the risks through the most appropriate options.

Communication and monitoring and review are ongoing processes in AS/NZS 4360 that inter-relate with all of the five steps.

5.13.4 Risk management in the public sector

Risk management in public and private sectors are little different. In the UK, HM Treasury (2004) produced 'The Orange Book – Management of Risk: Principles and Concepts'. This contrasted the private sector pursuit of shareholder value with the purpose of government being the delivery of service or the delivery of a beneficial outcome in the public interest. The task of (public sector) management is to respond to risks so as to maximise the likelihood of achieving the purpose, recognising that the resources available for doing so are finite, so the aim is to achieve an optimum response to risk, prioritised in accordance with an evaluation of the risks.

A hierarchy of risks is established, encompassing strategic, programme and project levels, and a public sector model of risk management is presented. However, while the HM Treasury document uses slightly different terminology but follows the same principles as are described throughout this chapter.

5.13.5   Comparison of approaches

Whilst all four approaches are similar, the IRM standard and the CIMA cycle provide only brief guidance rather than the detailed supporting information that is available from COSO (in a separate Application Techniques document) and AS/NZS 4360 (in their Guidelines document).

AIRMIC (the Association of Insurance and Risk Managers) has carried out a comparison of the COSO, IRM and AS/NZS 4360 standards. They found minor differences in terminology and the sequence in which the approach to risk management is presented. Both the IRM and COSO standards are more explicit than AS/NZS 4360 about the role of the Board of Directors, the risk management function and internal auditors. COSO's more detailed Application Techniques is more financially oriented than the other approaches, whilst AS/NZS 4360 emphasises qualitative, semi-quantitative and quantitative techniques to estimate likelihood and consequences.

The rest of this chapter takes a generic approach that does not rely on any particular model. We consider in turn:

- Risk assessment: how risks are identified;
- Risk reporting: monitoring the operations of the risk management system
- Risk treatment: how we respond to risks
- Residual risk reporting

5.14   Risk assessment

Risk assessment comprises the analysis and evaluation of risk through processes of identification, description and estimation.

5.14.1   Risk identification

Risk identification aims to determine an organisation's exposure to uncertainty, which requires an excellent knowledge of the organisation's objectives, its product/services and markets and the legal, political, economic, social and technological environment in which it exists. Risk identification needs to be methodical to ensure that all significant activities within the organisation have been identified and all risks flowing from those activities defined. Risk identification involves perceiving hazards, identifying failures and recognising adverse consequences.

5.14.2   Methods of identifying risk

The organisation may adopt either a top down (management knows best) or a bottom up (operatives know best) approach to identifying risk, or a combination of these methods.

Examples of methods of identifying risk are:

- brainstorming
- workshops
- stakeholder consultations
- benchmarking
- checklists
- scenario analysis

- incident investigation
- auditing and inspection
- hazard and operability studies (HAZOP)
- fish bone: breaking down a business process into its component parts to examine all the risks to that process
- questionnaires/surveys
- interviews.

5.14.3 Risk description

Risk description displays the identified risks in a structured format, by using a table which can be used to facilitate the description and assessment of risk. Table 5.1 gives an example of the information that could be shown against each risk.

5.14.4 Risk estimation

Risk estimation can be quantitative, semi-quantitative or qualitative in terms of the likelihood of occurrence and the possible consequences.

5.14.5 Methods of estimating risk

Various methods may be used to assess the severity of each risk once they are identified. Examples include:

- information gathering (e.g. market survey, research and development)
- scenario planning
- soft systems analysis
- computer simulations, e.g. Monte Carlo
- decision trees

Table 5.1 Risk descriptions

1. Name of risk	
2. Scope of risk	Qualitative description of the events, their size, type, number and dependencies
3. Nature of risk	For example strategic, operational, financial, knowledge or compliance
4. Stakeholders	Stakeholders and their expectations
5. Quantification of risk	Significance and probability
6. Risk tolerance/appetite	Loss potential and financial impact of loss
	Value at risk
	Probability and size of potential losses/gains
	Objectives for control of the risk and desired level of performance
7. Risk treatment and control mechanisms	Primary means by which the risk is currently managed
	Levels of confidence in existing control
	Identification of protocols for monitoring and review
8. Potential action for improvement	Recommendations to reduce risk
9. Strategy and policy developments	Identification of function responsible for developing strategy and policy

Source: Institute of Risk Management (2002), *A Risk Management Standard*.

- root cause analysis
- fault tree/event tree analysis
- dependency modelling
- failure mode and effect analysis (FMEA)
- human reliability analysis
- sensitivity analysis
- cost-benefit and risk-benefit analysis
- real option modelling
- software packages
- Delphi method
- risk map
- SWOT or PEST analysis
- HAZOP
- statistical inference
- measures of central tendency and dispersion.

A description of several of these methods is given below.

Probability

Many text books assume that managers gauge the probability (or likelihood or chance) of some event occurring by assigning a range of numeric probabilities. For example, a business may consider a range of estimated weekly sales figures and assign to each a probability:

Sales level (£)	Probability (%)
90,000	10
100,000	50
110,000	30
120,000	10

calculating the probability results in a probability-weighted estimate of £104,000 even though there is no expected level of sales of £104,000.

Failure mode and effects analysis

FMEA is systematic brainstorming aimed at finding out what could go wrong with a system or process by breaking it down into its component parts. Under FMEA, for each component of a system, the effect of its failure is identified, together with the consequential failure on the rest of the system. The likelihood and consequence of failure can then be estimated.

Fault tree analysis and event tree analysis

Fault tree analysis (FTA) and event tree analysis (ETA) are systematic methods to encourage better understanding of how a particular condition could arise, allowing causes and outcomes of events to be identified. This is a graphical technique that uses logic diagrams to identify causes (the fault tree) and consequences (the event tree) of potential failures.

FMEA and fault tree/event tree analysis are used in complex manufacturing, such as the automotive industry.

Hazard and operability studies

HAZOP is a brainstorming technique commonly used in oil and chemical industries. It uses terms such as 'none', 'more than', 'less than', etc. to identify problems in systems design.

Cost-benefit and risk-benefit analysis

Cost-benefit analysis is a technique that compares the advantages and disadvantages which would result from particular choices. Each advantage and disadvantage is assigned a monetary value, taking probabilities into account and often utilising discounted cash flow techniques.

Risk-benefit analysis balances the expected benefits that would arise from a particular choice with the expected risks. These may be either monetary or expressed in terms of injuries. This type of analysis was reportedly used by Railtrack to determine whether investments in train braking systems should be made.

Root cause analysis

This method investigates the cause of incidents by working backwards and considering all possible causes, continually asking 'Why?'

Human reliability analysis

Human reliability analysis (HRA) aims to identify failures due to human interaction. Processes are broken down into decision points at which correct or incorrect performance can result.

Delphi method

This is a group technique for aggregating the opinions of a number of experts. Questionnaires may be completed independently, and these are then circulated anonymously between the panel members. The process is repeated several times to achieve a convergence of opinion.

Sensitivity analysis

Sensitivity analysis is used to ask 'what if?' questions to test the robustness of a plan. Altering variables one at a time identifies the impact of that variable.

Simulations and Monte Carlo

Computer simulations of scenarios enable a consideration of actions against different events. The Monte Carlo technique uses probability distributions of different variables to simulate a wide range of events.

Soft systems analysis

Soft systems analysis is less concerned with issues beyond tangible, quantifiable information and is more concerned with feelings, attitudes, perceptions of individuals and groups and how conflict emerges and is treated.

5.14.6 Critique of methods

Research for CIMA by Collier, Berry & Burke (2007) found that the risk management methods in highest use were the more subjective ones (intuition, hindsight and experience), with quantitative methods used least of all.

The degree to which these methods were observed to be effective in helping respondents' organisations to manage risk was highly correlated with their degree of use, as might be expected. If a method was not perceived as effective it was unlikely to continue in use. An exception was that there was less confidence in experience, intuition, hindsight and judgement with only 48% of respondents believing that these were the most effective methods, compared with the 70% of respondents who used those methods.

Many of the quantitative methods are reductionist in nature (e.g. FMEA, FTA/ETA, HAZOP, root cause, HRA), that is, although the methods provide a formal structure for estimating risk, they assume linear cause–effect relationships rather than holistic or whole system relationships.

However, many methods are subjective and rely on individual perceptions of risk (e.g. soft systems analysis, brainstorming, cost-benefit and risk-benefit analysis, Delphi etc). Others are a mixture of the two, with subjective judgements reflected in probabilities (e.g. Monte Carlo simulations, sensitivity analysis).

It appeared from interview responses to the Collier, Berry & Burke research, that while quantitative methods of risk management were used, these were evident at lower organisational levels, rather than at corporate level, where the methods used were more subjective.

The most frequent example of how risks were assessed was through a matrix of likelihood and consequences.

5.14.7   Risk mapping: the likelihood/ consequences matrix

Whichever method of estimating risk is used, the most common way of assessing those risks is through the likelihood/impact matrix. This process is commonly called risk mapping. The likelihood or probability of occurrence may be high, medium or low. Similarly, impact or consequences in terms of downside risk (threats) or upside risk (opportunities) may be high, medium or low. For many organisations a 3×3 matrix of high/medium/low will suit their needs, while for others a 5×5 matrix (or even 7×7) may be more suitable.

Table 5.2 shows one way in which criteria can be assessed using a 5×5 matrix.

Table 5.2   Measures of likelihood and consequence

Likelihood Probability	
Almost certain	Expected to occur
Likely	Will probably occur
Moderate	Could occur at some time and may be difficult to control
Unlikely	Not expected to occur
Remote	May occur only in exceptional circumstances
Consequence Impact	
Extreme	Would threaten the survival or viability of the business unit or extreme political or community sensitivity or major impairment of reputation
Very high	Would threaten the continued operation of the business unit or significant impact on achieving business objectives or significant political or community sensitivity or significant impact on reputation
Medium	Would lead to significant review and change to the business unit or moderate impact on achieving business objectives or moderate political or community sensitivity or moderate impact on reputation
Low	Would threaten efficiency or effectiveness of some aspect of the business, although this could be dealt with internally, or minimal impact on achieving business objectives or low political or community sensitivity or little impact on reputation
Negligible	The consequences are dealt with by routine operations

However many categories are selected, care needs to be taken in placing risks in the middle category so it is useful to define what is meant by each risk category, either in terms of a quantified financial impact, or the number of times an event may occur. The difficulty in deciding categories is one reason why some organisations have expanded to the 5 × 5 or 7 × 7 matrix.

An example of a risk matrix is shown in Figure 5.8. This shows the area of highest risk.

By considering the consequence and probability of each of the risks it should be possible for organisations to prioritise the key risks. A typical risk description table may look like Table 5.3.

5.14.8 The Risk Register

Once risks are identified, described, estimated through using one or other quantitative or qualitative technique, and mapped according to their likelihood and consequence, many organizations record their risks in a Risk Register. This may contain as much information as may be considered useful for monitoring purposes. Examples of data to be included in a risk register are:

- Risk number (unique identifier)
- Risk category (see earlier in this chapter)
- Description of risk

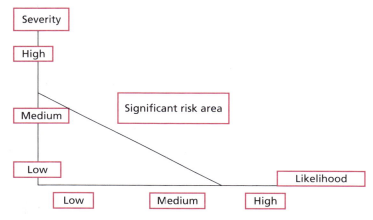

Figure 5.8 Risk matrix

Table 5.3 Risk matrix

	Low likelihood	**Medium likelihood**	**High likelihood**
High Impact	Failure of information systems	Subcontractors fail to meet commitments	Government intervention in markets
	Serious accident	Failure of project planning system	Entry of new competitor
Medium Impact	Loss of certificates or licences	Insufficient capacity leads to delays	Management overload
	Shortcomings in succession planning	Excess capacity leads to losses	Poor employee morale leads to resignations
Low Impact	Supplier failure	Profit shortfall	Inadequate R&D
		Cost overruns	Legal claims

- Date risk identified
- Name of person who identified risk
- Likelihood
- Consequences
- A monetary value, if such can be allocated to the risk
- Interdependencies with other risks.

As will be seen later in this chapter, the risk register will later be updated with the risk treatment (or response) decided by management. This will enable risk monitoring through the organization's risk strategy and by the board.

5.14.9   Risk evaluation

Risk evaluation is used to make decisions about the significance of risks to the organisation and whether each specific risk should be accepted or treated.

When risk analysis (identification, description and estimation) has been completed, the risks faced by the organisation need to be compared against its risk profile, i.e. the array of opportunities and exposures to the organisation and its preferences towards taking or avoiding risks.

Risk evaluation is concerned with making decisions about the significance of risks to the organisation and whether those risks should be accepted or whether there should be an appropriate treatment or response.

5.14.10   Case study: Risk in an Engineering Consultancy

This organisation is privately owned with 3,500 employees. A review of its financial performance had revealed that the estimated cost of project over-runs, non-productive time and contractual penalties incurred was about 2% of annual turnover. This represented an opportunity loss of about £3 million per annum against reported profits of about £5 million.

However, the main driver behind risk management was to address the rapidly increasing premium for professional indemnity that had increased premiums to several million pounds and had seen its excess increase from £5,000 to £500,000 per annum over the last few years. The organisation had appointed a risk manager; adopted an offshore 'captive' insurer and implemented a management development programme to improve the skills of all its managers. This had included a substantial content on risk awareness.

One of the ways in which it was helping its managers to understand risk was to undertake risk assessments as part of every project bid and to reflect each risk in pricing. During contract negotiations, each risk could be discussed between the lead consultant and the client when the value of the risk could be discussed in terms of the control devices that could be put in place by the client to reduce the risk and hence reduce that component of the project price that reflected the risk.

It was anticipated that this collaboration between consultant and client would reduce risk and lead to a more profitable outcome for both parties.

5.15 Risk reporting

Risk reporting includes:

- A systematic review of the risk forecast at least annually.
- A review of the management responses to the significant risks and risk strategy.
- A monitoring and feedback loop on action taken and variance in the assessment of the significant risks.
- An 'early warning system' to indicate material change in the risk profile, or circumstances, which could increase exposures or threaten areas of opportunity.
- The inclusion of audit work as part of the communication and reporting process.

Reporting needs to address:

- The control systems in place for risk management.
- The processes used to identify and respond to risks.
- The methods used to manage significant risks.
- The monitoring and review system.

5.16 Risk treatment (or risk response)

Risk treatment (also called risk response) is the process of selecting and implementing measures to modify the risk. This may include risk control/mitigation, risk avoidance, risk transfer, risk financing (e.g. insurance), etc.

Risk response involves:

- Setting a policy defining the organisation's attitude to a particular risk and the objectives of the risk response;
- Individual accountability for the management of the risk, with the nominated person having the expertise and authority to effectively manage the risk;
- The management processes currently used to manage the risk;
- Recommended business processes to reduce the residual risk to an acceptable level;
- Key performance measures to enable management to assess and monitor risk;
- Independent expertise to assess the adequacy of the risk response;
- Contingency plans to manage or mitigate a major loss following the occurrence of an event.

5.16.1 Risk mapping and risk response

Risk maps assess risks in terms of their likelihhod and probability. This provides a useful framework to determine an appropriate risk response. Figure 5.9 shows the COSO ERM approach to risk response based on the risk map.

Risk response may be:

- *Avoidance*: action is taken to exit the activities giving rise to risk, such as a product line or a geographical market, or a whole business unit. These are high risk events.
- *Reduction*: action is taken to mitigate (i.e. reduce) the risk likelihood or impact, or both, generally via internal controls. These risks occur more frequently but have less impact.

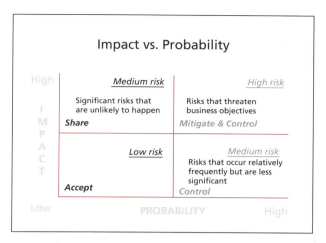

Figure 5.9 Risk mapping and response

Source: COSO (2004) Enterprise Risk Management – Integrated Framework.

- *Sharing*: Action is taken to transfer a portion of the risk through, for example, insurance, pooling risks, hedging or outsourcing. These are significant risks, which occur rarely.
- *Acceptance*: no action is taken to affect likelihood or impact. These have low impact even when they do occur, which may be frequent.

Each response needs to be considered in terms of its effect on reducing the likelihood and/or impact of the risk. Risk response also needs to consider the costs and benefits of alternative risk responses.

5.16.2 Portfolio

In establishing a portfolio view of risk responses, management will recognise the diversity of responses and the effect on the entity's risk tolerances. The basic principle of portfolio theory is that it is less risky to have diverse sources of income through a portfolio of assets or investments. Spreading investments reduces risk. This may be achieved by a combination of market expansion or diversification.

Types of market expansion include:

- Extension to market segments not currently served;
- Development of new uses for existing products;
- Geographic expansion, either nationally or internationally.

Types of diversification include:

- *Backward*: activities concerned with inputs to business processes within the same industry in which the organisation operates, e.g. production, raw materials;
- *Forward*: activities concerned with outputs from business processes within the same industry in which the organisation operates, e.g. transport, distribution, servicing;
- *Horizontal*: activities that are competitive with, or complementary to present activities, such as airlines providing car rental services;
- *Unrelated diversification*: opportunities beyond the current product/service or customer base of the organisation. These opportunities may be a result of exploiting core competencies or developing new ones.

The portfolio approach to risk management enables risk to be spread over a wider range of investments, thus reducing the impact of an event in one of those business areas on the whole business.

5.16.3   Insurance

Insurance involves protection against hazards by taking out an insurance policy against an uncertain event. Insurance involves payment of a premium to an insurer, who will pay the sum assured to recompense loss suffered by the insured. An insurer is able to offer such cover on the basis of probabilities assigned to particular events and the pooling of risks by many insured parties. The premium cost will be influenced by the extent of risk management carried out by the insured in order to prevent or mitigate risk, such as compliance with fire safety precautions and health and safety practices.

5.16.4   Derivatives and hedging

A *derivative* is an asset whose performance is based on the behaviour of an underlying asset (commonly called underlyings, e.g. shares, bonds, commodities, currencies, exchange rates). Derivative *instruments* include options, forward contracts, futures, forward rate agreements and swaps. *Hedging* protects assets against unfavourable movements in the underlying while retaining the ability to benefit from favourable movements. The instruments bought as a hedge tend to have opposite-value movements to the underlying and are used to transfer risk. Derivatives and hedging are covered in chapters 11–14.

5.16.5   Disclosure

A study by Solomon et al. (2000) emphasised that little guidance was available in the Combined Code as to what information about risks companies should disclose in their annual reports. They suggested a framework for corporate risk disclosure comprising:

- The voluntary or mandatory nature of disclosure
- Investors' attitudes towards risk disclosure
- Forms of risk disclosure, i.e. reported separately or grouped
- Disclosure preference, i.e. whether all risks had equal importance
- Location of disclosure, in the Operating & Financial Review, or elsewhere
- Level of risk disclosure, whether current levels were adequate or if increased disclosure would help decision-making.

Solomon et al. surveyed institutional investors during 1999. They found that almost a third of institutional investors agreed that increased risk disclosure would help their portfolio decision-making. They also found that institutional investors saw a strong link between corporate governance reform and risk disclosure. Solomon et al. recommended that the current voluntary framework be retained.

The Operating and Financial Review (OFR) provides a discussion and analysis of the performance of the business and the main trends and factors underlying the results and financial position and which are likely to affect future performance. This includes a discussion of the major risks facing the organization.

Linsley and Shrives (2006) studied risk disclosure in 79 UK company annual reports. They found a significant association between the number of risk disclosures and company size. However, they found no association between risk disclosures and measures of risk using financial ratios. There were few monetary assessments of risk but companies did disclose forward-looking risk information. Linsley and Shrives concluded that the dominance of general statements of risk management policy and a lack of coherence in risk narratives implied that stakeholders would be unable to adequately assess the risk profile of a company from its annual report.

The Appendix to this Chapter provides examples of how risk is disclosed in the annual reports of Adidas, Nestle SA, and Sony Corporation.

5.17 Residual risk reporting

Effective risk treatment will enable the board to consider:

- The nature and extent of risks facing the organisation;
- The extent and categories of risk which it regards as acceptable for the organisation to bear (the risk strategy);
- The likelihood of risks materialising;
- The costs and benefits of risk responses.

The assessment of risk significance can be further categorised to show how well the existing risk treatment techniques have reduced the overall exposure to the organisation (or increased the opportunities available to it).

Gross risk involves the assessment of risk before the application of any controls, transfer or management responses.

Net risk involves the assessment of risk, taking into account the application of any controls, transfer or management response to the risk under consideration.

An example of risk assessment using gross and net risk assessments is shown in Figure 5.10.

A comparison of gross and net risk enables a review of risk response effectiveness and possible alternative management options.

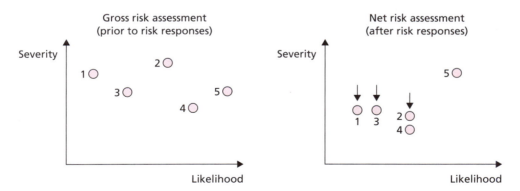

Figure 5.10 Gross and net risk assessments

Source: Association of Insurance and Risk Managers (2001), *A Guide to Developing a Risk Management Process*, p. 18, reproduced with permission © Association of Insurance and Risk Managers, 2001.

5.18 Case study: Risk in a Retail Chain

The group has 480 stores and sales of £1.5 billion. Risk management was part of the internal audit function. The internal auditor/risk manager said that the motivation for risk management was to 'establish best practice in corporate governance'. However, he commented that the business recently had 'problems with its fundamental controls' when 'senior management were looking at refinancing so took their eye off the ball'.

The process commenced with a brainstorming by the internal audit team of 'risk drivers' to identify what could go wrong and what controls could be put in place to address risks. The internal audit team held interviews with all managers to determine a measure of the effectiveness of these controls on a scale from 1 to 5. The threat of the control gap was identified and recommendations were made. This list looked like a risk register, although the group did not call it that. The internal auditor/risk manager did not see value in a risk register but rather saw risk management as high level.

The Risk Management Committee (RMC) meets every 2 months, comprising all business (executive) directors. The list given by the internal audit team to RMC showed the monetary value of a 'fundamental control breakdown', from which was deducted the monetary value arising from controls implemented to give a 'residual risk' (i.e. the risk after controls) to which was assigned a probability. These values were admittedly subjective. The RMC consider the risk maps, which showed the percentage probability of a threat arising and the residual monetary risk after taking account of controls. The whole process has been centrally driven, with a concern for 'high level' risks.

The big risks identified through this process were: supply chain, suppliers, people management, rebates, cost base, key processes, property management, market share, product offering and pricing, brand management, strategic management, integration and change, systems and business continuity.

The most recent development is a Key Control Improvement Plan (KCIP) that provides recommendations to address the risks. It summarises each risk (the example of supply chain failure was given) and the 'mitigating factors' (i.e. controls) and what still needs to be done.

The Audit Committee (AC) of the Board has four non-executive directors, the external auditors, the finance director and the internal auditor/risk manager and monitors progress in relation to the risk maps. The risk maps also drive the audit plan which is agreed on by the AC, business directors and RMC. The 'big nasties' are picked off, for example, purchase ordering and goods received, new stores, margins. Results are provided to the RMC and AC where the value of the report is greater than £250,000. Internal audit now had more exposure to decision-makers, as the risk management role had given them a high profile.

In the future, the internal auditor/risk manager wants to implement a Risk Intelligence Report to provide early warning of risks, by looking at key performance indicators to identify what the business should be concerned with. He also wanted to introduce a Risk Management Marketing Plan to help communicate risk and to pass on the responsibility to other managers with senior managers making presentations to RMC.

The internal auditor/risk manager expects it to take another 2 years to establish risk management in the organisation. More 'bottom up' controls need to be introduced and risk management needs to be embedded at the cultural level.

5.19 Summary

- Risk has been typically defined as a chance or possibility of adverse consequences. Historically, risk was associated with not knowing what future events will happen, but having the ability to estimate the odds, while uncertainty was not even knowing the odds.

- Risks can be classified as business or operational; financial; environmental or reputation. International risk has both economic and political dimensions.

- Risk can be understood as hazard or threat; as uncertainty or as opportunity.

- There is a natural progression in managing risk from managing the risk associated with compliance and prevention (the downside); through managing to minimise the risks of uncertainty; to managing opportunity risks (the upside) needed to increase and sustain shareholder value.

- Many risks are not objectively identifiable and measurable but subjective and qualitative. Risk can be thought about by reference to the existence of internal or external events; the visibility of those events; managerial perception about events and information and how organisations establish tacit/informal or explicit/formal ways of dealing with risk.

- Risk can impact on organisational culture through a shock or crisis; compliance with corporate governance regulations or where those in control can see business benefits in risk management.

- Not everyone, even in the same organisation, will see risk in the same way, and risks will almost certainly be seen differently by people in different organisations, even in the same industry. To aid in understanding different people's attitudes to risk, Adams identified four rationalities: fatalists; hierarchists; individualists and egalitarians. This has implications for risk appetite and risk culture. Adams' 'risk thermostat' (see Figure 5.3) is useful in understanding this.

- The new approach to risk management is about 'seeking the upside while managing the downside'. Risk management can be seen as linked closely with achieving business objectives; addressing both 'upside' and 'downside' risks; involving the identification and treatment of risks and reducing both uncertainties and the probability of failure. Enterprise risk management aligns risk management with business strategy and embeds a risk management culture into business operations.

- There are many benefits of risk management (see Section 5.9.2).

- The roles and responsibilities for risk management are spread across the Board, the chief risk officer, a risk management group and individual business units to all employees, through the organisation's culture.

- There are several approaches to risk management: COSO's Enterprise Risk Management framework; The Institute of Risk Management's Risk Management Standard; CIMA's risk management cycle; the AS/NZS 4350 Standard; and the Orange Book for Risk Management in the Public Sector. All have more in common than there are differences.

- Risk assessment comprises the analysis and evaluation of risk through processes of identification, description and estimation. There are various methods of identifying risk (see Section 5.14.2) and estimating risk (Section 5.14.5). The most common way of assessing risks is through the likelihood/impact matrix (see Section 5.14.7). Risk evaluation is used to make decisions about the significance of risks to the organisation and whether each specific risk should be accepted or treated.

- Risk treatment (also called risk response) is the process of selecting and implementing measures to modify the risk. There are a number of approaches to risk treatment (see Section 5.16).
- Risk reporting is concerned with regular reports to the Board and to stakeholders setting out the organisation's policies in relation to risk and enabling the monitoring of the effectiveness of those policies. Residual risk reporting involves a comparison of gross and net risk which enables a review of risk response effectiveness and possible alternative management options.

References

Students are encouraged to read:

Chartered Institute of Management Accountants & International Federation of Accountants (2004), *Enterprise Governance: Getting the Balance Right.*

Chartered Institute of Management Accountants (2002), *Risk Management: A Guide to Good Practice*. London: CIMA Publishing.

Collier, P.M., Berry, A.J. and Burke, G.T. (2007), *Risk and Management Accounting: Best Practice Guidelines for Enterprise-wide Internal Control Procedures*. Oxford: Elsevier/CIMA Publishing.

Committee of Sponsoring Organizations of the Treadway Commission (COSO) (2004). *Enterprise Risk Management – Integrated Framework*. www.coso.org

Institute of Risk Management (2002), *A Risk Management Standard*. London: IRM.

International Federation of Accountants (1999), Enhancing Shareholder Wealth by Better Managing Business Risk. Rep. *International Management Accounting Study No. 9.*

Linsley, P.M. and Shrives, P.J. (2006), 'Risk reporting: A study of risk disclosures in the annual reports of UK companies'. *British Accounting Review*, Vol. 38, No. 4, pp. 387–404.

Students are also encouraged to consult the websites of the large professional firms for details of their publications about risk management. The example in this chapter is:

Ernst and Young. (2001), *Risk Management Guide: Managing Risk To Protect And Grow Shareholder Value.*

Those students who would like to read about broader approaches to risk management may also like to read:

Adams, J. (1995), *Risk*. UCL Press.

Beck, U. (1986, 1992 in translation), *Risk Society*. London: Sage.

Douglas, M. and Wildavsky, A. (1983), *Risk and Culture: An Essay on the Selection of Technological and Environmental Dangers*. University of California Press.

It is not necessary to consult the following references for examination purposes; they are provided for those students who wish to explore various aspects of risk in more detail.

Bettis, R.A. and Thomas, H. (1990), *Risk, Strategy, and Management*. JAI Press.

Committee of Sponsoring Organizations of the Treadway Commission (COSO) (2003), *Enterprise Risk Management Framework.*

Hofstede, G. (1980), *Culture's Consequences: International Differences in Work Related Values*. Beverly Hills: Sage Publications.

Institute of Chartered Accountants in England & Wales (1999), *Internal Control: Guidance for Directors on the Combined Code*. (Turnbull Report).

International Federation of Accountants (1999), Enhancing Shareholder Wealth by Better Managing Business Risk. Rep. International Management Accounting Study No. 9.

March, J.G. and Shapira, Z. (1987), 'Managerial Perspectives on Risk and Risk Taking'. *Management Science*, Vol. 33, pp. 1404–18.

Porter, M.E. (1985), *Competitive Advantage: Creating and Sustaining Superior Performance*. New York: Free Press.

Solomon, J.F., Solomon, A. and Norton, S.D. (2000), 'A Conceptual Framework for Corporate Risk Disclosure Emerging from the Agenda for Corporate Governance Reform'. *British Accounting Review*, Vol. 32, pp. 447–78.

Weber, E.U. and Hsee, C. (1998), 'Cross-cultural Differences in Risk Perception, but Cross-cultural Similarities in Attitudes Towards Perceived Risk'. *Management Science*, Vol. 44, pp. 1205–17.

Weber, E.U. and Milliman, R.A. (1997), 'Perceived Risk Attitudes: Relating Risk Perception to Risky Choice'. *Management Science*, Vol. 43, pp. 123–44.

Appendix

5

The case of Northern Rock – a failure of risk management

Perhaps the most interesting example of 2007 for students of risk and control was the case of Northern Rock. In September 2007 Northern Rock plc was a top five UK mortgage lender, on the FTSE 100 index with over £100 billion in assets. Northern Rock raised over 70% of the money it used in its growing mortgage lending business from banks and other financial institutions. Following the global credit crunch that resulted from the crisis in the US sub-prime (high risk) mortgage sector, banks stopped lending to each other and Northern Rock could not raise sufficient cash to cover its liabilities.

A bank run (the first on a UK bank for 150 years) on Northern Rock by its customers led to the government providing 'lender of last resort' funding and guarantees for the bank's depositors totalling about £20 billion. The result has been a 90% fall in the bank's share price, a deteriorating credit rating and a loss of reputation. The CEO has resigned and several directors have also left the board. The most likely scenario is that Northern Rock will be taken over by another bank or financial institution.

Northern Rock had a formal approach to risk management, including liquidity, credit, operational and market risk, fully described in its Securities and Exchange Commission filings. Northern Rock's assets were sound so there was no significant credit risk. Market risk was also well managed in terms of interest rate and foreign exchange exposure. However, despite formal procedures and a demonstrated compliance with regulations, there was an assumption by managers that access to funds would continue unimpeded. The US sub-prime crisis led to liquidity risk materialising, causing the Northern Rock problems. The consequence was also the loss of reputation that followed press reports which blamed the bank's management for not having a contingency plan to cover the possibility of disruption to its funding, an operational risk. It is likely that the board of Northern Rock failed in both monitoring liquidity risk and in monitoring the effectiveness of the existing controls. CIMA members and students should also keep up-to-date on changes in corporate governance and should be aware of three recent developments.

Perhaps this case best illustrates the importance of balancing conformance with performance, as promoted by CIMA's *Enterprise Governance – Getting the Balance Right*.[1]

---

[1] http://www.cimaglobal.com/cps/rde/xbcr/SID-0AAAC544-CB9F2ECA/live/tech_execrep_enterprise_governance_getting_the_balance_right_feb_2004.pdf

Conformance takes place through assurance, ensuring that the organisation understands and is managing its risks effectively. Performance identifies the need to take risks to achieve objectives, and in order to do this, risk management needs to be integrated with decision-making at each organisational level. Northern Rock's SEC filings give the impression that its concern was primarily with demonstrating conformance with regulation, rather than with its overall control environment.

CIMA members and students need to be continually aware of the need to identify, evaluate, mitigate and monitor risks in their organisations. Business strategy, financial strategy, and risk and control strategy (not limited to financial risk) are distinguishing features of the CIMA syllabus, as identified in CIMA's report *The CIMA difference: our relevance to business*[2] which concluded (p. 31) that 'CIMA people go way beyond accountancy – they use their skills to provide analysis, decision support, value creation and risk management'.

The lesson of Northern Rock is that we need to move beyond the tick-box approach to compliance and that good governance requires a more insightful approach to risk management and internal control. This also shows the value of students and practitioners alike becoming more familiar with the subject matter of *Performance Strategy*.

---

[2] http://www.cimaglobal.com/cps/rde/xbcr/SID-0AAAC544-CB9F2ECA/live/brand_cimadifference_090807.pdf

Revision Questions

❓ Question 1

This question is a modified version of a question in the May 2006 P3 examination.

LMN is a charity that provides low-cost housing for people on low incomes. The government has privatized much of the home building, maintenance and management in this sector. The sector is heavily regulated and receives some government money but there are significant funds borrowed from banks to invest in new housing developments, on the security of future rent receipts. Social security benefits fund much of the rental cost for low-income residents.

The board and senior management have identified the major risks to LMN as: having insufficient housing stock of a suitable type to meet the needs of local people on low incomes; making poor property investment decisions; having dissatisfied tenants due to inadequate property maintenance; failing to comply with the requirements of the regulator; having a poor credit rating with lenders; poor cost control; incurring bad debts for rental; and having vacant properties that are not earning income. LMN has produced a risk register as part of its risk management process. The risk register identifies, for each of more than 200 individual risks, a description of the risk and the (high, medium or low) likelihood of the risk eventuating and the (high, medium or low) consequences for the organisation if the risk does eventuate.

The management of LMN is carried out by professionally qualified housing executives with wide experience in property development, housing management and maintenance, and financial management. The board of LMN is composed of volunteers with wide experience and an interest in social welfare. The board is representative of the community, tenants and the local authority, any of whom may be shareholders (the company is limited by guarantee, such that shareholdings are nominal and the company pays no dividends). The local authority has overall responsibility for housing and social welfare in the area. The audit committee of the board of LMN, which has responsibility for risk management as well as internal control, wants to move towards a system of internal controls that are more closely related to risks identified in the risk register.

Requirements

For an organisation like LMN, discuss

(a) the purposes of risk management,
(b) the importance of risk management, and
(c) its relationship with the internal control system.

Question 2

This question is a modified version of a question in the May 2005 P3 examination.
BJP is an organisation involved in making business-to-business sales of industrial products. BJP employs a sales team of 40 representatives and assigns each a geographic territory that is quite large. Sales representatives search for new business and follow up sales leads to win new business, and maintain contact with the existing customer base.

The sales representatives spend almost all their time travelling in order to visit clients. The only time when they are not doing this is on one day each month when they are required to attend their regional offices for a sales meeting. Sales representatives incur expenses. They have a mobile telephone and a fully maintained company car and a corporate credit card which can be used to pay for vehicle expenses, accommodation and meals and the cost of entertaining potential and existing clients.

The performance appraisal system for each sales representative is based on the number and value of new clients and existing clients in their territory. All sales representatives are required to submit a weekly report to their regional managers which gives details of the new and existing clients that they have visited during that week. The regional managers do not get involved in the daily routines of sales representatives if they are generating sufficient sales. Consequently, sales representatives have a large amount of freedom.

Head Office Finance department, to whom regional managers have a reporting relationship, analyse the volume and value of business won by sales representatives and collect details of their expenses which are reported back monthly to regional managers. At the last meeting of regional managers, Head Office Finance department highlighted the increase in sales representatives' expenses as a proportion of sales revenue over the last two years and instructed regional managers to improve their control over the work representatives carry out and the expenses they incur.

Requirement
Advise regional managers as to the risks facing BJP as a result of the lack of apparent control over sales representatives and their expenses and recommend the controls that should be implemented by regional managers to rectify this situation.

 Question 3

Revisit the case study of Crashcarts in the revision question at the end of Chapter 1, which was the 50-mark case study in the pilot examination for Risk & Control Strategy.
Answer the following questions:

(a) Discuss the increase in importance of risk management to all companies (with an emphasis on listed ones) over the last few years and the role of management accountants in risk management.   **(10 marks)**
(b) Advise the Crashcarts Call Centre on methods for analysing its risks.   **(5 marks)**
(c) Apply appropriate methods to identify and quantify the major risks facing Crashcarts at both parent level and subsidiary level.   **(20 marks)**

Note: The question and answer for part (d) worth 15 marks is included in Chapter 1.

Question 4

This question is adapted from the May 2007 examination.

ACB is a stock exchange listed company that designs and assembles small passenger aircraft which it sells to regional airlines throughout the world. ACB is highly regarded by its airline customers for the quality of its aircraft. ACB is also recognised for meeting contractual commitments through on-time delivery. The company generates profits before interest and taxes of about 5% of sales. However, due to the depressed nature of the airline industry and competition from foreign manufacturers the company has modest growth targets.

Marketing

About 60 aircrafts are delivered each year. The company's competitive advantage is its ability to take a standard aircraft design and customise it to the varying needs of its customers. This includes changes in engine size, passenger capacity, configuration, electronic equipment, etc. The cycle time from signed order to delivery is about 18 months. ACB sells its completed aircraft in the customer's currency. The fixed price is converted to ACB's home currency using exchange rates applicable at the time contracts are signed. Progress payments are made on order and throughout the production process, but the balance of approximately 60% of the selling price of the aircraft is made on delivery to the airline. This purchase price is typically paid by finance companies that provide lease finance to the airlines. Any delivery delay to the airline is a breach of ACB's contract and will result in significant financial penalties to ACB.

Production and supply chain

The manufacture of all the aircraft components has been subcontracted to about 200 suppliers located across several continents. The cost of purchased components constitutes 70% of the final aircraft selling price. Suppliers are selected on the basis of quality, reliability and cost. Contracts with each supplier include prices established in the supplier's currency and incorporate price increases and anticipated efficiency savings over the next 2 years. This enables accurate forecasting of material costs by ACB. As each component is produced to satisfy the differing requirements of each aircraft, any delay in receipt of any component will delay final assembly. A distribution company has the contract to transport all components to ACB's factory and barcoding together with satellite tracking technology enables the location of all components to be identified from despatch from supplier premises until receipt by ACB.

There are five major production operations at ACB's factory: four relate to component assembly and one to final assembly. The four component assembly operations are fuselage, wings, engines and electronics. All four component assemblies are brought together in a large hangar where the final aircraft assembly takes place. ACB operates its factory on a just in time (JIT) basis to minimise inventory. Production scheduling for each of the four component assembly operations must be integrated so that the final assembly can take place on schedule.

IT support

ACB uses a sophisticated enterprise resource planning system (ERPS) to manage its supply chain, purchase ordering, production scheduling, accounting and performance management and customer relationship management. The company also relies on an electronic data interchange (EDI) system to track component purchase orders from their despatch by suppliers to receipt at ACB's factory.

Quality control

Aircraft manufacture is highly regulated with stringent quality control and safety requirements. ACB has always maintained the highest standards. The government's Aircraft Inspection Agency undertakes regular inspections of component and final assembly quality in order to ensure annual re-licensing of ACB as an aircraft manufacturer.

Costing and pricing

The cost of each aircraft is estimated from a bill of materials for components and a labour routing, both of which take into account the customisation of each aircraft. Price negotiations follow the cost estimation process and discounts are given for quantity and the significance of the customer to ACB in terms of past and anticipated sales.

Overhead costs are traced to products through an activity-based cost system, based on cost drivers established for eight significant business processes. Profits are calculated for each aircraft and each order (which may be for several aircraft) and customer profitability analysis is used to support future sales efforts.

Risk management and governance

The company has a Risk Management Group at senior management level that maintains a register of major risks, carries out risk assessments in terms of their likelihood and consequences, identifies appropriate risk responses and reports to each meeting of the Audit Committee. IT risks and foreign currency exposures require highly specialised attention, and responsibility for these risks is delegated to the IT Department and Treasury Department respectively.

The ERPS and EDI systems are managed by the in-house IT department which has long-serving and highly skilled staff who have developed comprehensive operating procedures and business continuity plans. ACB's Treasury department primarily uses matching techniques to offset foreign exchange exposures in each currency but does use forward contracts where exposures in some currencies are deemed unacceptable.

The Board of Directors emphasises strategy and monitors sales and delivery performance. It aims to ensure that sales are spread evenly over different regions so as not to be disproportionately affected by political or economic changes. The general approach to risk management is to have a portfolio of customers, products and suppliers, so as to minimise sensitivity to any one factor that might jeopardise the company's success. The Board reviews assessments made by the Aircraft Inspection Agency and is actively involved in rectifying any problems identified.

The company's Audit Committee, composed of independent directors, monitors the risk assessments made by managers, ensures that internal controls are adequate and approves the company's internal audit plan each year. The Audit Committee also monitors all monthly financial performance information while the internal audit function spends a considerable proportion of its resources ensuring that financial performance information produced by the ERPS is accurate for management decision-making and financial reporting purposes.

Requirements

(a) State the recommended components of any organisation's risk management strategy and evaluate ACB's approach to risk management in terms of those components.

(12 marks)

(b) Identify the major categories of risk facing ACB and evaluate the controls adopted by ACB in relation to each category. **(28 marks)**

(c) Risk treatment (or risk response) is an important component of risk management strategy. Explain what is meant by risk treatment and its benefits to a Board of Directors.

(10 marks)

(Total = 50 marks)

Solutions to Revision Questions

5

✓ Solution 1

(a) *Purpose of risk management*:

Risk management is the process of identifying risks facing an organization, assessing the scale of the risk (in terms of likelihood and consequences). A risk response strategy is determined for each risk that takes into account the organisation's risk appetite, and a system of controls are put in place for the reporting and management of risks. There needs to be a risk treatment or response strategy whereby risks are managed through alternative courses of action: stopping an activity; influencing either or both the likelihood or impact of the risk; sharing risk through techniques such as insurance; or the risk may be accepted. One of the strategies for managing risk is internal control.

(b) *Importance of risk management*:

As for most businesses, risk may be business/operational, financial, environmental or reputational. Risk management is important to a non-profit organisation like LMN because it helps to enable the business to be successful both financially and in achieving its social goals. Risk management improves the ability to respond to and mitigate risks that occur; it minimizes surprises; enables advantage to be taken of opportunities; maintains the organisation's reputation; and helps the organisation to be socially responsible and be seen as a good corporate citizen. It is important, while recognizing all 200+ risks, to especially emphasise risk management for the major identified risks identified in the scenario.

(c) *Relationship of risk management with internal control system*:

An internal control system includes all the policies and procedures necessary to ensure that organisational objectives are achieved including the orderly and efficient conduct of the business; the safeguarding of assets; the prevention and detection of fraud and error; the accuracy and completeness of the accounting records; and the timely preparation of reliable financial information.

Risk management is an important precursor to internal control as it allows the internal controls to be focused on the most significant risks. In the United States, Committee of Sponsoring Organizations of the Treadway Commission (COSO) developed a model of internal control containing five elements:

1. A control environment that includes management values, operating style, organisation structure, authority, and policies, etc.
2. The risk assessment of internal and external risks.
3. Control activities which should be integrated with risk assessment.

4. A system for monitoring the effectiveness of the system of controls.

5. Means by which information can be captured and communicated.

Therefore, risks are assessed and control activities are determined that relate to the assessed risks. These internal controls comprise financial and other controls, including internal audit, established in order to provide reasonable assurance of effective and efficient operation; internal financial control; and compliance with laws and regulations (CIMA *Official Terminology*). Internal controls comprise the whole set of financial controls; non-financial quantitative controls; and non-financial qualitative controls.

In LMN, internal controls should address issues of demand and capacity management of housing stock; financial evaluation techniques (such as DCF) for property investment decisions; tenant satisfaction surveys; monitoring of response to maintenance requests; establishing strong liaison with the regulator and lenders; financial reporting; cost control; debt collection procedures; and management of vacant properties.

 ## Solution 2

The risks facing BJP can be considered in two areas: first, the lack of control over the activities of sales representatives that may result in them not spending their time efficiently and effectively on business activities; and second, the incurrence of costs that are unauthorised or unnecessary. The first results in paying salaries for representatives but obtaining inadequate or inappropriate efforts from them. This has both a financial and an opportunity cost. The second results in excessive financial costs. Both are largely a problem of agency in which there is information asymmetry between the sales representative and regional manager. There is also an issue of moral hazard in which there is the potential for 'shirking' behaviour.

Risks may be classified either as business risks where value for money is not obtained (i.e. waste) or fraud risk in which there is a deliberate attempt to use business time and/or expenses for non-business purposes. These risks are particularly important where there are staff working without direct supervision and where regional management is remote from staff and from Head Office.

Risk management practices involve assessing the likelihood and consequences of risk and putting in place appropriate management. Prior to the approach by Finance to regional managers, there appears to have been no assessment, reporting or mitigation of risk in BJP.

The controls that should be introduced cover sales activities, and expenses. In relation to sales activities:

- Contract of employment and policies covering expectations of sales representative performance e.g. planning calls to minimise mileage and accommodation, number of calls expected per day, etc.
- Setting targets for the number of sales calls and volume and value of business generated by each representative;
- Setting of appropriate bonus schemes to ensure that incremental effort is rewarded and that bonuses are not paid on business that would be generated in any event;
- Monitoring of sales call reports by regional manager to ensure workload is adequate;
- Confirming with customers that visits have taken place and customer is satisfied with the quality of the visit;
- Determining success rates by representatives in turning prospects into customers;
- Monitoring comparative performance between individual representatives.

In relation to expenses

- Expense policies to specify what costs can be incurred and charged to the business and what constitute private expenditure, e.g. use of mobile phone for private calls, private use of motor vehicle;
- Procedures for negotiating with hotel chains, petrol stations and similar suppliers to obtain quantity and loyalty discounts;
- Setting of a budget for expenses, possibly as a percentage of sales revenue;
- Setting limits for individual items of expenditure;
- Monthly expense reporting for each representative showing the cost incurred and the reason for its incurrence, including the customer/prospective customer the expense was incurred in relation to;
- The company should strive to pay, wherever possible, for expenses directly via invoicing or corporate credit card rather than reimbursing expenses to representatives.
- Monitoring of expenses by regional manager and pre-authorisation of expenses over agreed limits;
- Reduction of bonuses by a factor reflecting the level of representative expenses incurred;
- Comparison of budget and actual expenditure and investigation of material variances;
- Monitoring of vehicle mileage, maintenance, insurance claims, parking and speeding penalties and mileage rates by representative to identify higher than expected use or careless driving;
- Monitoring of comparative expenditure by individual representatives;
- Representative expenses should be subject to internal audit.

All expenses must be documented, authorised, necessary for business purposes, and not private expenditure which the employee seeks to have paid for by the organisation. Organisations need to establish policies and procedures to recover business expenditure used for private purposes, e.g. private mileage, use of business telephones for personal calls, etc.

Generally in relation to personnel controls

- Effective recruitment including checking of prior references;
- Performance appraisal covering both sales activities and results and expenses;
- Appropriate training programmes to ensure effective sales techniques;
- Awareness, and influencing, of the informal socialisation processes in the organisation, especially where the culture of sales representatives may encourage behaviour not consistent with policies;
- Disciplinary process and appropriate rewards and sanctions to support other processes.

✔ Solution 3

(a) Answers must address the Combined Code and especially the Turnbull report. This includes the need for internal controls as part of corporate governance processes. The Turnbull report (ICAEW, 1999) recognised that profits were in part a reward for successful risk taking, and that the purpose of internal control was to help manage and control risk, rather than eliminate it. The report requires a risk-based approach to establishing a system of internal control. The report requires all listed companies to have an embedded internal control system that monitors important threats. Risks are defined as any events that might affect a listed company's performance, including environmental, ethical and social risks. For each risk, Boards need to consider the risks and the extent to which they are acceptable, the likelihood of risk materialising and the ability of the organisation to reduce the incidence and impact of the risk. A major responsibility of the Board is to review the effectiveness of internal control. It is required to make a statement on internal control, i.e. the process for identifying, evaluating and managing significant risks.

Management accountants have a role in developing and maintaining management control systems that accommodate both strategic and budgetary (feed forward) and financial and non-financial performance control (feedback) mechanisms. While this typically emphasizes a concern with variance (between plan and expectation, or between plan and actual result), management accountants can play a part in identifying risk, assessing the consequences of risk through the application of quantification and analytic techniques, developing internal control systems to help manage risk and incorporating risk reporting into management information systems.

(b) There are various methods of identifying, evaluating and managing risk that Crashcarts could employ. Methods include using experience and judgement, brainstorming, scenario analysis, PEST/SWOT analysis, interviews and surveys, and statistical analysis. Some organisations use professional risk managers, either as internal consultants or as bought-in advisers. A common method is the Risk Register which lists each significant risk and the management action taken in relation to each risk. A simple but appropriate method for assessing risk is the likelihood/ consequences matrix (see below). However, this simple version can be enhanced by Crashcarts using a 3 × 3 or larger matrix. The risks can be assessed by using probability techniques to assess likelihood and financial and non-financial performance information to quantify the consequences.

(c) Methods for analysing risk

The *likelihood/consequences matrix* is the simplest and most effective method to categorise risk and prioritise risk management.

		Consequences	
		Low	*High*
	High	Spare operator capacity Staffing changes	Loss of clients at end of 5 years out of stocks
Likelihood	*Low*	Reduced line items	Reduced orders Failure of Suppliers Systems failure

Quantification can be used to identify for example, the impact of gaining/losing a customer, price changes, changes in the out-of-stock rate, etc. The impact of spare operator capacity and out of stocks on lost income is shown below:

	2001	2002	2003
Spare Capacity			
No. of operators	70	80	80
Capacity (operators × orders)	1,050,000	1,200,000	1,200,000
Actual number of orders	1,000,000	1,100,000	1,150,000
Spare capacity (orders)	50,000	100,000	50,000
Cost per order (Operator costs/order capacity)	£1.48	£1.60	£1.82
Cost of spare capacity	£73,810	£160,000	£90,833
Out of stocks			
No. of incoming calls received	1,200,000	1,300,000	1,350,000
No. of orders processed	1,000,000	1,100,000	1,150,000
Out of stocks – orders	200,000	200,000	200,000
Average no. of line items per order	3.0	2.9	2.8
Out of stocks – line items	600,000	581,818	565,217
Income per order processed	£2.50	£2.75	£3.00
Income per line item processed	£0.20	£0.15	£0.12
Lost income per order	£500,000	£550,000	£600,000
Lost income per line item	£120,000	£87,273	£67,826
Total lost income from out of stocks	£620,000	£637,273	£667,826

NB: Different results may be presented as a result of rounding differences.

Although both are risks, the financial consequences of out-of-stocks are much higher than spare capacity.

The major risks facing the subsidiary are:

- The loss of clients and the inability to win replacement (in the event of loss) and/or new clients (increased business), particularly in an environment where call centre operations are increasingly being transferred to lower cost off-shore locations.
- The number of out-of-stock situations in its retail clients, which are causing substantial lost income, both to Crashcarts and to its retail clients, although there may be a need to increase staffing if the number of out of stocks was reduced. The question implies that lost orders are solely a result of the difference between calls received and orders placed.

Both of these represent significant lost opportunities.

- A further issue is the need to replace or update the technology after five years (or even before!)

The major risks facing the parent are:

- Reputation risk may face Crashcarts Group if the Call Centre subsidiary lets its clients down by not being able to provide its service, as it is heavily reliant on external suppliers to maintain its infrastructure. As an IT consultancy to the retail sector, Crashcarts Group may also face a reputation loss if its subsidiary is unsuccessful.
- Given the reducing profits of the subsidiary, Crashcarts may also face impairment of its goodwill, which may need to be reflected in its Balance Sheet under FRS10.
- Fraud in the subsidiary is also a major risk, given the subsidiary's ability to obtain credit and debit card information from the retail stores' customers.

The diversification into Call Centre operations presents a risk to the parent that needs to be assessed, monitored and managed. There is a need to protect shareholders' investment (reputation, physical assets, profitability, etc.) as well as interests of clients.

The major risks to the subsidiary are not carried through to the parent as the consequences of failure of the subsidiary will not impact the parent significantly (goodwill is fairly minor in relation to group turnover), other than the reputation risk.

☑ Solution 4

(a) Risk management strategy

All organisations should develop a risk management strategy, which will include:

- the risk appetite of the organisation, i.e. the level of risk it finds acceptable;
- the risk assessment and evaluation processes the organisation practices;
- its preferred options for risk treatment (e.g. retention, avoidance, reduction, transfer);
- who is responsible in the organisation for risk management;
- how reporting and monitoring processes take place.

There is no evidence of individuals or a group being charged with actively identifying risks. It is insufficient to simply react to risks that become generally apparent.

There is no evidence of an explicit determination of ACB's risk appetite which would provide a consistent reference point. The method of risk treatment adopted seems to rely on a portfolio approach. However, there is potential for significant risks to eventuate due to the company's exposure to its supply chain, information technology and foreign exchange.

The company's Risk Management Group does carry out risk assessments, treatment and reporting. However, it is not clear from the scenario whether internal controls are related to risk or whether more traditional methods of internal control are in use.

IT risks appear to be managed by the IT department and foreign exchange risks by the Treasury department but there appears to be little oversight of these risks by the Risk Management Group or the Audit Committee.

There is an internal audit process but again, it is unclear the extent to which this is linked to risk assessment as the main emphasis seems to be on financial controls. Consequently, it seems likely that improvements could be made in internal controls, internal audit and reporting processes to support the established risk management function.

The risk management process is managed by the audit committee of ACB. While governance does appear to incorporate risk management, internal controls and internal audit, it may be that the audit committee is overly reliant on financial rather than non-financial information.

(b) Risk and controls

Supply chain risk

A major risk faced by ACB is a failure of its supply chain which would stop aircraft production and result in significant penalties from airlines where delivery dates are not met. Although the board does seem to monitor ACB's delivery performance, any potential failure of suppliers or the logistics company constitutes a significant risk. There is no evidence that there is dual sourcing of either component or logistics suppliers or of any contingency back-up capacity for transport or production line operations.

Reputation risk

Failure of ACB's supply chain will cause delays in delivery which will not only incur financial penalties but future orders may be lost resulting in a loss of reputation and lower profits in the future.

The stringent quality and safety requirements are being maintained but any reduction in standards due to either supplier failure in component manufacture or assembly problems would result in a loss of ACBs licence and consequently its inability to trade. Although there is active involvement by the Board in rectifying problems once they have been identified by the Inspection Agency, little is known of any internal controls for maintaining quality and safety standards. Any serious problems will also result in a significant effect on ACB's reputation.

Economic and political risk

There are economic and political risks resulting from trade with different countries over long time periods, although the Board's adoption of a portfolio approach may be effective in offsetting risks. It is evident that the market in which ACB sells is depressed and there is significant competition, but apart from conservative growth estimates, ACB appears to have no risk management strategy to cope with potentially declining performance over time.

There are also industry-specific risks. Even if ACB maintains its market share, terrorism, fuel costs or restrictive regulations and taxes could result in industry stagnation. Consideration may therefore be given to whether some form of diversification might be appropriate and/or research and development activity into reducing the environmental impact of the aircraft produced.

IT risk

Allied to the supply chain risk is the risk of failure of IT systems on which ACB is so dependent. ERPS take a whole of business approach and capture accounting, operational, customer and supplier data in data warehouses from which management reports are produced. ERPS is the central method by which companies manage their supply chain, customer relationship management, activity-based costing and performance measurement. It is assumed that ACB's ERPS carries out these functions. Consequently, ACB is highly reliant on data accuracy and information security to support its operations.

While operating procedures and continuity plans appear to be in existence, it is unclear whether or not these have been tested. There is a dependence on highly skilled IT staff who may leave ACB's employment.

Even though responsibility is delegated to the IT Department, there still needs to be some form of accountability to the Audit Committee by specialists from IT who are able to report, in plain language on IT matters.

Exchange rate fluctuations

A major risk is from exchange rate fluctuations for purchased components, which are paid for in the currency of each supplier's country. Offsetting or exacerbating this risk is that of exchange rate fluctuations for the supply of completed aircraft, as a result of exchange rate changes between the date on which contracts are signed and when progress payments or final deliveries are made. Internal hedging could take place by invoicing in ACB's home currency. External hedging techniques such as forward exchange contracts could be used to provide more extensive risk management of this exposure.

Even though responsibilility is delegated to the Treasury Department, there still needs to be some form of accountability to the Audit Committee by specialists from Treasury who are able to report, in plain language on currency risk exposure.

Cost control

A further risk relates to cost control. Bill of materials and labour routings exist, and provided these are kept up-to-date, cost estimates should be accurate. However, customisation results in variable costs per aircraft. These are estimated at the time prices are negotiated. Cost increases need to be taken into account, especially as the cycle time is so long. This appears to be covered in supplier agreements but there is a risk of labour and overhead cost increases (comprising 25% of the selling price). While backflushing eliminates routine accounting tasks, it will not necessarily identify cost overruns in labour or components between standard and actual costs. Overhead cost control is necessary, even under an activity-based costing system. Product and customer profitability analysis will assist in identifying problems, but these will only be after the event.

Other risks may be identified that are generally applicable to businesses, such as personnel risks relating to senior management recruitment and retention, fraud, asset loss, etc.

(c) Risk treatment

Risk treatment (also called risk response) is the process of selecting and implementing measures to modify risk that has been identified. This may include risk control/mitigation, risk avoidance, risk transfer, risk financing (e.g. insurance), etc.

Risk response involves determining and documenting:

- A policy of defining the organisation's attitude to a particular risk and the objectives of the risk response.
- Individual accountability for the management of the risk, with a nominated person having the expertise and authority to effectively manage the risk.
- The management processes currently used to manage the risk.
- Recommended business processes to reduce the residual risk to an acceptable level.
- Key performance measures to enable management to assess and monitor risk.
- Independent expertise to assess the adequacy of the risk response.
- Contingency plans to manage or mitigate a major loss following the occurrence of an event.

Risk treatment (or response) enables the Board to see easily which risks have been addressed and those where risk management procedures remain outstanding, and in both cases which individuals are responsible. This permits management by exception. It will enable a board of directors to better understand and react to:

- The nature and extent of risks facing the organization.
- The extent and categories of risk which it regards as acceptable for the organisation to bear (the risk strategy).
- The likelihood of risks materialising.
- The costs and benefits of risk responses.

Consideration of these factors enables the Board to have evidence that they have carried out their responsibilities for risk management.

Risk treatment (or response) may be:

- *Avoidance*: Action is taken to exit the activities giving rise to risk, such as a product line or a geographical market, or a whole business unit. These are high risk events.
- *Reduction*: Action is taken to mitigate (i.e. reduce) the risk likelihood or impact, or both, generally via internal controls. These risks occur more frequently but have less impact.
- *Sharing*: Action is taken to transfer a portion of the risk through, for example, insurance, pooling risks, hedging or outsourcing. These are significant risks, which occur rarely.
- *Acceptance*: No action is taken to affect likelihood or impact. These have low impact even when they do occur, which may be frequent.

Each response needs to be considered in terms of its effect on reducing the likelihood and/or impact of the risk. A comparison of gross and net risk enables a review of risk response effectiveness and possible alternative management options.

- *Gross risk* involves the assessment of risk before the application of any controls, transfer or management responses.
- *Net risk* involves the assessment of risk, taking into account the application of any controls, transfer or management response to the risk under consideration.

6

Internal Control

Internal Control

6.1 Introduction

The main purpose of this chapter is to define internal control and internal control systems, with its links to the Combined Code and the role of the board in internal control. Whilst Chapters 2 and 3 reviewed management and accounting controls generally, in terms of Section A of the *Performance Strategy* syllabus, this chapter is concerned more with the general principles of internal control as it relates to risk management, the subject of Part B of the syllabus. The chapter contains a discussion of the limitations and cost-benefit of internal control and addresses the board's responsibility for reviewing the effectiveness of internal control and board effectiveness.

6.2 Internal control

 Internal control is:

The whole system of internal controls, financial and otherwise, established in order to provide reasonable assurance of:

(a) effective and efficient operation;
(b) internal financial control;
(c) compliance with laws and regulations (CIMA *Official Terminology*).

This definition reflects the important business reasons for having a system of internal control: to maximise the reliability and timeliness of information for making decisions. It also reflects the need to comply with regulation (see below).

Whilst there are hundreds of different controls working in any organisation, they can be categorised into four main types:

1. **Detective**: These controls identify undesirable outcomes that have occurred and function after the event has happened. This means that they are suited when it is possible to accept the loss or damage incurred. An example of this type of control is a financial reconciliation (where unauthorised transactions are detected after they have occurred).
2. **Directive**: These controls 'direct' an activity towards a desired outcome. An example of this type of control would be training staff to work towards achieving particular objectives for the organisation or the existence of a strategy that informs employees to carry a particular series of acts.
3. **Preventative**: These controls limit or stop the possibility of an undesirable events happening. Examples include physical access controls, separation of duty controls or authorisation limits and levels.
4. **Corrective**: These correct undesirable outcomes after hey have happened. An example of this might be the terms and conditions of a contract to recover an overpayment from an employee.

6.3 Internal control system

> An internal control system
>
> includes all the policies and procedures (internal controls) adopted by the directors and management of an entity to assist in achieving their objectives of ensuring, as far as practicable, the orderly and efficient conduct of a business, including adherence to internal policies, the safeguarding of assets, the prevention and detection of fraud and error, the accuracy and completeness of the accounting records, and the timely preparation of reliable financial information (CIMA *Official Terminology*).

The Institute of Internal Auditors (IIA) describes the control system as:

The attitude and actions of management and the board regarding the significance of control within the organization. The control environment provides the discipline and structure for the achievement of the primary objectives of the system of internal control. The control environment includes the following elements: integrity and ethical values, management's philosophy and operating style, organizational structure, assignment of authority and responsibility, human resource policies and practices, and competence of personnel.

A further definition of an internal control system is:

The policies, procedures, practices and organizational structures, designed to provide reasonable assurance that business objectives will be achieved and that undesired events will be prevented, or detected and corrected (Information Systems Control & Audit Association (ISACA)).

An internal control system comprises the control environment and control procedures.

6.3.1 Control environment

> Control environment is:
>
> The overall attitude, awareness and actions of directors and management regarding internal controls and their importance to the entity … [it] encompasses the management style, and corporate culture and values shared by all employees. It provides a background against which the various other controls are operated (CIMA *Official Terminology*).

The Institute of Internal Auditors (IIA) describes the control environment as the attitude and actions of management and the Board regarding the significance of control within the organisation. The control environment provides the discipline and structure for the achievement of the primary objectives of the system of internal control. The control environment includes: integrity and ethical values, management's philosophy and operating style, organizational structure, assignment of authority and responsibility, human resource policies and practices, and competence of personnel (The Institute of Internal Auditors Inc, 2008 – The Glossary).

6.3.2 Control procedures

> Control procedures are:
>
> Those policies and procedures in addition to the control environment which are established to achieve the entity's specific objectives (CIMA *Official Terminology*).

Control procedures will include all those accounting, non-financial and qualitative controls that were described in Chapters 2 and 3.

6.4 COSO model of internal control

COSO defines internal control as a process, effected by an entity's board of directors, management and other personnel. This process is designed to provide reasonable assurance regarding the achievement of objectives in effectiveness and efficiency of operations, reliability of financial reporting, and compliance with applicable laws and regulations.

1. Internal control is a process. It is a means to an end, not an end in itself.
2. Internal control is not merely documented by policy manuals and forms. Rather, it is put in by people at every level of an organisation.
3. Internal control can provide only reasonable assurance, not absolute assurance, to an entity's management and board.

4. Internal control is geared to the achievement of objectives in one or more separate but overlapping categories.

Source: http://www.coso.org/resources.htm

COSO's *Enterprise Risk Management – Integrated Framework* (COSO, 2004) states that internal control is an integral part of enterprise risk management. This is described in COSO's *Internal Control – Integrated Framework* (COSO, 1992) which is encompassed within the ERM framework (see Chapter 5).

The COSO internal control framework contains five elements:

1. Control environment
2. Risk assessment
3. Control activities
4. Monitoring
5. Information and communication.

The control environment was discussed above. The risk assessment section of the model identifies the risks of failing to meet financial reporting objectives; failing to meet compliance and failing to meet operational objectives (see Chapter 5). This is consistent with the CIMA definition (above) of internal control. COSO recommends the identification of external and internal risks to the organisation and its activities beyond those typically considered as finance or accounting ones.

However, the risks of financial mis-reporting (in Sarbanex-Oxley terms) should not be under-emphasised. In mid-2006, COSO published *Internal Control over Financial Reporting – Guidance for Smaller Public Companies*[1], which provided 20 basic principles that would help ensure compliance with the Sarbanes-Oxley requirements for internal control over financial reporting. The principles cover the control environment, risk assessment, control activities, information and communication, and monitoring.

Control activities (or control procedures, see above) are the policies and procedures that help ensure management directives are carried out and objectives are achieved. These include both accounting and non-accounting controls.

Information and communications covers the need to capture relevant internal and external information about competition, economic and regulatory matters and the potential of strategic and integrated information systems.

Monitoring is concerned with the need for management to monitor the entire control system through specific evaluations. Control activities relate to the procedures carried out and the need to integrate these procedures with risk assessment.

The elements of the COSO model were described in detail in the previous chapter.

In September 2007 COSO produced a discussion document *Guidance on Monitoring Internal Control Systems* furthering its *Internal Control – Integrated Framework*. The discussion document provides guidance on monitoring internal control systems, arguing strongly that ineffective monitoring leads to control breakdown. This can happen if processes or risks change and controls do not adapt to those changes, or where previously effective controls cease to operate as they were originally designed. The COSO discussion document recommends that monitoring of controls takes place through a structure that includes: a control baseline or starting point, a change-identification process, a change-management

---

[1] http://www.coso.org/Publications/erm_sb/SB_EXECUTIVE_SUMMARY.PDF

process, and control reconfirmation through seeking various sources of evidence. The report discusses different types of information that can be used in monitoring dependent on the importance of the controls and the underlying likelihood and significance of the risks the controls relate to. COSO expects to release the final version of its report early in 2009.

6.5 Internal control and the Combined Code

Like the IFAC report (International Federation of Accountants, 1999), the Turnbull report (Institute of Chartered Accountants in England & Wales, 1999) emphasised that:

Since profits are, in part, the reward for successful risk-taking in business, the purpose of internal control is to help manage and control risk appropriately rather than to eliminate it.

Code C.2 of the Combined Code (Financial Reporting Council, 2003) relates to internal control. Code provision C.2.1 states:

The board should, at least annually, conduct a review of the effectiveness of the group's system of internal controls and should report to shareholders that they have done so. The review should cover all material controls, including financial, operational and compliance controls and risk management systems.

The Combined Code encompasses the Turnbull Guidance (Institute of Chartered Accountants in England & Wales, 1999), which provides guidance further to Code C.2, that:

The board should maintain a sound system of internal control to safeguard shareholders' investment and the company's assets.

The Turnbull Guidance:

Is based on the adoption by a company's board of a risk-based approach to establishing a sound system of internal control and reviewing its effectiveness (para. 9).

6.6 Governance, risk and control: the 'state of play'

The publication by the International Federation of Accountants (IFAC) in August 2006 of *Internal Controls – A Review of Current Developments* is a timely reminder that candidates for *Performance Strategy* examinations need to be aware of the current 'state of play' of governance, risk and control in preparation for their examinations.

An important role of a board of directors is to understand the significant risks an organisation faces and ensure controls are in place in relation to those risks. The IFAC report emphasises the risk-based approach to internal control as encompassing all an organisation's activities, an approach that is much wider than those related to financial reporting. Under this approach, internal control is a fundamental part of risk management, and risks are defined broadly, covering not just what might go wrong, but as importantly, the risk of not achieving organisational objectives.

This approach is evident in the US by the Committee of Sponsoring Organizations of the Treadway Commission (COSO) in their reports on *Internal Control Integrated Framework* (1992) and *Enterprise Risk Management Integrated Framework* (2004), and in the UK by the Turnbull report, now part of the Financial Reporting Council's (FRC) *Combined Code on Corporate Governance*. COSO has also influenced the approach taken in relation to IT governance in the *Control Objectives for Information and Related Techno*logy (COBIT), the latest version of which was published in 2005 (COBIT is described in Chapter 9). The COSO/Turnbull approach has been adopted in Canada (the *Criteria of Control Board Guidance on Control*, or CoCo), in Hong Kong by the Hong Kong Stock Exchange, and in Europe by the Fédération des Experts Comptables Européens (FEE). Similar approaches have also been adopted in South Africa (the King Report, commonly referred to as King II) and despite a two-tier Board system, also in the Netherlands. In each of these countries, the approach taken in the US has been rejected. Similarly, Australia largely follows the UK model in its Company Law Economic Reform Program (CLERP9).

The principles-based approach adopted by COSO and the FRC, where risk management and internal control is embedded in organisational processes, is in contrast with the narrow and more rules-based approach taken by the Sarbanes-Oxley (SOX) Act, passed in 2002 and which applies to all organisations listed in the US. SOX, in particular sections 302 and 404, takes an approach that is limited to internal control over financial reporting. Under SOX, annual reports have to include a statement that management is responsible for establishing and maintaining adequate internal controls for financial reporting; and an assessment of the effectiveness of those internal controls. In addition, auditors have to attest to and report on management's assessment. This is reported to have increased both management compliance costs and audit costs in US-listed corporations. In the UK, there is no requirement for auditors to express a view publicly on the effectiveness of a company's internal controls.

SOX is extremely important as it affects all companies registered with the US Securities and Exchange Commission (SEC). However, the IFAC report recognises that the emphasis in SOX on internal control over financial reporting may be detrimental to broader aspects of internal control and risk management as it may lead organisations to see internal control as a compliance issue rather than as a part of managing a successful organisation.

Interestingly, even though in the UK the *Combined Code on Corporate Governance* applies only to companies listed on the Stock Exchange, the Code is seen as an example of best practice and there are many examples of the principles being adopted by many privately-owned organisations, by the public sector and by non-profit organisations.

The full IFAC report can be downloaded from http://www.ifac.org/Store/Details. tmpl?SID=11559337241982775&Cart=1157581557690125

6.7 Role of the board in relation to internal control

Although the role of the Board was covered in detail in Chapter 4, it is worthwhile repeating some of the key points here. In determining its policies for a system of internal control, boards need to consider:

- The nature and extent of the risks facing the company
- The extent and types of risk which are acceptable for the company to bear
- The likelihood of the risks materialising
- The ability of the company to reduce the incidence and severity of risks that do materialise
- The costs of operating controls compared with the benefit obtained in managing the risk.

The board is responsible for the company's system of internal control and should set policies on internal control and seek assurance that the system is working effectively and is effective in managing risks. It is management's role to identify and evaluate the risks faced by the company for consideration by the board. Management must also implement board policies on risk and control by designing, operating and monitoring a suitable system of internal control.

The Turnbull Guidance identified the elements of a sound system of internal control as the policies, processes, tasks and behaviours that:

- facilitate its effective and efficient operation by enabling it to respond appropriately to significant business, operational, financial, compliance and other risks to achieving the company's objectives;
- help ensure the quality of internal and external reporting;
- help ensure compliance with laws and regulations and with internal policies about the conduct of the business.

A system of internal control will reflect its control environment and include:

- Control activities
- Information and communication processes
- Processes for monitoring the effectiveness of the internal control system.

The system of internal control should:

- be embedded in the operations of the company and form part of its culture,
- be capable of responding quickly to evolving risks,
- include procedures for reporting immediately to appropriate levels of management any significant control failings or weaknesses.

However, while a system of internal control can reduce, it cannot eliminate the following:

- Poor judgement in decision-making
- Human error
- The deliberate circumvention of control processes
- The over-riding of controls by management
- Unforeseeable circumstances.

The Turnbull guidance summarises:

A sound system of internal control therefore provides reasonable, but not absolute, assurance that a company will not be hindered in achieving its business objectives, or in the orderly and legitimate conduct of its business, by circumstances which may reasonably be foreseen. A system of internal control cannot, however, provide protection with certainty against a company failing to meet its business objectives or all material errors, fraud, or breaches of laws or regulations (para. 24).

6.8 Management review of controls

Although the Board has overall responsibility for guiding and evaluating management controls, it is the primary function of management to ensure that a system of management controls is in place. The appropriate system should be within the organisational risk appetite as determined by the Board, take into account the organisation's objectives and the risks faced by the organisation. The controls should encompass financial, quantitative and qualitative controls. Management has the responsibility to review these controls on a regular basis and to report to the Board on the results of their review.

Reports from management to the board should:

Provide a balanced assessment of the significant risks and the effectiveness of the system of internal control in managing those risks. Any significant control failings or weaknesses identified should be discussed in the reports, including the impact that they have had, could have had, or may have, on the company and the actions being taken to rectify them (Turnbull Guidance, para. 30: Institute of Chartered Accountants in England & Wales, 1999).

The Smith Guidance notes:

The company's management is responsible for the identification, assessment, management and monitoring of risk, for developing, operating and monitoring the system of internal control and for providing assurance to the board that it has done so ... the audit committee should receive reports from management on the effectiveness of the systems they have established and the conclusions of any testing carried out by internal and external auditors (para. 4.6).

6.9 Board's assessment of internal control

Reviewing the effectiveness of internal control is one of the board's responsibilities (which may be delegated to the audit committee) and needs to be carried out on a continuous basis. The audit committee should review the company's internal financial controls and, unless expressly addressed by a separate board risk committee composed of independent directors, the company's internal control and risk management systems.

Directors are expected to apply the same standard of care when reviewing the effectiveness of internal control as when exercising their general duties. The Board should regularly review reports on internal control in order to carry out an annual assessment for the purpose of making its public statement on internal control to ensure that it has considered all significant aspects of internal control. It is important that a review of internal controls is not limited to financial controls.

When reviewing management reports on internal control, the board should:

- consider what are the significant risks and assess how they have been identified, evaluated and managed;
- assess the effectiveness of internal controls in managing the significant risks, having regard to any significant weaknesses in internal control;
- consider whether necessary actions are being taken promptly to remedy any weaknesses;
- consider whether the findings indicate a need for more exhaustive monitoring of the system of internal control.

The Financial Reporting Council established a group to review the impact of the Turnbull Guidance and to determine whether it needed to be updated. The revised guidance (Financial Reporting Council, 2005) included the requirement to confirm in the annual report that necessary action has been or is being taken to remedy any significant failings or weaknesses identified from their review of the effectiveness of the internal control system, and to include in the annual report such information as considered necessary to assist shareholders' understanding of the main features of the company's risk management processes and system of internal control.

6.10 Checklist for Board/Audit Committee's Assessment of Internal Control

The Turnbull Guidance includes a series of questions that boards may consider when reviewing management reports and carrying out the annual assessment of internal control.

Risk assessment:

- Does the company have clear objectives with measurable targets and indicators that have been communicated so as to provide effective direction to employees on risk assessment and control issues?
- Are the significant internal and external operational, financial, compliance and other risks identified and assessed on an ongoing basis?
- Is there a clear understanding by management and others within the company of what risks are acceptable to the board?

Control environment and control activities:

- Does the board have clear strategies for dealing with the significant risks that have been identified? Is there a policy on how to manage these risks?
- Do the company's culture, code of conduct, human resource policies and performance reward systems support the business objectives and risk management and internal control system?
- Does senior management demonstrate, through actions and policies, the necessary commitment to competence, integrity and fostering a climate of trust within the company?
- Are authority, responsibility and accountability defined clearly such that decisions are made and actions taken by the appropriate people? Are the decisions and actions of different parts of the company appropriately co-ordinated?
- Does the company communicate to employees what is expected of them and the scope of their freedom to act?
- Do people in the company (and its outsourced service providers) have the knowledge, skill and tools to support the achievement of the company's objectives and to manage effectively risks to their achievement?
- How are processes/controls adjusted to reflect new or changing risks, or operational deficiencies?

Information and communication:

- Do management and the board receive timely, relevant and reliable reports on progress against business objectives and the related risks that provide them with the information needed for decision-making and management review purposes?
- Are information needs and related information systems re-assessed as objectives and related risks change or as reporting deficiencies are identified?
- Are periodic reporting procedures effective in communicating a balanced and understandable account of the company's position and prospects?
- Are there established channels of communication for individuals to report suspected breaches of laws or regulations or other improprieties?

Monitoring:

- Are there ongoing processes embedded within the company's overall business operations which monitor the effective application of the policies, processes and activities related to internal control and risk management?

- Do these processes monitor the company's ability to re-evaluate risks and adjust controls effectively in response to changes in its objectives, its business and its external environment?
- Are there effective follow-up procedures to ensure that appropriate change or action occurs in response to changes in risk and control assessments?
- Is there appropriate communication to the board on the effectiveness of the ongoing monitoring processes on risk and control matters?
- Are there specific arrangements for management monitoring and reporting to the board on risk and control matters of particular importance?

6.11 Limitations of internal control

Internal control can provide reasonable, but not absolute assurance that the objectives of an organisation will be met. There are limitations to internal control that need to be understood:

1. Management, not auditors, have responsibility for internal controls, although the board is responsible for reviewing the adequacy of those controls.
2. Internal controls provide a reasonable assurance, not an absolute guarantee.
3. Internal controls should be independent of the method of data processing. The specific controls may vary depending on the methods in use but the objectives should be independent of those methods.
4. There is always the possibility of error in any accounting system. This may include the deliberate circumvention of controls by a determined person; the overriding of controls by management; the internal controls may not have kept pace with changing business conditions.

6.12 Cost-benefit of internal control

The benefits of internal control are identified throughout this chapter. It is relatively easy to quantify losses incurred from ineffective internal control. What is more difficult is identifying the benefits of controls that prevent losses from occurring. This may be largely a confidence factor that controls are effective because losses are being avoided, although some measurement may be possible of the likely loss that might have been incurred based on problems identified by the internal control system that are corrected before any loss eventuates.

The costs of internal control will comprise the people and system costs involved in all aspects of control. This will be particularly evident in the cost of internal audit services. However, it is difficult to differentiate between internal controls and that which is simply good business practice, for example, human resource practices and accounting procedures.

6.13 Internal control and risk management

Organisations will adopt internal controls in accordance with their risks, which as we have seen in Chapter 5, may vary considerably between companies and industries. In the

Appendix to this chapter are examples of two board statements in relation to internal control and risk management:

1. Arriva plc
2. BAE Systems

These provide a good example of the variety of controls that organisations may adopt, and how their risk management systems work. However, as with many statutory reports, you may notice similarities in wording and the high level at which these reports are written.

6.14 Summary

- Internal control is the whole system of internal controls, financial and otherwise, established in order to provide reasonable assurance of effective and efficient operation; internal financial control and compliance with laws and regulations.
- Internal controls mat be categorised as detective; directive; preventative, or corrective.
- An internal control system (defined in Section 6.3) comprises the control environment and control procedures.
- The COSO model of internal control includes the control environment; risk assessment; control activities; monitoring and information and communication.
- The Combined Code holds the board responsible to safeguard shareholders' investment and the company's assets by adopting a risk-based approach to establishing a sound system of internal control and for conducting a review of the effectiveness of the group's system of internal controls, including financial, operational and compliance controls and risk management systems.
- Boards need to consider the nature and extent of the risks; the extent and types of risk which are acceptable for the company to bear; the likelihood of the risks materialising; the ability of the company to reduce the incidence and severity of risks that do materialise and the costs of operating controls compared with the benefit obtained in managing the risk.
- An effective system of internal control should be embedded in the operations of the company and form part of its culture; be capable of responding quickly to evolving risks and include procedures for the immediate reporting of any significant control failings or weaknesses.
- The board's statement on internal control should disclose that there is an ongoing process for identifying, evaluating and managing the significant risks faced by the company, that it has been in place for the year and up to the date of approval of the annual report and accounts, and that it has been regularly reviewed by the board and conforms to the Turnbull Guidance.
- Boards/audit committees need to satisfy themselves that there is a proper system and allocation of responsibilities for the day-to-day monitoring of financial controls but they should not seek to do the monitoring themselves. The audit committee should review the significant financial reporting issues and judgements made in connection with the preparation of the company's financial statements, interim reports, preliminary announcements and other related statements.
- The Board/audit committee should also review the company's internal financial controls and, unless expressly addressed by a separate board risk committee composed of independent directors, the company's internal control and risk management systems.

A checklist (see Section 6.10) provides a series of questions that boards may consider in reviewing management reports and carrying out their annual assessment of internal controls.

- There are limitations to internal control: management, not auditors, have responsibility for internal controls, although the board is responsible for reviewing the adequacy of those controls; internal controls provide a reasonable assurance, not an absolute guarantee; internal controls should be independent of the method of data processing and there is always the possibility of error in any accounting system.

References

Students are encouraged to read:

Financial Reporting Council (2003), *The Combined Code on Corporate Governance*.

Institute of Chartered Accountants in England & Wales (1999), *Internal Control: Guidance for Directors on the Combined Code (Turnbull Report)*. Note that the Combined Code incorporates the Turnbull Report guidance.

Committee of Sponsoring Organizations of the Treadway Commission (COSO) (1992), *Internal Control – Integrated Framework*.

International Federation of Accountants (1999), Enhancing Shareholder Wealth by Better Managing Business Risk. Rep. *International Management Accounting Study No. 9*.

Johnson, H.T. and Kaplan, R.S. (1987), *Relevance Lost: The Rise and Fall of Management Accounting*. Boston: Harvard Business School Press.

Kaplan, R.S. and Norton, D.P. (2001), *The Strategy-Focused Organization: How Balanced Scorecard Companies Thrive in the New Business Environment*. Boston, MA: Harvard Business School Press.

Parker, L.D. (2001), 'Back to the Future: The Broadening Accounting Trajectory.' *British Accounting Review*, Vol. 33, pp. 421–53.

Appendix to Chapter 6 – Extracts from Annual Reports

6

Arriva plc

Management Review

Principal risks and uncertainties

The Board recognises that any commercial opportunity brings with it a degree of risk and, like any business, Arriva must manage a range of risks in the course of its activities. An impact assessment of the scale and probability of the principal risks affecting the business is reviewed annually.

As part of the ongoing programme of risk assessment and management, the following actual and potential risks have been identified as those which the directors believe could have a material impact on the long-term value generation of the group. The factors described below are not intended to form a definitive list of all risks and uncertainties.

1. Market risks
2. Operational risks
3. Commercial risks
4. Financial risks
5. Other risks

1. Market risks

Changes in national public transport budgets

A considerable proportion of the group's income is derived directly or indirectly from national public transport budgets. Changes in these budgets can have positive or negative impacts on the group's prospects. The group continues to monitor national public transport budgetary policies in the countries where it operates, and ensures it is strategically aware in order to understand possible changes and react to them in a timely fashion.

2. Operational risks

Meeting health, safety and environmental standards

The Board recognises the importance to the business, as a public transport operator, of maintaining high standards and the consequences of failing to do so. A Safety Committee of the Board oversees the group's safety policy and the arrangements of its implementation and reporting (see Corporate responsibility).

INTERNAL CONTROL

Mobilisation of large new rail franchises

We aim to use the knowledge gained in the successful rail mobilisation processes we have been involved in to date for other new rail franchises won by the group. The mobilisation of the CrossCountry contract from November 2007 went smoothly, benefiting from our previous experience both in the UK and abroad.

3. Commercial risks

Franchise / tender / acquisition costing and revenue forecasting

Errors or inaccurate assumptions in tenders or acquisitions represent a risk to the business. A number of procedures are in place to mitigate the risk.

The Board monitors all material new franchise, tender and acquisition submissions across the group's operations, whilst the executive directors review other bids on an ongoing basis in line with delegated authority limits. Standard tender models are in use across the business. Significant bus and train tender contracts are compared with current experience to identify weaknesses and potential improvements in the tender process. Post-investment appraisals are carried out through quarterly business review meetings.

One of the most significant set of assumptions which may be required in constructing a franchise bid relates to general economic factors influencing the market concerned. Arriva's balanced portfolio of operations, between bus and rail, and between different countries, minimises its exposure to any downturn in any individual market sector. The revenue risk associated with any potential loss of consumer demand from the travelling public is mitigated by the substantial proportion of the group's revenues which flow from non-passenger sources (see Spreading our net).

Most tendered net cost contracts (see Hold on tight) require the operator to deliver specified services whilst retaining the income from passengers. In contracts where passenger income represents a significant proportion of total revenue, the group is exposed to the risk of passenger revenue being higher or lower than anticipated. Historically, passenger revenue growth is highly correlated with growth in local economies. The recently started UK CrossCountry rail contract is a particularly large contract with these characteristics; Arriva is committed to reducing government financial support on this franchise to almost zero before the end of the franchise in 2016. To deliver anticipated returns, over 8% annual revenue growth in real terms will be required, a considerable proportion of which is dependent on economic growth. However, in the fourth year of the franchise, the financial risk is partially mitigated by a revenue risk sharing mechanism in the contract.

The actual conditions are complex but the principal financial arrangements are:

Percentage shortfall on target revenue	Revenue support
0–2%	Nil
2–6%	50%
6% and higher	80%

These risk mitigating factors are mirrored by potential payments to the UK Government when targeted revenue is exceeded.

Throughout the franchise, revenue support may also be available if the dominant cause of a qualifying revenue shortfall is a 'Force Majeure' event, such as severe flooding.

Acquisitions

Arriva has clearly defined guidelines for due diligence work and internal reporting on potential acquisitions, which require the monitoring of such items by the executive directors subject to delegated authority limits. Sale and Purchase Agreements include price adjustment mechanisms and warranties as appropriate.

4. Financial risks

As detailed in the Financial Review, the group's financial risks are managed by the group treasury function in accordance with a formal Board approved treasury policy.

Interest rate risk

Fluctuations in interest rates are managed through the use of interest rate derivatives and fixed rate debt.

Commodity risk

The group's policy is to maintain fuel price fixes at least 12 to 15 months ahead, on a rolling basis.

Currency translation risk

The group policy on foreign exchange exposure is that the risk of translating non-UK assets and liabilities into pounds sterling should be reduced to insignificant levels.

Retirement benefit obligations

Increased retirement benefit obligations may require additional contributions to be made by companies to state or other schemes. Such contributions could have a material impact on the group. We perform regular pension strategy reviews with the group's pension advisors, and monitor developments in group pension schemes and state schemes where we operate.

5. Other risks

Changes in transport legislation and/or regulation.

This is a risk that faces Arriva in every country in which it operates.

The group has procedures in place to ensure effective liaison with appropriate national and European Union officials and monitoring of developments in this area for timely reporting to senior management.

In the UK, the Government is currently planning changes to transport legislation with an expected implementation date in late 2008 or early 2009. The Government is also considering amendments to the Bus Service Operators Grant. These planned and potential changes could have significant impact on the UK bus industry.

Arriva, alongside other UK operators, is monitoring the development of legislation in this area and representing the best long-term interests of the industry.

Succession planning for key managerial positions.

Arriva is a fast-growing company in many markets. The group has a stable senior management population but any inability to fill a significant proportion of senior vacancies could have an adverse impact on the group's future development. Succession planning is already in place, as is a process for identifying emerging management talent. We are developing an executive development programme.

http://www.arriva.co.uk/annualreport2007/management/group_level_risk/

INTERNAL CONTROL

Arriva plc

Management Review

Treasury and financial risk management

The group's financial risks are managed by the group treasury function in accordance with a formal Board-approved treasury policy. The policy sets a range of formal targets for managing the group's exposure to fuel prices, interest rate changes and foreign currency movements. These targets are achieved through the use of forward fuel price fixes, interest rate and exchange rate swaps, and fixed rate finance. In addition, foreign acquisitions and operations are funded in local currency where possible. The result of this policy has been to reduce to insignificant levels the foreign exchange risk when translating overseas assets and liabilities into sterling and to increase euro borrowings as the group expands in mainland Europe.

- Commodity risk
- Interest rate risk
- Foreign currency risk
- Credit risk
- Liquidity risk
- Capital risk

Commodity risk

The group's general policy is to maintain fuel price fixes at least 12 to 15 months ahead on a rolling basis. The requirement to fix fuel is determined after taking into account the extent to which businesses are protected from fuel price volatility through contract price indexation. Following the award of the CrossCountry contract, a fuel fix was put in place covering 75% of the anticipated fuel usage of the contract up to its expiry. The group's forward fixing of fuel, excluding associates for 2008 and 2009, at 25 February 2008, compared with 2007, was:

Commodity risk

	2007 %	2008 %	2009 %
Protected by indexation arrangements	8.8	10.4	9.7
Forward purchased*	85.2	81.1	34.3
Subject to spot or future forward purchase	6.0	8.5	56.0
	100.0	100.0	100.0
***Average price per litre of forward purchased fuel, excluding fuel taxation and delivery**	28.1 pence	27.2 pence	29.1 pence

On a like-for-like basis, fuel costs, excluding fuel taxation, are likely therefore to decrease moderately in 2008, but with the prospect of an increase in 2009 if current prices in the market are maintained. The total fuel consumption in 2007 was approximately 365 million litres. The CrossCountry franchise is anticipated to consume around 100 million litres of fuel per annum.

Interest rate risk

Fluctuations in interest rates are managed by a combination of interest rate swaps and use of fixed rate debt. Actual hedged debt at 31 December 2007 was 83%. The target level of hedged debt is 80% of group net debt, achieved within a banding of 65–95% of net debt. Hedged debt for this purpose represents fixed rate finance and swaps over 1 year's duration at inception.

Foreign currency risk

As noted previously, the group policy on foreign exchange exposure is that the risk of translating non-UK assets and liabilities into pounds sterling should be reduced to insignificant levels. At 31 December 2007, the exposure was 6% of non-UK assets. The risk is managed through the use of funding in local currencies and by entering into foreign currency swaps of durations up to 3 years. The majority of such swaps also encompass fixed interest rates, thus also providing interest rate protection between EURIBOR, LIBOR and CIBOR. The group also enters into foreign exchange forward contracts to hedge specific cash flows arising with overseas suppliers. The fair value of the group's cross currency swaps and foreign exchange forward contracts at 31 December 2007 was a liability of £23.1 million.

Credit risk

Credit risk arising from operational suppliers and customers is managed at a local level and is subject to periodic reviews by central management and the group's internal audit function. Credit limits are in place for customers, many of which are local authorities or local transport authorities. Due to the nature of certain contractual arrangements, particularly where the agreement and settlement of allocations of passenger revenues between multiple service providers can take more than 1 year to complete, certain customer debts can often exceed 1 year before settlement. This is common, and the incidence of impairment of such debt is both rare and immaterial. The group also manages its exposure to debit risk in respect of financial institutions that provide credit to the group. The group nominates and approves banks and lease providers with whom it will deal with. All group companies are required to bank with the nominated bankers, which change from time to time due to group refinancing, entry into new markets and changes to credit ratings.

Liquidity risk

In addition to daily local monitoring, the liquidity of the group is monitored fortnightly, via group net debt reports showing the level of drawdown compared to available facilities for all components of net debt, and monthly against forecasts and budget. Future liquidity is monitored through detailed 3-month cash forecasts prepared on a rolling monthly basis, and through forecasts for each financial year updated approximately quarterly throughout the year. At a strategic level, long-term liquidity is assessed as part of the 5-year strategic planning process, which is updated annually. The above reviews support compliance with group policy, which is to maintain an average weighted maturity of hedged debt of at least 18 months at any point in time, and to maintain a 12-month in advance, foreseeable level of unutilised available facilities of more than £100 million. At 31 December 2007, hedged debt maturity was 19 months and headroom on facilities was approximately £470 million.

Capital risk

The group monitors its capital risk on a continuous basis to ensure that, having regard to the anticipated and possible future requirements, sufficient capital exists to fund operations and provide returns to shareholders, and that the Weighted Average Cost of Capital (WACC) of the group is optimised. There are a number of alternative methods of calculating WACC and there are also variations caused by doing business in the different markets in Europe in which we operate. Our current assessment is that the group WACC is around 7%.

http://www.arriva.co.uk/annualreport2007/management/financial_review/risk/

INTERNAL CONTROL

BAE Systems

Extract from Directors' Report

Group management of risks

Effective management of risk and opportunity is essential to the delivery of the Group's objectives, achievement of sustainable shareholder value and protection of its reputation. The Group's approach to risk management is to remove or reduce the likelihood and effect of risks before they occur, and deal effectively with problems if they arise. The Group is committed to the protection of its assets, which include human, property and financial resources, through an effective risk management process, underpinned where appropriate by insurance.

The management of risk is linked into the Group's strategy, the environment in which it operates, the Group's appetite for risk and the delivery of the Group's business objectives. The underlying principles are that risks are continuously monitored, associated action plans reviewed, appropriate contingencies are provisioned and this information is reported through established management control procedures.

To enable this process, BAE Systems has developed a system of internal control, the 'Operational Framework' (OF), that encompasses, amongst other things, the mandated policies and core business processes that provide a common framework for how we do business and what it means to be part of BAE Systems.

The Board has overall responsibility for ensuring that risk is effectively managed across the Group and has delegated to the Audit Committee, the responsibility for reviewing in detail the effectiveness of the Group's system of internal controls. During the year, the Executive Committee has further enhanced its oversight of material non-financial risks including, in particular, those arising in connection with safety and ethical issues. Close attention has been paid to analysing risks associated with the conduct of international business and new policies and processes have been implemented seeking to provide the highest levels of assurance. The Executive Committee advises the Corporate Responsibility Committee of all matters within the latter's remit.

In order to assist the Committees and the Board in their review, the Group has a self-assessment Operational Assurance Statement (OAS) process. The OAS is in two parts: a self-assessment of compliance with appropriate parts of the OF; and a report showing the key risks for the relevant business. Together with independent reviews undertaken by Internal Audit, and the work of the external auditors, the OAS forms the Group's process for reviewing the effectiveness of the system of internal controls.

Reporting within the Group is structured so that key issues are escalated through the management team, ultimately to the Board if appropriate. The responsibility for risk identification, analysis, evaluation, mitigation, reporting and monitoring rests with line management. Both the Audit Committee and the Corporate Responsibility Committee report the findings of their reviews to the Board so that the Board can form a view.

Five core processes and 27 policies are mandated by the OF, enabling the business to respond appropriately to material risks faced by the Group. As with any system of internal control, the policies and processes that are mandated in the OF are designed to manage rather than eliminate the risk of failure to achieve business objectives, and can only provide reasonable, and not absolute, assurance against material misstatement or loss.

http://production.investis.com/annualreport07/performance/riskman/groupman/

BAE Systems

Extract from Directors' Report
Summary of principal risks

Defence spending

The Group is dependent on defence spending and reductions in such spending could adversely affect the Group.

The Group's core businesses are primarily defence-related, selling products and services directly and indirectly primarily to the US, the UK, the Saudi Arabian and other national governments. In any single market, defence spending depends on a complex mix of political considerations, budgetary constraints and the ability of the armed forces to meet specific threats and perform certain missions. Because of these factors, defence spending may be subject to significant fluctuations from year to year.

Although the Group expects growth in US defence spending to slow, it believes it is well placed to support the US Department of Defense's likely emphasis on force sustainment, readiness and affordable transformation. The UK defence equipment budget is expected to continue to be constrained, having potential implications for the sustainability of long-term funding for future defence technologies and engineering capabilities in the UK.

Impact

A decrease in defence purchases by the Group's major customers could have a material adverse effect on the Group's future results of operations and financial condition.

Action

The Board regularly reviews the Group's performance in these markets, and the Executive Committee continues to work closely with customers to ensure the Group strategy is aligned with theirs (refer to the strategy section).

Certain parts of the Group's business are dependent on a small number of large contracts.

A significant proportion of the Group's revenue comes from a small number of large contracts. These contracts individually are typically worth or potentially worth £1 billion or more including, but not limited to, those contracts in the Programmes and Support business group.

Impact

The loss, expiration, suspension, cancellation or termination of any one of these contracts, for any reason, could have a material adverse effect on the Group's future results of operations and financial condition.

Action

The Board regularly reviews the Group's performance in these markets, and the Executive Committee continues to work closely with customers to ensure the Group strategy is aligned with theirs (refer to the strategy section).

The Group's largest customer contracts are government contracts.

The governments of the UK, the US and the Kingdom of Saudi Arabia are the Group's three largest end customers. Any significant disruption or deterioration in the relationship with these governments and a corresponding reduction in government contracts would significantly reduce the Group's revenues. Moreover, companies engaged in the supply of defence-related equipment and services to government agencies are subject to certain business risks particular to the defence industry. These governments could unilaterally cancel, suspend or amend their contractors' funding under existing contracts or eligibility for new contracts potentially at short notice. Terms and risk sharing agreements can also be amended. In addition, the Group, as a government contractor, is subject to financial audits and other reviews by some of its governmental customers with respect to the performance of, and the accounting and general practices relating to, government contracts. As a result of these audits and reviews, costs and prices under these contracts may be subject to adjustment.

Impact
The termination of one or more of the contracts for the Group's programmes by governments, or the failure of the relevant agencies to obtain expected funding appropriations for the Group's programmes, could have a material adverse effect on the Group's future results of operations and financial condition.

Action
The Board regularly reviews the Group's performance in these markets, and the Executive Committee continues to work closely with customers to ensure the Group strategy is aligned with theirs (refer to the strategy section).

The timing of contracts could materially affect the Group's future results of operations and financial condition.

The Group's operating performance and cash flows are dependent, to a significant extent, on the award of defence contracts and its performance in delivering these contracts.

Impact
Because the amounts payable under these contracts can be substantial, the award or completion of one or more contracts, the timing for manufacturing and delivery of products under these contracts or the failure to receive anticipated orders could materially affect the Group's operating results and cash flow for the periods affected.

Action
The Board regularly reviews the Group's performance in these markets, and the Executive Committee continues to work closely with customers to ensure the Group strategy is aligned with theirs (refer to the strategy section).

Fixed-price contracts
The Group has fixed-price contracts.

A significant portion of the Group's revenues are derived from fixed-price contracts, although the Group has reduced its exposure to fixed-priced design and development activity which is in general more risk intensive than fixed-price production activity. An inherent risk in these fixed-price contracts is that actual performance costs may exceed the projected costs on which the fixed prices for such contracts are agreed.

Impact
The Group's failure to anticipate technical problems, estimate costs accurately or control costs during performance of a fixed-priced contract may reduce the profitability of such a contract or result in a loss.

Action
To manage contract-related risks and uncertainties, contracts are managed through the application of the Group's mandated Lifecycle Management (LCM) business process at the operational level and the consistent application of metrics is used to support the review of individual contract performance (refer to the Resources page for further information on LCM).

Global Market

The Group is exposed to risks inherent in operating in a global market.

BAE Systems is a global company which conducts business in a number of regions, including the Middle East, and, as a result, assumes certain risks associated with businesses with a broad geographical reach. In some countries these risks include, and are not limited to, the following: government regulations and administrative policies could change quickly and restraints on the movement of capital could be imposed; governments could expropriate the Group's assets; burdensome taxes or tariffs could be introduced; political changes could lead to changes in the business environment in which the Group operates; and economic downturns, political instability and civil disturbances could disrupt the Group's business activities.

Impact

The occurrence of any such events could have a material adverse effect on the Group's future operational performance and financial condition.

Action

The Group has a balanced portfolio with six home markets.

Export controls and other restrictions

The Group is subject to export controls and other restrictions.

A portion of the Group's sales is derived from the export of its products. Many of the products the Group designs and manufactures for military or dual use are considered to be of national strategic interest. The export of such products outside of the jurisdictions in which they are produced is normally subject to licensing and export controls and other restrictions. No assurance can be given that the export controls to which the Group is subject will not become more restrictive, that new generations of the Group's products will not also be subject to similar or more stringent controls, or that political factors or changing international circumstances will not result in the Group being unable to obtain necessary export licences.

Impact

Reduced access to export markets could have a material adverse effect on the Group's future results of operations and financial condition.

Failure to comply with export controls and wider regulations could expose the Group to fines and other penalties, including potential restrictions on trading.

Action

The Group has formal systems and policies in place to ensure adherence to regulatory requirements and to identify any restrictions that could adversely impact the Group's future activities.

Competition

The Group's business is subject to significant competition.

Most of the Group's businesses are focused on the defence industry and subject to competition from multinational firms with substantial resources and capital and many contracts are obtained through a competitive bidding process. The Group's ability to compete for contracts depends to a large extent on the effectiveness and innovation of its research and development programmes, its ability to offer better programme performance than its competitors at a lower cost to its customers, and the readiness of its facilities, equipment and personnel to undertake the programmes for which it competes.

Additionally, in some instances, governments direct to a single supplier all work for a particular programme, commonly known as a sole-source programme. Although governments have historically awarded certain programmes to the Group on a sole-source basis, they may in the future determine to open such programmes to a competitive bidding process.

Government contracts for defence-related products can, in certain countries, be awarded on the basis of home country preference. Therefore, other defence companies may have an advantage over the Group for some defence-related contracts on the basis of the jurisdiction in which they are organised, where the majority of their assets are located or where their officers or directors are located.

Impact

In the event that the Group is unable adequately to compete in the markets in which it operates, the Group's business and results of operations may be adversely affected.

Action

The Group's strong global market positioning, balanced portfolio, leading capabilities and performance continue to address this risk (refer to strategy section page for further information on the Group's positioning and portfolio).

Consortia and joint ventures

The Group is involved in consortia, joint ventures and equity holdings where it does not have control.

The Group participates in various consortia, joint ventures and equity holdings, exercising varying and evolving degrees of control. While the Group seeks to participate only in ventures in which its interests are aligned with those of its partners, the risk of disagreement is inherent in any jointly controlled entity, and particularly in those entities that require the unanimous consent of all members with regard to major decisions, and that specify restricted rights.

Impact

In the event of disagreement within a consortia, joint venture or equity holding and the business arrangement fails to meet its strategic objectives or expected benefits, the Group's business and results of operations may be adversely affected.

Action

The Group has formal systems and procedures in place to monitor the performance of such business arrangements and identity and manage any adverse scenario arising.

Pension funding

The Group is exposed to funding risks in relation to the defined benefits under its pension schemes.

The Group operates certain defined benefit pension schemes. At present, in aggregate, there is an actuarial deficit between the value of projected liabilities of these schemes and the value of the assets they hold. The Group has put in place and is implementing deficit recovery plans in line with agreements reached with the respective scheme trustees based on actuarial advice and the valuation results.

Impact

The amount of the deficits may be adversely affected by a number of factors, including lower than assumed investment returns, changes in long-term interest rate and price inflation expectations, and greater than anticipated improvements in members' longevity. An increase in pension scheme deficits may require the Group to increase the amount of cash contributions payable to these schemes, thereby reducing cash available to meet the Group's other obligations or business needs.

Action

The performance of the Group's pension schemes and deficit recovery plans are regularly reviewed by both the Group and the Trustees of the schemes taking actuarial and investment advice as applicable. The results of these reviews are discussed with the Board and appropriate action taken (refer to Notes to the Group accounts for further details on the Group's retirement benefit plans).

Acquisitions

The Group has experienced growth through acquisitions. Anticipated benefits of acquisitions may not be realised.

The Group has experienced growth through acquisitions and continues to pursue acquisitions in order to meet its strategic objectives. Integrating the operations and personnel of acquired businesses is a complex process. The Group may not be able to integrate the operations of acquired businesses with existing operations rapidly or without encountering difficulties.

Impact

The diversion of management attention to integration efforts and any difficulties encountered in combining operations could adversely affect the Group's business. The failure to manage growth by acquisition while at the same time maintaining adequate focus on the existing assets of the Group, could have a material adverse effect on the Group's business, future results of operations or financial condition. In addition, failure to integrate acquisitions appropriately creates the risk of impairments arising on goodwill and other intangible assets.

Action

The Group has an established methodology in place to deliver the effective integration of acquisitions. The Group has an established policy for monitoring impairment risks.

Regional Aircraft

The Group holds a number of regional aircraft on its balance sheet and has provided residual value guarantees in respect of certain regional aircraft sold.

These aircraft are leased, or have been sold, to airline operators.

Impact

Values of regional aircraft are impacted by a range of factors including the financial strength of regional aircraft operators, market demands for regional aircraft and the impact of economic factors on aircraft operating costs. Reductions in the valuations of these aircraft could result in impairment charges against the carrying value of the aircraft or additional provisions against the guarantees given.

Action

The Group's primary action is to operate an efficient asset management organisation. Much of the leasing business was underpinned by the Group's Financial Risk Insurance Programme, which makes good shortfalls in actual lease income against originally estimated future income for a 15-year period from 1998 to 2013. Since 2006 BAE Systems and the reinsurers have been in dispute over several areas of the policy. During 2007, agreement was reached with almost all reinsurers and settlements have been paid by them based on the net present value of estimated future claims. Arbitration proceedings are ongoing in relation to several claims advanced by one reinsurer who has a maximum potential liability under the policy of $145 million. These claims are being vigorously defended.

Laws and regulations

The Group is subject to risk from a failure to comply with laws and regulations.

The Group's operations are subject to numerous domestic and international laws, regulations and restrictions. Non-compliance with these laws, regulations and restrictions could expose the Group to fines, penalties, suspension or debarment, which could have a material adverse effect on the Group. The Group has contracts and operations in many parts of the world and operates in a highly regulated environment. The Group is subject to the laws and regulations of many jurisdictions, including those of the UK and US. These include, without limitation, regulations relating to import-export controls, money-laundering, false accounting, anti-bribery and anti-boycott provisions. From time to time, the Group is subject to government investigations relating to its operations.

Impact

Failure by the Group or its sales representatives, marketing advisers or others acting on its behalf to comply with these laws and regulations could result in administrative, civil or criminal liabilities resulting in significant fines and penalties and/or result in the suspension or debarment of the Group from government contracts for some period of time or suspension of the Group's export privileges.

Action

During the year, the Group has devoted additional resource and further enhanced its mandated procedures designed to ensure compliance with its policies relating to the conduct of international business. The Executive Committee maintains a list of approved export markets arrived at on the basis of a market risk assessment utilising input from externally developed risk assessments. A panel of experts scrutinises all adviser appointments within the Group. Findings of the panel of experts are reviewed by members of the Executive Committee and material market or programme risks are discussed by the Board.

The investigation by the Serious Fraud Office into suspected false accounting and corruption is continuing and the Group continues to co-operate with this investigation. In June 2007, the Company was notified by the US Department of Justice that it had commenced a formal investigation relating to the Group's compliance with anti-corruption laws, including its business concerning the Kingdom of Saudi Arabia.

Exchange rates

The Group is exposed to volatility in currency exchange rates.

The global nature of the Group's business means it is exposed to volatility in currency exchange rates in respect of foreign currency denominated transactions, and the translation of net assets and income statements of foreign subsidiaries and equity accounted investments. The Group is exposed to a number of foreign currencies, the most significant being the US dollar.

Impact

Significant fluctuations in exchange rates to which the Group is exposed could have a material adverse effect on the Group's future results of operations and financial condition.

Action

In order to protect itself against currency fluctuations, the Group's policy is to hedge all material firm transactional exposures, unless otherwise approved as an exception by the Treasury Review Management Committee, as well as to manage anticipated economic cash flow exposures over the medium term. The Group aims, where possible, to apply hedge accounting treatment for all derivatives that hedge material foreign currency exposures. The Group does not hedge the translation effect of exchange rate movements on the income statement or balance sheet of overseas subsidiaries and equity accounted investments it regards as long-term investments. Hedges are, however, undertaken in respect of investments that are not considered long term or core to the Group.

Additional risks and uncertainties currently unknown to the Group, or which the Group currently deems immaterial, may also have an adverse effect on the financial condition or business of the Group.

http://production.investis.com/annualreport07/performance/riskman/prinrisks/

INTERNAL CONTROL

BAE Systems

Extract from Corporate Governance Statement

Internal control

The Board has conducted a review of the effectiveness of the Group's system of internal controls, including financial, operational and compliance controls and risk management systems, in accordance with the Combined Code and the Turnbull Guidance (as revised).

BAE Systems has developed a system of internal control that was in place throughout 2007 and to the date of this report, that encompasses, amongst other things, the policies, processes, tasks and behaviours that taken together, seek to:

- facilitate the effective and efficient operation of the Company by enabling it to respond appropriately to significant operational, financial, compliance and other risks that it faces in carrying out its business;
- assist in ensuring that internal and external reporting is accurate and timely and based on the maintenance of proper records supported by robust information gathering processes; and
- assist in ensuring that the Company complies with applicable laws and regulations at all times and also internal policies in respect of the standards of behaviour and conduct mandated by the Board.

Reporting within the Company is structured so that key issues are escalated through the management team ultimately to the Board if appropriate. The Operational Framework provides a common framework across the Company for operational and financial controls and is reviewed on a regular basis by the Board. The business policies and processes detailed within the Operational Framework draw on global best practice and their application is mandated across the organisation. Lifecycle Management (LCM) is such a process and promotes the application of best practice programme execution and facilitates continuous improvement across the Group. It considers the whole life of projects from inception to delivery into service and eventual disposal, and its application is critical to our capability in delivering projects to schedule and cost.

Further key processes are Integrated Business Planning (IBP), Quarterly Business Reviews (QBR) and Performance Centred Leadership (PCL). The IBP, approved annually by the Board, results in an agreed long-term strategy for each business group, together with detailed near-term budgets. The QBRs, chaired by the Chief Operating Officers, evaluate progress against the IBP and business performance against objectives, measures and milestones. PCL drives business success by linking individual goals to those of the organisation enabling employees to understand how their own success contributes to the success of the whole business.

Whilst the quality of the control processes is fundamental to the overall control environment, the consistent application of these processes is equally important. The consistent application of world-class control processes is a key management objective.

The Company is committed to the protection of its assets, which include human, property and financial resources, through an effective risk management process, underpinned where appropriate by insurance.

The Internal Audit team independently reviews the risk identification procedures and control processes implemented by management. It provides objective assurance as to the operation and validity of the systems of internal control through a programme of cyclical reviews making recommendations for business and control improvements as required.

The Board has delegated to the Audit Committee responsibility for reviewing in detail the effectiveness of the Company's system of internal controls. Having undertaken such reviews, the Committee reports to the Board on its findings so that the Board as a whole can take a view on this matter. In order to assist the Audit Committee and the Board in this review, the Company has developed the Operational Assurance Statement (OAS) process. This has been subject to regular review over a number of years, which has resulted in a number of refinements being made.

The OAS requires that each part of the business completes a formal review of its compliance against the Operational Framework, including operational and financial controls and risk management processes. It is signed-off by the managing director of every line of business and relevant functional directors. The OAS is completed every 6 months and includes a formal assessment of business risk.

The overall responsibility for the system of internal control within BAE Systems rests with the directors of the Company. Responsibility for establishing and operating detailed control procedures lies with the line leaders of each operating business.

In line with any system of internal control, the policies and processes that are mandated in the Operational Framework are designed to manage rather than eliminate the risk of failure to achieve business objectives, and can only provide reasonable and not absolute assurance against material misstatement or loss.

The responsibility for internal control procedures with joint ventures and other collaborations rests, on the whole, with the senior management of those operations. The Company monitors its investments and exerts influence through Board representation.

http://production.investis.com/annualreport07/governance/corpgov/

Revision Questions

Note: These questions also require candidates to review the content of Chapters 2 and 3.

? Question 1

The following question is adapted from the May 2006 examination for P3.

HIJ is a new professional services firm carrying out a range of business services on behalf of small business clients. Apart from the principal, a qualified accountant who owns 100% of the business, there are four professionally qualified and two support staff. The business model adopted by HIJ is to charge an annually-negotiated fixed monthly retainer to its clients in return for advice and assistance in relation to budgeting, costing, cash management, receivables and inventory control, and monthly and annual management reporting. The work involves weekly visits to each client by a member of staff and a monthly review between HIJ's principal and the chief executive of the client company. In delivering its client services, HIJ makes extensive use of specialist accounting software.

The principal continually carries out marketing activity to identify and win new clients. This involves advertising, production of brochures and attending conferences, exhibitions, and various business events where potential clients may be located.

The management of HIJ by its principal is based on strict cost control, maximising the chargeable hours of staff and ensuring that the retainers charged are sufficient to cover the hours worked for each client over the financial year.

Requirements

(a) Recommend management controls that would be appropriate for the principal to have in place for HIJ.
(b) Evaluate the likely costs and benefits of an internal control system for HIJ

? Question 2

This question is a modified one based on the May 2005 examination for P3.

(a) Explain the meaning of an internal control system, and how it relates to the control environment.
(b) Advise senior management as to the costs, benefits and limitations of any internal control system.

Question 3

This question is a modified one based on the November 2007 examination for P3.

EWC is a large company in an unregulated sector of the telecommunications industry. It has ambitious plans for sales growth to increase profitability and returns to shareholders. In support of these goals, senior management has established a flat management structure. Budget targets place employees under considerable pressure but success in achieving and surpassing sales and profitability targets is rewarded by bonuses and share options. Employees who do not achieve their targets do not remain with the company for long.

Performance targets exist for expanding EWC's customer base, sales value and profitability per customer, and geographic and product-based expansion. EWC zealously pursues cost reduction with continual efforts to drive down suppliers' prices. The company aims to eliminate any wasteful practices in management and administration. EWC considers any expenditure that does not lead directly to sales growth to be wasteful and the company minimises its corporate policies and procedures. As a result, EWC has tended to overlook unscrupulous practices in its employees' dealings with customers, competitors and suppliers in the pursuit of its goals. The company is unlisted and reports its profits to shareholders once per year.

Requirements

(a) Identify the major types of risk facing EWC that arise from its style of management. Give reasons to support your answer. **(10 marks)**
(b) Explain the significance of the control environment in EWC. **(5 marks)**
(c) From the perspective of a newly appointed non-executive director, evaluate the financial, non-financial quantitative, and qualitative controls in EWC in the context of EWC's goals and the risks facing EWC. **(10 marks)**

Total = 25 marks

 # Question 4

This question has been adapted from the May 2006 examination.

(a) Discuss the principles of good corporate governance as they apply to the Board's role in (i) conducting a review of internal controls and (ii) reporting on compliance.
(b) Explain the importance of management's review of controls for the audit committee.

 # Question 5

This question has been adapted from the May 2007 examination.

The PKG High School has 900 pupils, 40 teachers, 10 support staff and a budget of $3 million per annum, 85% of which represents salary and salary-related costs. The Local Authority[2] for PKG's area is responsible for 34 schools, of which six are high schools. The Local Authority allocates government funding for education to schools based on the

---

[2] NOTE: A Local Authority (or council) carries out services for the local community and levies local taxes (or council rates) to fund much of its operations. Many of the Local Authority functions are regulated by central government and considerable funding also comes from that source. The range of Local Authority services include education, community health, refuse collection, maintenance of footpaths and public parks, etc.

number of pupils. It ensures that the government-approved curriculum is taught in all schools in its area with the aim of achieving government targets. All schools, including PKG, are subject to an independent financial audit as well as a scrutiny of their educational provision by the Local Authority, and reports of both are presented to the school Governing Body.

The number of pupils determines the approximate number of teachers, based on class sizes of approximately 30 pupils. The salary costs for teachers are determined nationally although the scale of pay means that more experienced teachers receive higher salaries. In addition, some teachers receive school-specific responsibility allowances.

PKG is managed on a day-to-day basis by the Head Teacher. On matters such as building maintenance the Head Teacher will seek expert advice from the Local Authority. The governance of each school is carried out by a Governing Body comprising the Head Teacher, elected representatives of parents of pupils, and members appointed by the Local Authority. The Governing Body holds the Head Teacher accountable for day-to-day school management. The principles of good corporate governance apply to school Governing Bodies which are accountable to parents and the Local Authority for the performance of the school.

The Governing Body meets quarterly and has as its main responsibilities budgetary management, appointment of staff, and educational standards. The main control mechanisms exercised by the Governing Body include scrutiny of a monthly financial report, a quarterly non-financial performance report, teacher recruitment and approval of all purchases over $1,000. The Head Teacher has expenditure authority below this level.

The monthly financial report is presented to each meeting of the Governing Body. It shows the Local Authority's budget allocation to the school for the year, the expenditure incurred for each month and year-to-date, and any unspent balances. Although there is no external financial reporting requirement for the school, the Local Authority will not allow any school to overspend its budget allocation in any financial year.

PKG's budget allocation is only just sufficient to provide adequate educational facilities. Additional funds are always required for teaching resources, building maintenance, and to upgrade computer equipment. The only flexibility the school has in budget management is to limit responsibility allowances and delay teacher recruitment. However, this increases individual teachers' pupil-contact time which forces teachers to undertake preparation, marking and administration after school hours.

Requirement

Evaluate the effectiveness of the Governing Body's control over PKG High School and recommend ways in which it might be improved.

(This section of the question was worth 20 marks).

Solutions to Revision Questions

6

✓ Solution 1

(a) There are three types of control that should be implemented: financial, non-financial quantitative and qualitative.

Financial controls help the achievement of organisation objectives by monitoring performance, informing strategic decisions, controlling expenditure and providing reasonable assurance of the safeguarding of assets and the maintenance of proper accounting records. The main forms of financial control are:

- Budgets, which for HIJ should establish income targets and planned hours for each client, projected new business and expenses (mainly salaries, travel, marketing and office expenses).
- Periodic reporting, comparing actual and budget income and planned hours for each client and actual versus budget expenditure for salaries, travel, marketing and office expenses. Variances should be investigated. This enables the principal to have confidence in reported financial results.
- Cash controls will ensure that profits are reflected in cash flow, work-in-progress and debtors are managed effectively and that recruitment and capital investment decisions undergo proper appraisal and approval.

Financial controls should be complemented by non-financial controls which provide leading indicators of business performance. A Balanced Scorecard-type system could include measures relating to customer, process, learning/growth as well as financial perspectives. Customer measures may include customer retention and satisfaction data. Process measures may include time recording systems showing the time spent on each client as well as non-chargeable time, the average charge-out rate per hour (as the retainer is fixed but hours may vary), a quality assessment based on review by the principal, and whether deadlines for the production of information for clients are achieved. Learning/growth measures may include new business, employee retention and satisfaction, professional development activities, etc. Financial controls will largely be focused on achieving profitability and cash flow targets, therefore control of debtor days outstanding will be important.

Qualitative controls will comprise the formal reporting structure (e.g. do all employees report to the principal, or is there an intermediate structure?); informal methods of socialisation and control (i.e. developing a culture for the firm); policies and procedures; physical controls over access to buildings, equipment, and data (especially in relation to the security and back-up of its specialist IT software); recruitment, induction, training and appraisal processes and incentives and rewards for employees; constant monitoring of the work schedule to ensure there is adequate but not excessive capacity. Of particular importance will be a contract of employment that prevents employees from 'poaching' clients, either for themselves or for a new employer.

(b) Internal controls are not a discretionary item but an essential part of being in business. All businesses inevitably have some controls. The cost of these controls will increase as the costs become more sophisticated and there may be diminishing marginal benefit in those controls.

The major cost associated with internal controls is their establishment: the design and set-up of policies and procedures. The cost of internal controls is that they require administrative support to develop and maintain budgeting and accounting systems, debtors and cash control, Balanced Scorecard measures, time management recording, policies and procedures, employment processes, etc. There will also be a cost in providing secure back-up facilities for computer systems and data, and in the use of independent advisers in relation to personnel procedures and marketing. These processes can consume time and incur costs of external advisers, support staff as well as for the principal. There is an opportunity cost that time spent by the principal equates to time not being spent with existing clients or developing new business. It should also be recognised that internal controls provide a reasonable safeguard but not an absolute guarantee.

The main benefit of a system of internal control is the avoidance of losses. The main losses that HIJ could face in the absence of effective controls include loss of clients, inadequate fixed sum retainer, loss of key staff, lack of expense control (salaries, travel, marketing and office costs), poor control over debtors and inadequate cash to fund the business.

However, many of these controls are not merely to avoid losses. For example, good human resource practices are necessary to recruit, train, motivate and retain skilled employees, who are HIJ's most important resource. Good accounting practices are necessary not only for control but for reporting to the taxation authorities.

✓ Solution 2

(a) Internal control is the whole system of financial and other internal controls established in order to: provide reasonable assurance of effective and efficient operation, internal financial control and compliance with laws and regulations. While the internal control system includes all the policies and procedures, the control environment is the overall attitude, awareness and actions of directors and management regarding internal controls and their importance to the organisation and encompassing management style, corporate culture and values.

A system of internal control will reflect its control environment and include: control activities, information and communication processes, and processes for monitoring the effectiveness of the internal control system. The system of internal control should be embedded in the operations of the company and form part of its culture; be capable of responding quickly to evolving risks; and include procedures for reporting immediately to appropriate levels of management any significant control failings or weaknesses.

(b) The costs of internal control will comprise the time of regional managers and any opportunity costs resulting from this plus costs associated with introducing and operating new systems and reports. However, it is difficult to differentiate between internal controls and policies and procedures that are simply good business practice (e.g. human resource practices and accounting procedures). A cost of internal control may be restrictions on the flexibility, creativity and responsiveness of the organisation.

The benefits of internal control may be difficult to identify but can be largely considered to be an improvement in the efficiency and effectiveness by which sales representatives use their time to win business, and the improved management of costs associated with their activities. These are largely concerned with eliminating both waste and fraud. Losses incurred from ineffective internal control can be estimated based on their level compared to targets or by benchmarking representatives against each other or by observing the trend over time. To the extent that effective internal control provides assurance to external auditors it can be used in negotiations to reduce the external audit fee.

A system of internal control cannot eliminate: poor judgement in decision-making; human error; the deliberate circumvention of control processes (especially where collusion occurs); the over-riding of, or lack of emphasis on, controls by senior management; and unforeseeable circumstances.

✅ Solution 3

(a) The major risks facing EWC are reputational, business and reporting.

Reputational risks arise because EWC is overlooking unscrupulous practices in dealings with customers, competitors and suppliers. These will most likely impact on future business as unscrupulous practices are brought to the attention of the press and public. This attention is also likely to affect customer retention and make winning new customers more difficult, and may lead to difficulties in obtaining supply. It may also make it difficult to attract employees to the company, especially ethical ones.

Business risk arises as a consequence of poor reputation. However, business risk may also arise from the single-minded pursuit of growth and low costs. EWC may find that its cost reduction process results in a lack of ability to deliver what it has sold to customers, or that quality declines, customer service is poor or inadequate management leads to poor decision-making. The major business risk is therefore not achieving the sales and profitability targets that have been set, leading to unsatisfactory shareholder returns. The constant price pressure placed on suppliers by EWC could cause the financial failure of those suppliers and lead to an interruption to EWC's supply chain. The attention to supplier profitability is important. A further business risk arises from the flat management structure and the potential inability to deal with unexpected events such as business shocks or the resignation of key staff. Given its emphasis on sales growth, EWC also faces the risk of overtrading which could lead to pressure on working capital and inadequate financing.

Reporting risk, that is inaccurate or late financial results may follow from inadequate administration. There is also the possibility that the approach to growth and profits, together with the rewards associated with that, will lead to the fabrication of financial results, as occurred with Enron, WorldCom and others.

(b) The control environment is the attitude, awareness and actions of directors and managers in relation to the importance of internal controls, including the organisation's culture and values and the style of management. The control environment is the necessary background for internal control procedures to be developed and operate effectively.

The culture within EWC is one that allows unscrupulous practices and minimises administration. There are likely to be few internal controls given the limited attention to policies and procedures. However, any internal controls that do exist may well be undermined by this culture and the single-minded pursuit of growth and profits to the exclusion it seems, of other factors. The reward and penalty systems in place are likely to support unscrupulous practices and it is likely that over time, the majority of employees will tend to behave in unethical ways.

The control environment in EWC evidenced by the culture that top management subscribes to is therefore likely to accentuate reputational, business and reporting risks.

(c) A non-executive director (NED) is expected to take an independent, distanced and longer-term responsibility for looking after the interests of shareholders and broader stakeholders. EWC appears to take a very short-term view. Financial controls express financial targets and spending limits. These appear to dominate in EWC. Budget targets are stretching and this may demotivate some employees, whilst encouraging others to engage in any practices that will lead to those results being achieved. Cost reduction is also likely to lead to poor practices. Management accounts should be produced regularly to enable monitoring of financial performance by the Board.

Non-financial quantitative controls comprise targets and measures that support financial goals. The idea of the Balanced Scorecard and similar models is that financial results are lagging indicators of performance. Leading indicators of performance focus on customers, process efficiency and innovation. However, in EWC those non-financial targets that exist are exclusively focused on customers and markets. It seems that in terms of targets and measures, processes are not considered important, nor is innovation, beyond cost reduction. This may result in poor quality, late deliveries and inefficiency. The scorecard used by EWC is therefore seriously unbalanced.

Qualitative controls comprise the formal and informal structures; the policies and procedures; plans; incentives and personnel controls. In EWC, these controls all support the objective of sales growth and profitability. There is a flat management structure and formal policies and procedures are minimised. The dominant form of qualitative control is the incentive system that encourages the achievement of targets and discourages failure by facilitating those deemed unsuccessful to leave the company (although how this is done is unclear from the scenario).

One positive aspect of the controls that are in place is that they support EWC's goals of sales growth and profitability. Whether these goals are in the medium or longer term realistic or achievable is one matter, but the controls do support growth. However, these controls do not take reputational, business and reporting risks into consideration and may in fact accentuate those risks rather than mitigate them.

While it is not necessarily the role of a NED to monitor all such control data, it is their responsibility to ensure that such controls are in place and are being monitored by the executive directors and managers.

Although it is management's responsibility to identify and manage risks, to effectively assess the adequacy of internal controls, internal auditors need to have expertise in risk management: how risks are identified, assessed and managed. The risk management system will itself need to be audited in order to ensure that it can be relied upon. Internal audit matches its audit programme with the degree of risk maturity in the organisation. Risk management will inform the priorities for the internal audit plan. In particular, internal audit should identify high risk matters and control deficiencies so that actions can be taken to improve those controls and so avoid, reduce or mitigate risks.

 # Solution 4

(a) *(i) Review of internal controls*

The Combined Code states that the board should maintain a sound system of internal control to safeguard shareholders' investment and the company's assets. The Turnbull Guidance recommended that companies adopt a risk-based approach to establishing a sound system of internal control and reviewing its effectiveness.

Reviewing the effectiveness of internal control is one of the responsibilities of the Board and reviewing the adequacy of internal controls needs to be carried out on a continuous basis. The Combined Code suggests that no less than three audit committee meetings should be held annually. It is important that a review of internal controls is not limited to financial controls. While this role is delegated to audit committees, the Board as a whole remains responsible.

Through their audit committees, boards need to consider the nature and extent of the risks facing the company; the extent and types of risk which are acceptable for the company to bear; the likelihood of the risks materialising; the ability of the company to reduce the incidence and severity of risks that do materialise; and the costs of operating controls compared with the benefit obtained in managing the risk.

When reviewing management reports on internal control, the board should consider the significant risks and assess how they have been identified, evaluated and managed; assess the effectiveness of internal controls in managing the significant risks, having regard to any significant weaknesses in internal control; consider whether necessary actions are being taken promptly to remedy any weaknesses; and consider whether the findings indicate a need for more exhaustive monitoring of the system of internal control.

The audit committee should regularly communicate the results of the monitoring to the board which enables it to build up a cumulative assessment of the state of control in the company and the effectiveness with which risk is being managed, including any weaknesses. The Board should regularly review reports on internal control from management in order to carry out the annual assessment that is required so that the Board can comply with the Combined Code.

(ii) Reporting on compliance

The Board should, at least annually, conduct a review of the effectiveness of the company's system of internal controls and should report that they have done so to shareholders. The Board's review should cover financial, operational and compliance controls and risk management systems.

The Board's annual statement to shareholders on internal control should disclose that there is an ongoing process for identifying, evaluating and managing the significant risks faced by the company, that it has been in place for the year and up to the date of approval of the annual report and accounts, and that it has been regularly reviewed by the board and conforms to the Turnbull Guidance.

INTERNAL CONTROL

The Board's annual assessment should address the following issues:

- Changes over the past year in the nature and extent of significant risks and the organisation's ability to respond to those risks.
- The quality of management's monitoring of risks, the system of internal control, the internal audit function and other providers of assurance.
- Frequency of reporting to the Board in relation to risks and controls.
- Any significant control weaknesses identified during the period.
- The effectiveness of reporting information to stakeholders.

The board must acknowledge in its annual statement that it is responsible for the company's system of internal control and for reviewing its effectiveness. It should also explain that the system is designed to manage rather than eliminate the risk of failure to achieve business objectives, and can only provide reasonable but not absolute assurance against material misstatement or loss.

(b) The audit committee should receive reports from management on the effectiveness of the systems they have established and the conclusions of any testing carried out by internal and external auditors. These reports provide one mechanism by which audit committees (and through them, Boards) receive assurances about the adequacy and effectiveness of the system of internal controls. However, the Board should receive reports from a number of independent sources to corroborate the management assurances.

The Smith Guidance contained within the Combined Code on Corporate Governance emphasises that a company's management is responsible for the identification, assessment, management and monitoring of risk; for developing, operating and monitoring the system of internal control; and for providing assurance to the board that it has done so.

The Turnbull Guidance within the Combined Code suggests that reports from management to the board should provide a balanced assessment of the significant risks and the effectiveness of the system of internal control in managing those risks. Any significant control failings or weaknesses identified should be discussed in the reports, including the impact that they have had, could have had, or may have, on the company and the actions being taken to rectify them.

While management is responsible for the review of controls, this is only one of the forms of assurance that the Board and audit committee should rely on.

 Solution 5

In PKG's case, the role of the Governing Body is to provide assurance that the main risks (adequacy of educational provision and budgetary control) are being managed and that internal controls are operating effectively. The adequacy of educational provision is assessed by the local authority. The accuracy of financial records needs to be audited to ensure that budgetary allocations are not overspent.

The Governing Body receives annual reports on educational provision from the local authority and a financial audit report. While these will be useful in evaluating risk and control, the annual nature of the reports means that problems that emerge during the year may not be recognised. These reports are also unlikely to address the issues under a performance (VFM) or management audit.

PKG's Governing Body relies on the monthly financial report and its prior approval of staff recruitment and significant expenditure decisions as its main form of controls. An analysis of the budget into different expense categories should be carried out.

The monthly financial report needs to be checked for accuracy. This would include the accuracy of budget phasing and whether expenditure is on a cash or accruals basis and whether commitments of expenditure are recognised before goods/services are delivered to the school. These factors can significantly affect the reliability of financial controls. This is particularly important in relation to the requirement not to overspend the school's budget allocation. These aspects, particularly throughout the year, may not be reviewed by the financial audit.

The Head Teacher can approve expenditure below $1,000 however it is possible that this authority may be abused by larger items of expenditure being split over several payments, each below $1,000. Expenditure approved by the Head Teacher should be monitored and approved retrospectively by the Governing Body.

The most important control is that over staff recruitment and strict headcount control is required. It is essential that the headcount control is reconciled with the salary budget, given the variation in rates of pay between staff of different experience, and that the Governing Body does in fact approve all recruitment decisions before they are made.

Other personnel controls include:

- The need for 10 support staff needs to be questioned. This would require an independent evaluation of their roles and responsibilities as well as their individual effectiveness. Should the number of support staff be increased to provide more effective support for teachers? Can the number of staff be reduced with reallocation of any savings to teaching staff or maintenance/teaching resources? The impact of any support staff change on the administrative load on teachers needs to be assessed.
- More experienced teachers receive higher salaries so PKG can control costs by recruiting less experienced teachers on lower salary levels, although this may have an impact on the quality of educational provision. There should be a balance of staff of different levels of experience to ensure adequate educational provision within budget limitations.
- Class sizes can be increased above 30 to provide some flexibility in staffing, although this may have an impact on the quality of educational provision.
- The impact of higher teacher/pupil contact time is likely to have industrial relations repercussions and may have an impact on the quality of educational provision.
- A means for monitoring the morale of staff, with teacher representation on the Governing Body.

There appears to be a lack of any strategic plan which would form the basis for devolving explicit goals and ways of achieving those goals.

Financial flexibility appears to be weak given the procedures determined by the local authority. TO avoid over-spending at year end, the school may have to be cautious and possibly underspend. This could be improved by the Governing Body building a contingency fund into the budget.

7

Internal Audit and the Auditing Process

Internal Audit and the Auditing Process

7.1 Introduction

The main purpose of this chapter is to identify types of audit, and the role of and need for internal audit. Internal audit is differentiated from external audit. The chapter describes in detail the relationship between risk management and internal auditing, different types of risk and risk assessment in auditing. The audit plan and various techniques for analytical review are then introduced together with methods of evaluation and reporting the findings of internal audit. The chapter concludes with the ethical principles that are relevant to internal audit.

7.2 Audit

 Audit is

A systematic examination of the activities and status of an entity, based primarily on investigation and analysis of its systems, controls and records (CIMA *Official Terminology*).

An audit is intended to objectively evaluate evidence about matters of importance, to judge the degree of correspondence between those matters and some criteria and to communicate the results of that judgement to interested parties.

In accounting, matters of importance may be financial statements and internal controls in relation to those financial statement. The criteria against which those are assessed may include 'true and fair view' and accounting standards for financial reports.

There are some important elements to these definitions:

- The systematic process avoids random actions. An audit focuses on the objectives of the audit and involves a plan of activities to achieve the audit objectives.
- Obtaining and evaluating evidence may be through observation, interviews, reviews of reports, recalculations, confirmation and analysis.
- The judgement must be based on the evidence as to whether pre-determined criteria have been met.
- Communication through an audit report presents an opinion as to whether the criteria were met.

7.3 Types of audit

External auditors are independent firms of accountants who conduct audits on behalf of their client organisations and report to the board and shareholders. Internal auditors may be employees of the organisation (or the role may be subcontracted to an accounting or professional services firm) who carry out more detailed activities on behalf of, and as prescribed by, the board of directors. External auditors will typically rely on the work of internal auditors as a form of evidence to satisfy themselves about the adequacy of internal controls. Whilst internal auditors may conduct a wide range of types of audit, external auditors are mainly concerned with forming an opinion in relation to the annual financial statements. However, external auditors may also be commissioned to carry out other forms of audit, although this practice is increasingly rare due to the separation of audit and non-audit duties.

Types of audit include:

A financial audit is one where typically external auditors express an opinion on whether financial statements present a true and fair view and comply with applicable accounting standards.

Compliance audit is an audit of specific activities in order to determine whether performance is in conformity with a predetermined contractual, regulatory or statutory requirement (CIMA *Official Terminology*). An example is compliance with company procedures for evaluating tenders.

Transactions audit: The checking of a sample of transactions against documentary evidence. This method can be used where controls are weak or where transactions are high risk, for example, mortgage lending.

Systems-based audit: This approach concentrates on the functioning of the accounting system, rather than the accuracy of accounting records and the evaluation of controls and control systems (see later in this chapter for a fuller description).

Risk-based audit: This approach reviews the risk management process: how the organisation manages risk and takes action to mitigate risks, including the use of controls (see later in this chapter for a fuller description).

Performance audit (also called operational audits, or value for money audits): Provides an evaluation of organisational or business unit performance. These are typically carried out by internal auditors through a consulting role.

Best value audit (previously known as *Value for Money* (VFM) audits): A version of performance audits, predominantly used in the public sector, VFM audits are concerned with calculating and evaluating the economy, efficiency and effectiveness of operations, in the absence of any profit or shareholder value measure. Best Value audits in the public sector require an evaluation of operations in terms of the four Cs: *c*hallenge (why something is done); *c*onsult (with the community and users about service expectations); *c*ompare (benchmark to similar organisations) and *c*ompete (apply market mechanisms such as outsourcing where this would be more cost-effective).

Post-completion audit: This is an objective and independent appraisal of the measure of success of a capital expenditure project in progressing the business as planned. It should cover the implementation of the project from authorisation to commissioning and its technical and commercial performance after commissioning. The information provided is also used by management as feedback which aids the implementation and control of future risk projects (CIMA *Official Terminology*).

Environmental audit: This is a systematic, documented, periodic and objective evaluation of how well an organisation, its management and equipment are performing, with the aim of helping to safeguard the environment by facilitating management control of environmental practices; and assessing compliance with company policies and external regulation (CIMA *Official Terminology*).

Management audit is an objective and independent appraisal of the effectiveness of managers and the corporate structure in the achievement of entity objectives and policies. Its aim is to identify existing and potential management weaknesses and to recommend ways to rectify them (CIMA *Official Terminology*).

While there are substantial differences between the purposes and focus of each type of audit, the general principles described in this chapter are similar, so far as they affect the Performance Strategy syllabus.

7.3.1 Case study: Enron

In December 2001, US energy trader Enron collapsed. Enron was the largest bankruptcy in US history. Even though the United States was believed by many to be the most regulated financial market in the world, it was evident from Enron's collapse that investors were not properly informed about the significance of off-balance sheet transactions. US accounting rules may have contributed to this, in that they are concerned with the strict legal ownership of investment vehicles rather than with their control. By contrast, International Accounting Standards follow the principle of 'substance over form'. There were some indications that Enron may have actively lobbied against changing the treatment in US financial reporting of special purpose entities used in off-balance sheet financing. Overall, there was a clear need for greater transparency and trust in reporting.

The failure of Enron also highlighted the over-dependence of an auditor on one particular client, the employment of staff by Enron who had previously worked for the auditors, the process of audit appointments and re-appointments, the rotation of audit partners and how auditors are monitored and regulated.

As a consequence of the failure of Enron and WorldCom, the United States has introduced Sarbanes-Oxley legislation to address many of the criticisms of reporting and auditing practice. In their comments on the failure of Enron, the Association of Certified Chartered Accountants recommended the need for global financial markets to have a global set of principles-based financial reporting standards and a global code of corporate governance, arguing that legalistic, rules-based standards encourage creative, loophole-based practice.

Former chief executive Kenneth Lay died in 2006 before he could stand trial. Enron's former chief financial officer Andrew Fastow was sentenced in late 2006 to six years in prison for stealing from Enron and devising schemes to deceive investors about the energy company's true financial condition.

Lawyers have to date won settlements totaling $US 7.3 billion from banks including JPMorgan Chase, Bank of America, Citigroup, etc.

7.4 Internal auditing

 Internal audit is

An independent appraisal function established within an organisation to examine and evaluate its activities ... The objective ... is to assist members of the organisation in the effective discharge of their responsibilities (CIMA *Official Terminology*).

The Institute of Internal Auditors defines internal auditing as:

An independent, objective assurance and consulting activity designed to add value and improve an organisation's operations. It helps an organisation accomplish its objectives by bringing a systematic, disciplined approach to evaluate and improve the effectiveness of risk management, control and governance processes.

The core role of internal audit is to provide assurance that the main business risks are being managed and that internal controls are operating effectively.

Internal audit differs from external audit in that it does not focus only on financial reports and financial risks but extends to a more holistic review of risk and control. However, internal and external auditors need to work closely together to provide the board with the assurances it needs to satisfy corporate governance requirements.

Internal audit should operate under a written charter which indicates the purpose, authorities and responsibilities of the internal audit function. An example of a Charter for Internal Audit produced by the Chartered Institute of Management Accountants (1999) is shown below.

7.4.1 Example of a Charter for Internal Audit

CIMA, 1999, *Internal Audit – A Guide to Good Practice for Internal Auditors and their Customers*

Function

1. Internal Audit is an independent review function set up within the organisation as a service to the Board and all levels of management. The Head of Internal Audit is responsible for effective review of all aspects of risk management and control throughout the organisation's activities.

Independence

2. Internal Audit is independent of the activities which it audits to ensure the unbiased judgements essential to its proper conduct and impartial advice to management.

Role and scope

3. The role of Internal Audit is to understand the key risks of the organisation and to examine and evaluate the adequacy and effectiveness of the system of risk management and internal control as operated by the organisation. Internal Audit, therefore, has unrestricted access to all activities undertaken in the organisation, in order to review, appraise and report on:

(a) the adequacy and effectiveness of the systems of financial, operational and management control and their operation in practice in relation to the business risks to be addressed;

(b) the extent of compliance with, relevance of, and financial effect of, policies, standards, plans and procedures established by the Board and the extent of compliance with external laws and regulations, including reporting requirements of regulatory bodies;

(c) the extent to which the assets and interests are acquired economically, used efficiently, accounted for and safeguarded from losses of all kinds arising from waste, extravagance, inefficient administration, poor value for money, fraud or other cause and that adequate business continuity plans exist;

(d) the suitability, accuracy, reliability and integrity of financial and other management information and the means used to identify measure, classify and report such information;

(e) the integrity of processes and systems, including those under development, to ensure that controls offer adequate protection against error, fraud and loss of all kinds; and that the process aligns with the organisation's strategic goals;

(f) the suitability of the organisation of the units audited for carrying out their functions, and to ensure that services are provided in a way which is economical, efficient and effective;

(g) the follow-up action taken to remedy weaknesses identified by Internal Audit review, ensuring that good practice is identified and communicated widely;

(h) the operation of the organisation's corporate governance arrangements.

This monitoring of Internal Audit's processes should be carried out on a regular basis by Internal Audit management and business management may rely on the professional expertise of the Head of Internal Audit to provide assurance. From time to time independent reviews should be carried out: for example, peer reviews by another Internal Audit function or review by External Audit. Testing compliance with the standards laid down in the audit manual is an essential approach to such a review.

Reporting

4. Internal Audit reports regularly on the results of its work to the Audit Committee, which is a Board subcommittee. The Head of Internal Audit is accountable to the Audit Committee for:

(a) providing regular assessments of the adequacy and effectiveness of the organisation's systems of risk management and internal control based on the work of Internal Audit;

(b) reporting significant control issues and potential for improving risk management and control processes;

(c) providing periodically information on the status and results of the annual audit plan and the sufficiency of Internal Audit resources.

Responsibility

5. The Head of Internal Audit is responsible for:

  (a) developing an annual audit plan based on an understanding of the significant risks to which the organisation is exposed;
  (b) submitting the plan to the Audit Committee for review and agreement;
  (c) implementing the agreed audit plan;
  (d) maintaining a professional audit staff with sufficient knowledge, skills and experience to carry out the plan;
  (e) developing audit staff for redeployment elsewhere in the organisation.

Note: Some Internal Audit functions, because they have appropriate skills, also carry out value for money reviews (see 3(f) above), which go further than a normal audit. They question the continued provision of the particular service in its present form with its present objectives, and recommend other ways in which the service might be provided, e.g. by organisational change or outsourcing.

7.4.2 Internal audit standards

Internal audit standards are defined by the Financial Reporting Council (FRC) took over responsibility for the setting of audit standards through the Auditing Practices Board in 2004. The FRC is also charged with monitoring and enforcing these auditing standards. Auditing standards are called Statements of Auditing Standards (SASs). 'Generally Accepted Auditing Standards' (GAS) are a set of formal and informal rules acknowledged as the basis for auditors to conduct their work and have the quality of their work assessed by. These include legislation, pronouncements from professional or standard setting bodies, legal judgements in cases involving auditors and practitioners, and 'internal' standards that are accepted practice even when no formal public pronouncements have been issued.

The most widely accepted standards for internal audit are those produced by the Institute of Internal Auditors (IIA). The IIA issued its revised and updated *International Standards for the Professional Practice of Internal Auditing*, in 2004 (see http://www.theiia. org/?doc_id = 1499). The UK version of these is the Code of Ethics and International Standards for the Professional Practice of Internal Auditing (Institute of Internal Auditors UK and Ireland, 2004a).

As risk management has become more widespread and has taken on the mantle of enterprise risk management, the role of internal audit, previously seen as part of the system of internal control, has become transformed into a broader process designed to provide objective assurance on the effectiveness of that system, with the Institute of Internal Auditors becoming the predominant body, in competition with the accounting profession. Risk-based approaches have also been adopted by external auditors, particularly those subject to Sarbanes-Oxley requirements in relation to the specific risk of mis-reporting in financial statements.

In addition, the audit of public sector organisations is governed by Government Internal Audit Standards (GIAS: HM Treasury, 2001).

7.5 Need for internal audit

The primary responsibility for providing assurance on the adequacy of controls and risk management lies with management. Audit committees need independent and objective assurance to validate management's assurances. Objectivity relates to having the ability to make unbiased judgements and avoid situations where judgement may be compromised.

The need for an internal audit function will depend on the scale, diversity and complexity of business activities and a comparison of costs and benefits of an internal audit function. Companies that do not have an internal audit function should review the need for one on an annual basis. Changes in the external environment, organisational restructuring or adverse trends evident from monitoring internal control systems should be considered as part of this review. An internal audit may be carried out by staff employed by the company or be outsourced to a third party.

In the absence of an internal audit function, management needs to apply other monitoring processes in order to assure itself and the board that the system of internal control is functioning effectively. The board will need to assess whether those processes provide sufficient and objective assurance.

Where there is an internal audit function, its scope of work, authority and resources should be reviewed annually. Internal audit should also monitor and report on management's agreed responses to findings and whether internal audit recommendations have been implemented.

The relationship between internal and external audit is an important one as the work of the internal auditor will be sued by the external auditor in forming a view about the effectiveness of organizational control.

7.6 Scope of internal audit

The role of internal audit is to understand the key risks of the organisation and to examine and evaluate the adequacy and effectiveness of the system of risk management and internal control in the organisation. Therefore, the internal audit function needs to have unrestricted access to all activities in the organisation and is expected to review and report on:

1. The adequacy and effectiveness of systems of financial, operational and management control in relation to business risks.
2. The extent of compliance with, and the effect of policies, plans and procedures established by the board and the extent of compliance with laws and regulations.
3. The extent to which the assets are acquired economically, used efficiently and safeguarded from losses (including waste, extravagance, inefficiency, poor value for money, fraud, etc.).
4. The suitability, accuracy, reliability and integrity of financial and non-financial performance information.
5. The integrity of processes and systems (including those under development) to ensure that controls offer adequate protection against error, fraud and loss.
6. The suitability of the organisation of each business unit for carrying out its functions economically, efficiently and effectively.
7. The follow-up action taken to remedy weaknesses identified by internal audit reviews and ensuring that good practice is identified and communicated widely.
8. The operation of the organisation's corporate governance arrangements.

Good practice is to have an independent review of internal audit, either through peer review by another internal audit function or by the external auditors.

7.7 Head of internal audit

The Head of Internal Audit should be appointed by the audit committee and is responsible for:

- Developing an annual audit plan based on an assessment of the significant risks to which the organisation is exposed.
- Submitting the plan to the audit committee for approval.
- Implementing the agreed audit plan.
- Maintaining a professional audit team with sufficient knowledge, skills and experience to carry out the plan.

The Head of Internal Audit should, wherever possible, be independent of the chief financial officer but should report to the audit committee with a 'dotted line' relationship to the finance function.

The Institute of Internal Auditors (IIA) is the professional body for those involved in the practice of internal auditing. The IIA's *International Standards for the Professional Practice of Internal Auditing* has been endorsed by the Smith Guidance in the Combined Code.

7.8 Systems-based auditing

Transaction-based auditing was a process that aimed to validate the accurate recording of transactions. This gave way to systems-based auditing which is concerned with the functioning of the accounting system, rather than the accuracy of accounting records.

Under the systems-based auditing approach, auditors and management identify all financial and non-financial auditable systems and processes. These are prioritised against risk assessments and the resources needed to audit and an audit frequency is determined. For each system or process, the auditor:

- Identifies the objective of the system or process.
- Identifies the prescribed procedures to achieve the system objective and corporate objectives.
- Identifies the risk to the achievement of objectives.
- Identifies the way management has determined to manage the risks.
- Decides whether the controls in place are appropriate.
- Tests to see whether the controls are operating effectively in practice.
- Reports on the findings and monitors the implementation of agreed recommendations.

The systems audit is cost-effective because it focuses on risks and controls; offers better assurance that a system is currently achieving and will continue to achieve its objectives.

7.9 Risk-based internal auditing

Internal audit has shifted from a focus on systems and processes to a risk-based approach. The objective of risk-based internal auditing (RBIA) is to provide assurance to the board that:

- The risk management processes which management has put in place are operating as intended. This includes all risk management processes at corporate, divisional, business unit and business process levels.
- These risk management processes are part of a sound design.

● The responses that management has made to risks which they wish to treat are adequate and effective in reducing those risks to a level acceptable to the board.
● A sound framework of controls is in place to mitigate those risks which management wishes to treat.

RBIA begins with management's approach to the risks that may prevent the business objectives from being achieved. Internal audit assesses the extent to which a robust risk management process is in place. An RBIA approach enables internal audit to link directly with risk management.

The RBIA approach is shown in Figure 7.1.

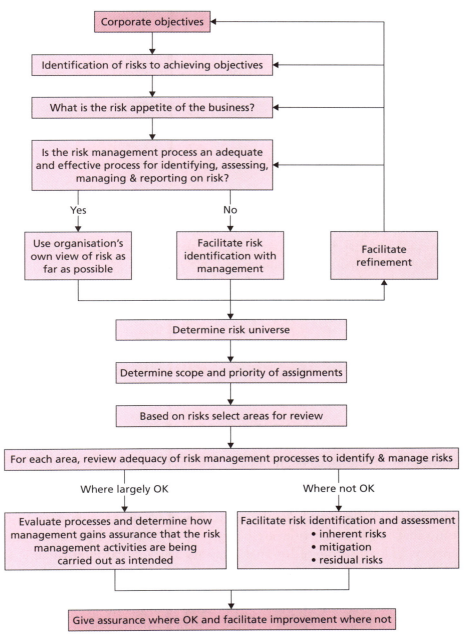

Figure 7.1   Risk-based internal auditing approach

Source: Institute of Internal Auditors UK and Ireland (2003), *Risk Based Internal Auditing*.

Reproduced with permission © Institute of Internal Auditors UK and Ireland 2003.

Table 7.1 Internal audit approach for different levels of risk maturity

Risk maturity	Key characteristics	Internal audit approach
Risk naive	No formal approach developed for risk management	Promote risk management and rely on audit risk assessment
Risk aware	Scattered silo-based approach to risk management	Promote enterprise-wide approach to risk management and rely on audit risk assessment
Risk defined	Strategy and policies are in place and communicated Risk appetite defined	Facilitate risk management and/or liaise with risk management and use management assessment of risk where appropriate
Risk managed	Enterprise-wide approach to risk management developed and communicated	Audit risk management processes and use management assessment of risk as appropriate
Risk enabled	Risk management and internal control fully embedded into the operations	Audit risk management processes and use management assessment of risks as appropriate

Source: Institute of Internal Auditors (2003), Risk Based Internal Auditing.

Different organisations are at different stages of maturity in relation to risk management. The internal audit function needs to match its programme, particularly how it assesses risk, according to the degree of risk maturity.

The Institute of Internal Auditors has suggested the internal audit approach appropriate to different levels of risk maturity, as shown in Table 7.1.

While many of the principles of external and internal auditing are common, this chapter emphasises the auditing process as it relates to internal auditing and in particular adopts a risk-based auditing approach.

7.10 Differentiating risk management and internal audit

The relationship between the risk management and internal audit functions in an organisation is a two-way one. Risk management will inform the priorities for the internal audit plan. However, the risk management system will itself need to be audited, in order to ensure that it can be relied on.

The core role of internal auditing in enterprise risk management (ERM) is to provide objective assurance to the Board on the effectiveness of an organisation's ERM activities to ensure that key business risks are being properly managed and that internal controls are effective. The Institute of Internal Auditors believes that internal auditors should not set the risk appetite, impose risk management processes, give the assurance on risk that is the role of management, make decisions about or implement risk response, or be accountable for risk management. However, internal auditors do provide advice to management and the Board, and challenge or support management decisions in relation to risk management.

Internal auditors will not just focus on financial control but on risk management and broader internal control systems. Internal auditors should focus on matters of high risk and where significant control deficiencies have been found, to identify actions taken to address them.

Internal auditors are specialists in systems for risk management and control, but managing individual risks is the role of line managers, with that role being co-ordinated by the Chief Risk Officer. Internal auditors assess how risks are identified, analysed and managed and give independent advice on how to embed risk management practices into business activities. Internal auditors can provide advice to the Board in relation to:

- The identification of key risks
- The effectiveness of processes to identify and analyse threats to the business
- The controls in place to manage the most important risks
- The culture in relation to risk and control
- The adequacy and reliability of financial and non-financial reporting
- The effectiveness of management in directing and controlling the business
- The degree of compliance with legislation
- The safeguarding of business assets
- The control of change including systems development.

7.11 Different types of risk in auditing

Some risks are *inherent risks*, that is, they follow from the nature of the business and its environment, such as market demand, competitive conditions, natural disasters, human error, fraud and theft and strategic mismanagement such as failure to respond to market change or expansion into unprofitable markets.

Other risks are related to the *failure of controls* and control systems, such as failure to control password access to computer systems, failure to comply with established procedures, having inadequate insurance cover or not reconciling balance sheet accounts regularly.

However, controls do not guarantee the elimination of risk. Changing circumstances lead to control systems being out of date, the actions of people are unpredictable and the cost of control may outweigh the benefit. The *residual risk* is that risk which remains after controls have been implemented and it is for management to decide whether the level of residual risk is acceptable. The auditor's responsibility is to ensure that managers understand the consequences of the level of residual risk that they implicitly or explicitly accept.

Auditing cannot provide complete assurance that systems and processes are all operating effectively. *Audit risk* relates to the inability of the audit process to detect control failures.

7.12 Risk assessment in auditing

Assessing risk is an important element in planning and implementing audit. Risk can be assessed through three methods:

- Intuitive or judgemental assessment;
- Risk assessment matrix;
- Risk ranking.

7.12.1 Intuitive or judgemental risk assessment

The chief internal auditor, working with his audit team or independently, will carry out a risk assessment based on past experience and professional training. This method is difficult to justify to an audit committee as being objective or based on sound assessment criteria and its effectiveness depends on the skill and experience of the auditor and his/her knowledge of the organisation.

7.12.2 Risk assessment matrix

This method identifies risk factors, assigns each a measure of the value to the organisation and provides a weighting to emphasise the importance of some factors more than others. These factors and weightings are then applied to each of the organisation's systems in order to calculate a total risk index.

Risk factors include:

- Transaction volume
- Impact on business continuity
- Adequacy of existing controls
- Whether systems are new or long-established
- Quality and experience of staff and management
- Susceptibility to fraud.

The measure of value to the organisation may be based, for example, on the number of transactions (for transaction volume); on the number of days during which the business may not be able to process transactions due to a failure (for business continuity) and an assessment (e.g. on a scale of 1–5) of the quality of internal controls. The weighting is based on an assessment of the relative importance of each risk factor.

The example in Table 7.2 provides the risk factors, measures of value and weightings for two systems.

In this example, sales order processing has a higher risk index and therefore would receive a higher assessment of risk for audit purposes than purchase order processing. While this method provides a more objective assessment than the intuitive or judgemental

Table 7.2 Risk factors and weightings for two systems

Risk factor	Measure of value	Weighting (range 1–5)	Sales order processing	Purchase order processing
Transaction volume	Up to 500 = 1 1,000–2,000 = 2 over 2,000 = 3	3	1,500 transactions $2 \times 3 = 6$	500 transactions $1 \times 3 = 3$
Business continuity	1 day = 1 2 days = 2 5 days = 4	5	2 days $2 \times 5 = 10$	1 day $1 \times 5 = 5$
Quality of internal controls	Good = 1 Adequate = 2 Poor = 3	2	Quality 2 $2 \times 2 = 4$	Quality 3 $3 \times 2 = 6$
Total risk index			20	14

Table 7.3 Audit risk ranking using likelihood/consequences matrix

		Consequences	
		High	**Low**
Likelihood	**High**	Risks to be managed by reduction or avoidance, e.g. having an adequate computer back-up facility	Risks to be managed and controlled, e.g. by introducing control systems
	Low	Risks to be managed by transfer or reduction, e.g. insurance	Risks that might be considered and accepted as insignificant

one, it should be noted that the risk factors, measures of value and weightings are all subjective judgements.

7.12.3 Risk ranking

As for risk assessment for the business as a whole (described in an earlier chapter), the likelihood/consequences matrix is a useful method of ranking risks. An example is shown in Table 7.3.

7.13 Risk management in auditing

Internal auditors need to make judgements about the measures that can be taken against risk:

- *Transferring the risk*: by insurance, hedging, use of partners, joint ventures, networks, etc.
- *Reducing the likelihood of risk*: by the introduction of controls, such as requiring purchase invoices to be signed by budget holders only after comparison with the purchase order and goods received documentation.
- *Reducing exposure to risk*: by the introduction of controls, such as not allowing any staff to accept cash payments from customers, other than cashiers.
- *Detecting occurrences*: by feedback mechanisms, such as comparison between authorised and actual spending levels.
- *Recovering from occurrences*: by adequate contingency planning.

7.14 Audit planning

Audit planning takes place at both the long-term (2–5 years) and short-term (annual) levels. Within these timeframes, detailed plans need to be developed to cover each individual audit assignment. Planning is necessary to allocate audit resources to the highest risk areas. The audit plan is circulated to management for comment before being sent to the audit committee for approval. Any shortfalls in audit resource to address risks will need to be brought to the attention of the audit committee.

Long-term audit planning is based on the objectives of the organisation, the risk management system in place and the relative risks of each area to be audited. This leads to the prioritisation of each area to be audited and an allocation of time (and therefore cost) to each area.

The short-term or annual plan sets out the areas to be audited over the next 12 months with an explanation as to why those areas were selected and the risk assessed for those areas. There may be a particular emphasis to be covered in depth. A more detailed plan will involve a month-by-month schedule of work to be undertaken by members of the internal audit staff, taking into account holidays and other commitments.

Each audit must also be carefully planned. This begins with a preliminary survey to obtain background information about the area to be audited, and to judge the scope and depth of audit work to be undertaken, based on the complexity of the area to be audited. The survey will identify the objectives, scope and timing of the audit and the audit resources (staff days, other costs, skills and experience) required.

The survey will include:

- Review of previous internal audit reports and files.
- Consideration of changes in the business environment, e.g. legislation, board decisions, strategy, competition, computer system changes, reorganisation of the department.
- Review of recent work carried out by external auditors or other bodies, e.g. Health and Safety inspections, consultants.
- Discussions with local managers to determine any issues or concerns.
- Identification of local risks.
- Identification of audit objectives.

The audit plan will set out:

- Terms of reference for the audit.
- Description of the system or process to be audited, identifying its boundaries and connections to other systems and processes.
- Risks that need special attention.
- Scope of work to be carried out, identifying any areas not to be audited.
- Milestone dates for completion and resources allocated to the audit.
- Reporting and review procedure.
- Audit programme and techniques to be applied.
- Audit staff allocated to the assignment.

Audit planning has clear advantages in terms of professionalism and co-ordination of different audit activities; resource allocation and prioritisation; workload and staff planning; clear documentation of what is/is not to be done.

The disadvantages of audit planning are that it is time consuming, can stifle initiative and may lead to inflexibility in responding to management concerns as they arise.

7.15 Audit testing and statistical sampling

Testing is used to provide evidence to the auditor as to how a system or process is operating, in order to arrive at an opinion about the adequacy of internal controls. There are three types of test:

1. Walk-through
2. Compliance
3. Substantive.

Walk-through tests

Walk-through tests follow several transactions through the system from their origination to the end of the process, at each stage identifying the process in use and the controls in place.

Compliance tests

Compliance tests, or tests of control determine whether system controls are operating as intended. They are based on a sample of transactions. Examples of compliance tests are:

- Whether loan applications have been authorised in accordance with procedures.
- Whether customer payments are allocated against outstanding invoices and the debtors account reconciled each month.

Substantive tests

Substantive tests aim to establish the validity of the outcome of transactions. They may be used more extensively when compliance tests indicate weak controls or when fraud is suspected. They are based on a sample. Examples of substantive tests are:

- Checking fixed assets in the fixed assets register to ensure that new assets are correctly recorded from purchase invoices, assets are depreciated correctly, disposals are properly recorded and assets physically exist and are being used by the organisation.
- Deliveries of goods to customers are checked to ensure there is a valid customer order, goods issued documents were issued, the goods were signed for by the customer, the invoice was properly raised and the payment was received.

The scope and depth of testing will be determined by the risk assessment, audit objectives and the time available for the audit. More testing may occur if controls are weak; management have expressed concerns about systems or processes; previous audit work identifies a weakness or there are material items that may affect the organisation.

Internal controls are often tested using attributes sampling. This involves selecting a sample of transactions from a population of data and testing for the presence or absence of certain attributes or qualities. For example, a sample of accounts payable transactions may be checked to ensure that each has been approved for payment.

A sampling plan provides information about the population and helps to avoid testing the wrong population or a non-representative sample.

In an article in The Internal Auditor, Martin (2004) identifies a 10-step model for developing a sampling plan to minimise the risk of error and help increase the validity of the data selected for testing.

1. *Conduct pre-sampling research*: Internal auditors need to understand what they're testing. A test on an examination results database which has experienced errors would involve learning where the source data comes from, and how the data base is updated.
2. *Define the objective*: Using the same example, the result of the audit test should be to identify the database problems.

3. *Define the population*: Internal auditors need to identify what is to be included and excluded from the population, for example, by specifying beginning and ending dates, or by identifying problems with a particular examination question.

4. *Examine the population*: Standard statistical tests such as mean, median and mode and standard deviations can be used to understand the population and to determine if data is distributed evenly or skewed. For example, the marks for one question may be skewed away from the average.

5. *Define a sampling unit*: A sampling unit is an individual item of the population selected for sampling. The sample selected for testing needs to contain a significant number of sampling units that supports the test objective. If the sample includes few sampling units from questions that are not skewed, then the sample will not be representative.

6. *Select the number of sampling units*: Counting the number of sampling units that meet the definition described in step 5.

7. *Define the sample selection method*: How will the random sample be selected? By what factor will it be randomised? Will the sample be computer generated?

8. *Determine the sample size*: Sample size is determined by population size, acceptable sampling risk and degree of reliance on results.

9. *Select the sample*: Computer aided audit software provides guidance on selecting a sample, or a random number generator can be used to assign a random number to each sampling unit.

10. *Check the sample*: Check that the sample looks like the total population and that the size and spread of the sample is similar to that of the population.

7.16 Analytic review

Analytic review is an audit technique used to help analyse data to identify trends, errors, fraud, inefficiency and inconsistency. Its purpose is to understand what has happened in a system, to compare this with a standard and to identify weaknesses in practice or unusual situations that may require further investigation.

The main methods of analytic review are

- ratio analysis to identify trends
- non-financial performance analysis
- internal and external benchmarking

The purpose of analytical review in external audit is to understand financial performance and position and to identify areas for more in-depth audit treatment.

In internal audit, analytical review aims to better understand the control environment and identify potential control weaknesses.

7.16.1 Ratio analysis

Ratio analysis, as those used in published accounts, but using internal management accounting data. These ratios should be compared over time (trend analysis) and compared with industry averages or the performance of competitors (benchmarking). Ratios are useful means by which questions can be generated in order to obtain explanations about trends and relative performance.

7.16.2 Benchmarking

 Benchmarking is

The establishment, through data gathering, of targets and comparators, through whose use relative levels of performance (and particularly areas of underperformance) can be identified. By the adoption of identified best practices it is hoped that performance will improve (CIMA Official Terminology).

Types of benchmarking include:

- *Internal*: comparing the performance of a business unit with one in another company in the same industry.
- *Functional*: comparing the performance of a business unit with those regarded as best practice, even if they are in a different industry.
- *Competitive*: comparing performance with a direct competitor.
- *Strategic*: competitive benchmarking aimed at strategic change.

The limitations of benchmarking are that:

- It assumes consistent and accurate data analysis;
- It will only identify significant errors or variations;
- There needs to be a standard against which performance is judged;
- It is less effective during times of change;
- It is more reliable for disaggregated data where comparisons are possible, rather than for aggregated data.

7.17 Other methods of internal audit

Various audit methods, derived from external audit, can be used as part of the internal audit process. These include:

- Physical inspection may take place, for example, counting stock to compare to inventory records or observing the amount of work being done on a construction contract.
- Corroboration involves obtaining facts confirmed by a third party, such as having customers verify the debt due by them or having banks confirm the loan securities they are holding.
- Re-calculation involves checking accuracy by repeating a calculation, for example, pricing a supplier's invoice or ensuring that a spreadsheet report is added correctly. Reconciliation involves agreeing different sets of figures, for example, reconciling the differences between the profit shown in the final monthly management accounts for a year and the published financial reports; and reconciling the organisation's accounting records with bank statements.
- Surveys can be used to establish various facts, especially where there are many locations for a business unit and a comparison is needed, or to assess a particular aspect of internal control, for example, whether a routine report is received regularly and whether it is used.

- Narratives are written descriptions of processes or systems obtained from interviews with those responsible for, or working with systems or processes, whether as users or customers. Narratives can also be generated from observations made by auditors about systems or processes. These observations usually come about as a result of testing processes (see below). Narratives provide an explanation about how processes or systems work and their strengths and weaknesses and enable comparison with formal documented procedures for those processes or systems. Narratives tend to be long and wordy and may be difficult to follow where processes or systems are complex. Narratives tend to be used by auditors mainly to record the results of interviews with people in relation to the area being audited, as they provide clarification of issues, responses to errors and a record of recent changes or unusual events.
- Flowcharting involves showing, in diagrammatic form, the inputs (e.g. source documents), processes (e.g. activities) and outputs (e.g. reports). Flowcharting can be carried out for a business process (e.g. purchasing) or a system (e.g. a payroll processing system). Flowcharting can identify overlaps and gaps in systems/processes and the interface between different systems and processes (e.g. between purchasing and inventory control or between payroll and financial reporting).

There are various types of flowcharts:

- *Data flow*: The logical flow of data through a system, e.g. how a sale is processed to invoicing stage.
- *Procedures*: The procedures carried out, and the responsibilities for carrying out those procedures, e.g. for approval of overtime.
- *Program*: Computer programming operations, e.g. an inventory control system.
- *Document*: The flow of documents or physical resources between areas of responsibility, e.g. how goods are issued from a store, or how a loan application is processed by a financial services organisation.
- *System*: A high-level description of major elements of a system, e.g. accounts payable.

Flowcharts provide precise descriptions, identify inconsistencies and problems, provide a record of the system or process, are a visual method of presentation leading to easier understanding and are easy to update.

7.18 Internal control questionnaires

An internal control questionnaire is a checklist of the specific internal control techniques that should be present in a particular system to provide assurances about internal control. They are an important element in forming an audit judgement about the adequacy of internal controls. The internal control evaluation questionnaire (ICEQ) provides high-level assurance that controls are adequate, while the internal control questionnaire (ICQ) provides the more detailed checklists. Both can be developed from models available through professional bodies or by developing an organisation-specific checklist.

7.19 Evaluation of audit findings

The audit should provide an understanding of the system or process; identify strengths and weaknesses, including gaps and overlaps and a comparison between the system or process in operation with that documented in formal manuals and procedures. The evaluation will be based on the use of internal control questionnaires. The auditor may identify variances between:

- The system documented in formal manuals and procedures;
- The system that staff believes is operating, based on answers to questions recorded in narratives;
- The system that is operating, based on flowcharts and other observational evidence, including testing.

It may be that systems or processes have developed over time to meet changing circumstances, in which case, documented manuals and procedures may need alteration. However, it may be that changes in practice, however caused, have led to internal control weaknesses that need to be corrected by changes in activities. This is an audit opinion which needs to be presented to management to obtain their response.

7.20   Audit working papers

Working papers are an essential record of the work carried out by internal auditors and provide the evidence base that leads to conclusions and recommendations being made. They may comprise a combination of techniques such as ratio analysis, benchmarking, narratives, flowcharts and testing.

Increasingly, the formalisation of audit work and its importance as an evidence base has led to standardisation in working papers. The content of working papers will often include:

- Scope of the audit and the type of audit (e.g. compliance, systems, Best Value)
- Report from previous audit and recommendations outstanding
- Timetable for the audit and resources allocated to the audit
- Work programme including analytical methods used
- Evidence collected from ratio analysis, benchmarking, narratives, flowcharts and testing
- Interpretation of the evidence and significant findings
- Conclusions
- Recommendations
- Final Report.

7.21   Internal audit reporting

The auditor writes a draft report of findings, conclusions and recommendations and presents this to management for their response. A plan of action is agreed between the auditor and management, which is incorporated into the final audit report and presented to the audit committee. The auditor subsequently follows up whether the agreed action plan has been implemented. Any unimplemented recommendations need to be reported to the audit committee as do any recurring themes emerging from different audits.

The Head of Internal Audit should report to the Audit Committee of the Board in relation to:

- Providing regular assessments of the adequacy and effectiveness of systems of risk management and internal control;

- Reporting significant internal control issues and potential for improving risk management and control;
- Providing information on the status and results of the annual audit plan and the adequacy of resources for internal audit.

7.22   The audit committee and internal audit

The audit committee should review and approve the scope of work of the internal audit function, with regard to the complementary roles of internal and external audit. The audit committee should ensure that the internal audit function has access to the information it needs and the resources necessary to carry out its function. The audit committee should approve the appointment or termination of the head of internal audit. The audit committee should, at least annually, meet the external and internal auditors, without management being present, to discuss the scope of work of the auditors and any issues arising from the audit.

In its review of the work of internal audit, the audit committee should:

- Ensure that the internal auditor is accountable to the audit committee and has direct access to the board chairman and audit committee
- Review and assess the internal audit work plan
- Receive regular reports on the results of the work of the internal auditor
- Review and monitor management's responsiveness to the internal auditor's findings and recommendations
- Monitor and assess the role and effectiveness of the internal audit function in the overall context of the company's risk management system.

7.23   The audit committee and the external auditor

The audit committee is also responsible for making a recommendation on the appointment, re-appointment and removal of the external auditors and oversight of relations between the company and the external auditor. Each year the audit committee should assess the qualification, expertise, resources and independence of the external auditors and the effectiveness of the audit process. This should include obtaining a report on the audit firm's own internal quality control procedures. If the external auditor resigns, the audit committee should investigate the reasons and consider whether any further action is required.

The audit committee should approve the terms of engagement and remuneration of the external auditor and should review and agree with the engagement letter issued by the external auditor at the start of each audit, ensuring that it has been updated to reflect any changed circumstances. The scope of the audit work should be reviewed by the audit committee and if unsatisfied with its adequacy, it should arrange for additional work to be done.

The audit committee should have procedures to ensure the objectivity and independence of the external auditor, taking into account professional requirements. This assessment should consider all relationships between the external auditor and the company, including any non-audit services carried out by the external auditor for the company.

The audit committee should monitor the audit firm's compliance with ethical guidance in relation to the rotation of audit partners, the level of fees the company pays to the external auditor in proportion to the total fee income of the firm, office and partner.

The audit committee should also agree with the Board on the company's policy for the employment of former employees of the external auditor, especially those who were part of the audit team and moved directly to the company, with consideration given to the ethical guidelines of the accounting profession. Consideration needs to be given in respect of any former employees of the external auditor currently employed by the company as to whether there has been any impairment (or appearance of impairment) of the auditor's judgement or independence in respect of the audit.

The audit committee should review with the external auditors their findings and should in particular:

- Discuss major issues that arose during the audit and have subsequently been resolved and those issues that remain unresolved
- Review key accounting and audit judgements
- Review levels of error identified during the audit, obtaining explanations from management and the external auditors, as to any errors that remain unadjusted

At the end of the audit cycle, the audit committee should review the effectiveness of the audit by:

- Reviewing whether the auditor has met the agreed audit plan, and understood why any changes have been made to that plan
- Considering the robustness and perceptiveness of the auditors in their handling of the key accounting and audit judgements; in responding to questions from the audit committee and in their commentary on the systems of internal control
- Obtaining feedback about the conduct of the audit from key people involved, notably the finance director and head of internal audit
- Reviewing and monitoring the content of the external auditor's management letter, in order to assess whether it is based on a good understanding of the company's business and establish whether recommendations have been acted upon

The chairman of the audit committee should be present at the annual general meeting to answer questions on the report of the audit committee's activities and matters within the scope of the audit committee's responsibilities.

7.24 The effectiveness of internal audit

The effectiveness of internal audit can be judged by answering the following questions:

- Has the purpose, authority and responsibility of the internal audit function been formally defined and approved by the audit committee?
- Can internal audit carry out consulting services without compromising its primary role?
- Does the head of internal audit report directly to the audit committee?
- Is the head of internal audit free of any operational responsibility that might impair objectivity?
- Does the head of internal audit have direct access to the chair of the board?
- Have any members of the internal audit team given assurance on business areas for which they were previously responsible?

- Has any consulting activity carried out by internal audit detracted from the primary role?
- Does the internal audit team have sufficient technical expertise, qualifications and experience to provide the required levels of assurance? If not, how is competent advice and support obtained?
- Is internal audit capable of identifying the indicators of fraud?
- Has the work of internal audit considered all important business risks?
- Has internal audit considered the cost of control and assurance and balanced that cost against the benefits?
- Does internal audit demonstrate an understanding of the organisation and its key processes and related risks?
- Has there been any significant control breakdown in areas that have been reviewed by internal audit?
- Does internal audit measure its effectiveness and its value for money?
- Does internal audit undertake a programme of continuous improvement?
- Does internal audit respond satisfactorily to feedback it receives?
- Is internal audit seen as a valuable contribution by business units?
- Is an independent assessment of internal audit performed every 5 years?
- Are internal audit practices benchmarked against best practice?
- Does internal audit carry out its role in accordance with the IIA's *International Standards for the Professional Practice of Internal Auditing?*
- Does internal audit focus on the key issues that concern the board?
- Does internal audit cover all risk areas (financial, operational, technological, behavioural, etc.) in its work programme?
- Can internal audit respond quickly to organisational change?
- Does internal audit have the necessary resources and access to information to enable it to carry out its role?
- Do internal audit reports contain an opinion on the adequacy of control?
- Is internal audit effective in communicating its findings and recommendations and obtaining agreed outcomes?
- Does internal audit stimulate debate and improvements in key risk areas?
- Are significant control issues raised at an appropriate level in the organisation?
- Does management feel that recommendations made by internal audit are useful, realistic and forward looking?

Source: Institute of Internal Auditors (2003), *Appraising Internal Audit*.

A useful document is the guide for audit committees in evaluating auditors (Institute of Chartered Accountants in England and Wales, 2003).

7.25 Case study: Barings Bank

Barings Bank was Britain's oldest bank, having existed for 200 years before it collapsed as a result of uncontrolled derivatives trading by Nick Leeson in the bank's Singapore office.

The collapse of Barings Bank in 1995 was caused by Nick Leeson, a 26-year-old dealer who lost £800 million in unauthorised dealings in derivatives trading from his base in Singapore. Leeson suppressed information on account '88888' which he used for trading between 1992 and 1995, which management was unaware of. The losses wiped out the Bank's capital.

As only a small amount of money (a margin) is needed to establish a derivatives position, it is possible to face financial obligations beyond an organisation's ability to pay. Therefore, strict controls are needed. There are many risk management and control lessons to be learned from the failure of Barings.

Barings had placed Nick Leeson in charge of both the dealing desk and the back office. The back office records, confirms and settles trades made by the front office and provides the necessary checks to prevent unauthorised trading and minimise the potential for fraud and embezzlement. In this dual position, Leeson was able to relay false information back to London.

An internal audit report in August 1994 concluded that Leeson's dual responsibility for both the front and back office was an excessive concentration of powers and warned of the risk that Leeson could override controls. The internal auditors' responsibility was to make sure the directors were aware of the risk they were facing by not implementing the separation of duties. However, directors did not implement these recommendations. Their response was that there was insufficient work for a full-time treasury and risk manager. There was also a lack of supervision of Leeson by Barings' managers, either in Singapore or London.

Senior managers of Barings had a superficial knowledge of derivatives, did not understand the risks of the business, did not articulate the bank's risk appetite or implement strategies and control procedures appropriate to those risks.

When the Singapore exchange made margin demands on Barings, large amounts of cash had to be paid out but still no steps were taken by the London head office to investigate the matter. Eventually, the amounts required were so great that Barings were forced to call in receivers. The trading positions taken out by Leeson were unhedged and the cost of closing out the open contracts was US$1.4 billion.

The information in this case study comes from the *Report of the Board of Banking Supervision (BoBS) Inquiry into the Circumstances of the Collapse of Barings.*

7.26 Summary

- Audit involves a systematic process, aimed at a providing a defined level of assurance. The audit process is to obtain and evaluate evidence through a variety of techniques in order to make a judgement based on that evidence, and to present an opinion through an audit report.
- There are various types of audit: financial, compliance, transactions, systems based, risk based, performance, value for money or best value, post completion, environmental, and management (see Section 7.3).
- The primary responsibility for providing assurance on the adequacy of controls and risk management lies with management. Audit committees need independent and objective assurance to validate management's assurances.
- The role of internal audit is to understand the key risks of the organisation and to examine and evaluate the adequacy and effectiveness of the system of risk management and internal control in the organisation.

- The Head of Internal Audit should be appointed by the audit committee. S/he is responsible for developing an annual audit plan based on an assessment of significant risks; submitting the plan to the audit committee for approval; implementing the agreed audit plan and maintaining a professional audit team with sufficient knowledge, skills and experience to carry out the plan.

- Transaction-based auditing aims to validate the accurate recording of transactions. Systems-based auditing is concerned with the functioning of the accounting system, rather than the accuracy of accounting records.

- RBIA provides assurance to the board that: the risk management processes which management has put in place are operating as intended; these risk management processes are part of a sound design; the responses that management has made to risks which they wish to treat are adequate and effective in reducing those risks to a level acceptable to the board and a sound framework of controls is in place to mitigate those risks which management wishes to treat.

- Different organisations are at different stages of maturity in relation to risk management. The internal audit function needs to match its programme, particularly how it assesses risk, according to the degree of maturity.

- Internal auditors will not just focus on financial control but on risk management and broader internal control systems. Internal auditors should focus on matters of high risk and, where significant control deficiencies have been found, identify actions taken to address them.

- Internal auditors can provide advice to the board in relation to: the identification of key risks; the effectiveness of processes to identify and analyse threats to the business; the controls in place to manage the most important risks; the culture in relation to risk and control; the adequacy and reliability of financial and non-financial reporting; the effectiveness of management in directing and controlling the business; the degree of compliance with legislation; the safeguarding of business assets and the control of change including systems development.

- Inherent risks follow from the nature of the business; other risks are related to the failure of controls; residual risk is that risk which remains after controls have been implemented and audit risk relates to the inability of the audit process to detect control failures.

- Risk assessment in internal auditing can be assessed through three methods: intuitive or judgemental assessment; risk assessment matrix or risk ranking.

- Internal auditors need to make judgements about the measures that can be taken against risk: transferring the risk; reducing the likelihood of risk; reducing exposure to risk; detecting occurrences and recovering from occurrences.

- Audit planning is necessary to allocate audit resources to the highest risk areas and is based on the objectives of the organisation, the risk management system in place and the relative risks of each area to be audited.

- Each audit must be carefully planned, beginning with a preliminary survey to obtain background information about the area to be audited, and to judge the scope and depth of audit work to be undertaken.

- Statistical sampling is a technique to ensure that checking a sample of data is representative of the population, from which it is valid to draw conclusions about the total population.

- Analytic review is an important audit technique used to help analyse data to identify trends, errors, fraud, inefficiency and inconsistency. Its purpose is to understand what has happened in a system, to compare this with a standard and to identify weaknesses in practice or unusual situations that may require further examination. The main methods of analytic review are ratio analysis, benchmarking, physical inspection, corroboration, re-calculation and reconciliation, surveys and questionnaires, narratives, flowcharting and testing (see Section 7.15).

- Testing is used to provide evidence to the auditor as to how a system or process is operating, in order to arrive at an opinion about the adequacy of internal controls. There are three types of test: walk-through, compliance and substantive.
- An internal control questionnaire is a checklist of the specific internal control techniques that should be present in a particular system to provide assurances about internal control.
- The audit should provide an understanding of the system or process; identify strengths and weaknesses, including gaps and overlaps and a comparison between the system or process in operation with that documented in formal manuals and procedures.
- Working papers are an essential record of the work carried out by internal auditors and provide the evidence base that leads to conclusions and recommendations being made.
- The auditor writes a draft report of findings, conclusions and recommendations and presents this to management for their response. A plan of action is agreed between the auditor and management, which is incorporated into the final audit report and presented to the audit committee. The auditor subsequently follows up whether the agreed action plan has been implemented.
  - The audit committee should review and approve the scope of work of the internal audit function, with regard to the complementary roles of internal and external audit; should ensure that the internal audit function has access to the information it needs and the resources necessary to carry out its function; should approve the appointment or termination of the head of internal audit and should, at least annually, meet the external and internal auditors, without management being present, to discuss the scope of work of the auditors and any issues arising from the audit.
  - The audit committee is responsible for making a recommendation on the appointment, re-appointment and removal of the external auditors and oversight of relations between the company and the external auditor. The audit committee should approve the terms of engagement and remuneration of the external auditor; and should have procedures to ensure the objectivity and independence of the external auditor. At the end of the audit cycle, the audit committee should review the effectiveness of the audit.
- There are a number of ways by which to gauge the effectiveness of internal audit (see Section 7.24).

References

Chartered Institute of Management Accountants (2006), *Code of Ethics for Professional Accountants*.

Chartered Institute of Management Accountants (1999), *Internal Audit – A Guide to Good Practice for Internal Auditors and Their Customers*.

HM Treasury (2001), *Government Internal Audit Standards*.

Institute of Chartered Accountants in England and Wales (2003), *Guidance for audit committees: Evaluating your auditors*.

The Institute of Internal Auditors (1999). *The Definition of Internal Auditing*,

The Institute of Internal Auditors (2008). *The International Standards for the Professional Practice of Internal Auditing*

Institute of Internal Auditors UK & Ireland (2004a), *Code of Ethics and International Standards for the Professional Practice of Internal Auditing.*

Institute of Internal Auditors UK & Ireland (2004b), *Position Statement: The Role of Internal Audit in Enterprise-wide Risk Management.*

The Institute of Internal Auditors – UK and Ireland (2005). *An Approach to the Implementation of Risk Based Internal Auditing*

Martin, J.R. (2004), Sampling made simple. *The Internal Auditor*, Vol. 61, No. 4 (August), pp. 21–23.

Students should also consult the wide range of reports available from the website of the Institute of Internal Auditors in UK and Ireland at www.iia.org.uk.

Appendix

7

Risk, control and internal audit: A case study of ABC

ABC is a small listed company in the service sector. Its board of directors takes its responsibilities to shareholders seriously. Over recent years it has tried to improve its corporate governance processes in the light of the Combined Code. The management prepares monthly accounts for the board and annual accounts for investors. The annual accounts are audited.

Although ABC's board takes overall responsibility for the company's accounts, it has delegated the detail of supervising the quality of the information and liaising with the external auditors to the audit committee. Two years ago the board established its first audit committee. In its first year, the committee focused on improving confidence in the company's financial statements and formed a view that ABC's internal financial controls were effective. Its view was supported by the external auditors, who considered the company's financial management and reporting to be sound.

ABC had an approach to internal control that allowed delegated decision-making within a framework of policies and financial regulations. It had made a lot of effort to recruit and train the best people, but the complexity of service provision and high staff turnover owing to industry competition meant that key work practices were documented as standard procedures and a quality management system had been introduced. Budgetary control was also quite strict.

The audit committee relied on a wide range of evidence in considering the effectiveness of ABC's internal controls. These included reports by external and internal auditors; management assurances about risk management and controls; the results of Inland Revenue and HM Customs & Excise inspections; the performance measurement system; the quality assurance system; the business planning and budgeting process; and contingency planning relating to the possible loss of information systems. The committee recognized that it had relied heavily on financial controls and was unsure whether the non-financial controls gave the board enough of an assurance that risk was being managed effectively.

A major form of internal control for ABC was its internal audit function. The company had thought for many years that it was more likely to achieve objective and cost-effective judgments about its internal controls by outsourcing this to a professional accounting firm.

Although the internal audit provided a lot of assurance about financial controls and the quality of financial statements, ABC's board became increasingly concerned with broader issues of control over the business operations. This was partly a reflection of the importance placed by the Turnbull report on risk management and its adoption into the Combined Code. As a result, it was decided that the remit of the audit committee should be extended to encompass risk management.

In the audit committee's second year of existence, ABC appointed a risk manager who implemented a comprehensive system of identifying and assessing risks, and of developing a risk register, which was reported regularly to the board.

Although the board was satisfied with the risk management processes that were in place, the audit committee felt that it didn't have a sufficient independent and objective assurance that the risk management system and internal controls were effective. The audit committee asked the internal audit provider to spend less time auditing financial systems and more time auditing the broader risk management system and internal controls – ie, to take a more risk-based internal audit approach.

Over the next year, ABC's audit committee became disillusioned with the internal audit provider, which had continued to take an overly traditional financial systems approach, rather than focusing on broader risk management issues. The committee considered that the major risk facing the company was a failure to achieve its business objectives, which could cause ABC to lose its market position in a competitive environment. The internal audit provider had failed to respond to these concerns, so the committee decided to put the work out to tender as a risk-based internal audit.

It soon appointed a new internal firm, which reviewed ABC's risk management system and recommended a new internal audit plan based on an assessment of the major risks. The risk register was improved and the audit committee received a higher level of assurance that controls were effective and that risks were being managed in accordance with ABC's appetite for risk. Financial controls remained important, but they no longer dominated internal audit, while many non-financial controls came to be seen as just as important as the financial ones.

Financial reports and systems are crucial for all organizations. But in ABC's case there were far more important risks facing the organization and a need for controls beyond the traditional financial ones. Once an organization has sound financial controls and can rely on its systems for timely and accurate financial reports, all risks need to be assessed – particularly those relating to the achievement of organisational objectives. Internal controls need to be put in place to manage those risks and a risk-based internal audit approach should support risk management and internal controls by providing assurances to the audit committee about their effectiveness. Only through a combination of risk management, internal controls, and internal and external audit can a board of directors fulfil its governance responsibilities. Focusing on accounting alone is simply not enough.

Revision Questions

? Question 1

The following question is adapted from the November 2007 examination for P3
"Effective internal control, internal audit, audit committee and corporate governance are all inter-related". Discuss this statement with reference to:

(a) How internal audit should contribute to the effectiveness of internal control.

(7 marks)

(b) How an audit committee should contribute to the effectiveness of internal audit.

(9 marks)

? Question 2

The following question has been adapted from the November 2007 examination for P3.

EWC is a large company in an unregulated sector of the telecommunications industry. It has ambitious plans for sales growth to increase profitability and returns to shareholders. In support of these goals, senior management has established a flat management structure. Budget targets place employees under considerable pressure but success in achieving and surpassing sales and profitability targets is rewarded by bonuses and share options. Employees who do not achieve their targets do not remain with the company for long.

Performance targets exist for expanding EWC's customer base, sales value and profitability per customer, and geographic-and product-based expansion. EWC zealously pursues cost reduction with continual efforts to drive down suppliers' prices. The company aims to eliminate any wasteful practices in management and administration. EWC considers any expenditure that does not lead directly to sales growth to be wasteful and the company minimises its corporate policies and procedures. As a result, EWC has tended to overlook unscrupulous practices in its employees' dealings with customers, competitors and suppliers in the pursuit of its goals. The company is unlisted and reports its profits to shareholders once per year.

Requirements

(a) Identify the major types of risk facing EWC that arise from its style of management. Give reasons to support your answer. **(10 marks)**

(b) Explain the significance of the control environment in EWC. **(5 marks)**

(c) From the perspective of a newly appointed non-executive director, evaluate the financial, non-financial quantitative, and qualitative controls in EWC in the context of EWC's goals and the risks facing EWC. **(10 marks)**

Total = 25 marks

? Question 3

This question has been adapted from the May 2008 examination for P3.

Recommend the tests or techniques, both manual and computerised, that internal auditors can use in assessing the adequacy of inventory controls.

(10 marks)

Solutions to Revision Questions

7

✔ Solution 1

(a) An internal audit contributes to the effectiveness of internal controls by ensuring that internal controls take into account the risks facing the organisation and that risks are reduced to a level acceptable to the board. The focus of risk-based internal auditing is to be able to provide assurances to the audit committee that risk management processes are operating as intended. This is achieved by ensuring that the risk management system has a sound design; that management's responses to risks are adequate and effective in reducing risks to an acceptable level; and that a framework of controls is in place to mitigate risks.

Whilst managers are expected to put in place controls to mitigate risk, they are also expected to deliver financial performance and this may place managers in a conflict of interest. This may lead them to minimise controls where they see these as unnecessary, costly or restrictive. As a result of this potential conflict, the internal audit function has an important role to play in ensuring that controls are in place.

Although it is management's responsibility to identify and manage risks, to effectively assess the adequacy of internal controls, internal auditors need to have expertise in risk management: how risks are identified, assessed and managed. The risk management system will itself need to be audited in order to ensure that it can be relied upon. Internal audit matches its audit programme with the degree of risk maturity in the organisation. Risk management will inform the priorities for the internal audit plan. In particular, internal audit should identify high risk matters and control deficiencies so that actions can be taken to improve those controls and so avoid, reduce or mitigate risks.

(b) The primary responsibility for providing assurance on the adequacy of controls and risk management lies with management. However, audit committees require independent and objective assurance to validate the assurances they are receiving from management.

Internal audit is an independent and objective function which may be a department of an organisation or an outsourced function which examines and evaluates risk management, internal control and governance processes. The core role of internal audit is to provide assurance that the main business risks are being managed and that internal controls are operating effectively. Internal audit should have a charter which describes its purpose, authority and responsibility, which should be reviewed annually.

The Head of Internal Audit should be appointed by and report to the audit committee and be independent of the chief financial officer (CFO), although the Head will have to work closely with the CFO. The Head should develop an internal audit plan based on risk assessments, submit internal audit plans to the audit committee for approval, implement the approved plan, and maintain a team with knowledge and capacity to carry out the plan.

An audit committee contributes to the effectiveness of the internal audit function by ensuring that

- the internal audit charter is adequate,
- the Head of Internal Audit is independent and objective,
- there are adequate internal audit resources to provide the necessary support for management assurances and enable the audit committee to advise the board so that the board can give its report to shareholders.

The audit committee must also approve internal audit plans and exercise its own expertise and judgement that risks have been properly assessed and that internal audit plans address the most significant risks. The audit committee must also carefully consider internal audit reports and ensure that the organisation implements recommendations that have the audit committee's support. Finally, the audit committee should monitor and review the effectiveness of internal audit and may seek the opinion of external auditors in making that assessment.

☑ Solution 2

(a) The major risks facing EWC are reputational, business and reporting.

Reputational risks arise because EWC is overlooking unscrupulous practices in dealings with customers, competitors and suppliers. These will most likely impact on future business as unscrupulous practices are brought to the attention of the press and public. This attention is also likely to affect customer retention and make winning new customers more difficult, and may lead to difficulties in obtaining supply. It may also make it difficult to attract employees to the company, especially ethical ones.

Business risk arises as a consequence of poor reputation. However, business risk may also arise from the single-minded pursuit of growth and low costs. EWC may find that its cost reduction process results in a lack of ability to deliver what it has sold to customers, or that quality declines, customer service is poor or inadequate management leads to poor decision-making. The major business risk is therefore not achieving the sales and profitability targets that have been set, leading to unsatisfactory shareholder returns. The constant price pressure placed on suppliers by EWC could cause the financial failure of those suppliers and lead to an interruption to EWC's supply chain. The attention to supplier profitability is important. A further business risk arises from the flat management structure and the potential inability to deal with unexpected events such as business shocks or the resignation of key staff. Given its emphasis on sales growth, EWC also faces the risk of overtrading which could lead to pressure on working capital and inadequate financing.

Reporting risk, i.e. inaccurate or late financial results may follow from inadequate administration. There is also the possibility that the approach to growth and profits, together with the rewards associated with that, will lead to the fabrication of financial results, as occurred with Enron, WorldCom and others.

(b) The control environment is the attitude, awareness and actions of directors and managers in relation to the importance of internal controls, including the organisation's culture and values and the style of management. The control environment is the necessary background for internal control procedures to be developed and operate effectively.

The culture within EWC is one that allows unscrupulous practices and minimises administration. There are likely to be few internal controls given the limited attention to policies and procedures. However, any internal controls that do exist may well be undermined by this culture and the single-minded pursuit of growth and profits to the exclusion it seems, of other factors. The reward and penalty systems in place are likely to support unscrupulous practices and it is likely that over time, the majority of employees will tend to behave in unethical ways.

The control environment in EWC evidenced by the culture that top management subscribes to is therefore likely to accentuate reputational, business and reporting risks.

(c) A non-executive director (NED) is expected to take an independent, distanced, and longer-term responsibility for looking after the interests of shareholders and broader stakeholders. EWC appears to take a very short-term view. Financial controls express financial targets and spending limits. These appear to dominate in EWC. Budget targets are stretching and this may demotivate some employees, whilst encouraging others to engage in any practices that will lead to those results being achieved. Cost reduction is also likely to lead to poor practices. Management accounts should be produced regularly to enable monitoring of financial performance by the Board.

Non-financial quantitative controls comprise targets and measures that support financial goals. The idea of the Balanced Scorecard and similar models is that financial results are lagging indicators of performance. Leading indicators of performance focus on customers, process efficiency and innovation. However, in EWC those non-financial targets that exist are exclusively focused on customers and markets. It seems that in terms of targets and measures, processes are not considered important, nor is innovation, beyond cost reduction. This may result in poor quality, late deliveries and inefficiency. The scorecard used by EWC is therefore seriously unbalanced.

Qualitative controls comprise the formal and informal structures; the policies and procedures; plans; incentives and personnel controls. In EWC, these controls all support the objective of sales growth and profitability. There is a flat management structure and formal policies and procedures are minimised. The dominant form of qualitative control is the incentive system that encourages the achievement of targets and discourages failure by facilitating those deemed unsuccessful to leave the company (although how this is done is unclear from the scenario).

One positive aspect of the controls that are in place is that they support EWC's goals of sales growth and profitability. Whether these goals are in the medium or longer term realistic or achievable is one matter, but the controls do support growth. However, these controls do not take reputational, business and reporting risks into consideration and may in fact accentuate those risks rather than mitigate them.

While it is not necessarily the role of an NED to monitor all such control data, it is their responsibility to ensure that such controls are in place and are being monitored by the executive directors and managers.

Solution 3

Auditing IT systems is particularly important given the reliance on computer systems for inventory control.

- Computer assisted audit techniques (CAATs) may be used. Test data can be used to compare the results of inventory processing through the computer system with manual processing to ensure accurate processing by computer.
- Embedded audit facilities allow for a continuous audit review by, for example, an integrated test facility using a false entity, software code comparison programmes to detect programme changes, and logical path analysis programmes which convert software code into flowcharts.
- Audit interrogation software allows auditors to access the inventory system and check large volumes of data by extracting data from computer files, performing calculations, verifying data and comparing it with management reports, and identifying any items that do not comply with system rules.
- Resident audit software permits real-time auditing by tagging items so they can be selected by the auditor at a later date or copied to a system control and review file (SCARF) for later analysis.

8

Information Systems and Systems Development

Information Systems and Systems Development

8

LEARNING OUTCOMES

After completing this chapter you should be able to:

▶ Advise managers on the development of information management (IM), information systems (IS) and information technology (IT) strategies that support management and internal control requirements.

▶ Evaluate IS/IT systems appropriate to an organisation's needs for operational and control information.

▶ Evaluate benefits and risks in the structuring and organisation of the IS/IT function and its integration with the rest of the business.

▶ Recommend improvements to the control of information systems.

8.1 Introduction

The main purpose of this chapter is to identify alternative information strategies and the links between them. This includes the cost-benefits of information, methods of data collection and presenting management information. Various types of information systems are described, from transaction systems to expert systems and the growth of information linked to e-commerce. An overview of outsourcing IT is also included. The chapter then contains a major section on information systems development and controls over that development, concluding with a consideration of IT department structure.

8.2 Information and information systems

Information is different from raw data because it has been made usable by some form of analysis. For example, sales data can be summarised and analysed by customer and/or product/service and becomes meaningful management information – a monthly sales analysis – which can then be used for decision-making. Information needs to be relevant, timely, accurate, complete, concise and understandable.

An information system is a system that collects information and presents it, usually in summarised form for management. Information is also an essential tool of management control. The International Organization for Standardization (ISO) has developed a new standard: ISO/IEC 38500 Corporate Governance in Information Technology. The new standard contains guidelines for corporate governance in terms of the values and principles of management and effective monitoring of undesirable developments in relation to IT technology. The standard recognises that IT systems can adversely affect performance and competitiveness in organisations and in some cases may even breach legislation.

ISO/IEC 38500 contains six principles of corporate governance: responsibility, strategy, acquisition, performance, conformity and human behaviour. The goal of the standard is to offer a basis with which to evaluate corporate governance, to inform leaders about how they can regulate the use of IT in their organisations, and build trust in corporate governance.

8.3 Information strategies

Organisations have three different strategies relating to information:

- Information systems (IS)
- Information technology (IT)
- Information management (IM)

8.3.1 Information systems strategy

IS strategy determines the long-term information requirements of a business and provides an 'umbrella' for different information technologies that may exist. The IS strategy follows the organisational business strategy and needs to ensure that the appropriate information is acquired, retained, shared and available for use in strategy implementation such as financial, non-financial, competitive, human resources.

8.3.2 Information technology strategy

IT strategy defines the specific systems that are required to satisfy the information needs of the organisation, including the hardware, software, operating systems, etc. Each IT system must be capable of obtaining, processing, summarising and reporting the required information. The most sophisticated forms of IT system are the Enterprise Resource Planning System (ERPS) and Executive Information System (EIS) described later in this chapter.

IT strategy is required because:

- IT involves high costs and a strategy will result in a budgetary allocation and budgetary control.
- IT is critical to business success and so systems must be reliable and accessible at all times.
- IT is necessary to build and retain competitive advantage, e.g. by using customer information for targeted marketing.
- IT results in cost reductions, e.g. the use of e-mail has reduced postal and telephone charges.
- IT is necessary to assist managers by providing information for planning, decision-making and control.

8.3.3 Information management strategy

IM strategy is concerned with methods by which information is stored and available for access. This will consider methods of flat or relational database use, data warehousing, back-up facilities, etc. The IM strategy will ensure that information is being provided to users and that redundant information is not produced.

8.3.4 Linking information strategies

IS strategies are focused on the business unit, enabling it to satisfy (internal or external) customer demand. IT strategies are supply-oriented, focused on activities and the technology needed to support those activities. IM strategies are management-focused at the whole organisation level.

IS, IT and IM strategies will change over time as a result of:

- Changes in organisational objectives
- Development of new information technologies
- Updating of hardware and software
- Business growth and diversification.

8.4 Cost-benefit of information

The collection, processing, analysis and reporting of information can be an expensive process, and care needs to be taken that the value of the information obtained is greater than the cost of that information.

The cost of information may include computer hardware and software, implementation costs (e.g. the project team) and training associated with a new systems development. The day-to-day costs associated with information systems include salaries, office accommodation, depreciation or lease payments, utilities, maintenance, consumables, financing costs, etc. Quantifying the cost of information involves estimating likely costs and applying techniques such as discounted cash flow, payback or accounting rate of return.

The benefits of information may include improved decision-making, customer service, product/service quality, productivity, reduced staffing, etc. Quantifying the benefits of information is usually more difficult than quantifying costs as it involves making judgements about market growth, market share, competitive advantage and the effect on sales and profitability. Reduced staffing is easier to quantify, but as organisations grow, achieving staff savings is often more difficult in practice. Often the benefits of information will be qualitative, such as improved knowledge about the market, customers and competitors.

8.5 Methods of data collection

Most data collection in organisations takes place as a by-product of transaction recording through computer systems. For example, in retail businesses:

Electronic point of sale (EPOS): uses bar code scanning to price goods and also to reduce inventory and identify margins by linking the sale price to the cost of goods sold. Over a time period (day, week or month) the outputs from such a system include cash receipts, business volume (number of customers, number of items sold, etc.) sales analysis, product profitability and inventory re-order requirements. A cash register docket is printed for the customer. Additional benefits of EPOS include information about peak sales times during each day, products that may need to be discounted, sales locations that may need to be expanded, etc.

Electronic funds transfer at point of sale (EFTPOS): enables customers to pay for their purchases by debit or credit card. Although there is a cost charged by banks to retailers for this service, retailers avoid the cost and risk associated with handling large volumes of cash.

Loyalty cards: enable retailers to maintain a detailed knowledge of their customers' purchasing habits to enable targeted promotional campaigns aimed at specific customers.

Internet purchasing: For many products and services, purchasing over the internet enables customers to carry out the data processing previously carried out by the retailer's own employees. Customers make their own selection, provide delivery details, and pay by debit or credit card. The retailer automatically obtains a detailed history of the customer's spending habits for later targeted marketing. Examples of the use of on-line purchasing are for books, food, clothing, travel, etc. Companies such as Amazon save costs by not needing expensive retail premises or staff taking customer orders.

Electronic data interchange (EDI): In businesses selling products to other businesses, transactions are processed over the internet using EDI. Supplier and customer systems are linked by a common data format (EDI) so that purchase orders raised by the customer are automatically converted into sales orders on the supplier. For example, in the automotive industry, orders from the vehicle assemblers are placed on suppliers. These orders are expected to be delivered against a strict Just-in-Time (JIT) delivery schedule. EDI transactions enable the supplier to confirm being able to meet the order. Goods are despatched by the supplier and the location of the goods can be identified by the logistics organisation delivering the product through barcode tracking. Accurate delivery is linked to the sequencing of multiple components in a prescribed order to meet the requirements of the vehicle assembly line, as any delay or out-of-sequence component can stop the assembly line. The use of EDI enables automatic generation of invoicing by the supplier, tracing of deliveries by the logistics supplier and receipt of goods by the vehicle assembler, ultimately leading to payment to the supplier.

Document imaging: The reduction of paper in organisations has led to improved efficiency and lower costs. Customer orders can be processed through a document imaging system which scans an image and creates an electronic document. This enables faster response to customers, improved service levels, reduced staff costs, faster access to records and fewer errors caused by lost documents.

8.6 Methods of presenting management information

8.6.1 Periodic reports

The most common form of delivering management information to users is the hard copy report, a computer-generated report that may list transactions (a transaction report), exceptions (an exception report), or a summarised periodic report. However, screen displays of key performance data with graphical representation are becoming increasingly common.

- *Transaction reports* or audit trails are a detailed listing of all transactions for a period, such as all invoices generated for a week.

- *Exception reports* list exceptions to predetermined rules, such as those customers who have exceeded their credit limit or those products that are out of stock.
- *Summarised periodic reports* are produced at regular intervals, usually weekly or monthly, and include both financial (profit and loss account, balance sheet, aged debtors analysis, etc.) reports and non-financial reports (e.g. manpower or staffing levels, productivity and repeat orders).

The major problem of periodic reports is that the content is largely quantitative, is focused on short-term performance, ignores external factors and it is difficult to distinguish key performance information from the volume of data presented.

8.6.2 Briefing book

Increasingly, management needs focused information linked to business objectives, identifying key trends. An example is the briefing book, a series of one-page summaries produced monthly that contain key financial or non-financial information, identifying trends, typically also represented in graphical form, with a brief narrative explanation of variations to budget or trends.

However, the content of the briefing book is frequently determined by the producer of the information rather than the user, so key performance information may not be included, the content may not be relevant to all managers at different levels in different parts of the organisation and the narrative information may quickly become obsolete.

On-line information generated to meet the specific needs of individual managers as information users with up-to-date information is available through executive information systems which can be interrogated by managers, rather than relying on the production of standard reports by information producers. Often, these electronic versions, whether on screen or on paper, are presented with 'traffic lights'. Traffic lights (red/amber/green) draw attention to those aspects of performance which are meeting target (green), those which are in need of urgent attention (red) and those that need to be considered as they are borderline (amber). Such 'electronic briefing books' have different names but may be Balanced Scorecards or dashboards (see Chapter 3 for a discussion of non-financial performance measures).

8.7 Types of IS

There are various types of IS each with a different purpose:

- Transaction processing systems
- Management information systems
- Enterprise resource planning systems
- Strategic enterprise management
- Decision support systems
- Executive information systems
- Expert systems.

8.7.1 Transaction processing systems

Transaction processing systems collect source data about each business transaction, for example, customer order, sales, purchases, stock movements, payments, receipts. These are reported on a regular basis. Transaction processing reports are important for control and audit purposes but provide little usable management information.

8.7.2 Management information systems

Management information systems (MIS) provide managers with information for decision-making and for control. Data are drawn from transaction processing systems and produced as reports (described earlier in this chapter). Reports tend to be standard but information usually requires additional processing. It is quite common for information to be extracted from standard reports and transferred to a spreadsheet for manipulation and analysis by managers. MIS are not particularly helpful for planning purposes.

8.7.3 Enterprise resource planning system

An enterprise resource planning (ERP) system helps to integrate data flow and access to information over the whole range of a company's activities. ERP systems typically capture transaction data for accounting purposes, operational data, customer and supplier data which are then made available through data warehouses against which custom-designed reports can be produced. ERP systems are a development of older-style materials requirement planning (MRP), manufacturing resource planning (MRPII) and distribution resource planning (DRP) systems. ERP systems take a whole-of-business approach. ERP system data can be used to update performance measures in a Balanced Scorecard system and can be used for activity-based costing, shareholder value, strategic planning, customer relationship management and supply chain management. ERP systems are being developed in three directions:

1. Supplier facing to meet the needs of supply chains;
2. Customer facing with a customer relationship management (CRM) function;
3. Management facing to support the information and decision-making needs of managers through strategic enterprise management (SEM).

8.7.4 Strategic enterprise management

SEM is an IS providing the support needed for the strategic management process. It is based on data stored in a data warehouse which is then used by a range of analytical tools, such as shareholder value management, activity-based management and the Balanced Scorecard. SEM can be an important driver of organisational performance as it enables faster and better decision-making at all organisational levels.

8.7.5 Decision support systems

Decision support systems (DSS) contain data analysis models that provide the ability for managers to simulate, or ask 'What if?' questions so that different options can be considered and information can be obtained to aid in decision-making. DSS may be contained in a spreadsheet or in a complex software package. A simple example of a DSS is a spreadsheet containing cost, volume and profit data. Managers can manipulate, for example, selling prices to see the effect on volume and profit as part of their decision-making about pricing and product profitability. A further example is a spreadsheet containing expected cash flows to support a capital investment appraisal. Discounted cash flow techniques can be applied by using probabilities to produce alternative cash forecasts with varying costs of capital.

8.7.6 Executive information systems

Executive information systems (EIS) are systems used for decision support, which incorporate access to summarised data, often in graphical form, to enable senior managers to evaluate information about the organisation and its environment. An EIS utilises a 'drill down' facility to move from aggregated data down to a more specific and detailed level (e.g. customer, product, business unit). Information is typically also available from external sources, for example, public databases. Ease of use is an important feature so that enquiries can be made without a detailed knowledge of the underlying data structures.

8.7.7 Expert systems

Expert systems store data relevant to a specialist area gained from experts and retained in a structured format or knowledge base. Expert systems provide solutions to problems that require discretionary judgement. Users access data through a graphical user interface (GUI) to ask questions of the system, which will prompt the user for more information. Various rules are then applied by the expert system to make decisions. The best example of an expert system is that used for credit approval. Information is entered to the system in response to prompts, such as postcode, telephone number, age, employment history, which is compared with confidential data held by credit reference agencies to make an automated judgement about an applicant's credit worthiness and the allocation of a credit limit.

8.8 Information and the web

8.8.1 Internet

The internet comprises the computers, web servers, communication lines and communications software that allow users access to data held on multiple computers through the World Wide Web (www). The main internet software is TCP/IP (transmission control protocol/internet protocol) which is the standard for communications software and HTML (Hypertext Mark-up Language), the programming language allowing the creation of links between data items on the World Wide Web. Web browsers are software applications that enable the use of hypertext together with searching and moving around the Internet. The most common browsers are Microsoft Internet Explorer and Netscape Navigator. Users subscribe to the internet through an Internet Service Provider (ISP). It is estimated that there are almost 300 million users of the Internet worldwide. E-mail (electronic mail) and chat rooms are the most popular uses of the internet in addition to browsing (or 'surfing') the web.

8.8.2 Intranets and extranets

An intranet is the in-house version of an internet, operated by a single organisation. Intranets can be used for sharing all types of information within an organisation, such as:

- Telephone lists
- Procedure manuals
- Reference material

- Staff recruitment vacancies
- Staff newsletters.

  An intranet requires:

- A network capable of fast transmission of data to all users
- Web browser software
- Use of hypertext
- E-mail software.

An extranet is a system that links the intranets of related organisations – for example, within a supply chain – for their mutual benefit. Extranets can be used to share:

- Stock availability
- Price information
- Delivery schedules.

The difficulties involved with using extranets include the loss of confidentiality and the incompatibility between systems.

8.8.3 E-commerce

Electronic commerce (or e-commerce) describes the purchase and sale of goods and services, and the conduct of financial services, through the internet. Organisations can use the internet for:

- Public relations. Websites can contain details about the company including its products, staff, locations, financial information, etc. They can be used to initiate contact with the organisation.
- Information. An electronic product/service brochure can be contained within an organisation's web pages or can be downloaded as a separate file. Many organisations store quite detailed reports on their websites, often as PDF (portable document format) files.
- Retailing. Customers can order and pay for goods through the Internet (see earlier in this chapter).

The major benefits of e-commerce are the potential growth in sales volume through the global marketplace; and the reduction in transaction costs compared with other methods of distribution. However, there are additional control and security problems associated with allowing others access to computer systems and permitting remote real-time processing.

8.9   IS outsourcing and facilities management

Historically, computer bureaux provided computer systems for a variety of clients who could not afford their own systems. As the power of computers increased and their size and cost reduced, organisations acquired their own computer systems and developed their own in-house IT expertise.

Outsourcing (or sub-contracting) non-core or support activities has become increasingly common in organisations. This is particularly so in relation to the provision of IT services. Outsourcing enables organisations to concentrate on their core activities while subcontracting support activities to those organisations who are specialists. Outsourcing of IT can range from the whole IT department to specific elements, the most common ones being programming, maintenance and disaster recovery. The services are provided to an agreed level of service, at an agreed cost and for an agreed period of time.

The main advantages of outsourcing for IT are:

- The more accurate prediction of costs, and therefore more accurate budgetary control
- Using services only when necessary (IT staff may 'create' work to keep themselves busy)
- Improving quality and service
- Higher standard of service because of the specialisation of the service provider
- Economies of scale available to the outsource service provider
- The organisation is relieved of the burden of managing specialist staff, especially where there is little promotional opportunity and/or high staff turnover
- The outsourced service supplier has a better knowledge of changing technologies.

The main disadvantages of outsourcing for IT are:

- The difficulty of agreeing on a service level agreement (SLA) that clearly identifies the obligations of each party
- The loss of flexibility and inability to quickly respond to changing circumstances as the outsourced service is no longer under the control of the organisation
- Risk of unsatisfactory quality and service, or even failure of supplier
- Short-term cost-savings focus at expense of long-term strategy considerations
- Ignoring unchanged overhead burden
- Poor management of the changeover
- Poor management of outsource supplier
- Increasing costs of outsource provision and difficulty of changing the outsourced supplier or of returning to an in-house provision.

Facilities management (FM) is a development of outsourcing in which the management and operation of part or all of an organisation's IT services is carried out by an external party. Frequently with FM, external staff works within the client organisation's premises and using its equipment.

An outsourcing or FM decision needs to be carried out on the basis of a competitive bidding process and the information systems development process described later in this chapter needs to be followed.

The risk of outsourcing and FM can be partly offset by retaining a small group of IT specialists in-house to monitor and work with the outsource supplier. Risk can also be reduced by building a long-term partnership or joint venture between both companies.

Another option is to organise an outsourcing contract such that a member of the supplier's staff is permanently located at the organisation's premises to act as liaison between client and contractor. This is sometimes called an 'implant'.

8.9.1   IT and shared services centres

Shared services centres (or SSCs) provide services needed by several, if not all, business units within an organisation. The distinctive features of shared service centres for IT (as for other functions such as finance and human resources) are that they offer a common service provision of IT functions including systems design, data processing, IT security, generation of reports, etc. Shared services centres are service-focused, enabling the customers of the shared service to specify the level and nature of the service. This is typically established, as for any outsourced service, through an SLA.

The fact that the service is specified by the customer or user distinguishes a SSC from traditional centralisation of activities. With centralised services there is a focus on control and central requirements, with policy and direction being enforced from a Head Office and information requirements being determined by the centre. The ethos of shared service centres is different, with the focus being on quality and customer service and the pooling of resources to achieve common aims. SSCs differ from outsourcing in that whilst a split is maintained between provider and client, the IT services are retained in-house.

8.10 IS development

In an environment of continual business change and emerging information technologies, organisations will frequently need to improve or change their information systems. However, there is a significant risk in IS development of obtaining a product that does not meet user needs, is late or costs more than was estimated. Therefore, it is important to have strong controls over systems development.

A comprehensive coverage of information systems project management and systems development is outside the scope of this subject. However, the key elements of IS project management are:

- Project planning and definition
- Management support
- Project organisation: role and responsibilities of the steering committee, project board and project manager
- Resource planning and allocation
- Quality control and progress monitoring
- Risk management (identification, assessment and management of risks)
- Systems design and approval
- System testing and implementation
- User participation and involvement
- Communication and co-ordination
- User education and training.

8.11 Systems design and approval

One approach to systems design is the Systems Development Life Cycle (SDLC). An abbreviated version of the SDLC for systems development is based on:

- *Feasibility study*: identifying the needs and objectives of the system by identifying current problems and the technical, operational and economic feasibility of the proposed solution.
- *Systems analysis*: the processes necessary to generate the specification for the system through a methodical investigation of a problem and the identification and ranking of alternative solutions through obtaining more information than was contained in the feasibility study. This will result in a tender specification and a choice between in-house versus outsourced provision.
- *Systems design*: the conversion of specifications into a workable design including source data, input layout, file structure, reports, and interfaces with other systems, etc. Increasingly, computer-assisted software engineering (CASE) tools are used for systems analysis and design in many organisations.

- *Implementation*: the use of project management techniques for hardware, software, testing, documentation and training and conversion from existing systems.
- *Systems operation and maintenance*: Maintenance involves the correction or enhancement of systems once they are in operation. There should also be a post-implementation review.

8.12   Systems development controls

Systems development projects need to be reviewed to determine compliance with standard performance criteria. In particular:

- At the *feasibility study* stage, there should be a clear understanding about the objectives of the new system, the deliverables, its cost and its time to completion.
- At the *system design* stage, there need to be rules with regard to data security and levels of authorisation which need to be built into the system design. At this stage, the auditor needs to review system documentation, interfaces with other systems, and acceptance of design by all in the project team, especially users.
- At the *testing* stage, there must be comprehensive testing by systems development staff, programmers, users and internal auditors. Auditors need to review the specifications, flowcharts, test data and operating instructions.
- At the *implementation* stage, there needs to be a review of training and documentation, file conversion and operational issues, e.g. staffing and supervision.

A steering committee is important in bringing together

- the sponsor of the project – a senior manager who has been involved in authorising the project and is committed to its success;
- the project manager – responsible for the day-to-day delivery of the project;
- specialist IT staff with responsibility for delivering the project;
- user representatives with responsibility for accepting the system;
- internal audit representative with responsibility for ensuring the adequacy of internal controls and system testing in conjunction with users.

The steering committee monitors the system implementation in comparison with the plan and ensures that specific deliverables are accepted at each stage of systems development. It has overall responsibility to ensure that the system meets requirements in terms of quality, time and cost.

8.13   Case study: Criminal Records Bureau

The objective of the Criminal Records Bureau (CRB) is to widen access to criminal records so that employers could make better informed recruitment decisions, especially in relation to the protection of children and vulnerable adults. The CRB is a Public Private Partnership with Capita plc which operates a call centre, inputs applications for checking, collects fees, develops and maintains the IT infrastructure and issues disclosures.

Planning for the CRB commenced in 1999 and live access began in March 2002, seven months later than planned caused by problems in business and technical development and the decision to conduct more extensive testing prior to live operations.

There were weaknesses in the business assumptions made by Capita. In particular, the assumption that 70–85 per cent of people would apply by telephone to a call centre or on-line was incorrect and not based on adequate research with potential users, 80 per cent of whom preferred paper applications. However, data entry screens had been designed for input from a telephone call, not from paper forms, and Optical Character Recognition (OCR) systems did not have the capacity to handle the volume of paper applications. Also, systems had been designed around receipt of individual applications and could not cope when batched applications were received. The processes were also unable to cope with the volume of errors and exceptions on paper applications.

Since June 2003 the CRB has met service standards in terms of turnaround times and backlogs have been eliminated. A House of Commons Report concluded that 'the key to running a complex, Greenfield operation with a private sector partner is to work together as a team to solve operational problems'.

Source: House of Commons, Criminal Records Bureau: Delivering Safer Recruitment? (HC266), 2004

8.14   Systems implementation

An implementation plan will cover parallel running, where the new system is operated in conjunction with the existing system until such time as the new system is proven to work by reconciling outputs from both systems and ensuring that users are satisfied with the new system and are confident about discontinuing the existing system. If there is a change-over without parallel running, then testing prior to implementation becomes more important and additional monitoring may be needed during the early stages of implementation.

Particular care needs to be taken in converting data from existing systems. This needs to be properly planned and sufficient resources allocated to carry out the conversion. Adequate controls need to be implemented to ensure the consistency of data as they are transferred between systems, identifying any duplications and omissions.

The auditor may be required to sign off the system before implementation. This involves forming a professional opinion that the system:

- Meets user requirements
- Functions satisfactorily
- Has been developed with adequate built-in controls
- Is auditable
- Master files and data files have been converted and are complete and accurate
- Implementation plan is realistic.

8.15   Post-implementation review

A thorough review of the new system should be carried out after implementation, by the project team, to establish whether the system is operating as intended and to confirm that user needs are being satisfied. The outcomes of the post-implementation review are to:

- Establish whether the new system satisfies users' needs.
- Evaluate the actual performance of the system compared with the system specification.

- Make recommendations for improvement or alteration.
- Ascertain the quality of the project management for the systems implementation and any learning points for future projects.
- Recommend improvements to system development procedures.
- Compare actual costs with budgeted project costs and ascertain whether planned benefits have been achieved.

The internal audit team should ensure that the post-implementation review has been properly carried out by the project team.

8.16   IT structure and support services

The size and structure of the IT department will depend on the size of the organisation, its information needs and the extent to which IT provision, especially new systems development, is in-house or outsourced. The organisation needs to have

- the desired ability to develop new systems,
- the desired ability to maintain and modify existing systems,
- the ability to support users,
- adequate systems controls.

Information centres have become the most common way of organising the IT function. An information centre carries out some or all of the following functions, as required to satisfy IT, IS and IM strategies:

- Help desk to resolve user problems with the use of software, involving the use of remote diagnostic software, and so offer advice to the user.
- Advice on hardware and software purchase and the standards necessary for integration of systems, especially where ERP, SEM, DSS or EIS are in use.
- Advice on application development, either in-house or using outsourced contractors. This will involve advice in relation to the systems development process to be followed.
- Monitoring network usage, central processor usage and disk storage to ensure adequate capacity; and carrying out routine backup of data.
- Maintaining corporate databases or data warehouse.
- System maintenance and testing; user training and systems and user documentation.
- Maintaining IT security.

8.17   Information Technology Infrastructure Library

The Information Technology Infrastructure Library (ITIL) is an internationally accepted best practice model in the public domain that guides business users through the planning, delivery and management of quality IT services. ITIL assists organisations in aligning IT services with business requirements. ITIL is based on a core set of ten processes and one function. There are five processes targeted at service support and five processes focused on service delivery. The Service Desk function interfaces to all ten processes to provide a single point of contact from customers to IT.

The Service Support processes and goals are:

- *Configuration Management*: To identify record and report on all IT components.
- *Incident Management*: To restore normal service operation as quickly as possible and minimise the adverse impact on business operations.
- *Change Management*: To ensure that standardised methods and procedures are used for efficient and prompt handling of all changes to minimise the impact of change-related incidents and improve day-to-day operations.
- *Problem Management*: To minimise the adverse impact of incidents and problems on the business that are caused by errors in the IT infrastructure and to prevent recurrence of incidents related to these errors. Problem Management seeks to get to the root cause and initiate action to remove the error.
- *Release Management*: Release Management takes a holistic view of a change to an IT service and should ensure that all aspects of a release, both technical and non-technical, are considered together.

The Service Delivery processes and goals are:

- *Service Level Management*: To maintain and improve IT service quality through a constant cycle of agreeing, monitoring and reporting to meet the customers' business objectives.
- *Availability Management*: To optimise the capability of the IT infrastructure, services and supporting organisation to deliver a cost-effective and sustained level of availability enabling the business to meet its objectives.
- *Capacity Management*: To ensure that all the current and future capacity and performance aspects of the business requirements are provided cost-effectively.
- *IT Service Continuity Management*: To ensure that the required IT technical and services facilities can be recovered within required and agreed timescales. This is a systematic approach to the creation of a plan and/or procedures to prevent, cope with and recover from the loss of critical services for extended periods.
- *Financial Management*: To provide cost-effective stewardship of the IT assets and resources used in providing IT services.

The Service Desk function and goals are:

- To provide a single point of contact for customers and an operational single point of contact for managing incidents to resolution.
- To facilitate the restoration of normal operational service with minimal business impact on the customer within agreed service levels and business priorities.

8.18　Summary

- Information is different from raw data because it has been made usable by some form of analysis. An IS is a system that collects information and presents it, usually in summarised form for management.
- Organisations have three different strategies relating to information: information systems (IS) strategy, information technology (IT) strategy, and information management (IM) strategy. IS strategy determines the long-term information requirements of a business and provides an 'umbrella' for different information technologies. IT strategy defines the specific hardware and software required to satisfy the information needs of the organisation.

IM strategy is concerned with methods by which information is stored and available for access.

- The collection, processing, analysis and reporting of information can be an expensive process, and care needs to be taken that the value of the information obtained is greater than the cost of that information. However, despite the relative ease of calculating the cost of information, the benefits will often be qualitative, such as improved knowledge about the market, customers and competitors.

- Most data collection in organisations takes place as a by-product of transaction recording through computer systems. Examples include EPOS, EFTPOS, loyalty cards, internet purchasing, EDI and document imaging.

- The most common form of delivering management information to users is the hard copy report. These may be reports on transactions, exceptions or summarised periodic reports. The Briefing Book provides focused information linked to business objectives, typically represented in graphical form, with a brief narrative explanation of variations to budget or trends.

- There are various types of information systems: transaction processing systems; management information systems; enterprise resource planning systems; strategic enterprise management; decision support systems; executive information systems and expert systems (see Section 8.7).

- The World Wide Web has enabled information to be transmitted over the internet, intranets and extranets and has supported the growth of e-commerce. The major benefits of e-commerce are the potential growth in sales volume through the global marketplace; and the reduction in transaction costs compared with other methods of distribution. However, there are additional control and security problems associated with allowing others access to computer systems and permitting remote real-time processing.

- Outsourcing non-core or support activities has become increasingly common in organisations. This is particularly so in relation to the provision of IT services, for which there are many advantages and disadvantages (see Section 8.9). Some of the benefits of outsourcing, whilst retaining key knowledge in-house, can be obtained through using shared services centres.

- Organisations will frequently need to improve or change their information systems. It is important to have strong controls over systems development because there is a significant risk in IS development of obtaining a product that does not meet user needs, is late or costs more than was estimated. This control needs to cover the feasibility study, systems design, testing and implementation phases.

- The key elements of information systems project management are: project planning and definition; management support; project organisation – steering committee, project board and project manager; resource planning and allocation; quality control and progress monitoring; risk management; systems design and approval; testing and implementation; user participation; communication and co-ordination and education and training.

- A post-implementation review needs to establish whether the new system satisfies users' needs; evaluate the actual performance of the system compared with the system specification; make recommendations for improvement or alteration; ascertain the quality of the project management for the systems implementation and any learning points for future projects; recommend improvements to system development procedures; and compare actual costs with budgeted project costs and ascertain whether planned benefits have been achieved.

- Information centres have become the most common way of organising the IT function. They typically include a help desk; advice on hardware and software purchase and integration; advice on application development, either in-house or using outsourced contractors; monitoring system usage and capacity and performing routine backups; maintaining corporate databases; system maintenance, testing, training and documentation and IT security.

- The ITIL model guides business users through the planning, delivery and management of quality IT services. It is based on a set of five processes targeted at service support and five processes focused on service delivery. The Service Desk function interfaces to all ten processes to provide a single point of contact from customers to IT.

References

Fahy, M. (2001a), *Enterprise Resource Planning Systems: Leveraging the Benefits for Business*. London: CIMA.

Fahy, M. (2001b), *Strategic Enterprise Management Systems: Tools for the 21st Century*. London: CIMA.

Revision Questions

? Question 1

This question is taken from the May 2005 P3 examination.

AMF is a market leading, high technology manufacturing organisation producing components for the computer industry. AMF has adopted a 'lean' approach to all its functions and has already made a decision to implement a new enterprise resource planning system (ERPS) to support the management of its customers, suppliers, inventory, capacity planning, production scheduling, distribution and accounting functions. The Board of AMF is considering the outsourcing of the design, delivery, implementation and operation of the ERPS to a specialist contractor that has an excellent reputation within the computer industry.

Requirement

Write a report to the Board of AMF:

- Comparing and contrasting the advantages and disadvantages of outsourcing the ERPS system as suggested above. **(5 marks)**
- Evaluating the main risks involved in outsourcing the ERPS and suggesting how these risks might be mitigated. **(10 marks)**
- Recommending the processes and controls that AMF should adopt to achieve a successful transition to a chosen outsource supplier should that be the decision of the Board.

(5 marks)

(Total = 25 marks including 5 marks for style, coherence and presentation of the report)

Note: 5 marks are allocated to answers requiring a report style. Marks are allocated for structure (introduction, body, conclusion), addressing, headings and a clear and coherent style of presentation.

? Question 2

This question is taken from the pilot examination for P3.

The Information Systems strategy within the MG organisation has been developed over a number of years. However, the basic approach has always remained unchanged. An IT budget is agreed by the Board each year. The budget is normally 5% to 10% higher than the previous year's to allow for increases in prices and upgrades to computer systems.

Systems are upgraded in accordance with user requirements. Most users see IT systems as tools for recording day-to-day transactions and providing access to accounting and other information as necessary. There is no Enterprise Resource Planning System (ERPS) or Executive Information System (EIS).

The Board tends to rely on reports from junior managers to control the business. While these reports generally provide the information requested by the Board, they are focused at a tactical level and do not contribute to strategy formulation or implementation.

Requirements

(a) Compare and contrast Information Systems strategy, Information Technology strategy and Information Management strategy and explain how these contribute to the business. **(10 marks)**

(b) Advise the Board on how an ERPS and EIS could provide benefits over and above those provided by transaction processing systems. **(10 marks)**

(c) Recommend to the Board how it should go about improving its budgetary allocations for IT and how it should evaluate the benefits of ERPS and EIS. **(5 marks)**

(Total = 25 marks)

 # Question 3

This question is taken from the November 2008 examination for P3

FDS is a large diversified company whose information technology and information management activities are carried out by a shared service centre. FDS25 is one of many business units operating as an investment centre within FDS. FDS25 has developed a new business strategy which requires a major new investment in information technology to support its business strategy. FDS25 needs to implement the new system as quickly as possible and within budget in order to meet its objectives.

Requirements

(a) Recommend the controls that could be implemented by a business unit like FDS25 to mitigate against risk at each stage of information system design and implementation. **(15 marks)**

(b) From the perspective of FDS25, identify the risk management advantages and disadvantages of each of -

(i) utilising the shared service centre, and

(ii) outsourcing for the design and implementation of a new information system. **(10 marks)**

(Total = 25 marks)

Solutions to Revision Questions

8

 Solution 1

Report to Board of Directors

Introduction: Context and Purpose of the Report

AMF has already decided to implement an enterprise resource planning (ERP) system. ERP systems take a whole-of-business approach by capturing transaction data for accounting purposes, operational data, and customer and supplier data which are then made available through a data warehouse against which custom-designed reports can be produced. ERP system data can be used to update performance measures in a Balanced Scorecard system and can be used for activity-based costing, shareholder value, strategic planning, customer relationship management and supply chain management.

Outsourcing enables organisations to concentrate on their core activities while subcontracting support activities to those organisations which are specialists. Services are provided to an agreed level of service, at an agreed cost and for an agreed period of time.

AMF's decision as to whether or not to outsource should be within the context of its information systems (IS), information technology (IT) and information management (IM) strategies. IS strategies are focused on the business unit, enabling it to satisfy internal and external customer demand. IT strategies are supply oriented, focusing on business activities and the technology needed to support those activities. IM strategies are management focused and concerned with the methods by which information is stored and available for access.

Advantages and disadvantages of outsourcing

The main potential advantages of outsourcing IT are: more accurate prediction of costs and more accurate budgetary control; using services only when necessary; improved quality and service; economies of scale available to the outsource service provider; the organisation is relieved of the burden of recruiting and managing specialist staff, especially where skills are in short supply; the outsourced service supplier has a better knowledge of changing technologies; saving management time and effort.

The main disadvantages of outsourcing IT are: the difficulty of agreeing an SLA that clearly identifies the obligations of each party; the loss of flexibility and inability to quickly respond to changing circumstances and the possibility of ending up with a less customised system; the risk of unsatisfactory quality and service, or even failure of the supplier; the risk of a lack of security over confidential or critical information; a short-term cost-savings focus may be at the expense of long-term strategy considerations; ignoring an unchanged overhead burden; poor management of the changeover or of the supplier; increasing costs of outsource provision over time, difficulty of changing the outsourced supplier or of returning to an in-house provision, and a loss of internal IM/IT/IS capability leading to dependence on outside suppliers.

In cost terms, the costs of in-house provision need to be compared with outsourcing. The costs of in-house provision can be estimated quite easily, comprising staffing and equipment costs, maintenance, accommodation, etc. For outsourcing, cost estimation is more complex because many costs are 'hidden'. A transactions cost approach will consider not only the direct costs of the outsource supplier but also costs associated with negotiation, monitoring, administration, insurance, etc. These hidden costs involve time commitments, opportunity costs and are associated with legal, moral and power conditions. Understanding these costs and conditions may reveal that it is more economic to carry out an activity in-house than to accept a market price which appears less costly but which may incur transaction costs that are hidden in overhead costs.

Evaluation of Risks associated with outsourcing
The major risks facing AMF are business, financial and reputation. The risk of poor performance or failure of the supplier or the ERPS such that AMF is not able to support its business operations may lead to a failure to satisfy customers. This may well incur a financial loss. There is a consequential reputation risk to AMF if the failure of the ERPS causes it to fail to meet its business obligations.

However, there is also likely to be a risk even if AMF carries out the ERPS function in-house. The outsource supplier may be in a better position to identify, assess, and manage the risks than can AMF due to its expertise.

It may mitigate risks if AMF retains some in-house IT expertise, although this will be at a cost to AMF. The size and structure of the IT department retained by AMF will depend on its SLA with the outsource supplier and its assessment of risk. AMF needs to consider its ability to maintain and modify existing systems, its ability to support users, and the adequacy of system controls. The risk of outsourcing can be partly offset by retaining a small group of IT specialists in-house to monitor and work with the outsource supplier. Another option is to include in the SLA a requirement that a member of the supplier's staff (an 'implant') is permanently located at AMF's premises to act as liaison between client and contractor. Risk can also be reduced by building a long-term partnership between both companies rather than merely a contractor/client relationship.

Mitigation of risk through internal controls and internal audit
In an information systems environment, there are four types of control, and AMF or its outsource supplier needs to ensure the adequacy of:

- General controls to ensure appropriate use of computer systems and security from loss of data. This will be a responsibility both of AMF and the outsource supplier for controls over personnel recruitment, training and supervision and the separation of duties. Logical and physical access controls through password and other security devices will be important at both the supplier's and AMF's site. Business continuity planning will be the responsibility of the outsource supplier but AMF's risk management needs to assess its adequacy.
- Application controls for input, processing and output are necessary for each individual ERPS application and are designed to prevent, detect and correct transaction processing errors. These need to be developed jointly by AMF and the outsource supplier and be reviewed by AMF's internal audit.

- Software controls ensure that software used by the organisation is authorised. This is the outsource supplier's responsibility.
- Network controls must exist to prevent unauthorised access to data transmitted over networks and to secure the integrity of data. This is especially important to prevent hacking, viruses, eavesdropping, errors, or malfunctions between the outsource supplier's site and that of AMF.

Mitigation of risk could also be carried out by AMF:

- seeking legal guarantees from the outsource supplier;
- monitoring the financial health of the outsource supplier;
- seeking assurances as to the appropriateness of staff employed by the outsource supplier on the implementation and operation of their systems.

AMF's own internal audit function needs to be involved during system design (as described above) and continuously thereafter to ensure that risks are adequately addressed by controls designed-in during the development phase; to ensure that financial and non-financial information is accurate and complete and suitable for its intended purpose; to identify potential problems in data collection, input, processing and output; to ensure an adequate audit trail; and to review the scope for possible fraud. Internal audit can only achieve these by working closely with the in-house and outsourced project team and steering committee. Internal audit should also be involved in a post-completion audit of the project. It is essential that AMF's internal auditors have access to the outsourced supplier's site, staff and databases to enable the necessary audit functions to be carried out on AMF's data.

Processes and controls to achieve successful transition
If the Board decides to outsource the ERPS, there are two main issues to be addressed:

1. Management of the implementation of the new ERPS by the outsource supplier; and
2. The changeover from the existing system.

The processes and controls that AMF should adopt to achieve a successful transition to the outsource supplier should be embedded in a project with a project team, project manager and steering committee. The project team should have responsibility for:

- Project planning and definition of user needs
- Obtaining management support throughout AMF
- Resource planning and allocation to support the system
- Quality control and progress monitoring
- Liaising with AMF's suppliers and customers about how the way they interface with AMF will be affected by the changes
- Identification, assessment and management of risks
- Detailed systems design and approval
- System testing and implementation
- User participation and involvement
- Communication and co-ordination
- User education and training.

A steering committee is important in bringing together the sponsor of the project who should be a senior manager who has been involved in authorising the project and is committed to its success; the project manager who is responsible for the day-to-day delivery of the project; specialist IT staff both in-house and from the outsource supplier with responsibility for delivering the project; user representatives with responsibility for accepting the system; and an internal audit representative with responsibility for ensuring the adequacy of internal controls and system testing in conjunction with users.

While many of the technical tasks may be carried out by the outsource supplier, it is essential that the management of the project remain within AMF.

The changeover from the existing system requires an implementation plan which will cover parallel running, where the ERPS is operated in conjunction with AMF's existing system until such time as users are satisfied with the new system and are confident about discontinuing the existing system. If there is a changeover without parallel running, as will be the case in new features of ERPS that do not exist within existing systems, then testing prior to implementation becomes more important and additional monitoring may be needed during the early stages of implementation.

Particular care needs to be taken in converting data from existing systems. This needs to be properly planned and sufficient resources allocated to carry out the conversion. Adequate controls need to be implemented to ensure the consistency of data as it is transferred from the old to the new system, identifying any duplications and omissions.

Conclusion

An ERP system is to a large extent integrated into the daily working practices of an organisation and AMF will become highly dependent on the system for the management of its customers, suppliers, inventory, capacity planning, production scheduling, distribution and accounting functions as well as for the information that will flow to management from the ERPS data warehouse.

Therefore, the question for management becomes how best risk can be managed and how the advantages of cost, quality and staffing can be balanced with disadvantages of loss of flexibility and the need to manage the outsource supplier.

An outsourcing decision needs to be carried out on the basis of a competitive bidding process and implemented according to the information systems development process described above. Adequate internal controls need to be established and the involvement of AMF's internal audit function is essential.

Solution 2

(a) Information systems (IS) strategy determines the information requirements of a business and provides an 'umbrella' for different information technologies that may exist. The IS strategy follows the organisational business strategy and needs to ensure that the appropriate information is acquired, retained, shared and made available for use in strategy implementation such as financial, non-financial, competitive, human resources, etc.

Information technology (IT) strategy defines the specific systems that are required to satisfy the information needs of the organisation, including the hardware, software, operating systems, etc. Each IT system must be capable of obtaining, processing, summarising and reporting the required information. The most sophisticated forms of IT system are the Enterprise Resource Planning System (ERPS) and Executive Information System (EIS).

Information management (IM) strategy is concerned with methods by which information is stored and available for access. This will consider methods of flat or relational database use, data warehousing, back-up facilities, etc. The IM strategy will ensure that information is being provided to users and that redundant information is not produced.

(b) Transaction processing systems typically collect data from sales and purchase invoices, stock movements, payments and receipts, etc. in order to provide the information necessary for accounting systems (debtors, creditors, stock) and financial reports. They are largely oriented to line item reporting and profit reporting based on the organisational structure. They rarely provide profitability information by product/service groups, customers, etc.

A more outward-focused approach may help the business to be more competitive, either by looking more broadly along its supply chain and/or by considering information available from the market place generally or from specific competitors. This is a *strategic* management accounting approach. The reports from junior managers suggest a lack of strategic planning and a lack of top management consideration of 'big picture' matters. Applying Porter, for example, the company needs to determine whether its strategy is cost leadership, differentiation or focus, and how its IT can support that strategy.

An ERPS helps to integrate data flow and access to information over the whole range of a company's activities. ERPS typically capture transaction data for accounting purposes, operational data, customer and supplier data which is then made available through data warehouses against which custom-designed reports can be produced. ERPS data can be used to update performance measures in a Balanced Scorecard system, can be used for activity-based costing, shareholder value, strategic planning, customer relationship management and supply chain management.

Executive Information Systems (EIS) provide high level views of an organisation by aggregating data from various sources from within the organisation and from external sources. Ad hoc enquiries generate performance data and trend analysis for top level management. Ease of use is an important feature so that enquiries can be made without a detailed knowledge of the underlying data structures.

(c) The IT budget is increased annually without any links to the services provided by IT. Answers should mention activity-based or zero-based budgeting compared with incremental methods. The introduction of ERPS and EIS would require a business case with all hardware, software, facilities and personnel costs identified, together with the benefits that could be achieved by the company from the information those systems would generate.

Best practice for both IT budgets and for an ERPS/EIS business case would be to determine user requirements in the light of the organisational strategy and need for information (the IS strategy). User requirements should lead to the design of systems (hardware and software) needed to meet those requirements (IT strategy). The type of system and the risks faced would then determine system design and security considerations (the IM strategy). A best practice model such as Information Technology Infrastructure Library (ITIL) should be used in design, development, testing and management phases of any IT development.

✔ Solution 3

(a) There is a significant risk in IS development of obtaining a system that does not meet the needs of the user in terms of functionality, or is delivered later than scheduled due to delays in systems development or testing, or where costs exceed budget. As FDS25 is an investment centre, there is also the risk that the shared service centre may want to pursue its own goals rather than those of the other FDS business units. Therefore, it is important to have strong controls over systems development.

Although there are several approaches to systems design and implementation, a commonly used approach is the Systems Development Life Cycle (SDLC). The key elements of the SDLC and the controls that could be introduced at each stage are:

- *Feasibility study*: identifying the needs and objectives of the system by identifying current problems and the technical, operational and economic feasibility of the proposed solution. Control: To avoid the risk of developing an unsuitable new system, at feasibility stage there should be a clear understanding of the objectives of the new system, the deliverables, its cost and its time to completion.
- *Systems analysis*: the processes necessary to generate the specification for the system through a methodical investigation of a problem and the identification and ranking of alternative solutions through obtaining more information than was contained in the feasibility study. This will result in a tender specification and a choice between in-house versus outsourced design. Control: The most significant risk here is the failure of the design process to understand the needs of the business unit users and not meet functionality required in terms of the business unit's business strategy. This problem can only be overcome by the analysts fully understanding the business and through close communication between analysts and users.
- *Systems design*: the conversion of specifications into a workable design including source data, input layout, file structure, reports, and interfaces with other systems, etc. Control: Data security needs to be defined and the auditor needs to review system documentation, interfaces with other systems and ensure that there has been acceptance of design by all in the project team, but especially by users.
- *Implementation*: this includes both hardware and software, testing, documentation and training and conversion from existing systems. Controls: Comprehensive testing needs to take place by systems development staff, programmers, users and internal auditors. There also needs to be a review of training and documentation, file conversion and operational issues (e.g. staffing and supervision). An implementation plan will also cover parallel running, where the new system is operated in conjunction with the existing system until such time as the new system is proven to work. IT also involves ensuring that users are satisfied with the new system and are confident about discontinuing the existing system.
- *Systems operation and maintenance*: The correction or enhancement of systems once they are in operation. Controls: A thorough post-implementation review of the new system should be carried out after implementation, by the project team, to establish whether the system is operating as intended and to confirm that user needs are being satisfied.

An important control throughout the design and implementation process is the establishment of a steering committee. The steering committee monitors the system implementation in comparison with the plan and ensures that specific deliverables are accepted at each stage of systems development. It has overall responsibility to ensure that the system meets requirements in terms of quality, time and cost. The steering committee brings together the sponsor of the project; the project manager who is responsible for the day-to-day delivery of the project; specialist IT staff with responsibility for delivering the project; user representatives with responsibility for accepting the system; and internal auditors with responsibility for ensuring the adequacy of internal controls and system testing in conjunction with users.

(b) The major risk faced by FDS25 is that the system delivered does not achieve the planned functionality, is late or exceeds the cost budget. This may then have a serious impact on the ability of FDS25 to achieve its new business strategy.

(i) Shared services centres (or SSCs) provide services needed by business units within an organisation. Shared service centres for IT offer a common service provision including systems design, data processing, IT security, generation of reports, etc. They are service-focused, enabling the internal business unit customers of the shared service centre to specify the level and nature of the service which is typically established, as for other outsourced services, through a Service Level Agreement (SLA). Unlike outsourcing, whilst a split is maintained between provider and client, the IT services are retained in-house. Shared service centres have a focus on quality and customer service and the pooling of resources to achieve common aims.

If IT and IM services are provided in-house, the in-house providers need to have the ability to develop new systems, the ability to maintain and modify existing systems, the ability to support users, and adequate systems controls. In-house IT provision has the benefit of meeting corporate IT requirements in terms of information needed, controls and auditability. However, in an SSC there may be a focus on control with policy and direction focused on Head Office information requirements. In the context of risk, corporate requirements may impede achieving the requirements of a particular business unit. A further risk of developing IT and IM in-house is that the company may not have the resources or skills to undertake a major new systems development function that meets business unit requirements in terms of functionality, time and cost. Corporate requirements and competing business unit priorities may take precedence over the needs of a particular business unit.

(ii) Outsourcing (or subcontracting) support activities have become increasingly common in organisations, especially in relation to the provision of IT services. Outsourcing enables organisations to concentrate on their core activities while subcontracting support activities to specialists. Outsourced services are provided to an agreed level of service, at an agreed cost and for an agreed period of time. The main advantages of outsourcing for IT are the more accurate prediction of costs, and therefore more accurate budgetary control; a higher standard of service because of the specialisation of the service provider; economies of scale available to the outsource service provider; the outsourced service supplier may have a better knowledge of changing technologies.

The main risks of outsourcing IT are the difficulty of agreeing on a service level agreement (SLA) that clearly identifies the obligations of each party; the loss of flexibility and inability to quickly respond to changing circumstances as the outsourced service is no longer under the control of the organisation; the risk of unsatisfactory quality and service, or even failure of supplier; poor management of the outsource supplier.

Risks are also involved in the tendering process, selecting a supplier and agreeing terms. There is also the risk of failure of the outsource supplier and of a lack of compatibility between the system used by FDS25 and that used by the rest of the FDS group.

The risk of outsourcing and FM can be partly offset by retaining a small group of IT specialists in-house to monitor and work with the outsource supplier. Risk can also be reduced by building a long-term partnership or joint venture between both companies.

Another option is to organise an outsourcing contract such that a member of the supplier's staff is permanently located at the organisation's premises to act as liaison between client and contractor. This is sometimes called an 'implant'.

9

Information Systems
Control and
Auditing

Information Systems Control and Auditing

9.1   Introduction

Following from Chapter 8, the main purpose of this chapter is to describe methods of internal control and auditing in an information systems environment. The chapter begins with the framework of information security and reviews models of internal control in an IS environment. It also considers various control strategies and classifications, focusing on general controls, application controls, software controls and network controls. The chapter then considers internal controls and methods of auditing computer systems including computer assisted auditing techniques.

9.2   Information security

Systems and data are vulnerable to loss by human error, fraud, theft or hacking. Information security is about protecting the information resource of an organisation. Information security needs to be based on a risk assessment and the controls in place to mitigate those risks. BS 7799 (ISO 17799) provides a best practice checklist in relation to information security:

• *Security policy*: defines security, allocates responsibility, defines reporting mechanisms for suspected breaches. All staff should be aware of the policy and training should be provided.

- *Security organisation*: a management structure should exist with managerial roles defined and documented, covering authorisation of hardware and software purchases, prevention systems for unauthorised access and third party access to data.
- *Asset classification and control*: an asset register of all hardware and software should be maintained. The owners of data bases should also be catalogued.
- *Personnel security*: security staff should be responsible for ensuring that systems are in place and monitored to minimise risks from error, fraud, theft or hacking.
- *Physical and environmental security*: controls should be in place to restrict access. Disposal of equipment, data files and paper reports should be carried out securely. Fire protection should be in place.
- *Computer and network management*: systems and data should be protected against attack from viruses, malicious software, denial of service attacks, etc. Anti-virus software, intruder detection systems, firewalls (see later in this chapter) should be in place and policies should exist for the use of e-mail and access to websites.
- *Systems access controls*: physical access, passwords, authentication of remote users should be documented and maintained with terminals protected by screen savers and time-outs.
- *Systems development and maintenance*: all systems should be developed in accordance with standards, tested and documented with segregated areas for development, test and live systems. Change control systems should be in place to control all development and maintenance work.
- *Business continuity and disaster recovery*: a plan should exist to cover all information systems including backup, offsite fireproof storage and alternative hardware, software and building site requirements for recovery. Adequate insurance should be taken out.
- *Compliance*: organisations should be aware of their legal and contractual obligations and comply with relevant legislation, e.g. Data Protection Act 1998; Computer Misuse Act 1990.

9.3 Internal controls in an IT environment

There are a number of control models associated with IT systems. The main ones considered here are:

- CobiT
- SAC and eSAC.

The third model, COSO, was described in a previous chapter.

9.3.1 CobiT

IT governance has been defined by the National Computing Centre as

A structure of relationships and processes to direct and control enterprise in order to achieve the goals of a business by adding value while balancing risk versus return over IT and its processes.

An important tool for IT governance is CobiT®, Control Objectives for Information and Related Technology. CobiT was developed by the Information Systems Audit and Control Foundation in 1996 and is now operated by the IT Governance Institute. CobiT:

- Is designed to help management balance risk and control investment in an unpredictable IT environment;

- Addresses concerns about performance measurement, IT control profiling, awareness and benchmarking;
- Is a synthesis of global best practice.

CobiT addresses three audiences: management, users and auditors. It groups IT processes into four categories:

1. Planning and organisation
2. Acquisition and implementation
3. Delivery and support
4. Monitoring.

CobiT defines high-level Business Control Objectives for the processes which are linked to business objectives and supports these with Detailed Control Objectives to provide management assurance and/or advice for improvement. The Control Objectives are supported by Audit Guidelines. Figure 9.1 shows the CobiT framework.

The CobiT Management Guidelines use the principles of the *Balanced Scorecard* and define:

- Benchmarks for IT control practices, known as Maturity Models. Using Maturity Models, the organisation can compare itself against the best in the industry, international standards and where the organisation wants to be. A method of scoring can be used against thirty-four IT processes so that an organisation can score itself from 0 (non-existent) to 5 (optimised).
- Critical success factors for getting IT processes under control. These define the most important things management must do: strategically, technically, organisationally and procedurally.

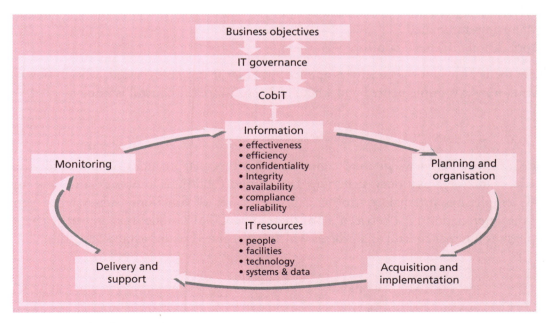

Figure 9.1 CobiT framework

Source: National Computing Centre, www.ncc.co.uk/ncc/myitadviser/archive/issue8/business_processes.cfm.

- Key goal indicators determine (by feedback) whether an IT process has achieved its business requirements in terms of availability of information; absence of integrity and confidentiality risks; cost-efficiency; and confirmation of reliability, effectiveness and compliance.
- Key performance indicators use measures to determine (by feed forward) how well the IT process is performing in enabling the goal to be reached and are indicators of capabilities, practices and skills.

9.3.2 SAC and eSAC

Systems Auditability and Control (SAC) and, with the growth of e-commerce, its development into Electronic Systems Assurance and Control (eSAC) is aimed at understanding, monitoring, assessing and mitigating technology risk.

Risks in eSAC are defined as fraud, errors, business interruptions and inefficient and ineffective use of resources. Control objectives reduce these risks and assure information integrity, security and compliance. Information integrity is guarded by input, processing, output and software quality controls. Security measures include data, physical and program security controls. Compliance controls ensure conformance with laws and regulations, accounting and auditing standards and internal policies and procedures.

Under eSAC, internal controls have three components:

- Control environment
- Manual and automated systems
- Control procedures.

Control procedures consist of general, application and compensating controls. These can be classified as:

- Preventive, detective or corrective
- Discretionary or non-discretionary
- Voluntary or mandatory
- Manual or automated
- Application or general control.

These focus on when the control is applied, whether it can be bypassed, who imposes the control, how it is implemented and where in the software the control is implemented.

9.3.3 Comparing the models

The CobiT model views internal control as a process that includes policies, procedures, practices and organisational structures that support business processes and objectives. eSAC emphasises internal control as a system, a set of functions, sub-systems, people and the interrelationships between all of these. The COSO model (see an earlier chapter) emphasises internal control as a process which is integrated with business activities.

9.3.4 IT control objectives

The IT Governance Institute, the research arm of the Information Systems Audit and Control Association (ISACA), has published *IT Control Objectives for Sarbanes-Oxley* to help bridge the gaps among business risks, technical issues, control needs, and performance-measurement requirements. Emphasizing the importance of information technology in the design, implementation, and sustainability of internal controls over disclosure and financial reporting, the document is designed to reflect the latest thinking on this increasingly global topic.

Based on the concepts of Control Objectives for Information and Related Technology (COBIT), the primary focus of ISACA's guidance relates to IT controls in relation to financial reporting, which is critical to compliance with the requirements of the U.S. Sarbanes-Oxley Act.

Auditors need to understand the flow of transactions, including how transactions are initiated, authorized, recorded, processed, and reported. Because such transaction flow commonly involves the use of application systems, networks, databases, and operating systems involved in the financial reporting process, IT processes should be considered in the design and evaluation of internal control.

The guidance relates to the controls that should be considered in evaluating an organization's internal controls, including controls over program development, program changes, computer operations, and access to programs and data.

To ensure that IT general controls and application controls exist and support the objectives of the organization, the guidance includes:

— Mapping the internal control and financial reporting process of IT systems that support the financial statements.
— Identifying risks related to the IT systems.
— Designing, implementing, and assessing controls to mitigate identified risks and monitoring them for continued effectiveness.
— Documenting and testing IT controls.
— Ensuring that IT controls are updated and changed, as necessary, to correspond with changes in internal control or financial reporting processes.
— Evaluating the extent of IT dependence at the various locations or business units and the degree of consistency in processes and procedures.

When performing an IT risk assessment, the degree of impact – the effect of a risk-related event – and the probability or likelihood that a potential event will occur should be considered. Some of the factors to consider when looking at impact and probability include:

— A failure of security failure in reporting financial information.
— Implementation of an unapproved change.
— Lack of availability of the system or application.
— Failure to maintain the system or application.
— Failure in the integrity of information managed by the application, such as calculation accuracy, and completeness.
— Volume of transactions running through the system or application.
— Complexity of the technology and the application.
— Volume and complexity of changes made.
— Age of the system or application.
— Past history of issues related to the system or application.
— Custom in-house programming versus off-the-shelf packages.

9.4   Control strategies and classifications

There are a number of different ways in which controls can be classified in an IT environment. Controls must exist in every information system. These can be broadly classified as:

- *Security controls*: the prevention of unauthorised access, modification or destruction of stored data.
- *Integrity controls*: data must be accurate, consistent and free from accidental corruption.
- *Contingency controls*: if security or integrity controls fail, there must be a back-up facility and a contingency plan to restore business operations as quickly as possible.

There are four types of control strategy:

1. *Predictive controls*: identify likely problems and introduce appropriate controls. This can be addressed by pre-employment checks on employees and early warning systems of potential hacking.
2. *Preventive controls*: minimise the possibility of a risk occurring. A firewall may prevent unauthorised access.
3. *Detective controls*: to detect unauthorised access after it has occurred.
4. *Corrective controls*: to provide the means to correct the results of unauthorised access.

In an information systems environment, there are four types of control, although there is some overlap between the various types:

1. General controls ensure the effectiveness of the organisation's controls over its information systems as a whole. The aim of general controls is to ensure appropriate use of computer systems and security from loss of data.
2. Application controls are designed for each individual application, such as payroll, accounting, inventory control, etc. The aim of application controls is to prevent, detect and correct transaction processing errors.
3. Software controls ensure that software used by the organisation is authorised.
4. Network controls have arisen in response to the growth of distributed processing and e-commerce.

This chapter uses the last classification of general, application, software and network controls to explore the controls necessary in an information systems environment.

9.5   General controls

General controls are considered in terms of controls over

- Personnel
- Logical access
- Facility
- Business continuity.

9.5.1   Personnel controls

Recruitment, training and supervision needs to be in place to ensure the competency of those responsible for programming and data entry. Personnel controls include the separation of duties within departments and the separation of data processing between departments.

For example, those with responsibility for programming should not also be responsible for data entry. Controls must extend to staff leaving the organisation, when all access rights need to be stopped immediately.

9.5.2 Logical access controls

Logical access controls provide security over unauthorised access to data. The most common form of access security is through password authorisation.

Effective password control requires:

- Regular changes to passwords
- Format including a minimum length and a combination of alpha and numeric characters
- Prevention of screen display of password during typing
- Encryption
- Prevention of access after multiple unsuccessful log-in attempts
- Time-outs after a terminal has been unused for a predetermined period
- Logging of access, particularly to remote terminals, sensitive files, operating system and utility programs.

Many people use combinations of personal information in their passwords. Computer programmes exist to access personal details and to continually attempt log-ins using combinations of data until access is granted.

Following password entry, operators should only have access to those programmes for which they have authorisation, and other programmes should not be displayed. Different levels of authorisation will also exist, for example, between entering payment data to BACS (Bank Automated Clearing System) and authorising payment.

9.5.3 Facility controls

Security over physical computer security is necessary to avoid loss through damage (intentional or accidental) or theft. Facility controls include those over location and those over physical access.

- Locating computer facilities above ground (to avoid flooding) and away from public access. Controls such as fire alarms and smoke detectors should be used.
- Physical access controls should prevent physical access to computer equipment, such as through swipe cards, voice recognition, security officers. To reduce the risk of breaking passwords (see logical access above), information security may increasingly rely on methods such as fingerprint or eye scanning.

9.5.4 Business continuity

Business continuity management is defined by the Business Continuity Institute as a process

that identifies potential impacts that threaten an organisation and provides a framework for building resilience and the capability for an effective response that safeguards the interests of its key stakeholders, reputation, brand and value creating activities.

Business continuity planning or disaster recovery planning takes place in order to recover information systems (both physical and data) from business critical events after they have happened. This may be a result of natural disaster (fire, flood, earthquake) or a result of a deliberate criminal or terrorist attack.

Business continuity planning involves

- Making a risk assessment
- Developing a contingency plan to address those risks.

The continuity or disaster recovery plan should identify:

- The roles and responsibilities of key individuals;
- Back-up facilities for all data;
- Alternative sites for data processing;
- Equipment providers;
- Staffing;
- The work necessary to restore business-critical information to enable the organisation to continue operating;
- The time involved to restore computer systems and business-critical information.

The Business Continuity Institute has established a business continuity life cycle with six stages:

1. Understanding the business through business impact analysis and risk assessment and control.
2. Establishing business continuity management (BCM) strategies.
3. Developing and implementing BCM response including detailed plans; relationships with other organisations; crisis management; sourcing and outsourcing; emergency response; communications and public relations.
4. Building and embedding a BCM culture through education, training and awareness.
5. Exercising, maintenance and audit through rehearsals and testing, and audit processes.
6. Implementing a BCM programme with Board commitment and participation, strategy, policies, accountabilities, resources, information systems, etc.

9.6 Application controls

Application controls are specific to each application but can be grouped into

- Input
- Processing
- Output

controls.

9.6.1 Input controls

Input controls are designed to detect and prevent errors during transaction data entry to ensure that the data entered are complete and accurate. The main input controls are:

- Authorisation of transactions prior to data entry, e.g. approval of supplier invoices, usually after matching invoices with goods received documents and purchase orders.
- Password access to data entry screens.
- Data entry screens prescribe the format for data entry with operators not allowed to skip mandatory fields, e.g. a reason code must be used for credit notes.

- On-line verification of codes, e.g. the system validates customer numbers on entry of invoices.
- On-line verification of limits, e.g. the system validates credit limits before accepting a customer order.
- Reasonableness checks, e.g. payroll data are checked so that amounts to be paid are within normal upper limits.
- Documentation and approval of all adjustments, e.g. all journal adjustments should be documented and approved.

9.6.2   Processing controls

Processing controls ensure that processing has occurred according to the organisation's requirements and that no transactions have been omitted or processed incorrectly. The main processing controls are:

- Standardisation, e.g. the use of a chart of accounts.
- Control totals, e.g. the total value of cash banked is agreed with the amount processed during data entry.
- Balancing, e.g. agreeing the balance on subsidiary ledgers with the general ledger.

9.6.3   Output controls

Output controls ensure that input and processing activities have been carried out and that the information produced is reliable and distributed to users. The main output controls are:

- *Transaction listing*: a list of all transactions that provides an audit trail of data entry.
- *Exception reports*: information that falls outside pre-determined upper and lower limits, e.g. customers who have exceeded their credit terms; inventory below minimum levels.
- *Forms control*: the use of pre-printed and pre-numbered stationery, e.g. cheques, purchase orders.
- *Suspense accounts*: temporary holding accounts for unprocessed transactions need to be reconciled and corrected on a regular basis.
- *Distribution lists*: standing lists of those people who have access to each routine report, which will depend on the sensitivity of the information.

9.7   Software control and software piracy

Software is protected by copyright and intellectual property legislation. Software control prevents making or installing unauthorised copies of software. Illegal software is more likely to fail; comes without warranties or support; can place computer systems at an increased risk of viruses and the use of illegal software can result in significant financial penalties and sometimes criminal prosecutions which carry with it an associated reputation risk.

Software can be controlled by

- Buying only from reputable dealers
- Ensuring that the original disks/CDs come with the software
- Ensuring that licences are received for all software
- Retaining all original disks/CDs and documentation.

A physical inventory of all software should be taken regularly. The Business Software Alliance (www.bsa.org) has tools to assist in a software audit and identify installed software. These tools are available free of charge. The inventory should include

- Product name
- Version number
- Serial number.

The inventory can then be compared with the licences held by the organisation, taking account of multiple users of the software and any home use of the software by employees.
    Software piracy can take place through:

- *Counterfeiting*: the illegal duplication and sale of copyright material with the intention of imitating the copyrighted product. The software may appear genuine and may include packaging, documentation.
- *'Gold' CDs*: compilation CDs of software sold through black-market channels, which do not have the appearance of being genuine.
- *Hard disk loading*: computer resellers may load unauthorised copies of software onto computers as an added incentive to buy. This is different from legitimate preinstalled software as a result of agreements between computer suppliers and software suppliers.
- *End-user piracy*: making unauthorised copies of software for use on multiple computers, taking advantage of upgrades without a legal copy of the previous version or swapping disks with other people.
- *On-line piracy*: downloading copies of computer program from the Internet.

Management should institute a policy that affirms management commitment to comply with copyright laws. This policy needs to be communicated to all employees.

9.8   Network controls

Particular problems for computer and data security have resulted from the growth of distributed data processing and e-commerce. The main risks are:

- Hacking via the Internet
- Computer virus or worm
- Electronic eavesdropping into confidential information
- Customers who deny orders were placed via the Internet and rejection of payments made on credit card transactions via the Internet
- The accidental or deliberate alteration of data transferred over the network
- Human error
- Computer system malfunction
- Natural disasters.

Controls must exist to prevent unauthorised access to data transmitted over networks and to secure the integrity of data. This is particularly important with the increase in e-commerce. Methods may include:

- Firewalls
- Data encryption
- Authorisation

- Virus prevention
- Protection and detection of hacking
- Technical, formal and informal controls.

Competitive intensity has increased so protecting customer databases from competitor access is important. The Data Protection Act has also made it essential to maintain the confidentiality of data. There is an increased availability of tools for hackers through the Internet and an increasing number of disgruntled ex-employees who may have difficulty in finding another comparable job and want to take revenge on their last employer.

The increased use of e-commerce by businesses has increased the potential for hacking. Users visiting an organisation's web site are electronic rather than personal visitors so security is more difficult. The control used to restrict access to an organisation's computer system over the Internet is a firewall.

9.8.1 Firewalls

A firewall comprises a combination of hardware and software located between the company's private network (intranet) and the public network. It is a set of control procedures established to allow public access to some parts of the organisation's computer system (i.e. outside the firewall) while restricting access to other parts of the system (i.e. inside the firewall).

Components of a firewall include:

- Placing software and files for public use on a dedicated web server to which access is limited.
- Requiring all users to enter the site through a single gateway from the main system to the web server.
- Establishing user names and passwords to control access from the web server to the rest of the system.
- Scanning all traffic through the gateway for the presence of viruses and spam mail.

9.8.2 Data encryption

Data are converted into a non-readable format before transmission and then re-converted after transmission. The data can only be read by a receiver with a matching encryption key. This method is commonly used for on-line purchases using credit cards. Digital envelopes can send the encryption key in a message separately to the encrypted message.

9.8.3 Authorisation

Registration of customers by identification and password. Digital signatures may also be required using encryption devices.

9.8.4 Virus protection

A virus is a computer program that is capable of self-replication, which allows it to spread between infected computers. The virus can alter or delete files or even erase the entire contents of a computer hard disk drive. A worm can randomly over-write or change pieces of data within a file. The main ways in which a virus can spread is through:

- Files on removable disks or CD's
- Files downloaded from the Internet
- E-mail attachments
- Hacking.

The main controls that can be used against viruses are:

- Use of virus detection and protection software: the software scans for viruses, alerts the user and removes the virus. Detection and prevention software must be regularly updated.
- Establish and enforce information security policies. Staff awareness needs to be increased about the threats involved and should not be permitted to use unauthorised software, and data on floppy disks and CDs must be checked before opening files. Attachments to e-mails from unknown sources must similarly be treated with caution.

9.8.5 Prevention and detection of hacking

Hacking refers to the ability to obtain unauthorised access to a computer system. Hacking can take many forms:

- A denial of service attack that overloads a website with a well organised increase in traffic can force the website offline and result in lost revenue as well as a loss of brand image and reputation.
- Access to systems by breach of password security and tampering with files.
- Insertion of viruses.

Because experienced hackers can find ways around firewalls and avoid, at least in the short-term, virus protection software, additional security to prevent hacking has become more important. The methods include:

- Vulnerability or penetration testing: deliberate attempts to breach security;
- Intrusion detection: determining when the network is being attacked by regular monitoring and the alertness and vigilance of staff;
- Scanning of all e-mails received.

The real aim of information security is to increase the cost in time and money to hackers who want to gain unauthorised access to the network. Network forensics is a new science that can be used after a security breach to find out how the network was compromised, from where the attack originated and what the hacker was able to do. Evidence can be used to protect against similar attempts in the future and may assist a prosecution.

Glossary of hacking terms (*Source*: Royal Bank of Scotland):

- *Hacker*: An individual attempting to gain unauthorized access to computer systems for the purpose of stealing and/or corrupting data.
- *Keystroke logger*: Software that captures the keys pressed on a keyboard and send a log of these to the hacker via the Internet. It is used to capture passwords and is often included in Trojans.

- *Phishing*: The use of 'spoof' emails and fraudulent websites designed to trick recipients into divulging personal financial data such as credit card numbers, passwords, etc.
- *Trojans*: Apparently harmless software that contains malicious code designed to give control of your computer to a hacker.

9.9 Auditing in an information systems environment

The development of large computer systems in the 1970s and 1980s were often associated with a centralised location; detailed systems and procedures, standard methods of processing transactions, typically after the transaction had taken place, in batches with batch totals; slow systems change with additional specification, flowcharting and programming.

However, information systems now exhibit a much different situation: distributed processing, often PC-based, has led to the decentralisation of data processing; systems and procedures are sometimes flexible and changing in response to changing business conditions; transactions are often processed in real-time, with the production of documents (e.g. invoices, cheques) as a by-product of data entry; quick systems change as a result of sophisticated programming tools and the availability of relational database systems and data warehousing.

The growth of computerisation has resulted in the need for auditors to recognise the additional or different control problems associated with information systems and to consider the appropriateness of the tools and techniques they use. There are two main elements of auditing in an information systems environment:

1. Systems development auditing, and
2. Auditing computer systems.

9.10 Systems development auditing

An important area of internal control and internal audit is in relation to the development of new IS. Internal audit needs to:

- Ensure that risks are adequately addressed by controls designed-in during the development phase, as it is more expensive to add controls once a system is operational.
- Ensure that financial and non-financial information is accurate and complete and suitable for its intended purpose.
- Identify potential problems in data collection, input, processing and output.
- Ensure an adequate audit trail.
- Review the scope for possible fraud.

Internal audit can only achieve these by working closely with the systems development team. In addition, the internal auditor may be involved in a post-completion audit of the systems development project itself.

Those involved in a computer implementation project are usually committed to its success, but may fail to recognise any warning signals. Often, cost escalation and delay are noticed but if the system does not work at all, there may be a fundamental risk to the business operations which are dependent on effective information systems.

A systems development audit is carried out to ensure that there has been compliance with predetermined performance standards for new systems development; and to ensure that adequate controls have been built into the system design to ensure its reliability, security and auditability.

The main features of auditing systems development are:

- Ensuring that the project is led by a senior operational manager who will have responsibility for the system being designed and has a sound understanding of IT.
- Establishing a project team representing those who are responsible for designing the system, users and the accounting department.
- Ensuring that the Head of IT in the organisation has sufficient skill and experience to manage systems development.
- Ensuring that alternative approaches to the business problem have been considered (e.g. outsourcing).
- Ensuring that the objectives of the system are clearly stated and agreed; that the project has been costed accurately and that there is a clear financial or other justification for the project.
- Ensuring that suppliers and contractors are reliable, financially sound and that contracts are legally checked.
- Obtaining independent professional advice on the project.
- Monitoring the progress of the project in terms of cost, meeting scheduled dates and quality criteria.
- Regular reporting to the board where the project is of a large scale or critical.
- Including project development in internal audit programme.
- Considering whether the audit committee ought to monitor the project.
- Making provision for a post-completion audit.

9.11 Auditing computer systems

The basic principles of auditing a computer system are:

- Understanding the system.
- Identifying how the system can be tested, e.g. by the use of test data (see below); or by tagging predesignated transactions for later evaluation.
- Reviewing security including effective password control and limiting access, both physical and logical.
- Encryption of data.
- Accuracy of information generated by the system.
- Authorising transactions and amendments and maintaining database integrity. This can be achieved through recording the process, i.e. a separate image of transaction data and amendments, preferably by operator or workstation to identify the location of any errors.
- Acknowledgement or confirmation systems, e.g. for customer orders, e.g. hotel and airline bookings.
- Data validity checking, e.g. reasonableness checks against the size of a transaction, valid codes.
- Backup of data files on a regular (at least daily) basis and logs of the day's transactions to enable recovery.
- Recovery procedures especially failures over networks and messages in transit.

9.12   Computer assisted audit techniques

Computer assisted audit techniques (CAATs) are used in most audits involving computer systems. There are two types of CAATs:

1. Techniques used to review system controls; and
2. Techniques used to review actual data.

The main techniques are the use of test data and embedded audit facilities.

9.12.1   Test data

Test data are a set of data that are processed by a computer system. The results are compared with expected results based on manual processing, to ensure that the computer system has processed the data accurately. It is time consuming to prepare test data for a complex system. Test data are also difficult with real-time systems as the test data need to be reversed, although the data can be run against a separate copy of the data files. For these reasons, test data are most commonly associated with the testing of a system before it is implemented, or after program modifications.

9.12.2   Embedded audit facilities

Embedded audit facilities allow a continuous audit review of data and its processing. They consist of audit programs that are built into the organisation's accounting system, such as an integrated test facility.

An integrated test facility involves the creation of a false entity within an existing system. Transactions are posted to the false entity together with all of the normal transactions. The normal processing cycle results are then compared with what should have been produced by the system, determined, as for test data, by alternative means. Care must be taken to ensure that the false entities do not become part of the organisation's real financial data.

Other embedded audit facilities include

- Code comparison programmes which are used to compare two versions of a program (the standard approved one and the one in current use) and identify any differences between them;
- Logical path analysis programs which convert a source program into a logic path which can be printed, sometimes as a flowchart, and compared with documented process maps.

9.13   Techniques used to review actual data

Techniques available for auditors to review actual data include audit interrogation software, resident audit software, integrated audit monitors and simulation.

9.13.1   Audit interrogation software

Audit interrogation software allows auditors to access the system as a separate activity. The software allows the auditor to carry out routine procedures that might otherwise have to be carried out manually. Audit software allows the auditor to check large volumes of data, enabling the auditor to concentrate on analysis and investigation rather than routine data extraction. Audit interrogation software:

- Allows extraction of data from files for further audit work.
- Allows the auditor to interrogate computer files and extract the required information.
- Can perform complex calculations quickly and accurately, allowing statistical analysis.
- Provides verification of data by comparing data extracted and manipulated by the audit package for comparison with management reports.
- Identifies items that do not comply with system rules or that seem to be unreasonable.

9.13.2 Resident audit software

Resident audit software is a real-time version of audit interrogation software that allows real-time auditing of real-time systems. It is a program that is built into the operational program or incorporated into the operating system. The software selects items and prints them for later investigation; tags items so that they can be selected by the auditor at a later date or copies items to a systems control and review file (SCARF) for later analysis.

9.13.3 Integrated audit monitors

Integrated audit monitors allow auditors to select accounts within the financial accounting system and designate those accounts for monitoring. The audit monitoring software will then monitor all transactions on the specified accounts and select items outside the parameters set by the auditor. Items selected are tagged or copied to a SCARF.

9.13.4 Simulation

Simulation entails the preparation of a separate program that simulates the operation of the organisation's real system. It is used to test the operation of the real system.

9.14 Control self-assessment

Control self-assessment (CSA) or self-audit is performed by line managers as a means of raising awareness of control systems. CSA also provides the ability for internal audit to meet management's identified needs (based on the self-assessment of weaknesses and strengths) while controlling audit costs.

9.15 Auditing systems maintenance

The internal auditor needs to review the procedures in the IT department, looking for a systematic approach to maintenance. This could be evidenced by documentation, authorisation of modifications, and a systematic approach to collecting and analysing systems performance data. Change control systems should be in place to control all development and maintenance work.

9.16 Summary

- Systems and data are vulnerable to loss by human error, fraud, theft or hacking. Information security is about protecting the information resource of an organisation. Information security needs to be based on a risk assessment and the controls in place to mitigate those risks.

- There are a number of control models associated with IT systems. The CobiT model views internal control as a process that includes policies, procedures, practices and organisational structures that support business processes and objectives. eSAC emphasises internal control as a system, a set of functions, sub-systems, people and the inter-relationships between all of these. The COSO model (described in an earlier chapter) emphasises internal control as a process which is integrated with business activities.

- *IT Control Objectives for Sarbanes-Oxley* has been produced to help bridge the gaps among business risks, technical issues, control needs, and performance-measurement requirements in IT environments.

- There are four types of control strategy: predictive, preventive, detective and corrective controls.

- Controls can be broadly classified as: security controls – the prevention of unauthorised access, modification or destruction of stored data; integrity controls – data must be accurate, consistent and free from accidental corruption; and contingency controls – a back-up facility and a contingency plan to restore business operations.

- General controls ensure the effectiveness of the organisation's controls over its information systems as a whole, the aim being to ensure appropriate use of computer systems and security from loss of data. General controls are considered in terms of controls over personnel; logical access; facilities and business continuity.

- Application controls are designed for each individual application, the aim of which is to prevent, detect and correct transaction processing errors. Application controls are specific to each application but can be grouped into input, processing and output controls.

- Software is protected by copyright and intellectual property legislation. Software control prevents making or installing unauthorised copies of software.

- Network controls have arisen in response to the growth of distributed processing and e-commerce. Controls must exist to prevent unauthorised access to data transmitted over networks and to secure the integrity of data. Methods may include firewalls, data encryption, authorisation, virus protection, protection and detection of hacking and technical, formal and informal controls.

- A systems development audit is carried out to ensure that there has been compliance with predetermined performance standards for new systems development; and to ensure that adequate controls have been built into the system design to ensure its reliability, security and auditability. Systems development auditing involves ensuring: That risks are adequately addressed by controls designed-in during the development phase; That financial and non-financial information is accurate and complete and suitable for its intended purpose; That potential problems in data collection, input, processing and output are identified; That there is an adequate audit trail and That scope for possible fraud has been considered.

- The growth of computerisation has resulted in the need for auditors to recognise the additional or different control problems associated with information systems and to consider the appropriateness of the tools and techniques they use. The two main elements of auditing in an information systems environment are systems development auditing (covered in the previous chapter) and auditing computer systems.

- CAATs are used in most audits involving computer systems. There are two types of CAATs: techniques used to review system controls and techniques used to review actual data. The main techniques used to review system controls are the use of test data and embedded audit facilities. Techniques available for auditors to review actual data include audit interrogation software, resident audit software, integrated audit monitors and simulation.

References

Students are encouraged to look at the web sites of the
Business Continuity Institute (www.thebci.org)
IT Governance Institute (http://www.itgi.org/)
Information Systems Audit & Control Association (www.isaca.org).

Revision Questions

? Question 1

The following question is adapted from the November 2005 examination for P3 and was included in the revision questions for Chapter 7

As a CIMA member, you have recently been appointed as the Head of Internal Audit for SPQ, a multinational listed company that carries out a large volume of internet sales to customers who place their orders using their home or work computers. You report to the Chief Executive although you work closely with the Finance Director. You have direct access to the Chair of the audit committee whenever you consider it necessary.

One of your internal audit teams has been conducting a review of IT security for a system which has been in operation for 18 months and which is integral to internet sales. The audit was included in the internal audit plan following a request by the Chief Accountant. Sample testing by the internal audit team has revealed several transactions over the last three months which have raised concerns about possible hacking or fraudulent access to the customer/order database. Each of these transactions has disappeared from the database after deliveries have been made but without sales being recorded or funds collected from the customer. Each of the identified transactions was for a different customer and there seems to be no relationship between any of the transactions.

You have received the draft report from the internal audit manager responsible for this audit which suggests serious weaknesses in the design of the system. You have discussed this informally with senior managers who have told you that such a report will be politically very unpopular with the Chief Executive as he was significantly involved in the design and approval of the new system and insisted it be implemented earlier than the IT department considered was advisable. No post-implementation review of the system has taken place.

You have been informally advised by several senior managers to lessen the criticism and work with the IT department to correct any deficiencies within the system and to produce a report to the Audit Committee that is less critical and merely identifies the need for some improvement. They suggest that these actions would avoid criticism of the Chief Executive by the Board of SPQ.

Requirement

Analyse the potential risks faced by SPQ that have been exposed by the review of IT security and recommend controls that should be implemented to reduce them.

Question 2

The following question is adapted from the November 2007 examination for P3

VWS is a company manufacturing and selling a wide range of industrial products to a large number of businesses throughout the country. VWS is a significant local employer, with 2,500 people working out of several locations around the region, all linked by a networked computer system.

VWS purchases numerous components from 750 local and regional suppliers, receiving these into a central warehouse. The company carries about 10,000 different inventory items, placing 25,000 orders with its suppliers each year.

The Accounts Payable Department of VWS has six staff who process all supplier invoices through the company's computer system and make payment to suppliers by cheque or electronic remittance.

Requirement

Identify the information systems controls that should be in place for Accounts Payable in a company like VWS. **(10 marks)**

Solutions to Revision Questions

✓ Solution 1

There seems to be a serious weakness in the design and/or operation of the present system. There may be a lack of controls over the information system as a whole, over specific applications such as the order entry system identified as the weakness here or over the network allowing customer access, or a combination of these. The most likely sources of the problem in this case are: poor systems development controls; poor network controls; or fraud by employees.

The potential risks faced by SPQ include: financial loss due to loss of customers; loss of orders; reputation loss; and fraud. The risk here may be only the one that has become evident. Broader risks that have not yet been identified may be a consequence of the failure of system development controls and the lack of proper testing and acceptance of the system by users; or failures in the operation of systems via the network leading to loss of other transactions.

Reducing the likelihood of risk is only possible through effective systems design and operating controls, and protection against fraud.

Systems development

Systems development controls should involve comprehensive system design and testing with sign-off by all parties before implementation. This involves being satisfied that the system meets user requirements, functions satisfactorily, has adequate controls, and is auditable. Such a sign-off does not appear to have taken place in this case as the IT department advised against implementation and there has been no post-implementation review. Poor integrity controls can result in corruption of data within the system, and the absence of contingency controls can fail to identify lost transactions.

Network or operating controls

The risks faced by the company may be a consequence of poor security controls that fail to prevent unauthorised access, modification or destruction of data. Network controls avoid risks such as hacking, a computer virus/worm or accidental or deliberate customer alteration of data. There should be warning alarms in relation to attempted hacking. Preventive controls such as a firewall may also prevent unauthorised access. Examples of controls include data encryption, transaction authorisation, virus prevention, hacking detection, etc.

Reducing exposure to risk is possible through controls which, for example, ensure that all sales are delivered and funds are collected and that all transactions that enter the system are fully completed.

Computer audit techniques such as using test data or embedded audit facilities or audit interrogation software can be used to detect irregularities and can lead to recovery action if errors are quickly identified, enabling corrections to be effected.

Fraud
The problem may be evidence of employee fraud, with funds being diverted, however this topic is covered in Chapter 10.

 ## Solution 2

A number of general controls are particularly important in a distributed information systems environment. Personnel controls cover recruitment, training, supervision and the separation of duties. Physical access controls limit access to computer systems, whilst logical access controls prevent unauthorised access to data through password controls. Business continuity or disaster recovery puts procedures in place to recover physical computer systems and data if a critical business event such as a fire or flood occurs.

In addition, specific input, processing and output controls will apply to each software application. These will include input controls covering transaction authorisation, completeness and accuracy of data entry, on-line code verification, reasonableness checks and supporting evidence for all adjustments. Processing controls cover standardised coding and processes, control totals, and balancing between subsidiary and general ledgers. Output controls include transaction lists, exception reports, forms control and suspense accounts.

Network controls in a distributed processing environment provide protection against hacking, viruses and unauthorised access through firewalls, data encryption and virus protection software.

Ethics and Fraud

Ethics and Fraud

10

LEARNING OUTCOMES

After completing this chapter you should be able to:

▶ Evaluate ethical issues as a source of risk to the organisation and recommend control mechanisms for their detection and resolution.

Section B of the syllabus includes ethical issues identified in the CIMA *Code of Ethics for Professional Accountants*.

You should also be able to:

▶ Discuss the importance of exercising ethical principles in conducting and reporting on internal reviews.

Section C of the syllabus includes the particular relevance of the fundamental principles in CIMA's *Ethical Guidelines*.

The topic of fraud recurs in the indicative syllabus content for *Performance Strategy*. After completing this chapter you should understand:

▶ Fraud as a source of risk
▶ Fraud related to sources of finance
▶ Minimising the risk of fraud including computer-based fraud
▶ Detection and investigation of fraud

These relate to Section B, C & E of the syllabus

10.1 Introduction

This chapter has two main purposes:

1. to introduce the importance of CIMA's ethical principles in terms of risk, control and audit as part of the *Performance Strategy* syllabus.
2. to describe fraud through its different forms, the opportunity for fraud, indicators of fraud and identifying the risk of fraud. Risk management strategy in relation to fraud is covered through methods of fraud prevention, identification and response. The chapter also includes a discussion of fraud using computer systems and other types of fraud.

10.2 Professional ethics

In 2006, CIMA adopted a new *Code of Ethics for Professional Accountants*, based on the International Federation of Accountants (IFAC) Code of Ethics, issued in June 2005. It is clear from the Code that a professional accountant's responsibility is not exclusively to satisfy the needs of an individual client or employer. Professional accountants must act in the public interest and in order to do so, should observe and comply with the ethical requirements of this Code.

The Code is in three parts.

- Part A establishes the fundamental principles of professional ethics for professional accountants and provides a conceptual framework which provides guidance on fundamental ethical principles.
- Part B applies to professional accountants in public practice.
- Part C applies to professional accountants in business.

Parts B and C illustrate how the conceptual framework is to be applied in specific situations.

10.2.1 Fundamental principles

A professional accountant is required to comply with the following fundamental principles:

(a) *Integrity*
A professional accountant should be straightforward and honest in all professional and business relationships.

(b) *Objectivity*
A professional accountant should not allow bias, conflict of interest or undue influence of others to override professional or business judgements.

(c) *Professional Competence and Due Care*
A professional accountant has a continuing duty to maintain professional knowledge and skill at the level required to ensure that a client or employer receives competent professional service based on current developments in practice, legislation and techniques. A professional accountant should act diligently and in accordance with applicable technical and professional standards when providing professional services.

(d) *Confidentiality*
A professional accountant should respect the confidentiality of information acquired as a result of professional and business relationships and should not disclose any such information to third parties without proper and specific authority unless there is a legal or professional right or duty to disclose.

(e) *Professional Behaviour*
A professional accountant should comply with relevant laws and regulations and should avoid any action that discredits the profession.

10.2.2 Conceptual framework

The conceptual framework requires a professional accountant identify, evaluate and address threats to compliance with the fundamental principles, rather than merely comply with a set of specific rules. Compliance with the fundamental principles may potentially be threatened by a broad range of circumstances. Many threats fall into the following categories:

(a) Self-interest threats, which may occur as a result of the financial or other interests of a professional accountant or of an immediate or close family member.
(b) Self-review threats, which may occur when a previous judgement needs to be re-evaluated by the professional accountant responsible for that judgement.
(c) Advocacy threats, which may occur when a professional accountant promotes a position or opinion to the point that subsequent objectivity may be compromised.
(d) Familiarity threats, which may occur when, because of a close relationship, a professional accountant becomes too sympathetic to the interests of others.
(e) Intimidation threats, which may occur when a professional accountant may be deterred from acting objectively by threats, actual or perceived.

Safeguards to these threats include:

- Educational, training and experience requirements for entry into the profession.
- Continuing professional development requirements.
- Corporate governance regulations.
- Professional standards.
- Professional or regulatory monitoring and disciplinary procedures.
- External review by a legally empowered third party of the information produced by a professional accountant.
- Effective, well publicised complaints systems operated by the employing organisation, the profession or a regulator, which enable colleagues, employers and members of the public to draw attention to unprofessional or unethical behaviour.
- An explicitly stated duty to report breaches of ethical requirements.

10.3   Resolution of ethical conflicts

When initiating either a formal or informal conflict resolution process, a professional accountant should consider the following, either individually or together with others, as part of the resolution process:

(a) Relevant facts
(b) Ethical issues involved
(c) Fundamental principles related to the matter in question
(d) Established internal procedures
(e) Alternative courses of action.

A professional accountant should determine the appropriate course of action that is consistent with the fundamental principles identified. The professional accountant should also weigh the consequences of each possible course of action. It may be in the best interests of the professional accountant to document the substance of the issue and details of any discussions held or decisions taken, concerning that issue. Where a matter involves a conflict with, or within, an organisation, a professional accountant should also consider consulting with those charged with governance of the organisation, such as the Board of Directors or the audit committee.

   If a significant conflict cannot be resolved, a professional accountant may wish to obtain professional advice from the relevant professional body or legal advisors, and thereby obtain guidance on ethical issues without breaching confidentiality. The professional accountant should consider obtaining legal advice to determine whether there is a legal requirement to report.

If, after exhausting all relevant possibilities, the ethical conflict remains unresolved, a professional accountant should, where possible, refuse to remain associated with the matter creating the conflict. The professional accountant may determine that, in the circumstances, it is appropriate to withdraw from the specific assignment, or to resign altogether from the engagement, the firm or the employing organisation.

Detailed advice is contained within the CIMA (2006) publication *Code of Ethics for Professional Accountants*.

10.4 Case study: Ethics and CIMA

Going downhill fast

Danielle Cohen shares the true story of a CIMA member who contacted the institute's ethics helpline for advice, His problem stemmed from allowing what seemed, on the face of it, a minor issue to snowball into a job-threatening situation.

Andrew was the management accountant of a small firm that was part of a plc. His boss, Chris, was the firm's CEO. Several months ago Chris has approached him with a query about the month-end figures that Andrew has produced, saying that they must be wrong. At the time there was a certain amount of confusion, because their firm had just taken over another small company, so Andrew adjusted them as instructed.

Next month Chris questioned the numbers again, and Andrew duly changed them once more. This happened at several more month-ends until he began to suspect that Chris's reasons for changing the numbers might not be valid – and that the business was simply not performing. He raised the issue with his boss, who assured him that he would sort everything out. Relieved that Chris has recognized that the matter needed to be dealt with, Andrew dropped it.

At the end of the firm's financial year, Chris announced that he had, as promised, found a solution to the problem of the ongoing adjustments. Unfortunately, this was very different from what Andrew was expecting. Chris proposed that he own up to the discrepancies, admit that they were the result of a simple error and then resign to prevent any further questions from being asked. In return for carrying the can, Andrew would receive a glowing reference – on the understanding, of course, that he kept quiet about the whole affair.

Shocked and unsure about what to do, Andrew contacted CIMA's ethics helpline. He had gone from accepting a small month-end adjustment to his figures to finding himself about to lose a job. Our guidance to Andrew was that he should consider taking the problem to more senior people in the group, since raising it with Chris wasn't an option. Andrew has some concerns about the possible repercussions of doing this, particularly because Chris was well respected in the group, and he was worried that his version of events would not be believed. The lack of an internal grievance or whistle blowing procedure made it hard for him to predict how his case would be handled.

Given all these factors, Andrew questioned whether quitting was an acceptable solution. A good reference has been promised, but was this pledge worth anything coming from Chris? And how would he explain to any future employer why he had left? And what would happen if a colleague were to complain to CIMA about his lack of competence? If this were to happen, he could potentially lose his membership. Even worse, lying to accept responsibility that wasn't his would be another breach of CIMA's code of ethics. If discovered, this would also have consequences for his membership.

After further discussion, Andrew identified a potential ally (a financial controller) at group level. He arranged a meeting through a trusted colleague in order to minimize the chances of discovery by Chris.

We suggested that Andrew should speak to the institute's legal advice line for expert guidance on his legal obligations and employment rights, and also to the whistle-blowing advice line for free, confidential, independent advice on raising his concerns.

Andrew spoke to the financial controller and Chris was eventually forced to resign. But Andrew's ongoing compliance with his boss's wishes was enough to have tarnished his reputation. A few months later he resigned of his own accord.

Andrew's case is a reminder of how crucial it is to use your professional judgment, heed the warning signs and establish the facts at the first sign of an ethical dilemma. Armed with these and CIMA's code of ethics, you can decide whether or not you need to act and, if so, what that action should be.

So how exactly do you know when an ethical dilemma is an ethical dilemma? As Oscar Whilde observed: 'Morality, like art, means drawing a line someplace.' When the amount of money is not material, the report is only for internal purposes or when no one else seems to think there's an issue, how can you be sure where that line is?

Taking time to consider the situation from all angles will help you to know for sure. In the code of ethics, the line is where a threat to our fundamental principles is anything more than trivial. Although the changes that Andrew made to the numbers in that first month might not have been material, the pattern that they established was. If he had stood up to Chris the first time he was asked to adjust the figures, the situation might never have developed.

Danielle Cohen is CIMA's ethics manager.
This article appeared in Financial Management, Novermber 2007.

10.5 Fraud

Fraud is dishonestly obtaining an advantage, avoiding an obligation or causing a loss to another party. It includes:

- Crimes against customers and clients (e.g. misrepresenting the quality of goods, pyramid trading schemes).
- Employee fraud against employers (e.g. payroll fraud, falsifying expense claims, theft of cash).
- Crimes by small business against customers and employees (e.g. selling counterfeit goods, not paying over tax and national insurance contributions).

- Crimes against financial institutions (e.g. using lost or stolen credit cards, fraudulent insurance claims).
- Crimes by individuals against government (e.g. social security benefit claims fraud, tax evasion).
- Crimes by professional criminals against major organisations (e.g. counterfeiting, money laundering, advance fee fraud).

Those committing fraud may be managers, employees or third parties (sometimes customers or suppliers). People commit fraud because of:

- The perceived suitability of targets for fraud
- The incapability of potential fraud victims to look after their interests
- The motivation of potential offenders.

A major reason why people commit fraud is because they are allowed to do so. The likelihood that fraud will be committed will be decreased if the potential fraudster believes that the rewards will be modest, that they will be detected or that the potential punishment will be unacceptably high. Therefore, a comprehensive system of control is needed to reduce the opportunity for fraud and increase the likelihood of detection.

10.6 The opportunity for fraud

As for most property-related crimes, there are three prerequisites for fraud to occur: dishonesty on the part of the perpetrator; the opportunity for fraud to occur and a motive for the fraud. Each can be dealt with through fraud prevention techniques:

- Dishonesty
  - Pre-employment checks on all new staff (especially references)
  - Careful scrutiny of staff by supervision and lifestyles that are not supported by salaries
  - Severe discipline for offenders
  - Effective moral leadership.

- Opportunity
  - Separation of duties where possible
  - Controls over inputs (especially cash)
  - Controls over processing
  - Controls over outputs
  - Physical security of assets.

- Motive
  - Good employment conditions
  - Instant dismissals where necessary
  - Sympathetic complaints procedure.

An analysis of 100 fraud cases by KPMG Forensic and published in *Accountancy Age* (29 April, 2004, p.4) revealed that 72% involved men only and 32% had worked for the company between 10 and 25 years. Culprits were most likely to be aged 36–55. Staff aged between 18 and 25 accounted for only 1% of frauds and females were identified in 7% of cases.

Forty per cent of fraud involved employees from the finance department with 12% from procurement, the next most likely. In 51% of cases, the fraudsters were acting in partnership with up to 4 other people. Directors and senior managers committed almost two thirds of the 100 cases.

10.6.1 Indicators of fraud risk

The following warning signs may indicate the presence of fraud risk.

- Absence of an anti-fraud culture
- Failure of management to implement a sound system of internal controls
- Lack of financial management expertise and professionalism in key accounting principles, the review of management reports and the review of significant cost estimates
- A history of legal or regulatory violations or claims alleging violations
- Strained relationships between management and internal or external auditors
- Lack of supervision of staff
- Inadequate recruitment processes
- Redundancies
- Dissatisfied employees with access to desirable assets
- Unusual staff behaviour
- Personal financial pressures on key staff
- Discrepancy between earnings and lifestyle
- Low salary levels of key staff
- Employees working unsocial hours unsupervised
- Employees not taking annual leave entitlements
- Lack of job segregation and independent checking of key transactions
- Lack of identification of assets
- Poor management accountability and reporting
- Alteration of documents and records
- Photocopies of documents replacing originals
- Missing authorisations
- Poor physical security of assets
- Poor access controls to physical assets and IT security systems
- Inadequacy of internal controls
- Poor documentation of internal controls
- Poor documentary support for transactions, especially credit notes
- Large cash transactions
- Management compensation highly dependent on meeting aggressive performance targets
- Significant pressure on management to obtain additional finance
- Extensive use of tax havens without clear business justification
- Complex transactions
- Complex legal ownership and/or organisational structure
- Rapid changes in profitability
- Existence of personal or corporate guarantees
- Highly competitive market conditions and decreasing profitability levels within the organisation

- The organisation operating in a declining business sector and facing possible business failure
- Rapid technological change which may increase potential for product obsolescence
- New accounting or regulatory requirements which could significantly alter reported results.

Fraud in the purchasing function is a particular risk. Examples of indicators of procurement fraud include:

- Disqualification of suitable tenderers
- Unchanging list of preferred suppliers
- Constant use of single source contracts
- Contracts that include specifications that only one supplier can satisfy
- Personal relationships between staff and suppliers
- Withdrawal of a lower bid without explanation
- Acceptance of late bids
- Changes to specifications after bids have been opened
- Poor documentation of contract award process
- Consistent favouring of one firm over another
- Unexplained changes to contract after its award
- Contract awarded to supplier with poor performance record
- Split contracts to circumvent controls

Example of indicators of fraud in the selling process

- Overcharging from an approved price list
- Short-changing by not delivering the correct quantity or quality
- Diversion of orders to a competitor or associate
- Bribery of a customer by sales representative
- Bribery of customer by a competitor
- Insider information by knowing competitor's prices
- Warranty claims that are false
- Over-selling of goods or services that are not necessary
- Free samples that are not necessary

10.7 Fraud risk management strategy

Fraud risk arises out of errors or events in transaction processing or other business operations where those errors or events could be the result of a deliberate act designed to benefit the perpetrator.

As for all other risks, a risk management strategy needs to be developed for fraud. This strategy should include:

- Fraud prevention
- Identifying fraud
- Responding to fraud.

10.8   Fraud prevention

The existence of a fraud strategy is itself a deterrent. This can be achieved through:

- Anti-fraud culture
- Risk awareness
- Whistle blowing
- Sound internal control systems.

10.8.1   Anti-fraud culture

Where minor unethical practices are overlooked, for example, expenses or time recording, this may lead to a culture in which larger frauds occur. High ethical standards bring long-term benefits as customers, suppliers, employees and the community realise they are dealing with a trustworthy organisation. Guiding principles could include:

- Not acting in a way that could bring the organisation into disrepute
- Acting with integrity towards colleagues, customers, suppliers and the public
- Ensuring that business objectives are clearly stated and communicated
- Ensuring that benefits (whether to shareholders, customers or employees) are distributed fairly and impartially
- Safeguarding the confidentiality of personal data
- Complying with legal requirements.

10.8.2   Risk awareness

Fraud should never be discounted, and there should be awareness among all staff that there is always the possibility that fraud is taking place. It is important to raise awareness through training programmes. Particular attention should be given to training and awareness among those people involved in receiving cash, purchasing and paying suppliers.

Publicity can also be given to fraud that has been exposed. This serves as a reminder to those who may be tempted to commit fraud and a warning to those responsible for the management of controls.

10.8.3   Whistle blowing

Fraud may be suspected by those who are not personally involved. People must be encouraged to raise the alarm about fraud. An anti-fraud culture will be important in reinforcing the need for employees to express their concerns. However, management must realise that loyalties among workers, fear of the consequences and having unsubstantiated suspicions will prevent people from coming forward. Of course, management has to be aware of the risk of malicious accusations or of suspicions that prove unfounded, whether anonymous or otherwise. The Public Interest Disclosure Act of 1999 provides some protection for whistleblowers and guidance to management.

10.8.4   Sound internal control systems

As described in earlier chapters, sound systems of internal control should monitor fraud by identifying risks and then putting into place procedures to monitor and report on those risks.

10.8.5   A 16-Step Fraud Prevention Plan

1. Consider fraud risk as an integral part of your overall corporate risk-management strategy.
2. Develop an integrated strategy for both fraud prevention and control.
3. Develop an 'ownership structure' from the top to the bottom of the organisation.
4. Introduce a fraud policy statement.
5. Introduce an ethics policy statement.
6. Actively promote these policies through the organisation.
7. Establish a control environment.
8. Establish sound operational control procedures.
9. Introduce a fraud education, training and awareness programme.
10. Introduce a fraud response plan as an integral part of the organisation's contingency plans.
11. Introduce a whistle-blowing policy.
12. Introduce a 'reporting hotline'.
13. Constantly review all anti-fraud policies and procedures.
14. Constantly monitor adherence to controls and procedures.
15. Establish a 'learn from experience' group.
16. Develop appropriate informance and communication systems.

Source: http://www.dti.gov.uk/ccp/scams/page1.htm

10.9   Identifying fraud

External auditors do not generally find fraud; in fact, their letters of engagement typically identify that it is not one of their roles to look for fraud. Most frauds are discovered accidentally or as a result of information received. A survey carried out by Ernst and Young revealed that most fraudulent activity was identified as a result of normal procedures, outside information and internal investigation.

   Some methods of discovering fraud are:

- Performing regular checks (e.g. stocktaking and cash counts)
- Warning signals: late payments, backlogs of work, holidays not being taken, extravagant lifestyles, multiple and/or complex interlocking company structures, payments to countries with different standards (e.g. Swiss banking law has different privacy rules), missing audit trails, large transfers before public holidays, etc.
- Whistleblowers

   The response to any suspicion of fraud is that an investigation team should be put in place. The actions will be driven by the organisation's policy as to whether internal disciplinary, civil or criminal proceedings are expected. This will influence the method of collection, storage and documentation of physical evidence and interview statements.

10.10   Responding to fraud

The fraud response plan sets down the arrangements for dealing with suspected cases of fraud, theft or corruption. It provides procedures for evidence gathering to enable decision-making and that will subsequently be admissible in any legal action. The fraud response plan also has a deterrent value. The fraud response plan should reinforce the organisation's commitment to high legal, ethical and moral standards and its approach to those who fail to meet those standards.

The organisation's response to fraud may include:

- Internal disciplinary action, in accordance with personnel policies
- Civil litigation for recovery of the loss
- Criminal prosecution through the police.
  Individual responsibilities should be allocated to:
- Managers, to whom employees should report their suspicions. Managers should have an agreed, standard response in relation to any reported incidence of fraud.
- Director of Finance, who has overall responsibility for the organisational response to fraud including the investigation. This role may be delegated to a fraud officer or internal security officer.
- Personnel, who will have responsibility for disciplinary procedures and issues of employment law and practice.
- Audit committee, who should review the details of all frauds, and to whom notice of any significant fraud needs to be reported.
- Internal auditors, who will most likely have the task of investigating the fraud.
- External auditors, to obtain expertise.
- Legal advisers, in relation to internal disciplinary, civil or criminal responses.
- Public relations, if the fraud is sufficiently large that it will come to public attention.
- Police, where it is policy to prosecute all those suspected of fraud.
- Insurers, where there is likely to be a claim.

10.11   Fraud using computer systems

Computer fraud may be easier to commit because of the centralisation of large databases and their accessibility by operators; because the segregation of duties possible with manual systems is not always possible with computer systems; and because technology makes access easier. Computer records are not visible and therefore it is more difficult to trace fraud and detect the deletion of files. The complexity of modern computer systems places those with expert knowledge in a privileged position if they are susceptible to fraudulent intentions. Increased control also reduces efficiency and increases cost.

Particular controls in relation to computer fraud are:

- Control and testing of program changes
- Physical security of computer systems
- Password controls
- Control over issue of output forms, especially cheques.

The increased use of the Internet has increased the possibility of fraud for many organisations. Users visiting an organisation's website are electronic rather than personal visitors so security is more difficult. Control of computer systems was covered in the previous chapter.

10.12 Management fraud

Many of the large corporate failures of the last decade have involved management (Enron, Parmalat, etc.). Management may manipulate accounting records to improve performance or to gain a personal advantage (especially where bonuses or share options are issued as rewards). This could be achieved through:

- Deliberate distortion of cut-off procedures to shift profits between years
- Capitalisation of expenses
- Under-provisions
- Over-valuation of inventory.

Management may also manipulate records to hide their incompetence; or they may pay inflated prices to suppliers in return for bribes; or employment of family members or charging personal expenses to the organisation.

10.12.1 Case study: WorldCom

WorldCom filed for bankruptcy protection in June 2002. It was the biggest corporate fraud in history, largely a result of treating operating expenses as capital expenditure.

WorldCom (now renamed MCI) admitted in March 2004 that the total amount by which it had misled investors over the previous 10 years was almost US$75 billion (£42 billion) and reduced its stated pre-tax profits for 2001 and 2002 by that amount.

WorldCom stock began falling in late 1999 as businesses slashed spending on telecom services and equipment. A series of debt downgrades had raised borrowing costs for the company, struggling with about US$32 billion in debt. WorldCom used accounting tricks to conceal a deteriorating financial condition and to inflate profits.

Former WorldCom chief executive Bernie Ebbers resigned in April 2002 amid questions about US$366 million in personal loans from the company and a federal probe of its accounting practices. Ebbers was subsequently charged with conspiracy to commit securities fraud, and filing misleading data with the Securities and Exchange Commission (SEC). Scott Sullivan, former chief financial officer, pleaded guilty to three criminal charges.

The SEC said WorldCom had committed 'accounting improprieties of unprecedented magnitude' – proof, it said, of the need for reform in the regulation of corporate accounting.

10.12.2 Case study: Parmalat

In December 2003, Italian dairy-foods group Parmalat, with 36,000 employees in 30 countries, went into bankruptcy protection with US$ 8–10 billion of vanished assets. The company was 51% owned by the Tanzi family.

Parmalat defaulted on a US$185 million bond payment that prompted auditors and banks to scrutinise company accounts. Thirty-eight per cent of Parmalat's assets were supposedly held in a bank account in the Cayman Islands but no such account ever existed. Letters received from the bank by auditors were forgeries.

Parmalat has been one of the largest financial frauds in history. The company falsified its accounts over a 15-year period. This was not identified by two firms of auditors, Grant Thornton and Deloitte Touche Tohmatsu. At least 20 people have been involved in the fraud, including members of the Tanzi family, the chief financial officer, board members and the company's lawyers. Calisto Tanzi the founder and chief executive was arrested on suspicion of fraud, embezzlement, false accounting and misleading investors.

Tanzi admitted that he knew the accounts were falsified to hide losses and the falsified balance sheet was used to enable Parmalat to continue borrowing. He also confessed to misappropriating US$620 million, although prosecutors believe it could be as much as US$1 billion.

10.13 Other types of fraud

Advance fee fraud or '419' fraud (named after the relevant section of the Nigerian Criminal Code) is a popular crime with West African criminals. There are a myriad of schemes and scams – mail, faxed and telephone promises designed to obtain money from victims. All involve requests to help move large sums of money with the promise of a substantial share of the cash in return. Similar types of fraud include High Yield Investment fraud and Prime Bank fraud.

Identity theft is the unlawful taking of another person's details without their permission. The information stolen can be used to obtain financial services, goods and other forms of identification, for example, passports and driving licences. The information stolen can range from a copy of birth certificate to copies of discarded bank or credit card statements and utility bills. Once the criminals have copies of someone's identity they can embark on criminal activity in their name with the knowledge that any follow-up investigations will not lead to them. This makes it difficult for organisations to know who they really are dealing with.

Pyramid schemes are a system of selling goods in which agency rights are sold to an increasing number of distributors at successively lower levels. Distributors pay for these rights which become worthless as the pyramid grows.

10.14 Summary

- The fundamental ethical principles for CIMA members are integrity, objectivity, professional competence and due care, confidentiality, and professional behaviour.
- .CIMA members should be constantly conscious of, and be alert to factors which give rise to conflicts of interest and the resolution of ethical conflicts. Members should follow the CIMA *Code of Ethics for Professional Accountants*.
- Fraud is dishonestly obtaining an advantage, avoiding an obligation or causing a loss to another party.
- Those committing fraud may be managers, employees or third parties (sometimes customers or suppliers).
- There are three prerequisites for fraud to occur: dishonesty on the part of the perpetrator; the opportunity for fraud to occur and a motive for the fraud.
- Warning signs may indicate the presence of fraud risk.
- A risk management strategy needs to be developed for fraud which should include fraud prevention, identifying fraud and responding to fraud.
- Prevention can take place through an anti-fraud culture in the organisation, risk awareness of fraud, a whistle blowing policy and sound internal control systems.
- Most frauds are discovered accidentally or as a result of information received. External auditors rarely uncover fraud.
- The organisation's response to fraud may include internal disciplinary action; civil litigation for recovery of the loss and criminal prosecution through the police.
- Computer fraud may be easier to commit because of the centralisation of large databases and their accessibility to operators; because the segregation of duties possible with manual systems is not always possible with computer systems and because technology makes access easier.
- The increased use of the Internet has increased the possibility of fraud for many organisations. Users visiting an organisation's website are electronic rather than personal visitors, so security is more difficult.
- Many of the large corporate failures of the last decade have involved management who may manipulate accounting records to improve performance or to gain a personal advantage.
- Other frauds include advance fee fraud, pyramid schemes and identity fraud.

References

Chartered Institute of Management Accountants (2006), *Code of Ethics for Professional Accountants*.

Chartered Institute of Management Accountants (2001), *Fraud Risk Management – A Guide to Good Practice*.

A number of useful websites exist in relation to fraud, including

Metropolitan Police: http://www.met.police.uk/fraudalert/index.htm

Department of Trade & Industry: http://www.dti.gov.uk/ccp/scams/page1.htm

Revision Questions

? Question 1

Recommend to management the major causes of fraud and the major controls that should be in place to reduce fraud.

? Question 2

Discuss the elements of a fraud risk management strategy.

? Question 3

This question is adapted from the November 2007 examination for P3

VWS is a company manufacturing and selling a wide range of industrial products to a large number of businesses throughout the country. VWS is a significant local employer, with 2,500 people working out of several locations around the region, all linked by a networked computer system.

VWS purchases numerous components from 750 local and regional suppliers, receiving these into a central warehouse. The company carries about 10,000 different inventory items, placing 25,000 orders with its suppliers each year.

The Accounts Payable Department of VWS has six staff who process all supplier invoices through the company's computer system and make payment to suppliers by cheque or electronic remittance.

Requirement

Explain the risk of fraud in Accounts Payable for a company like VWS and how that risk can be mitigated. **(5 marks)**

? Question 4

The following question is adapted from the November 2005 examination for P3

As a CIMA member, you have recently been appointed as the Head of Internal Audit for SPQ, a multinational listed company that carries out a large volume of Internet sales to customers who place their orders using their home or work computers. You report to the Chief Executive although you work closely with the Finance Director. You have direct access to the Chair of the audit committee whenever you consider it necessary.

One of your internal audit teams has been conducting a review of IT security for a system which has been in operation for 18 months and which is integral to Internet sales. The audit was included in the internal audit plan following a request by the Chief Accountant. Sample testing by the internal audit team has revealed several transactions over the last three months which have raised concerns about possible hacking or fraudulent access to the customer/order database. Each of these transactions has disappeared from the database after deliveries have been made but without sales being recorded or funds collected from the customer. Each of the identified transactions was for a different customer and there seems to be no relationship between any of the transactions.

You have received the draft report from the internal audit manager responsible for this audit which suggests serious weaknesses in the design of the system. You have discussed this informally with senior managers who have told you that such a report will be politically very unpopular with the Chief Executive as he was significantly involved in the design and approval of the new system and insisted it be implemented earlier than the IT department considered was advisable. No post-implementation review of the system has taken place.

You have been informally advised by several senior managers to lessen the criticism and work with the IT department to correct any deficiencies within the system and to produce a report to the Audit Committee that is less critical and merely identifies the need for some improvement. They suggest that these actions would avoid criticism of the Chief Executive by the Board of SPQ.

Requirement

Explain the ethical principles that you should apply as the Head of Internal Audit for SPQ when reporting the results of this internal review and how any ethical conflicts should be resolved.

(**7 marks**)

 ## Question 5

HFD is a registered charity with 100 employees and 250 volunteers providing in-home care for elderly persons who are unable to fully take care of themselves. The company structure has no shareholders in a practical sense although a small number of issued shares are held by the sponsors who established the charity many years previously. HFD is governed by a seven-member Board of Directors. The Chief Executive Officer (CEO) chairs the board which comprises the chief financial officer (CFO) and five independent, unpaid non-executive directors who were appointed by the CEO based on past business relationships. You are one of the independent members of HFD's board.

The CEO/Chair sets the board agendas, distributes board papers in advance of meetings and briefs board members in relation to each agenda item. At each of its quarterly meetings the Board reviews the financial reports of the charity in some detail and the CFO answers questions. Other issues that regularly appear as agenda items include new government funding initiatives for the client group, and the results of proposals that have been submitted to funding agencies, of which about 25% are successful. There is rarely any discussion of operational matters relating to the charity as the CEO believes these are outside the directors' experience and the executive management team is more than capable of managing the delivery of the in-home care services.

The Board has no separate audit committee but relies on the annual management letter from the external auditors to provide assurance that financial controls are operating effectively. The external auditors were appointed by the CEO many years previously.

HFD's Board believes that its corporate governance could be improved by following the principles applicable to listed companies.

Requirements

(a) Recommend how HFD's Board should be restructured to comply with the principles of good corporate governance. **(16 marks)**

(b) Explain the aspects of CIMA's ethical principles and the conceptual framework underlying those principles which you would consider relevant to continuing in your role as an independent member of HFD's Board. **(9 marks)**

Total = 25 marks

Solutions to Revision Questions

✔ Solution 1

Fraud is dishonestly obtaining an advantage, avoiding an obligation or causing a loss to another party. Those committing fraud may be managers, employees or third parties, including customers and suppliers.

There are three conditions for fraud to occur: dishonesty, opportunity and motive. Controls to prevent dishonesty include pre-employment checks; scrutiny of staff by effective supervision; severe discipline for offenders and strong moral leadership. Opportunity can be reduced by the separation of duties, controls over inputs, processing and outputs and by the physical security of assets, especially cash. Motive can be influenced by providing good employment conditions, a sympathetic complaints procedure, but dismissing staff instantaneously where it is warranted.

A major reason why people commit fraud is because they are allowed to do so. The likelihood of fraud will be decreased if the potential fraudster believes that the rewards will be modest, or that the chance of detection or punishment will be unacceptably high. Therefore, a comprehensive system of control is needed to reduce the opportunity for fraud and increase the likelihood of detection.

Fraud risk arises out of errors or events in transaction processing or other business operations where those errors or events could be the result of a deliberate act designed to benefit the perpetrator (see Sections 10.2 and 10.3).

✔ Solution 2

As for all other risks, a risk management strategy needs to be developed for fraud. This strategy should include fraud prevention; the identification and detection of fraud, and responses to fraud.

The existence of a fraud strategy is itself a deterrent. This can be achieved through an anti-fraud culture and the maintenance of high ethical standards throughout the organisation; risk awareness among employees through training and publicity; a whistle-blowing policy that encourages staff to raise the alarm about fraud and sound internal control systems.

The identification of fraud is often a result of performing regular checks during internal audit. There may be warning signals such as late payments, backlogs of work, holidays not being taken, extravagant lifestyles, missing audit trails, etc. Whistleblowers sometimes identify the existence of fraud. Little fraud is discovered by external auditors. The response to any suspicion of fraud is that an investigation team should be put in place.

ETHICS AND FRAUD

Responses to fraud may be internal disciplinary, civil or criminal proceedings and this will influence the method of evidence collection. The fraud response plan should reinforce the organisation's commitment to high standards and its approach to those who fail to meet those standards. Individual responsibilities should be allocated to managers for management of the investigation, response (personnel, police, etc.) and other follow-up action (such as publicity, legal, insurance) (see Sections 10.5–10.8).

 ## Solution 3

Computer systems provide a particular opportunity for fraud, although this requires dishonesty by employees, opportunity to commit fraud, and motive. Accounts Payable in particular presents the opportunity for unscrupulous suppliers to claim payment for goods not delivered or services not supplied, or to overcharge. It also provides the opportunity for employees to redirect payments to themselves or third parties rather than to the intended supplier, either alone or in concert with third parties.

Some controls are preventative to limit or prevent an event from occurring. This could include physical access control over the computer system, selection and training of staff, separation of duties between invoice and payment processing or authorisation levels for invoices and payments. Other controls are detective: they identify events that have already occurred, through, for example, the reconciliation of invoices to a supplier statement. Internal audit, based on risk identification and assessment procedures have an important role to play in detective controls. Finally, corrective controls correct events after they have occurred (e.g. recovering overpayments from suppliers, or seeking recompense from employees under a fraud response plan).

It is particularly important that strong controls exist over programme alterations to accounts payable software, physical and logical access controls to accounts payable systems, authorisation levels for invoices and payments and control over forms such as cheques and electronic bank remittances.

The risk of fraud can be reduced through fraud prevention, identification and response policies. Fraud prevention requires an anti-fraud culture and risk awareness which is part of the control environment; sound control systems; and an effective whistle-blowing policy.

Fraud can be identified through regular internal audit checks, warning signals such as late payments, work backlogs, untaken annual leave, and the lifestyle of staff where it is incommensurate with their salary. Fraud response should include disciplinary action under human resource policies, civil litigation for recovery and criminal prosecution.

Solution 4

The fundamental principles that relate to the work of accountants as internal auditors are integrity (acting honestly and avoiding misleading statements); objectivity (impartiality and freedom from conflicts of interest); professional competence and due care; confidentiality; professional behaviour and the avoidance of conduct that might bring discredit to CIMA; and technical competence (the presentation of information fully, honestly and professionally).

Most of these principles apply in the present case. If the evidence justifies it, integrity and objectivity require that it be brought to the audit committee's attention. However, professional and technical competence requires that the Head of Internal Audit be confident in the audit findings before doing so.

CIMA's *Ethical Guidelines* describe the process for resolving ethical conflicts. Accountants working in organisations may encounter situations which give rise to conflicts of interest, ranging from fraud and illegal activities to relatively minor situations. An ethical conflict is not the same as an honest difference of opinion.

CIMA members should be constantly conscious of, and be alert to factors which give rise to conflicts of interest. In the present case, the ethical conflict is the real or perceived pressure placed on the Head of Internal Audit not to embarrass the Chief Executive. There is also the question of divided loyalty to the Chief Executive, to the audit committee, and to the Head of Internal Audit's professional responsibilities as a CIMA member.

Although it has not been suggested to the Head of Internal Audit that the matter not be reported, there is a suggestion that the report be softened and that work carry on behind the scenes to improve the system.

However, it is important that a draft report be produced and submitted for comment before it is sent to the audit committee. This presents the opportunity for other views to be aired. One course of action may be to discuss the matter with the Finance Director to determine his/her view and with the Chief Executive to determine that person's reactions to the draft audit report.

When faced with ethical conflicts, members should:

- Follow the organisation's grievance procedure
- Discuss the matter with the member's superior and successive levels of management, always with the member's superior's knowledge (unless that person is involved).

Discussion with an objective adviser or the professional body may be useful to clarify the issues involved and alternative courses of action that are available, without breaching any duty of confidentiality. Throughout, the member should maintain a detailed record of the problem and the steps taken to resolve it.

If an ethical conflict still exists after fully exhausting all levels of internal review, the member may have no recourse on significant matters other than to resign and report the matter to the organisation. Except when seeking advice from CIMA or when legally required to do so, communication of information regarding the problem to persons outside the employing organisation is not considered appropriate.

✔ Solution 5

(a) The principles of corporate governance that are in the Combined Code are equally applicable to public sector and third sector (not-for-profit) organisations. They are applicable whether a charity is limited by shares or limited by guarantee. There are 6 categories of corporate governance in the Combined Code: directors, remuneration, accountability and audit, relations with shareholders, institutional shareholders, and disclosure. The main principles applicable to HFD are in relation to directors, accountability and audit, and disclosure. Remuneration and relations with shareholders are not relevant to HFD.

Good corporate governance requires that a company be headed by an effective board with a clear division of responsibilities between running the board and running the company /charity with no individual having unfettered decision-making power. There should be a balance of executive and non-executive directors so that no individual or group can dominate the board. There should be a formal and rigorous process for the appointment of directors who should receive induction training. Information should be supplied in a timely manner to board members so that the board can discharge its duties. The board should then evaluate its performance both individually and collectively each year.

These principles do not seem to be applied for HFD as it is dominated by the chief executive who also acts as chair and appears to dominate the board through his appointment of non-executive directors and his control over the agenda. To meet the principles of good corporate governance, HFD should:

- Separate the roles of chief executive and chairman with the chairman being a non-executive director
- Ensure that all directors are independent of influence by the chief executive. Positions should be advertised with interviews being conducted, perhaps initially by an independent person. Appointments should be for a defined period, after which directors should stand for re-election
- Provide induction training to new board members in the goals and operations of the charity
- Annually evaluate the performance of each director and the board as a whole.

Accountability and audit principles of good corporate governance require that a board should be able to present a balanced and understandable assessment of the company's position and prospects, should maintain a sound system of internal control and maintain an appropriate relationship with the company's auditors.

HFD's Board does not seem to be able to make a balanced and understandable assessment of the company's position and prospects, given the narrow confines of what the CEO/Chair allows it. The CEOs relationship with the external auditors is not appropriate.

To meet the principles of good corporate governance, HFD should:

- Set an agenda for board meetings that encompasses a wide variety of strategic matters including the charity's strategy, operations, risk management, internal controls and not be limited to financial reports and proposals for funding
- Consider meeting more frequently than quarterly
- Obtain an independent assessment of the company's internal controls by appointing a firm to act as (outsourced) internal auditor
- Affirm the reporting relationship of the external auditors to the board as a whole, and not to the CEO. The external auditors may need to be changed if they are unwilling to accept this changed relationship
- Although it is good practice, it is not necessary to have a separate audit committee, but if not, the functions of the audit committee should be carried out by the full board itself

The disclosure principle requires that a company's annual report contains a high level statement of how the board operates and the decisions taken by the board and management, details of board members, meetings, performance evaluation, etc.

- HFD should provide adequate disclosure of board functioning in its annual report to make this aspect of the charity transparent.

(b) CIMA's *Code of Ethics for Professional Accountants* makes clear that an accountant's responsibility is more than satisfying the needs of a client, s/he must also act in the public interest. It is irrelevant whether or not the CIMA member is paid for his/her services, which are still expected to comply with the ethical principles.

There are 5 fundamental principles in the Code of Ethics: integrity, objectivity, professional competence and due care, confidentiality and professional behaviour.

Of particular relevance to HFD are objectivity, and professional competence and due care. Objectivity may be impeded due to bias because of his/her appointment by the CEO or the influence of the CEO or other persons on the board who may align themselves with the CEO.

The demands of professional competence and due care means that the accountant must look beyond the narrow agenda set by the CEO to a broader perspective than financial statements to non-financial risks (mainly in relation to the charities operation) and the adequacy of internal controls (as it is insufficient to rely wholly on the external auditor's annual management letter).

The conceptual framework underlying CIMA's ethical principles requires accountants to risk manage their own position in relation to the work they are performing and in so doing to identify, evaluate and mitigate any risks they face. The main risks faced by an accountant include those relating to self-interested behaviour, self-review, advocacy, familiarity and intimidation.

The major threats faced in relation to HFD are familiarity and intimidation. The accountant has been appointed to the board as a result of some prior business relationship which may affect his/her objectivity. The CEO/Chair of HFD also appears to be a dominating individual and the accountant may be intimidated by this individual, resulting in the accountant's views not being presented accurately and/or forcefully.

The accountant as board member needs to identify and evaluate the risks of familiarity and/or intimidation that s/he faces, and ensure that s/he takes appropriate action (ultimately resignation from the board) to maintain his/her independence and objectivity.

Introduction to Risk Management and Derivatives

Introduction to Risk Management and Derivatives

11

LEARNING OUTCOMES

After completing this chapter you should be able to

▶ appreciate the purpose and functions of a treasury department;

▶ identify and evaluate reasons for corporate hedging;

▶ explain the various steps in the financial risk management process;

▶ identify and explain basic derivatives and their uses.

11.1 Introduction

The main purpose of this chapter is to introduce students to derivatives and financial risk management. It lays the groundwork for the subsequent chapters where we apply the concepts introduced in this chapter. We begin by giving a brief background to recent developments in financial markets that have resulted in the need for financial risk management. Then, we describe the functions of the corporate treasurer and discuss arguments in favour of and against corporate hedging activities. We also provide a brief overview of derivatives and outline different ways in which derivative instruments can be used. The chapter concludes with a brief summary.

11.2 Recent developments in financial markets

The financial environment in which companies operate has undergone substantial changes in recent times, including increased globalisation and changes in the regulatory environment of financial and capital markets. These have resulted in more and more companies trading and investing outside their home countries and increased volatility in interest rates and foreign exchange rates. As the environment changes, companies all over the world are exposed to new opportunities as well as new risks and uncertainties. The sources of uncertainty cover a wide area but it is worth noting that economic and political trends are major contributory factors. In particular, in the 1980s the move away from using interest rates to manage demand (Keynesian economics) to their use in controlling the money supply led to increased interest-rate volatility around the world, particularly in the United Kingdom and the United States, and this had a knock-on effect with exchange rates, as international capital moved to countries with increasing interest rates boosting the exchange rate.

Businesses wish to reduce their exposure to risk in all its forms; hence, risk management has become an area of increasing importance in financial management. Traditionally, the treasury department or the corporate treasurer has responsibility for managing financial risk.

11.3 The treasury function

The treasury function exists in every business, though in small businesses it may form part of a department covering other functions, such as accounting or company secretarial work. In a larger company, it is likely to be a separate department reporting to the chief financial officer, but communications with the rest of the organisation need to be in good order if an effective service is to be provided.

The *treasury function* represents one of the two main aspects of financial management, the other being *financial control*.

> *Treasury* is concerned with the relationship between the entity and its financial stakeholders, which include shareholders, fund lenders and taxation authorities, while *financial control* provides the relationship with other stakeholders such as customers, suppliers and employees.

The establishment of a specialist treasury function within the finance department can be traced back to the late 1960s. Developments in technology, the breakdown of exchange controls, increasing volatility in interest rates and exchange rates, combined with the increasing globalisation of business, have all contributed to greater opportunities and risks for businesses over the last three decades. To survive in today's complex financial environment, businesses need to be able to actively manage both their ability to undertake these opportunities and their exposure to risks.

Businesses have become more aware of the expanding range of hybrid capital instruments (e.g. convertible preference shares issued by a multinational company in the name of a subsidiary registered in the Dutch Antilles) and financial instruments (such as forward markets and the various derivatives markets) and need to be able to select from these the ones that are appropriate to the business's needs in the prevailing circumstances.

In larger companies and groups, the treasury function will usually be centralised at the head office, providing a service to all the various units of the entity and thereby achieving economies of scale, for example, by obtaining better borrowing rates, or netting-off balances.

The main functions of the treasurer can be classified as follows:

- *Banking*: The Treasurer will be responsible for managing relationships with the banks. In this book we view this function as an integral part of the three other functions identified below.
- *Liquidity management*: This will involve working capital and money management. The treasurer will need to ensure that the business has the liquid funds it needs, and invests surplus funds.

- *Funding management*: Funding management is concerned with identifying suitable sources of funds, which requires knowledge of the sources available, the cost of those sources, whether any security is required and management of interest-rate risks.
- *Currency management*: The treasurer would be responsible for providing the business with forecasts of exchange rate movements, which in turn will determine the procedures adopted to manage exchange rate risks. Dealing in the foreign exchange markets and day-to-day management of foreign exchange risks becomes a key function for the treasurer.

The treasurer's key tasks can also be categorised according to the three levels of management:

1. *strategic*, for example matters concerning the capital structure of the business and distribution/retention policies, the actual raising of capital, including share issues, the assessment of the likely return from each source and the appropriate proportions of funds from each source, the decision as to the level of dividends and consideration of alternative forms of finance;
2. *tactical*, for example the management of cash/investments and decisions as to the hedging of currency or interest-rate risk;
3. *operational*, for example the transmission of cash, placing of 'surplus' cash and other dealings with banks.

Treasurers require specialist skills to be able to handle effectively an ever-growing range of capital instruments, and to determine the most suitable way to protect their company from foreign exchange risk, which demands a good knowledge of forward markets and an ability to select the most appropriate methods of hedging and foreign exchange cover. They also need knowledge of taxation in all areas in which the group operates and, deriving from that, the ability to advise effectively on policies such as transfer pricing in permissible ways to minimise overall tax liability, and to be able to liaise competently with the group taxation department.

The capacity to make large gains or losses is enormous: a treasurer can wipe out, in a few hours, all the profit made from making and selling things over several months. It is important, therefore, that authority and responsibility associated with the treasury function are carefully defined and monitored. This becomes even more important as the range of derivative instruments increases. The board and senior managers need to be aware of which risks are being carried, which laid off, and, where appropriate, taken on. There is also growing pressure for companies to disclose, in their annual reports, more information about their treasury policies, and their 'use of derivatives and other financial instruments' as at the balance sheet date.

11.3.1 Cost centre or profit centre

An area for debate is whether the treasury activities should be accounted for simply as a cost centre or as a profit centre. Some companies use derivatives for hedging as well as trading in their own right, seeking to make a profit out of their trading activities.

Below are some examples of Corporate Treasury Policy and Financial Risk Management practices.

Marks and Spencer

Marks and Spencer operates a centralised treasury function to manage the Group's external/internal funding requirements and financial risks in line with the Board approved treasury policies and procedures, and delegated authorities therein given. ... Group Treasury also enters into derivative transactions, principally interest rate and currency swaps and forward currency contracts. The purpose of these transactions is to manage the interest-rate and currency risks arising from the Group's operations and financing. It remains Group policy not to hold or issue financial instruments for trading purposes, except where financial constraints necessitate the need to liquidate any outstanding investments. The treasury function is managed as a cost centre and does not engage in speculative trading.

Marks and Spencer Plc. *Annual Report 2008,* p. 82.

SABMiller (formerly South African Breweries)

The directors are ultimately responsible for the establishment and oversight of the group's risk management framework. An essential part of this framework is the role undertaken by the audit committee of the Board, supported by the internal audit function, and by the Chief Financial Officer, who in this regard is supported by the treasury committee and the group treasury function. Amongst other responsibilities, the audit committee reviews the internal control environment and risk management systems within the group and it reports its activities to the Board. The Board also receives a quarterly report on treasury activities, including confirmation of compliance with treasury risk management policies.

… Some of the risk management strategies include the use of derivatives, principally in the form of forward foreign currency contracts, cross currency swaps, interest rate swaps and exchange traded futures contracts, in order to manage the currency, interest rate and commodities exposures arising from the group's operations. … It is group policy that no trading in financial instruments be taken.

SABMiller Plc, *Annual Report 2008,* p. 97.

Hutchison Whampoa Limited

The Group's treasury function sets financial risk management policies in accordance with policies and procedures approved by its Executive Directors, which are also subject to periodic review by the Group's internal audit function. The Group's treasury policies are designed to mitigate the impact of fluctuations in interest rates and exchange rates and to minimise the Group's financial risks. The Group's treasury function operates as a centralised service for managing financial risks including interest rate and foreign exchange risks, and for providing cost efficient funding to the Group and its companies. … The Group cautiously uses derivatives, principally interest rate and foreign currency swaps and forward currency contracts as appropriate for risk management purposes only, for hedging transactions and managing the Group's assets and liabilities. It is the Group's policy not to enter into derivative transaction for speculative purposes. It is also the Group's policy not to invest liquidity in financial products, including hedge funds or similar vehicles, with significant underlying leverage or derivative exposure.

Hutchison Whampoa Limited, *Annual Report 2007,* p. 190.

BP Plc

The group is exposed to a number of different financial risks arising from natural business exposures as well as its use of financial instruments including market risks relating to commodity prices, foreign currency exchange rates, interest rates and equity prices, credit risk and liquidity risk. The group financial risk committee (GFRC) advises the group chief financial officer (CFO) who oversees the management of these risks. … The committee provides assurance to the CFO and the group chief executive (GCE), and via the GCE to the board, that the group's financial risk-taking activity is governed by appropriate policies and procedures and that financial risks are identified, measured and managed in accordance with group policies and group risk appetite. … All derivative activity, whether for risk management or entrepreneurial purposes, is carried out by specialist teams that have the appropriate skills, experience and supervision.

BP Plc, *Annual Report 2007,* p. 136.

The examples above illustrate how different companies organise their treasury and financial risk management operations. BP Plc uses derivatives for both risk management and trading purposes. However, most non-financial companies will only use derivatives for risk management purposes. The fact that the risk management practices of these companies differ, does not make one better than the other. The choice depends on many factors, including

- the company's objectives;
- the risk profile and risk appetite of the company;
- the resources including personnel, time and money available for the risk management function.

Most of the companies above managed the treasury function as a cost centre. The main advantages of operating the treasury as a profit centre rather than as a cost centre are as follows:

- Individual business units of the entity can be charged a market rate for the service provided, thereby making their operating costs more realistic.
- The treasurer is motivated to provide services as effectively and economically as possible to ensure that a profit is made at the market rate, for example in managing hedging activities for a subsidiary, thereby benefiting the group as a whole.

The main disadvantages are as follows:

- The profit concept is a temptation to speculate, for example by swapping funds from currencies expected to depreciate into ones expected to appreciate.
- Management time is unduly spent in arguments with business units over charges for services, even though market rates may have been impartially checked (say, by internal audit department).
- Additional administrative costs may be excessive.

The decision whether to operate the treasury function as a profit centre or not may well depend on the particular 'style' of the company and the extent of centralisation or decentralisation of its activities. Many large companies, however, operate a centralised treasury which has both merits and limitations:

- Centralisation facilitates intra-company netting of opposing transactions that occur across the different units of the company. For example, the South African subsidiary of a UK multinational company may have payables in dollars in 6 months time with their Brazilian subsidiary expecting a receipt of dollars. If each subsidiary were to manage its own treasury activities it might lead to unnecessary hedging costs.
- Centralisation reduces overlap and duplication of treasury activities.
- Centralisation can also achieve lower transaction costs through economies of scale compared to a decentralised treasury. A small number of large volume transactions will be cheaper than a greater number of small transactions.
- Centralisation will ensure the concentration of specialist skills and expertise. Lack of necessary expertise in the decentralised units can increase risk of abuse and misuse of financial insruments such as derivatives.
- Centralisation ensures uniformity of procedures and senior managers will have better knowledge of the company's activities for better monitoring and control.
- A centralised treasury may be slow in responding to the treasury needs of the localised units.

11.4 Overview of financial risk management

Companies are exposed to various types of risks in the course of their business operations that affect the company's cash flows and/or cost of capital. These risks can generally be classified into two main categories:

Firm-specific risks: These risks are specific to the particular activities of the company such as fire, lawsuits and fraud. Although firm-specific risks are diversifiable from an investor's perspective, it is possible, however, for the company to manage many sources of these risks with adequate internal controls and insurance contracts. These issues have already been addressed in the earlier chapters.

Market-wide risks: Market risk is the risk or uncertainty associated with the economic environment in which all companies operate, including changes in interest rates, exchange rates and commodity prices. (e.g. oil and gas prices). Changes in these variables can have a significant impact on the future performance of many companies. These are the risks we consider in this chapter and the subsequent three chapters.

This section addresses general issues associated with financial risk management. In particular, we will look at the ongoing debate on why companies hedge and steps in the risk management process.

A hedge is a transaction to reduce or eliminate an exposure to risk (CIMA *Official Terminology*, 2005).

11.4.1 Why do companies manage financial risk?

Decades ago, Modigliani and Miller, two Nobel Prize winning economists, showed that if financial markets were perfect, then financial policy would not increase the value of the company. If financial policy is to increase company value, then it must be because it either increases the expected future cash flows of the company or lowers the company's cost of capital in a way that cannot be replicated by individual investors. Financial risk management is largely a process to alter the financing mechanism of the company, and a number of surveys show that most companies are actively managing their exposures to financial risk. So, why do companies bother with financial risk management? Can it increase the value of the firm?

The perfect market assumptions underlying the Modigliani and Miller irrelevance proposition imply that companies as well as individual investors have equal access to information and hedging instruments. However, in the real world, information asymmetries exist and there are transaction costs. Companies may have better information and access to financial markets than individual investors (e.g. for prices on commodities, interest rate and foreign exchange). It is therefore less costly for the firm to hedge than for individuals to hedge. Other arguments in favour of corporate hedging also include the following:

Hedging reduces the probability and cost of financial distress (bankruptcy): Corporate hedging can reduce the variability of the company's cash flows and therefore the probability that the company will encounter financial distress. The reduced probability lowers the expected cost of financial distress.

Hedging reduces taxes: If a company faces a convex (progressive) tax schedule, reducing the variability of the pre-tax earnings can reduce the company's expected tax bill. Thus, a company that hedges can achieve a higher expected profit after tax.

Hedging and investment decisions: Reducing the volatility of cash flows can increase the value of a company by improving management's incentive to undertake all profitable investment projects. In addition, if hedging reduces the probability and the expected cost of financial distress, it would also increase the company's debt capacity and lower the cost of borrowing. Together, they lead to the acceptance of positive NPV projects that would have been otherwise rejected and the availability of funds to take on the investment.

Managerial incentive to hedge: Managers of a company are less well diversified than shareholders in that they stand to lose more in the event of bankruptcy. Risk-averse managers will thus prefer to hedge to protect their job. Consequently, hedging can reduce contracting costs as it reduces the risk faced by managers.

While there are reasons to hedge, there are also reasons why companies may not hedge their financial risks. In addition to the perfect market arguments as described above, other arguments against hedging include

Shareholder diversification: If shareholders hedge their investment risk by holding a diversified portfolio, then further hedging by the company may harm rather than enhance shareholders' interests. Furthermore, if investors do not want the exposure to the volatility inherent in the company, they can take action to mitigate those risks themselves.

Transaction costs: The costs associated with derivative products such as brokerage fees and commissions may discourage managers from actively managing their exposures. Risk management is valuable only if the benefits outweigh the costs.

Resistance by board or senior management: Senior management may lack the necessary expertise to exercise their oversight responsibility to monitor and evaluate the cost and benefits of the range of hedging methods and instruments available.

Accounting and tax issues: The complexities associated with the tax and accounting consequences of derivative transactions may discourage some companies from using these instruments. In particular, IAS 39 issued by the International Accounting Standards Board has increased requirements for companies to disclose their use of derivative instruments, which may complicate reporting. The implications of IAS 39 are discussed later in a separate section.

11.4.2 The financial risk management process

Companies may manage their financial risk in many different ways. This depends on the activities of the company, its attitude to risk and the level of risk it is prepared to accept. In this sense, the directors of the company will need to identify, assess and decide whether the company needs to manage the risks identified.

Stages in the financial risk management process entail the following.

Identify the risk exposures

The company should identify which types of risks it is exposed to in the course of its operations and whether these risks are significant to the circumstances of the company and therefore of concern. For example, how does changes in commodity prices, interest rates or exchange rates affect the company operations and what risks arise from these changes? For an airline company, such as British Airways, unanticipated increases in oil prices can pose a significant risk as they increase its costs and reduce its profits, while changes in foreign exchange rates can lead to loss of competitiveness for UK manufacturers.

Quantify the exposure

Quantification of risk is important in understanding the extent and significance of the exposure. This can be done by measuring the impact of the risk factor on the value of the company or individual items such as cash flows, income or cost. Several different techniques can be employed including regression analysis, simulation analysis and value at risk. Risk exposure can also be measured by calculating the standard deviation of relevant income items.

Regression method

> Regression analysis can be used to measure the company's exposure to various risk factors. This can be done by regressing changes in the company's cash flows against the various risk factors such as changes in interest rates, changes in the exchange rate of a particular currency or basket of currencies and changes in the price of a major input, say oil. The regression model could be expressed as

$$R = \alpha + \beta_1 \text{INT} + \beta_2 \text{FX} + \beta_3 \text{OIL} + e$$

where

R represents changes in the company's cash flows;
INT represents changes in interest rates;
FX represents changes in exchange rates;
OIL represents changes in oil prices.

The coefficients β_1, β_2 and β_3 represent the sensitivity of the company's cash flows or stock price to the risk factors. The company's stock price can also be used instead of cash flows as the dependent variable in the regression model as an alternative approach.

Simulation method

> Simulation analysis is used to evaluate the sensitivity of the value of the company or the company's cash flows to a variety of simulated values of the various risk factors based on the probability distribution of the risk factors that is believed to capture or approximate the possible changes in the risk factors. Based on the probability distribution of each of the risk factors that influence the company's value, a possible value for each element is selected at random and the relevant cash flow is calculated. This procedure is repeated a number of times to obtain the range of values that can be achieved. Calculate the mean and standard deviation of the range of values obtained to give the expected value and a measure of the risk. The greater the standard deviation, the greater the risk associated with the expected cash flows or value. The simulation method is therefore a forward-looking method and superior to regression analysis which is based on historical values. However, unlike regression analysis it does not specify the relationship between the value of the company or the company's cash flows and the various risk factors.

Expected value and standard deviation

Suppose the cash flow of a UK exporter depends on the strength of the pound relative to the currency of its major clients. The company's cash flow over the year is predicted as follows:

Cash flow (£)	Probability
10 million	0.3
12 million	0.4
14 million	0.3

Generally, the expected value of a random variable X, $E(X)$, is calculated as the sum of the products obtained by multiplying each possible outcome by the corresponding probability. This can be expressed as

$$E(X) = \Sigma P_i X_i$$

where X_i represents possible values of the random variable X and P_i is the corresponding probability that X_i would occur.

The expected value or mean cash flow is calculated as

$$0.3 \times £10 \text{ million} + 0.4 \times £12 \text{ million} + 0.3 \times £14 \text{ million} = £12 \text{ million}$$

The standard deviation, denoted as σ, is a measure of the dispersion of the possible values from the expected value or mean. This can be calculated as

$$\pi \quad \sigma = \sqrt{\Sigma P_i [X_i - E(X)]^2}$$

where $E(X)$ is the expected value or mean calculated as above.

As the standard deviation measures the variability of possible outcomes from the expected value, it gives an indication of the risk involved. *For a given expected value, the greater the standard deviation the greater the risk involved.*

Using the example above, the standard deviation can be calculated as

$$\sigma = \sqrt{0.3(10 \times 12)^2 + 0.4(12 \times 12)^2 + 0.3(14 \times 12)^2}$$
$$\sigma = \sqrt{1.2 + 0 + 1.2}$$
$$\sigma = \sqrt{2.4} = 1.549$$

Thus, the cash flows have an expected value of £12 million and a standard deviation of £1.549 million.

Value at risk

Value at risk (VaR) measures the maximum loss possible due to normal market movements in a given period of time with a stated probability. The given holding period can be 1 day, 1 week, 1 month or longer. Under normal market conditions, losses greater than the value at risk occur with a very small probability. It was first used by the major financial institutions to measure the risks of their trading portfolios, but VaR has now become an industry standard for measuring exposure to financial price risks.

The VaR measure depends on two critical parameters:

1. the holding period and
2. the confidence level.

A key assumption underlying the calculation of VaR is that possible changes from time to time in the value of the underlying asset or portfolio are independent of each other and follow a normal distribution with a mean of zero. It is common in practice for VaR to be calculated on a daily basis. Let X% be the required confidence level, then a daily X% VaR can be calculated using these three steps.

1. Calculate the daily volatility (standard deviation) of the underlying asset.
2. Using statistical tables, determine the standard normal value (Z) associated with the given one-tail confidence level, X%.
3. Multiply the result in point (1) by the result in point (2) to obtain the daily X% VaR.

Note that to calculate the daily VaR, the standard deviation would have to be stated in daily terms. If you have been given volatility for a period other than daily, then convert the given volatility into daily volatility before using the steps above. For example, suppose σ_W is the weekly volatility of the underlying asset. There are 5 working days in the week. Then the daily volatility, σ_D, can be calculated as:

$$\sigma_D = \sigma_W \div \sqrt{5}$$

Example 11.A

Suppose a UK company expects to receive $14 million from a US customer. The value in pounds to the UK company will depend on the exchange rate between the dollar and pounds resulting in gains or losses as the exchange rate changes. Assume that the exchange rate today is $1.75/£ and that the daily volatility of the pound/dollar exchange rate is 0.5%. Calculate the

(a) 1-day 95% VaR
(b) 1-day 99% VaR.

Solution

The value of the $14 million today is £8 million ($14 million ÷ $1.75/£) with a daily standard deviation of £40,000 (0.5% × £8 million).

(a) The standard normal value (Z) associated with the one-tail 95% confidence level is 1.645. Hence, the 1-day 95% VaR is 1.645 × £40,000 = £65,800. This means that we are 95% confident that the maximum daily loss will not exceed £65,800. Alternatively, we could also say that there is a 5% (1 out of 20) chance that the loss would exceed £65,800.
(b) The standard normal value (Z) associated with the one-tail 99% confidence level is 2.326. Hence, the 1-day 99% VaR is 2.326 × £40,000 = £93,040. Thus, there is a 1% (1 out of 100) chance that the loss would exceed £93,040.

Given the 1-day VaR, we can easily calculate the VaR for longer holding periods as

N-day VaR = 1-day VaR × √N

Thus, from Example 11.A, we can calculate the 5-day 95% VaR as

5-day 95% VaR = 1-day 95% VaR × √5
= £65,800 × √5
= £147,129

There is a 5% chance that the company's foreign exchange loss would exceed £147,129 over the next 5 days.

Similarly, the 30-day 99% VaR would be

$$30\text{-day } 99\% \text{ VaR} = 1\text{-day } 99\% \text{ VaR} \times \sqrt{30}$$
$$= £93,040 \times \sqrt{30}$$
$$= £509,601$$

Notice that for a given confidence level, the VaR increases with the holding period. Thus, the longer the holding period, the greater the VaR. Also, for a given holding period VaR increases with the confidence level.

Sensitivity and scenario analysis

Other methods of quantifying risk exposure include the use of sensitivity and scenario analysis.

Sensitivity analysis is a modelling and risk assessment procedure in which changes are made to significant variables in order to determine the effect of these changes on the planned outcome. Particular attention is thereafter paid to variables identified as being of special significance (CIMA *Official Terminology*, 2005). In many cases, changes in key variables (e.g. foreign exchange rate) cannot be known with certainty so forecasts of possible alternative values can be used to determine the effect of such changes on planned outcomes. For example, to quantify interest rate exposure we might look at the impact of a 1% change in interest rate on a company's assets, liabilities, income statement or expected future cash flows. One limitation of sensitivity analysis is that it assumes the key variable of interest can change independently of all other variables which is unlikely in practice. Scenario analysis on the other hand looks at the effect of simultaneous changes in a number of key variables on planned outcomes. In both cases, however, the extent of changes in the key variables assumed are subjective and arbitrary.

Pros and Cons of the alternative approaches

In this section we have outlined a number of alternative approaches that may be used to identify and quantify exposure to risk. The advantages and disadvantages of the various approaches can be looked at in terms of their complexity and ease of implementation, ease of understanding and interpretation to senior management and reliability of any underlying assumptions. Table 11.1 summarises how the different approaches differ on these characteristics.

Deciding whether to hedge

Once the risks have been identified and quantified, the company then decides whether to hedge each of the significant exposures. The decision needs to be made within the context of the established goals and objectives of the company and the environment within which the resulting risk management strategies will be implemented. The company's decision to hedge will depend on the company's appetite for risk. The company may decide to either accept or modify the risk exposure quantified as being inherent. Thus, the company's strategies for managing the exposures may include one or more of the following:

- Accepting the risk and doing nothing. Although some risks are necessary if the company has to make some profits, doing nothing can also be speculative. Hence, there is the need to ensure that these are acceptable risks and that the company is not being reckless.
- Managing the risk using internal (operating) techniques. As many exposures are completely or partially offsetting, at a minimum, non-derivative internal hedging strategies should be exhausted before utilising derivatives.

Table 11.1 Comparing the alternative approaches

Method	Ease of implementation	Ease of understanding	Reliability of underlying assumptions
Regression Method	Easy to implement	Familiar and easy to understanding	Based on historical data, thus depending on the availability of reliable data for the relevant variables
		Easier to explain to non-specialist managers	Analysis based on the past period may not be typical of the risks faced by the company in the future
Simulation	Complex and difficult to implement	Conceptually complex and thus difficult to explain to non-specialists	Dynamic and can be adapted to different assumptions and circumstances
	Computations can be time consuming		Useful if a complete distribution of cash flows is required
	However, standard computer software packages are available to ease implementation		Generally assumes a particular probability distribution for the risk factor, for example a normal distribution, but the actual distribution may be different from the assumed distribution
Value at Risk	Many variants of VaR computations. Some of these may be complex and difficult statistical assumptions to implement	Easier to understand and communicate to non-specialist managers as the risk is presented as a single number and in monetary terms	Depends on underlying assumptions, e.g. the holding period, and cannot be regarded as an accurate measure
	However, standard computer software packages are available to ease implementation	Gives and indication of the materiality of the risk and can be used to prioritise risks	May not capture extreme scenarios – e.g. market crashes

- Managing the risk using external (derivative) hedging techniques. There are a wide range of derivative products that can be used to manage or reduce risk exposure. The treasurer needs to examine the various products and select the most cost-effective product that is appropriate for the company's exposure and risk preference. There are, basically, four derivative products, Forwards, Futures, Swaps and Options. These are considered in the next section.

Implement and monitor the hedging program

Finally, once a decision has been made to manage the exposure, the treasurer needs to put in place a proper monitoring and evaluation strategy taking into consideration reporting and oversight issues. The monitoring framework should include clear roles and responsibilities of the treasury team, authorisation, counterparty exposure, dealing limits and reporting guidelines. Regular reports to the board on risk management activities, including confirmation of compliance with the risk management policies set by the board is a good practice. Note that current financial reporting standards – SFAS 133 issued by the Financial Accounting Standards Board, IFRS 7 and IAS 39 issued by the international Accounting Standards Board – require that gains and losses associated with the use of derivatives are properly disclosed in the financial statements.

11.5   Introduction to derivatives

🔑 A *derivative* is a financial instrument whose value depends on the price of some other financial assets or some underlying factors. The underlying variables may be commodities such as oil and gold, stocks, interest rates, currencies or some abstract conditions such as the weather. Derivatives are useful instruments that can be used to manage or reduce risk. There are four basic types of derivatives: forward contracts, futures contract, options contract and swaps. These are the building blocks for more complex derivatives such as swaptions. Derivative products can also be classified into exchange-traded derivatives and over-the-counter (OTC) derivatives. Exchange-traded products trade on organised exchanges such as the London International Financial Futures and Options Exchange (LIFFE), Chicago Board of Trade (CBOT) and Singapore International Monetary Exchange (SIMEX). On the other hand, OTC derivatives are individually negotiated between the buyer and the seller. Below is a general description of the basic derivative instruments. The operations and specific characteristics of interest-rate derivatives and currency derivatives and how they are used in managing risks are discussed in the subsequent chapters.

11.5.1   Forward contracts

🔑 A *forward contract* is a legally binding agreement between two parties to buy or sell a specified asset at a specified future date and at a specified price agreed today. Consequently, the party that has agreed to buy commits to take delivery at the future date, while the seller commits to deliver at the future date at the agreed price regardless of the price at the future date. The buyer is said to have a long position and the seller is said to have a short position.

For example, in February 200X, a UK confectionery enters into a forward contract with a Ghanaian cocoa merchant to buy 1,000 tons of cocoa in 6 months at a price of £2,000 per ton. In this case, regardless of the price of cocoa in 6 months' time, the Ghanaian cocoa merchant is obliged to deliver the 1,000 tons of cocoa and the UK confectioner is obliged to pay £2,000,000 (i.e. £2,000 per ton) on delivery.

Forward contracts are arranged in the OTC market and exist on a wide variety of underlying assets. For example, there are forward markets for commodities (e.g. oil, electricity and gold), interest rates and currencies. A forward contract can be used to lock in the price of the underlying asset. For example, the UK confectionery can use the forward contract on cocoa to protect itself against unexpected increases in the future price of cocoa. Similarly, a company can use a forward contract on currencies to protect itself against unfavourable exchange rate movements.

A gain or a loss on the forward contract occurs when the price of the underlying asset at maturity differs from the forward price. Suppose the price of cocoa in 6 months' time is £2,100 per ton instead of the £2,000 per ton agreed under the forward contract. Then the UK confectioner (long forward) gains £100 per ton under the contract as the company pays £2,000 for a product that is trading at £2,100. The Ghanaian cocoa merchant (short forward) loses £100, as they have to accept £2,000 for a product that can be sold for £2,100. Similarly, if the price of cocoa in 6 months' time were £1,800, then the UK confectioner would have lost £200 for agreeing to pay £2,000 for a product that is now trading at £1,800. The cocoa merchant would have gained £200. Table 11.2 shows the gain or loss on the forward contract for different prices of cocoa at maturity.

Table 11.2 Gains and losses on a forward contract

Price at maturity (£)	Gain/(loss) for long position	Gain/(loss) for short position
1600	(400)	400
1700	(300)	300
1800	(200)	200
1900	(100)	100
2000	0	0
2100	100	(100)
2200	200	(200)
2300	300	(300)
2400	400	(400)

Figure 11.1 shows the payoff profile of the forward contract. The profile for the long position shows the gains and the loses of the buyer of the forward contract whilst the short position illustrates the gains and the losses of the seller of the forward. Generally, the buyer losses on the forward if the price of the underlying asset at maturity falls below the contract price and gains if the price of the underlying rises above the contract price. Notice that the gains of the buyer equal the losses of the seller and vice versa.

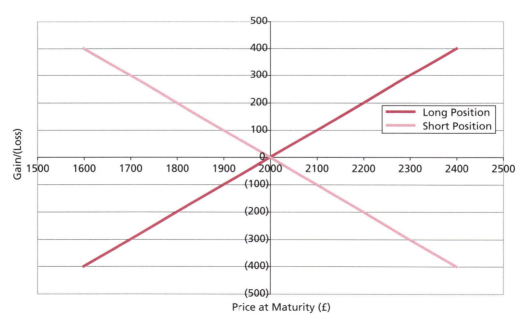

Figure 11.1 Payoff profile of a forward contract

11.5.2 Futures contracts

> 🔑 A *futures contract* is a contract relating to currencies, interest rates, commodities or shares that obliges the buyer (seller) to purchase (sell) the specified quantity of the item represented in the contract at a predetermined price at the expiration of the contract (CIMA *Official Terminology*, 2005).

Although both forwards and futures call for the delivery of an asset at a future date at a given price, futures contracts usually trade on organised exchanges while forwards are OTC contracts. Like all exchange-traded products, futures contracts are standardised in terms of products, contract sizes and delivery dates. Thus, a futures contract calls for the delivery of a standardised quantity of an asset, on a standardised delivery date in the future at a given price. For example, oil futures on New York Mercantile Exchange (NYMEX) are made for 1,000 barrels of oil and British Pound contracts on Chicago Mercantile exchange are made for £62,500 per contract. Note that you cannot trade fractional contracts. In order to minimise counterparty risk, futures contracts are also settled daily and any gains or losses paid through the life of the contract. This is known as daily marking-to-market.

Similar to forward contracts, a futures contract can be used to lock in to the price of the underlying asset. The payoff profile for a futures contract is similar to that of the forward contract.

In most cases, the appropriate number of contracts required to hedge an underlying position can be calculated as: size of underlying exposure divided by the futures contract size. For example, an oil refinery company imports crude oil for refinery every quarter. The company has a need for one million barrels of crude oil in 3 months time and wants to hedge this exposure using crude oil futures. The contract size for the crude oil futures is 1,000 barrels. The refinery company will need 1,000 crude oil futures contracts (1,000,000 ÷ 1,000) in order to fully hedge the exposure. In this case, the underlying exposure (crude oil) matches the hedge instrument (crude oil futures) hence a change in the price of a barrel of crude oil futures will match (albeit not fully) the price change in the crude oil to be purchased by the refinery. The hedge ratio is therefore 1:1 but this is not always the case.

In some cases, there could be a mismatch between the underlying asset and the hedge which would affect the hedge ratio. Consider the case of a bus company that requires 100,000 barrels of gasoline in the next 3 months. Local supplies of gasoline currently cost $80 per barrel. The bus company is worried that gasoline prices may rise and want to hedge this exposure using crude oil futures. Crude oil futures for delivery in 3 month's time is trading at $35 per barrel (contract size = 1,000 barrels). How many futures contracts should the company buy to hedge this exposure?

In this case, the price of the underlying exposure (gasoline) does not match the price of the futures (crude oil), thus a change in the price of a barrel of crude oil futures will not match a change in the price of a barrel of gasoline. In this case, the number of contracts required can be calculated as:

$$\frac{\text{Value of underlying exposure}}{\text{Value of futures contract}} = \frac{100,000}{1,000} \times \frac{82}{35} = 234.3 \text{ contracts}$$

Thus, the bus company will need 234 crude oil contracts (234,000 barrels) to hedge the exposure. A common mistake is to calculate the number of contracts required in this case as: 100,000 barrels ÷ 1,000 barrels per contract = 100 contracts.

11.5.3 Swaps

A *swap* is an agreement between two parties to exchange one series of cash flow for another at specified future times. For example, in an interest-rate swap, one party agrees to pay a fixed interest rate on a notional amount to the other party and receive from the other party a floating interest rate on the same amount, based on a reference rate, say the London Inter-Bank Offer Rate (LIBOR). A swap is arranged in the OTC market and can be considered as a long-term forward contract with a series of settlement dates compared to a simple forward that has only one settlement date. For example, a company may enter into an agreement with another party to receive 6-month LIBOR and pay a fixed rate of 5 per cent per annum every 6 months for 3 years on a notional principal of £100 million. Interest-rate swaps and currency swaps are the two major types of swaps. In a currency swap, one party exchanges a stream of payments in one currency for another. The growth in the swap market is huge and the total value of outstanding swap agreements amounts to trillions of dollars.

11.5.4 Options

In forward and futures contracts both the buyer and the seller have the obligation to honour their side of the contract. An *option* is the right of an option holder to buy or sell a specific asset on predetermined terms on, or before, a future date (CIMA *Official Terminology*, 2005).

A European style option is an option that can be exercised only at the expiration date (CIMA *Official Terminology*, 2005).

An American style option is an option that can be exercised at any time prior to expiration (CIMA *Official Terminology*, 2005).

The right granted to the option holder attracts a fee called the *option premium*. There are two types of options, a call option and a put option.

A *call option* is the option to buy a specified underlying asset at a specified price on, or before, a specified exercise date (CIMA *Official Terminology*, 2005).

A *put option* is the option to sell a specified underlying asset at a specified price on, or before, a specified exercise date (CIMA *Official Terminology*, 2005).

Option contracts, both calls and puts, are available on a wide range of underlying assets. There are stock options where the underlying asset being traded is a company stock, currency options where the asset being traded is a foreign currency or interest-rate options where the underlying asset is interest rate. Some options are traded on organised exchanges but other option contracts can be arranged in the OTC market.

Options can also be used by companies to manage exposure to the underlying asset. As the option gives the right but not the obligation to buy or sell the underlying asset, it can be used to reduce the downside risk whilst leaving the potential to benefit from favourable movements in the price of the underlying asset.

Payoff profile of a call option

Suppose, instead of entering into a forward contract to buy cocoa, the UK confectioner buys a 6-month call option on cocoa at a strike price of £2,000 per ton, for a premium of £50 per ton. The premium is paid upfront but the UK confectioner has the right but not the obligation to buy the cocoa at £2,000 per ton in 6 months' time. If the price of cocoa is £2,100 in 6 months' time, the option will be exercised and the UK confectioner would realise a net gain of £50, considering the premium paid for the option (£2,100 – £2,000 – £50). On the other hand if the price of cocoa in 6 months' time is £1,900, the option will not be exercised, but given the premium paid the UK confectioner would lose £50. For prices lower than or equal to £2,000, the UK confectioner loses only the premium paid. A call option can thus be used to lock in to a maximum cost. Tables 11.3 and 11.4 show the profit/loss for the buyer and writer, respectively, of the call option.

Figure 11.2 illustrates the gains and the losses of the buyer and writer of the call option. The loss of the buyer is limited to the premium paid but the gains are unlimited and depend on the price of the underlying asset (in this case cocoa) at the expiration of the contract. On the other hand, the gains of the writer are limited to the premium received but the losses are unlimited.

Table 11.3 Gain/loss of the buyer of the call option

Cocoa price at maturity	Gain/(loss) on contract	Premium paid	Net gain/(loss)
1600	0	50	(50)
1700	0	50	(50)
1800	0	50	(50)
1900	0	50	(50)
2000	0	50	(50)
2100	100	50	50
2200	200	50	150
2300	300	50	250
2400	400	50	350

Table 11.4 Gain/loss of the writer of the call option

Cocoa price at maturity	Gain/(loss) on contract	Premium paid	Net gain/(loss)
1600	0	50	50
1700	0	50	50
1800	0	50	50
1900	0	50	50
2000	0	50	50
2100	(100)	50	(50)
2200	(200)	50	(150)
2300	(300)	50	(250)
2400	(400)	50	(350)

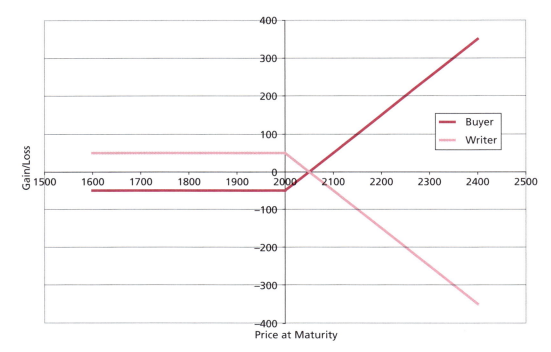

Figure 11.2 Payoff profile of a call option

Table 11.5 Gain/loss of the buyer of the put option

Cocoa price at maturity	Gain/(loss) on contract	Premium paid	Net gain/(loss)
1600	400	40	360
1700	300	40	260
1800	200	40	160
1900	100	40	60
2000	0	40	(40)
2100	0	40	(40)
2200	0	40	(40)
2300	0	40	(40)
2400	0	40	(40)

Payoff profile of a put option

Suppose, instead of using the forward market the cocoa merchant buys a put option on cocoa at a strike price of £2,000 per ton, for a premium of £40 per ton. This offers the cocoa merchant the right but not the obligation to sell cocoa at £2,000 per ton in 6 months' time. If the price of cocoa is £2,100 in 6 months' time, the put option will not be exercised and the cocoa merchant would lose £40 being the premium paid upfront. On the other hand, if the price of cocoa in 6 months' time is £1,900, the option will be exercised and considering the premium paid, the cocoa merchant would realise a net gain of £60 (£2,000 – £1,900 – £40). Tables 11.5 and 11.6 show the gain/loss of the buyer and seller of the put option at different prices.

Figure 11.3 illustrates the payoff profile of the buyer and writer of the put option. The loss of the buyer is limited to the premium paid and the maximum gain occurs when the price of the underlying falls to zero. Once again, note that the gains of the buyer are the losses of the seller and vice versa.

Table 11.6 Gain/loss of the seller of the put option

Cocoa price at maturity	Gain/(loss) on contract	Premium received	Net gain/(loss)
1600	(400)	40	(360)
1700	(300)	40	(260)
1800	(200)	40	(160)
1900	(100)	40	(60)
2000	0	40	40
2100	0	40	40
2200	0	40	40
2300	0	40	40
2400	0	40	40

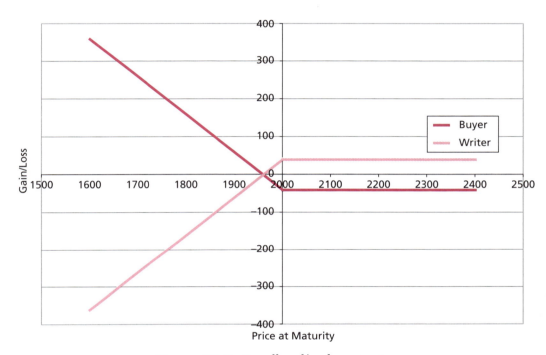

Figure 11.3 Payoff profile of a put option

Call and put options can be used to lock in to a maximum cost or a minimum income but unlike forward and futures, they also offer the opportunity to benefit from favourable price movements.

11.5.5 Uses of derivatives

The common reasons for using derivatives are to hedge risks, to speculate or to lock in an arbitrage profit. The directors of an organisation will need to determine their goals and attitude to risk and decide how the use of derivatives would meet their needs.

- *Hedging* involves the reduction or elimination of financial risk by passing that risk on to someone else. The person that takes on the risk acts as a speculator, and in the financial markets it is the trader or dealer in a financial institution with whom one carries out the hedging activity. The treasurer will normally be involved only in hedging activities and will not be a speculator or an arbitrageur. This is typical of a cost centre treasury since its overall objective is risk minimisation. As an example, Sainsbury's 2005 Annual Report states that 'Group policy permits the use of derivative instruments but only for reducing exposures arising from underlying business activity and not for speculative purposes.'

- *Speculation* is where a view is taken of the market and the speculator hopes to make a profit by pre-judging the direction in which the underlying asset will move. A classic example of this would be buying a foreign currency and hoping that the currency will appreciate. The speculator takes on risk by buying the currency because he or she does not know whether the currency will appreciate or depreciate.
- *Arbitrage* is the simultaneous purchase and sale of a security in different markets with the aim of making a risk-free profit through the exploitation of any price difference between the markets (CIMA *Official Terminology*, 2005).

For instance, it may be possible to buy virtually instantaneously a security from one source at, say, £4, and to sell them on elsewhere at £4.10. This activity is normally carried out by market professionals who spend their day dealing in the markets. The activity of arbitrageurs helps to keep prices for similar financial instruments more similar around the world.

These three categories can be summarised with reference to risk:

1. a speculator seeks or takes on risks;
2. an arbitrageur is risk-neutral;
3. a hedger avoids or reduces risk by passing it on to someone else.

11.5.6 Derivatives and financial reporting

There are special accounting provisions that relate to the corporate use of derivatives and other financial instruments. It is important for you to appreciate the demands of these provisions if you are going to be involved in derivative transactions.

In the United States, accounting for derivatives and hedge instruments is governed by the Financial Accounting Standards Board Standard No. 133 (FASB 133). The FASB 133 requires that all derivative instruments whether they are assets or liabilities should be disclosed on the company's balance sheet at fair value. Similar standards have been issued by the International Accounting Standards Board (See for example IAS 39 *Financial Instruments: Recognition and Measurement* and IFRS 7 *Financial Instruments: Disclosures*. These are to ensure greater transparency about the risks that companies suffer in the use of financial instruments. It is expected that these disclosures will provide better information for investors and other users of financial statements to make informed decisions about risk and return.

The main issues are that

- all financial assets and financial liabilities, including derivatives, are to be recognised on the balance sheet at fair market value. This means that financial instruments such as swaps, which may have been off-balance sheet previously, would have to be recognised and marked to market.
- changes in the fair market values of financial instruments are to be recognised in the income statement for the period.

These rules also apply to embedded derivatives. These are derivatives embedded in other financial instruments or other contracts. For example, a contract by an airline company to purchase aviation fuel at a fixed price for delivery at a future date contains an embedded derivative. It is therefore important that contracts are assessed for any embedded derivatives.

The IAS 39 also provides for different treatments in accounting for derivatives used for hedging and derivatives used for trading purposes. For hedge accounting to be used there must be a highly effective hedging relationship between the derivative instrument and the underlying exposure it is required to offset. Any derivative that does not meet these criteria should be classified as being held for trading purposes. Where derivatives are held for trading purposes, all realised and unrealised gains and losses (resulting from changes in the fair value) need to be recognised in the period in which they occur. Furthermore, the implementation of these reporting standards may possibly have significant implications for share price volatility, especially for companies using derivatives and derivative-embedded instruments. As the fair values of financial instruments fluctuate from one period to another, these could lead to increased volatility of reported earnings, and hence increased share price volatility as investors incorporate earnings information into share price valuation. It is also argued that disclosures of fair value impairments could be misunderstood leading to further risks, especially for financial institutions. In this regard, fair value accounting has been blamed in recent times, albeit unfairly, for contributing to the current financial crisis.

11.6 Summary

This chapter examines some key issues in financial risk management and introduces the basic derivatives contracts: forwards, futures, swaps and options. Financial risk management has become increasingly important to corporate treasurers. We have examined why companies hedge and how the financial risk management process can be managed. Although hedging risk is the primary use of derivatives by corporate treasurers, derivatives can also be used for speculation and arbitrage. Corporate treasurers using derivatives should take into consideration the valuation, monitoring and reporting issues in using derivatives.

Revision Questions 11

This chapter simply introduces the background and various concepts required to understand the subsequent chapters on managing interest-rate and foreign-exchange risks. The questions below are self-review questions designed to remind students what they have studied in the chapter and to check their own understanding. Check your answers to these questions against the relevant sections of the text.

❓ Question 1

What are the main areas of concern for the corporate treasurer?
  (Check your answer against Section 11.3 – The treasury function)

❓ Question 2

Identify and explain the arguments for and against hedging corporate financial risk exposure.
  (Check your answer against Section 11.4.1 – Why do companies manage financial risk?)

❓ Question 3

Identify and evaluate the alternative methods of quantifying risk.
  (Check your answer against Table 11.1 – Comparing the alternative approaches)

❓ Question 4

Identify and explain the four basic types of derivatives.
  (Check your answer against Section 11.5 – Introduction to derivatives)

❓ Question 5

Identify and explain the different ways in which derivatives may be used.
  (Check your answer against Section 11.5.5 – Uses of derivatives)

12

Interest Rate Management

Interest Rate Management

12

LEARNING OUTCOMES

After completing this chapter you should be able to:

▶ identify and evaluate interest-rate risks facing an organisation;

▶ identify and evaluate appropriate methods for managing interest-rate risk;

▶ demonstrate how and when to convert fixed-rate to floating-rate interest;

▶ evaluate the effects of alternative methods of interest-rate risk management such as swaps, forward-rate agreements, futures, options and swaptions, and make appropriate recommendations.

12.1   Introduction

The main purpose of this chapter is to introduce interest-rate risk management. Interest-rate risk has received increased attention as an important source of corporate risk in recent times. Interest-rate movements may affect present and future cash flows of the company. We begin by examining the various sources of interest-rate risks and their impact on the company. We then examine how these risks can be managed using a range of interest-rate management techniques including the use of interest-rate products such as forward-rate agreements, interest-rate swaps, futures and options. The chapter concludes with a brief summary.

12.2   Sources of interest-rate risk

Interest-rate risk can be defined as the risk to the profitability or value of a company resulting from changes in interest rates. Fluctuations in interest rates may affect different companies in different ways but almost every company is affected by changes in interest rates.

A company's debt or an investment of surplus funds can be made at a fixed rate of interest or at a floating (variable) rate. A fixed rate debt (or investment) offers a fixed interest payment (or receipt), say 8 per cent per annum, whereas the interest payment (or receipt) of a floating-rate debt (or investment) varies through the life of the loan (or investment). Floating rates are usually expressed as a given percentage over an agreed reference rate and are reset at regular intervals, usually every 3–6 months. For example, a floating interest rate may be quoted as LIBOR + 3 per cent. LIBOR is an acronym for the London Interbank Offer Rate, an important reference rate in the financial market.

For a floating-rate debt (or investment), changes in short-term interest rates can have a significant impact on the interest paid on the debt (or interest received on the investment). Whilst rising interest rates increase the cost of borrowing, falling interest rates reduce interest income from the investment. Thus, although a floating-rate debt (investment) provides some flexibility, the company may lose out if interest rates rise in the case of the debt (or if interest rate falls in the case of the investment).

Fixed rates, on the other hand, provide certainty as interest payments or receipts are known regardless of future interest-rate movements. However, there are also risks associated with fixed-rate debts (or investments). Short-term fixed-rate debts (or investments) may have the same risks as floating-rate debts (or investments) if they are rolled over periodically. For long-term debts (or investments) the company risks being locked in to a high (low) interest rate, if interest rate falls (or rises) in the future.

Thus companies may face interest-rate risks from the interest-rate sensitivity of their debts and/or from the interest-rate sensitivity of their investments. However, for most non-financial companies the risks from interest-rate sensitivity of their debts would outweigh the risks from their investments.

In addition, interest-rate movements can impact indirectly on present and future cash flows. For example, an increase in interest rates could adversely affect the business if customers are reluctant to make purchases in a high-interest-rate environment because they have less disposable income or it increases the time it takes its customers to pay for goods supplied. Examples from the real estate industry suggest that demand for housing declines with increases in interest rates.

Companies may also suffer from high interest rates if suppliers increase their prices to cover the increase in their funding costs but the extent will vary from one company to another. For example, a supermarket may notice its costs rising in a high-interest-rate environment, but it is unlikely to lose its customer base. A luxury-goods maker, on the other hand, would be in a worse position. As interest rates rise, input costs will rise as well as its funding costs; at the same time the higher interest rates may encourage consumers to postpone their purchases on non-essential goods. Thus, the luxury-goods manufacturer is likely to be highly sensitive to interest-rate rises and will have more to gain from managing effectively its interest costs.

Generally, the impact of interest rates on the business will depend on the choice of funding:

- the mix between equity capital and debt
- the mix between fixed- and floating-rate debt
- the mix between short-term and long-term debt.

In any case, business needs to pay as little interest as possible on the liability or funding side, and earn as much as possible on the asset or deposit side. Companies should choose a funding structure that suits their business requirements and operations.

12.3 Fixed versus floating interest rates

As discussed above, it is important to recognise that there are inherent risks in both fixed-rate and floating-rate exposures. There are a number of factors that need to be considered when deciding between fixed-rate and floating-rate instruments (debt or investment). These include

- expectation of future interest-rate movements. If interest rates are expected to fall, a floating rate would be more attractive to a borrower.
- term of the loan or investment. Interest-rate changes would be easier to predict in the short-term than in the long-term.
- differences between the fixed rate and the floating rate.
- company policy and risk appetite.
- existing levels and mix of interest-rate exposure. Adequate mix of fixed- and floating-rate instruments ensures diversification of interest rate exposure and acts as a natural hedge.

12.4 Internal hedging techniques

Although a number of financial products are available for managing interest-rate risk, the company may not always hedge their exposure or, in certain cases, may use various operating (internal) strategies to reduce exposure to interest rates. To hedge or not to hedge depends on a number of factors including

- the company's objectives
- the risk profile and risk appetite of the company
- the resources including personnel, time and money available for the risk management function
- availability of appropriate products
- the amount of exposure compared to the size of the company. An exposure of £1,000,000 may be considered insignificant by a company with £20 billion in assets, for example
- the treasurer has a strong view that rates are going to move in their favour
- the cost of hedging. The treasurer may choose not to hedge if the cost appears too high relative to the exposure.

Operating or internal hedging strategies for managing interest-rate risk involve restructuring the company's assets and liabilities in a way that it minimises interest-rate exposure. These include

- *Smoothing*: The company tries to maintain a certain balance between its fixed-rate and floating-rate borrowing. The portfolio of fixed- and floating-rate debts thus provides a natural hedge against changes in interest rates.
- *Matching*: The company matches its assets and liabilities to have a common interest rate. If a company borrows to finance an investment receiving a floating interest rate, the loan will be taken at floating interest rate.
- *Netting*: In netting the company aggregates all positions, both assets and liabilities to determine the net exposure. If a company has interest bearing investments of, say, £50 million and a loan of, say, £100 million, then the company would only hedge the net exposure of £50 million as the interest-rate risk on the investment would offset the risk on the loan.

Example 12.A Mark and Spencer's funding and interest rate hedging policy

The Group's funding strategy is to ensure a mix of financing methods offering flexibility and cost effectiveness to match the requirements of the Group ... Interest rate risk primarily occurs with the movement of sterling interest rates in relation to the Group's floating rate financial assets and liabilities. Group policy for interest rate management is to maintain a mix of fixed and floating rate borrowings. Interest rate risk in respect of debt on the balance sheet is reviewed on a regular basis against forecast interest costs and covenants. A number of interest rate swaps have been entered into to redesignate fixed and floating debt.

On the whole, internal hedging strategies work well if the company operates a centralised treasury system. In spite of the benefits of internal hedging, companies, particularly non-financial companies, are limited in the amount of interest-rate risk they can manage using internal methods. It is, therefore, often necessary to use derivative (external) hedging techniques in managing interest-rate exposure. These are discussed in the next section.

12.5 Derivatives (external) hedging techniques

An enterprise may wish to take precautions against interest rates moving up or down in the future, or may wish to change the existing structure of its funding or deposits, for instance from a fixed rate of interest to a floating rate. With the development of the financial markets and, in particular, the financial derivatives markets, a number of derivative instruments have arisen which allow the treasurer to hedge interest-rate risk. We examined derivatives in general in Chapter 11. This section looks at interest-rate derivatives – derivatives for which the underlying asset being traced is interest rate.

12.5.1 Interest-rate swaps

An interest-rate swap is simply the exchange of one stream of interest payments for another in the same currency. As an example, a company may have obtained funding through the issue, 3 years ago, of a 10-year debenture paying a fixed rate of interest of 10 per cent per annum. It may now be more suitable to its needs to pay an interest rate based on current market rates (usually the London interbank offer rate, LIBOR). As shown in Figure 12.1, instead of redeeming the debenture (if indeed possible) and obtaining floating-rate finance, it could simply undertake a 7-year swap (being the original 10 years less the 3 years already expired). It will pay the swaps counterparty a floating rate of interest based on LIBOR, on a notional principal, and receive a fixed amount of 10 per cent per annum on the same principal. The interest received from the swap will then be used to pay the interest due to the debenture holders. Thus, the company can synthetically manufacture its remaining 7-year, fixed-rate loan into one paying current market interest rates. It is much cheaper and easier for a treasurer to transact a swap than to renegotiate existing debt. Similarly, the company could have changed a floating-rate liability into a fixed-rate one, or a fixed- or floating-rate asset stream into a different cash flow profile. Interest-rate swaps are the most common interest-rate product used today. Note that the notional principal is not exchanged but only used in calculating the interest to be paid.

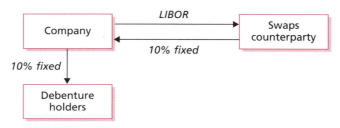

Figure 12.1 Interest-rate swaps

Example 12.B

Lockwood plc has a high credit rating. It can borrow at a fixed rate of 10% or at a variable interest rate of LIBOR + 0.3%. It would like to borrow at a variable rate.

Thomas plc has a lower credit rating. It can borrow at a fixed rate of 11% or at a variable rate of LIBOR + 0.5%. It would like to borrow at a fixed rate.

The information in Example 12.B can be summarised as

	Lockwood Plc	Thomas Plc	Quality spread
Fixed rate (%)	10	11	1
Floating rate	LIBOR + 0.3%	LIBOR + 0.5%	+0.2%
Quality spread differential (%)			0.8

The *quality spread* is the premium paid by the borrower with a low credit rating over the rate paid by the borrower with a high credit rating. Note that, in this example, Lockwood Plc with its high credit rating has absolute interest cost advantage in both the fixed- and floating-rate markets. However, Thomas Plc has a comparative advantage in the floating-rate market. The quality spread in the floating-rate market (0.2%) is not as wide as the spread in the fixed-rate market (1%). The quality spread differential (QSD) is the difference between the quality spreads in the fixed- and floating-rate markets. The QSD of 0.8% (or 80 basis points − 100 basis points equal 1%) is the benefit that would arise from any swap arrangement and could be shared among all parties including intermediaries such as banks. In this example, there is no intermediary and if the benefit (QSD) is shared equally each of the parties benefit by 0.4% (or 40 basis points). Note that the existence of a QSD is necessary for a swap to take place.

Thus, if each company borrows from the market where it has the comparative advantage, the total interest payment would be lower and both parties could benefit from a swap arrangement, whereby

(i) Lockwood plc borrows at a fixed rate of 10%;
(ii) Thomas plc borrows at a variable rate of LIBOR + 0.5%;
(iii) the parties agree a rate for swapping their interest commitments with, perhaps, Thomas plc paying a fixed rate of 10.1% to Lockwood plc, and Lockwood plc paying a variable rate of LIBOR to Thomas plc.

As illustrated in Figure 12.2, the outcome would be as follows:

Lockwood plc	
Borrows at	10%
Receives from Thomas plc	(10.1%)
Pays to Thomas plc	LIBOR
Net interest cost	LIBOR − 0.1% (a saving of 0.4%)

Thomas plc	
Borrows at	LIBOR + 0.5%
Receives from Lockwood plc	(LIBOR)
Pays to Lockwood plc	10.1%
Net interest cost	10.6% (a saving of 0.4%)

In this example, both companies benefit from lower interest costs. The example is shown in diagrammatical form in Figure 12.2.

So far, we have ignored the role of any intermediaries, for example swap brokers, in this arrangement or that there are no payments to the intermediary. Usually, there is an intermediary who arranges the swap between the

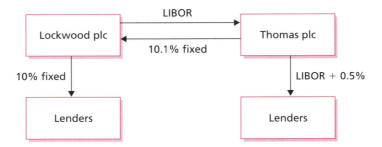

Figure 12.2 Interest-rate swaps (Example 12.B)

two parties for a fee. When interest rates are falling, the risk of default from the fixed rate payer under the swap (in this case Thomas Plc) is high, whereas the risk of default from the floating-rate payer (in this example Lockwood Plc) is high if interest rate continues to rise. Because of the risk of default, the credit worthiness of your counterparty in a swap arrangement is very important. The intermediary may be able to find you a suitable counterparty that matches your needs. The use of an intermediary also offers a choice of currencies, notional amount and maturity.

Now, suppose a swap broker charged a commission of 20 basis points for arranging the deal above. Then the quality spread differential of 0.8% would be shared among the three parties as follows: 0.2% to the swap broker, 0.3% to Lockwood Plc and 0.3% to Thomas Plc. With a saving of 0.3% each, the net interest cost for Lockwood Plc and Thomas Plc would be LIBOR and 10.7% respectively, as illustrated below.

Lockwood plc		
Borrows at	10%	
Receives from Swap dealer	(10%)	
Pays to Swap dealer	LIBOR	
Net interest cost	LIBOR	(a saving of 0.3%)
Thomas plc		
Borrows at	LIBOR + 0.5%	
Receives from Swap dealer	(LIBOR)	
Pays to Swap dealer	10.2%	
Net interest cost	10.7%	(a saving of 0.3%)

Figure 12.3 shows the transactions involved in diagrammatical form.

Figure 12.3 Swaps arrangement when the intermediary is paid 20 basis points

Interest-rate swaps are used for purposes other than exploiting comparative advantage of the parties in different markets to obtaining a cheaper financing rate. They could, for example, be used to

- change future cash flows by converting floating-rate interest payments (receipts) into fixed-rate interest payments (receipts) and vice versa. As in the case of Marks and Spencer in the example above, they use interest-rate swaps to redesignate fixed- and floating-rate debt (i.e. to change a floating-rate debt into a fixed and vice versa).

- enhance returns by taking a position on interest rates in the market. Note that the motivation in this case is purely speculative and could therefore increase instead of reducing risk.

The relative advantages of interest-rate swaps are that as an OTC product they can be customised to meet the company's needs in terms of amount and duration. It has lower transaction costs as no premiums are required compared to interest-rate options. Additionally, they are useful in hedging long-term exposures. On the other hand, as the swap arrangement is binding on both parties regardless of whatever happens in the future, the company is unable to benefit if interest rate moves in its favour. In spite of recent improvements in liquidity in the SWAP market, it has yet to mature to a point where all market participants can freely trade and unwind contracts of all maturities. As an OTC product, there is higher counterparty risk as the performance of the contract is not guaranteed. Trading in swaps is thus restricted to highly rated market participants. In addition, it could be difficult to liquidate the contract if the swap were no longer required. If a company wished to unwind its position it would have to enter into another swap that is equal but opposite to the original transaction. As swaps are not exchange-traded, sometimes it might be difficult to find a counterparty that is willing to take the other side of the transaction.

12.5.2 Forward-rate agreements

A forward-rate agreement (FRA) is an agreement whereby an enterprise can lock in an interest rate today for a period of time starting in the future. On the future date the two parties (the buyer and the seller) in the FRA settle up and, depending on which way rates go, one will pay an amount of money to the other representing the difference between the FRA rate and the actual rate.

The buyer of the FRA pays fixed and receives floating, whilst the seller pays floating to receive fixed. A company will buy FRAs to hedge against rising interest rates (the case of a net borrower) and sell FRAs to hedge against falling interest rates (the case of a net investor).

Example 12.C

Thompson plc has a £1m loan outstanding, on which the interest rate is reset every 6 months for the following 6 months, and the interest is payable at the end of that 6-month period.

The next 6-monthly reset period may now be just 3 months away, but the treasurer of Thompson plc thinks that interest rates are likely to rise between now and then. Current 6-month rates are 8% and the treasurer can get a rate of 8.1% for a 6-month FRA starting in 3 months' time. By transacting an FRA the treasurer can lock in a rate of 8.1% today. If interest rates rise as expected to, say, 9%, Thompson plc has reduced its interest charge as it will pay the current 9% rate on its loan but will receive from the FRA counterparty the difference between 9 and 8.1%.

If, however, rates drop to 7%, Thompson plc will still end up paying an effective rate of 8.1% because, although the interest rate on the loan is lower, the company will pay the FRA counterparty the difference between the 7 and the 8.1%.

If rates are 9% in 3 months' time,

	£
Interest payable on the loan 9% × £1m × $\frac{6}{12}$	45,000
Amount receivable on FRA (9% − 8.1%) × £1m × $\frac{6}{12}$	(4,500)
Net amount	40,500

The £40,500 is the net amount payable, giving an effective rate of 8.1%.

If rates are 7% in 3 months' time,

	£
Interest payable on the loan 7% × £1m × $\frac{6}{12}$	35,000
Amount payable on FRA (8.1% − 7%) × £1m × $\frac{6}{12}$	5,500
Net amount	40,500

The £40,500 is the net amount payable, again giving an effective rate of 8.1%.

The FRAs do not involve any actual lending or investment of the principal sum. They are agreements on interest rate only, and fix the rate payable or receivable on a notional principal amount.

The FRAs are usually for at least $1m (or equivalent in other major currencies). They are essentially a short-term hedging instrument, typically with a starting date of up to 12 months ahead and for a notional lending term of up to 1 year. They can be arranged for up to 2 or 3 years in the future, although swaps are more suitable for hedging interest rates for longer periods.

As in forward contracts, FRAs are OTC agreements negotiated individually with a bank, so they can create an exact hedge for both the amount and the timing of interest-rate exposure. FRAs, like interest rate futures, are binding agreements on both parties. However, because FRAs are not exchange-traded instruments they are less flexible to unwind compared to interest-rate futures.

12.5.3 Interest-rate futures

Interest-rate futures are standardised traded forms of FRAs, and the above FRA example could also have been used for an interest rate future. Table 12.1 summarises some of the differences between FRAs and interest-rate futures. The FRAs are normally transacted with banks and other financial institutions, and because of this they are tailor-made to suit the dates and amounts that each individual company requires. However, interest-rate futures are exchange traded and each contract is for a pre-specified amount and a pre-specified date. In the United Kingdom, interest-rate futures are traded on the London International Financial Futures and Options Exchange (LIFFE).

If a company does not need a specific amount or set dates, then futures are useful. For most organisations, however, they are not so convenient. There are also administrative and cash-flow problems associated with the use of interest-rate futures, as profits and losses are settled daily, which many organisations find burdensome. However, futures contracts are very liquid – it is easy to liquidate a contract. This is not so common with FRAs. In Example 12.C the treasurer could not have easily sold on his FRA if it was no longer required before it

Table 12.1 FRAs and futures compared

	FRAs	**Futures**
Amount	Any amount	Only standard round-sum amounts
Dates	Any dates	Only pre-specified dates – normally March, June, September and December
Payments	One only on settlement date	Initial and thereafter daily variation margin payments
Delivery	As per contract	Most are liquidated before maturity
Credit	With the counterparty	Very limited risk because of margin payments and the exchange acts as buyer and seller of every contract
Market	OTC	Exchange traded

matures, but would have needed to take out a second FRA with the reverse effect of the first. However, in practice many organisations use FRAs; relatively few use interest-rate futures.

Interest-rate futures can be grouped into two types:

1. short-term interest-rate futures (shorts).
2. long-term interest-rate futures (bond futures).

The underlying item for short-term interest-rate futures is a notional money market deposit (typically a 3-month deposit) or a standard quantity of money market instruments (e.g. $1m of 90-day US Treasury bills). The underlying item for long-term interest-rate futures is a standard quantity of notional government bonds (e.g. £50,000 (nominal value) of notional 9 per cent UK government bonds).

Pricing interest-rate futures

The price of short-term interest-rate futures reflects the interest rate on the underlying financial instrument, and is quoted at a discount to a par value of 100. A price of 96.40, for example, would indicate that the underlying money market instrument is being traded at a rate of 3.6 per cent per annum (i.e. $100 - 96.40$).

The price of long-term interest-rate futures reflects market prices of the underlying notional bonds. A price of 100 equals par (e.g. a price of £100 for bonds with a nominal value of £100). The interest rate is implied in the price. For example, if a long-term 9 per cent notional gilt futures contract has a price of 118.00, the implied interest rate on long-term sterling bonds is approximately $\frac{100}{118} \times 9\% = 7.7$ per cent per annum.

Ticks

The minimum amount by which the price of an interest-rate futures contract can move is called a tick, which has a known and measurable value.

The minimum price movement for a short-term interest-rate future is 0.01 which means that if the price of the interest-rate future were to be 96.40 (i.e. an implied interest rate of 3.60%) then the minimum price movement would be 96.41 (implied rate of 3.59%) or 96.39 (implied rate of 3.51%). Thus the minimum price change of 0.01 is equivalent to a minimum change of 0.01% or 1 basis point in the implied interest rate. In the case of a 3-month sterling future, the amount of the underlying instrument is a £500,000, 3-month deposit. As a tick is 0.01 (i.e. an implied interest rate of 0.01%), the value of a tick can be calculated as

$$£500,000 \times 0.01\% \times \frac{3}{12} = £12.50$$

(Note: Tick size of Short Sterling futures was reduced from 1 basis point to 0.5 basis points in March 2008 but this is expected to move back to 1 basis point soon)

With the move towards decimalisation, the minimum price movement for most long-term interest-rate futures is also 0.01 (i.e. 0.01%). For example, the tick size (previously quoted in fractions) for UK long gilts futures traded on Euronext-Liffe is 0.01 with a notional contract size of £100,000. The value of a tick of long gilt is therefore $£100,000 \times 0.01\% = £10$.

Example 12.D

The December 3-month sterling futures price rose from 95.90 to 96.55. Ateyo plc has a long position (a buyer) of ten of these contracts. What is the profit or loss for the company on the futures contracts?

Solution

Increase in price (96.55 − 95.90) = 0.65	65 ticks
Value of one tick	£12.50
Increase in value of one contract (65 × £12.50)	£812.50

Ateyo plc is a buyer of ten contracts and would gain £8,125.00 (=£812.50 × 10).

Example 12.E

The September long gilts contract rose in price from 118.31 to 119.12. Kazloui plc has a short position (a seller) of twenty of these contracts. What is the profit or loss for the company on the futures contracts?

Solution

Increase in price (119.12 − 118.31)	81 ticks
Value of one tick	£10.00
Increase in value of one contract (81 × £10.00)	£810.00

Kazloui plc is a seller of twenty contracts and would lose £16,200 (= £810 × 20)

Hedging using interest-rate futures

Notice that the price of interest-rate futures increases if interest rate falls and the price falls if interest rate rises. As a result, short-term interest-rate futures can be used to lock in to an interest rate for short-term borrowing by selling futures. Companies expecting to invest or lend can lock in a short-term rate by buying futures.

Example 12.F

Kolb plc expects to borrow £5m for 3 months, starting next month in early December, and expects to pay interest at LIBOR plus 0.5%. The company wishes to use 3-month sterling futures to hedge the exposure to increasing interest rates.

Kolb plc sells ten December 3-month sterling futures at a price of 96.26 (ten contracts × £500,000 per contract = £5m). Kolb plc subsequently closes the position in early December at a price of 95.55. At the same time the company borrows £5m at 4.95%, which is the current 3-month LIBOR rate of 4.45 plus 0.5%.

Kolb plc has locked in an interest rate of 3.74% (=100 − 96.26) for LIBOR for its £5m loan through selling ten December 3-month sterling futures at a price of 96.26. The total interest rate of LIBOR plus 0.5% is therefore 4.24% (=3.74 + 0.5).

The interest cost for a 3-month loan of £5m at 4.24% would be

$$£5m \times 4.24\% \times \tfrac{3}{12} = £53,000$$

In early December, Kolb plc borrows £5m at 4.95% and will pay interest of £61,875 (£5m × 4.95% × $\tfrac{3}{12}$). This is offset by the profit made on its futures position:

Decrease in price (96.26 − 95.55) = 0.71	71 ticks
Value of one tick	£12.50
Decrease in value of one contract (71 × £12.50)	£887.50

Kolb plc is a seller of ten contracts and would gain £8,875 (=£887.50 × 10).
The net cost of borrowing is therefore

Interest payable	£61,875
Profit on futures	(£8,875)
	£53,000

This is equal to borrowing £5m for 3 months at 4.24%, the rate locked in by the original futures transaction.

In practice it is often not possible to achieve a perfect hedge with interest-rate futures. Interest rates that are reflected in the price of futures may differ from interest rates in the 'cash market', due to speculation or arbitrage activities. This is called *basis risk*.

In Example 12.F, we have assumed that the interest rate on the cash market, 4.45 per cent, is the same interest rate reflected in the futures price. Suppose the futures closed at 95.70, instead of 95.55, reflecting an interest rate of 4.3 per cent. The difference between the interest rate on the cash market and the rate reflected in the futures price creates a basis risk. Mismatches between the maturity on the cash market and the futures market would also cause basis risk.

Hedge efficiency measures how successful a hedge instrument offsets the underlying risk. In the example above, suppose the futures price in December reflects LIBOR. Thus LIBOR equals 3.74 per cent. If LIBOR rose to 4.45 in 3 months, then Kolb would lose (4.95% − 4.24%) × £5m × 3/12 = £8,875. This is exactly matched by the profit on the futures market of £8,875 yielding a hedge efficiency of (8,875 ÷ 8,875) × 100 = 100 per cent. If, on the other hand, the futures closed at 95.70, instead of 95.55, then the gains from the futures contract would be £7,000 (i.e. 56 ticks × £12.50 × 10 contracts). In this case the hedge efficiency is (7,000 ÷ 8,875) × 100 = 78.9%. The hedge efficiency is low if basis risk is high.

Hedge efficiency would also be affected if the underlying exposure is not a perfect multiple of the futures contract size. As with all futures contracts, the need to trade in standardised contract sizes makes it difficult to achieve a perfect hedge.

Example 12.G

In example 12F the underlying amount (£5m) was a perfect multiple of the contract size for sterling futures (£500,000). Now suppose the underlying amount was £4.8m instead of £5m.
   Then number of futures contract required = £4.8m/500,000 = 9.6.

Cash market:

   The interest cost of borrowing £4,800,000 × 4.95% × $\frac{3}{12}$ = £59,400

On the futures market:

   Sell December contracts at 96.26
   Buy December contracts at 95.55
   Gain in price = (96.26 − 95.55) = 71 ticks
   Gain per contract = 71 × £12.50 = £887.50
   Total Gain on the futures = 9 × £887.50 = £7,987.50

Thus the effective interest payable is £59,400 − £7,987.50 = 51,412.50
If LIBOR rose to 4.45 in 3 months, then Kolb would lose (4.95% − 4.24%) × £4.8m × $\frac{3}{12}$ = £8,520. Compared with the profit from the futures market, the hedge offsets 93.75% (7,987.50/8,520) of the additional cost. Thus the hedge efficiency in this case is about 94%.

In calculating the number of contracts required in Examples 12.F and 12.G, we have made two implicit assumptions: (1) that the interest rate on the hedge instrument (LIBOR) and the underlying exposure are the same and (2) that the period of the exposure (3 months) matches the maturity of the hedge instrument (also 3 months in this case). Where either of the two or both conditions are not met, then adjustments should be made to take account of the mismatch.

Example 12.H

Suppose now, Kolb plc expects to borrow £5m for 4 months (instead of 3 months as in Example 12.F), starting next month in early December, and expects to pay interest at LIBOR plus 0.5%. The company wishes to use

3-month sterling futures to hedge the exposure to increasing interest rates. Suppose Kolb plc sells December 3-month sterling futures at a price of 96.26 and subsequently closes the position in early December at a price of 95.55. At the same time the company borrows £5 m at 4.95%, which is the current 3-month LIBOR rate of 4.45 plus 0.5%.

In this case there is a mismatch in the period of exposure and the futures maturity. The number of contracts required to hedge the exposure will be:

$$\frac{\text{Underlying Exposure}}{\text{Futures contract size}} \times \frac{\text{Period of Exposure}}{\text{Futures maturity}} = \frac{5,000,000}{500,000} \times \frac{4}{3} = 13.33$$

Kolb plc will thus sell 13 sterling interest rate futures to hedge this exposure.
The interest cost of the 4-month loan is:

$$£5,000,000 \times 4.95\% \times \frac{4}{12} = £82,500$$

This is then offset by the profit made on its futures position:

Decrease in price (96.26 − 95.55) = 0.71	= 71 ticks
Value of one tick	£12.50
Decrease in value of one contract (71 × £12.50)	= £887.50

Kolb plc is a seller of 13 contracts and would gain £11,537.50 (= £887.50 × 13).
The net cost of borrowing is therefore:

Interest payable	£82,500.00
Profit on futures	(£11,537.50)
	£70,962.50

Thus the effective interest payable is £70,962.50. The effective annualised interest rate achieved is therefore 4.32%. That is:

$$\left(1 + \frac{£70,962.5}{£5,000,000}\right)^{12/4} - 1 = 0.0432 \text{ or } 4.32\%$$

If LIBOR were to remain at 3.74%, the interest cost on the 4-month loan would have been:

$$£5,000,000 \times 4.24\% \times \frac{4}{12} = £70,667$$

Therefore, Kolb plc would have lost (£82,500 − £70,667) = £11,833. This loss is offset by the gain of £11,537.50 on the futures contract. Hence the hedge efficiency in this case is 97.5% (i.e. 11,537.50/11.833).

If Kolb had used only 10 contracts (instead of the 13) they would have gained only £8,875. In that case, given the 4-month exposure, the efficiency of the hedge would be 75% (i.e. 8,875/11,833).

12.5.4 Interest-rate options

> 🔑 An option is the right, but not the obligation, to carry out a transaction at a price set today, at some time in the future. Swaps, FRAs and futures are all contracts which two parties agree to transact and which must be carried out even if circumstances change. An option, however, gives the buyer the choice of whether to transact or not. A company would generally buy an option from an option seller. An option is a form of insurance, and as such a premium is paid at the time the option is taken out, for the period of the option.

Example 12.I

Let us suppose that instead of buying the FRA in Example 12.C, an option was bought, entitling the buyer of the option to pay the same interest rate of 8.1%. This is known as the strike price. The period of the option is for 3 months, which is when the renewal period for the loan starts. Suppose that the option premium paid today is £1,000. In 3 months' time we could have the same two scenarios.

If rates are 9% in 3 months' time,

	£
Interest payable on the loan 9% × £1m × $^6/_{12}$	45,000
Exercise the option at a strike price of 8.1%, receive	(4,500)
Plus premium paid	1,000
Net amount	41,500

If the rates are 7% in 3 months' time,

	£
Interest payable on the loan 7% × £1m × $^6/_{12}$	35,000
Plus premium paid	1,000
Net amount	36,000

Thus, if interest rates are 9% in 3 months' time, Thompson plc will pay a net amount of £41,500 in interest over the 6-month period, which is more than with the FRA because of the option premium. However, if rates fall to 7%, only £36,000 will be paid, as the company does not need to exercise the option. An option is thus not quite so favourable relative to FRAs and interest rate futures when rates go as expected, but much better when rates move in the opposite direction. Thus, with an option a company can take advantage of favourable interest-rate movements.

Caps, floors and collars

Caps, floors and collars are longer-term interest-rate options, which potentially appeal to borrowers with medium-term floating-rate loans or lenders with medium-term variable-rate deposits.

Example 12.J

A company can currently borrow at 11%, but is concerned that interest rates may rise in the near future to 14% or more.

In this situation the company could buy an interest-rate cap from a bank which will fix the maximum rate for borrowing. The bank will reimburse the company if market interest rates rise above the cap rate. As part of the arrangement, the company may also agree that it will pay a floor rate of, say, 10%. The bank will pay a premium to the company for agreeing to this floor rate.

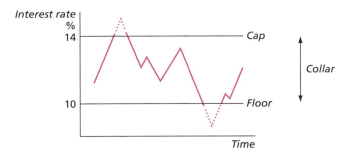

Figure 12.4 Caps, floors and collars

Exchange-traded interest-rate options

The options described above are all OTC options, negotiated individually with a bank. The only exchange-traded interest-rate options are options on interest-rate futures, which give the holder the right to buy (call option) or sell (put option) a futures contract on or before the expiry of the option at a specified price. Options on interest-rate futures are traded on futures exchanges, such as LIFFE and the Chicago Mercantile Exchange (CME).

Options on futures are mainly used by banks to hedge their exposures in the futures markets. Companies could use options on futures as an alternative to buying or selling futures themselves. A company could buy a put option to lock into a maximum cost of borrowing rather than selling futures. Equally, a company could buy call options to lock into a minimum rate for investments as an alternative to buying futures.

12.5.5   Swaptions

A swaption is an option on a swap. It gives the holder of the swaption the right, but not the obligation, to enter into a swap agreement with the seller of the swaption, on or before a fixed future date. There are two basic types of swaptions: a payer swaption and a receiver swaption.

A 'payer' swaption when exercised gives the holder the right to enter the swap agreement as a fixed-rate payer whilst a 'receiver' swaption gives the holder the right to enter the swap agreement to receive fixed and pay floating-rate interest.

Swaptions can be bought to secure a worst-case interest rate for a future swap agreement. For example, a company that is planning to issue a floating-rate bond some time in the future can buy a payer swaption that offers the opportunity to convert the floating rate to fixed rate should interest rates rise. If the swaption is exercised, the company will pay the strike rate and receive floating under the swap. In this case the swaption guarantees a maximum interest payable. Similarly, a receiver swaption can be used to lock in a minimum interest rate receivable.

A swaption can also be used to effectively terminate an existing swap arrangement when exercised. Suppose a company has an existing swap arrangement in which it pays fixed, say 7 per cent, to receive floating but is concerned that interest rates may fall. The company can buy a receiver swaption at a strike rate of 7 per cent, which gives the company the right to enter into a swap as a floating-rate payer and receive 7 per cent fixed. The receiver swaption at the strike rate of 7 per cent when exercised will effectively terminate the company's swap arrangements.

12.5.6   Selecting a hedging method

The content of this chapter can be summarised using a comprehensive example, in which alternative methods of hedging interest-rate risk are evaluated.

Example 12.K

(a) It is 31 December 20X1 and the corporate treasurer of Omniown plc is concerned about the volatility of interest rates. His company needs in 3 months' time to borrow £5m for a 6-month period. Current interest rates are 14% per year for the type of loan that Omniown plc would use, and the treasurer does not wish to pay more than this. He is considering using (i) an FRA, (ii) interest-rate futures or (iii) an interest-rate option.

Requirement
Explain briefly how each of these three alternatives might be useful to Omniown plc.

(b) At 31 December 20X1, the corporate treasurers of Omniown plc expects interest rates to increase by two percentage points during the next 3 months, and has decided to hedge the interest-rate risk using interest-rate futures.
At March 20X2 sterling deposit futures are priced at 86.25. The standard contract size is £500,000, and the minimum price movement is one tick (the value of one tick is 0.01% per year of the contract size).

Requirements

Show the effect of using the futures market to hedge against interest-rate movements:
   (i) if interest rates increase by two percentage points and the futures market price also moves by two percentage points;
   (ii) if interest rates increase by two percentage points and the futures market moves by 1.5 percentage points;
   (iii) if interest rates fall by one percentage point and the futures market moves by 0.75 percentage points. In each case, estimate the hedge efficiency.

Taxation, margin requirements and the time value of money are to be ignored.

(c) If, as an alternative to interest-rate futures, the corporate treasurer had been able to purchase interest-rate guarantees at 14% for a premium of 0.2% of the size of the loan to be guaranteed, calculate whether the total cost of the loan after hedging in each of the situations (i)–(iii) in part (b) would have been less with the futures hedge or the guarantee. The guarantee would be effective for the entire 6-month period of the loan. Taxation, margin requirements and the time value of money are to be ignored.

Solution

(a) (i) Forward-rate agreements offer companies the facility to fix future interest rates on either borrowing or lending for a specific period. For example, a company might wish to invest £10m in 6 months' time at a guaranteed interest rate of 10% per year. The company might wish to enter into an FRA with a bank at the agreed rate of 10% per year, whereby if actual interest rates are lower than 10% the bank will pay the company the difference between 10% and the actual rate. If the interest rate is above 10%, then the company will have to compensate the bank for the difference between the actual rate and 10%. No matter what level market interest rates move to, the yield to the company remains at 10%. The FRAs do not involve any actual lending or investment of the principal sum. The FRAs are usually for at least US$ 1m (or equivalent in other major currencies) and can be arranged for up to 2 or 3 years in the future. As Omniown plc wishes to fix borrowing costs in 3 months' time, FRAs would be a suitable means of managing the interest-rate exposure. The actual borrowing of the £5m would need to be arranged separately from the FRA.

   (ii) Interest-rate futures are binding contracts between seller and buyer to make and take, respectively, delivery of a specified interest-rate commitment on an agreed date and at an agreed price. They can be used to protect against expected rises in interest rates by means of a 'short hedge', and are available for a maximum of 1–2 years. With a short hedge, futures contracts are sold now in the expectation that as interest rates rise the contract value will fall, and they can then be purchased at a lower price, generating a profit on the futures deal. This profit compensates for actual rises in interest rates experienced by companies that have borrowed funds from banks and elsewhere. If interest rates move in the opposite direction to that expected, a futures loss will occur but this will, to some extent, be offset by gains from cheaper interest costs in the cash market. Only a limited range of interest-rate futures contracts exist, the most important on LIFFE being 3-month sterling time deposits, 3-month Eurodollar, 20-year gilts and 20-year US government Treasury bonds. All contracts require a small initial deposit or margin. Interest-rate futures should allow Omniown plc to hedge successfully against most of the exposure from interest-rate movements, although 100% protection (a perfect hedge) is rare.

   (iii) Interest-rate options such as caps, collars and floors guarantee that the interest rate will not rise above (alternatively, fall below) an agreed fixed level during a specified period commencing some time in the near future. The interest-rate protection for a borrower worried about interest rates is, therefore, similar to that given by an FRA. However, there are major differences between interest-rate options and FRAs. Interest-rate options involve the payment of a premium to the seller of the option, whether or not the option is exercised. No premium is payable with an FRA (although interest compensation may be payable, as described above). The second major difference is that interest-rate options, while protecting against downside risk (i.e. an interest-rate rise for Omniown plc), offer the option holder the opportunity to take full advantage of favourable interest-rate movements. For example, if interest rates fall, the guarantee is not used and the company borrows in the cash market at the lower interest rate. Neither FRAs nor interest-rate futures allow the company to take full advantage of favourable interest-rate movements. Omniown could use an interest-rate guarantee to protect against rising interest rates but could still benefit if interest rates fall. However, the premium cost of interest-rate options is considered to be expensive by many companies.

(b) (i) The value of one tick is

$$0.0001 \times £500,000 \times \frac{3}{12} = £12.50$$

A movement of two percentage points is a 200-tick movement. Omniown needs to borrow £5m for 6 months. An expected increase of two percentage points in interest rates would result in extra interest costs of

$$£5m \times 2\% \times \frac{6}{12} = £50,000$$

Omniown plc needs to hedge with sufficient contracts to generate an expected £50,000 gain. A 200-tick movement on one contract would result in an expected gain of $200 \times £12.50$, or £2,500. For £50,000, a twenty-contract hedge would be required.

- 31 December 20X1: sell twenty £500,000 March sterling time-deposit contracts at 86.25 (effectively 13.75% per year interest).
- March 20X2 (or whenever interest rates have changed): buy twenty £500,000 March sterling time-deposit contracts at 84.25 (effectively, 15.75% per year interest).

This closes out the position. The gain is

$$20 \times 200 \text{ ticks} \times £12.50 = £50,000$$

or

$$£10m \text{ (i.e. twenty contracts)} \times 2\% \times \frac{3}{12} = £50,000$$

This is a perfect hedge with 100% hedge efficiency.

(ii) In this case the futures gain will be

$$20 \times 150 \text{ ticks} \times £12.50 = £37,500$$

or

$$£10m \times 1.5\% \times \frac{3}{12} = £37,500$$

This is a hedge efficiency of £37,500/£50,000, or 75%.

(iii) In this case there is a cash-market gain as interest rates fall, but a loss on the futures-market hedge. The cash-market gain is

$$£5m \times 1\% \times \frac{6}{12} = £25,000$$

The futures-market loss results from selling at 86.25 and closing out the position at 87.00. The loss is

$$20 \times 75 \text{ ticks} \times £12.50 = £18,750$$

or

$$£10m \times 0.75\% \times \frac{3}{12} = £18,750$$

This is a hedge efficiency of £25,000/£18,750, or 133%.

(c) The total costs with the futures hedge are

(i) Interest $£5m \times 16\% \times \frac{6}{12} = £400,000$, less gain £50,000 = £350,000
(ii) Interest £400,000, less gain £37,500 = £362,500
(iii) Interest $£5m \times 13\% \times \frac{6}{12} = £325,000$, plus loss £18,750 = £343,750

The cost (premium) of the guarantee is $£5m \times 0.2\% = £10,000$, payable whether or not the guarantee is 'exercised'.

The total cost with (i) and (ii) when the guarantee will be used and will limit interest rates to 14% is

$$£5m \times 14\% \times \frac{6}{12} = £350,000, \text{ plus } £10,000 \text{ premium} = £360,000$$

This is more expensive than the futures hedge for (i) and cheaper than for (ii).

The total cost for (iii), where the guarantee is not used and the interest rate is 13%, is

$$£5m \times 13\% \times \frac{6}{12} = £325,000, \text{ plus } £10,000 \text{ premium} = £335,000$$

This is cheaper than the futures hedge as the guarantee has allowed the company to take advantage of lower cash-market interest rates.

12.6 Summary

Interest-rate risk is a problem faced by all companies with gearing. Given the past volatility of interest rates, an awareness of the risks of interest-rate movements is important. In this chapter we have considered some of the influences on interest-rate movement, and identified a range of techniques that may be used to reduce exposure to interest-rate risk, such as interest-rate swaps, forward-rate agreements, futures, options and swaptions.

The advantages and disadvantages of the various instruments can be summarised as follows.

	FRA	FUTURES	SWAPS	OTC OPTIONS	EXCHANGE-TRADED OPTIONS
Exchange-traded product	✗	✓	✗	✗	✓
Can be customised to meet customer's needs in terms of amount and duration	✓	✗	✓	✓	✗
No upfront fees (premiums) to be paid	✓	✓	✓	✗	✗
Settlement at maturity – no intermediate cash flow problems	✓	✗	✓	✓	✓
Potential to benefit from favourable price changes	✗	✗	✗	✓	✓
Price transparency – availability of price information to enable clients determine best prices	✗	✓	✗	✗	✓
Lower counterparty (default) risk	✗	✓	✗	✗	✓
Easy to liquidate position – active greater liquidity secondary market ensures greater liquidity	✗	✓	✗	✗	✓

Note that the relative advantages and disadvantages of these products depend critically on two main issues:

1. whether the product is exchange-traded or OTC traded; and
2. whether the instrument provides certainty, such that regardless of whatever happens in the future the outcome is known, or it provides insurance such that it protects downside risk but offers the potential to benefit from favourable movements in which case an upfront fee (premium) is expected.

Revision Questions

❓ Question 1

Explain the term 'risk management' in respect of interest rates and discuss how interest-rate risk might be managed. **(8 marks)**

❓ Question 2

(a) Official statistics show that over the past 4–5 years, overdraft usage has been falling by around 5 per cent per annum and is being replaced by other forms of asset-based lending.

You are required to explain the main uses of overdraft facilities as part of a company's working capital management policy and discuss the alternative sources of finance which are available. **(10 marks)**

(b) The following comments were overhead at a recent conference of financial managers and directors:

(i) All our company's borrowings are at fixed rates of interest, so we do not have any interest-rate risk.'

(ii) 'A consultant's recent report has suggested we should investigate the use of derivatives to manage our interest-rate risk. My view is that derivatives are too risky.'

You are required to discuss the management of interest-rate risk. Include in your answer an explanation of why the comments quoted above might not necessarily be correct. **(10 marks)**

(Total marks = 20)

Questions 3 and 4 are taken from Paper 5 (Money Management) of the examinations of the Association of Corporate Treasurers (ACT).

Question 3

Games plc manufactures popular board games and toys for sale in the United Kingdom and continental Europe. Extracts from the last financial statements show the following:

	£m
Balance sheet	
Shareholders' funds	250
Long-term funding	200
Short-term funding	50
Profit and loss account	
Turnover	600
PBIT	50

The company has a loan covenant with PBIT/interest three times.

As treasurer, you are concerned about the effect of a possible rise in interest rates on the results of the company and are considering hedging the interest risk on a £100m floating-rate sterling loan (at 6-month LIBOR plus twenty basis points) for the next 2-year period.

Today is 1 January 20X1, a fixing date on the loan.

Hedging strategies under consideration:

(i) a 2-year 5.5 per cent cap against 6-month LIBOR at a premium of 0.5 per cent p.a.;
(ii) a 2-year zero-cost collar against 6-month LIBOR with a floor of 4.5 per cent and a cap of 6.5 per cent.

In order to assist in the evaluation of these hedging strategies, you have obtained the following forecast for 6-month LIBOR for the next 2 years.

LIBOR Six-month forecast

Requirements

(a) Explain what factors you would take into account, what additional information you would collect and how such information would be used in drawing up an interest-rate policy for this company. **(5 marks)**
(b) From the interest-rate forecast provided, identify the forecast rate for 6-month LIBOR at each interest-rate fixing date for the £100m loan in the calendar years 20X1 and 20X2. **(1 mark)**

(c) Use the rates calculated in part (b) to calculate the overall interest rate that would be achieved for the loan for each 6-month period in calendar years 20X1 and 20X2 for each of the following:

 (i) no-hedge scenario

 (ii) capped loan

 (iii) loan with collar hedge. **(6 marks)**

(d) Plot your results from part (c) onto two graphs, as follows:

 1. *Graph A*: capped loan and no-hedge scenario

 2. *Graph B*: loan with collar hedge and no-hedge scenario.

 Use your graphs to illustrate the success of each hedge strategy and discuss your findings. Which hedge strategy gives the best overall result? **(8 marks)**

(e) Explain whether the cap or collar would give the best result under each of the following outturn interest-rate scenarios:

 (i) low fluctuation in rates (5 ± 0.5%)

 (ii) highly volatile rates (up or down). **(5 marks)**

(Total marks = 25)

? Question 4

(a) Two companies are able to borrow at different rates as follows:

	Floating	*Fixed*
Big Widget	LIBOR + 0.5%	6%
Small Widget	LIBOR + 1.5%	8%

Construct a swap to show how these companies could co-operate to their mutual benefit while both are raising external funding. Assume that Big Widget requires floating-rate finance and Small Widget requires fixed-rate finance. Illustrate your answer by including a flowchart showing the cash flows involved. **(8 marks)**

(b) What are the pros and cons of arranging a swap through a bank as intermediary rather than with a counterparty directly? **(7 marks)**

(Total marks = 15)

? Question 5

Assume you are the financial manager with GH plc, a large, multinational company. The company wishes to raise finance to fund an increase in working capital requirements, caused by a decision to implement a more aggressive sales and marketing policy. Its current finance is largely US dollars–denominated although it has some borrowing in pounds sterling. The company treasurer believes there are advantages to borrowing at a floating rate of interest in the Eurobond market and entering into a swap arrangement with JJ plc, a UK-based company in the same industry but which, because of its smaller size, has a lower credit rating. JJ plc would prefer to borrow at fixed rates to finance an acquisition.

GH plc currently has a credit rating of AAA and is able to raise fixed-rate finance in the Eurobond market at 8.5 per cent and floating-rate finance at LIBOR + 0.5 per cent. The smaller company can raise fixed-rate finance at 10.5 per cent and floating-rate finance at LIBOR + 1.1 per cent. The swap will be arranged through GH plc's bank, which will charge fees of 0.15 per cent of the principal sums. The bank is suggesting the following swap terms to open negotiations:

- JJ plc will pay 9 per cent fixed to GH plc;
- GH plc will pay LIBOR + 0.0 per cent to JJ plc.

Requirements

(a) Discuss the advantages and disadvantages of fixed- and floating-rate finance in general and in the context of this scenario. Comment also on the advantages and disadvantages to GH plc of raising money in the Eurobond market as compared with the bond market in the United States. **(8 marks)**

(b) Discuss, in the context of the scenario, the principles and benefits of interest-rate swaps and the financial advantages to both GH plc and JJ plc that will result from the swap's interest-rate effects. **(12 marks)**

(c) GH plc currently invoices all its customers in US dollars. Assume it raises new finance in US dollars in the Eurobond market to fund its more aggressive sales and marketing policy. Discuss the implications for its invoicing policy. **(5 marks)**

(Total marks = 25)

Solutions to Revision Questions

12

✔ Solution 1

Interest-rate risk management requires a company treasurer to use techniques to reduce the risk to his company caused by its vulnerability to changes in interest rates and the need to pay higher returns to lenders. There are other risks – such as the possibility of rates increasing shortly before the launch of new capital – but these are matters for good judgement rather than risk management issues.

In respect of the management of rate changes during the life of a loan, there are three main techniques: interest-rate swaps, interest-rate options and interest-rate futures. These three techniques are commented on below. The company could also consider covering the risk itself and not managing it in an active way.

Interest-rate swaps

1. The ability to obtain finance, or cheaper finance than by borrowing directly in the market, if one company has a comparative advantage in terms of credit rating. This provides an arbitrage opportunity which can be shared by the participants to the swap.
2. Interest-rate commitments can be altered without redeeming old debt or issuing new debt, which is an expensive procedure.
3. Swaps can be developed to meet specific needs, and there are many innovative products on the markets – for example, zero-coupon swaps or 'swaptions'.

Interest-rate options

Where an organisation can arrange, for example, for a bank to purchase, lend or borrow at a guaranteed interest rate at some specified future time. A premium would be payable for this. If interest rates are adversely lower or higher than the guaranteed rate at the date of the option, the organisation can allow the option to lapse.

Interest-rate futures

The organisation buys or sells interest-rate futures. Interest-rate movements will be offset by the value of the futures.

INTEREST RATE MANAGEMENT

 # Solution 2

(a) The idea of an overdraft, originally, was to cover the normal fluctuations in a company's balance of payments. Neither receipts from customers nor payments to suppliers and employees rise at a steady rate, so operational cash flow is quite volatile. Add to this, such periodic payments as value added tax, corporation tax and dividends and it is clear that the company's capital requirement can vary considerably across one financial year.

Say, for example, that the requirement varies from £2m to £2.4m. The idea would be that the lower figure would be matched by long-term capital (shares, debentures, loans) and the balance by a fluctuating overdraft. Since it would reflect a movement in net current assets (e.g. higher debtors or stocks) the banks would classify it as low risk and therefore be prepared to lend at a relatively low interest rate. In some situations they might seek a floating charge over the current assets.

The other forms of short-term finance which are available are mainly asset-based. Perhaps the most well known is invoice discounting, in which a factoring company will advance 80 per cent of the face value of an invoice within 24 hours, subject to an interest charge at a similar level to overdrafts (reflecting the security, reinforced by the factor having the right to refuse to accept any accounts seen as doubtful). The attraction is that the facility increases automatically as sales increase, as opposed to having to negotiate a higher overdraft limit, but the reverse applies also.

Other forms are geared in a similar way to the level of investment in stock. A company which buys an annual crop, for example, can have it financed by a bank, paying only as the stock is used.

Finally, customers and suppliers can be a source of short-term funds, by agreeing (for a limited period) to pay earlier or accept payment later, respectively.

(b) Interest-rate risk arises from the uncertainty associated with the level of future interest rates. It is mainly thought of in terms of interest receivable or payable, but can also affect other aspects of the business (e.g. reduced demand, as a consequence of higher interest rates in the economy generally).

In respect of the two statements, the following comments apply:

(i) *Interest-rate risk*

If interest rates are fixed, they are by definition predictable. Thus, to the extent that borrowing requirements can be predicted, interest payments can be predicted with complete accuracy. However, there is more to risk than that.

Say, for example, that interest rates fell substantially. Competitors would find that a smaller proportion of their cash flows was pre-empted for the payment of interest, and their cost of capital would be reduced. This would make growth opportunities look more valuable. This could prompt them to lower their selling prices, or invest in volume building strategies (e.g. advertising and selling) which our company would feel it could not afford. We would lose market share and, probably, absolute volume making us less competitive and ushering in a downward spiral. A key step in financial strategy is therefore to ask what would be the consequences of significant changes in interest rates. If they are substantial, then methods of hedging should be considered.

(ii) *The use of derivatives*

Generally speaking, hedging mechanisms do not eliminate all risk, so much as to enable one to choose which risks to bear. Were we to negotiate fixed rates of interest, for example, that would give us protection against the possibility of interest-rate increases, but leave us vulnerable to falls (e.g. if we are competing with an organisation with variable rate borrowings).

It is for this reason that more elaborate hedging mechanisms have been developed. Options, for example, require some front-end investment (the premium) but then give the right but not the obligation to buy or sell. An option which effectively fixes interest payable, for example, will be exercised if interest rates increase but will be allowed to lapse if they go down. This sounds attractive but it is always worth noting the residual risk, for example, in this case, that premium is a cost which a competitor who chooses not to hedge will not bear, and is therefore a drag on competitiveness.

✓ Solution 3

(a) Factors to take into account:
- critical factor here is the three-times interest cover
- impact on bottom line
- treasury experience in handling derivatives.

Additional information:
- forecast PBIT for the next 2–5 years
- sensitivity of profit forecasts
- overall interest-rate profile of the company (effect of interest-rate changes on income stream and purchase and other costs)
- view on rate movements
- competitors' position.

The above information would be used
- to analyse impact of rate changes on results, including 'best' and 'worst' scenarios
- to determine risk appetite – to what extent is the group willing or able to accept certain risks
- to choose appropriate hedging instruments
- to set limits.

(b)

1 January 20X1	5.50%
1 July 20X1	7.00%
1 January 20X2	5.50%
1 July 20X2	3.50%

(c)

Period	*(i)* No hedge	*(ii)* Cap	*(ii)* Collar
1 Jan. 20X1	5.7 (5.5 + 0.2)	6.2 (5.5 + 0.5 + 0.2)	5.7 (5.5 + 0.2)
1 Jul. 20X1	7.2 (7.0 + 0.2)	6.2 (5.5 + 0.5 + 0.2)	6.7 (6.5 + 0.2)
1 Jan. 20X2	5.7 (5.5 + 0.2)	6.2 (5.5 + 0.5 + 0.2)	5.7 (5.5 + 0.2)
1 Jul. 20X2	3.7 (3.5 + 0.2)	4.2 (3.5 + 0.5 + 0.2)	4.7 (4.5 + 0.2)

INTEREST RATE MANAGEMENT

(d) *Graph A*: Comparison of cap and no-hedge strategies

The cap is worse than doing nothing since the benefit of capping the interest rate in period 2 is outweighed by the extra cost of the premium when the cap was not required in periods 1, 3 and 4 (i.e. area A is less than area (B1 + B2 + B3)).

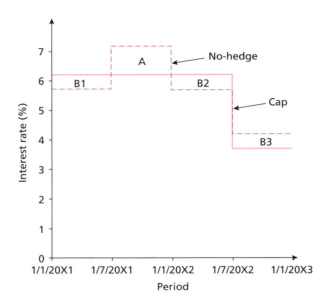

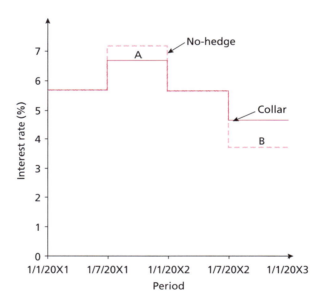

Graph B: Comparison of cap and no-hedge strategies

A collar is worse than doing nothing since the benefit of capping the interest rate in period 2 is outweighed by the cost of the floor in quarter 4.

Overall, no hedge gives the best result (average 5.575% p.a.) and the collar and cap give identical results (both average 5.7% p.a.).

(e) (i) Low fluctuation in rates: recommend collar, as no premium.

(ii) Highly volatile rates: recommend cap, as protects from higher rates but allows the company to benefit from favourable rates.

Solution 4

(a) A swap for mutual benefit

	Big Widget	Small Widget
Receives	Fixed 6%	Floating LIBOR
Pays	Fixed 6%	Floating LIBOR + 1.5
Pays	Floating LIBOR	Fixed 6%
Net result	Pays LIBOR	Pays 7.5%
Net benefit	0.5%	0.5%

(b)

	Advantage of using bank	Advantage of direct relationship
Choice of maturity, currency, etc.	✓	✗
Cost	✗	✓
Credit risk	✓*	
Ease of unwinding	✓	✗
Speed of dealing	✓	✗

*(but depends on relative credit rating).

 Solution 5

(a) *Fixed versus floating rates*

Fixed-rate finance may be preferred because interest payment commitments are known. This type of finance will be especially useful if interest rates are expected to rise. Floating-rate finance would be preferred if interest rates are expected to fall, or if the company has floating assets which will provide a better match, for example debtors.

Eurobonds: A Eurobond is a bearer bond, issued in a euro currency, usually Euro dollars, which are US dollars deposited with, or borrowed from, a bank outside the United States.

A key advantage of the Eurobond market is that it allows for a greater range of potential investors. From the investor's point of view, the bearer bond format may be attractive, although this raises considerations for the safe keeping of the documents.

Other benefits from the company's point of view are as follows:

- they are usually cheaper than equivalent domestic bonds
- the market is more flexible, allowing tailor-made financial instruments
- they may provide a hedge against interest rate or currency movements
- the cost of the issue may be lower than with the US corporate bond market.

The one main disadvantage for the use of Eurobonds is that the market is restricted to large bond issues for internationally recognised companies, although this would not be a problem for GH plc.

(b) *Principles and benefits of interest-rate swaps and financial advantages to GH plc and JJ plc*

The two firms, GH plc and JJ plc, have unequal access to capital. Although GH plc can borrow at a fixed rate of 8.5 per cent, JJ plc must pay 10.5 per cent because of its slightly lower credit rating. Both firms can also borrow at floating rates, GH plc at LIBOR + 0.5% and JJ plc at LIBOR + 1.1%. Each firm has its own *comparative* advantage in access to capital. GH plc can borrow at a full 2 per cent less than JJ plc at fixed rates, but that also means JJ plc has a comparative advantage in borrowing floating-rate funds. Although JJ plc must pay more for floating-rate funds than GH plc, it pays only 0.6 per cent more for floating, whereas it must pay a full 2 per cent more for fixed.

Each firm borrows in its advantaged market, GH plc at fixed rates and JJ plc at floating rates. They then swap debt service obligations, on the basis of their agreed terms. The gains to be shared are as follows:

Fixed rate:	10.5% − 8.5%	2.0%
Less:	Floating rate 1.1% − 0.5%	0.6%
Gains to be shared		1.4%

JJ plc has been requested to make fixed interest payments of 9 per cent to GH plc and GH plc will cover JJ plc's floating-rate payments. The final negotiated interest-rate swap benefits all three parties, including the bank. GH plc will make floating-rate payments at LIB OR + 0%, which is cheaper than it could acquire on its own. Similarly, JJ plc will make fixed-rate payments at 9 per cent, cheaper than what it could acquire on its own (10.5%).

Each of the borrowers will benefit from the interest-rate swap by being able to borrow capital in the preferred interest-rate structure and at a lower rate than obtainable on their own, as follows:

GH plc	
Fixed 9.0% − 8.5%	0.5% gain
Floating 0.5% − 0.0%	0.5% gain
Total gain	1.0%
JJ plc	
Fixed 10.5% − 9.0%	1.5% gain
Floating 1.1% − 0.0%	1.1% loss
Total gain	0.4%

The bank receives its own share of 0.15 per cent for facilitating the transaction and accepting some financial risk. Clearly GH plc has the strongest bargaining power and can probably negotiate to receive the highest proportion of the gains.

(c) *GH plc invoices its customers in US dollars*

Assuming these customers are worldwide, the company is simply transferring its exchange rate risk to its customers. The policy decision to adopt a more aggressive sales and marketing policy is separate from its decision on how to finance that policy, although they are connected when the effect on the overall risk of the policy change is considered. If GH plc finances the change with a floating-rate Eurobond loan, this in itself should have no effect on invoicing policy.

However, there will be a benefit from currency matching, which, plus any benefits from reduced debt payments, may allow GH plc to improve its credit terms to its customers.

An interest-rate *cap* is an option which sets a maximum interest rate on future borrowings for an agreed length of time. A *floor* is an option that sets a minimum interest rate. A *collar* arises when a borrower buys an interest-rate cap and at the same time sells an interest-rate floor (Fig. 12.4). The premium received from selling the floor will reduce the cost of the premium paid for the cap.

13

Foreign Exchange: Relationships and Risks

Foreign Exchange: Relationships and Risks

13

LEARNING OUTCOMES

After completing this chapter you should be able to:

▶ explain and distinguish between purchasing power parity, interest-rate parity and the international Fisher effect theories;

▶ calculate the impact of differential inflation and interest rates on forecasting exchange rates;

▶ identify and explain the different types of foreign exchange risks;

▶ identify and evaluate appropriate strategies of minimising political risks.

13.1 Introduction

The main purpose of this chapter is to introduce the mechanics of the foreign exchange market and to discuss the relationship between inflation, interest rate and exchange rates according to the purchasing power parity (PPP) theory, interest-rate parity (IRP) and the international Fisher effect (IFE). We then examine the different types of exposures to foreign exchange risk; transaction exposure, translation exposure and economic exposure. The chapter concludes with a brief summary.

13.2 The foreign exchange market

The basic principles of international financial management are, of course, the same as those for financial management in general, the complicating factor being the need to deal with different currencies, economies and governments. One role of a company treasurer is to manage foreign exchange dealings in a way that contributes to the maximisation of shareholder wealth without taking undue risk. How much risk is 'undue' risk is, of course, for the individual company to decide, but most non-financial businesses choose to hedge exchange-rate risks. Before we can examine ways of managing foreign exchange risk, we

375

need to understand the basics of the foreign exchange market and the factors that affect movements in foreign exchange rates.

13.2.1 Exchange rates

Exchange rates tell us how many units of one currency may be bought or sold for one unit of another currency. They therefore show the price of a currency relative to the price of another currency. They may be expressed in two ways.

1. A *direct quote* is the number of domestic currency units needed to buy one unit of a foreign currency. For example, a French person looking up the value of the Euro against the US dollar would find from Table 13.1, a direct quote of €0.7803 per US dollar.
2. An *indirect quote* is the number of foreign currency units needed to buy one unit of the domestic currency. It is simply the reciprocal of a direct quote (i.e Indirect quote = 1 ÷ direct quote). To use the French example given above, the indirect quote would be US$1.2815 per euro (1 ÷ 0.7803 = 1.2815).

Note that €0.7803 per US dollar is the same as US$1.2815 per euro which can be a little confusing. It is therefore important to keep in mind the type of quotation when forecasting exchange rates using the formulae for interest-rate parity and purchasing power parity. The mathematical tables in the preliminary pages of this Study System show both. In general, if you are using sterling as the domestic currency, then you will use the indirect formula. Most countries use direct quotes. For mainly historical reasons, Britain and Ireland use indirect quotes. In Britain, therefore, the exchange rate for sterling against the US dollar would be quoted as, say, US$1.4417 = £1. It is, of course, quite simple to calculate the direct quote: 1/1.4417 = 0.6936, which states that US$1 is worth 69.4p.

Table 13.1 shows exchange cross-rates for some selected currencies derived from information published in the *Financial Times* on Friday, 30 January 2009. The published rates relate to closing prices at the last trading day (i.e. Thursday 29 January 2009). These rates tell us how many units of one currency can be bought for one (or more – see below) units of another. The cross-rate of Swiss francs to the US dollar can be used to provide an example. If we take the column of information for Switzerland (column 16) and read down until we reach the exchange rate for US dollar (row 19) we get the direct quote of SFr1.1607 = US$1. If we then take the column of information for the US dollar (last column) and read down until we reach the exchange rate for Swiss francs (third row from the bottom) we get the direct quote of US$0.8615 = SFr1.

Appreciation or depreciation of a currency

Suppose as at today the exchange rate for sterling against the US dollar is quoted as US$1.4417/£ (which is the same as £0.6936/US$). Suppose the exchange rate a year ago was US$1.400/£ (£0.7143/US$), then sterling is said to have appreciated or strengthened. On the other hand, if the exchange rate a year ago was US$2.0000/£ (£0.5000/US$), then sterling is said to have depreciated or weakened against the dollar. In general, a *currency A*

Table 13.1 Exchange cross-rates – 30 January 2009

Column/ Row	1	2	3	4	5	6	7	8	9	10	11	12	13	14	15	16	17	18	19
		(Peso)	(A$)	(R$)	(C$)	(DKr)	(Euro)	(HK$)	(Rs)	(Y)	(M$)	(NKr)	(S$)	(R)	(SKr)	(SFr)	(Bt)	(£)	($)
2	Argentina (Peso)	1	0.4510	0.6664	0.3556	1.6685	0.2238	2.2242	14.0198	25.7593	1.0347	1.9823	0.4333	2.9263	2.3792	0.3329	10.0315	0.1989	0.2868
3	Australia (A$)	2.2171	1	1.4774	0.7884	3.6991	0.4962	4.9311	31.0825	57.1097	2.2940	4.3949	0.9607	6.4877	5.2749	0.7381	22.2404	0.4411	0.6359
4	Brazil (R$)	1.5007	0.6769	1	0.5337	2.5038	0.3359	3.3378	21.0391	38.6562	1.5528	2.9748	0.6503	4.3914	3.5704	0.4996	15.0540	0.2986	0.4304
5	Canada (C$)	2.8120	1.2684	1.8738	1	4.6917	0.6294	6.2545	39.4239	72.4358	2.9097	5.5743	1.2186	8.2288	6.6905	0.9362	28.2090	0.5594	0.8065
6	Denmark (DKr)	0.5994	0.2703	0.3994	0.2131	1	0.1341	1.3331	8.4028	15.4390	0.6202	1.1881	0.2597	1.7539	1.4260	0.1995	6.0125	0.1192	0.1719
7	Euro (Euro)	4.4680	2.0153	2.9773	1.5889	7.4547	1	9.9377	62.6403	115.0924	4.6231	8.8570	1.9362	13.0747	10.6304	1.4875	44.8209	0.8889	1.2815
8	Hong Kong (HK$)	0.4496	0.2028	0.2996	0.1599	0.7501	0.1006	1	6.3033	11.5814	0.4652	0.8913	0.1948	1.3157	1.0697	0.1497	4.5102	0.0894	0.1290
9	India (Rs)	0.0713	0.0322	0.0475	0.0254	0.1190	0.0160	0.1586	1	1.8374	0.0738	0.1414	0.0309	0.2087	0.1697	0.0237	0.7155	0.0142	0.0205
10	Japan (Y)	0.0388	0.0175	0.0259	0.0138	0.0648	0.0087	0.0863	0.5443	1	0.0402	0.0770	0.0168	0.1136	0.0924	0.0129	0.3894	0.0077	0.0111
11	Malaysia (M$)	0.9664	0.4359	0.6440	0.3437	1.6125	0.2163	2.1496	13.5494	24.8950	1	1.9158	0.4188	2.8281	2.2994	0.3217	9.6950	0.1923	0.2772
12	Norway (NKr)	0.5045	0.2275	0.3362	0.1794	0.8417	0.1129	1.1220	7.0724	12.9946	0.5220	1	0.2186	1.4762	1.2002	0.1679	5.0605	0.1004	0.1447
13	Singapore (S$)	2.3076	1.0409	1.5377	0.8206	3.8502	0.5165	5.1326	32.3525	59.4431	2.3878	4.5745	1	6.7528	5.4904	0.7682	23.1492	0.4591	0.6619
14	South Africa (R)	0.3417	0.1541	0.2277	0.1215	0.5702	0.0765	0.7601	4.7910	8.8027	0.3536	0.6774	0.1481	1	0.8131	0.1138	3.4281	0.0680	0.0980
15	Sweden (SKr)	0.4203	0.1896	0.2801	0.1495	0.7013	0.0941	0.9348	5.8926	10.8267	0.4349	0.8332	0.1821	1.2299	1	0.1399	4.2163	0.0836	0.1206
16	Switzerland (SFr)	3.0038	1.3548	2.0016	1.0682	5.0117	0.6723	6.6809	42.1120	77.3748	3.1080	5.9544	1.3017	8.7899	7.1466	1	30.1324	0.5976	0.8615
17	Thailand (Bt)	0.0997	0.0450	0.0664	0.0354	0.1663	0.0223	0.2217	1.3976	2.5678	0.1031	0.1976	0.0432	0.2917	0.2372	0.0332	1	0.0198	0.0286
18	UK (£)	5.0265	2.2672	3.3495	1.7875	8.3865	1.1250	11.1799	70.4703	129.4790	5.2010	9.9641	2.1782	14.7090	11.9592	1.6734	50.4235	1	1.4417
19	USA ($)	3.4865	1.5726	2.3233	1.2399	5.8171	0.7803	7.7547	48.8800	89.8099	3.6075	6.9114	1.5109	10.2025	8.2952	1.1607	34.9750	0.6936	1

Source: Cross rates derived from the Financial Times closing mid-point rates of 30 January 20099.

is said to have strengthened (appreciated) relative to another currency B if you now need to give less units of currency A to purchase a unit of currency B. Currency B would therefore weaken (depreciate) relative to currency A. It is quite possible for one currency to strengthen against a second currency while weakening against a third. To understand why this has happened would, of course, require an examination of the underlying economic, and possibly political, factors in the three countries.

Cross-exchange rates

We can infer the implied exchange rate between two currencies if each of these currencies is quoted against a third currency. For example, in Table 13.1 the exchange rates for the US dollar and the euro in terms of the British pound are quoted as \$1.4417/£ and €1.1250/£, respectively. The implied cross-rate of dollars per euro is given by

$$\frac{\text{dollars per pound}}{\text{euros per pound}} = \frac{1.4417}{1.1250} = 1.2815 \text{ dollars per euro}$$

Implied cross rates can be useful when we want to compare two currencies which are not actively traded against each other.

13.2.2 The meaning of spot and forward rates

> 🔑 The spot rate is the exchange price for transactions for immediate delivery. In practice this means to be settled within a very short period of time, usually 2 or 3 days, although settlement may take up to a week.

The forward rate applies to a deal which is agreed upon now but where the actual exchange of currency is not due to take place until some future date. The exchange of currencies at the future date will be at the rate agreed upon now.

Table 13.2 shows the value of sterling spot and forward against other major currencies. The table gives the closing mid-point exchange rate and other information about currency movements on Thursday, 29 January 2009. However, deals are done either side of this mid-point, depending on whether the dealer is buying or selling the currency.

Bid-Ask spread (also known as Bid-Offer spread) difference between the buying and the selling prices of a traded commodity or financial instrument (CIMA *Official Terminology*, 2005).

In the case of exchange rates, exchange rate dealers would buy a currency from you at the bid rate and sell at the ask or offer rate. Thus the dealer's offer rate will always be greater than the bid rate. For example, the closing mid-point spot rate for the Hong Kong dollar against sterling on 29 January 2009 was 11.1799. The bid-offer spread was quoted as 780–818. This means that a person who wishes to buy Hong Kong dollars for pounds (or wishes to sell UK pounds for Hong Kong dollars) will receive a rate of 11.1780HK\$/£. On the other hand, a person who wishes to sell Hong Kong dollars for pounds (or wishes to buy UK pounds for Hong Kong dollars) will receive a rate of 11.1818HK\$/£. The difference between the buying and the selling prices represents profit for the bank. The size of the bid-offer spread depends on a number of factors including processing cost, storage cost, the volatility of the currency and the volume of transactions in the market. The higher the volatility, and the lower the volume of transactions, in a particular currency, the

Table 13.2 Pound spot and forward rates* – 30 January 2009

	Closing mid-point	Change on day	Bid/offer spread†	Day's mid		One month		Three month		One year		Bank of England Index
				High	Low	Rate	% p. a.	Rate	% p. a.	Rate	% p.a.	
Argentina (Peso)	5.0265	0.0331	236–293	5.0424	4.9509	5.1426	−27.1	5.4085	−28.3	6.5252	−23.0	–
Australia (A$)	2.2672	0.0928	662–682	2.2709	2.1907	2.2713	−2.2	2.2782	−1.9	2.3006	−1.5	73.1
Brazil (R$)	3.3495	0.0764	472–517	3.3596	3.2448	3.3791	−10.5	3.4378	−10.3	3.6268	−7.6	–
Canada (C$)	1.7875	0.0463	869–881	1.7906	1.7395	1.7875	0.0	1.7868	0.2	1.7854	0.1	92.2
Denmark (DKr)	8.3865	0.2264	838–892	8.3994	8.2053	8.3965	−1.4	8.4138	−1.3	8.4443	−0.7	–
Euro (Euro)	1.1250	0.0299	247–253	1.1267	1.1008	1.1251	−0.1	1.1253	−0.1	1.1259	−0.1	98.6
Hong Kong (HK$)	11.1799	0.0699	780–818	11.2203	11.0058	11.1745	0.6	11.1678	0.4	11.1688	0.1	–
India (Rs)	70.4703	0.3019	461–945	70.4710	68.8560	70.6546	−3.1	70.9818	−2.9	71.8287	−1.9	–
Japan (Y)	129.479	0.6939	432–526	129.980	126.750	129.370	1.0	129.130	1.1	128.199	1.0	164.1
Malaysia (M$)	5.2010	0.0461	966–053	5.2161	5.1233	5.2060	−1.2	5.2054	−0.3	5.1944	0.1	–
Norway (NKr)	9.9641	0.299	585–697	9.9737	9.7737	9.9760	−1.4	10.0003	−1.4	10.0249	−0.6	96.2
Singapore (S$)	2.1782	0.0228	774–789	2.1850	2.1406	2.1781	0.0	2.1771	0.2	2.1749	0.1	–
South Africa (R)	14.7090	0.4683	957–222	14.7807	14.2485	14.8198	−9.0	15.0368	−8.7	15.7321	−6.5	–
Sweden (SKr)	11.9592	0.4286	521–662	12.0263	11.6607	11.9618	−0.3	11.9586	0.0	11.9411	0.2	72.2
Switzerland (SFr)	1.6734	0.0332	726–742	1.6778	1.6379	1.6722	0.9	1.6700	0.8	1.6589	0.9	119.3
Thailand (Bt)	50.4235	0.4219	948–521	50.5840	49.5810	50.5546	−3.1	50.7692	−2.7	51.5329	−2.2	–
UK (£)	–	–		–	–	–		–		–	–	100.0
USA ($)	1.4417	0.0094	415–419	1.4469	1.4190	1.4411	0.5	1.4407	0.3	1.4415	0.0	90.3

*This is an extract from the full table.
†Bid/offer spreads in the Pound spot table show only the last three decimal places.
Source: Financial Times, 30 January 2009.

greater the spread. Higher processing and storage costs would also lead to wider bid-offer spreads.

Notice that when the bank sells, a customer is buying and vice versa. The use of the terms *bid* and *offer* can therefore be confusing, but remember that the dealer always wins and a company (the customer) will always have to trade at the rate least favourable to itself. In the example here, if a company was buying Hong Kong dollars with pounds it would receive the lower rate of 11.1780 HK$ for every £1. If it was selling Hong Kong dollars for UK pounds it would have to give the dealer the higher rate of 11.1818 HK$ for every £1.

Table 13.2 also shows forward rates and the percentage premium or discount against the spot rate for most major currencies. It should be noted that forward quotes are not available in all currencies. Looking at the 3-month forward rates, we can see that on 29 January 2009 most of the currencies were trading at a discount to sterling. The Canadian dollar, the Japanese yen and the US dollar among others were trading at a premium (shown as positive values under the '3 months % p.a.' column). *Note that because the quote is indirect, an increase in the exchange rate against the pound shows a depreciation of the foreign currency relative to sterling. It is always important to use the terms appreciation (strengthening) or depreciation (weakening) when dealing with currencies and not higher or lower because an increase in the exchange rate does not necessarily mean an appreciation.* Two worked examples are shown below to demonstrate the relationship.

Example 13.A

Using a UK *indirect* quote:

- the spot rate for Swiss francs is SFr1.6734 = £1;
- the 3-month forward rate is SFr1.6700 = £1.

Is the Swiss franc trading at a premium or at a discount relative to sterling, and what is the annual percentage premium or discount?

Solution

If you transact to receive Swiss francs in 3 months' time, you receive fewer Swiss francs for your pound than if you buy now at spot. The Swiss franc is therefore trading at a forward *premium*, sterling at a forward *discount* against each other. We could say that the Swiss franc is expensive and sterling cheap in relation to each other.

Looked at using direct quotes,' the spot rate would be

$$1 \div SFr1.6734/£ = £0.5976/SFr$$

and the forward rate would be

$$1 \div SFr1.6700/£ = £0.5988/SFr$$

Forward Swiss francs are more expensive than spot ones: you need 59.88p to buy one Swiss franc in 3 months' time but only 59.76p to buy one now. However, the forward rate is not necessarily the future spot rate. This is discussed in more detail later in this chapter.

To calculate the annual percentage premium or discount, the formula used depends on whether the currency is quoted in direct or indirect terms. If the exchange rate is quoted in indirect terms then the appropriate formula would be

$$\% \text{ Forward Permium/Discount} = \frac{360}{n} \times \frac{\text{Spot rate} - \text{Forward rate}}{\text{Forward rate}} \times 100$$

On the other hand, if the rates are quoted in direct terms then the appropriate formula would be

$$\% \text{ Forward Permium/Discount} = \frac{360}{n} \times \frac{\text{Forward rate} - \text{Spot rate}}{\text{Forward rate}} \times 100$$

where *n* is the number of days forward.

If the pound is the home currency, then the rates in Table 13.2 are quoted in indirect terms. Hence, the annual rate of appreciation of Swiss francs is (approximately)

$$\% \text{ Forward Premium Discount} = \frac{360}{90} \times \left(\frac{1.6734 - 1.6700}{1.6700} \right) \times 100 = 0.81$$

This corresponds with the '3 months % p.a.' column for Switzerland in Table 13.2.

Example 13.B

This example uses the South African rand. The spot rate for South African rand is 14.7090 rands = £1, the 3-month forward rate is 15.0368. In 3 months' time you receive more rands for your pound than if you buy spot. The South African rand is therefore trading at a forward *discount* and sterling at a forward *premium* against each other.

What is the annual rate of sterling appreciation?

Solution

The annual rate is (approximately)

$$\% \text{ Forward Premium Discount} = \frac{360}{90} \times \left(\frac{14.7090 - 15.0368}{14.7090} \right) \times 100 = -8.7$$

which again corresponds to the 'Three months % p.a.' column for South African rand in Table 13.2.

If the forward rate is the same as the spot rate, the currency is said to be trading at *par*. There are no currencies in the table trading at par 3 months forward against sterling on 29 January 2009.

Forward rates, instead of being quoted outright, say $1.4450/£ − $1.4470, can also be quoted as forward points that is added to or subtracted from the spot rates to obtain the outright forward quotes. The forward points are just the difference between the forward and the spot quotes.

If the forward points are in ascending order (say 20–30), it suggests a forward premium and would be added to the spot quotes. If on the other hand, the forward points are in descending order (say 45–30) then that suggests a forward discount and would subtracted from the spot rates.

Consider the following quotes:

spot rates	$1.4500/£ − $1.4510 /£
forward points	30–20
outright forward rates	$1.4470/£ − $1.4490/£

In this case the forward points indicate a forward discount so they have been subtracted from the spot quotes to obtain the forward outright quotes.

Suppose we have the following quotes for a 3-month forward on Australian dollars against the pound.

spot rates	A$2.2660/£ − A$2.2680 /£
forward points	100–120

Because the forward points are in ascending order, they will be added to the spot quotes to obtain the outright forward quote of A$2.2760/£ − A$2.2800/£. Note that, the bid-ask spread of the forward rates will always be bigger than that of the spot rates due to the increased risk in the forward market to the dealer relative to the spot market.

13.3 Theoretical foreign exchange relationships

Currency volatility is one of the major risks faced by businesses today. It is necessary to understand the theoretical reasons why a currency's value may change from time to time.

There are a number of factors that influence a currency's exchange rate:

- *Speculation.* Speculators enter into foreign exchange transactions not because they have a need for the currency but with a view to profit from their expectations of the currency's future movements. If speculators expect a currency to devalue, they will short sell the currency with the hope of buying it back cheaply in the future. *A* good example of how speculation can affect currency values occurred in 1992, when the UK government was forced to devalue sterling by the actions of speculators in the market who sold huge sums of sterling short (i.e. sold currency they did not own in the hope of buying it back more cheaply). The Bank of England was buying in the market in an attempt to maintain the value of sterling and base rates of interest were raised twice in 1 day. The speculators won, however. The United Kingdom withdrew from the European exchange rate mechanism and sterling was effectively devalued. Speculation also played a major role in the Argentinian and Asian currency crises.
- *Balance of payments.* The net effect of importing and exporting will result in a demand for or a supply of the country's currency.
- *Government policy.* Governments from time to time may wish to change the value of their currency. This can be achieved directly by devaluation/revaluation or via the use of 'the foreign exchange markets'.
- *Interest-rate differentials. A* higher rate of interest can obviously create a demand for that particular currency: investors will buy that currency in order to hold financial securities in the currency with the higher interest rate.
- *Inflation-rate differentials.* Where countries have different inflation rates the value of one country's currency is falling *in real terms* in comparison with the other. This will result in a change in the exchange rate.

Let us now consider a number of theoretical foreign-exchange relationships which underpin changes in a currency's exchange rate.

13.3.1 Interest-rate parity

Interest-rate parity theory is a method of predicting exchange rates based on the hypothesis that the difference between the interest rates in two countries should offset the difference between the spot rates and the forward foreign exchange rates over the same period (CIMA *Official Terminology*, 2005).

Interest rates within a country are determined in the money market. The price of money, like anything else, is determined by supply and demand, although in many countries governments do try to manage the interest rate. There is a strong relationship between the foreign exchange market and the money market. The relationship between the interest rates in two countries affects the rate of exchange, and in particular the relationship between the *spot rate* of exchange and the *forward rate* of exchange.

As identified above, there are many factors other than interest rates that affect movements in exchange rate over time. However, all things being equal, the currency with the higher interest rate will sell at a discount in the forward market against the currency with the lower interest rate. The reasoning behind the interest-rate parity relationship is that if a country has a higher domestic rate of interest than its trading partner, it will find that this interest-rate differential attracts foreign investors, and their desire to invest in that country will lead them to purchase the domestic currency, thus increasing that currency's spot rate.

However, assuming that the foreign investors will eventually wish to transfer their investment back into their own domestic currency, they will also engage in a forward contract. This is done at the same time as buying the foreign currency spot: they engage in a forward contract to convert the currency back into their own domestic currency, at some specified date in the future.

If, for example, the UK interest rate was 3 per cent higher than the US rate, in the spot transactions sterling would be bought and the spot rate for sterling would increase (as investors wanted to take advantage of the higher rate of interest). But sterling would also be sold in the forward market, so the forward rate for sterling would be brought down. Eventually, an equilibrium state is achieved where the forward premium/discount offsets the interest-rate differential.

Suppose the US nominal interest rate is $r_\$$ and that of the UK is $r_£$, then the interest-rate parity relationship can be expressed as

$$\frac{F_{\$/£} - S_{\$/£}}{S_{\$/£}} = \frac{r_\$ - r_£}{1 + r_£}$$

where $F_{\$/£}$ = forward rate now and $S_{\$/£}$ = spot rate now.

This formula can be rearranged as follows:

$$\frac{F_{\$/£}}{S_{\$/£}} = \frac{1 + r_\$}{1 + r_£} \quad \text{or} \quad F_{\$/£} = \frac{1 + r_\$}{1 + r_£} \times S_{\$/£}$$

Try to exercise some care with the way the parity relations are written. They may be written differently in some textbooks depending on how the exchange rate is quoted. The formula here assumes that the exchange rate is quoted as $\$/£$. In this case, the dollar is the numerator currency and the pound is the denominator currency. Hence, the dollar interest rate will be the numerator divided by the expression containing the pound interest rate. If the exchange rates were quoted as $£/\$$, then the forward rate would be calculated as $F_{£/\$} = \frac{1 + r_£}{1 + r_\$} \times S_{£/\$}$. Notice that this time because the pound is the numerator currency ($£/\$$), the expression containing the pound interest rate appears as the numerator.

These points can best be illustrated by way of an example.

Example 13.C

Suppose interest-rate on US dollar deposits is 8% and interest rate on euro deposits in 5%. If interest-rate parity holds, what would the 1-year forward rate be if the spot rate is €0.92/$.

Solution

Based on the exchange-rate quote, the euro is the numerator currency with the dollar being the denominator. Therefore, interest-rate on the euro, $1 + r_€$, would appear as the numerator in the interest-rate parity relationship:

$$\frac{1 + r_€}{1 + r_\$} \times S_{€/\$} = F_{€/\$}$$

$$\frac{1 + 0.05}{1 + 0.08} \times 0.92 = 0.8944 \approx 0.89$$

Example 13.D

Suppose that on 1 January 20X1 the spot rate is £1 = $1.90 and the UK and the US interest rates are 6% and 4% per annum, respectively, what would we expect the 1-year forward rate to be?

Solution

$$\frac{1 + r_\$}{1 + r_£} \times S_{\$/£} = F_{\$/£}$$

$$\frac{1.04}{1.06} \times 1.90 = 1.8642 \approx \$1.86/£$$

Proof

$$\frac{F_{\$/£} - S_{\$/£}}{S_{\$/£}} = \frac{r_\$ - r_£}{1 + r_£}$$

$$\frac{1.8642 - 1.90}{1.90} = \frac{0.04 - 0.06}{1.06}$$

$$-0.019 = 0.019$$

Interest-rate parity ensures that depositing funds abroad should earn the same return as a similar investment at home. In an attempt to explain the above theory let us consider the sequence of events that would take place if an investor in the United States was attracted by the high interest rate in the United Kingdom.

Assume that $100 was available for investment.

1 January 20X1	Sell dollars and buy sterling: $100/1.90 = £52.63
	Invest £52.63 for 12 months at 6%:
	£52.63 × 6% = £3.16
	Total pound holding (£52.63 + £3.16) = £55.79
	Enter into a 1-year forward contract to sell pounds at $1.8642/£
31 December 20X1	Sell pounds and by back dollars:
	55.79 × $1.8642 = $104

If, however, the money had been left in the US:

1 January 20X1	Invest $100 for 12 months at 4%:
	$100 × 4% = $4
31 December 20X1	Total US investment ($100 + $4) = $104

Now let us consider whether a UK investor will earn more by investing funds in the US in an attempt to take advantage of the forward premium on the dollar. Assume that £100 was available for investment.

1 January 20X1	Sell dollars and buy sterling: 100 × $1.90 = $190
	Invest £190 for 12 months at 4%:
	$190 × 4% = $7.60
	Total pound holding ($190 + $7.60) = $197.60
	Enter into a 1-year forward contract to sell pounds at $1.8642/£
31 December 20X1	Sell pounds and by back sterling:
	197.60/1.8642 = £106

If, however, the money had been left in the UK:

1 January 20X1	Invest £100 for 12 months at 6%:
	£100 × 6% = £6
31 December 20X1	Total UK investment (£100 + £6) = £106

Thus neither the US investor nor the UK investor benefits from investing their funds abroad.

Note that interest rates are normally quoted annualised unless otherwise specified. So, if the period of investment is not 12 months, simply adjust the interest rate proportionately. For example, if the interest rate is quoted as 8% per annum, and you are interested in the 6-month forward rate, the relevant interest rate to use in the formula is 8% × 6/12 = 4%

Example 13.E

Suppose that on 1 January 20X1 the spot rate is £1 = $1.90 and the UK and the US interest rates are 6% and 4% per annum, respectively, what would we expect the 6-month forward rate to be?

Solution

For a 6-month forward rate, the relevant interest rate for the period would be 3% in the United Kingdom and 2% in the United States. Thus the 6-month forward would be:

$$\frac{1+r_\$}{1+r_£} \times S_{\$/£} = F_{\$/£}$$

$$\frac{1.02}{1.03} \times 1.90 = 1.8816 \approx \$1.88/£$$

Now try the exercise below. (It assumes a limited knowledge of hedging techniques, which are covered more fully in Chapter 14.)

 ## Exercise 13.1

Exporters plc, a UK company, is due to receive 500,000 Northland dollars in 6 months' time for goods supplied. The company decides to hedge its currency exposure by using the forward market. The short-term interest rate in the United Kingdom is 12% per annum and the equivalent rate in Northland is 15%. The spot rate of exchange is N$2.5 = £1.

You are required to calculate how much Exporters plc actually gains or loses as a result of the hedging transaction if, at the end of 6 months, sterling, in relation to the Northland dollar, has (i) gained 4%, (ii) lost 2% or (iii) remained stable.

You may assume that the forward rate of exchange simply reflects the interest differential in the two countries (i.e. it reflects the interest-rate parity analysis of forward rates).

 ## Solution

If interest rate parity holds, then the forward rate can be calculated using the following formula:

$$\frac{1+r_{N\$}}{1+r_£} \times S_{N\$/£} = F_{N\$/£}$$

The interest rates for 6 months are 15% × 6/12 = 0.075 and 12% × 6/12 = 0.06.

$$\frac{1.075}{1.06} \times N\$2.5 = N\$2.535$$

The 6-month forward exchange rate is therefore N$2.535.

(i) If the spot rate strengthens by 4% (i.e. from N\$2.50 to N\$2.60), then the company, had it secured the forward rate provided by the forward exchange market, would have saved £4,931.

	£
N\$500,000/2.535	197,239
N\$500,000/2.60	192,308
	4,931

(ii) If the spot rate weakens by 2% (i.e. from N\$2.50 to N\$2.45), then the company, had it secured the forward rate provided by the forward exchange market, would have lost £6,843.

	£
N\$500,000/2.45	204,082
N\$500,000/2.535	197,239
	6,843

(iii) If the spot rate remained unchanged at 2.50, then the company, had it secured the forward rate provided by the forward exchange market, would have lost £2,761.

	£
N\$500,000/2.50	200,000
N\$500,000/2.535	197,239
	2,761

13.3.2 Purchasing power parity

Purchasing power parity (PPP) theory is the theory stating that the exchange rate between two currencies is in equilibrium when the purchasing power of currency is the same in each country (CIMA *Official Terminology*, 2005). There are two versions of the PPP theory.

In its **absolute form**, PPP suggests that in the absence of transactions costs, the price of a similar basket of goods when measured in a common currency should be the same across different countries. If this parity does not hold, then arbitrage will take place until equilibrium is achieved.

If PPP holds, then the exchange rate between the two countries should be equal to the ratio of price levels in the two countries. For example, suppose a basket of goods costs £400 in the United Kingdom. The same basket of goods costs ¥82,800 in Japan. If PPP holds, then the exchange rate between the Japanese yen and the UK pound is ¥207/£ (¥82,800 ÷ £400).

In its *relative form* PPP suggests that inflation differentials are offset by changes in exchange rates. Consequently, if the rate of inflation was, say, higher in the United Kingdom than in a foreign country, say Japan, then we would expect the pound to depreciate against the yen.

This relationship can best be illustrated by reference to the following formula:

$$\frac{S_t - S_0}{S_0} = \frac{i_F - i_{UK}}{1 + i_{UK}}$$

where i_F and i_{UK} = inflation rate in the foreign country and in the United Kingdom, respectively; S_t = spot rate at a future time and S_0 = spot rate now.

The formula can be rearranged to give a method of predicting future spot exchange rates:

$$S_t = S_0 \times \frac{1 + i_F}{1 + i_{UK}}$$

Note that once again the formula given above assumes the exchange rate is quoted as foreign currency per unit of UK pound. Hence, the UK inflation appears in the denominator, as the pound is the denominator currency in the exchange-rate quotation.

Consider the following example.

Example 13.F

Bradbury cricket bats cost £100 in the United Kingdom and A$2.50 in Australia. The current exchange rate is A$2.50 = £1. Explain what happens to the exchange rate if inflation, which is presently zero in both the United Kingdom and Australia, increases to 10% in Australia?

Solution

The exchange rate becomes

$$\frac{1.10}{1} \times 2.50 = 2.75$$

The cost of a bat in the United Kingdom remains at £100; in Australia it rises to A$275.

This can also simply be shown by looking at the relative values of the goods:

	UK £	Australia A$	Exchange rate
Cricket bat: cost	100	250	250/100 = A$2.50
Inflation	0 (10%)	25 (10%)	
	100	275	275/100 = A$2.75

In reality, purchasing-power parity – or the *law of one price* – does not hold, but comparing the price of an identical good in different countries enables us to study the factors in those countries which might influence exchange rates and price differentials.

Every year since 1986, the *Economist* publishes the Big Mac Index where they use the relative prices of the MacDonald's Big Mac burger in their outlets around the world. The relative prices are used to determine whether the currencies of these countries are trading at their PPP implied rates, overvalued or undervalued. Although not a perfect measure, it is nonetheless a light-hearted approach to explaining a difficult economic concept. In the 2007 version, the price of a Big Mac in the United States is quoted as $3.22, and in the euro area as €2.94. The official exchange rate used in the article is $1.30/€. The exchange rate implied by the relative prices of Big Macs in the United States and the euro area is $1.10/€ (i.e. 3.22/2.94). Given the official exchange rate Big Mac costs the equivalent of $3.82 in the Eurozone. This implies that the euro is approximately 19% overvalued against the dollar (3.82/3.22 − 1) × 100%.

The reasons for the big difference in price are likely to be market imperfections such as taxes, transaction costs, transport costs between markets, government intervention in exchange rates, McDonald's promotional activity in selected markets, and differences in non-traded costs such as rent and labour costs. However, over time the 'Big Mac Index' has been shown to be a useful predictor of exchange rates in the long term.

13.3.3 The Fisher effect

The Fisher effect concentrates on the relationship between interest rates and inflation expectation between trading partners. Generally speaking, countries with higher rates of inflation will have higher nominal interest rates – both as a means of combating the inflationary pressure and as a way of counteracting the high inflation to provide investors with an adequate real rate of return. It is the second point which is stressed in the Fisher effect. This is based on the basic Fisherian principle of interest rates that

$$(1 + \text{real rate})(1 + \text{inflation rate}) = 1 + \text{monetary rate of interest}$$

For example, a building society might offer a rate of interest of 6.09 per cent per year. If inflation is currently at 3 per cent per year, then the 'real' rate of interest is 3 per cent (1.0609/1.03 = 1.03). In other words, out of the 6.09 per cent interest rate, 3 per cent protects against inflation, and the remaining 3 per cent is the reward for investing for a year. Note that the extra 0.09 per cent is as a result of compounding.

This principle also rests on the assumption that the expected real rate is the same in any two countries, so the change in interest rates is determined by the expected change in inflation rates.

Real interest rates are more likely to be the same in the international Eurocurrency markets than in the domestic capital markets. But any differences in real rates in different countries should not last very long. As people transfer holdings to foreign countries for higher real rates, all rates will be driven into equilibrium, so no one benefits. However, evidence has shown that the difference in interest rates exaggerates the likely differences in inflation rates.

13.3.4 The international Fisher effect

The international Fisher effect holds that interest-rate differentials should reflect the expected movement in the spot exchange rate. The parity condition is derived from the two already discussed: the PPP theory and the generalised Fisher effect.

Countries that have higher nominal interest rates than their trading partners are expected to experience currency depreciation: hence, the high nominal interest rates are seen by foreign investors as a compensating payment for future currency depreciation (because once depreciation occurs, conversion of the foreign currency to the domestic currency will be lower). The country with the higher nominal interest rate is starting from a higher base relative to the country with the lower interest rate and if capital is internationally mobile, then it is believed that the real rate of return between countries will be equalised by the movements in the spot exchange rate in the appropriate direction. This means that interest-rate differences between trading partners are offset by the spot exchange rate changing over time in the appropriate way.

For example, if the United Kingdom has 5 per cent higher interest rates than the United States, then, to equalise the rates of return between the two nations, sterling should depreciate in value by a proportionate (5%) amount against the dollar.

This relationship can be shown as

$$\frac{S_t}{S_0} = \frac{1 + r_{US}}{1 + r_{UK}}$$

where r_{US} and r_{UK} = interest rate in the United States and the United Kingdom, respectively (in dollars and pounds); S_t = spot rate ($/£) at a future time; and S_0 = spot rate ($/£) now.

13.3.5 Expectations theory

The relationship between interest rate and the Forward rate is addressed in Section 13.3.1. This section relates to the 'unbiased expectations hypothesis' which is a different concept from the interest rate parity relation in Section 13.3.1. The 'unbiased expectations hypothesis' states that the forward/futures rate is what the market expects the spot rate to be at delivery. Suppose it is March 200X, then under the expectations hypothesis the market's expected spot rate in 3-months (i.e. June 200X) is the 3-month forward rate today. Thus, if the 3-month forward rate for the A$/£ is A$2.50/£, then this means that the market expects the A$ to trade at A$2.50/£ in June. Note that this is the market's expectation; it does not mean this should be the exact rate in 3-months time. The spot rate in June could be different from the 3-month forward rate we know today (A$2.50/£). However, there should be no systematic deviations-the sum of the deviations over time must equal to zero. Over time, the forward rate should under-estimate as much as it over-estimates the future spot rate. If the forward/futures rate consistently over-estimate (under-estimate) the future spot rate then there will be arbitrage opportunities. Speculators/arbitrageurs will buy (sell) the forward today and sell (buy) at spot at the future spot rate if the forward rate consistently underestimate (overestimate) the future spot rate.

The implication of the Expectations hypothesis is that the best estimate of the A$/£ spot rate in 3-months time is the 3-month forward/futures rate today. For example, if the forward rate is less than today's spot rate, the odds are only a little better than evens that the spot rate will increase in the future. Therefore, we can use these and other relationships presented to predict in broad terms what will happen in the long run to exchange rates, but short-term changes are more difficult to forecast.

13.3.6 Implications of these theories

Interest-rate parity and purchasing power parity rely heavily on arbitrage arguments. These theories must hold if there are a large number of quick-acting buyers and sellers and small transaction costs. Although these theories might not hold consistently in practice, they provide a useful way (on average over a period of time!) in forecasting the direction of *exchange-rate risk* (i.e. whether a currency is likely to appreciate or depreciate).

13.4 Foreign exchange risk exposure

Changes in the global economy have resulted in the liberalisation of international trade and financial flows. Many companies now regularly raise finance overseas and also import and/or export goods overseas. Others open up subsidiaries and production facilities abroad in order to reduce production costs and remain competitive. Increased global activity, however, come with additional risks due to changes in the foreign exchange rate as well as changes in the political, social and economic climate in the countries in which the company operates.

The previous section reviewed the fundamental determinants of exchange rates. Changes in exchange rates have a significant effect on expected cash flows (receipts and payments) denominated in a foreign currency. This section discusses foreign exchange risks to which companies are exposed.

Exchange-rate risk may be classified into transaction risk, economic risk and translation risk. These are discussed in turn below. Various techniques of managing these risks are examined in Chapter 14.

13.4.1 Transaction risk

> Transaction risk occurs from the effect of changes in nominal exchange rates the company's contractual cash flows in foreign currencies. It relates to contracts already entered into but have yet to be settled. Thus, a company is subject to transaction risk whenever it imports goods from or export goods abroad to be paid at a later date, borrows or invests in a foreign currency or uses a certain derivatives denominated in a foreign currency.

By way of illustration, consider a company based in the United Kingdom:

- On 1 November, the company took delivery of some materials, manufactured in Australia and invoiced at A\$600,000, payable at the end of January. The spot rate on 1 November was A\$2.50 = £1, so the goods were entered into the books at £240,000. But what if sterling were to weaken, relative to the Australian dollar, to the point that the spot rate at the end of January reached A\$2.40 = £1? Then, it would cost £250,000 to buy the Australian dollars with which to settle the invoice, that is an extra cost of £10,000.
- The company spent £210,000 on converting the materials into finished goods, which were despatched to the United States on 1 December, and invoiced at \$900,000, due for payment at the end of January. The spot rate on 1 December was \$1.80 = £1, so the sale was booked at £500,000. But what if sterling were to strengthen relative to the dollar to the point that the spot rate at the end of January reached \$2.00 = £1? Then the dollars would be sold for only £450,000, that is a reduction in revenue of £50,000.

As far as accounting is concerned, the items had to be booked at the spot rate at the time the transaction was documented, that is when the material was received and when the goods were despatched, and a profit of £500,000 − £240,000 − £210,000, that is £50,000, was recorded. If the company's financial year ended on 31 December, then that would be the position shown in the accounts. In the event, the actual flows of cash would have been found to have been £450,000 − £250,000 − £210,000, that is a loss of £10,000.

Note how, as in this example, it is possible for one currency (sterling in this case) to weaken against another (the Australian dollar), yet strengthen against a third (the US dollar).

Just as net short-term cash flows represent only a small proportion of the value of an entity, so its transaction risk is likely to represent only a small proportion of its total currency exposure. The bulk will normally be in the category called economic risk, to which we now turn.

13.4.2 Economic risk

Economic risk refers to the degree to which the value of the firm's future cash flows can be influenced by exchange rate fluctuations. These are essentially the foreign exchange risks which affect a business before a transaction actually takes place, and are not therefore measurable in an accounting sense. Even purely domestic companies may be subject to economic risk if they face foreign competition within the local markets, losing competitiveness if the domestic currency appreciates against that of its major competitors.

Economic risk is a much broader and subjective concept as it involves the effect of exchange rate changes on expected future cash flows on all aspects of the companies operations. It is sometimes referred to as competitive risk and it is the most relevant risk, from the long-term perspective of the company. Generally, gains and losses associated with transaction and translation risks appear in the financial statements of the company. However, those associated with economic exposure do not appear in the financial statements, as they are more subjective and hence difficult to measure. Examples of events that can lead to economic risk for a UK-based company include:

- Insisting on dealing in only the home currency – sterling – thereby avoiding transaction risk, but this may affect the foreign demand for its products if the pound appreciates or their relationship with suppliers if the pound weakens.
- Investing in a marketing campaign in, say, Spain with a view to supplying goods or services, in competition with local producers a few months hence. If sterling were to strengthen relative to the euro, the appropriate euro price might not convert into enough sterling to make it worthwhile.
- Equally important, but often overlooked, consider a UK company exporting goods or services to Spain, in competition with (say) US companies. In this case, if the US dollar weakens relative to the euro (even if the pound remains unchanged against the euro), it will become cheaper for the Spanish customers to import those goods and services from the US supplier if the order is denominated in the foreign currency. Even if the order is denominated in euros (the Spanish currency) the euro price from the US supplier might not convert into enough sterling to make it worthwhile for the UK company.
- Deciding to acquire resources, say equipment in Italy, with a view to supplying goods or services to the UK market. In this case the company's costs are in euros with expected revenues in sterling. If sterling were to weaken against the euro, the costs of the operation could become uneconomic.

It is perhaps because these items do not appear in the accounts (because the business is lost to competitors), they are less well understood. The fact is that, in today's conditions – as the last example showed – you do not even have to be importing or exporting to have an exposure to foreign currency risk. Identifying, and quantifying (with inevitable margins of error), economic risk calls for a thorough appreciation of the competitive position and prospects of the company.

13.4.3 Translation risk

> Translation risk is the susceptibility of the balance sheet and income statement to the effect of foreign exchange rate changes (CIMA *Official Terminology*, 2005). It relates to the situation in which, for the purposes of preparing a consolidated financial statement for publication, overseas assets and liabilities are translated into the currency of the country in which the company is domiciled. For example, overseas assets and liabilities will be converted into sterling for a UK-registered company. If sterling has weakened, overseas assets and liabilities will be translated into higher sterling figures; if sterling has strengthened, then they will be translated into smaller sterling figures. Translation risk does not affect the cash flows of the company, but nevertheless attracts considerable treasury attention.

Taking the first of those possibilities, let us imagine that a UK company borrows 10 million Danish krones, at a time when £1 is worth 10 krones. At that time, the borrowings would appear on the company's balance sheet at £1 million. Over the ensuing year, however, the pound falls in value to 8 krones; the borrowings would now be translated at £1.25 million, that is an apparent loss of £0.25/krones. If this were assumed to be a permanent change in the pound-krone rate, it might be argued that this was a genuine loss of value, in the sense that more sterling would be needed to pay the interest and repay the loan in due course. The problem is that, in this age of discontinuity, it is unreasonable to assume that the change is a permanent one. It could be reversed, reduced or increased in the next and subsequent years.

Meanwhile, the change in parity will have affected reported profits (and hence earnings per share), total assets, borrowings, net worth (and hence gearing) but – to repeat – it will not have affected the measured cash flow in the period being reported on.

Academic theory argues that translation risk, of itself, need not concern financial managers, but in practice, there are two strong arguments in favour of the relevance of translation risk:

1. Although it does not affect the value of the entity as a whole, it can affect the attribution of that value between the different stakeholders. Higher gearing may lead to higher interest rates being charged on bank loans, either directly in accordance with clauses in borrowing agreements or indirectly as a result of the company's credit rating being reduced. The banks benefit at the expense of the equity investors in the business. If the treasurer is pursuing an objective of maximising shareholder wealth, he will want to manage this risk.
2. If the accounts are being used 'beyond their design specification', for example as the basis for calculating bonus payments for directors and senior managers, then there is a temptation to protect the current year's figures, even though it is known that doing so has a long-term cost. This is comparable to pulling profit into the current year, knowing that it will both reduce next year's profit and result in tax being paid earlier than necessary.

The former is a good reason, the latter is often the real reason for managing translation risk.

13.4.4 Attitudes to risk

The examples quoted above tended to emphasise the downside risks, that is, leading to an adverse effect on performance or potential. At this stage we need to recognise the upsides too: if sterling weakens after you have invoiced in dollars, for example, your sterling income increases.

This prompts the recognition of a spectrum of attitudes to risk, including:

- Choosing to open up risks, that is to get into a position to benefit from exchange-rate volatility, for example buying currencies which are expected to strengthen, writing options for other businesses. This is speculation and should be avoided by a non-financial company if the company does not use derivatives for trading purposes.
- Accepting the risks which arise in the normal course of business as an inevitable element thereof, on a par with competitors discovering new ways of delivering the goods or services.
- Taking a view on currency movements and finding a way to cover some (i.e. take some offsetting action) but not others. If you are confident that sterling can only weaken against the dollar, leave dollar receipts uncovered, but cover all payables, and vice versa. The basis for taking the view might be an econometric forecast, chartism or simply sentiment. As a general rule, however, confidence is misplaced at least as often as it is justified, as some embarrassing annual reports have shown.
- Cover all identified risks in certain categories, for example all liabilities, all transaction exposures, all economic exposures included in the current 12-month forecast.
- Hedge (i.e. cover a predetermined proportion of) identified exposures, for example 60 per cent of transaction risks, 40 per cent of economic risks included in the current 12-month forecast.
- Match opposite risks, for example those associated with importing and exporting – actively seeking matches by leading and lagging, perhaps, and covering or hedging only the net balance.

In organisational terms, there have been the usual debates as to whether currency risk management should be centralised or decentralised, and if the former, whether a profit centre or cost centre approach is appropriate. As time goes by, opinion seems to be hardening in favour of

- decentralising the responsibility for identifying risk;
- transferring identified risks to the centre at the market rate;
- giving (within defined limits) the centre discretion as to whether they actually take cover in the market;
- measuring their performance against the cost or benefit of covering everything at the market rate (i.e. they have to beat the market to be in credit).

13.5 Political risk

> Political risk is the unwanted consequence of political activities such as changes in government, political instability or changes in legislation that will have a detrimental effect on the value of the company's investments.

Companies that enter foreign markets are also exposed to political risks. Political risks are risks and uncertainties arising from political actions and governmental policies that could affect the future operations and hence the financial position of a company. For example, as a result of new laws and regulations a company could be required to cease certain operations, or could incur additional costs. Examples of actions that can have a detrimental effect on the value of the company's investments include:

- Expropriation – A company's assets may be seized with little or no compensation.
- Disruption of operations due to civil unrest, conflicts and war or due to the activities of social, environmental and other non-governmental organizations.
- Renegotiation of contractual terms of agreements signed by a previous government with the company.
- Policies and regulations that require the use of domestic labour and supplies or limit foreign ownership.
- Policies and regulations requiring the approval of certain mergers, acquisition and joint ventures which could restrict a company's ability to operate or acquire new businesses in certain countries. The case of Dubai Ports World's acquisition of P&O, where US port security concerns forced DP World to sell P&O's operations in the US, is a classic example. This case also shows that political risks are not limited to developing countries.
- Corrupt practices that may cause delays in the approval of licenses and other permits necessary to operate.
- Placing restrictions on the repatriation of dividends, profits or capital – blocked funds.
- Imposition of price controls, tax increases and introduction of new taxes, tariffs and restrictions on imports and exports.
- Discrimination against foreign businesses.

High political risk does not necessarily mean that a company should not invest in a particular country. It may be that the high political risk does not affect the firm's industry. Even if the project is affected by high political risk, the level of returns available may be large enough to justify taking on that risk.

13.5.1 Managing political risk

There are various strategies that can be employed to limit a company's exposure to political risks. Some of the more common strategies include:

- Pre-investment negotiations prior to investment. An agreement that states the duties and obligations of the company and the host government should be arranged. This would normally cover issues such as repatriation of funds, transfer pricing, use of expatriate personnel and provisions for settling any disputes.
- Use of risk-adjusted cash flows and discount rates. It is also important to consider political risks at the pre-investment capital budgeting analysis stage. Project cash flows and/or discount rates should be adjusted to reflect the potential risks. For example, potential cash flows may be discounted at a higher than normal rate if the potential for political risk is high.

When the proposed foreign investment is accepted, strategies that the company can employ to manage its exposure to political risks include:

- Use local labour and supplies. Using local labour and supplies has the potential to reducing exposure to expropriation. However, issues like reliability and quality of the local supplies could adversely affect the company's operations.
- **Borrowing from local banks**. If the subsidiary company is financed with a minimal equity contribution from the parent and a large local borrowing from local banks, it reduces the risk of host government takeover as local banks also have an interest in the survival of the company.
- Use joint ventures. As above joint ventures could also reduce exposure to political risks but control of the company may be an issue.
- Using loans from governmental and other multilateral agencies (e.g. The World Bank) can also reduce the risk of expropriation. It is less likely that the host government would take any action that would cause a row between that government and the other agencies involved.
- Informal and formal lobbying of the host government through diplomatic channels can also be used to reduce adverse political interventions.
- Adherence to corporate social responsibility and ethical standards. Maintaining strict corporate social responsibility and ethical standards would reduce potential conflicts with civil society groups and other non-governmental organisations. For example, provision of social and public amenities – schools, hospitals, etc., can be helpful in reducing tension between the company and the local community in which it operates.
- **Political risk insurance**. Many export credit agencies (such as the Export Credit Guarantee Department in the UK and Australia's Export Finance and Insurance Corporation) provide insurance cover for companies in their home countries that operate in other markets. The World Bank Group also offers a range of investment guarantees and political risk insurance products for direct foreign investment in developing countries. A company investing overseas can take out insurance to manage its exposure to political risks such as expropriation, inconvertibility of the host currency and war and civil disturbances.
- **Control of technology, markets and patents**. Control of technology, patents and trademarks can reduce the risk of expropriation, if the host government cannot operate the business without access to the patents, trademarks, and the technical know-how. This can be achieved by diversifying the operational structure of the company, such as research and development, production, and supply chains are not located in the same country.

Other measures that can also be used to manage the issue of blocked funds include:

- Transfer pricing. Adjustments to inter-subsidiary transfer pricing of goods and services can be used to move funds from the subsidiary to the parent company thus bypassing any restrictions on remittances. For example, goods from the country with blocked funds to other affiliates could be priced lower but goods received from other subsidiaries would be at a higher priced. The host government may intervene to determine a fair price if they view the pricing policy as inappropriate.
- Adjustments to fees and royalties. Fees and service charges due to the parent company, for the use of licences, patents and trademarks, may be increased. Parent will thus continue to receive income from the subsidiary.
- Create exports earnings. Blocked funds can be used to purchase local materials, for export. Foreign exchange earned from these exports can then be used by the company.

- Local sourcing. If possible the company might use the blocked funds to purchase raw materials and other services needed by other subsidiaries or the parent company.
- Local new investments or expansions. The blocked funds could be used to finance new investments or expansions to existing business.
- Parallel or back-to-back loans. The blocked funds could be lent to a local company which in turn would arrange an equivalent amount in loan to the parent company or one of its subsidiaries.

13.6 Summary

The theoretical foreign exchange relationships that we have considered in this chapter are important, as they help to explain why exchange rates between currencies tend to change.

Once the reasons for exchange-rate movement have been identified, foreign exchange risks can be fully understood and techniques to hedge these risks may be developed. In this chapter we have identified the main types of foreign exchange risk. Techniques to manage these risks are covered in the next chapter.

Revision Questions

13

? Question 1

Explain the meaning of 'economic risk' and distinguish it from transaction risk. **(5 marks)**

? Question 2

How reliable are forward rates as estimates of future spot rates? **(5 marks)**

? Question 3

Explain and exemplify the nature of foreign exchange transaction exposures. **(5 marks)**

? Question 4

A dealer working for a major commercial bank which deals in international currencies finds the following quotations for US dollars to Swiss francs:

Spot	$0.8313/SF1
Six months forward	$0.8447/SF1

The annualised 6-month dollar interest rate is 5.33% and the annualised 6-month Swiss franc rate is 2.4%.

Interest rates are annualised by semi- (half-yearly) compounding.

The dealer is authorised to buy or sell up to US$5 million, or its equivalent in other currencies. Other relevant information is as follows:

Transaction costs for dealing in hard currencies are US$5,500 per transaction, paid at the end of the 6-month period.

The final profits, if any, are held in sterling.

Borrowing and lending can be done at the rates given above.

The current exchange rate for US$ to sterling is 2.00.

Requirements

(a) Explain the term 'arbitrage profits' and discuss the reasons why such profits might be available in the scenario given above. **(6 marks)**

(b) Describe, with the aid of suitable calculations, the actions necessary for the dealer to take advantage of such possibilities. **(8 marks)**

(c) Discuss other types of arbitrage opportunities that are available to, and suitable for
- financial institutions such as a major commercial bank;
- non-financial organisations with established treasury departments, such as a manufacturing company. **(6 marks)**
(Total marks = 20)

Questions 5 and 6 are taken from Paper 5 (Money Management) of the examinations of the Association of Corporate Treasurers (ACT).

Question 5

Equip plc is a major exporter of agricultural equipment to Australia, New Zealand and throughout Europe. All production facilities are in the United Kingdom. The majority of raw materials and tools are also sourced in the United Kingdom, with a few imports from Eire, priced in sterling. Major competitors are based in the United States and Germany. There are plans to set up a manufacturing subsidiary in Australia, funded in part by an Australian dollar loan to be taken out by Equip plc. The new manufacturing facility would be used to source the Australian and New Zealand markets.

Requirements
(a) Describe the potential currency exposures faced by this company before setting up the manufacturing subsidiary. **(7 marks)**

(b) Consider the effects of setting up the new manufacturing subsidiary in Australia.
 (i) Will any of the exposures identified in (a) above be reduced?
 (ii) What new currency exposures will the group face? **(8 marks)**
(Total marks = 15)

Question 6

(a) If the long-term prospects for inflation in the United Kingdom and Australia are 2 and 6% p.a., respectively, what changes would you expect to observe in the following rates over the next 12 months:
 (i) sterling/A$ spot rate (currently £/A$2.68)?
 (ii) UK and Australian 3-month interest rates (currently 6% for sterling and 8% for Australian dollars)?
 Explain your results. **(10 marks)**

(b) Exchange rates for US dollars to Japanese yen are currently quoted as follows:

Maturity	US$/JP¥	A$/US$
Spot	123.40/50	0.5255/60
3 months	0.12/0.02	4.7/4.9
6 months	0.13/0.03	4.7/4.9

Requirement

At what rate would the bank buy Japanese yen and sell Australian dollars 6 months' forward?

(5 marks)

(Total marks = 15)

 # Question 7

Mango Plc is a UK-based manufacturer of electrical equipments. The company exports regularly to countries in the Euro zone, Switzerland and South Africa denominated in the currency of the customer.

Requirements

(a) Discuss the foreign exchange risks that Mango Plc might face in its operations.

(10 marks)

(b) Assume the following information is available:

	Spot Rates against the Pound (£)	
Country (Currency)	**Spot rate at today**	**Expected spot rate in 6 months**
Euro zone (Euro)	1.4955	1.4565
Switzerland (SFr)	2.3283	2.2328
South Africa (Rand)	11.5831	12.0815

Explain the theory of purchasing power parity (PPP). Based on this theory would you expect the 1-year inflation rates of the countries above to be higher or lower than UK inflation rate? [No calculations required] **(8 marks)**

(c) How does the change in exchange rates in (b) above, affect Mango Plc? **(7 marks)**

(Total marks = 25)

Solutions to Revision Questions

13

✅ Solution 1

Theoretically 'economic risk' is the risk that the value of the business expressed as the net present value of its future cash flows will be affected by exchange-rate movements. To a practitioner of currency risk management, economic exposure is concerned with the strategic evaluation of foreign transactions and relationships and the impact of exchange-rate fluctuations on the competitive position of the firm in its markets. The consequences can be direct, through the effect on the value of future remittances, overseas investments, cost structures and profit margins; or indirect, through the changes in economic conditions brought about by exchange-rate changes. The identification of economic exposure is crucial to strategic planning in companies and will require the use of simulation techniques to explore the impact, over varying time frames, of the relationship between the firm's performance and possible currency movements.

Transaction risk in contrast focuses on the gains or losses which arise when actual transactions involving a currency conversion take place. It is therefore concerned with actual cash flows rather than estimated future flows, although obviously many of the economic exposures identified will end up as transaction exposures.

✅ Solution 2

Forward rates regarded as estimates of future spot rates can only be as reliable as the best prediction the market can make based on the underlying technical information available at a point of time. This would include assessment of the interest differential for the period involved.

✅ Solution 3

Foreign exchange rates fluctuate according to the demand for and supply of a currency. A home exporter or importer who enters into a contract in a currency other than his home currency, where the currency passes at a future time, opens himself to foreign exchange transaction risk.

For example, a UK company enters into a contract with a US company to purchase a machine for $40,000, the amount being payable on delivery in 2 months' time. The exchange rate at the contract date was £1 to $2.00, which would entail the UK company paying an amount of £20,000 if the debt was settled immediately. However, the actual sterling outflow will depend on the rate of exchange in 2 months' time. If the rate is £1 to

$1.90, £21,053 will be paid; if £1 to $2.10, £19,048 will be paid. The cash outflow depends on a future event.

The risk occurs because the spot exchange rate on a future date is unknown today, thereby making the future spot rate a random variable. The variability of the exchange rate leads to variability in future cash flows.

 Solution 4

(a) The expression 'arbitrage profits' relates to the gain made by exploiting differences in market rates, for instance interest rates and forward currency rates. If, for example, a forward currency rate is at a higher premium than is warranted by the differences in the respective local interest rates, then a profit can be made by borrowing in one currency and depositing in the other. Given the advanced state of communications, however, such simple differences are rarely available.

More recently, therefore, it has been applied to much more speculative positions, for example selling particular bonds forwards and buying others which, it is believed, will increase in price relative to the bonds sold (so they can be bought back leaving a net profit). The so-called 'hedge funds' build up big positions of this kind, but at considerable risk.

In the scenario provided, there is a possibility of profiting by entering into arbitrage, because the interest-rate differentials are not precisely matched by the premium implicit in the forward rates.

(b) The actions which would be necessary to take advantage of this are as follows:
1. borrow $5 million at 5.33% p.a. for 6 months, at a cost of $131,520;
2. buy $5 million of Swiss francs at 1.2029 per dollar, that is 6,014,500 Swiss francs;
3. invest this amount at 2.4% p.a. for 6 months ($\sqrt{1.024} - 1$) to earn 71,745 Swiss francs, bringing the total to 6,086,245 Swiss francs;
4. sell this amount forward at 0.8447 to yield $5,141,051;
5. pay off the original loan, which has accumulated to $5,131,520 to yield a gross profit of $9,531, or $4,031 net of the transaction costs (equivalent to £2,016 at today's exchange rate).

The original loan is $5 million, plus accumulated interest of $131,520, as in item (1) above. The profit is the amount sold forward less the payment of the loan plus interest:

$$\$5,141,051 - \$5,131,520 = \$9,531$$

An equally acceptable answer was one starting with the borrowing of only $4,871,870, that is equivalent to $5 million in 6 months' time. On that basis, the net profit would have been $3,958 (equivalent to £1,979 at today's exchange rate).

(c) Arbitrage is an important element in the working of the market, in the sense that it exploits apparent inefficiencies in that market, in a way which almost invariably has the effect of reducing the inefficiencies, that is moving the market in the direction of equilibrium.

Traders in financial organisations will have up-to-date information on many markets which are managed separately, but the movements in which are perceived as being correlated. For example, interest rates within common currency areas should be the same. If they are higher in country B than country A, then it will pay to borrow A's currency and deposit in B's. In macroeconomic terms, however, the inflow of cash into B will have a downward impact on interest rates.

Another example concerns the prices at which bonds are trading. If one bond is priced higher than another seen as being of a similar maturity and risk, there is a case for selling the first short, and buying the second. Selling a future and buying the underlying asset is another – both of these, again, being likely to influence the prices of the instruments concerned.

Whereas financial institutions (from banks to so-called 'hedge funds') are in the business of making money out of money, other organisations have primary objectives in other markets. It is rare, therefore, for them to indulge in arbitrage on the broad scale available to the banks.

However, their knowledge of particular markets could give them opportunities to follow a similar path. A company involved in manufacturing products derived from traded commodities, for example, will need to have a detailed knowledge of the respective commodity markets, and will see opportunities where

- the prices quoted in different geographical markets are not the same, when translated at current exchange rates (action, buy in the market where prices are low in international terms and sell where they are high);
- the different positions in the market do not reflect the prevailing rate of interest (e.g. if the 12-month price exceeds the 6-month price by more than 6 months' interest, buy the 6-month position and sell the 12-month one).

The unit margins available to arbitrageurs are usually small, and large positions need to be taken to cover transaction costs. In most cases, there are risks (e.g. that the market does not return to equilibrium); hence, a sound knowledge of the market is an essential prerequisite.

 ## Solution 5

(a) *Transaction risk*
- Sales revenue denominated in Australian dollars, New Zealand dollars euros, other.

Economic risk
- Purchase costs denominated in sterling but sourced from Eire.
- Price pressure from competitors in the United States and Germany (this will be affected by the currency cost base of these companies).

Translation risk
- Minor as Equip Plc has no foreign subsidiaries – just retranslation of year-end currency debtors.

Overall assessment
- Mismatch of sterling cost base versus exposed sales revenue.

(b) (i) Reduction in exposure:
Australian dollar transaction risk
Australian dollar economic risk
Exposure from competitors is not eliminated.

(ii) New exposures, to the extent that they do not net out:
translation risk from incorporating subsidiary accounts;
translation risk arising from the Australian dollar debt;
transaction risk as a result of the Australian dollar dividend payments to the UK.

The end result will depend on the success of the Australian operation, the actual figures involved and any increase in local sales that may naturally result from a greater presence in Australia. For example, exposure to New Zealand dollars could increase if sales to New Zealand were to increase.

 ## Solution 6

(a) (i) *Purchasing power parity*

Using the formula in Section 13.3.2 of the study material, the expected spot rate in 1 year is

$$\frac{1 + i_{\text{AUST}}}{1 + i_{\text{UK}}} \times S_0 = S_t$$

Therefore,

$$\frac{1.06}{1.02} \times 2.68 = 2.7851$$

(ii) *The Fisher effect*

The real rate of return should be the same in each country

UK: real rate–1.06/1.02 − 1 = 3.921% p.a.
Australia: real rate = 1.08/1.06 − 1 = 1.887% p.a.

Therefore a reduction can be expected in UK interest rates, or an increase in Australian rates to bring them in line, depending on levels of real returns in other currencies. However, this is from a long-term perspective; interest rates are commonly used as a tool in controlling inflation and so the position in the economic cycle and success at meeting inflation targets may have more impact on the level of interest rates in the shorter term.

As inflation rates in Australia are forecast to be higher than that in the United Kingdom, we would expect the Australian dollar to *weaken* against the pound sterling. Therefore, in 12 months' time you would expect to receive more Australian dollars for your pounds sterling.

(b) As both currencies (A$ and JP¥) are quoted against the US$, what we need is the cross rate (A$ and JP¥). This is the same as selling A$ for US$ and using the US$ to buy JP¥. The outright ask rate on US$, on the A$/US$ leg, is 0.5260 + 0.00049 = 0.52649. Note that the points are added because they appear in ascending order in the quote. The outright bid rate on US$, on the JP¥/US$ leg, is 123.40 − 0.13 = 123.27. In this case the points are subtracted because they appear in descending order in the quote.

Thus, A$/JP¥ = 123.47 × 0.52649 = 65.0057.

 ## Solution 7

(a) As the company's exports are denominated in the foreign currency Mango Plc is exposed to transaction risk. Its income from the exports would be adversely affected if the UK pound should depreciate against any of the three currencies. However, the extent of the exposure will depend on how the three currencies are correlated. If the currencies are positively correlated, then the level of transaction risk is likely to be higher. If some of the currencies are negatively correlated, then this mitigates the extent of the transaction risk as the negative effect of depreciation in some currencies would be offset by an appreciation of the others.

Mango also faces economic risks due to the mismatch in the currency of their costs and that of their revenue. Should those currencies depreciate in the long run against the pound, revenue from their exports when converted into pounds may not be enough to cover their cost which is fixed in pounds. This might also lose competitiveness if the currency of these countries should depreciate against the pound whilst appreciating against the currency of Mango's competitors in other countries such as Japan and the United States.

(b) PPP suggests that the purchasing power of a consumer will be similar whether purchasing goods in a foreign country or in the home country. The rational behind this argument is that when inflation is high in a particular country, foreign demand for goods in that country and hence its currency will decrease. In addition, that country's demand for foreign goods should increase. As a result, the currency of that country will weaken.

In general, currencies in countries with high inflation would weaken according to PPP, causing the purchasing power of goods in the home country versus that of the foreign country to be similar.

As both the euro and the Swiss franc are expected to appreciate against the pound, we would expect inflation in the Euro-zone and Switzerland to be lower than inflation in the United Kingdom. However, we would expect inflation in South Africa to be higher than inflation in the United Kingdom as the SA rand is expected to depreciate against the pound.

(c) The revenues of Mango Plc from its sales to South Africa would be adversely affected as the depreciation of the South African Rand means the sales will convert into fewer pounds. On the other hand, the depreciation of the pound against the euro and the Swiss franc means would benefit Mango Plc as sales now convert to more pounds. The net effect on Mango Plc will depend on the amount of sales to the various countries.

14

Foreign Exchange
Risk Management

Foreign Exchange Risk Management

14

LEARNING OUTCOMES

After completing this chapter you should be able to:

► identify and evaluate foreign exchange risk facing an organisation;

► identify and evaluate appropriate methods for managing foreign exchange risk.

The topics covered in this chapter are

► hedging export credit risk;

► forward contracts;

► money market hedges;

► internal hedging techniques;

► currency swaps;

► currency futures and options.

14.1 Introduction

The main purpose of this chapter is to introduce foreign exchange instruments and outline how they are used in the management of foreign exchange risk. Exchange rate movements affect present as well as future cash flows of the company. We begin by examining the various internal hedging techniques. We then examine ways of managing foreign exchange risk using forward contracts, money market hedge, currency futures and currency options. Most of the methods described will be aimed at reducing transaction risk.

14.2 Hedging exchange-rate risk

Transaction risk (Figure 14.1) occurs when there is a time delay between the sale of goods and the receipt of the payments, and it will occur in all foreign trading. The question is, who carries it?

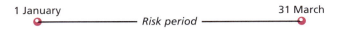

Figure 14.1 Transaction risk

If the spot rate was £1 = $1.50 and $1,500 worth of goods were sold on 1 January, the risk period is the 3 months till 31 March.

The exchange rate could move to £1 = $2, thus changing the sterling value received from £1,000 (1,500/1.50) to £750 (1,500/2.00): a loss of £250.

Companies exposed to transaction risk can either run the risk of exchange-rate movements or they can take steps to protect their future cash flows from exchange-rate fluctuation. If they have sold goods abroad and are prepared to gamble they could, in addition to the profit on the sale of the goods, find that they had made a currency gain. This would happen if the rate of exchange had moved in their favour between the time that they delivered the goods and the time when they are paid. However, it could be that the rate of exchange moves the other way, giving them a currency loss (as indicated above), perhaps meaning that the payment they receive when converted into their own currency does not cover their costs. It is to avoid this possibility that many businessmen seek to avoid the risks of currency movements by hedging.

Once an enterprise has decided to hedge a particular foreign currency risk, there are a number of methods to consider. They can be grouped as *internal* and *external* hedging techniques.

14.3 Internal hedging techniques

Internal hedging means using techniques available within the company or group to manage exchange-rate risks. These techniques do not operate through the foreign exchange markets and therefore they avoid the associated costs. However, this does not mean they are costless.

14.3.1 Invoicing in the home currency

Here, the company simply invoices in its own currency. The exchange rate risk is not avoided, it is merely transferred to the customer. This technique may not always be possible, given that the company may well be competing with local industries invoicing in the local currency, and, as such, the overseas quote may become uncompetitive.

14.3.2 Bilateral and multilateral netting

This is a form of matching appropriate for multinational groups or companies with subsidiaries or branches in a number of overseas countries. Bilateral netting applies where pairs of companies in the same group net off their own positions regarding payables and receivables, often without the involvement of a central treasury department. Multilateral netting is performed by a central treasury department where several subsidiaries are involved and interact with head office.

The process is based on determining a base currency, for example sterling or US dollars, so that the intra-group transactions are recorded only in that currency; each group company reports its obligations to other group companies to a central, say UK, treasury department, which then informs each subsidiary of the net receipt or payment needed to settle their foreign exchange intra-group positions.

While this procedure undoubtedly reduces transaction costs by reducing the number of transactions and also reduces exchange-rate risk by reducing currency flows, the difficulties are that there are regulations in certain countries which severely limit or even prohibit netting, and there may also be cross-border legal and taxation problems to overcome as well as the extra administrative costs of the centralised treasury operation.

Example 14.A

Certain organisational and policy adjustments may be made internally by a business for the purpose of minimising the effects of transactions in foreign currencies.

A group of companies controlled from the United Kingdom includes subsidiaries in India, South Africa and the United States. It is forecast that, at the end of the month, inter-company indebtedness will be as follows:

- The Indian subsidiary will be owed 144,381,000 Indian rupee (Rs) by the South African subsidiary and will owe the US subsidiary $1,060,070.
- The South African subsidiary will be owed 14,438,000 South African rands (R) by the US subsidiary and will owe it $800,000.

It is a function of the central treasury department to net off inter-company balances as far as possible and to issue instructions for settlement of the net balances. For this purpose, the relevant exchange rates in terms of £1 are $1.415; R10.215; Rs 68.10.

What are the net payments to be made in respect of the above balances, and what are the possible advantages and disadvantages of such multilateral netting?

Solution

First set out the table in the separate currencies:

	India	South Africa	US
India	–	Rs144,381,000	($1,060,070)
South Africa	(Rs144,381,000)	–	R14,438,000
			($800,000)
US	$1,060,070	(R14,438,000)	
		$800,000	

Now convert to sterling:

	India £	South Africa £	US £	Total £
India	–	2,120,132	(749,166)	1,370,966
South Africa	(2,120,132)	–	1,413,412	(1,272,091)
			(565,371)	
US	749,166	(1,413,412)	–	(98,875)
		565,371		
	(1,370,966)	1,272,091	98,875	–

Central treasury department will instruct the South Africa subsidiary to pay the Indian subsidiary £1,272,091, and the US subsidiary to pay the Indian subsidiary £98,875. Figure 14.2 illustrates the cash flows involved.

Possible advantages of this procedure are

- lower transaction costs as a result of fewer transactions;
- regular settlements may reduce intra-company exposure risks.

FOREIGN EXCHANGE RISK MANAGEMENT

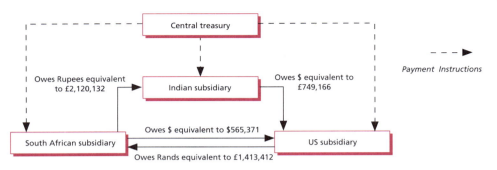

Figure 14.2 Multilateral netting

Possible disadvantages are that

- if the base currency is generally weak against other currencies for a sustained period, subsidiary company results could be significantly distorted;
- if a particular subsidiary is suffering from cash-flow problems, the centre may have to arrange for it to have additional funds for settlements, thereby offsetting some or all of the transaction cost benefits and possibly incurring exchange losses;
- the central treasury may have difficulties in exercising the strict control that the procedure demands;
- tax considerations may be adverse.

14.3.3 Leading and lagging

This method involves changing the timing of payments in an attempt to take advantage of changes in the relative value of the currencies involved.

Leading could, for example, be a requirement by a payee for immediate or short-term payment where the payee's currency, representing the basis for settlement, is weakening against the payer's currency. *Lagging*, on the other hand, is an arrangement whereby the payee grants longer-term credit or defer payments to another party in anticipation of exchange rate changes.

The technique can be used only when exchange-rate forecasts can be made with some degree of confidence, while interest rates would also need to be taken into account in granting long-term credit. The procedure is used mainly for settlement of intra-company balances, but it can also be used externally, for example, between two companies in different countries which carry on extensive trade with each other.

14.3.4 Matching

This is the use of receipts in a particular currency to match payment obligations in the same currency.

A UK company may have a substantial trade with another country overseas, involving both debtor and creditor transactions, for example, where goods are exported and invoiced in a foreign currency and the overseas sales transacted are also paid for in that currency. The UK company may well benefit from operating a foreign currency account, whereby its exchange risk is limited to any conversions of the net account balance into sterling. Sometimes, a company may be able to reduce its transaction exposure by pricing some of its exports in the same currency as that needed to pay for its imports.

Companies with foreign subsidiaries can also reduce their translation exposure, by matching assets in the foreign subsidiary with liabilities in the currency of the subsidiary.

If monetary assets in the foreign subsidiary equal liabilities in the foreign currency, the net exposure of the parent company from currency fluctuations will be zero. There may be difficulties, however, such as restrictions on borrowing limits in the foreign country, in achieving this objective.

14.3.5 Restructuring

The firm can also reduce its long-term exposure to exchange rate fluctuations by restructuring its operations. Restructuring may involve

- increasing or reducing sales in new or existing foreign markets;
- increasing or reducing dependency on foreign suppliers;
- establishing or eliminating production facilities in foreign markets; and/or
- increasing or reducing the level of debt denominated in foreign currencies.

14.4 External hedging techniques

External techniques mean using the financial markets to hedge foreign-currency movements. These include the use of forwards, futures, options and swaps on currencies. As much as possible, the relative advantages and disadvantages of these products are similar to those of their interest-rate counterparts presented in Chapter 12. Important considerations in the selection of an appropriate external hedging technique would be cost and flexibility of the hedge, the company's attitude to risk, the currency to be hedged and the size and certainty of the exposure.

14.4.1 Forward markets

A forward contract is one in which one party agrees to buy 'something', and another party agrees to sell that same 'something' at a designated date in the future. For example, in the case of a forward exchange contract, one party agrees to deliver a specified amount of one currency for another at a specified exchange rate at a designated date in the future. The specified exchange rate is called the *forward rate*. The designated date at which the parties must transact is called the *settlement date* or *delivery date*.

When an investor takes a position in the market by buying a forward contract, the investor is said to be in a *long position*. If, instead, the investor's opening position is the sale of a forward contract, the investor is said to be in a *short position*.

The foreign exchange forward market is an interbank market. Most forward contracts have a maturity of less than 2 years. For longer-dated forward contracts, the bid – ask spread – increases; that is, the size of the spread for a given currency increases with the maturity. Consequently, forward contracts become less attractive for hedging long-dated foreign currency exposure.

Fixed forward exchange contract

A fixed forward exchange contract is an agreement, entered into today, to purchase or sell a fixed quantity of a commodity, currency or other financial instrument on a fixed future date at a price fixed today. They are tailor-made to meet the exact requirements of the contract, and once entered into, the c ontract must be completed. A major problem with a forward contract is the fixed settlement date. By using an option forward contract this can be overcome.

Example 14.B

Suppose Karen's Shoe Shops plc, a UK company, has to pay an American supplier $200,000 in 1 month's time and the forward rate and spot rates are $1.9255 = £1 and $1.9295 = £1, respectively.

There are a number of options available:

- *Forward contract.* If Karen's Shoe Shops plc entered into a forward contract to buy dollars, the amount the company would have to pay in a month's time would be,

$$\text{Forward rate} = \frac{200,000}{1.9255} = £103,869.13$$

- *Spot in 1 month.* Alternatively, the company could wait for a month and transact at the prevailing spot price. If the forward rate is the best estimate of the future spot rate, then the amount payable would be the same as above, that is £103,869.13.
- *Lead payment.* The third possibility is to make a lead payment – settle the amount now. This will cost,

$$\frac{200,000}{1.9255} = £103,653.80$$

If interest payments are ignored, the lead payment proves the cheapest method.

Example 14.C

The Kidwelly Sweetie Company exports confectionery to a number of department stores in the United States and Europe. It is due to receive $12,000 in 6 months' time from goods supplied to a US customer.

The 6-month US$ forward rate is 1.9550–1.9600. The spot rate is 1.9960–1.9990.

What is the sterling receipt if the company decides to hedge using a forward exchange contract?

Solution

Reminder: When deciding which rate to use, it will always be the one that gives the lower sterling value for receipts and the highest sterling value for payments.

$12,000/1.9550 = £6,138
$12,000/1.9600 = £6,122

Therefore the sterling receipt is £6,122, as this is the lower of the two.

Option forward exchange contract

An option forward exchange contract is not the same as a currency option contract.

An option forward exchange contract offers the same arrangement as a fixed forward contract except that there is a choice of dates on which the user can exercise the contract. This is either: on any date up to a specified date or at any time between two future dates. In either case the forward rate that applies would be the forward rate, in the period in which the contract can be exercised, that is *least favourable* to the purchaser of the contract. If transaction dates are unknown, then an option forward contract offers more flexibility than a forward contract but at a higher cost.

Problems with forward contracts

Note that a forward exchange contract is binding. If, for example, an importer discovers eventually that he or she has contracted to buy more currency than he or she needs to pay his or her supplier, he or she is required to take up the full contractual amount at the agreed forward rate. He or she can then sell back any surplus to the bank at the spot rate on the day he or she settles. This is known as *closing out* the contract.

Similarly, an exporter who has contracted to sell forward more currency than he or she actually receives from his or her customer will be required to buy an extra amount at spot in order to close out his or her contract.

14.4.2 Money market hedge

The use of the forward market as a 'hedge' against variations in exchange rates was – illustrated above. Using the forward market it was possible to ensure that the exchange rate applying at some future date was known with certainty. Another way of achieving this is to use the money market. More steps are involved and they are illustrated below.

To hedge payments in a foreign currency, you would borrow at home, which would then be changed into the required foreign currency and invested until the payment is due. On the other hand, to hedge receipts you will borrow the foreign currency and invest the amount in the home currency. If there is no forward market for a given currency, the money market hedge provides a useful alternative. If interest-rate parity holds, then the money market hedge will achieve the same result as using the forward market. However, because the money market hedge requires two transactions (borrowing and investing) it can be relatively costly compared to the forward rate. Example 14.D illustrates the use of the money market to hedge receivables.

Example 14.D

Details are the same as in Example 14.C, with the following additional information on interest rates:

	Borrow	Lend
US	12%	–
UK	–	10%

Solution

(i) Borrow from the bank at the discounted value:

$$\frac{\$12,000}{1.06^*} = \$11,320$$

*Note that interest rate is always quoted annualised unless stated otherwise. Borrowing at 12% per annum is equivalent to 6% for 6-months (that is 12% ÷ 2).

(ii) Convert at the sterling spot rate:

$$\frac{11,320}{1.9990} = £5,663$$

(iii) Invest at the sterling interest rate:

£5,663 × 1.05* = £5,946

*Investing at 10% per annum is equivalent to 5% for 6-months (that is 10% ÷ 2).

This is only necessary so that comparisons can be made with forward exchange contracts. This amount is less than the forward exchange contract (see Example 14.C) and therefore the company should hedge using the forward exchange contract, and receive £6,122.

In reality, the money may well be invested elsewhere within the business, or used to pay off outstanding liabilities.

Now attempt Exercise 14.1, dealing with foreign exchange. The exercise is about the identification of foreign exchange risks and alternative strategies for managing the risk.

 Exercise 14.1

F plc, a merchandising company operating mainly in the United Kingdom, undertakes import and export transactions with firms in a less well-developed country, Freiland.

Many of these transactions are necessarily conducted in the local currency, the freimark (Fm).

F plc also has a small subsidiary company in Freiland, concerned wholly with servicing equipment sold in that country.

The sterling value of the freimark has fluctuated frequently over the past 12 months, between Fm12.50 = £1 and Fm27.50 = £1.

The exchange rate currently stands at Fm25.00.

The treasurer of F plc has prepared the following cash-flow forecast of transactions in Fm over the next 6 months:

	Month 1 Fm'000	Month 2 Fm'000	Month 3 Fm'000	Month 4 Fm'000	Month 5 Fm'000	Month 6 Fm'000
Receipts in respect of sales invoiced from UK	37,400	48,500	35,000	77,300	62,600	46,700
Remittances from subsidiary co. balances in excess of agreed float	3,200	1,600	2,000	2,700	2,400	1,800
Total receipts	40,600	50,100	37,000	80,000	65,000	48,500
Payment for goods imported from Freiland	38,200	55,500	44,200	36,800	53,000	49,500
Purchase of fixed assets in Freiland for subsidiary company				40,000	5,000	
	38,200	55,500	44,200	76,800	58,000	49,500
Net receipts/(payments)	2,400	(5,400)	(7,200)	3,200	7,000	(1,000)

Requirements

(a) State and explain the various factors that should be taken into account before the company decides to take any action to reduce its foreign exchange transaction exposure.

(b) Describe three techniques of exposure management that might be available to F plc under the circumstances of this question.

(c) Explain the meaning of 'economic exposure' and distinguish it from transaction exposure.

Solution

(a) Factors which should be taken into account include

- *Future exchange-rate movement*: The currency is extremely volatile and has moved between Fm12.50 = £1 and Fm27.50 = £1. Future movements will depend on a number of factors, including economic growth, interest rates, movements in money aggregates and reserves, central bank actions, inflation rates and taxation rates. Principally, the factors will relate to national economic events in the United Kingdom and Freiland. However, exchange-rate movements also have a wider international dimension which cannot wholly be ignored.

- *Corporate philosophy and policy*: This covers matters such as
  - the enterprise's attitude towards foreign currency transactions and the importance of overseas trading;
  - the ability of the firm to absorb foreign exchange losses;
  - the attitude of the firm to risk and whether there is a policy actively to arrange positions with a view to profiting from foreign exchange, or whether currency management is viewed as risk reduction, through close-out strategies which provide certainty as to home currency values;
  - competitors' views and reactions to currency fluctuations – comprising exporters from the United Kingdom and other countries and domestic market competitors.
- *Other currency flows in the group*: Possible links between Freimark and other currencies in which the firm has dealings should be investigated. The links may be formal, through systems such as the European Monetary System (EMS), or informal, where historically close trading links have led to the behaviour of currencies mirroring each other.
- *Forecast beyond the 6-month time horizon*: At present, the currency flows in freimarks almost match each other over the 6 months, with the deficit of freimarks rising up to Month 3, before falling.
- *Expertise within the firm*: Forecasting exchange-rate trends, assessing risks and taking management *action* requires the commitment of resources and the existence of skilled personnel.

(b) Three techniques of exposure management which F plc might apply are as follows:
- *Currency bank account*: Open a freimark bank account in the United Kingdom and open an overdraft facility sufficient to cover the maximum indebtedness (Fm9,200 in month 3). All payments and receipts are put through the account and the company will pay interest (only for the period when the account is overdrawn) and bank charges.
- *Leading and lagging*: A mechanism whereby a company accelerates or delays payments or receipts in anticipation of exchange rate movements (leads and lags respectively). For example, consider payments for imported goods. If the current rate of Fm25 = £1 is unlikely to hold, and the forecast is for a fall to Fm15 = £1, the company could lead its payments so that they are made when sterling is strong. Similarly, receipts of freimarks could be timed for when sterling is weak – in the case of a fall, lagged until it is Fm15 = £1.
- *Forward exchange contracts*: The company could enter into six forward exchange contracts, timed at 1, 2, 3, 4, 5 and 6 months, purchasing or selling the company's future currency commitments in the forward market. This would provide certainty as to the future value of the net receipts or payments, provided always that the cash-flow forecast is accurate, since the company would be required to fulfil the contract. This may necessitate buying or selling currency to meet the contract and it is possible that a forward-option contract, where the company has discretion as to the exact date on which the contract is to be fulfilled, may be the most appropriate.

(c) Theoretically, 'economic exposure' is the risk that the value of the business expressed as the net present value of its future cash flows will be affected by exchange-rate movements. To a practitioner of currency risk management, economic exposure is concerned with the strategic evaluation of foreign transactions and relationships, and the impact of exchange-rate fluctuations on the competitive position of the firm in its markets. The consequences can be direct, through the effect on the value of future remittances, overseas investments, cost structures or profit margins; or indirect, through the changes in economic conditions brought about by exchange rate changes.

The identification of economic exposure is crucial to strategic planning in companies, and will require the use of simulation techniques to explore the impact, over varying time frames, of the relationship between the firm's performance and possible currency movements.

In contrast, transaction exposure focuses on the gains or losses which arise when actual transactions involving a currency conversion take place. It is therefore concerned with actual cash flows rather than estimated future cash flows, although obviously many of the economic exposures identified will end up as transaction exposures.

14.4.3 Futures

> Financial futures in foreign exchange rates are contracts to buy or sell an amount of foreign currency at a future date, and are traded on futures exchanges such as the Chicago Mercantile Exchange (CME), which has a London office. The futures exchange quotes a price for each contract on every trading day, so that contracts are saleable before their delivery date. Although this makes them flexible, there are restrictions in that contracts have to be for specific amounts of currency (e.g. £62,500 blocks for a currency future against the US dollar) and delivery dates are limited.

You would sell currency futures to hedge receivables in a foreign currency, and buy currency futures to hedge foreign currency payments if the foreign currency is the underlying currency of the futures. Thus a US exporter expecting to receive £1 million from a UK customer in 3 months will sell sterling futures to protect itself against the pound depreciating relative to the dollar.

Example 14.E

A UK company Clark plc sells goods to Smith Inc. in the United States to the value of $2,650,000. The sale takes place in June with payment due in August. The finance director of Clark plc is concerned that sterling will strengthen against the dollar which would reduce the sterling value of the contract. The spot rate in June is $1.9050 = £1.

Assume that in June a September $/£ futures contract is quoted at $1.9000. This means that the futures market will buy or sell sterling for dollars for future delivery, in September, at an exchange rate of $1.9000 = £1.

To hedge against the risk of sterling strengthening against the dollar, Clark plc would need to buy an appropriate number of $/£ futures contracts. This means that Clark plc has agreed to buy sterling for dollars on the future delivery date at the exchange rate specified by the price of the futures contract. The sterling futures contracts which are traded on the CME are for £62,500.

The number of contracts that Clark plc would need to buy is

$$\frac{2,650,000}{1.9000 \times 62,500} = 22.32 \text{ contracts}$$

Only a whole number of contracts can be traded, so Clark plc would need to buy either twenty-two or twenty-three contracts. We will assume twenty-two contracts, although this will leave a small amount unhedged.

In August, just before Smith Inc. is due to pay, the futures contract price has changed to $1.9200 and the spot rate has also moved to $1.9200 = £1.

Clark plc will now close out its position in the futures contracts by selling the futures contracts:

Profit on futures ($)	
$(1.9200 - 1.9000) \times 62,500 = \$1,250$ per contract × 28 contracts	27,500
Received from Smith Inc. ($)	2,650,000
	2,677,500

The total receipts of $2,677,500 will be sold on the spot market to give a sterling receipt of $\frac{2,677,500}{1.9200} = £1,394,531$

and an effective exchange rate for the $2,650,000 received of $\frac{2,650,000}{1,394,531} = \$1.9903/£$.

Alternatively we could calculate the net receipts as follows:

The 22 contracts cover $2,612,500 ($1.900 \times 62,500 \times 22$) of the exposure leaving $37,500 ($2,650,000 − $2,612,500) unhedged. The hedged amount will be converted at the agreed futures rate but the unhedged part will be converted at the prevailing spot rate on receipt of the money. Thus, the net receipt in pounds will be

Hedged	22 × 62,500 =	£1,375,000
Unhedged	37,500/1.9200 =	£19,531
Total Receipt		£1,394,531

In practice, the profit on the futures contracts would be received as it arose during the period from June to August.

Note also that if sterling had weakened against the dollar, a loss would have been made on the futures contract, but this would have been offset by receiving more sterling in the spot market in August.

Example 14.F

A UK company, Coopers Plc, imports electronic components from the United States. Assume it is June and Coopers has just received a consignment from the United States valued at $5,200,000 payable in August. The spot rate today is $1.9050 = £1 and a September $/£ futures contract is quoted at $1.9000 (contract size = £62,500).

To hedge against the risk of sterling weakening against the dollar, Coopers plc would need to sell an appropriate number of $/£ futures contracts.

The number of contracts that Coopers would need to sell is

$$\frac{5,200,000}{1.9000 \times 62,500} = 43.79 = 43 \text{ contracts}$$

Suppose in August, the futures contract price has changed to $1.9200 and the spot rate has also moved to $1.9200 = £1.

Coopers will now close out its position in the futures contracts by buying the futures contracts:

Loss on futures ($)	
(1.9200 − 1.9000) × 62,500 = $1,250 per contract × 43 contracts	53,750
Amount due to US supplier ($)	5,200,000
	5,253,750

The total amount payable of $5,253,750 will be purchased on the spot market to give a sterling cost of

$$\frac{5,253,750}{1.9200} = £2,736,328 \text{ and an effective exchange of } \frac{5,200,000}{2,736,328} = \$1.9004/£$$

Alternatively, the net cost of the import can be calculated as follows:

The 43 contracts cover $5,106,250 ($1.900 \times 62,500 \times 43$) of the exposure leaving $93,750 ($5,200,000 − $5,106,250) unhedged. The hedged amount will be converted at the agreed futures rate but the unhedged part will be converted at the spot rate on the payment date. The net cost in pounds will be

Hedged	43 × 62,500 =	£2,687,500
Unhedged	93,750/1.9200 =	£48,828
Total Receipt		£2,736,328

14.4.4 Options

> 🔑 Options give the client the right – but not the obligation – to buy ('call') or sell ('put') a specific amount of currency at a specific price on a specific date. The banks take into account the costs of buying and selling currencies and the potential profits, and distil them all into the premium payable for the option.

The level of premium depends on a number of factors:

- The *strike price*: This might be
  - 'at the money', that is the agreed price corresponds with that currently available (spot or forward);
  - 'in the money', that is the agreed price is more favourable to the client than is currently available (but then the premium would be higher);
  - 'out of the money', that is the price is less favourable to the client than is currently available (but then the premium would be low – possibly zero).
- The *maturity*: The premium follows the line of a diminishing returns curve, for example a 6-month option will not be twice as expensive as a 3-month option.
- The *volatility* of the spot rate, that is the greater the volatility, the greater the premium.
- *Interest-rate differentials*, which affect the banks' carrying costs.
- *Liquidity* in the market, sentiment and other judgemental factors.

Example 14.G

A company is tendering for the sale of equipment to a US company for $3 m, settlement due in 3 months' time. The current spot rate is $1.95 = £1. However, the company is worried about the dollar weakening against the pound, thus making the sale less profitable.

The company has been offered a 3-month put option on US dollars at $1.97 = £1, costing 0.02 cents per pound. What is the company's position?

Solution

The sterling amount received if the option is exercised:

$3,000,000/$1.97 = 1,522,843

In addition, the cost of the option itself must be considered. This is quoted in cost per foreign currency unit:

0.02 cents × £1,522,843 = $30,457

This is payable regardless of whether the option itself is exercised. Hence the net sterling amount:

	£
To sell $3m	1,522,843
Cost of option (at spot): $30,457/$1.95	(15,619)
	1,507,224

Suppose in 3 months' time the dollar appreciated and the new spot rate is $1.92/£. Then the option will not be exercised, but the premium would have been paid already. Hence the net sterling amount:

	£
To sell $3m at spot of $1.92/£	1,562,500
Cost of option (at spot): $30,457/$1.95	(15,619)
	1,546,881

Clearly the advantage here is that if the spot rate moves in the company's favour (say, to $1.92), then the option can be abandoned and the dollars sold on the spot market. The option offers the company the opportunity to benefit from favourable movements in the currency. Second, if the tender is not won, the company has no binding obligation to deliver dollars in 3 months' time.

Observation suggests that the option route is becoming increasingly popular. It sits comfortably alongside a situation in which the cash flows themselves are subject to considerable uncertainty, for example the tactical component of economic risk. If you cannot be sure that the dollars will be received, you do not want to be committed to delivering them to the bank at a fixed price!

There are rules and products to deal with delays in currency becoming available and, of course, the options have a (positive or negative) value at a point in time. This can be left unrealised, or could be realised by selling the option or taking up an opposing position in the market. The scope for switching profit between accounting periods is enormous.

There are various other products available on the futures markets, and there are various combinations of these products, called derivatives. You can, for example, get a lower-cost (or even zero-cost) option by agreeing to forego some of the 'upside' potential' or take some of the 'downside' risk. There are caps, floors, collars and swap agreements. These derivatives can be extremely important in financial management, but the above is probably sufficient to introduce the products and their underlying logic. Selection and monitoring in this area have become very specialised skills, given the need to be aware of developments, not only new instruments, but also the security of the company writing them.

Many banks seized the opportunity to diversify into these products as their core credit intermediation businesses were going through difficult times, and capital adequacy ratios were being tightened. In this case the banks were doing this not as hedgers but speculators. They and the regulators are not sure they fully understand the products and are able to manage this level of complexity. Likewise, there are some concerns regarding the rapid spread of computerised trading systems and the increasing interdependence of markets: problems in one area could easily spread to others. It does not help that the accounting legal and taxation framework has not been able to keep pace.

14.5 Selecting a hedging method

When a company has an outstanding foreign currency payable or receivable, it may choose to hedge against the currency risk by using the forward markets or the money markets. The method selected should be the one which leads to the smallest payment in sterling terms, or the highest receivable in sterling terms.

 Exercise 14.2

This past examination question requires you to demonstrate both a written and a numerical understanding of foreign exchange hedging techniques.

(a) Define a forward exchange contract and explain the differences between fixed forward exchange contracts and option forward exchange contracts.

(b) PQ plc, a UK company, has a substantial proportion of its trade with US and German companies. It has recently invoiced a US customer the sum of $5 m, receivable in 1 year's time. PQ plc's finance director is considering two methods of hedging the exchange risk.

- *Method 1.* Borrowing $5 m now for 1 year, converting the amount into sterling and repaying the loan out of eventual receipts.
- *Method 2.* Entering into a 12-month forward exchange contract with the company's bank to sell the $5 m and meanwhile borrowing an equivalent amount in sterling.

  The spot rate of exchange is £1 = US$1.9455.

  The 12-month forward rate of exchange is £1 = US$1.9065.

  Interest rates for 12 months are US: 3.5% and UK: 5.75%.

You are required

(i) to calculate the net proceeds in sterling under both methods and advise the management of PQ plc on the most advantageous method. Ignore bank commissions.

(ii) to explain the meaning of the terms 'spot rates' and 'forward rates', and comment on the reliability of forward rates as estimators of future spot rates.

(c) PQ plc decides to proceed with Method 2 by entering into a forward exchange contract through the foreign exchange department of its bank. Its US customer is disputing payment.

You are required to explain the procedures the bank might take if PQ plc cannot satisfy its obligations under the contract because of this dispute.

 Solution

(a) A forward exchange contract is a firm and binding agreement for the purchase/sale of a specified quantity of currency, at a specified price:
- on a specified date – for example 28 February next – in which case it is known as a *fixed* forward exchange contract; or
- within a specified period – for example any time in February, or any time between now and 28 February next – in which case it is known as an *option* fixed exchange contract.

(b) Note that this is not a pure money market hedge, as no discounting takes place in order for the amount borrowed to equal the amount due.

(i)

Method 1	£
Borrow $5 m now and convert into sterling (5,000,000/1.9455)	2,570,033
Expect to pay interest of 3.5% thereon, that is $5m × 3.5% = $175,000	
Net proceeds depend on spot rate in 12 months' time, for example, if it is as today's forward rate (1.9065) $175,000 dollars will require:	91,791
On this basis, net proceeds in 12 months' time:	2,478,242
Method 2	
Sell $5m forward at 1.9065: that is for	2,622,607
Borrow $5m/1.9455, that is £2,570,033 and expect to pay interest of 5.75% thereon	147,777
On this basis, net proceeds in 12 months' time:	2,474,820

Method 2 gives £3,412 less than Method 1, a difference which represents the bank's gross profit. Ignoring transaction costs, Method 1 is therefore preferable.

(ii) The spot rate is today's rate. In this question, $1.9455 could be exchanged for £1 today.

The forward rate is the rate which could be agreed for delivery at some specified future date. In this question the bank is agreeing to purchase $1.9065 for £1 in 12 months' time.

The relationship between the two is a function of interest-rate differentials. In effect, the bank would protect its position by borrowing $1.9455, paying interest at 3.5 per cent bringing it up to $2.0134, then, lending £1 on which it would earn interest of 5.75 per cent, bringing it up to £1.0575. $2.0134/£1.0575 = $1.9041 per pound. The bank divides by a higher figure to earn a margin.

Exchange rates and interest rates are subject to such volatility that it is not safe to regard the forward rate as a reliable predictor of what the spot rate will be at the appropriate future date. If future spot rates were predictable there would be no need to hedge. However, it is argued that in the long term the various rates are reconcilable; for example, a country with relatively high interest rates will cede growth opportunities to others, and its economy will weaken.

(c) If the dispute is expected to be settled in due course, then the bank is likely to be willing to extend the arrangement – but at a price which reflects the exchange rate at the time originally specified. If there is no hope of the debt being settled, then PQ plc will have to buy currency at the spot rate and deliver it to the bank on the agreed basis. The actual solution could, of course, be anywhere between these two extremes, and a 'mixed' solution reached.

 Exercise 14.3

Shengal Ltd is a company based in Singapore. The company has recently concluded negotiations for the purchase of equipment from a Swiss manufacturer valued at SFr 2,000,000. Payment is due in 6 months' time and the board of Shengal is worried about possible depreciation of the Singapore dollar (S$) against the Swiss franc. The following information is available:

Exchange rate market:
    Spot exchange rate: S$1.300/SFr–S$1.350/SFr
    3-month forward rate: S$1.285/SFr–S$1.335/SFr

Interest rates are as follows:

	Switzerland	Singapore
6-month borrowing rate (per annum)	8.0%	6.0%
6-month deposit rate (per annum)	6.0%	4.0%

Options:
    An OTC call option on SFr that expires in 6 months has an exercise price of S$1.33 and a premium of S$0.03
    An OTC put option on SFr that expires in 6 months has an exercise price of S$1.34 and a premium of S$0.02

Four alternatives available to manage the exposure are

 (i) Remain unhedged (do nothing)
(ii) Hedge in the forward market
(iii) Hedge in the money market
(iv) Hedge in the options market.

Requirements

Determine the outcome of each of the four alternatives if the spot exchange rate in 6 months is

(a) Spot: 1.285S$/SFr–1.320S$/SFr
(b) Spot: 1.450S$/SFr–1.500S$/SFr

 ## Solution

Today, the cost of the equipment is 2,000,000 × S$1.350 = S$2,700,000
  6 months' time:

(i) If Shengal decides to do nothing (Remain unhedged), then
   (a) Cost of equipment if spot rate is S$1.320/SFr
       = 2,000,000 × S$1.320
       = S$2,640,000
   (b) Cost of equipment if spot rate is S$1.500/SFr
       = 2,000,000 × S$1.500
       = S$3,000,000

(ii) If Shengal decides to use the forward market, irrespective of the future spot rate, the cost of the equipment is S$2,670,000 = 2,000,000 × S$1.335

(iii) Using the money market hedge:

Today:
Determine how many euros to be invested so that after 6 months we have exactly SFr2,000,000 to cover the payment required.

$$\frac{2,000,000}{(1 + 0.06 \times 0.5)} = 1,941,748$$

With spot rate of S$1.350/SFr:
  Amount required = 1,941,748 × S$1.350
                  = S$2,621,359

Thus Borrow S$2,621,359 at 6.0% for 6 months.
Convert S$2,621,359 at S$1.350/SFr into Swiss francs
S$2,621,359/S$1.350/SFr = SFr1,941,748
Invest SFr1,941,748 for 6 months at 6% p.a.

6 months' time:
Receive SFr investment + interest: SFr1,941,748 × (1 + 6% × 0.5) = SFr2,000,000 to pay off the cost of the equipment.

We then pay off the S$ Loan + interest:
S$2,621,359 × (1 + × 6% × 0.5) = S$2,700,000

The net result is a home-made forward rate of
S$2,700,000/SFr2,000,000 = 1.350S$/SFr

Thus cost of the equipment is fixed at S$2,700,000 regardless of the spot rate in 6 months.

(iv) Using the options hedge:

Shengal would buy a call option on SFr with an exercise rate of S$1.33 at a premium of S$0.03.

Hence the premium paid = S$0.03 × 2,000,000 = S$60,000

(a) In 6 months' time if the spot rate is S$1.320/SFr, the call will not be exercised.
The net payment is

Equipment cost at spot = S$2,640,000
Option premium paid = S$60,000
Net payment = S$2,700,000

(b) In 6 months' time if the spot rate is S$1.500/SFr the call will be exercised.
The net payment is

Equipment cost at spot at S$1.33/SFr = S$2,660,000
Option premium paid = S$60,000
Net payment = S$2,720,000

14.6 Currency swaps

A currency swap is the regular exchange of interest or cash flows in one currency for that of another currency. Unlike an interest-rate swap there is an exchange of principal at the beginning and at the end of the swap contract. Currency swaps are useful for medium- to long-term hedging as futures, forward contracts and currency options are generally only suitable for hedging up to 1 year ahead.

Example 14.H

Consider a UK company that wants to set up a new subsidiary in the United States. It borrows £10m from its bank in the United Kingdom (a UK company would find it easiest to borrow in the United Kingdom), for a period of 10 years, paying 7% interest. The company would need to convert the £10m into US dollars for use in the United States. The future earnings of the US subsidiary will be in US dollars, but the interest payments on the loan will be in sterling. The company could enter into a 10-year swap contract, to swap the £10m received from the loan for a current amount of US dollars, say $15m (Figure 14.3). The company can then use the dollars to build up its new US operation.

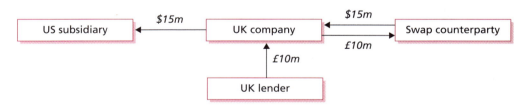

Figure 14.3 Principal payments

Suppose that under the terms of the swap contract 7% interest is paid on the sterling amount and 5% on the US dollar principal. During the lifetime of the loan and the swap, the US subsidiary earns US dollar revenue and remits US dollars to the parent. The parent uses the dollars to pay the US dollar amounts on the swap: 5% of $15m being $750,000. In return, £700,000 sterling is received and this is used to pay the interest on the loan (Figure 14.4). This occurs annually over the 10-year period.

Figure 14.4 Interest payments

At the end of the 10-year period the original swap cash flows are reversed, with the parent paying $15m back to the swap counterparty and receiving £10m sterling, which is in turn used to repay the loan. Using the swaps market, the company could raise finance in any currency to obtain the required currency funding.

This example is the only use of a currency swap. They can be used whenever there are regular receipts or payments in foreign currencies.

14.7 Cross-currency hedging

Exchange-traded currency derivatives are only available in a limited number of currencies. Thus, sometimes a company is unable to hedge an exposure to a given currency using financial instruments in that currency. For example, a UK company may not be able to hedge an exposure to the New Zealand dollar. The company may therefore decide to hedge the exposure using derivatives denominated in another currency that is highly correlated to the New Zealand dollar.

14.8 Summary

This chapter has considered a range of potential techniques for hedging foreign currency risk. Most of these are aimed at hedging transaction risks, but the technique of matching may equally be used to hedge transaction or translation risk.

Financial managers need to be aware of the range of hedging techniques available to them and the relative attractions of each. Techniques for managing financial risk can be classified into internal and external techniques. Note that internal hedging techniques work well if the company has a centralised treasury system. This enables the company to have control over timing, maturity and amount of the exposure. Companies use internal hedging techniques first to reduce exposure before applying external techniques. The choice of an appropriate external hedging technique would depend on the cost and flexibility of the hedge, the company's attitude to risk, the currency to be hedged and the size and certainty of the exposure.

Revision Questions 14

Question 1

Expo plc is an importer/exporter of textiles and textile machinery. It is based in the United Kingdom but trades extensively with countries throughout Europe. It has a small subsidiary based in Switzerland. The company is about to invoice a customer in Switzerland SFr750,000, payable in 3 months' time. Expo plc's treasurer is considering two methods of hedging the exchange risk:

- *Method 1.* Borrow SFr750,000 for 3 months, convert the loan into sterling and repay the loan out of eventual receipts.
- *Method 2.* Enter into a 3-month forward exchange contract with the company's bank to sell SFr750,000.

The spot rate of exchange is SFr2.3834 to the £1.

The 3-month forward rate of exchange is SFr2.3688 to the £1.

Annual interest rates for 3 months' borrowing are – Switzerland: 3 per cent, UK: 6 per cent.

Requirements

(a) Advise the treasurer on
  (i) which of the two methods is the most financially advantageous for Expo plc; and
  (ii) the factors to consider before deciding whether to hedge the risk using the foreign currency markets.
  Include relevant calculations in your advice. **(14 marks)**

(b) Assume that Expo plc is trading in and with developing countries rather than Europe and has a subsidiary in a country with no developed capital or currency markets. Expo plc is now about to invoice a customer in that country in the local currency. Advise Expo plc's treasurer about ways in which the risk can be managed in these circumstances.

  Note: No calculations are required for this part of the question. **(6 marks)**
  (Total marks = 20)

Question 2

(a) You have been retained by the management of a nationalised industry to advise on the management of its foreign exchange exposure.

You are required to

  (i) explain the main types of foreign exchange exposure and comment on those which are most likely to affect a nationalised industry;

 (ii) advise on policies which a corporate treasurer could consider to provide valid and relevant methods of reducing exposure to foreign exchange risk. **(15 marks)**

(b) Discuss how the financial management of an organisation in the public sector is likely to be different from that of a company in the private sector. **(10 marks)**

(Total marks = 25)

? Question 3

RP plc is a medium-sized importer and exporter of textile and other heavy machinery. It sells its products worldwide and has a policy of hedging all its overseas transactions in excess of a sterling equivalent of £100,000. Typically, the company uses money market hedges of forward contracts. Below £100,000, the company bears the exchange risk itself.

The company's profits after interest for the past 2 years were as follows:

Year	30 September 20X1	30 September 20X2
Profit after interest (£m)	2.919	2.026

If the company had not hedged its currency risks, the profits would have been £2.141 m in 20X1 and £2.373 m in 20X2.

The chief executive is concerned about the effect hedging costs have had on the bottom line, especially as a hedging operation for a large contract is currently being arranged. He has asked for a report with a view to considering changing the company's policy on hedging.

The details of the proposed hedge are as follows:

The company is due to pay a Chinese supplier Y2.5m in 3 months' time for machinery for which RP plc has already found a buyer within the United Kingdom for £300,000. Today's exchange rate is Y8.9321 to the £1. On the advice of the treasurer, the company is proposing to take out a contract to purchase Y2.5m in 3 months' time at the forward rate of Y8.8820.

Requirement

As financial manager with RP plc, write a report to the chief executive explaining:

- the purpose of hedging and the advantages and disadvantages of the company's current policy;
- the financial implications of the hedging contract currently being considered. For the purposes of illustration and comparison, assume the Chinese reminbi (a) weakens against the pound sterling in 3 months' time to 8.9975, and (b) strengthens against the pound to 8.6500;
- the factors the company should consider before changing its policy, in particular taking a decision not to hedge future foreign currency transactions;
- alternative methods of managing currency risks which might be available to the company.

(20 marks)

Question 4

Bailey Small plc is an importer/exporter of heavy machinery for a variety of industries. It is based in the United Kingdom but trades extensively with the United States. Assume that you are a newly appointed management accountant with Bailey Small plc. The company does not have a separate treasury function and it is part of your duties to assess and manage currency risks. You are concerned about the recent fluctuations in the exchange rate between the US dollar and sterling and are considering various methods of hedging the exchange risk involved. Assume it is now the end of March. The following transactions are expected on 30 June.

	($)
Sales receipts	450,000
Purchases payable	250,000

Economic data

- The spot rate of exchange is US$1.9540–1.9590 to the pound.
- The US dollar premium on the 3-month forward rate of exchange is 0.82–0.77 cents.
- Annual interest rates for 3 months' borrowing are – USA: 6 per cent; UK: 9 per cent.
- Annual interest rates for 3 months' lending are – USA: 4 per cent; UK: 6.5 per cent.
- Option prices (cents per £, contract size £12,500):

Exercise price ($)	Calls	Puts
1.90	–	1.20
1.95	2.65	3.45
2.00	1.70	5.25

Assume that there are 3 months from now to expiry of the June contracts.

Requirements

(a) Calculate the net sterling receipts that Bailey Small plc can expect from its transactions if the company hedges the exchange rate risk using each of the following alternatives:
  (i) the forward foreign exchange market;
  (ii) the money market.

  Accompany your calculations with brief explanations of your approach and recommend the most financially advantageous alternative for Bailey Small plc. Assume transaction costs would be 0.2 per cent of the US dollar transaction value under either method, paid at the beginning of the transaction (i.e. now). **(8 marks)**

(b) Explain the factors the company should consider before deciding to hedge the risk using the foreign-currency markets, and identify any alternative actions available to minimise risk. **(5 marks)**

(c) Discuss the relative advantages and disadvantages of using foreign currency options compared with fixed forward contracts. To illustrate your arguments assume that the actual spot rate in 3 months' time is 1.9460–1.9520, and assess whether Bailey Small plc would have been better advised to hedge using options, rather than a fixed forward contract. **(12 marks)**

(Total marks = 25)

Question 5

AB plc is a UK-based construction company that operates internationally, mainly in the Middle and Far East. It has recently obtained a contract to build a number of electricity generating stations (EGSs) in an Eastern European country (EE). The EGSs will be paid for by the EE government at a fixed price of 2,000 million EE marks 12 months after the start of the contract. AB plc will need to spend 750 million EE marks immediately and an additional 750 million EE marks in 6 months' time. The company has not worked in Eastern Europe before and has no other business in this region. Its opportunity cost of capital in the United Kingdom is 15 per cent each year.

The treasurer of AB plc is discussing the possibility of a fixed-rate currency swap with an EE-based company that trades in the United Kingdom. The swap would be taken out immediately for the full expected expenditure of 1,500m EE marks at a swap rate of 15 EE marks to £1.

Interest of 20 per cent each year would be payable on the full 1,500m EE mark swap by AB plc to the EE-based company. Payment would be in EE marks. The EE-based company will pay interest to AB plc on the sterling value of the swap at 12 per cent. Payment would be in sterling. Assume that interest payments are made annually at the end of the year.

There are no formal capital markets in the EE country and therefore no forward rates are available for the EE mark against sterling. Forecasts of inflation rates for the next year are 3 per cent in the United Kingdom and 25 per cent in the EE country. Assume the value of the EE mark is allowed to float freely by the EE government. The current spot rate is 18 EE marks to £1.

Requirements

(a) Explain the procedure for a currency swap, and recommend, with appropriate supporting calculations, whether AB plc should enter into the currency swap with the EE-based company. **(15 marks)**

(b) Discuss the advantages and disadvantages to a company such as AB plc of using swap arrangements as part of its treasury management strategies, in general and in the circumstances of the proposed contract. Explain, briefly, the risks involved in using swap techniques. **(10 marks)**

(Total marks = 25)

 Question 6

PS is a medium-sized UK-based company that trades mainly in the United Kingdom and the United States. In the past, PS has not hedged its currency risks but movements in the exchange rate have recently become more volatile. Assume it is now 30 September. The company expects net cash inflow in US dollars (sales receipts less purchases) on 31 December, that is US$2,350,000.

The current quoted spot rate of exchange is US$1.4180–1.4220 to the £1.

The US$ discount on the 3-month forward rate of exchange is 0.36–0.46 cents.

Option prices (cents per pound, payable on purchase of the option, contract size £31,250):

	September contracts	
Exercise price ($)	Calls	Puts
1.41	2.28	1.69
1.42	1.77	2.19
1.43	1.36	2.68

Assume there are 3 months from now to the expiry of the September contracts.

The company is risk averse and plans to hedge the risk using either a fixed forward contract or a European currency option. Ignore transaction costs.

Requirement

Recommend, with reasons, the most appropriate methods for PS to use to hedge its foreign exchange risk for the next 3 months. Your answer should include appropriate calculations to support your recommendation. **(15 marks)**

? Question 7

Assume you are the newly appointed treasurer of ZY Ltd, a medium-sized exporter and importer of goods, based in Singapore. The company imports mainly from Australia and New Zealand and exports to the United States. It has a subsidiary based in Melbourne, Australia, which is partly financed by a loan from a local (Australian) bank. ZY Ltd usually hedges its foreign currency exposure by using the forward or money markets. Most customers are allowed, or take, 3 months' credit.

You have received the following memo from your managing director.

Memorandum

From: The Managing Director
To: The Treasurer
Date: 21 May 20X1

I have been reading the financial section of the daily newspaper and note the following in respect of exchange rates and other economic data:

Exchange rates	Sing$/US$	A$/US$	
Spot rate	1.8126	2.0367	
1-month forward rate	1.8101	2.0350	
	Singapore	USA	Australia
Central bank base rate annum	2.25%	4.25%	3.75%

A recent economic forecast for the South East Asia region, published in a local business journal, suggested that annual inflation over the next 12 months in Singapore is expected to be 1%, while in the United States it is expected to be 3.25%. I have a number of questions:

(1) As interest rates are higher in the United States than here, surely the US dollar should be trading forward at a premium to the Singapore dollar, not at a discount?

(2) The newspaper did not quote a 3-month forward rate. We have recently sold equipment to a customer in the United States valued at US$ 2 million. What 3-month forward rate of exchange is implied by the information we do have, and therefore what Singapore dollar receipts can we expect in 3 months' time?

(3) If we buy Australian dollars on the spot market as and when we need them to pay for our imports rather than taking out forward contracts, it should surely save us a lot of money?

(4) Would a potential policy be to buy Australian dollars on the spot market now and place them on deposit until we need them?

(5) Would it be in our interests to borrow Singapore dollars and pay off our Australian dollar loan? This would save us money on interest payments.

Please let me have your comments.

Requirement

Write a report to the managing director evaluating and answering each of his questions. Include appropriate calculations, where relevant, to aid your discussion.   **(25 marks)**

Questions 8–10 have been adapted from the examinations of the Association of Corporate Treasurers (ACT).

? Question 8

East West plc has a 1-year contract to construct highways in a South Asian country, for which payment would be made in the local currency, the kaasa. Payment of 1,500m kaasas from the local government in the South Asian country is expected to be received at the end of the year. The project requires the immediate investment of 1,200m kaasas, and East West has been offered a 1-year currency swap for this amount at a swap rate of 40 kaasas/£. East West would be required to pay net interest of 10 per cent per year under the swap, payable at the end of the swap period. The current spot exchange rate is 44 kaasas/£, and the 1-year forward exchange rate is 50 kaasas/£. The opportunity cost of funds for East West in the United Kingdom is 7 per cent per annum. The company does not have access to funds in the South Asian country.

Requirements

(a) On the basis of the information provided, evaluate whether it is likely to be more cost-effective for East West to agree to the currency swap or to hedge the risk through the forward market.   **(7 marks)**

(b) Discuss the major categories of risk that East West would be exposed to when exporting to an overseas client as opposed to a domestic client. What are the main additional risks that East West would face if it were to accept the swap agreement?

(8 marks)
(Total marks = 15)

? Question 9

Requirements

(a) Compare and contrast the main features of currency futures and forward contracts. Who are the main users of each instrument?   **(6 marks)**

(b) Construct a hedge for a one-off receipt of EUR775,000 due on 1 May 20x1, 3 months from today, using
   (i) forward contracts
   (ii) currency futures.

   Schedule the cash flows arising and comment on your results. For the purpose of this question, assume that variation margins are settled on the maturity or disposal of the futures contract.

Market information as at today, 1 February 20X1:

Exchange rates EUR/GBP		Euro currency futures EUR/GBP, contract size EUR100,000		
			Price	Initial margin (£)
Spot	0.6203/08			
1-month forward	3/8	February	0.6210	1,000
3-month forward	11/16	May	0.6223	1,500

Outturn market rates as at 1 May 20X1:

Exchange rates EUR/GBP	EURO currency futures EUR/GBP		
Spot	0.6244/49		
		May	0.6248

(10 marks)

 Question 10

The following is an extract from the Notes to the Accounts of Wood plc for the year ended 31 July 20X1 in accordance with FRS 13.

Interest and currency profile
The current value of interest bearing assets, borrowings and off balance sheet contracts is as follows:

Currency	Interest bearing assets (£m)	Borrowings (£m)	Off-balance sheet contracts (£m)	Net (£m)	Floating (£m)	Fixed (£m)	Total (£m)	Weighted average fixed interest Rate (%)	Weighted average time for which rate is fixed (years)
Sterling	20.2	(0.5)	156.0	175.7	175.7	–	175.7	–	–
US dollars	50.1	(536.0)	(155.7)	(641.6)	(466.2)	(175.4)	(641.6)	4.9	2.2
Euros	41.1	(118.1)	–	(77.0)	(62.9)	(14.1)	(77.0)	3.6	1.5
Other	146.3	(297.1)	–	(150.8)	(150.8)	–	(150.8)	–	–
Total	257.7	(951.7)	0.3	(693.7)	(504.2)	(189.5)	(693.7)		

Off-balance sheet contracts are currency and interest-rate swaps.
The group has entered into interest-rate swaps and forward-rate agreements with the following net effect:

Amount	Expiry date	Wood receives	Wood pays
EUR23m	January 20x4	6-month EURIBOR	3.58–3.60%
US$75m	January 20x4	6-month LIBOR	4.605–4.69%
US$75m	August 20x4	6-month LIBOR	5.14–5.36%
US$100m	May 20x4	6-month LIBOR	4.685–5.09%
£70m	September 20x2	3-month LIBOR	5.94%

Year-end exchange rate: USD/GBP 1.4252 EUR/GBP 1.6289

Requirements

(a) Quantify, in broad terms, the effect of the currency and interest rate-swaps and FRAs on the interest-rate and currency profile of the group and discuss your results.

(9 marks)

(b) Describe all the factors that you would take into account in order to determine an appropriate mix of fixed- and floating-rate debt.

(5 marks)

(Total marks = 20)

Solutions to Revision Questions

14

✔ Solution 1

(a) (i)

	£
Method 1	
If we borrow SFr750,000, this will convert, at SFr2.3834 per £, into	314,677
At 3% p.a. for 3 months, this will (cost) in interest, SFr5,625	
At the forward rate of SFr2.3688 per £, this is worth	(2,374)
The sterling deposit, at 6% p.a. will earn/save	4,720
So that, in 3 months' time, we shall have a total of	317,023
Method 2	
At a forward rate of SFr2.3688 per £, the sale of SFr750,000 will be worth	316,616

Advice:

The borrow/deposit approach, on this occasion, is the more attractive, but by a small margin only.

(ii) Before deciding to hedge, the following factors might be considered:
- the extent of the aversion of the management to risk (e.g. if already borrowed up to the limit, further uncertainty would be unacceptable and the stronger the case for hedging would be);
- the size of the deal, relative to expected cash flows (the greater the size of the deal, the stronger the case for hedging);
- the wider context (e.g. possible offsets elsewhere in the group);
- the transaction costs – the spread and the commission;
- alternatives to forward rates, for example futures, options, swaps.

(b) The growing popularity of the concept of customer orientation means that, increasingly, sales are invoiced in the currency of the customer. Where there are active markets in the currency (as with those of the major countries) it is possible to hedge the risk of exchange rate fluctuations by using forward rates, futures, options, and so on. In the case of the less widely traded currencies, however, these are unlikely to be available.

In some cases, the local currency might be pegged to one of the major ones, and this could serve as the basis for hedging. In others, however, the only ways in which the risk can be managed is by action by the group itself, for example borrowing in the local currency, use of barter or countertrade, netting off.

FOREIGN EXCHANGE RISK MANAGEMENT

 Solution 2

(a) (i) Foreign currency risk management reflects the three levels of financial control: strategic, tactical and operational. In reverse order, and thinking of a group such as that mentioned in the question:

- *Operational control* brings risks associated with transactions (often, therefore, referred to as transaction risk). For example, products of a UK subsidiary might have been sold in dollars, but payment is not expected for a while; if the dollar weakens in the interim, fewer pounds will be received;

- *Tactical control* brings risks associated with short-term plans. For example, the same UK subsidiary might buy in some commodities, the world price of which is expected to rise. If sterling strengthens in the interim, it would be better to buy later at a lower sterling price;

- *Strategic control* brings risks associated with the really big decisions concerning the business to be in: where to locate facilities, which markets to serve, and so on, often referred to as economic risk. For example, the group might choose to invest in an Australian production facility to serve the UK market. If sterling weakens in the interim, the business could become uneconomic.

   In addition to the above, people also talk of translation risk: the fact that when a balance sheet is drawn up, amounts can be affected by the rate on that day. This is not a financial risk for the enterprise as a whole, but can affect the value of the equity investment, for example, where higher borrowing costs are triggered by higher reported gearing as a result of a strengthening of the currency in which they are denominated.

(ii) Treasury policies will be influenced by the enterprise's philosophy as to risk, which can get quite complex – for example leaving an exposure uncovered is obviously a risk, but selling receipts forward to cover the risk of a weakening of the currency induces the risk of missing the benefits of a strengthening. Matching receipts and payments is a popular technique, but so is letting positions build up in currencies which are confidently predicted to change. As the treasurer of Volkswagen found, a policy of covering half an exposure is bound to be criticised: in the event, either covering all or covering nothing will be found to be better!

   Neutrality involves buying currencies ahead of settling a liability and selling currencies ahead of a receipt, for example the company with a dollar debtor can sell the dollars forward and avoid any currency loss. This has the effect of swapping cash between the two currencies (and could be done directly by the company, rather than using the forward currency market), but either way the problem, as implied above, is that any currency gain is thereby avoided also. For the tactical exposures, therefore, it is increasingly the case that companies buy options to buy or sell at a predetermined price at a predetermined date. In this way, for a small premium, for the major currencies, the risk of loss is avoided, but the possibility of gain opened up. A further alternative, if the scale is large, is to trade futures in currencies, in the same way that commodity importers have always done.

   At the strategic level, the key decision is capital structure. A UK enterprise investing, say, in Australia to serve the UK market needs to arrange its affairs so that it effectively goes long of Australian dollars and short of sterling, so that if sterling weakens it has a currency profit to offset the loss of value in its normal trade.

(b) Any enterprise, whether it is in the private sector or the public sector, needs to conform with certain 'business imperatives': identifying needs, satisfying needs and persuading someone to provide the finance to fund the operation. It is the last of these which appears to differ according to sector. In the private sector, it boils down to offering the prospect of an adequate return on investment, which manifests itself in the form of a stream of payments of interest, dividends and, inevitably, taxation. In the public sector, it boils down to persuading a higher authority, and ultimately the Treasury, that the proposed activities represent value for taxpayers' money. This is often politically driven, rather than being based on an assessment of long-term financial health.

Another feature of the public sector is the overriding importance attached to the current fiscal year's cash flows: trading off between time frames, using the time value of money as the criterion, is not particularly well developed. The cost of capital, if used at all, is dictated by the Treasury and is likely to ignore embarrassing aspects like inflation and fluctuations in interest rates. Tax is also ignored, on the grounds that it is an internal transfer.

Accounting is also very different between the two sectors. The public sector eschews accrual accounting because of its facility for manipulation, and has different rules for recognising assets. A local authority shows the loan raised to build some flats as an asset even if the flats have been knocked down, but ignores industrial estates if the relevant borrowings have been repaid.

The worrying thing is that, ultimately, the resources used by the public sector are thereby not available to the private sector. It is to be hoped that as time goes by, the two approaches can be harmonised.

Solution 3

Report

To: Chief executive
From: Financial manager
Date: 23 November 20X2
Subject: Hedging

I have given some thought to the questions you asked at the Executive meeting, and would reply as follows:

- The purpose of hedging is to offload specific risks. By choosing to buy currency forward to the extent of a currency liability, we will be protected against the adverse effects of a weakening of sterling in the period between now and when the bill is due to be settled. We shall know that there will not be any unpleasant surprises. It is worth stressing, however, that we would also be turning our back on a possible pleasant surprise, that is having less sterling to pay because sterling had risen relative to the Chinese reminbi.

The main advantage of our present policy, therefore, is that it gives us certainty as to our costs and cash payments; the disadvantage is that it does not minimise them. As you know, we realised quite early in the year that our reported profits were going to be lower than the previous year. In the event, had we not hedged, we would have benefited from the currency movements – but we were not to know that.

We should, of course, keep our threshold of £100,000 under review. If we felt, for example, that sterling was entering a period of downward adjustment, we would want to hedge even smaller liabilities.

- The sterling value of the Chinese machinery, at today's spot rate, is Y2.5 m/8.9321, that is £279,889, and this is the figure at which it will be put into our books. If we buy the currency for the Chinese machinery forward, we are committing ourselves to paying Y2.5m/8.8820, that is £281,468.

This might appear to amount to incurring an unnecessary cost, but we have to consider the alternatives:

- We could buy Y2.5m now, and deposit them. The problem here is that the interest we would earn would be significantly less than the amount we would lose as a result of higher borrowings in sterling. The difference between sterling and reminbi interest rates is around 4 per cent per annum, and this is reflected in the premium associated with the forward reminbi. Likewise, if we were to seek a cash discount for payment now, the amount of the discount would look small compared with our interest rates.
- We could wait and buy reminbi in the spot market on the day we have to settle the invoice. The problem here is that the exchange rate will not be the same as today. If sterling were to strengthen to, say, Y8.9975, settlement would cost us £227,855, that is we would have gained £3,613 by waiting. If it were to weaken to, say, Y8.6500, settlement would cost us £289,017, that is we would have lost £7,549 by waiting.

The conventional wisdom is that the higher the interest rate, the weaker the economy and hence the greater the likelihood that the currency will depreciate. If we were to take this route, therefore, we would be gambling that, when we come to buy our reminbi, sterling will be no lower than 1 per cent below its current parity, which seems to be a very small tolerance. The factors which would need to be included in any review of policy would include the following:

- The potential volatility of the currencies in which the company deals. Generally, this seems to be increasing, but note the emergence of regional blocs, for example the countries participating in the euro.
- The market situation, including the domicile of major competitors.
- Hence, the scale of risk which the company faces.
- The extent of risk aversion of the directors. They may, for example, see that currency exposure offers the potential for gain as well as loss, and that this is part of the uncertainty associated with any business enterprise.
- The possibility of erecting long-term hedges, for example denominating an appropriate proportion of capital in foreign currency.
- As an importer, we are very much affected by the strength of sterling relative to other currencies. When the exchange rate is higher than that reflected in relative purchasing power/comparative costs, we are at a competitive advantage relative to domestic manufacturers, and vice versa. Conversely, as an exporter, we are at our most competitive advantage when the exchange rate is lower than that reflected in relative purchasing power/comparative costs.

Being in both importing and exporting gives us considerable scope as regards managing currency risk:

- At one extreme, we could form a view as to the likely movement of exchange rates. If we thought sterling would strengthen, for example, we would cover all our receivables (selling foreign currency forward) but leave our payables exposed – and vice versa if we thought sterling would weaken. The problem is that there is no foolproof method of forecasting exchange rates – the best are wrong at least as often as they are right.

- At the other extreme, we could choose to hedge all our exposures. Part may be naturally hedged, for example if we are buying and selling in the same currency, we can net off our assets and liabilities – perhaps augmented by some judicious leading and lagging. The balance can then be hedged in the normal way, that is by use of the forward market or by matching our capital structure to the flow of funds (e.g. if we are net exporters to Germany, arrange that an equivalent proportion of our borrowings are denominated in euros).

Nothing can guarantee that payments are minimised or receipts maximised but we might consider options. Under this arrangement, we pay a premium to the bank for the right but not the obligation – as far as imports are concerned – to buy at the forward rate (or, for a different premium, a different rate). Thus, if sterling has weakened, we shall exercise the option but, if it has strengthened, we shall let it lapse (but the premium will be a cost to us). The converse route would be taken for exports.

I hope that the above notes meet your need but, should you require any elaboration, please let me know.

Signed: Financial manager

 Solution 4

(a) The company needs only to hedge the net amount, that is $450,000 − $250,000 = $200,000.

Spot rates	1.6540	1.6590
Premium	−0.0082	−0.0077
Forward rates	1.6458	1.6513

(i) *Forward market cover*
Hedge the risk by selling dollar forward.

	£
The sterling proceeds in 3 months' time would be $200,000/1.6513	121,117
Less transaction costs of $200,000 × 0.002/1.6540	(242)
Net receipt	120,875

(ii) *Money market cover*
The company will receive dollars; therefore it is necessary to borrow an appropriate amount of dollars now and sell them at the spot rate. The dollar receipt repays the loan. Loan interest is paid at 3/12 of the annual rate, that is 6 per cent/4 = 1.5 per cent. We need to calculate the amount to be borrowed which, with interest payable, equals the dollar amount due:

	£	
$200,000/1.015 = $197,044, sold at spot to receive ($197,044/1.659)	118,772	
Deposit £118,772 at $\frac{3}{12}$ × 6.5% (1.625%) to receive	120,702	in 3 months' time
Less transaction cost	(242)	
Net receipt	120,460	

Receipts are therefore highest under method (i): fixed forward market cover.

Note: Dividing by four is not strictly correct if the interest rate is a percentage per annum but it is a close enough approximation.

(b) The factors to consider before hedging using foreign currency markets are as follows:
   - The costs involved, commissions, and so on.
   - The availability of a market for the currency in question.
   - The relative size of the deal compared with the size of the company. If this is small, then the company could probably afford to cover the risk itself.
   - The company's attitude to risk. Presumably, the company is not in business to speculate on exchange rates and should arguably not be taking undue risks with shareholders' money (if a listed company), but an alternative is always not to hedge.
   - The in-house expertise available. Bailey Small plc does not have a specialist treasury function, so it would probably be better to play safe and use relatively simple methods, such as fixed forward cover.
   - The possibility of swap contracts.

   The alternatives available could be internal techniques such as multilateral netting, banking in an overseas country and so on.

(c) A forward exchange contract is a firm and binding contract between a customer and a bank for the purchase or sale of a specified quantity of a stated foreign currency. The rate of exchange is fixed at the time the contract is made.

   Forward exchange contracts can be 'fixed' or 'option'. 'Fixed' means that performance will take place on a specified date in the future. 'Option' means that performance may take place at the option of the customer on a specified date, or at any time between two specified dates. The main advantage of options is clearly that they offer the firm the opportunity of not exercising the option. This would benefit the company in two ways:

   1. If the spot rate moves in the firm's favour, the company would allow the option to lapse. In the example here, if the dollar strengthens against sterling to, say, 1.60 then the company would be better off selling dollars on the spot market.
   2. If there is any uncertainty about when, or if, the transaction will arise.

   There are two main disadvantages. The first is the cost involved. The cost of an option is substantially higher than for fixed contracts, to reflect the risk of the writer of the option. The second is that options are sold in standard contract amounts. This indivisibility means that the buyer of the option may have to either use a fixed forward contract to cover a portion of the transaction amount or carry some risk.

   There are various types of option that could help minimise the cost, such as low-cost or zero-cost options, but the potential benefits are, of course, correspondingly reduced. Option futures could be used to overcome the indivisibility problem, but these also carry a cost.

Example

The company is looking to hedge the risk of exchange movements between now and the time when the money is due to be received. The company will need to buy sterling call options for the sterling equivalent of the dollar amount expected. At any rate less than 1.6590 the company would be better off by selling on the spot market. An option contract at an exercise price of 1.65 would not seem sensible. The company would, therefore, buy options at an exercise price of $1.7: £1, option price 1.70 cents.

As the money is due in 3 months' time, European options would be bought, that is, to be exercised on a fixed date in the future. The question does not really require an explanation of the difference between European and American options.

The first step is to determine the number of contracts needed:

$$\frac{200,000}{1.70 \times 12,500} = 9.4$$

The company can either take out nine contracts and cover the remainder of the transaction risk with a fixed forward contract or money market hedge, or bear the risk itself. In the case here, nine contracts would cover $191,250 (£12,500 × 9 × 1.7), leaving a balance of $8,750. For such a small amount, the company would probably bear the risk itself.

The sterling receipts, if the options were exercised, would be

	£
Nine contracts at £12,500	112,500
$8,750 sold at spot (1.6513)	5,299
Total	117,799
Less option costs (note 1)	
£ 12,500 × 9 × 1.70 cents = $1,912 at 1.654	(1,156)
Net receipts	116,643

Note:
Costs are payable when the option is taken out. If the option costs have to be paid in dollars, the exchange rate to use would be the current spot buying price (assuming that the company had to buy the dollars). Any sensible assumption here would be acceptable.

Clearly, the company would allow the options to lapse and sell the $200,000 on the spot market at 1.6513 (to receive £121,117). The option costs of £ 1,156 would have been paid, but this is the total extent of the 'loss'. The net receipts after costs would be £119,961.

With the benefit of hindsight, the company would not hedge this risk. However, if it had had to choose between fixed and option forward contracts, fixed forward would have been preferable. The key point here is that with a fixed forward contract the company is locked into the deal. Even if the exchange rate fell dramatically to, say, 1.50, the company is committed to selling at 1.6513 and could not take advantage of the windfall profits arising from currency fluctuations.

 Solution 5

(a) The procedure for a swap will be
  1. Exchange of principal at spot (either notional or physical transfer – in this case probably physical) in order to provide the basis for computing interest.
  2. Exchange of interest streams.
  3. Re-exchange of principal on terms agreed at the outset.

  The currency swap will provide some protection against the likely depreciation of the EE mark. A total of 1,500 m EE marks will be swapped, with the swap reversed at the year-end. At a swap rate of 15 EE marks: £1 the principal involved in the swap will be

  EE marks 1,500 million/15 = £100 million

  At the end of the year, 1,500 m EE marks can be swapped back at the same rate of 15 EE marks: £1.500 m EE marks – the profit in the contract – is therefore still exposed to currency risk.

  The expected level of inflation in the United Kingdom is 3 per cent and in the EE country 25 per cent. In the absence of available forward rates, the purchasing power parity (PPP) theory can be used to estimate an exchange rate at the end of the year. PPP states that if the rate of inflation in one country is greater than the rate of inflation in another country, exchange rates will adjust to offset the differential; therefore, the cost of living in each country would be the same.

Using PPP, sterling is expected to strengthen against the EE mark. The expected year-end exchange rate is therefore,

$18 \times (1.25/1.03) = 21.85$ EE marks : £1

The interest cost of the swap is

1,500 million EE marks $\times$ 20% = 300 million EE marks

	£m
EE marks to be remitted at the spot rate at the year-end:	
$(2,000 - 1,500 - 300)/21.85$	9.15
Interest received from the EE-based company:	
£100 $\times$ 12%	12.00
Total net sterling receipts	21.15
Note: AB plc also has 750 m EE marks tied up for 6 months	
Opportunity cost attached to this which should be offset against	
the interest receipts: 750 m EE marks/18 = £41.67 m $\times$ 15%/2	
assuming simple bi-annual interest	3.12
Total receipts after opportunity costs	18.03

If the company can invest the 750 m EE marks in some way, the receipts can be off-set against the opportunity cost of £3.12 m. If the swap is not used, the entire 2,000 m EE marks is exposed to currency risk.

Sterling costs are

	£m
750 m EE marks at 18:£1	(41.67)
Exchanged immediately	(37.63)
750 m EE marks at 19.93:£1	
Exchanged in 6 months and assuming the exchange rate	
EE mark/£ moves downward at a constant rate	
throughout the year:	
Year-end receipt of 2,000 m EE marks at 21.85:£1 =	91.53
Total	12.23

Recommendation

1. The swap option appears the most advantageous.
2. The opportunity cost of total funds needs to be considered. However, assuming an investment appraisal has been done, this is a financing and risk management decision rather than an investment decision.
3. The creditworthiness of the EE-based company needs to be fully evaluated, as it is taking on significant risk itself on the interest payments.

(b) A swap is the exchange of one stream of future cash flows for another stream of future cash flows with different characteristics. Such opportunities generally exist because of imperfections in financial markets, although the difference here is unusually large to be explained in this way. In respect of interest-rate swaps, it is because risk premiums charged to a company in the fixed-rate borrowing market are not necessarily the same as the risk premiums charged in the floating-rate market. Currency swaps are contracts to exchange cash flows relating to debt obligations.

The potential benefits include

1. Ability to match financing with operations; for example, if the company has a high level of fixed interest debt, but its operational income is now correlated with short-term interest rates, it can enter into a swap arrangement with a company with the opposite profile.

2. Ability to obtain finance, or cheaper finance, than by borrowing directly in the market if AB plc has a comparative advantage in terms of credit rating. This provides an arbitrage opportunity that can be shared by the participants in the swap.

3. Hedging against foreign exchange risk – currency swaps can be particularly useful here, especially when dealing with countries with no formal capital markets or volatile exchange rates, such as is likely to be the case with the EE contract which involves a soft, depreciating currency.

4. Interest-rate commitments can be altered without redeeming old or issuing new debt, which is an expensive procedure.

5. Swaps can be developed to meet specific needs, for example zero coupon swaps or 'swaptions'.

However, there are disadvantages. Swaps are typically arranged through intermediaries, which creates opportunities for speculators. This is a high-risk business and should not be undertaken without extensive expertise. In the circumstances here, the company appears to have a treasurer with knowledge and perhaps expertise in this area. Swaps may well have a part to play in AB plc's treasury management.

 ## Solution 6
Supporting calculations

It is first necessary to calculate the forward rate using the information given. As the US dollar is trading at a discount against the pound, it is expected to weaken against the pound:

Spot rates	1.4180	1.4220
Discount	+0.0036	+0.0046
Forward rates	1.4216	1.4266

Method (i): forward market cover. Hedge the risk by selling dollar forward. The pound proceeds in 3 month's time would be:

$$\frac{\$2,350,000}{\$1.4266/£} = £1,647,273$$

Method (ii): option contracts. The company is looking to hedge the risk of exchange movements between now and the date when the money is due to be received. The company will need to buy sterling call options for the pound equivalent of the dollar amount expected. If the forward rate in 3 months' time is 1.4266, then at any rate less than this, the company would be better off selling on the spot market. An option contract at an exercise price of 1.41 or 1.42 would not seem sensible. The company would, therefore, buy options at an exercise price of $1.43 to the pound, option price 1.36 cents. The first step is to determine the number of contracts needed:

$2.350 million/$1.43/£31,250 = 52.59

The company can take out fifty-two contracts and cover the remainder of the transaction risk with a fixed forward contract, or bear the residual risk itself. In the case here, fifty-two contracts would cover $2,323,750, leaving a balance of $26,250. For such a relatively small amount, the company would probably bear the risk itself.

Author's note. A choice of fifty-three contracts would also be acceptable, but the calculations and procedure would be different.

The sterling receipts, if the options were exercised, would be

Fifty-two contracts at £31,250	1,625,000
$26,250 sold at spot in 3 months (1.4266)	18,400
Total	1,643,400
Less: Option costs	
£31,250 × 52 × 1.36 = $22,100/1.418	−15,585
Net receipts	1,627,815

Costs are payable when the option is taken out. If the option costs have to be paid in dollars, the exchange rate to use would be the current spot buying price (assuming the company had to buy the dollars).

The main advantage of options is clearly that they offer the company the opportunity of not exercising the option. The main benefit to the company here is that if the spot rate moves in the company's favour, the company would allow the option to lapse at any rate below 1.43. The option costs of £15,585 would have been paid, but this is the total extent of the 'loss'. In the example here, if the dollar strengthens against the pound to, say, 1.40, then the company would be better off selling the dollar on the spot market.

There are two main disadvantages. The first is the cost involved. The cost of an option is substantially higher than for fixed contracts to reflect the risk of the writer of the option. The second is that options are sold in standard contract amounts. This indivisibility means that the buyer of the option may have to use a fixed forward contract to cover a portion of the transaction amount and carry some risk themselves, but this is likely to be small.

With a fixed forward contract, the company is locked into the deal. So, that even if the exchange rate fell dramatically, say to 1.38, the company is committed to selling at 1.4266 and could not take advantage of the windfall profits arising from currency fluctuations. However, as the company is stated as risk-averse and as the money due to be received appears virtually certain, in dollar terms, a fixed forward contract would be the sensible choice.

 ## Solution 7

Report

To:	Managing Director
From:	Treasurer
Subject:	Hedging policies
Date:	21 May 20X1

I refer to your recent request to provide information on our hedging strategies. First of all, it might be useful to explain the main underlying theories about the relationship between interest rates, exchange rates and inflation. One of my key roles as company treasurer is to evaluate different financing strategies given the imperfections and inefficiencies that can exist in financial markets.

Purchasing power parity

This theory suggests that if the rate of inflation in one country is greater than the rate of inflation in another country, exchange rates will adjust to offset the differential; therefore, the cost of living in each country would be the same. Put another way, the expected difference in inflation rates between two countries equals, in equilibrium, the expected movement in spot rates.

Interest-rate parity

Interest rates are determined in the market by supply and demand (although we should note political interference). There is a relationship between foreign exchange and money markets. Other things being equal, the currency with the higher interest rate will sell at a discount in the forward market against the currency with the lower interest rate. This is because higher interest rates imply higher inflation, which is a negative indicator of economic strength.

I now respond to your specific points.

1. As noted above, higher interest rates in one country relative to another are indicative of a *relatively* weak economy in that country with implied higher rates of inflation. In the short term, it would be expected that the currency with the higher inflation would be trading at a discount to the currency from the stronger economy.

2. The rate implied by the information we already have is 1.8039. If we use interest-rate parity, as explained above, we can use the following formula to forecast forward rates as long as we know the spot rate and expected annual interest rates.

$$\frac{1 + r\text{Sing\$}}{1 + r\text{US\$}} = \frac{f\text{Sing\$/US\$}}{s\text{Sing\$/US\$}}$$

where

r = the interest rate expected in the country concerned for the period of the forward forecast;

f = the forward rate of one currency against another; and

s = the spot rate of one currency against the other.

In the example here, the figures are

$$\frac{1 + 0.0056}{1 + 0.0104} = \frac{f\text{Sing\$/US\$}}{1.8126}$$

The interest rates are for 3 months and are calculated as the fourth root of (1 + the published annual rate) − 1. That is $\sqrt[4]{1.0225} - 1$ and $\sqrt[4]{1.0425 - 1}$.

Examiner's note

Simply dividing the annual rate by 4 is also acceptable, and would gain credit.

Resolving the equation gives us a 3-month forward rate of 1.8039. This is an appreciation of 0.48 per cent in the exchange rate for the Singapore dollar against the US dollar over the 3-month period.

We could also use purchasing power parity and forecast rates of inflation to arrive at a forward rate. In theory, we should arrive at the same rate although slight imperfections in the market may cause minor distortions. To demonstrate, I replace interest rates with inflation rates and use the same formula given above.

$$\frac{1.0025}{1.0080} = \frac{f\text{Sing\$/US\$}}{1.8126}$$

As before, I use the fourth root of the annual inflation rate to arrive at a 3-month rate.

The solution here gives a 3-month forward rate of 1.8027. This suggests a slightly higher rate of appreciation of the Singapore dollar against the US dollar, but inflation forecasts are rather less precise and reliable than interest rates, in advanced countries at least.

If we use the rate of 1.8039, we can expect receipts of Sing$3,607,800 from our US customer in 3 months' time. If we were to receive the money today, we would receive Sing$3,625,200. To be sure of getting at least Sing$3,607,800, we should take out a forward contract or other form of hedge. I assume our pricing strategy takes into account the fact that we invoice our customers in US dollars, thereby exposing ourselves to exchange rate risk.

3. If we calculate cross rates for Sing$ to A$, we see that Sing$1 is worth A$1.1236 now and A$1.1242 in 3 months' time, an expected depreciation in the Australian dollar against the Singapore dollar. All other things being equal, the exchange of Singapore dollars for Australian dollars, in real terms, should be the same using spot rates or forward rates. Clearly, all other things are not always equal but forward contracts provide a hedge against the unexpected. However, using the spot market instead of the forward market as and when currency is needed is a valid strategy and could indeed save us money (or make us money), but it is high risk and we are not experts in foreign currency dealings or forecasting. We are also ignoring transaction costs here and these should perhaps be considered.

4. Buying Australian dollar on the spot market and placing them on deposit is a valid strategy, but theory suggests that there should be no financial gain in real terms, unless there are imperfections in the market. The company's currency risk management policies already allow for us to use money market hedges.

5. Presumably you think that because interest rates in Singapore are lower than in Australia, there would be a saving in interest payments. Interest-rate parity suggests that, in real terms, the interest payable on one currency is the same as in another, given equality of risk, irrespective of interest-rate differentials. This means that the interest rate in Singapore will be lower than in Australia if the Australian dollar is expected to depreciate against the Singapore dollar. The interest payable on the Singapore dollar loan, which will require Australian dollars cash flows to be converted into Singapore dollars to make the interest payments at the spot rate prevailing at the time, should, in theory, be the same as if interest was paid in Australian dollars on Australian dollar loans. However, imperfections in the market may offer opportunities for arbitrage or speculative ventures.

Signed: Treasurer

Solution 8

(a) If the swap is used, East West will receive 1200m kaasas immediately in exchange for 1200/40 = £30m

The opportunity cost of these funds is £30m ÷ 7% = £2.1m.

At the end of the year East west will receive 1500m kaasas as contract payment.

After setting off the swap repayment of 1200m kaasas, and the interest payment of 1200 × 10% = 1200m kaasas, the net amount received would be 1500 − 1200 − 120 = 180m kaasas.

Converted at the forward rate of 50 kaasas/£, the amount realised would be 180/50 = £3.6m.

After setting off the opportunity cost of £2.1m there would be surplus of £1.5m. If the swap is not used, East West will receive 1500m kaasas after 1 year.

Converted at the estimated future spot rate, the amount realised would be 1500/50 = £30m.

Against this, there would be an immediate investment of 1200m kaasas.

Converted at the spot rate, the sterling investment would be 1200/44 = £27.27m.

Including opportunity cost for 1 year, the investment would be 27.27 × 1.07 = £29.18m.

The surplus would therefore be 30 − 29.18 = £0.82m.

It would there be beneficial to use the swap.

(b) Risks that arise particularly in respect of export sales are

Currency risk

- Transaction exposure (risk of adverse currency movements affecting current contrast).
- Economic exposure (loss of competitive position due to long-term currency movements).

Political risk

- Exchange controls
- War
- Bureaucracy/corruption.

Commercial risk

- Transportation across frontiers
- Money transmissions
- Legal/jurisdiction.

Other acceptable points include cultural/language risks and so on.

The additional risks of entering into a swap agreement are

- Counterparty credit risk
- Position risk arising from movements of interest rate/exchange rate
- Basis risk (spread risk)
- May be difficult to unwind in the case of less popular currencies.

✅ Solution 9

(a)

Feature	Currency futures	Currency forward contracts
Source	Exchange traded	Banks
Contract terms	Standard contract sizes and specific delivery dates	Your choice of contract size and maturity date
Price	Price transparency and more competitive than forward contracts	Prices vary, phone round for bestquote
Liquidity	No problem, sell back to the market at any time	Fixed maturity contract
Counterparty risk	Practically zero as exposed to the credit lines exchange and does not take up bank credit lines	Greater exposure – and uses bank credit lines
Basis risk	Potential discrepancy between the cash market and the futures market	No such exposure
Administration	Complex system of margin calls and accounting	Simple to administer and account for
Main users	Banks, institutions and treasury departments of large corporates	Most treasury departments

(b)

	Forward contract	*Currency future*
Hedge construction	Enter into forward contract to sell EUR775,000 for sterling 3 months forward at a forward rate of 0.6214 (= 0.06203 + 0.0011)	Sell 8 May EURO futures contracts at 0.6223. Total contract value EUR800,000 (being the closest to EUR775,000)
Cash flow on 1 February 20X1	None	Pay initial margin on eight contracts at £1,500 per contract. Total payment £12,000
Cash flow on 1 May 20X1	Receive EUR775,000 Sell EUR775,000 Receive £481,585	Refunded initial margin of £12,000 plus interest Pay variation margin of £2,000 (= £250 price movement per contract × eight contracts) Receive EUR775,000 Sell EUR775,000 at spot of 0.6244 for sterling £483,910 Net sterling cashflow of £481,910

 Solution 10

(a) *Currency swaps*

Off-balance sheet column sterling £156m, US dollars (£155.7m).

This indicates that approximately £156m sterling loans were swapped into US dollar loans.

Comparison of the position before and after these currency swaps:

	£ Before	£ After
Sterling borrowings	156.5m	0.5m
US dollar borrowings	380.0m	536.0m

It can be seen that the currency swaps have increased the US dollar borrowings by 41 per cent and reduced the sterling borrowing to a negligible value. It is possible that the group has significant US dollar assets that have been hedged using US dollar borrowings.

Interest-rate swaps

The FRA (£70m) has limited impact on the interest-rate profile due to its short-term nature.

In addition, the group has entered into approximately £190m of interest-rate swaps, swapping borrowings from floating- to fixed-rate interest (or investments from fixed to floating rate).

Calculation:	
EUR	£14.1m (= EUR23/1.6289)
US dollar	£175.4m (= US $250/1.4552)
Total	£189.5m

Comparison of the position before and after the interest-rate swaps and FRAs:

	Before		After	
	£ Floating	£ Fixed	£ Floating	£ Fixed
Sterling	175.7	0	175.7	0
US dollar	(641.6)	0	(466.2)	(175.4)
Euros	(77.0)	0	(62.9)	(14.1)

This table shows that 27 per cent of US dollar borrowings and 18 per cent of Euro borrowings have been swapped from floating to fixed rate.

(b) Factors to take into account in order to determine an appropriate mix of fixed- and floating-rate debt:
- response of revenue stream to interest-rate changes;
- effect of interest-rate changes on cost base;
- balance sheet profile;
- competitor's interest risk profile;
- view on future rate changes;
- shape of yield curve;
- appetite for risk.

Guidance on
Examination
Preparation

Guidance on Examination Preparation

Studying and revision

When you receive your study system you need to allocate time to study each chapter and answer the questions contained in each chapter. You need to balance your time between study, work, family and personal commitments. When studying, you should find a quite place to study and do so at a regular time several times each week, when you are not tired or tensed. In studying, you need to highlight and underline key points and make notes in the margin where you can relate the concepts to your own practical experience, or to what you have learned in previous study. Read the Readings contained in the study system and access some of the recommended reading in the reading list. Summarise each chapter and apply what you have learned to answer the questions in each chapter before looking at the answer. Score yourself in terms of how well you have understood the question and applied your knowledge to answer it.

You should also allocate time, well in advance of the examination, to do revision. Your revision in preparation for the examination is an important element of studying. This means reviewing the main points of each chapter and answering the revision questions and looking at the pilot examination paper. Both of these integrate the individual topics in the study system. In revising, you need to concentrate on the main points and the linkages between topics. You should also concentrate on those areas that you think you are least confident about. Keep going back to the chapters in the study guide where you need to.

Each person has their own method of study. The more you understand, the more you will remember. Some tips for understanding include joining a study group with friends and discussing the concepts. You should also be reading the business press and relating what you read to the contents of the study system.

Format of the examination

There will be a written examination paper of 3 hours, plus 20 minutes of pre-examination question paper reading time. The examination paper will have the following sections:

Section A   50 marks
A maximum of four compulsory questions, totalling 50 marks, all relating to a pre-seen case study and further new unseen case material provided within the examination.

(Note: the pre-seen case study is common to all three of the Strategic level papers at each examination sitting i.e. paper E3, P3 and F3.)

Section B

50 marks

Two questions, from a choice of three, each worth 25 marks. Short scenarios will be given, to which some or all questions relate.

The pass mark for the examination is 50%.

Scope of the examination

The topic and study weighting for the syllabus is as follows.

Topic		Study weighting (%)
A	Management Control Systems	10
B	Risk and Internal Control	25
C	Review and Audit of Control Systems	15
D	Management of Financial Risk	35
E	Risk and Control in Information Systems	15

The percentage weighting for each topic is a guide as to the proportion of study time each topic requires. All topics must be studied as any examination question may examine more than one topic or carry a higher proportion of marks than the study weighting suggests. The weightings do not specify the number of marks that will be allocated to topics in the examination. The overall marks allocated in any single examination may vary from the study weightings shown above.

Management control, risk and internal control are inter-related. Therefore, examination questions are most likely to cross more than one of the above topics. For example, a question may ask you to advise, evaluate or recommend in relation to the review or audit (Topic C) of a management control system (Topic A) that is implemented as a result of risk management (Topic B) in relation to a financial risk (Topic D) with such controls being linked to the use of computer systems (Topic E). Revision, therefore, should aim as far as possible to integrate the ideas in each of the syllabus topics, rather than think about them as discrete topics.

Furthermore, the nature of a professional examination at strategic level is that students will be able to integrate and apply their knowledge from prior subjects in the management accounting pillar as well as from other subjects at the strategic level (Business Strategy and Financial Strategy).

The contexts in which examination questions are set will range from various business activities (manufacturing, retail, service, etc.) to public sector and not-for-profit activities. Answering examination questions will not depend on any knowledge of any particular industry or sector or any specific national context.

Learning outcomes define the skill or ability that a well-prepared student should be able to demonstrate, and identify the approach likely to be taken by examiners in setting questions. In revision, students need to focus on the learning outcomes as examination questions can be set in relation to any of these outcomes. It is important to note that the syllabus content is indicative only, that is it provides examples rather than an exhaustive list of what students should know. In particular, examination questions may be set in relation to content areas that are not listed in the syllabus but which fall within the scope of the learning outcomes.

Overall, about 25% of the content of the syllabus is numeric. While much of the numeric content is more likely to be in relation to examination questions for Topic D (Management of Financial Risk), numeric examples may be included in any question and students may be expected to interpret and evaluate numeric data (financial and non-financial) as well as perform relevant calculations. Formulae and tables will be included with each examination paper. However, the inclusion of tables and formulae does not necessarily indicate that they are required in order to answer any or all of the questions in the paper.

Examination technique

Students must strictly manage their time when answering examination questions. Time allocated to read, plan, answer and review each question (and each section of each question) should be proportional to the marks allocated for the question (and each section of each question). One-and-a-half hours should be allocated to Section A and 45 minutes to each of the questions in Section B of the examination paper. On average, each 5 marks allocated for an answer should be given a maximum of 9 minutes.

Students need to be aware of the differences between, and understand what examiners expect in using the hierarchy of verbs. At strategic level, students are being tested mainly in relation to evaluation (advising, evaluating and recommending) but also in relation to analysis (analysing, categorising, comparing and contrasting, constructing, discussing, interpreting and producing).

Answering examination questions involves several steps:

1. Read the question carefully and identify the issue for the organisation.
2. Determine what the question is asking you to do.
3. Allocate your time based on the marks available for each question and section of each question.
4. Make a list of points you want to cover in your answer, ensuring that you answer each section of the question.
5. Write your answer, keeping it legible, logical and concise.
6. Read over your answer carefully and correct any errors, omissions or ambiguities.

Some questions may expect students to write a report and some marks may be allocated for form and style, including the standard of English used. The marks for format and style will be indicated in the examination question.

Revision question mapping grid

Topic			Learning outcomes	Questions								
Management Control Systems	A	i	Evaluate and recommend appropriate control systems for the management of organizations		2a	3d			6a		8b	9a
		ii	Evaluate the control of activities and resources within the organisation		2c	3a	4c					9a
		iii	Recommend ways in which the problems associated with control systems can be avoided or solved			3b, 3d			6c			9c
		iv	Evaluate the appropriateness of an organisation's management accounting control systems and make recommendations for improvement		2b	3c			6b		8b	9c
Risk and Internal Control	B	i	Define and identify risks facing an organisation	1a	2c	3b		5b				9c
		ii	Explain ways of measuring and assessing risks facing an organisation, including the organisation's ability to bear such risks							7a		
		iii	Discuss the purposes and importance of internal control and risk management for an organization	1b	2c	3a					8a	
		iv	Evaluate risk management strategies							7b		9c
		v	Evaluate the essential features of internal control systems for identifying, assessing and managing risks	1b							8a	
		vi	Evaluate the costs and benefits of a particular internal control system	1c	2c							
		vii	Discuss the principles of good corporate governance for listed companies, particularly as regards the need for internal controls	1b		3a					8a	
Review and Audit of Control Systems	C	i	Explain the importance of management review of controls	1b	2a,c	3c	4a				8a	
		ii	Evaluate the process of internal audit			3c	4a					
		iii	Produce a plan for the audit of various organizational activities including management, accounting and information systems			3c	4b				8a,b	
		iv	Analyse problems associated with the audit of activities and systems, and recommend action to avoid or solve those problems				4a					
		v	Recommend action to improve the efficiency, effectiveness and control of activities		2c	3d	4a	5b			8b	9c
		vi	Discuss the principles of good corporate governance for listed companies, for conducting reviews of internal controls and reporting on compliance				4c				8a	
		vii	Discuss the importance of exercising ethical principles in conducting and reporting on Internal reviews				4a					

		Description												
Management of Financial Risk	D	i	Identify and evaluate financial risks facing an organization;	10a					15a		17a				21a
		ii	Identify and evaluate appropriate methods for managing financial risks;	10a,b,c	11a,b	12a,b	13a-e	14a-d	15b	16a,b	17b	18a,b	19a	20a,b	21b
		iii	Evaluate the effects of alternative methods of risk management and make recommendations accordingly;	10a	11a,b	12a,b	13a-e	14a-d	15b	16a,b	17b	18a,b	19a	20a,b	21b
		iv	Discuss exchange rate theory and demonstrate the impact of differential inflation rates on forecast exchange rates;							16b	17b	18b			
		v	Recommend risk management strategies and discuss their accounting implications.		11a,b		13a-e		15b		17a,b				
Risk and Control in Information Systems	E	i	Evaluate and advise managers on the development of IM, IS and IT strategies that support management and internal control requirements					5a							
		ii	Identify and evaluate IS/IT systems appropriate to an organisation's needs for operational and control information					5a	6b						
		iii	Evaluate benefits and risks in the structuring and organisation of the IS/IT function and its integration with the rest of the business			3b		5c	6a,b,c						
		iv	Evaluate and recommend improvements to the control of information systems	1b				5b	6c						
		v	Evaluate specific problems and opportunities associated with the audit and control of systems which use information technology				4b	5b							

Revision Questions

 Question 1

The operations division of ABC, a listed company, has responsibility to maintain and support the sophisticated computer systems used for call centres and customer database management which the organisation's retail customers rely on as much of their sales are dependent on access to these systems, which are accessed over the Internet.

Although there is no risk management department as such, ABC has a large number of staff in the operations division devoted to disaster recovery. Contingency plans are in operation and data are backed up regularly and stored off-site. However, pressures for short-term profits and cash flow have meant that there has been a continuing under-investment in capital equipment, which one manager was heard to comment as being 'a little like Railtrack'.

A review of disaster recovery found that although data were backed up there was a real risk that a severe catastrophe such as fire or flood would have wiped out computer hardware and although data back-up was offsite, there was no proven hardware facility the company could use. While managers have relied on consequential loss insurance, they appear to have overlooked the need to carry out actions themselves to avoid or mitigate any possible loss.

Requirements
(a) Advise the board as to the main business issue for ABC and the most significant risks that ABC faces. **(5 marks)**
(b) Advise the board as to its responsibilities for risk management and recommend a risk management system for ABC that would more effectively manage the risks of losing business continuity. **(15 marks)**
(c) Evaluate the likely benefits for ABC of an effective risk management system for business continuity. **(5 marks)**

(Total marks = 25)

 Question 2

A social services department in the public sector is funded by government with a fixed budget each year to cover its operating costs, which are primarily salaries. The department is referred clients who have problems such as inadequate welfare benefits, poor housing, anti-social behaviour of children and mental health problems. The department is staffed by experienced social workers who are overworked and there are long waiting lists of clients whose problems have neither been investigated nor resolved.

Due to the pressure of work, in terms of both the volume of work and the effect on social workers who regularly deal with difficult situations, there is significant absenteeism due to illness, a high staff turnover and recruitment is a continuous process. However, the social workers are hardworking and dedicated and the culture in the department is one of providing excellent client service despite the inadequate resources they have. Social workers are only really concerned with satisfying their clients and resolving the underlying problems rather than with financial reports or measures of efficiency.

The department maintains a control system that incorporates budget versus actual reporting of expenditure and the analysis of variances. There are also a set of non-financial performance indicators that measure actual performance against targets in relation to waiting times for clients; the cost per service (average time spent by staff advising and assisting clients); client satisfaction with the service received and the percentage of client problems that have been resolved. Actual spending in most periods is less than budget due to vacancies following staff turnover and actual performance is lower than the targets set by senior management.

Requirements

(a) Compare and contrast the rational-economic perspective with the interpretive perspective and apply these different perspectives to the management control system described in this scenario. **(5 marks)**

(b) Evaluate the limitations of budgetary systems, variance analysis and non-financial performance measures in the social services department and recommend improvements that could be made to the management control system. **(10 marks)**

(c) Recommend the internal controls which management should consider implementing in the social services department and the advantages of those controls. **(10 marks)**

(Total marks = 25)

? Question 3

SPM is a manufacturer and distributor of printed stationery products that are sold in a wide variety of retail stores around the country. There are two divisions: Manufacturing and Distribution. A very large inventory is held in the distribution warehouse to cope with orders from retailers who expect delivery within 48 hours of placing an order.

SPM's management accountant for the Manufacturing division charges the Distribution division for all goods transferred at the standard cost of manufacture which is agreed by each division during the annual budget cycle. The Manufacturing division makes a 10% profit on the cost of production but absorbs all production variances. The goods transferred to Distribution are therefore at a known cost and physically checked by both the Manufacturing and the Distribution division staff at the time of transfer.

The customer order process for SPM's Distribution division is as follows:

– SPM's customer service centre receives orders by telephone, post, fax, email and through a new on-line Internet ordering facility (a similar system to that used by Amazon). The customer service centre checks the creditworthiness of customers and bundles up orders several times each day to go to the despatch department.

– All orders received by the despatch department are input to SPM's computer system which checks stock availability and produces an invoice for the goods.

– Internet orders have been credit checked automatically and stock has been reserved as part of the order entry process carried out by the customer. Internet orders automatically result in an invoice being printed without additional input.
– The despatch department uses a copy of the invoice to select goods from the warehouse, which are then assembled in the loading dock for delivery using SPM's own fleet of delivery vehicles.
– When SPM's drivers deliver the goods to the customer, the customer signs for the receipt and the signed copy of the invoice is returned to the despatch office and then to the accounts department.

SPM's management accountant for the Distribution division produces monthly management reports based on the selling price of the goods less the standard cost of manufacture. The standard cost of manufacture is deducted from the inventory control total which is increased by the value of inventory transferred from the manufacturing division. The control total for inventory is compared with the monthly inventory valuation report and while there are differences, these are mainly the result of write-offs of damaged or obsolete stock, which are recorded on journal entry forms by the despatch department and sent to the accounts department.

Due to the size of inventory held, a physical stocktake is only taken once per annum by Distribution staff, at the end of the financial year. This has always revealed some stock losses, although these have been at an acceptable level. Both internal and external auditors are present during the stocktake and check selected items of stock with the despatch department staff. Due to the range of products held in the warehouse, the auditors rely on the despatch department staff to identify many of the products held.

Requirements

(a) Advise the board and the audit committee of SPM as to its responsibilities for internal control and for its relationship with both internal and external auditors. **(10 marks)**
(b) Evaluate any weaknesses in the risk management approach taken by SPM's Distribution division and how this might affect reported profitability. **(10 marks)**
(c) Advise the board about the role of internal and external audit and recommend an internal audit plan for SPM's Distribution division that is based on the risk assessment identified in (b) above. **(20 marks)**
(d) Recommend internal control improvements that would reduce the likelihood of risk.
(10 marks)
(Total marks = 50)

? Question 4

Qwerty has recently introduced a new computer system to handle its on-line travel bookings where customers can select a combination of flights, accommodation and insurance packages. Customers enquire into the availability of travel from their home or office computer and the system reserves their holiday requirements, for which the customer pays by credit card.

Qwerty's system is integrated with a major international booking system to ensure that travel sold is properly booked, with data being transferred via electronic data interchange (EDI). Qwerty therefore operates as a 'front office' for larger booking agencies. Qwerty's competitive advantage is its reputation for giving excellent customer service that has been built up over many years of manual operations. The introduction of the new computer system automates that process and is seen by the board and senior management to be far more cost-effective and has enabled Qwerty to reduce its staffing levels significantly. The computer implementation was managed in the main by Qwerty's IT Manager and has been considered to be a big success, despite some teething problems.

Qwerty's internal audit function has been sub-contracted to MNO, a firm of external accountants who are CIMA members. MNO are well acquainted with Qwerty's needs, having provided a range of IT consultancy services to Qwerty, including involvement in the feasibility study for the purchase of the new computer system. However, there was no internal audit involvement after the initial feasibility study. MNO have recently completed an internal audit which has included a review of Qwerty's new computer system.

MNO's report to Qwerty's board has identified the following strengths and weaknesses:

Table RQ1

Strengths	Weaknesses
(a) Excellent data security and authorisation of changes to master files	(a) Systems design problem leading to loss of some on-line customer bookings (continuing)
(b) Excellent operator training and systems documentation	(b) Inadequate control over conversion of manual systems to new computer system resulting in some duplication and some losses of data (now resolved)
(c) Excellent EDI links to international booking system	(c) Failure to adequately test and accept the system prior to live running
(d) The project was delivered to budget and to the expected timescale, although some issues of quality were not achieved (see Weaknesses)	(d) While the project management of the implementation was largely successful due to the IT Manager, no Steering Committe was established to oversee the project
	(e) No post-implementation review carried out

Requirements

(a) Evaluate MNO's audit report of management controls in Qwerty's new computer system against best practice for information systems development and make any necessary recommendations to the board. **(25 marks)**

(b) Recommend an internal audit approach that will provide assurance to the board that information system controls are adequate. **(10 marks)**

(c) Advise the board of Qwerty as to its corporate governance responsibilities for reviewing internal control and reporting on compliance. **(Total 15 marks)**

(Total marks = 50)

 ## Question 5

SupplyCo has recently acquired a new enterprise resource planning (ERP) system from a well-known supplier. The ERP system automates the tasks involved in performing a business process, from order fulfilment, which involves taking an order from a customer, shipping it and invoicing the customer. Previously, that order took a mostly paper-based journey from in-basket to in-basket around the company, often being keyed and re-keyed into different computer systems along the way.

With ERP, when customer service takes an order, all the necessary information to complete the order is available. This includes the customer's credit rating, the order history, inventory levels and delivery schedules. Everyone in the company sees the same information, from a single database. As each department carries out its function, the ERP system automatically routes the customer order to the next department.

However, SupplyCo is faced with the problem that the ERP software does not support an important business process. There are two solutions to this problem: change the way the company does business to fit the package, or modify the package to fit the business.

Requirements

(a) Compare and contrast strategies for information systems (IS), information technology (IT) and information management (IM). Discuss how an ERP system can be seen from the perspective of each of IS, IT and IM strategies. **(7 marks)**

(b) Discuss the IT-related risks that could be faced by SupplyCo in using an ERP system and recommend the control strategies that would be appropriate for an ERP environment. **(8 marks)**

(c) Advise SupplyCo as to whether it should change the way it does business to fit the ERP package, or modify the ERP package to fit its business needs. Recommend how management should go about deciding which solution to implement. **(10 marks)**

(Total marks = 25)

❓ Question 6

GDS is a small listed manufacturing company that has experienced difficulties in retaining qualified and experienced staff for the production of all its management accounting information. It has been approached by CMA, a professional accounting firm that has proposed to carry out a full outsourcing of the accounting function. This will include

– Backflushing of all labour and materials transactions as a result of the manufacturing process.
– Maintenance of inventory records for raw materials and finished goods.
– Processing of all sales invoicing and purchase invoices.
– Production of monthly management reports and end of year financial reports.
– Interpretation and advice to management based on the financial information.

This information will be processed on computer and access to all data will be available on GDS' own premises via an extranet. The payment of suppliers and non-creditor expenses, receipt of customer payments, maintenance of cash books and all payroll transactions will be retained in-house and carried out by GDS' own staff although the daily cash payment and receipt records will be processed by CMA.

The cost savings for GDS in existing staff more than compensate for the cost of outsourcing the accounting function to CMA.

Requirements

(a) Compare and contrast the advantages and disadvantages of outsourcing generally.
(7 marks)

(b) Advise GDS in relation to the outsourcing of the accounting function to CMA specifically. **(9 marks)**

(c) Recommend the methods by which a decision to outsource could be best controlled by GDS. **(9 marks)**

(Total marks = 25)

Question 7

MNO is a construction company involved in large engineering projects, often at a fixed price. MNO's target price is cost plus a 10% profit margin but the company includes in its cost estimates an allowance for risk based on an assessment of various circumstances that could cause cost overruns. However, as the industry is very price competitive, MNO frequently has to reduce its price below its target, thereby absorbing the risk of any cost overrun itself.

In one particular project for which MNO has to tender a fixed price, MNO has estimated its costs, risks and target profit as a range of possibilities, as shown below.

Table RQ2

Estimated cost of (£m)	Best estimate	Contractual delays	Planning delays	Site problems	Construction problems	Client readiness	Worst case
Materials	150.0	2.0	1.0	2.0	2.0	0.0	157.0
Labour (MNO own)	50.0	1.0	0.0	2.0	2.0	2.0	57.0
Sub-contract/ consultants	30.0	1.0	2.0	0.0	2.0	1.0	36.0
Total estimated cost	230.0	4.0	3.0	4.0	6.0	3.0	250.0
Profit margin 10%	23.0	0.4	0.3	0.4	0.6	0.3	25.0
Target price	253.0	4.4	3.3	4.4	6.6	3.3	275.0
Probability of occurrence (%)	50	15	10	10	5	5	5

MNO has estimated the probability of occurrence of each risk as shown above.

As can be seen, the lowest estimated cost for the project is £230 million. However, a range of risks could inflate this cost up to a maximum of £250 million. If a price of £253 million was tendered, it would virtually guarantee the tender being won. However, if £275 million was tendered, MNO would almost certainly lose the contract. If MNO tenders £253 million and the risks eventuate, the worst case outcome is income of £253 million and costs of £250 million, virtually wiping out all the profit on the project.

Requirements

(a) Recommend the price at which MNO should tender, with reasons, and if this tender is accepted, the best and worst case outcomes for MNO. **(10 marks)**

(b) Evaluate MNO's risk management strategy for its construction tenders and advise MNO as to any other approaches it could take to minimise risk and maximise its ability to earn its target profit margin. **(15 marks)**

(Total marks = 25)

 Question 8

JKL is a profitable but small FTSE 500 company in a technology-related service industry with annual sales of £150 million. Its gearing is 50% of total assets, secured by a mortgage over its main site. The industry is highly competitive but there are major barriers for entry to new competitors and the long-term future of JKL is considered by industry analysts to be sound.

The Board comprises a non-executive chairman, a chief executive who has a large shareholding, an executive finance director, operations director and marketing director and a non-executive director with wide knowledge of the industry and who retired from the company 3 years ago. There is only one committee of the board. The audit committee consists of the chairman, non-executive director and finance director.

There is no internal audit function in JKL but the external auditors are relied on to report on any weaknesses in control and their letter of engagement authorises them to carry out work over and above the financial audit in relation to internal control. The external auditors have always given a 'clean' audit report to the company and have reported that internal controls within JKL are sound. There is no formal risk management process in place in JKL although board meetings routinely consider risk during their deliberations.

The chairman and chief executive both believe that compliance with corporate governance reforms will not benefit JKL and is likely to be too costly. This is disclosed in JKL's Annual Report.

Requirements

Write a report to the Chairman

(a) evaluating the key reforms and best practice in
   - corporate governance **(7 marks)**
   - risk management **(8 marks)**

   that have taken place over the last few years and which affect JKL; and
(b) (with reasons), which (if any) of those reforms should be adopted by the company. **(5 marks)**

Five marks will be awarded for the quality of presentation and language in the report.

(Total marks = 25)

? Question 9

MAP is a manufacturer of automotive products and a supplier to some of the major motor vehicle assembly plants. It operates in a Just in Time (JIT) environment and uses sophisticated manufacturing technology for efficient production. MAP has adopted a lean manufacturing philosophy and has extended this to lean management accounting. The company's emphasis is on the elimination of waste and cost control in both manufacturing and support functions and generating continual incremental improvements in all that it does.

MAP uses a strategic enterprise management system (SEM) which integrates strategic, financial and operational information and is linked to MAP's executive information system (EIS) which enables senior managers to evaluate information about the organisation and its environment. The EIS incorporates a drill down facility to move from summarised to more specific and detailed operational and financial information.

MAP is organised around production, sales, design and accounting functions that are brought together in a number of semi-autonomous work groups. Each work group is focused on several similar products. Each MAP employee has a matrix reporting relationship, to its work group and to the functional hierarchy (production, sales, design and administration).

Although it is committed to waste reduction, MAP recognises that standardisation in its manufacturing is essential for the maintenance of quality and customer satisfaction.

It has carried this philosophy over into its support functions where it has established a strategic planning process focused on short-term profits and shareholder value, and policies and procedures for most support activities including human resource management (recruitment, training and appraisal, etc.). There is also a profit-sharing bonus scheme linked to MAP's overall performance.

The accounting-based control systems used by MAP include capital investment appraisal using discounted cash flow techniques with high hurdle rates for all decisions to increase manufacturing capacity. Budgets are extensively used as methods of controlling costs and ensuring that revenue targets are achieved. The chief executive relies on the finance director for accounting advice and the finance director is committed to capital investment and budget techniques. A suite of non-financial performance measures is also used to measure, for example quality, on-time delivery, production efficiency, customer satisfaction and employee morale.

The chief executive of MAP is an engineer by profession, a dominating individual, with a controlling interest in the company. He is obsessed with reducing waste and cutting costs to improve reported profits and most of the changes in philosophy, production technology, IT systems, reporting have been introduced by him. The chief executive uses the EIS to focus on work groups that need to improve their performance or that of their group of products. However, the management hierarchy is relatively flat and most managers are in staff positions rather than supervising production operations.

MAP is in a relatively stable business and its technological lead has assured it of long contractual relationships with its customers. It is a risk-averse business, evidenced by its strict controls, sophisticated information system and the hands-on role of the chief executive.

The culture of MAP is one of technological excellence and commitment to customer service although the perspective taken by employees is a long-term one. A team culture and commitment to working together is fostered by the work team structure and their relative autonomy from day-to-day management. Consequently, there is a relatively low staff turnover and generally high morale. The teams tend to carry out healthy competition between each other to see which team can produce the best performance each month.

However, surveys have shown that staff tend to be unhappy about the methods by which targets are set and believe that these are too demanding, which in turn affects their profit-related bonuses. They are also unhappy about the strict control over expenses and the way in which some of the non-financial performance measures are calculated. Many employees think that MAP has become too obsessive about cost and waste reduction.

Over the last year, the chief executive has become increasingly concerned as to whether he can rely on some of the capital investment appraisals, budget reports and non-financial performance measurement information he has been receiving.

Requirements

(a) Compare and contrast cybernetic and non-cybernetic forms of management control and how these apply in MAP. **(25 marks)**

(b) Evaluate the limitations of capital investment appraisal techniques, budgets and non-financial performance measures as methods of management control in MAP. **(15 marks)**

(c) Evaluate the effectiveness of MAP's risk management strategy in relation to its approach to management control. **(10 marks)**

(Total marks = 50)

Question 10

(a) A UK importer of Italian shoes needs to make a payment of €9,000,000 in 3 months time. The following market data is available:

Spot €/£ exchange rate is 1.49–1.52

3-month Euro interest rate is 6–8% per annum

3-month Sterling interest rate is 8–10% per annum

(i) Identify and explain the exchange rate risk facing the UK importer.

(ii) Show how this risk may be hedged using the money market hedge and calculate the cost of the import in pounds, to the UK importer, if the money market hedge is used. **(8 marks)**

(b) Assume it is June 2004 and a US company needs to pay SFr5,000,000 to a Swiss supplier in 3 months. Explain how the exchange rate risk may be hedged using September Swiss Franc futures, the current price is $0.67/SFr. The contract size for the Swiss Franc futures is SFr125,000.

Assume that the spot rate and the futures market rate for $/SFr are the same in September and that there is no basis risk. Calculate the effective cost to the US company in dollars if the rate at the time of payment in September is

(i) $0.65/SFr

(ii) $0.68/SFr **(7 marks)**

(c) Briefly discuss the problems faced when hedging with currency futures. **(5 marks)**

(Total marks = 20)

Question 11

(a) Bongoman, a US-based company, has delivered goods to a UK customer invoiced in UK pounds. Total payment of £2,000,000 is due in 3 months. You are given the following information (OTC means over-the-counter):

3-month forward rate ($/£)	1.860–1.900
3-month OTC call option on pounds strike price: $1.860/£	premium: 2.5 cents per pound
3-month OTC put option on pounds strike price: $1.860/£	premium: 3 cents per pound

(i) Based on the information available, advise Bongoman on how it can manage its exchange rate exposure. Calculate the effective revenue from the sale when the forward market is used and the effective minimum revenue from the sale when the option market is used. Evaluate your advice if the spot exchange rate in 3 months is

$1.82/£; $1.84/£; $1.86/£; $1.88/£; $1.90/£.

(ii) At what exchange rate would the put option hedge yield the same revenue as the forward market hedge? **(14 marks)**

(b) In view of the Black–Scholes option pricing model on a non-dividend paying stock, there are variables that influence the value of an option. Explain the relationship between each of these variables and the value of a call option. **(6 marks)**

(Total marks = 20)

Question 12

Banco Ltd, a UK manufacturer, has about 40% of its annual sales from Australia. The company's forecasts of cash flows indicate significant receipts of Australian dollars (A$) over the next 12-month period and a decision has been made to hedge the forecast exposure to protect the company's position. The following information has been obtained.

Forecast of A$ *cash flows*

6 months:	A$ 5,000,000
12 months:	A$ 8,000,000

Interest rates

	A$	GBP
6 months	5½–6¼%	7¼–8¼%
12 months	5¾–6½%	7½–8½%

Exchange rates A$/£

Spot	2.4520–2.4550
6 months	2.4230–2.4275
12 months	2.4115–2.4160

Requirements

(a) Explain how Banco Ltd could hedge the Australian dollar receipts due in 6 and 12 months' time given the information provided above and calculate the net receipt if the company chooses to hedge. **(14 marks)**

(b) Derivatives have been very successful innovations in capital markets. Three main types of users can be identified: hedgers, speculators and arbitrageurs. Distinguish between hedgers, speculators and arbitrageurs. **(6 marks)**

(Total marks = 20)

 # Question 13

Nelson & Co owes ¥70 million in 6 months for a recent import of Japanese tyres. The following market data is available:

Spot rate (¥/£):	192–196
6-month forward rate (¥/£)	190–194
6-month put option on pounds at ¥190/£	1% premium
6-month call option on pounds at ¥190/£	3% premium
U.K. pound 6-month interest rate (annualised):	8–10%
Yen 6-month interest rate (annualised):	4–6%

(a) Explain how this exposure could be hedged using the forward market hedge and calculate the hedged cost (to the nearest pound). **(3 marks)**

(b) Explain how Nelson & Co could hedge this exposure using the money market hedge and calculate the hedged cost (to the nearest pound). **(6 marks)**

(c) Explain how Nelson & co could hedge this exposure using currency options and calculate the hedged cost (to the nearest pound). **(5 marks)**

(d) At what exchange rate would the put option hedge yield the same cost as the forward market hedge? **(5 marks)**

(e) Based on your calculations above, what is the preferred alternative? In your opinion, should Nelson & Co hedge this exposure if they expect the pound to appreciate against the yen? **(6 marks)**

(Total marks = 25)

? Question 14

ABC Plc is a retailing company listed on the London Stock Exchange. ABC Plc has an excellent rating on the corporate bond market and is able to borrow at a fixed rate of 12% per annum or at a floating rate of LIBOR + 0.1%. The treasurer of ABC believes interest rate is likely to fall over the next 3 years, and therefore favour borrowing at a floating rate.

Zotor & Co is a small manufacturing company. It can borrow funds at a fixed rate of 13.4% per annum or at a floating rate of LIBOR + 0.6%. Zotor & Co wishes to borrow at a fixed rate. A bank is currently faced with the problem of arranging an interest rate swap which should benefit both companies equally. The bank's commission will be 10 basis points.

Requirements

(a) Briefly explain the motivations for interest rate swaps? **(6 marks)**

(b) Using a swap diagram, explain the course of actions needed to implement the swap being considered. What rates of interest will ABC Plc and Zotor & Co end up paying? **(10 marks)**

(c) If Zotor & Co defaults on the swap arrangement, the loss to the bank will be less than the expected loss from the default on a loan with the same principal. Do you agree with this statement? Explain. **(3 marks)**

(d) Interest rate swaps are over-the-counter (OTC) products. Briefly discuss the advantages and disadvantages of OTC products. **(6 marks)**

(Total marks = 25)

? Question 15

(a) Describe the main forms of currency risk faced by the following types of company and suggest possible methods of managing these risks:

 (i) international companies trading throughout the world;

 (ii) companies which make sales to customers within their home country only. **(8 marks)**

(b) LMN plc exports its products throughout the world. It has today received from a regular customer in France an order worth £350,000 at today's spot market exchange rate. It has also received from a new customer in Uganda an order worth £150,000 at today's spot rate. Both orders are to be paid in the respective importer's currency. Terms of trade are 60 days' credit. No discount is offered for early payment. Experience has shown that the French customer may take up to 90 days to pay.

Foreign exchange rates (mid rates)

	French francs/US$	*US$/£*	*Uganda shillings/£*
Spot	5.7485	1.4920	1,700
1 month forward	5.7622	1.4898	N/A
2 month forward	5.7727	1.4886	
3 month forward	5.7833	1.4873	

Money market rates (% per annum)

	Deposit	*Borrowing*
UK bank	5	8
Uganda bank	15	N/A
US domestic bank	3	6

These rates are fixed for a period of 2 or 3 months for immediate deposits or borrowings. LMN plc converts all foreign currency receipts into sterling immediately on receipt. Wherever possible, the company uses forward exchange contracts to hedge its currency risks.

In view of the lack of forward markets in Uganda, the Ugandan customer has offered to pay $US225,000 to LMN plc in 3 months' time, instead of Ugandan shillings in 60 days. The customer is able to do this as a result of his government's new economic liberalisation policies.

Requirements

(i) Calculate the sterling receipts that LMN plc can expect from its sales to the French customer, assuming that LMN plc hedges its risk using the forward market.

(ii) Calculate the expected sterling receipts from the Ugandan customer, assuming that its offer of payment in US$ is accepted. Assume that LMN plc hedges its risk using
- the forward market; or
- the money market;
and advise LMN plc on which method is most advantageous.

(iii) Advise LMN plc on whether the Ugandan customer's offer of payment in US$ should be accepted. **(12 marks)**

(Total marks = 20)

? Question 16

(a) Discuss the usefulness of interest rate swaps and currency swaps to the financial manager of a fast-growing business which is just beginning to trade internationally.

(8 marks)

(b) Assume that you are the treasurer of G Ltd, an importer of goods mainly from Germany. You have received the following memo from your managing director, who is not an accountant:

'I have been reading the *Financial Times* and note that the current spot rate for Deutschmarks is DM2.234 to the pound sterling. The 6-month forward rate is 2.196

and for 12 months it is even lower. I also note that interest rates in Germany are only 3.25% per annum whereas in the UK they are much higher. I have three suggestions:

1. If we buy Deutschmarks on the spot market as and when we need them to pay for our imports, rather than taking out forward contracts, as is our present policy, it should surely save us a lot of money.

2. An alternative policy, if you think that sterling will depreciate over the next 12 months, is to buy Deutschmarks on the spot market now and place them on deposit until we need them.

3. Would it not be in our interests to borrow Deutschmarks and pay off our sterling loans? This would save us money on interest payments.

   Please let me have your views.'

You are required to write a report to the managing director responding to each of his suggestions. **(12 marks)**

(Total marks = 20)

Question 17

(a) Assume that you are the treasurer of a medium-sized manufacturing company which trades throughout Europe. At a recent meeting to discuss the company's policy on foreign exchange management, the managing director, a non-accountant, makes the following statements:

   - *Statement 1*. 'Translation risk is concerned only with the effect of exchange rate changes on financial statements and is mainly an accounting issue. There is no need to hedge this risk unless we are close to our foreign currency borrowing limits.'

   - *Statement 2*. 'Transaction risk can easily be hedged using the forward market although I am inclined either not to hedge at all or to use internal hedging methods as they are cheaper.'

Requirements

   (i) In respect of statement 1, explain what the MD means when he says that there is no need to hedge unless the company is close to its foreign currency borrowing limits.
   (4 marks)

   (ii) In respect of statement 2, comment on whether the MD is right to consider not hedging as an appropriate strategy, and discuss, briefly, three internal hedging techniques which the company could consider. **(6 marks)**

(b) Assume that you are the treasurer of a multinational company based in Switzerland. Your company trades extensively with the United States. You have just received US$1m from a customer in the United States. As the company has no immediate need of capital you decide to invest the money in either US$ or Swiss francs for 12 months. The following information is relevant:

   - the spot rate of exchange is SFr1.3125 to US$1;
   - the 12-month forward rate is SFr1.275 to US$1;
   - the interest rate on a 1-year Swiss franc bond is $4\frac{9}{16}\%$;
   - the interest rate on a 1-year US$ bond is $7\frac{5}{8}\%$.

   Assume that investment in either currency is risk-free and ignore transaction costs.

Requirements

Calculate the returns under both options (investing in US$ or Swiss francs) and explain why there is so little difference between the two figures. **(10 marks)**

(Total marks = 20)

? Question 18

(a) Discuss how interest rate swaps and currency swaps might be of value to the corporate financial manager. **(10 marks)**

(b) Calvold plc has a 1-year contract to construct factories in a South American country. At the end of the year the factories will be paid for by the local government. The price has been fixed at 2,000 million pesos, payable in the South American currency.

   In order to fulfil the contract, Calvold will need to invest 1,000 million pesos in the project immediately, and a fixed additional sum of 500 million pesos in 6 months.

   The government of the South American country has offered Calvold a fixed-rate currency swap for 1 year for the full 1,500 million pesos at a swap rate of 20 pesos/£. Net interest of 10% per year would be payable in pesos by Calvold to the government.

   There is no forward foreign exchange market for the peso against the pound.

   Forecasts of inflation rates for the next year are as follows.

Probability	UK		South American country
0.25	4%	and	40%
0.50	5%	and	60%
0.25	7%	and	100%

   The peso is a freely floating currency which has not recently been subject to major government intervention.

   The current spot rate is 25 pesos/£. Calvold's opportunity cost of funds is 12% per year in the United Kingdom. The company has no access to funds in the South American country.

   Taxation, the risk of default, and discounting to allow for the timing of payments may be ignored.

Requirement

Evaluate whether it is likely to be beneficial for Calvold plc to agree to the currency swap.

(15 marks)

(Total marks = 25)

? Question 19

PG plc is considering investing in a new project in Canada which will have a life of 4 years. The initial investment is C$150,000, including working capital. The net after-tax cash flows which the project will generate are C$60,000 per annum for year 1, 2 and 3 and C$45,000 in year 4. The terminal value of the project is estimated at C$50,000, net of tax.

   The current spot rate for C$ against sterling is 1.7. Economic forecasters expect sterling to strengthen against the Canadian dollar by = per cent per annum over the next 4 years.

   The company evaluates UK projects of similar risk at 14%.

Requirements

(a) Calculate the NPV of the Canadian project using the following two methods:

   (i) convert the currency cash flows into sterling and discount the sterling cash flows at a sterling discount rate;

   (ii) discount the cash flows in C$ using an adjusted discount rate which incorporates the 12-month forecast spot rate;

   and explain briefly the theories and/or assumptions which underlie the use of the adjusted discount rate approach in point (ii). **(12 marks)**

(b) The company had originally planned to finance the project with internal funds generated in the United Kingdom. However, the finance director has suggested that there would be advantages in raising debt finance in Canada.

   You are required to discuss the advantages and disadvantages of matching investment and borrowing overseas as compared with UK-sourced debt or equity.

   Wherever possible, relate your answer to the details given in this question for PG plc.

(8 marks)
(Total marks = 20)

? Question 20

Assume you are a financial manager with HH, a multinational company based in the United States with subsidiaries in Germany and the United Kingdom. One of your responsibilities is cash management for the group of companies. You have received the following forecasts of surplus funds for the next 30 days from the financial mangers in the two subsidiaries:

Germany:	Euros (€) 10.5 million
UK:	£ Sterling 5.5 million

The US operation is forecasting a cash deficit of US$ 10 million.
You obtain the following exchange rate information from the financial press:

	€/US$	£/US$
Spot	1.131	0.695
30-day forward	1.126	0.700

Annual borrowing/deposit rates available to the group are as follows:

US$ 30-day	1.7%/1.6%
£ Sterling 30-day	4.1%/3.9%
€ 30-day	3.1%/3.0%

You are considering introducing a system of cash pooling whereby all funds are converted into US$ and the net balance invested or borrowed in US$ in the United States.

Ignore taxes and transaction costs.

Requirements

(a) Calculate the cash balance at the end of the 30-day period, in US$, for each company in the group (including the US parent) under each of the following two scenarios:

   (i) Each group company acts independently and invests/finances its own cash balances/deficits in its local currency.

  (ii) Cash balances are pooled immediately in the United States and the net $ balance invested/borrowed for the 30-day period.

     Based on your calculations, comment on which method is the most favourable in financial terms from the US parent's point of view.

     You should assume simple interest rates based on a year of 360 days.　**(13 marks)**

(b) Discuss the benefits and possible drawbacks to the parent company and to each subsidiary if a system of pooling were to be introduced as a general policy for the group.
(12 marks)

     A report format is not required in answering this question.　**(Total marks = 25)**

The following question is taken from the examinations of the Association of Corporate Treasurers (ACT).

Question 21

Bluechip Ltd is a manufacturing company based in the United Kingdom. Currently, all sales are priced in Sterling and all components and labour are sourced in the United Kingdom. Various business and market developments are being discussed at the next Board meeting and you have been asked to comment on the exchange rate risks that could arise in each case.

Requirements

(a) Write notes on the exchange rate risks that could result from each of the following developments, considering each one separately:

- Issuing an annual Euro price list to customers in Continental Europe.
- Increased competition in the US market from a US-based competitor.
- Plans to relocate 50% of the present manufacturing capacity to Italy under the legal framework of a subsidiary company.　**(9 marks)**

    Greenchip Ltd has a significant proportion of Euro debt and there is concern that the Euro will strengthen against Sterling before the next interest payment of EUR 1 million is due in 3 months' time. You have been asked to use option contracts to limit the potential loss to within = per cent of the cost represented by today's spot rate of EUR/GBP 0.6195/05.

    Redchip Ltd has a large Euro receipt of EUR500,000 due in 3 months' time. You have been asked to use an option contract to guarantee that the Sterling value of that receipt will not be lower than today's spot valuation before taking into account the cost of the premium.

Relevant market information – Today's spot rate: EUR/GBP 0.6195/05

3 month EUR/GBP option contracts priced as GBP per EUR

Strike price	Euro calls	Euro puts
0.5900	0.0330	0.0026
0.6200	0.0130	0.0120
0.6500	0.0033	0.0317

(b) Construct the hedges required by Greenchip Ltd and Redchip Ltd and calculate the premiums payable. **(5 marks)**

(c) Evaluate and compare the outcome of each hedge if the spot rate in 3 months' time is:

either (i) 0.7200/10
or   (ii) 0.6200/10
or   (iii) 0.5200/10

(6 marks)
(Total marks = 20)

Solutions to Revision Questions

☑ **Solution 1**

(a) A review of disaster recovery had identified a lack of hardware back-up as costs had been continually deferred from year to year to maintain current profits. This has an effect on business continuity for both ABC and its retail customers. Insurance is only one type of risk treatment and ABC has overlooked the need to address business continuity more proactively and comprehensively.

The pressure on short-term profits and cash flow is important to recognise but the short-term view may lead to medium- and long-term problems if under-investment continues. This needs to be the focus of a risk management exercise to properly assess, evaluate, report and treat the business continuity risk.

Although a severe catastrophe may have a small likelihood of occurrence, the impact will be severe and insurance cover is unlikely to be adequate as ABC will not have taken adequate steps to mitigate the loss. Customer awareness of the risk is likely to result in customers moving their business elsewhere. Public disclosure or a severe catastrophe will have a major impact on the reputation of ABC and on ABC's share price.

(b) The board is responsible for maintaining a sound system of internal control to safeguard shareholders' investment and the company's assets. When reviewing management reports on internal control, the board should consider the significant risks and assess how they have been identified, evaluated and managed; assess the effectiveness of internal controls in managing the significant risks, having regard to any significant weaknesses in internal control; consider whether necessary actions are being taken promptly to remedy any weaknesses and consider whether the findings indicate a need for more exhaustive monitoring of the system of internal control.

Risk management is the process by which organisations systematically identify and treat upside and downside risks with the goal of achieving organisational objectives. The goal of risk management is to manage, rather than eliminate risk. Initially, there needs to be a commitment from the board and top management in relation to risk management generally and business continuity in particular, even if this means a short-term detrimental impact on profitability. The board of ABC, through the audit committee, needs to be more involved in the risk management process. Individual responsibilities for risk management need to be assigned and sufficient resources need to be allocated to fund effective risk management for business continuity.

ABC needs to identify its appetite for risk, and a risk management policy needs to be formulated and agreed by the board. The risk management process needs to

477

identify and define risk, which needs to be assessed in terms of both likelihood and impact. For ABC, the risks have been clearly defined: a loss of business continuity caused by a major catastrophe and the consequent loss of reputation this would involve.

The likelihood of fire, flood, terrorist or criminal activity and so on needs to be assessed, particularly in terms of the risk avoidance processes that are already in place. For example, ABC needs to evaluate whether there has been flooding in the area before, whether water pipes run near the computer facility, whether fire prevention measures are in place, whether firewalls are in place and have been tested so as to reduce the likelihood of attack via the Internet. An assessment of probability of these and other catastrophes should be made. Although these may be low probability events, the impact on the business of any such catastrophe will be severe.

Risk evaluation determines the significance of risks to the organisation and whether each specific risk should be accepted or treated. It should be emphasised that these risks cannot be accepted but do need to be treated. Risk treatment (or risk response) is the process of selecting and implementing measures to reduce or limit the risk. The existing contingency plans need to be examined in detail. While data appear to be backed up regularly and stored off-site, there seems to be inadequate back-up for hardware. Risk treatment will involve deciding the most cost-effective method by which to manage the risk. A preferred solution given the reliance of ABC's customers on the system is to have a remote site equipped with a second system that data can be restored onto. While this is the most expensive option there may be business benefits in having two sites. A second solution may be to outsource the back-up facility so that ABC contracts with a third party to have a system available if one is needed. A third option is to negotiate with suppliers as to the availability of other sites and the replacement of equipment on a short notice basis. Finally, insurance coverage needs to be reviewed and the mitigation decided in consultation with ABC's insurers. The present method of risk management that relies only on off-site data back-up is inadequate to assure business continuity.

As business continuity is so important, the board and audit committee need to be involved in the decision-making process about risk treatment. There needs to be regular risk management reporting to assess the control systems in place to reduce risk; the processes used to identify and respond to risks; the methods used to manage significant risks and the monitoring and review system itself. Reporting should take place to business units, senior management, internal audit, the board and the audit committee.

(c) The benefits of effective risk management for ABC include the maintenance of profitability in the medium and longer term and the avoidance of sudden losses if business continuity is impeded. The major benefit for ABC in such a case is the avoidance of profit warnings and major exceptional items. Additional benefits may include more cost-effective insurance cover and reduced premium cost. If the recommendations are adopted, despite the increased costs that will almost necessarily be incurred, the board of ABC will have greater degree of assurance that business continuity will be safeguarded in the event of a catastrophe, will continue to satisfy its customers and will maintain its reputation with customers, the public and investors.

✅ Solution 2

(a) The rational-economic perspective views control as protecting the principals, in this case, government or the public, who pay taxes and want to see public monies spent efficiently and effectively. The perspective is reflected in the cybernetic management control system based on objective setting; measuring outputs; a predictive model of the business and taking actions to reduce deviations from objectives through feedback and feed forward processes. In this perspective, financial and non-financial performance measures portray an accurate representation of the organisation's results.

The interpretive perspective focuses on trying to understand and explain how managers think about and use management control systems. In the interpretive perspective, individuals act towards things on the basis of the meaning that things have for them. Meaning is brought to the situation by the individual and is socially constructed, as in the culture of social workers. In this perspective, accounting information is symbolic and ceremonial rather than on objective representation of reality. Although resources limit what can be done, providing services to the client is more important than what is reflected in management reports. Consequently, only some of the non-financial performance measures hold any importance for social workers.

(b) Budgets are used as forecasts of future events, as motivational targets and as standards for performance evaluation. Budgets provide a control mechanism through both feed forward and feedback loops. A major difficulty in budgeting is predicting the volume of activity, particularly in a public sector or not-for-profit organisation where client demand cannot be controlled but where the funding provided by government for service delivery is limited. Budgets are not effective in controlling what the social workers do.

The 'Beyond Budgeting' movement has criticised the limitations of budgets and proposes targets based on stretch goals linked to performance against world-class benchmarks and prior periods. It enables decision-making and performance accountability to be devolved to line managers and a culture of personal responsibility which leads to increased motivation, higher productivity and better customer service. This is likely to be a better model for a social services department, particularly given the spending below budget, which is most likely linked to the below target performance against non-financial measures.

Variance analysis involves comparing actual performance against plan, investigating the causes of the variance and taking corrective action to ensure that targets are achieved. Properly calculated, variations can identify poor budgeting practice, lack of cost control or variations in the usage or price of resources that need to result in corrective action. However, variance analysis is likely to be of little value in a social services department as costs, especially salary costs, are fixed and the volume of activity bears little relationship with budget costs. The cause of lower spending than budget is the inability to fill staff vacancies quickly.

Non-financial measures are better predictors of long-term performance and operational measures of performance may provide better control, especially in a public or not-for-profit organisation where financial results are unhelpful, other than as an expense limit that cannot be exceeded. Non-financial performance management requires a better understanding of the operational activities of the organisation and this understanding needs to be incorporated into control systems design.

Performance measurement through a Balanced Scorecard-type approach has become increasingly common in most organisations. The measures used by the social services department include client and efficiency measures. The waiting list, client satisfaction and resolution of problem measures are likely to be valued by both managers and social workers. However, in the efficiency measure used, the calculation of cost per service is also unlikely to be meaningful as resources are fixed but work pressures high, and it is unlikely that professional social workers would be influenced by measures of efficiency such as this.

Importantly, there is an absence in the non-financial measures used by the department of any improvement or staff-related measures. Given the circumstances described in the scenario, measures of absenteeism, staff turnover, staff satisfaction and vacancies may be important predictors of future performance and are important indicators of action management should undertake to resolve the internal problems in the department.

(c) An internal control system includes all the financial and non-financial controls, policies and procedures adopted by an organisation to assist in achieving organisational objectives; to provide reasonable assurance of effective and efficient operation; compliance with laws and regulations; safeguarding of assets; prevention and detection of fraud and error; the accuracy and completeness of the accounting records and the timely preparation of reliable financial information. A sound system of internal control provides reasonable, but not absolute, assurance that a company will not be hindered in achieving its business objectives, or in the orderly and legitimate conduct of its business, or by circumstances which may reasonably be foreseen.

The major risks identified in this scenario are financial risk if budgets are overspent; risk to clients and risk to employees. Internal controls need to be based on a risk assessment and the cost/benefit of controls.

Financial controls are essential to ensure that spending is contained within budget. However, continual spending below budget also identifies a problem. Recruitment activity needs to be improved to use available funds to replace social workers who have left, as this money is effectively lost by the department and contributes to below target performance on non-financial measures.

Non-financial performance measures are also important, subject to the comments made in Section (b) above. Additional measures need to be implemented to cover staffing and the reasons for below target performance need to be ascertained as there may either be operational problems, perhaps caused by shortages of staff, or the targets may be unrealistically high.

Non-financial qualitative controls influence behaviour to ensure that it is legally correct, co-ordinated and consistent throughout the organisation; linked to objectives; efficient and effective; fair and equitable. These controls include formal and informal structures; rules, policies and procedures; physical controls; strategic plans; incentives and rewards; project management and personnel controls.

Qualitative controls need to be emphasised in the social services department. Rules, policies and procedures are important elements of internal control as they guide behaviour. There is a trade-off between a longer waiting list for clients awaiting services and providing effective services to clients. Policies and procedures are based on prior experience and establish the most effective standards of service and procedures to be followed to ensure that each case is handled fairly, equitably and effectively.

Personnel controls are particularly important to ensure that social workers are properly recruited, trained and socialised into the organisation. Support needs to be provided to staff to help them cope with the volume and stress they face in their work. This has important health and safety considerations and improved controls might reduce staff turnover and absenteeism. Controls are also necessary over recruitment to improve the filling of vacancies which has led to lower than budget spending and probably contributes to the pressure on staff.

Solution 3

(a) The board is responsible for the company's system of internal control and for reviewing its effectiveness. An internal control system is designed to manage rather than eliminate the risk of failure to achieve business objectives, and can only provide reasonable but not absolute assurance against material misstatement or loss. The board should maintain a sound system of internal control to safeguard shareholders' investment and the company's assets, and should establish formal and transparent arrangements for considering how they should apply financial reporting and internal control principles and for maintaining an appropriate relationship with the company's auditors. The board or an audit committee need to satisfy themselves that there is a proper system and allocation of responsibilities for the day-to-day monitoring of financial controls but they should not seek to do the monitoring themselves.

The audit committee (or a separate risk committee) should review and approve the scope of work of the internal audit function; ensure that the internal audit function has access to the information it needs and the resources necessary to carry out its function; approve the appointment or termination of the head of internal audit and meet the external and the internal auditors at least annually, without management being present, to discuss the scope of work of the auditors and any issues arising from the audit.

When reviewing management reports on internal control, the board should consider the significant risks and assess how they have been identified, evaluated and managed; assess the effectiveness of internal controls in managing the significant risks, having regard to any significant weaknesses in internal control; consider whether necessary actions are being taken promptly to remedy any weaknesses and consider whether the findings indicate a need for more exhaustive monitoring of the system of internal control.

The audit committee should review with the external auditors their findings and should in particular discuss major issues that arose during the audit and have subsequently been resolved, and those issues that remain unresolved; review key accounting and audit judgements and review levels of error identified during the audit, obtaining explanations from management and the external auditors as to any errors that remain unadjusted.

(b) Risk management is the process by which organisations systematically identify and treat upside and downside risks across the portfolio of all activities with the goal of achieving organisational objectives. Risk management increases the probability of success, reduces both the probability of failure and the uncertainty of achieving the organisation's objectives. The goal of risk management is to manage, rather than eliminate risk. This is most effectively done through embedding a risk culture into the organisation.

For SPM's Distribution division, there is a risk of stock losses through theft, largely due to the lack of separation of duties. This lack of separation occurs because the Distribution Division:

- enters all orders to the computer;
- selects all stock from the warehouse;
- despatches all goods to customers;
- receives the signed paperwork evidencing delivery;
- writes off stock losses due to damage and obsolescence;
- carries out and to a large extent controls the annual physical stocktake.

This lack of separation of duties could result in stock losses or theft that is not identified or not recorded and any stock losses or theft may be disguised during the stocktake due to the expertise of the Distribution division which the auditors appear to rely on.

These stock losses or theft may not be accurately recorded and the reported profits of SPM may overstate profits if physical inventory does not match that shown in the accounting records. Stock of stationery is easy to dispose of and losses can easily happen due to error or carelessness, for instance through water damage, dropping and so on. The possibility of theft of stock which can readily be sold in retail stores is also high and the consequences of not identifying stock losses or theft might be severe over a period of time. There is a risk that inventory records may substantially overstate the physical stock. There is a serious limitation of accounting here as it relies on computer records and a stocktake process that may be severely impaired and hence there may be hidden losses not reflected in SPM's reported financial statements.

Fraud is dishonestly obtaining an advantage, avoiding an obligation or causing a loss to another party. Those committing fraud may be managers, employees or third parties, including customers and suppliers. There are three conditions for fraud to occur: dishonesty, opportunity and motive. If stock theft is occurring, the weakness in systems due to the lack of separation of duties provides an opportunity. Personnel policies and supervision may influence dishonesty and employment or social conditions among the workforce may influence motive.

As for all other risks, a risk management strategy needs to be developed for fraud. This strategy should include fraud prevention; the identification and detection of fraud and responses to fraud.

Existing risk treatment does not appear to be adequate due to the lack of separation of duties, the possibility of fraud and the reliance of internal and external auditors on the Distribution division's staff.

(c) External auditors cannot be relied on to provide assurance of stock accuracy. This is a role for management and in particular for internal audit. The board and the audit committee should recognise its responsibility for providing adequate controls. At the very least, SPM's management accountant and its internal auditors should have identified the weakness in control and brought this to the attention of the board.

An audit is a systematic examination of the activities of an organisation, based primarily on investigation and analysis of its systems, controls and records. It is intended to objectively evaluate evidence about matters of importance, to judge the degree of correspondence between those matters and some criteria or standard and to communicate the results of that judgement to interested parties.

Internal audit is an independent appraisal function established within an organisation to examine and evaluate its activities and designed to add value and improve an organisation's operations. The main role of internal audit is to provide assurance that the main business risks are being managed and that internal controls are operating effectively.

Risk-based internal auditing is linked directly with risk management. It begins with business objectives and focuses on those risks identified by management that may prevent the objectives from being achieved. Internal audit assesses the extent to which a robust risk management process is in place to reduce risks to a level acceptable to the board. It provides assurance to the board that the risk management processes which management has put in place are operating as intended; that the risk management processes are part of a sound design; that management's response to risks are adequate and effective in reducing those risks to a level acceptable to the board and that a sound framework of controls is in place to mitigate those risks which management wishes to treat. Internal auditors should focus on matters of high risk and where significant control deficiencies have been found, to identify actions taken to address them.

For SPM's Distribution division, the internal audit aim will be based on a risk assessment of the likelihood and consequences of unreported stock losses, whether caused by fraud or other loss.

An audit plan needs to be determined, commencing with a preliminary survey to obtain background information about the area to be audited, and to judge the scope and depth of audit work to be undertaken, based on the complexity of the area to be audited. The survey will identify the objectives, scope and timing of the audit and the audit resources (staff days, other costs, skills and experience) required.

Analytic review is the audit technique used to help analyse data to identify trends, errors, fraud, inefficiency and inconsistency. Its purpose is to understand what has happened in a system, to compare this with a standard and to identify weaknesses in practice or unusual situations that may require further examination.

The main methods of analytic review of relevance to this scenario include flowcharting systems and procedures and obtaining narrative explanations from staff. While this would provide background information, the main form of assurance will come from physical inspection of inventory against computer records and may also involve the re-calculation and reconciliation of stock movements to check accuracy and the physical testing of how the Distribution system is operating. This could be supplemented by benchmarking reported stock losses with similar organisations.

The audit should provide an understanding of the system or process; identify strengths and weaknesses and a comparison between the system or process in operation with that documented in formal manuals and procedures. The evaluation will be based on the use of internal control questionnaires to provide assurance that controls are adequate.

If stock theft is occurring, the weakness in systems due to the lack of separation of duties provides an opportunity. Personnel policies and supervision may influence dishonesty, and employment or social conditions among the workforce may influence motive. Internal audit needs to review the risk of dishonesty and motive as well as the opportunity provided by weak systems. There may be warning signals such as backlogs of work, holidays not being taken, extravagant lifestyles, missing audit trails.

The likely results of such an audit approach are three-fold. First, there would be an independent check on the accuracy of the physical stock, uncontaminated by the expertise of the Distribution staff. This would identify whether the reported financial results were accurate. Second, there would be a systematic review of systems and processes in use that would be the basis for recommendations for improved internal control. Third, a better understanding of the risk of fraud will be obtained and controls can then be revised to manage this risk.

(d) The main recommendation is for the separation of duties in SPM's distribution division. The customer service centre should process all customer orders, even though this may mean transferring staff from the despatch department. It may be more effective to use a document imaging system to reduce paperwork by the conversion of orders into electronic files that are capable of being read by computer programs and transferred to the despatch department. Further separation can be carried out by signed paperwork evidencing delivery being sent to the accounts department and for all writes offs of stock losses due to damage or obsolescence to be carried out by the accounts department. Finally, the reliance on Distribution staff for stocktaking needs to be reduced and accountants and internal auditors need to play a more prominent role in physical counting and reconciling to computer records.

The second recommendation is for greater emphasis on controls to prevent dishonesty. These include pre-employment checks; scrutiny of staff by effective supervision; severe discipline for offenders and strong moral leadership. Motive can be influenced by providing good employment conditions, a sympathetic complaints procedure, but dismissing staff instantaneously where it is warranted.

✓ Solution 4

(a) There are various good practice elements of information systems project management, and the systems development life cycle provides a framework for the control of new information systems. By the feasibility stage, there should be a clear understanding about the objectives of the new system, the deliverables, its cost and its time to completion.

Those involved in a computer implementation project are usually committed to its success, but may fail to recognise any warning signals. Often, cost escalation and delay are noticed but if the system does not work at all, there may be a fundamental risk to the business operations which are dependent on effective information systems.

However, a steering committee is important in bringing together the project sponsor, project manager, specialist IT staff, user representatives and internal audit. The steering committee monitors the system implementation in comparison with the plan and ensures that specific deliverables are accepted at each stage of systems development. It has overall responsibility to ensure that the system meets requirements in terms of quality, time and cost. A Steering Committee provides a consistent and systematic approach to implementing a new system. In Qwerty's case, the non-existence of a Steering Committee (Weakness d) has contributed to problems with conversion of data (Weakness b) and testing and acceptance (Weakness c). This has been compounded by a failure to carry out a post-implementation review (Weakness e). The IT Manager was clearly a key actor in the implementation but there may have been a trade-off between bringing the project to completion on time and to budget at the cost of quality (Strength d). Qwerty faced a substantial risk in leaving the responsibility for the implementation to one person, particularly if that person was incapable of the task, had resigned from the organisation or suffered from illness or accident.

Systems analysis is intended to generate the specification for the system through a methodical investigation of a problem and the identification and ranking of alternative solutions to aid in acquisition decisions. This is followed by systems design which involves the conversion of specifications into a workable design. At the conclusion of the system design stage, control should be evidenced in data security and levels of authorisation; system documentation; interfaces with other systems and acceptance of design by the project team, especially users.

The design of Qwerty's system is at the leading edge of technology. Internet purchasing enables customers to carry out the data processing previously carried out by the retailer's own employees by searching for and buying goods and paying for those goods by electronic funds transfer at point of sale (EFTPOS). Electronic data interchange (EDI) enables a common data format so that business transactions in one organisation can be automatically converted into transactions in another organisation via the Internet. The audit report has identified strengths in terms of both data security (Strength a) and EDI links (Strength c). However, there is a continuing systems design weakness (Weakness a) that has caused loss of customer bookings.

Implementation addresses testing, documentation and training and conversion from existing systems. There must be comprehensive testing by systems development staff, programmers, users and internal auditors. At the implementation stage, there needs to be a review of training and documentation, file conversion and operational issues, such as staffing and supervision. Systems operation and maintenance involve the correction or enhancement of systems once they are in operation. Finally, there needs to be a post-implementation review. The audit report has identified strengths in terms of training and documentation (Strength b). However, the report was critical of the conversion of data (Weakness b) and testing prior to implementation (Weakness c).

It is good practice for the internal auditor to sign off the system prior to implementation. This involves forming a professional opinion that the system meets user requirements; functions satisfactorily according to the agreed design; has been developed with adequate built-in controls; is auditable; files have been converted and are complete and accurate and the implementation plan is realistic.

There was no internal audit involvement during the systems implementation in Qwerty. Internal audit needs to ensure that risks are adequately addressed by controls designed-in during the development phase; ensure that financial and non-financial information is accurate and complete and suitable for its intended purpose; identify potential problems in data collection, input, processing and output; ensure an adequate audit trail; and review the scope for possible fraud. Internal audit can only achieve these functions by working closely with the systems development team. The internal auditor should also be involved in a post-completion audit of the systems development project. The absence of any internal audit involvement in MNO's implementation of a new computer system calls into question the financial and non-financial controls that may, or may not, exist.

Finally, CIMA's *Ethical Guidelines* recommend that members should be constantly conscious of, and alert to factors which give rise to conflicts of interest, whether from pressure from others, divided loyalty, or being a party to the issue of misleading information. The involvement by MNO in providing a range of IT consultancy services to Qwerty and their involvement in the feasibility study may impact their independence and objectivity in carrying out internal audit services for Qwerty, particularly those that are IT-related. Objectivity relates to the impartiality, intellectual honesty and freedom from conflicts of interest, while not allowing prejudice or bias or the influence of others to override objectivity. Consequently, Qwerty's board, while recognising the value of MNO's expertise, should be conscious of the impact their broader relationship may have on their reporting.

Recommendations to Qwerty's board will be to

- Thoroughly investigate the loss of on-line customer bookings and correct the design problem causing this problem.
- Undertake a post-implementation review with a view to documenting and learning from both successes and failures and in particular to identify any additional design weaknesses that may have been overlooked in the completion of the project.
- Undertake a comprehensive audit of the new computer system using computer-assisted audit techniques, in order to identify any other control weaknesses, on the basis that internal audit was not involved in systems design.
- Monitor the independence and objectivity of MNO in their internal audit role.

(b) The basic principles of auditing a computer system rely on understanding how the system works and how it can be tested. An IT environment has risks that are particular to the technology and structures adopted for business. The main features of modern computer systems that require controls are a result of the growth of networks where there is multi-user access from remote locations. In particular, external EDI links with other organisations and automated payment systems are a feature of e-commerce.

Data validity checking and acknowledgements or confirmations are important methods of ensuring control, particularly when, as for Qwerty, data are entered remotely via customer access over the Internet. Computer auditing also involves assessing security controls including physical and logical (password) access, again with the need to control remote access by customers, hence the importance of a firewall to insulate those records a customer can change from those that only employees can alter. Backup of data files needs to take place on a regular basis and logs of the day's transactions need to be maintained to enable recovery.

Computer-assisted audit techniques are used in most audits involving computer systems. These may be used to review system controls or to review actual data. System controls can be audited using test data that are processed by a computer system with the results compared with expected results, to ensure that the computer system has processed the data accurately. This might be difficult in an environment like Qwerty's where EDI is carried out with other computer systems. Embedded audit facilities allow a continuous audit review of data and its processing by using a fictitious business entity, which might be fictitious customers in Qwerty's case.

Audit interrogation software allows extraction of data from files for further audit work; enables the auditor to interrogate computer files and extract the required information; enables statistical analysis of data and provides verification of data by comparing data with management reports. It also identifies items that do not comply with system rules or that seem to be unreasonable. Selection of sample travel bookings from Qwerty's data files would enable further audit checking.

The internal auditor also needs to review the procedures in the IT department, looking for a systematic approach to maintenance and the analysis of systems performance data. Change control systems should be in place to control all development and maintenance work. Control self assessment enables managers to identify problems, such as Qwerty's loss of customer data that can be investigated.

(c) The board, usually through its audit committee, has a role to act independently of management to ensure that the interests of shareholders are properly protected in relation to financial reporting and internal control. The main role and responsibilities of the audit committee include monitoring the integrity of the company's financial statements; reviewing the company's internal control and risk management systems; monitoring and reviewing the effectiveness of the internal audit function; making recommendations to the board for the appointment, re-appointment and removal of the external auditor and approving the terms of engagement and remuneration of the external auditor, including the supply of any non-audit services; reviewing and monitoring the external auditor's independence and objectivity and the effectiveness of the audit process.

Reviewing the effectiveness of internal control is one of the board's responsibilities which needs to be carried out on a continuous basis. The Board should regularly review reports on internal control – both financial and non-financial – for the purpose of making its public statement on internal control.

The board must acknowledge that it is responsible for the company's system of internal control and for reviewing its effectiveness. It should also explain that the system is designed to manage rather than eliminate the risk of failure to achieve business objectives, and can only provide reasonable but not absolute assurance against material misstatement or loss. The board's statement on internal control should disclose that there is an ongoing process for identifying, evaluating and managing the significant risks faced by the company, that it has been in place for the year and up to the date of approval of the annual report and accounts, and that it has been regularly reviewed by the board and conforms to the Turnbull Guidance.

The board's annual assessment of risk and internal control should consider changes since the last annual assessment in the nature and extent of significant risks, and the company's ability to respond to changes in its business and the external environment; the scope and quality of management's ongoing monitoring of risks and of the system of internal control and the work of the internal audit function and other providers of assurance; the extent and frequency of the communication of the results of the monitoring to the board which enable it to build up a cumulative assessment of the state of control in the company and the effectiveness with which risk is being managed; the incidence of significant control weaknesses that have been identified during the period and the extent to which they have resulted in unforeseen outcomes that have had, or could have, a material impact on the company's financial performance and the effectiveness of the company's public reporting processes.

✔️ Solution 5

(a) Information systems (IS) strategies are focused on the business unit, enabling it to satisfy (internal or external) customer demand strategy. IS strategies determine the long-term information requirements of an organisation, providing an 'umbrella' for different information technologies that may exist. Information technology (IT) strategies are supply-oriented, focused on activities and the technology needed to support those activities. IT strategy defines the specific systems that are required to satisfy the information needs of the organisation, including the hardware, software and operating systems. Information management (IM) strategies are management focused at the whole organisation level. IM strategy will ensure that information is being provided to users, is securely stored and backed up and that redundant information is not produced.

Enterprise resource planning (ERP) systems integrate data flow across the organisation. They capture transaction data for accounting purposes, operational data, customer and supplier data, all of which are made available through data warehouses against which custom-designed reports can be produced. ERP systems are a development of older-style materials requirement planning (MRP), manufacturing resource planning (MRPII) and distribution resource planning (DRP) systems. ERP system data can be used to update performance measures in a Balanced Scorecard system and can be used for activity-based costing, shareholder value, strategic planning, customer relationship management and supply chain management.

From an IS perspective, ERP takes a whole supply chain view from supplier to customer, obtaining all of the information needs of SupplyCo, including customer, product, supplier, inventory, distribution, and so on and provides the foundation data for all business processes. From an IT perspective, the particular vendor selected and the hardware platform utilised for ERP will depend on the volume of business, extent of distributed processing, Internet access requirements (e.g. for EDI or EFTPOS), and so on. An ERP is likely to be used in larger organisations with substantial transaction and user volume. From an IM perspective, the shared data available on an ERP need to be accessible by all users, subject to information security policies and the need for business continuity. The complexity and scale of an ERP system will dictate its importance to the organisation and the reliance the organisation will place on secure and reliable IM strategy.

(b) An IT environment has risks that are particular to the technology and structures adopted for business. File structures in modern relational databases can be very complex as files have multiple purposes and methods of access. Also, real-time processing of data takes place, causing a greater risk for deliberate or accidental error. As much data entry takes place automatically, less documentation is evident, and this has implications for auditability and security. The dependence of SupplyCo on its ERP system will also dictate sophisticated business continuity procedures.

Security controls are aimed at preventing unauthorised access, modification or destruction of stored data. Integrity controls ensure that data are accurate, consistent and free from accidental corruption. Contingency controls operate so that a back-up facility and a contingency plan can be implemented to restore business operations as quickly as possible.

To address these risks, controls should exist over personnel, physical and logical access to systems, business continuity, and transaction input, processing and output. The extent of controls implemented will depend on a risk assessment process involving the likelihood/consequence of risk occurring and the organisation's risk appetite.

Personnel controls include those over recruitment, training, supervision, termination and separation of duties. Logical access controls provide security over unauthorised access to data through password authorisation. Facility controls include having a secure location from physical risk and controlling physical access to systems, remote or otherwise. Business continuity planning or disaster recovery planning takes place in order to recover information systems from critical events after they have happened.

Input controls are designed to detect and prevent errors during transaction data entry to ensure that the data entered are complete and accurate, such as through authorisation, verification and reasonableness checks. This is particularly important in an ERP environment where transactions update files that are accessed by multiple users for different purposes. Processing controls ensure that processing has occurred according to the organisation's requirements and that no transactions have been omitted or processed incorrectly. These can take place through control totals, standardisation and balancing procedures. Output controls ensure that input and processing activities have been carried out and that the information produced is reliable and distributed to users, such as transaction lists, exception reports, distribution lists and forms control.

(c) If SupplyCo changes the way it does business to fit the ERP package, it may impair its competitive advantage if it is providing something different to its competitors. If the company fits the package, companies will tend to be isomorphic (see institutional theory) with each other, with the computer system defining the way business processes are conducted for all companies using that system. This is dangerous as competitive advantage is likely to be eroded in pursuit of fitting in with a standard system, particularly when only two to three computer suppliers are likely to offer a suitable ERP product. Change is also likely to meet resistance from employees, suppliers or customers as they will be taken-for-granted ways of doing things that need to be altered. However, cost efficiency may dictate that there is a need to change a business process as, according to value chain principles, the cost of providing a benefit must be less than what the customer is prepared to pay for the added value.

If SupplyCo modifies the ERP package to fit the business this is likely to be an expensive option. Changing standard software involves a significant financial cost, increases implementation time and is likely to result in 'bugs' in the system. It could also result in unforeseen control problems that have been removed from the standard system but emerge in the modified system. Upgrading to the supplier's next version of the software is also likely to be much more difficult. Introducing a system as sophisticated as an ERP system requires a reconsideration of business processes. Companies that have merely automated existing business processes sometimes find that they have missed an opportunity to re-examine fundamental business processes and modify them to enhance their competitive advantage.

The ERP should be seen as a source of value. To release this value a rigorous business analysis is needed including addressing all existing business processes. Only by carrying out such a process with a cost-benefit analysis can a judgement be made about whether the package should be modified or whether business processes should be changed to fit the package.

✔ Solution 6

(a) Outsourcing enables organisations to concentrate on their core activities while subcontracting support activities to those organisations who are specialists. The main advantages of outsourcing are more effective budgetary control through the ability to predict costs; improved quality and service from a specialist supplier; relieving the organisation of the burden of managing specialist staff, especially where there is little promotional opportunity and/or high staff turnover and keeping up-to-date with changing techniques and practices.

The main disadvantages of outsourcing are the difficulty that may be experienced in obtaining a service level agreement that clearly identifies the obligations of each party; the loss of flexibility and inability to quickly respond to changing circumstances as the function is no longer under organisational control; the risk of unsatisfactory quality and service, or the failure of the supplier; poor management of the changeover or of the outsource supplier; increasing costs charged by the outsource supplier over time and the difficulty of changing the outsourced supplier or returning to in-house provision.

(b) Outsourcing the management accounting function is at first an appealing proposition, especially given the difficulties experienced by GDS in retaining qualified and experienced staff. Routine management accounting tasks are increasingly being carried out by computer systems, interpreting and managing detailed accounting information is increasingly decentred to non-accountants located in business units, and the more flexible use of budgets and non-financial performance measures in many organisations has led to a shift in the ownership of accounting reports from accountants to business managers. This supports the potential for outsourcing the accounting function.

Recent research has suggested a change in the way management accounting is used in organisations, from a traditional monitoring and control perspective to a more business- and support-oriented perspective. For example, the CIMA report on *Corporate Governance: History, Practice and Future* viewed the role of management accountants in corporate governance as providing the information to the chief executive and the board which allows their responsibilities to be effectively discharged. CIMA's *Risk Management: A Guide to Good Practice* suggested that management accountants can have a significant role to play in developing and implementing risk management and internal control systems within their organisations.

However, while this might be seen as conflicting with the outsourcing of the accounting function, given GDS' difficulties, they are unlikely to be obtaining consistently reliable and timely advice for management. Hence, outsourcing might provide a better quality of advice.

(c) To ensure that the outsourced accounting provision is cost-effective, it should be subject to a competitive bidding process and a comprehensive service level agreement needs to be formulated which sets out the rights and obligations of both parties. The preferred bidder's business references and credit worthiness need to be scrutinised in detail. A legal agreement needs to be drawn up addressing the ownership and privacy of the data.

The risk of outsourcing can be partly offset by retaining some in-house expertise to monitor and work with the outsource supplier, although given the difficulty GDS experiences already, this may not be possible. An alternative may be for an independent internal auditor to monitor their work and for the outsource supplier to accept this involvement and that of GDS' external auditor.

The maintenance of access to data by GDS will be beneficial for GDS management and will provide assurance that data are being processed in a timely manner. An implant from the outsource supplier working within GDS might also alleviate day-to-day problems, although this may not be practical given the size of GDS. However, regular visits by the outsource supplier and the maintenance of a strong working relationship over time will prove beneficial to both parties. Risk can be reduced by building a strategic partnership between both companies as opposed to a short-term supplier–contractor relationship. The board of GDS or its audit committee should monitor the outsource supplier's performance in terms of quality, reliability and cost of the service being provided compared with the service level agreement.

✔ Solution 7

(a) MNO has estimated the probabilities of each risk, so it has to calculate the total project cost for each possible outcome and then weight these total costs by the probability. The results are shown below.

Table RS1

(£m)	Best estimate	Contractual delays	Planning delays	Site problems	Construction problems	Client readiness	Worst case	Weighted
Total estimated cost	230.0	234.0	237.0	241.0	247.0	250.0	250.0	
Probability (%)	50	15	10	10	5	5	5	
Cost × probability	115.0	35.1	23.7	24.1	12.4	12.5	12.5	235.3
Profit margin 10%								23.5
Target price								258.8
Range of outcomes (£m)								
Tender price	258.5						258.5	
Actual costs	230.0						250.0	
Actual profit	28.5						8.5	

Based on estimated costs weighted by the probability of each risk, the estimated cost is £235.3 million, and with a 10% margin the target selling price for the tender is £258.8 million. The best case outcome if the tender is won at this price is a profit of £28.5 million if none of the risks eventuate, and a worst case outcome is a profit of £8.5 million if all of the risks eventuate. In the absence of any other information, a tender price of £258.5 million represents the best chance of the tender being won and the outcome being profitable.

(b) MNO's risk management strategy for its tenders is based on probabilities of various events occurring. For each of these probabilities the cost impact is estimated. However this is applied, MNO is trying to minimise downside risk, while maintaining an acceptable profit margin in a competitive industry.

A risk management strategy incorporates risk identification, estimation and evaluation followed by risk treatment. Risk identification aims to determine an organisation's exposure to uncertainty and tries to ensure that risk flowing from all significant activities within the organisation have been identified. This has largely been done already by MNO in the range of risks identified. Risk estimation is used to assess the severity of each risk once they have been identified. The methods of risk estimation used by MNO are quantitative, by assigning cost estimates to each risk. Risk evaluation is concerned with making decisions about the significance of risks to the organisation and whether those risks should be accepted or treated. MNO passes these risks onto the client without any risk treatment or response other than to reflect the risk in MNO's tender price.

The Institute of Risk Management and the International Federation of Accountants, together with the Turnbull Report, each recognise risk as opportunity, not just as threat and the need to manage both upside and downside risk for shareholder value. Risk appetite is the amount of risk an organisation is willing to accept, a consequence of organisational strategy and represented in the balance between risk and return. MNO needs to clearly identify its appetite for risk and the relationship it sees between risk and return. For example, MNO needs to judge whether the return suggested in answer (a) above is adequate to compensate MNO for the risk in the event of the worst case outcome.

Managing risk as threat or hazard means using management techniques to reduce the probability of the negative event (the downside) without undue cost. MNO's assignment of probabilities to the cost impact of risks is one way of taking likelihood and consequences into account when determining a selling price. However, no action is taken to reduce the probability through management, only to transfer the risk to the client in the tender price.

Risk as opportunity recognises the relationship between risk and return, a necessity for increasing shareholder value. Managing risk as opportunity means using techniques to maximise the upside while minimising the downside. An alternative approach for MNO is to base its costs on its best estimate of £230 million but to allow a higher profit margin than 10% because of the risks it is facing. MNO would then apply risk management techniques to identify, estimate and evaluate and treat each of those risks so as to minimise the likelihood of that risk occurring. Where MNO was unable to do so, the increased profit margin would provide a buffer. Where MNO was successful in managing the risks, the reward would be a higher profit margin.

Managing risk as uncertainty means reducing the variance between anticipated and actual outcomes. Taking a middle ground position, MNO could negotiate with its client over each risk to determine what actions the client could take to mitigate the risks for the project. Risk treatment or response may be action taken to exit the activities giving rise to risk (avoidance); to reduce the risk likelihood or impact (reduction); to transfer a portion of the risk to others (risk sharing) or no action may be taken if the risk is considered acceptable. By collaboration between MNO and the client to reduce these risks, the client is likely to get a lower price and MNO is likely to achieve its desired profit margin.

 Solution 8

Report
Dear Chairman,

Introduction

You have asked me to report on the key reforms in corporate governance and risk management that have taken place recently which affect JKL and to recommend (with reasons), which (if any) of those reforms should be adopted by JKL.

This report addresses the following issues: corporate governance, in particular non-executive directors and the audit committee; and risk management, internal control and internal audit. The recommendations are contained at the end of this report.

Corporate governance

Corporate governance in most of the western world is founded on the principle of enhancing shareholder value. Major corporate collapses have been a feature of recent business history in the United Kingdom and elsewhere, and the publicity surrounding these collapses and the actions of institutional investors have raised corporate governance to prominence.

The emergence of corporate governance can be seen as a result of regulatory action in response to past failings; changing financial markets including the desire of institutional investors to be more active and the dependence of an ageing population on pensions and savings which have been affected by declining confidence in stock markets.

The main principles of corporate governance are in relation to directors, the remuneration of directors, accountability and audit, relations with shareholders, and in particular with institutional shareholders and disclosure. The 'comply or explain' approach requires listed companies to disclose how they have applied the principles in the Combined Code and to either comply with the Code or to explain any departure from it.

Under the Combined Code, board effectiveness can be summarised as the effective splitting of the roles of chairman and chief effective; the role of non-executive directors and the role of remuneration, nomination and audit committees of the board. In JKL, the roles of chairman and chief executive are split but JKL does not comply with recommendations in relation to non-executive directors or the audit committee. I shall deal with each of these in turn.

Non-executive directors

The board should include a balance of executive and non-executive directors, and in particular 'independent' non-executives. It is recommended that a smaller company (outside FTSE 350) should have at least two independent non-executive directors. The notion of independence precludes non-executives from having recently been an employee of, or in a material business relationship with the company; receiving performance-related pay or a pension; having family ties or cross directorships; representing a substantial shareholder, or having been a board member for an excessive period of time.

Non-executive directors should be independent in judgement and have an enquiring mind. They need to be accepted by management as able to make a contribution; to be well informed about the company and its environment and be able to have a command of the issues facing the business. Non-executives need to insist that information provided by management is sufficient, accurate, clear and timely.

There should be a formal, rigorous and transparent procedure for the appointment of new directors to the board. Levels of remuneration should be sufficient to attract, retain and motivate directors of the quality required to run the company successfully. All directors should receive induction on joining the board and should regularly update and refresh their skills and knowledge. The board should undertake a formal and rigorous annual evaluation of its own performance and that of its committees and individual directors.

Audit committee

The Combined Code states that the board of smaller companies (below FTSE350) should establish an audit committee of at least two members, who should all be independent non-executive directors. At least one member of the audit committee should have recent and relevant financial experience.

The audit committee has a role to act independently of management to ensure that the interests of shareholders are properly protected in relation to financial reporting and internal control. The main role and responsibilities of the audit committee should include monitoring the integrity of the company's financial statements; reviewing the company's internal control and risk management systems; monitoring and reviewing the effectiveness of the internal audit function; making recommendations to the board for the appointment, re-appointment and removal of the external auditor and approving the terms of engagement and remuneration of the external auditor, including the supply of any non-audit services; reviewing and monitoring the external auditor's independence and objectivity and the effectiveness of the audit process.

There should be no less than three audit committee meetings each year held to coincide with key dates in the financial reporting and audit cycle as well as main board meetings. JKL's audit committees should have, as part of its terms of reference, the responsibility to assess risk management and internal control within JKL. Each of these is considered in turn.

Risk management

Risk management is the process by which organisations systematically identify, evaluate, treat and report risk with the goal of achieving organisational objectives. Risk management increases the probability of success, reduces both the probability of failure and the uncertainty of achieving the organisation's objectives.

A risk management strategy should include the risk profile of the organisation, that is the level of risk it finds acceptable; the risk assessment and evaluation processes the organisation practices; the preferred options for risk treatment; the responsibility for risk management and the reporting and monitoring processes that are required. Resources (money, experience and information, etc.) need to be allocated to risk management.

The benefits of effective risk management include being seen as profitable and successful with fewer surprises, predictable results without profit warnings or reporting major exceptional items. Being seen to have a system of risk management is also likely to be reflected in reputation and credit rating.

JKL has no clear risk management system in place and while the board considers risk, it does not do so systematically. Consequently, there may be risks faced by JKL that it has not recognised.

Internal control

The Combined Code incorporates what is known as the Turnbull Guidance, which recommends the adoption by a company's board of a risk-based approach to establishing a sound system of internal control and reviewing its effectiveness.

The board should acknowledge that it is responsible for the company's system of internal control and for reviewing its effectiveness. It should also explain that the system is designed to manage rather than eliminate the risk of failure to achieve business objectives, and can only provide reasonable but not absolute assurance against material mis-statement or loss. The board's statement on internal control should disclose that there is an ongoing process for identifying, evaluating and managing the significant risks faced by the company, that it has been in place for the year and up to the date of approval of the annual report and accounts, and that it has been regularly reviewed by the board and conforms to the Turnbull Guidance.

Reviewing the effectiveness of internal control is one of the board's responsibilities, which needs to be carried out on a continuous basis. The Board should regularly review reports on internal control – both financial and non-financial – for the purpose of making its public statement on internal control. When reviewing management reports on internal control, the board should consider the significant risks and assess how they have been identified, evaluated and managed; assess the effectiveness of internal controls in managing the significant risks, having regard to any significant weaknesses in internal control; consider whether necessary actions are being taken promptly to remedy any weaknesses and consider whether the findings indicate a need for more exhaustive monitoring of the system of internal control.

For risk management and for the board's assessment of the adequacy or otherwise of internal control, an internal audit function should be considered.

Internal audit

Internal audit is an independent appraisal function established within an organisation to examine and evaluate its activities and designed to add value and improve an organisation's operations. The main role of internal audit is to provide assurance that the main business risks are being managed and that internal controls are operating effectively.

The need for an internal audit function will depend on the scale, diversity and complexity of business activities and a comparison of costs and benefits of an internal audit function. Companies that do not have an internal audit function should review the need for one on an annual basis. Changes in the external environment, organisational restructuring or adverse trends evident from monitoring internal control systems should be considered as part of this review. An internal audit may be carried out by staff employed by the company or be outsourced to a third party.

In the absence of an internal audit function, management needs to apply other monitoring processes in order to assure itself and the board that the system of internal control is functioning effectively. The board will need to assess whether those processes provide sufficient and objective assurance.

Recommendations

- JKL's single non-executive director is not, under the Combined Code, considered to be independent. It is recommended that JKL appoint two independent non-executive directors to the board.
- In JKL, the audit committee currently consists of the chairman, non-executive director and finance director. It is recommended that the two newly appointed independent non-executives (recommended above) be appointed and that both the chairman and the finance director attend, but not be members of the audit committee.
- The audit committee should review JKL's risk management system and put in place an appropriate policy and system that reflects the risks faced.
- JKL's internal controls appear to be adequate based on the external auditor's report; however, it is recommended that JKL's board specifically consider the adequacy of the external audit report in reviewing the effectiveness of internal control in JKL.
- The audit committee should also consider the outcomes of the recommended risk management system before accepting the adequacy of internal controls.
- This report does not recommend the appointment of internal auditors separate to the external audit function. However, once the board has implemented a risk management system and assessed the adequacy of internal controls, the value of internal audit function should be reassessed.

Five marks are also awarded for the presentation and style of the report.

 # Solution 9

(a) Management control comprises the processes used by managers to ensure that organisational goals are achieved and procedures followed, and that the organisation responds to environmental change. Controls may be cybernetic or non-cybernetic.

In cybernetic systems, variations between targets and actual achievements are detected and result in corrective action, either through feedback or through feed forward processes. This involves target-setting level; the conversion of resource inputs into product/service outputs and the monitoring of outputs and comparison to performance targets. Text books normally recognise management control as a cybernetic system and this is reflected in the formal design of organisational structures and management accounting systems.

Importantly, control is not limited to financial control but extends to non-financial measures of performance. There are five major standards against which financial or non-financial performance can be compared: trends over time; benchmarking to similar organisations; estimates of future organisational performance (feed forward based on budget projections); estimates of what might have been achieved after the event (hindsight) and the performance necessary to achieve strategic goals.

Cybernetic management control ensures that the organisation or responsibility centre is efficient and effective. It can take place through budgetary control, variances from standard cost, non-financial measures of capacity utilisation, productivity, efficiency, quality, waste and so on. These types of control exist within MAP.

One problem with the cybernetic model is that actual and planned results and corrective action are not seen within organisations in a consistent manner. Despite accounting reports presenting a particular portrayal of organisational events, people interpret the same events differently. In MAP, there is no general agreement that the targets set are realistic. A second problem is that control can be seen not just as an objective regulator of activities to achieve goals, but in terms of the domination of one person or group over others within an organisation. In MAP, a dominant chief executive exerts his power and influence, not necessarily consistently with results reported by cybernetic control systems, particularly if targets are difficult to achieve.

The attributes of control systems vary due to the industry, size of organisation, management style, and so on. Fisher categorised different approaches to management control as tight versus loose; objective measurement versus subjective assessment; mechanistic versus organic evaluation of performance; short-term versus long-term focus; group versus business unit focus and so on. This is a contingent explanation of the design of control systems. In MAP, control systems are tight, objective, mechanistic and short-term focused.

The cybernetic form of control is based on an economic-rational view of the world. In the natural or non-rational perspective, informal relations between people are more important than the formal organisational structure of rules and roles. Non-cybernetic forms of control include intuition, judgement and the exercise of power, politics and influence.

Organisational structure is a form of control because the behaviour of people can be influenced by arranging them in a hierarchy with defined patterns of authority and responsibility. The business histories written by Chandler demonstrated that structure follows strategy. Organisations operate through a variety of organisational forms. The form of structure that is adopted (functional, divisionalised, matrix, network) will determine the type of management control. In MAP, the matrix structure is focused on identifying functional responsibilities with groups of products and supervision is relatively light touch, other than the 'strong arm' of the chief executive. Ouchi identified control through a bureaucracy of rules, markets and the informal social mechanism of the clan. The clan structure seems to be important for MAP.

The radical or critical perspective focuses on power and conflict in organisations in which management control systems are seen not as neutral mechanisms but as reinforcing particular power interests and class divisions in society and enabling the domination of one group in an organisation over another. In MAP, the chief executive uses his power and influence to set targets which may be unrealistic and uses the EIS to focus on areas for improvement.

Controls based on financial and non-financial performance measurement are supplemented by the 'softer' controls that are not measurable. These include formal and informal structures; rules, policies and procedures; physical controls; strategic plans; incentives and rewards; project management and personnel controls. MAP applies both formal matrix structures and clan or team cultures. There are many policies and procedures which may come into tension with the more flexible application of intuition and judgement. Human resource policies will dictate the type of employees recruited and how they are trained and socialised into MAP while incentives and rewards will reinforce what is important.

In Simons' terms, management control systems are the methods by which information is used to maintain or alter patterns in organisational activity. Simons found that the choice by top managers of control systems that actively monitor and intervene in the decisions of subordinates provides signals to organisational participants about what should be monitored and where new ideas should be proposed and tested. This can be seen to apply in MAP.

(b) The behavioural effects of accounting controls need to be understood by managers. Resistance to change is a common reaction, particularly where there are conflicts between the values of dominant managers and the culture of the organisation, which seems to be the case in MAP. These tensions are likely to lead to unintended consequences for MAP.

Despite the usefulness of capital investment techniques, the assumption has been that future cash flows can be predicted with some accuracy. Despite the apparent sophistication of techniques (particularly DCF), capital investment decisions are often made subjectively and then justified after the event by the application of financial techniques to subjectively 'guessed' cash flows which can be easily manipulated through sensitivity analysis in order to meet hurdle rates for ROI, payback or internal rate of return.

One of the most common dysfunctional consequences of budgeting is the creation of 'slack' resources. Budget expectations perceived to be unfair or exploitative, as in MAP, are not internalised by employees and can lead to lower motivation and performance. Similarly, the manipulation of data or its presentation to show performance in the best possible light is another common behaviour, particularly where performance is linked to rewards, as in MAP's bonus scheme. Dysfunctional behaviours include smoothing performance between periods; selective bias and focusing on particular aspects of performance at the expense of others; gaming, or producing the desired behaviour although this is detrimental to the organisation; filtering out undesirable aspects of performance and 'illegal' acts to bypass organisational accounting rules.

In non-financial performance measurement, there are similar dysfunctional consequences where targets are perceived to be too stretching, as is the case in MAP. Tunnel vision emphasises quantified results over qualitative performance. Sub-optimisation involves a focus on narrow local objectives rather than organisation-wide ones. Myopia is a focus on short-term performance rather than long-term consequences. Measure fixation emphasises measures rather than the underlying objective. Misrepresentation involves the deliberate manipulation of data with the aim to mislead. Misinterpretation is providing an inaccurate explanation about reported performance. Ossification inhibits innovation and leads to paralysis of action.

(c) A risk management strategy should include the risk profile of the organisation, that is the level of risk it finds acceptable; the risk assessment and evaluation processes the organisation practices; the preferred options for risk treatment; the responsibility for risk management and the reporting and monitoring processes that are required.

MAP has been identified as a risk-averse organisation. Its management control systems are aimed at reducing risk through continual attention to waste and cost control and focusing on work groups and products that need to be improved. The central role of the chief executive is critical in this process.

However, there is a significant risk that is overlooked by the chief executive's approach. This risk is a result of the tensions between cybernetic and non-cybernetic forms of control and the possible dysfunctional consequences that follow from MAP's use of capital investment appraisal, budgets and non-financial measurement. MAP's chief executive lives in a world dominated by the economic-rational perspective, while MAP's employees are as much social as rational actors. There are tensions between the values of the chief executive and the culture of the organisation.

The team culture in MAP and the socialisation pressures in the work groups are a clan that produces a power base of its own, less evident but capable of compensating for the dominating influence of the chief executive. There is suggestion of resistance to the chief executive's targets and his short-term focus on waste and cost reductions. The chief executive has raised concerns about the quality of financial and non-financial data he has been receiving and this may be due to a variety of techniques adopted by employees to show the results in a better light than they actually are. It is quite possible that data in capital investment evaluations have been massaged, that budgetary slack exists and that financial and non-financial performance is smoothed, biased, subject of gaming and so on.

MAP's risk management strategy is not perfect and some of the 'hard' controls may need to be relaxed in favour of a greater balance with 'soft' controls and seeking greater participation by employees in strategy, target-setting and performance measurement and adopting a focus that is not just short-term in nature. Continuing on the current path has the risk of increased employee dissatisfaction and greater resistance to and obfuscation of the system of management control.

✔ Solution 10

(a) The UK importer faces the risk that the £ will depreciate against the euro (euro will appreciate against the £) so that the cost of the €9,000,000 import in pounds might increase over the payment period.

To hedge in the money market, the UK importer would borrow a certain amount of pound today which when converted into euros, and invested in the Euro-zone would yield €9,000,000 to cover the payment in euros.

The relevant interest rates are as follows:

Euro lending rate: 6% × 3/12   = 1.5% or 0.015

Sterling borrowing rate: 10% × 3/12   = 2.5% or 0.025.

Thus, amount of euros required today = €9,000,000 ÷ 1.015 = €8,866,995.

To obtain €8,866,995 at €1.49/£ we would require

$$8{,}866{,}995 \div 1.49 = £5{,}951{,}003$$

Thus, the UK importer would borrow £5,951,003 for 3 months at 10% per annum:

$$\text{Cost} = £5{,}951{,}003 \times 1.025 = £6{,}099{,}778.$$

3 months later, the UK importer:

Receive € investment + interest: €9,000,000

Pay Italian supplier €9,000,000

Pay UK loan + interest = £6,099,778

Thus, the total cost in pounds when the money market hedge is used = £6,099,778

This yields an effective exchange rate = €9,000,000 ÷ £6,099,778

$$= €1.4755/£.$$

(b) The US company would buy September Swiss Franc Futures to hedge the risk that the Swiss Franc will appreciate during the payment period.

Number of contracts required = €5,000,000/€125,000

$$= 40 \text{ contracts.}$$

Thus, the company would buy 40 September SFr futures contracts at $0.67/SFr.

September 2004:

(i) If Spot price = 0.65$/SFr and   Futures price = 0.65$/SFr
profit/(loss) from futures   = (0.65 − 0.67) × 125,000 × 40
= ($100,000)

Dollar cost at spot   = 5,000,000 × 0.65$
= $3,250,000

Add loss from futures   = 100,000
Net Cost   = $3,350,000

(ii) If Spot price = 0.68$/SFr and   Futures price = 0.68$/SFr
profit/(loss) from futures   = (0.68 − 0.67) × 125,000 × 40
= $50,000

Dollar cost at spot   = 5,000,000 × 0.68$
= $3,400,000

Less profit from futures   = 50,000
Net Cost   = $3,350,000

Thus, regardless of the future exchange rate, the US company locks into a net cost of $3,350,000 when the futures market is used.

(c) There are a number of problems regarding the use of currency futures in hedging currency exposures. These include the following:

- The difficulty to achieve a perfect hedge due to
  - Standardised contract sizes – where the needs of the company fall between two contract amounts the value of cash flows associated with remaining unhedged amount cannot be determined with certainty.
  - Mismatch between spot market price and the futures price where the exchange rate on the futures market is different from the rate available on the spot market.
  - The standardised delivery dates may not match the needs of the company.
- Currency futures are also available for a limited number of currencies that may not suit the particular needs of the company.
- Currency futures are settled on a daily basis (marking-to-market) through the life of the contract. The intermediate settlement can cause cash flow problems to the company.

✔ Solution 11

(a) Bongoman can hedge its exposure to the pound by using either the
Forward market – by selling pounds forward at the forward rate of $1.860/£, or the
Options market – by buying a put option on pounds with an exercise price of $1.860/£ at a premium of 3 cents per pound.

(i) Forward market:
This locks in a dollar value of £2m × 1.860 = $3.72m regardless of the exchange rate in 3 months
Options market:
Premium paid = 2,000,000 × $0.03 = $60,000

For exchange rates between \$1.82/£ and \$1.86/£ the put option will be exercised and the £2,000,000 will yield £2,000,000 × \$1.86/£ = \$3,720,000.

For exchange rates above \$1.86/£ the option will not be exercised and the £2,000,000 will be exchanged at the spot rate. The net receipts are as follows:

Spot rate	$ receipts from £2,000,000	Premium ($)	Net receipt ($)
\$1.82/£: Put exercised at \$1.86/£	3,720,000	60,000	3,660,000
\$1.84/£: Put exercised at \$1.86/£	3,720,000	60,000	3,660,000
\$1.86/£: Put exercised at \$1.86/£	3,720,000	60,000	3,660,000
\$1.88/£: Put not exercised	3,760,000	60,000	3,700,000
\$1.90/£: Put not exercised	3,800,000	60,000	3,740,000

The currency option allows Bongoman to benefit from any favourable movements since the put option holder has the right but not the obligation to sell the pounds at the locked-in rate of \$1.86/£. But this option is at a cost via the premium. The minimum revenue is £3,660,000 but Bongoman has the opportunity to benefit if the dollar depreciates.

(ii) Regardless of the future exchange rate, the forward market hedge locks in a net receipt of £3.72m.

Let S^* be the exchange rate at which the options hedge yields the same net receipts as the forward market hedge. Then,

£2,000,000 × S^* − option premium paid = forward hedge receipts.

Thus,

£2,000,000 × S^* − \$60,000 = \$3,720,000
S^* = (\$3,720,000 + \$60,000) ÷ £2,000,000 = \$1.890/£.

Thus, for exchange rates below \$1.890/£, the forward market hedge is better than the option market hedge.

(b) With the Black–Scholes option pricing model on an asset that pays no dividends, the factors that influence the value of a call option are as follows:

- Exercise price – As the call option enables the holder to buy the underlying asset at the exercise price, the value of the call option decreases as the exercise price increases and vice versa.
- Stock price – If the current stock price increases, the greater the likelihood that the option will be exercised, hence the value of the call increases as the stock price increases.
- Volatility – Similarly, the greater the volatility of the underlying asset, the higher the value of the option. Thus the call value increases as volatility increases.
- Time to maturity – The more time the option has, the higher the likelihood that the option will be exercised, hence the value of the call increases as time to maturity increases.
- Risk free rate – The call value increases as the interest rate in the economy (or risk-free rate) increases.

✓ Solution 12

(a) Given the information provided, Banco Ltd can hedge the currency exposure using either the forward market or the money market.

Forward market:

For receipts due in 6 months, Banco would sell the A$5,000,000 forward at the rate of A$2.4275. This locks in a receipt of £2,059,732 (A$5,000,000 ÷ A$2.4275/£) in 6 months.

For receipts due in 12 months, Banco would sell the A$8,000,000 forward at the rate of A$2.4160. This locks in a receipt of £3,311,258 (A$8,000,000 ÷ A$2.4160/£) in 12 months.

Money market:

To hedge the foreign receipts using the money market, Banco would borrow Australian dollars, convert into pounds and invest the amount for the period the receipt is due.

For receipts due in 6 months, the relevant interest rates are as follows:

Australian $ borrowing rate: $6.25\% \times 6/12 = 3.125\%$ or 0.03125

Sterling lending rate: $7.25\% \times 6/12 = 3.625\%$ or 0.03625

Thus, the amount of A$ to be borrowed today = A$5,000,000 ÷ 1.03125

= A$4,848,485

Convert A$4,848,485 to pounds at the spot rate of A$2.4550/£:

= 4,848,485 ÷ 2.4550 = £1,974,943

Invest the amount at 7.25% for 6 months to yield,

£1,974,943 × 1.03625 = £2,046,535

6 months later, Banco Ltd would

Receipt A$ payments   A$5,000,000

Pay A$ loan + interest   A$5,000,000

Receive £ investment + interest: £2,046,535

The total receipt in pounds when the money market hedge is used = £2,046,535

For receipts due in 12 months, the relevant interest rates are

Australian $ borrowing rate: 6.5% or 0.065

Sterling lending rate: 7.5% or 0.075

Thus, the amount of A$ to be borrowed today = A$8,000,000 ÷ 1.065

= A$7,511,737

Convert A$7,511,737 to pounds at the spot rate of A$2.4160/£:

= 7,511,737 ÷ 2.4160 = £3,109,163

Invest the amount at 7.5% for 12 months to yield,

£3,109,163 × 1.075 = £3,342,350

12 months later, Banco Ltd would

Receive A$ payments   A$8,000,000

Pay A$ loan + interest   A$8,000,000

Receive £ investment + interest: £3,342,350

The total receipt in pounds when the money market hedge is used = £3,342,350

(b) Generally, derivatives can be used for hedging, speculation or arbitrage. Hedgers are individuals or companies who use derivatives to eliminate or reduce risk that they already have an exposure to. For example, a UK company that needs to pay an American supplier $10m in 3 months may decide to hedge the risk of the dollar appreciating against the pound by buying dollars forward. In this case, the UK company is using the forward contract to hedge an underlying exposure.

Unlike hedgers, Speculators may have no underlying exposure to offset but seek to profit from the future movements in the price of the underlying asset. For example, speculators would buy when they believe prices will rise and sell in anticipation of falling prices. Speculators willingly take on the risks that hedgers want to avoid.

Arbitrageurs, on the other hand, trade to take advantage of differences in prices in two or more different markets. Thus arbitrageurs help to bring price uniformity in financial markets.

✔ Solution 13

(a) Nelson & Co faces the risk that the yen may appreciate, increasing the cost in pounds. By buying yen forward, Nelson & Co can lock in the pound cost of 70,000,000 ÷ 190 = £368,421.

(b) To hedge in the money market, the company would borrow pounds today which when converted into yen and invested at 4% per annum would yield ¥70,000,000 to cover the payment.

The relevant interest rates are

Yen lending rate:	4% × 6/12	= 2% or 0.02
Sterling borrowing rate:	10% × 6/12	= 5% or 0.05

The amount of yen required today = ¥70,000,000 ÷ 1.02
= ¥68,627,451.

To obtain ¥68,627,451, we would require
¥68,627,451 ÷ 192 = £357,435.

Thus, Nelson & Co would borrow £357,435 for 6 months at 10% per annum:

Cost = £357,435 × 1.05 = £375,307.

6 months later, Nelson & Co would

Receive yen investment + interest:	¥70,000,000
Pay Japanese supplier	¥70,000,000
Pay UK loan + interest	£375,307

Thus, the total cost in pounds when the money market hedge is used = £375,307

Note that the result from this money market hedge is the equivalent of buying forward the ¥70 million at a forward rate of ¥70,000,000 ÷ £375,307 = ¥186.51/£. If interest rate parity holds and there are no transaction costs, the money market hedge would achieve the same result as using the forward market.

(c) Nelson & Co can hedge this exposure by buying a put option on pounds at the exercise rate of ¥190/£, paying a premium of 1%. At maturity, for exchange rates below ¥190/£, say ¥185/£, the put will be exercised and the pound will be sold at the strike rate of ¥190/£. For rates above ¥190/£, say ¥195/£, the put will not be exercised and the pound will be sold at the spot rate. This enables Nelson & Co to benefit from any favourable movements and thus reduce its cost. By buying a put option, Nelson & Co can lock in a maximum total cost of

put premium of (0.01 × 70,000,000 ÷ 192)	= £3,646
cost at exercise rate of ¥190/£(70,000,000 ÷ 190)	= £368,421
Total cost	= £372,067

(d) Using the forward market, Nelson & Co locks in a total cost of £368,421, regardless of the exchange rate in the future. For exchange rates below ¥190/£, the options hedge yields a total cost of £372,067. For exchange rates above ¥190/£, the total cost using options is

(¥70,000,000 ÷ Spot rate) + option premium paid

Let S^* be the exchange rate at which the options hedge yields the same cost as the forward market hedge. Then,

$$(¥70,000,000 ÷ S^*) + £3,646 = £368,421.$$

Thus,

$$(¥70,000,000 ÷ S^*) = £364,775.$$
$$S^* = ¥70,000,000 ÷ £364,775 = ¥191.90/£.$$

Thus, for exchange rates below ¥191.90/£, the forward market hedge is better than the option market hedge.

(e) The preferred alternative would be the forward contract because the amount of yen to be paid is known and produces the lowest cost compared to the other two alternatives.

The decision to hedge or not if they expect the pound to appreciate would depend on the company's attitude to risk. Since the cost is known, the company can use a currency forward to hedge this risk. Alternatively, the put option offers the opportunity to lower the cost if the yen depreciates against the pound. The issue then becomes whether the premium more or less offsets the potential benefit. It is only anticipated that the pound will appreciate against the yen which may or may not occur. A decision to hedge or not that is based on this expectation is speculation, which companies should avoid.

 ## Solution 14

(a) An interest rate swap is an agreement between two parties to exchange a series of interest rate payments over a period of time. The motivations for using interest rate swaps include

- Comparative advantage argument. Differential information in different markets and other market imperfections can create comparative advantages between the two parties in different markets, for one party may have better access to the floating-rate market than the other and vice versa. Interest rate swaps enables the parties to reduce their interest rate cost exploiting their comparative advantages on the different markets.
- Interest rate swaps offers companies new financing choices as it enables them to access other markets that otherwise would not be accessible.
- Asset/debt transformation. The parties may use interest rate swaps to change their interest receipts or payments from fixed to floating or vice versa. For example, if a company has an outstanding floating-rate loan, the company can change this floating-rate liability into a fixed-rate loan by entering into a swap arrangement as a fixed-rate payer to receive floating.

(b) Currently, ABC can borrow fixed at 12% and floating at LIBOR 10.1%, whilst Zotor can borrow fixed at 13.4% and floating LIBOR 10.6%. The quality spread differential is calculated as:

	Floating rate	Fixed rate
Zotor	LIBOR + 0.6%	13.4%
ABC	LIBOR + 0.1%	12%
Quality spread	0.5%	1.4%

Quality spread differential $= 1.4\% - 0.5\% = 0.9\%$.

Under the swap arrangement:

the quality spread differential will be shared as

Bank $- 0.1\%$, Zotor $- 0.4\%$ and Cashpro $- 0.4\%$

ABC would borrow fixed at 8%, whilst Zotor borrows floating at LIBOR + 0.6% given their comparative advantages in the different markets. ABC would then pay floating under the swap whilst Zotor pays fixed.

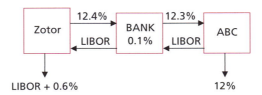

(c) Thus, effectively Zotor pays fixed at 13%:

LIBOR $+ 0.6\% + 12.4\% -$ LIBOR $= 13\%$

and ABC pays floating at LIBOR $- 0.3\%$:

LIBOR $+ 12\% - 12.3\% =$ LIBOR $- 0.3\%$.

(d) Yes. Default on the swap is on the interest payment only. The notional principal is not exchanged. However, in the case of a bank loan default is on both interest payments on the loan and the principal.

OTC products are contracts that are arranged between two parties outside of the organised trading exchanges. OTC markets, offer participant the advantage to determine the terms and conditions of the contract to their specific needs. In comparison, the organised exchanges offer standardised contract terms. In addition to developing tailor-made contracts, the OTC markets offer a certain amount of confidentiality as any transaction is a private arrangements between the two parties. The disadvantages of using these markets, however, are the lack of transparency and control. Trades on the OTC market are not regulated by any organised exchange so participants are exposed to counterparty risk. It is also difficult to close out your position if the contract taken is no longer required.

✓ Solution 15

This question aimed to examine knowledge of the main forms of currency risk when related to two different types of organisation. It further examined for the ability to use foreign exchange arithmetic and for an understanding of what other terms of trade might be considered by an exporter dealing with developing countries.

(a) (i) The main categories of currency risk (all of which might be induced by political or economic factors) are as follows:

- *transaction risk*, which affects the short-term cash flow of the entity, as a result of a movement in exchange rates between the delivery of goods/provision of service, and settlement;
- *economic risk*, which may be tactical or strategic, and relates to the projected cash flows of the business, as a result of a movement in exchange rates between a decision and its implementation;

- *translation risk*, which does not affect the cash flows of the entity, but can affect their attribution (e.g. higher interest payments as a consequence of higher gearing) and hence the value of the equity.

Methods of managing risk include offsetting borrowings or deposits, forward exchange contracts, currency options and – for long-term risks – an appropriate capital structure.

(ii) Domestic companies are not exposed to either transaction or translation risk. They are, however, exposed to economic risk, most notably

- the arrival of an overseas-based competitor, prompted by a strengthening of the domestic currency;
- movements in the world price of important commodities, compounded by movement in the value of the domestic currency vis-a-vis other currencies.

These are not easy to hedge. What opportunities will tend towards borrowing/raising capital denominated in foreign currencies; if domestic currency does strengthen, foreign currency gains will be made. Sources of supply from overseas might also help, but the problem could arise anywhere.

(b) (i) The exchange rate between sterling and the French franc can be calculated as follows:

Spot − 8.5768   2 months − 8.5932   3 months − 8.6015

The value of the first order is FFr 350,000 × 8.5768, that is FFr 3,001,880.

The forward contract appropriate to the situation described would be an option one, that is, for completion between 60 and 90 days. This would be priced at 8.6015, to yield FFr 3,001,880/8.6015, that is, £348,995.

(ii) The Uganda order is worth $225,000 in 3 months' time. This could be sold forward at 1.4873, to yield £151,281.

Alternatively, the exporter could borrow $221,675 and pay interest of $3,325, the total being repaid when the $225,000 is received from Uganda. The $221,675 would be worth £148,575, on which interest of £1,857 would be earned, bringing the total to £150,432.

On this basis, use of the forward exchange rate is the more beneficial.

(iii) Purely in terms of exchange rate risk, the exporter would be advised to accept the US dollar arrangement. This being a new customer, however, in a part of the world going through significant change, there may well be credit and political risks. The exporter should quantify these, and weigh them against the profitability of the product.

✔ Solution 16

This question tested for an ability to apply knowledge of developments in financial markets to a specific situation and for an understanding of theory and practice of foreign exchange dealings.

(a) *Swaps*

A swap is the exchange of one stream of future cash flows for another stream of future cash flows with different characteristics. Such opportunities exist because of imperfections in financial markets. In respect of interest rate swaps it is because risk premiums charged to a company in the fixed-rate borrowing market are not necessarily the same as the risk premiums charged in the floating-rate market. Currency swaps are contracts to exchange cash flows relating to debt obligations.

The potential benefits to an expanding company beginning to trade overseas include the following:

1. Ability to match financing with operations; for example, if the company has a high level of fixed interest debt but its operational income is now correlated with short-term interest rates, it can enter into a swap arrangement with a company with the opposite profile.

2. Ability to obtain finance, or cheaper finance, than by borrowing directly in the market if one company has a comparative advantage in terms of credit rating. This provides an arbitrage opportunity which can be shared by the participants to the swap. It is likely that the company in the scenario here will not have a high credit rating because it is expanding into new markets.

3. Hedging against foreign exchange risk – currency swaps can be particularly useful here.

4. Interest rate commitments can be altered without redeeming old or issuing new debt which is an expensive procedure.

5. Swaps can be developed to meet specific needs and there are many innovative products on the market, for example zero-coupon swaps or 'swaptions'.

However, there are disadvantages. Swaps are typically arranged through intermediaries which create opportunities for speculators. This is a high-risk business and should not be undertaken without extensive expertise. In the circumstances here, the company is inexperienced in foreign exchange and is unlikely to have in-house expertise. Swaps may not be suitable in these circumstances.

(b) *Hedging and forex*

Report

To: Managing director
From: Treasurer
Date:
Subject: Hedging policies

In response to your memo, you might find the following points helpful:

- *Purchasing power parity*: if the rate of inflation in one country is greater than the rate of inflation in another country, exchange rates will adjust to offset the differential, therefore the cost of living in each country would be the same.

- *Interest rate parity*: interest rates are determined in the market by supply and demand (although note political interference). There is a relationship between foreign exchange and money markets. Other things being equal, the currency with the higher interest rate will sell at a discount in the forward market against the currency with the lower interest rate.

- *Inflation* also affects the relationship between exchange rates and interest rates. This is that the expected difference in inflation rates between two countries equals, in equilibrium, the expected movement in spot rates.

Your comments can all be answered by referring to interest rate parity and purchasing power parity theories and market imperfections. The following specific points are relevant:

1. The fact that forward rates are lower than spot rates suggests that the market is expecting inflation in the United Kingdom to increase more than in Germany. All other

things being equal, the exchange of sterling for DM in real terms should be the same using spot rates or forward rates. Clearly, all other things are not always equal but forward contracts provide a hedge against the unexpected. However, using the spot market instead of the forward market as and when currency is needed is a valid, if high-risk, strategy.

2. Borrowing DM on the spot market and placing them on deposit is a valid strategy but theory suggests that there should be no financial gain in real terms unless there are imperfections in the market. One of the key roles of the company treasurer is to evaluate different financing strategies to attempt to benefit from these imperfections and inefficiencies.

3. It may be that you are under the impression that, because interest rates in Germany are lower than in the United Kingdom, this would give rise to a saving in interest payments. Interest rate parity suggests that in real terms the interest payable on one currency is the same as in another, given equality of risk, irrespective of interest rate differentials. This means that the interest rate in Germany will be lower than in the United Kingdom if sterling is expected to depreciate against the DM. The interest payable on the DM loan, which will require sterling cash flows to be converted into DM to make the interest payments at the spot rate prevailing at the time, should in theory be the same as if interest was paid in sterling on sterling loans. However, imperfections in the market may offer opportunities for arbitrage or speculative ventures.

Signed: Treasurer

 ## Solution 17

This question dealt with the management of foreign exchange risks. The first part requires discussion of two of the main types of risk (translation and transaction) and what type of hedging techniques, if any, might be appropriate. The second part of the question requires an understanding of basic foreign currency arithmetic and how the theories of interest rate parity and purchasing power parity attempt to explain the relationships between interest rates, exchange rates and inflation.

(a) (i) *Statement 1.* It is generally assumed that translation risk is an accounting issue and has no effect on the economic value of the firm. As a consequence there is no need to hedge as there is no real risk, other than the possible effects on performance measures and ratios. However, if a multinational company has extensive borrowings in foreign currencies and has agreed and approved limits for these borrowings, a major change in exchange rates could have an impact on the company's ability to borrow and cost of capital. For example, assume a company has borrowings in sterling and US dollars. Its capital structure is as follows:

	£m	
Equity	100	
Debt sterling	20	
Debt US$66m	40	(an implied exchange rate of 1.65)
Total	160	

If the US$/£ exchange rate falls substantially during the year to 1.4, the value of the debt in sterling rises to £47m. The gearing ratio has risen from 37.5% to over

40%, assuming no change in the other components of the capital structure. If the company has a maximum debt:debt 1 equity ratio of 40%, beyond which the UK shareholders and providers of debt will impose borrowing restrictions, the fall in the exchange rate has meant the company is now in breach of its debt contract. In reality this is unlikely to be a problem for most companies, although those with very heavy foreign currency denominated borrowings may suffer. It is also unlikely that the other variables will remain the same.

(ii) *Statement 2.* Transaction risk arises from delays in foreign currency payments – the risk is that customers do not pay their foreign currency–denominated bills immediately and the exchange rate moves against the supplier in the period between invoice and payment.

Hedging is a risk-reduction technique and as such has a cost. It could be argued that company treasurers are not employed to take risks with shareholders' money unless the company has a stated objective of making profits by speculating on the foreign currency markets. As the company here is a manufacturing company it is reasonable to assume it has no expertise in foreign currency speculation. Not hedging is a valid strategy, and carries no direct transaction cost, but it carries risk. It is up to the company's management to decide on the size of the risk and whether they should take that risk with shareholders' money.

Internal hedging techniques

- *Invoice in home currency.* Risk is not avoided, but merely transferred to the customer.
- *Multilateral netting.* Appropriate for multinational companies or groups of companies with subsidiaries or branches in a number of countries. This is highly complicated and requires a sophisticated accounting system to monitor the currency movements.
- *Leading and lagging.* Involves changing the timing of payments to take advantage of changes in the relative value of currencies. This is easier said than done and overseas customers might not appreciate your strategy if it means deferring payment.
- *Matching.* 'Matching' receipts in one currency with payment obligations in the same currency. This is also difficult to arrange and has similar problems to multilateral netting.

(b) If lending dollars at 7.625% interest, at the end of the year the lender will have

$$\$1m \times 1.07625 = 1,076,250$$

If lending Swiss francs the treasurer must first convert from dollars: at an exchange rate of 1.3125 this is SFr1,312,500, plus interest for 1 year at 4.5625% = SFr1,372,383.

The treasurer needs to consider what the exchange rate is going to be in 12 months' time. It will not matter if he sells Swiss francs forward as he is sure of receiving $1,076,379 at the end of the year (SFr1,372,383 4 1.275) when he converts back into dollars.

The investments give almost exactly the same rate of return, which is to be expected if the laws of purchasing power parity and interest rate parity hold.

Interest rate parity says that interest rates are determined in the market by supply and demand (although note political interference). There is a relationship between foreign exchange and money markets. Other things being equal, the currency with the higher interest rate will sell at a discount in the forward market against the currency with the lower interest rate.

Purchasing power parity (or the law of one price) says that if the rate of inflation in one country is greater than the rate of inflation in another country, exchange rates will adjust to offset the differential, therefore the cost of living in each country would be the same. This law does not always hold but an explanation is beyond the scope of this question.

Example (not required from candidates)

Spot rate SFr to US$1.3125
Inflation in Switzerland 1%
Inflation in USA 4%
Forward rate is $1.3125 \times 1.01/1.04 = 1.275$

Inflation also affects the relationship between exchange rates and interest rates. This is that the expected difference in inflation rates between two countries equals, in equilibrium, the expected movement in spot rates (proof not needed from candidates). Using the US and Swiss example: in theory, the expected real return on capital must be the same in both countries.

Therefore:

$$\frac{1.045625}{1.01} = 0.035 \text{ or} \sim 3.5\%$$

$$\frac{1.076250}{1.04} = 0.035 \text{ or} \sim 3.5\%$$

✓ Solution 18

(a) A swap is the exchange of one stream of future cash flows for another stream of future cash flows with different characteristics.

Interest rate and currency swaps offer many potential benefits to companies:

 (i) The ability to obtain finance cheaper than would be possible by borrowing directly in the relevant market.

   As companies with different credit ratings can borrow at different cost differentials in, for example, the fixed- and floating-rate markets, a company that borrows in the market where it has a comparative advantage (or least disadvantage) can, through swaps, reduce its borrowing costs. For example, a highly rated company might be able to borrow funds 1.5% cheaper in the fixed-rate market than a lower-rated company, and 0.80% cheaper in the floating-rate market. By using swaps, an arbitrage gain of 0.70% (1.5 − 0.80%) can be made and split between the participants in the swap.

 (ii) Hedging against foreign exchange risk. Swaps can be arranged for up to 10 years, which provide protection against exchange rate movements for much longer periods than the forward foreign exchange market. Currency swaps are especially useful when dealing with countries with exchange controls and/or volatile exchange rates.

(iii) The opportunity to effectively restructure a company's capital profile by altering the nature of interest commitments, without physically redeeming old debt or issuing new debt. This can save substantial redemption costs and issue costs. Interest commitments can be altered from fixed to floating rate or vice versa, or from one type of floating-rate debt to another, or from one currency to another.

(iv) Access to capital markets in which it is impossible to borrow directly. For example, companies with a relatively low credit rating might not have direct access to some fixed-rate markets, but can arrange to pay fixed-rate interest by using swaps.

    (v) The availability of many different types of swaps developed to meet a company's specific needs. These include amortising swaps, zero coupon swaps, callable, put-table or extendable swaps and swaptions.

(b) The currency swap will provide some protection against the likely depreciation in the value of the peso. 1,500 million pesos will be swapped, with the swap reversed at the year end at the same rate. At a swap rate of 20 pesos/£ the cost of the swap will be

$$\frac{1.500\text{m}}{20} = £75\text{m}$$

The opportunity cost of £75 million at 12% is £9m.

At the year end, 1,500 million pesos can be swapped back at the same rate of 20 pesos/£; 500 million pesos is exposed to currency risk.

The expected level of inflation in the United Kingdom is 5.25%, and in the South American country 65%. The purchasing power parity theory may be used to estimate an expected exchange rate at the end of the year, but it is likely to be more useful to Calvold to see the range of exchange rates that might occur, and evaluate their effects on sterling cash flows.

UK 7%, South America 100%

Using PPP the £ is expected to strengthen by

$$\frac{1 - 0.07}{1.07} = 0.8691 \text{ or } 86.91\%$$

The expected year-end exchange rate is 46.73 pesos/£ (25 × 1.8691).

UK 5%, South America 60%

$$\frac{0.60 - 0.05}{1.07} = 0.5238 \text{ or } 52.38\%$$

The expected exchange rate is 38.10 pesos/£.

UK 4%, South America 40%

$$\frac{0.40 - 0.04}{1.04} = 0.3462 \text{ or } 34.62\%$$

The expected exchange rate is 33.65 pesos/£.

The interest cost of the swap is:

1,500m × 10% = 150m pesos.

Deducting this, and the 1,500 million pesos in the swap from the year-end price of 2,000 million pesos, leaves 350 million pesos to be remitted at the spot rate at the year end.

Rate	Pesos (m)	£m
46.73	350	7.49
38.10	350	9.19
33.65	350	10.40

Given an opportunity cost of funds of £9 million, Calvold would only profit from the contract if inflation in South America does not move to 100%, the worst case scenario.

If the swap is not used, the full 2,000 million pesos is exposed to currency risk.

	£m
Sterling costs are immediately:	
1,000 million pesos at 25/£ =	(40.00)

In 6 months the sterling cost of 500 million pesos will depend upon inflation levels. A steady fall in the value of the peso is assumed.

UK 7% South America 100%	
6-month rate 35.86 pesos/£500m pesos	(13.94)
Year-end receipts at 46.73 pesos/£2,000m pesos	42.80
Net	(11.14)

UK 7% South America 60%	
Immediate cost	(40.00)
6 months' cost at 31.55 pesos/£	(15.85)
Year-end receipts at 33.65 pesos/£	52.49
Net	(3.36)

UK 4% South America 40%	
Immediate cost	(40.00)
6 months' cost at 29.33 pesos/£	(17.05)
Year-end receipts at 33.65 pesos/£	59.44
Net	2.39

However, the opportunity cost of funds in the United Kingdom is £40m at 12% is £4.8m, plus a further sum for a 6-month period.

Given the expected movements in exchange rates, in no circumstances will the contract be profitable if the swap is not used.

If Calvold is to proceed with this contract the currency swap should be used, but even with the swap there is risk that the contract will not be profitable if the South American country experiences a very high rate of inflation.

 ## Solution 19

(a) *Calculations*

Year	0	1	2	3	4
(i) Method 1					
C$ Initial investment	(150,000)				50,000
Other cash flows		60,000	60,000	60,000	45,000
Net cash flows	(150,000)	60,000	60,000	60,000	95,000
C$ per £	1.700	1.785	1.874	1.968	2.066
£	(88,235)	33,613	32,017	30,488	45,983
14% p.a. discount factors	1.000	0.877	0.769	0.675	0.592
Discounted £	(88,235)	29,479	24,621	20,579	27,222
Cumulative discount £	(88,235)	(58,756)	(34,135)	(13,556)	13,666
(ii) Method 2					
C$ net cash flows as above	(150,000)	60,000	60,000	60,000	95,000
19.7% p.a. discount factors	1.000	0.835	0.698	0.583	0.487
Discounted C$	(150,000)	50,100	41,888	34,980	46,265
Discounted £ (at C$ 1.700 per £)	(88,235)	29,479	24,621	20,579	27,222
Cumulative discounted £	(88,235)	(58,756)	(34,135)	(13,556)	13,666

For the two approaches to yield the same NPV, the discount rate applied to the Canadian $ cash flows needs to be the combination of the sterling discount rate (14% p.a.) and the projected strengthening of the pound (5% p.a.), that is 19.7% p.a. (1.14 × 1.05 being 1.197).

A forecast of a 5 per cent per annum strengthening of the pound against the dollar will, generally, be associated with UK inflation rates/interest rates being 5 percentage points per annum below the corresponding Canadian figures. It is surprising, therefore, to see that the Canadian cash flows are expected to be constant. It would be worth checking that they are nominal, and not inadvertently real.

(b) As the barriers to international trade come down, and globalisation becomes a reality, exchange rate risk management becomes a higher priority in financial management.

This particular project looks viable given the assumptions as regards future exchange rates. However, they are only forecasts and the actuals could turn out to be significantly different. If the pound were to strengthen by more than forecast, the value of the project to PG plc's shareholders would fall – and could even become negative. If PG plc's managers are sufficiently risk averse, they may wish to protect the company's cash flows against that possibility.

Borrowing Canadian dollars (as opposed to allowing UK borrowings to rise) would offer such protection in that, were sterling to strengthen, the number of pounds required to service/repay the loan would be fewer. Lower trading receipts, in other words, would be offset by lower financing payments. Covering the entire value of the project would mean borrowing its gross present value, that is $177,222, but they could choose to hedge a proportion, for example borrow $100,000 so as to offset more than half the risk.

The interest rate is likely to be different in the two countries – in the particular situation described, it could afford to be up to 5 percentage points per annum higher in Canada than in the United Kingdom before it adds to PG plc's costs. Interest payable is usually deductible in arriving at taxable profits, which could add further value. The other side of the coin, however, is that financing a project in the local currency could reduce its value if the currencies move in the opposite direction to that feared. In this case, for example, choosing not to borrow in Canada would be seen to have been the right move if sterling weakens against the dollar. It is most unlikely that additional UK equity would be raised for such a small (in the context of a plc) investment. It may, indirectly, affect the decision as to how much dividend to declare, but it is likely to be overwhelmed by other considerations.

 ## Solution 20

(a) Note: All figures in 000's

   (i) Subsidiaries alone

	Capital	Interest for 30 days	Local currency in 30 days	US$ in 30 days
US$	(10,000)	(14.17) $\left[\dfrac{(10,000) \times 0.017}{12}\right]$	(10,014)	(10,014)
Germany Euro	+10,500	+26.25 $\left[\dfrac{10,500 \times 0.03}{12}\right]$	+10,526 1.126	9,348
UK £	+5,500	+17.87 $\left[\dfrac{5,500 \times 0.039}{12}\right]$	+5,518 0.70	7,883
Total $ net receipts				7,217

(ii) If pooled

	US$ *amount now*	
US$	(10,000)	
Germany Euro	+9,284	$\left(\dfrac{10.5m}{1.131}\right)$
UK£	+7,914	$\left(\dfrac{5.5m}{0.695}\right)$
Total in US$	7,198	
Interest on $ for 30 days	10	
Total $ net receipts	7,208	

Not pooling, that is maintaining the existing system, is marginally preferable. It results in a gain of $9 million because of different interest rates; the US borrowing rate is well below investment rates in Germany and the United Kingdom. In reality, transaction costs might reduce any benefit. Also, the exchange rate data provided only shows mid-point exchange rates rather than buying and selling rates and this will account for some of the difference between the two approaches being considered.

It is also a relatively small difference, as might be expected given the efficiency of the markets in these currencies, and the decision will need to take into account other factors and wider consideration of the group's objectives.

(b) The benefits are
  - Better interest rates might be obtained for larger amounts, especially if they are planned in advance.
  - Possibly lower transaction costs, bank commissions and so on.
  - More control for the parent, more visibility of cash resources.
  - Possibly better management of cash resources.

The disadvantages are
  - Costs of converting money back and forward.
  - Risk of unexpected changes in exchange rates.
  - Possibly higher transaction costs.
  - Administrative complexities might make such a system difficult to operate effectively in practice, for example obtaining cash transfers in a timely manner.
  - A system would need to be in place to allow subsidiaries to obtain funds quickly should an unexpected, justifiable demand arise.

From the parent's point of view, the main benefit lies in control and reduced costs overall. From the subsidiaries perspective, they lose the flexibility of short-term investment and are constantly under the scrutiny of head office. The choice depends on the company's objectives and strategy towards both cash management policies and management of its subsidiaries.

✅ Solution 21

(a) Euro price list:
  - transaction exposure (firm order to settlement);
  - pre-transaction exposure (issue price list until receipt of firm order – quantities can only be estimated);
  - economic exposure (future sales exposed to rate of the Euro – extent difficult to quantify and may be the same as when prices were quoted in Sterling).

Increased competition from US-based competitor:

- customers would prefer to pay in US dollars and could therefore be forced to switch pricing to US dollars to avoid losing customers to US-based competitor selling in US dollars;
- increased exposure to the US dollar and competitor pricing strategy – if US dollar prices are held by competitor, a weakening dollar would reduce our Sterling-equivalent sales (whether or not we quote in US dollars).

Relocate manufacturing capacity to Italy:

- reduction in Euro transaction and economic exposure due to Euro costs;
- possibly new exposure to other currencies such as the Swiss France to take advantage of location and extend exports to countries outside Euroland;
- new translation exposure resulting from foreign subsidiary (translation of net investment and profit when consolidating accounts);
- new transaction/economic exposure arising from dividend payments.

(b) Greenchip Ltd
Strike price EUR/GBP 0.6500
Buy Euro call
Premium £0.0033 × 1 million = £3,300

Examiner's note: also accept a strike price of 0.6200 if pointed out that the premium of 0.0033 takes the effective rate on the option to 0.6533 which is greater than the required 5% limit on the loss

---

Redchip Ltd
Strike price EUR/GBP 0.6200
Buy Euro put
Premium £0.0120 × 500,000 = £6,000

(c)

	Outcome of hedge	
Outturn spot	*Greenchip*	*Redchip*
EUR/GBP 0.7200/10	Exercise and pay €1m × 0.65 + 3,300 = 653,300	Lapse and receive: €500,000 × 0.72 − 6,000 = 354,000
EUR/GBP 0.6200/10	Lapse and pay €1m × 0.6210 + 3,300 = 624,300	Indifferent to exercising or not €500,000 × 0.62 − 6,000 = 304,000
EUR/GBP 0.5200/10	Lapse and pay €1m × 0.5210 + 3,300 = 524,300	Exercise and receive: €500,000 × 0.62 − 6,000 = 304,000

Exam Q & As

At the time of publication there are no exam Q & As available for the 2010 syllabus. However, the latest specimen exam papers are available on the CIMA website. Actual exam Q & As will be available free of charge to CIMA students on the CIMA website from summer 2010 onwards.

Index

Index